D1404257

PSYCHOLOGY: A WAY TO GROW is designed to help students in an introductory psychology course in two ways. First, the book provides a solid foundation in the basic theories and principles of psychology. Second, it guides students toward a greater understanding of their own capacity for growth. Students who plan to take additional courses in psychology will thus have a solid basis on which to build. All students, however, will be able to benefit from the findings in a field that touches almost every aspect of their daily lives.

The book fits readily into most psychology courses. Traditional topics, such as personality, learning, and social psychology, are given proper attention. We have also included chapters on the brain and consciousness, child and adolescent development, and new frontiers in psychology. Special sections on research techniques, dreams, career opportunities, the troubled personality, and parapsychology all add interest and depth to the contents.

Several major themes run through PSYCHOLOGY: A WAY TO GROW. First, students are led toward self-understanding. Principles of behavior are illustrated by real-life situations that lie within the range of adolescent and young-adult experiences. As self-understanding grows, the student moves toward greater understanding of others. Connections among individuals, family, community, and society are probed for useful lessons and insights. Then, as understanding of self and others develops, readers begin to recognize opportunities for growth. Students become aware of self-defeating behaviors and counterproductive choices they sometimes make. From that point, they can then make more positive decisions about their lives.

No single school of psychology dominates this book. Freud receives respectful attention, but we are not Freudians. Neither are we biased toward behaviorism, humanistic psychology, existentialism, or any other specific viewpoint. When we discuss strategies for coping with problems of daily life in the special case studies in Chapter 16, our approach is totally pragmatic.

We made every effort to write a readable, easy-to-use text. Technical terms are defined in context, and the language is clear, direct, and personal. The layout is open and inviting. Each chapter starts with a lively "grabber" that sets the stage for the material to come. Pro & Con features involve the reader in a series of debates on controversial issues. Similarly, BioBoxes introduce readers to outstanding figures in the field (but not always to the most predictable ones). Other special features describe important experiments, summarize key ideas, and illustrate the people and events that make psychology so dynamic. Finally, carefully written summaries lead to an extensive set of end-of-chapter materials. These study aids include key terms, objective and discussion questions, student activities, and a reading list.

When all the theories, experiments, and debates are ended, what does psychology say to us? Perhaps Shakespeare put it best almost four hundred years ago. In *Hamlet*, he has old Polonius say:

> This above all, to thine own self be true;
> And it must follow, as the night the day,
> Thou canst not then be false to any man.

Psychology gives people the chance to know who they are and what they are. With that self-knowledge, they can go on to become mature and productive individuals.

Carl R. Green
William R. Sanford

ACKNOWLEDGMENTS

Grateful acknowledgment is made to the following sources for permission to use copyrighted materials in this book on the italicized pages indicated:

AFAR Publishers, A.G.: *Pages 40, 44:* Specified material from pp. 10–11 and 6 headings "common dream themes" (pp. 69–83) from *The Dream Game*, by Ann Faraday, Ph.D. Copyright © 1974 by AFAR Publishers, A.G. Reprinted by permission of Harper & Row, Publishers, Inc. For Canada: Reprinted by permission of Wallace & Sheil Agency, Inc. *Page 43:* Abridged and adapted from pp. 39–48 in *The Dream Game*, by Ann Faraday, Ph.D. Copyright © 1974 by AFAR Publishers, A.G. Reprinted by permission of Harper & Row, Publishers, Inc. For Canada: Reprinted by permission of Wallace & Sheil Agency, Inc.

A & W Publishers, Inc.: *Page 319:* Reprinted by permission of A & W Publishers, Inc. from *Understanding Yourself*, by Dr. Christopher Evans. Copyright © 1977 Phoebus Publishing Company/BPC Publishing Limited.

Arbor House Publishing Co.: *Page 233, pages 253–254:* From *The Making of a Psychiatrist*, by David Viscott. Copyright © 1972 by David S. Viscott. Used with permission of Arbor House Publishing Company.

Basic Books, Inc.: *Page 164:* From *The Origins of Psychoanalysis: Letters to Wilhelm Fliess: 1887–1902*, by Sigmund Freud, pp. 225–226, © 1954 by Basic Books, Inc., Publishers, New York. *Page 336:* From *The Roots of Psychology*, by Solomon Diamond, pp. 463–464, © 1974 by Basic Books, Inc., Publishers, New York.

Marshall Berges: *Page 208:* The material dealing with Rollo May was based on an article by Marshall Berges published in the *Los Angeles Times*, June 25, 1978. Copyright © 1978 by Marshall Berges. Reprinted by permission of the author.

Berkley Publishing Corp.: *Pages 272–273:* Richard G. Abell, M.D. with Corliss W. Abell, *Own Your Own Life* (New York: Berkley Publishing Corp. 1979, p. 21).

The Bobbs-Merrill Company, Inc.: *Page 259.* From *The Star Treatment*, by Dick Stelzer, copyright © 1977. Reprinted by permission of The Bobbs-Merrill Company, Inc.

Curtis Brown, Ltd.: *Pages 124–126:* Adapted from *I'm Owen Harrison Harding*, by James Whitfield Ellison. Reprinted by permission of Curtis Brown, Ltd. Copyright © 1955 by James Whitfield Ellison.

College Entrance Examination Board: *Page 496:* Adapted with permission from *How To Decide: A Guide for Women*, by Nelle Tumlin Scholz, Judith Sosebee Prince, and Gordon Porter Miller. Copyright © 1975 by College Entrance Examination Board, New York.

Coward, McCann & Geoghegan, Inc.: *Page 339:* Adapted by permission of Coward, McCann & Geoghegan, Inc. from *The IQ Cult*, by Evelyn Sharp. Copyright © 1972 by Evelyn Sharp.

Crown Publishers, Inc.: *Page 94:* Reprinted from *Birth: Facts and Legends*, by Caterine Milinaire. Copyright © 1974 by Caterine Milinaire. By permission of Harmony Books.

The Dial Press: *Page 471:* Excerpted from *When I Say No, I Feel Guilty*, by Manuel J. Smith. Copyright © 1975 by Manuel J. Smith. Reprinted by permission of The Dial Press.

Doubleday & Company, Inc.: *Pages 30–31:* Excerpts from *The Search for Bridey Murphey*, by Morey Bernstein. Copyright © 1956, 1965 by Morey Bernstein. Reprinted by permission of Doubleday & Company, Inc. *Page 70:* Excerpts from *The Mandarin Cypher*, by Adam Hall. Copyright © 1975 by Trevor Enterprises, Inc. Reprinted by permission of Doubleday & Company, Inc. For Canada: Extract from *The Mandarin Cypher*, by Adam Hall, reprinted by permission of William Collins & Sons, Ltd. *Page 135:* Excerpts from *Anne Frank: The Diary of a Young Girl*. Copyright © 1952 by Otto H. Frank. Reprinted by permission of Doubleday & Company, Inc. For Canada: By permission of Vallentine, Mitchell & Co. Ltd., London.

Arthur J. Dyck: *Page 389:* From "Questions for the Global Conscience," by Arthur J. Dyck, in

Readings in Social Psychology Today (Del Mar, CA: CRM Books, 1970), pp. 125–126.

M. Evans and Company, Inc.: *Page 366:* From *Body Language*, by Julius Fast. Reprinted by permission of the publisher, M. Evans and Company, Inc., New York.

Frederick Fell Publishers, Inc.: *Page 278:* From the book *I'll Cry Tomorrow*, by Lillian Roth, Gerold Frank, and Mike Connolly. Copyright © 1954 by Lillian Roth. Used by permission of Frederick Fell Publishers, Inc., New York.

W. H. Freeman and Company, Publishers: *Pages 91–92:* Reference: "Joey: A 'Mechanical Boy,'" by Bruno Bettelheim, *Scientific American*, March, 1959.

Grosset & Dunlap, Inc.: *Pages 155–156:* Adapted from *Exploring the Mind of Man*, by Lucy Freeman. Copyright © 1969 by Lucy Freeman. Used by permission of Grosset & Dunlap, Inc. *Pages 270–271:* From *Psychopoetry*, by Gilbert A. Schloss. Copyright © 1976 by Gilbert A. Schloss. Used by permission of Grosset & Dunlap, Inc.

Harcourt Brace Jovanovich, Inc.: *Page 265:* From *Mary Barnes: Two Accounts of a Journey Through Madness*, by Mary Barnes and Joseph Berke. Copyright © 1971 by Mary Barnes and Joseph Berke. Reprinted by permission of Harcourt Brace Jovanovich, Inc. *Page 410:* From *A Room of One's Own*, by Virginia Woolf. Copyright 1929 by Harcourt Brace Jovanovich, Inc. Copyright 1957 by Leonard Woolf. Reprinted by permission of Harcourt Brace Jovanovich, Inc. For Canada: Reprinted by permission of The Author's Literary Estate & The Hogarth Press.

Harper & Row, Publishers, Inc.: *Page 145:* From p. 6 and p. 46 of *The Art of Loving*, by Erich Fromm. Copyright © 1956 by Erich Fromm. Reprinted by permission of Harper & Row, Publishers, Inc. *Pages 188–189:* Excerpt from pp. 20–23 in *Brave New World*, by Aldous Huxley. Copyright 1932, 1960 by Aldous Huxley. Reprinted by permission of the publisher. For Canada: Reprinted by permission of Mrs. Laura Huxley and Chatto & Windus Ltd. *Page 219:* Specified material from pp. 142–143 in *The Bell Jar*, by Sylvia Plath. Copyright © 1971 by Harper & Row, Publishers, Inc. Reprinted by permission of the publisher. For Canada: Reprinted by permission of Faber and Faber Ltd., Publishers, London. *Page 220:* From pp. 1–3 of *Mania*, by L. M. Jayson. Copyright 1937 by Harper & Row, Publishers, Inc. Reprinted by

permission of Harper & Row, Publishers, Inc. *Page 425:* Text excerpt from pages 30–32 of *William's Doll* by Charlotte Zolotow. Copyright © 1972 by Charlotte Zolotow. By permission of Harper & Row, Publishers, Inc. *Page 513:* From p. 111 of *Your Erroneous Zones*, by Wayne Dyer. Copyright © 1976 by Wayne Dyer. Reprinted by permission of Harper & Row, Publishers, Inc.

Holt, Rinehart and Winston, Inc.: *Pages 240–241:* From *Varieties of Psychopathological Experience*, by Carney Landis. Copyright © 1964 by Holt, Rinehart and Winston, Inc. Reprinted by permission of Holt, Rinehart and Winston.

Humanities Press, Inc.: *Pages 454–456:* Adapted from *Lectures in Psychical Research*, by C. D. Broad. Copyright © 1962 by C. D. Broad. Humanities Press, Inc., New Jersey 07716. For Canada: Reprinted by permission of Routledge & Kegan Paul, Ltd.

International Creative Management: *Page 125:* "Thumbprint," from *It Doesn't Always Have To Rhyme*, by Eve Merriam. Reprinted by permission of Eve Merriam % International Creative Management. Copyright © 1965 by Eve Merriam.

Macmillan Publishing Co., Inc.: *Page 175:* Adapted with permission of Macmillan Publishing Co., Inc. from *All About Psychoanalysis*, by Joseph Rosner. Copyright © Joseph Rosner 1962. *Pages 219–220:* From *Lisa and David*, by Dr. Theodore I. Rubin (Copyright © Theodore Isaac Rubin 1961). *Page 392:* From *On Death and Dying*, by Elisabeth Kübler-Ross (Copyright © 1969 by Elisabeth Kübler-Ross). *Pages 491–492:* Adapted with permission of Macmillan Publishing Co., Inc., from *The Book of Hope*, by Helen A. DeRosis, M.D. and Victoria Y. Pellegrino. Copyright © 1976 by Helen A. DeRosis and Victoria Y. Pellegrino.

McGraw-Hill Book Company: *Page 418:* From *The Male Machine*, by Marc Fasteau. Copyright © 1974 by Marc Fasteau. Used with the permission of McGraw-Hill Book Company.

William Morrow and Company, Inc.: *Page 446:* Adapted from pp. 112–113, 114–115 in *The Relaxation Response*, by Herbert Benson, M.D., with Miriam Z. Klipper. Copyright © 1975 by William Morrow and Company, Inc. By permission of the publishers.

Ms. Magazine, Inc.: *Page 420:* From "Confessions of a Househusband," by Joel Roache, *Ms. Magazine*, November, 1972. Copyright © 1972 Ms. Foundation for Education and Communication. Reprinted by permission of Ms. Magazine, Inc.

The New York Times Company: *Page 40:* From "All you have to do is dream," by Ann Faraday, May 13, 1972. Copyright © 1972 by The New York Times Company. Reprinted by permission.

W. W. Norton & Company, Inc.: *Page 164:* From *An Autobiographical Study*, by Sigmund Freud, translated by James Strachey. Copyright 1935 by Sigmund Freud. Copyright 1952 by W. W. Norton & Company, Inc. Copyright renewed 1963 by James Strachey. Quotes used by permission of the publisher, W. W. Norton & Company, Inc. For Canada: Quoted from *An Autobiographical Study* in Volume 20 of *The Standard Edition of the Complete Psychological Works of Sigmund Freud*, translated and edited by James Strachey. Reprinted by permission of Sigmund Freud Copyrights Ltd., The Hogarth Press Ltd. and the Institute of Psychoanalysis. *Page 193:* From *Neurosis and Human Growth*, by Karen Horney. *Page 193:* From *The Neurotic Personality of Our Time*, by Karen Horney. *Page 412:* From *The Feminine Mystique*, by Betty Friedan. *Pages 416–417:* From *Raising Children in a Difficult Time*, by Benjamin Spock, M.D. Reprinted by permission of W. W. Norton & Company, Inc.

Plenum Press: *Page 375:* From p. 70 of *Confrontation: Psychology and the Problems of Today*, by Stanley Milgram. *Human Relations*, 1965, Tavistock Institute of Human Relations. Reprinted with permission of Plenum Press, New York.

The Psychological Corporation: *Pages 349–350:* Modified and reproduced by permission. Copyright © 1961, 1972–1975 by The Psychological Corporation. New York. All rights reserved.

G. P. Putnam's Sons: *Page 148:* From pp. 33–35 of *Mr. and Mrs. Bo Jo Jones*, by Ann Head. Copyright © 1967 by Ann Head. Reprinted by permission of G. P. Putnam's Sons.

Raines & Raines: *Page 468:* From p. 200 of *Please Touch*, by Jane Howard. Reprinted by permission of The Author and Her Agents, Raines & Raines. Copyright © 1970 by Jane Howard.

Random House, Inc.: *Pages 264, 506:* From *Knots*, by R. D. Laing. Copyright © 1970 by the R. D. Laing Trust. Reprinted by permission of Pantheon Books, a Division of Random House, Inc. For Canada: Tavistock Publications, Ltd. *Page 273:* Adapted from "Group Therapy: Let the Buyer Beware," by Everett L. Shostrum. From *Readings in Clinical Psychology Today*. Copyright © 1967, 1968, 1969, 1970 by Communications Research Machines, Inc. Reprinted by permission of Random House, Inc. *Page 348:* From *The Brain Watchers*, by Martin Gross. Copyright © 1962 by Martin L. Gross. Reprinted by permission of Random House, Inc. *Pages 352–353:* Adapted by permission of Random House, Inc., from *Getting In: A Guide to Acceptance at the College of Your Choice*, by Joel Levine and Lawrence May. Copyright © by Joel Levine and Lawrence May. *Page 444:* From *Powers of Mind*, by Adam Smith. Copyright © 1975 by Adam Smith. Reprinted by permission of Random House, Inc.

Science Digest: *Page 441:* Adapted from "Conduct Your Own Pyramid Experiments," by Marvin Grosswirth, *Science Digest*, February, 1976, Reprinted by permission from *Science Digest*. Copyright © 1976 The Hearst Corporation. All rights reserved.

Charles Scribner's Sons: *Page 127:* From pp. 596–597 of *Look Homeward, Angel*, by Thomas Wolfe. Copyright 1929 Charles Scribner's Sons; copyright renewed 1957, Edward C. Aswell, Administrator, C.T.A. Reprinted with the permission of Charles Scribner's Sons. *Page 138:* From pp. 426–428 of *The Yearling*, by Marjorie Kinnan Rawlings. Copyright 1938 Marjorie Kinnan Rawlings; copyright renewed 1966, Norton Baskin. Reprinted with the permission of Charles Scribner's Sons.

Simon & Schuster: *Page 54:* From *The Deep Self*, by John C. Lilly, M.D. Copyright © 1977 by Human Software, Inc. Reprinted by permission of Simon & Schuster, a Division of Gulf & Western Corporation. *Pages 416–417:* From *A Teenager's Guide to Life and Love*, by Benjamin Spock, M.D. Copyright © 1970, 1971 by John D. Houston II, Trustee. Reprinted by permission of

Simon & Schuster, a Division of Gulf & Western Corporation.

J. P. Tarcher, Inc.: *Pages 454–455:* From *The Probability of the Impossible*, by Dr. Thelma Moss, published by J. P. Tarcher, Inc., Los Angeles, 1974.

Charles C. Thomas, Publisher: *Pages 265–266, pages 271–272 (adapted):* From *Basic Approaches to Group Psychotherapy and Group Counseling* (Second Edition), by Gazda. Copyright © 1975 by Charles C. Thomas. Courtesy of Charles C. Thomas, Publisher, Springfield, Illinois.

University of North Carolina Press: *Page 143:* Adapted from *Sherwood Anderson's Memoirs*, edited by Ray Lewis White. Copyright 1942, 1969 Eleanor Anderson. Reprinted by permission of The University of North Carolina Press.

Viking Penguin, Inc.: *Page 223:* An excerpt from *The Vital Balance*, by Karl Menninger. Copyright © 1963 by Karl Menninger, M.D. Slightly adapted by permission of Viking Penguin, Inc.

Wyden Books: *Page 260:* From *A Psychiatrist's Head*, by Martin Shepard. Reprinted by permission of Wyden Books.

Ziff-Davis Publishing Company: *Pages 151–152:* From "The Erosion of the American Family," by Susan Byrne. Reprinted from *Psychology Today*, May, 1977. Copyright © 1977, Ziff-Davis Publishing Company. *Page 263:* From "Good! We Are Listening to You Talk About Your Sadness," by Charles W. Slack and Warner V. Slack. Adapted from *Psychology Today*, January, 1974. Copyright © 1974, Ziff-Davis Publishing Company. *Page 308:* Adapted from "Seven Quick Ways to Kid Yourself," by Carole Wade Offir. Reprinted from *Psychology Today*, April, 1975. Copyright © 1975, Ziff-Davis Publishing Company. *Page 357:* ADM test panel from "Attention Failure: A Test That Tells Who Is Accident Prone," by J. R. Block. Reprinted from *Psychology Today*, June, 1975. Copyright © 1975, Ziff-Davis Publishing Company. *Page 393:* From "The Child Will Always Be There; Real Love Doesn't Die," quote from interview with Elisabeth Kübler-Ross and Daniel Coleman. Reprinted from *Psychology Today*, September, 1976. Copyright © 1976, Ziff-Davis Publishing Company. *Page 393:* From "We Are Breaking the Silence About Death," by Daniel Coleman, poem by Richard Allen. Reprinted from *Psychology Today*, September, 1976. Copyright © 1976, Ziff-Davis Publishing Company.

Page 335: The estimates for Washington, Newton, Goethe are from John Wilson, *The Mind* (Alexandria, VA: Time-Life Books, 1964), pp. 126–127. The others are based on a study of biographical records by Sanford and Green, confirmed by checking with several educational psychologists. The original study was done by Dr. Catherine Morris Cox; Wilson's work was based on Cox's study.

CONTENTS

UNIT II HOW PEOPLE GROW

UNIT III PERSONALITY DEVELOPMENT

UNIT V HOW PEOPLE LEARN

UNIT I

THE MIND AT WORK

1

PSYCHOLOGY IS THE STUDY OF HUMAN BEHAVIOR

Does your life ever seem as though it's not working out the way you'd like? You'd give anything to be really happy, but fate keeps throwing you too many curve balls. Or just when things are going smoothly, you stumble over your own feet.

You're not alone. A lot of other people struggle with the same feelings. Take Bob and Susan, for example. You probably know a couple like them: sharp, talented people, the kind who get elected to class office and who wind up on the homecoming court. They show up at the best parties and always seem to wear the "in" clothes.

To look at Bob, you'd never know that his father is an alcoholic, would you? Or that Bob unconsciously fears that he might someday end up like his dad? No wonder he runs so hard. He's afraid something is gaining on him.

And Susan, honor student and part-time model—what torments her? Get to know her. You'll discover a lot of anxiety behind her easy manner and ready smile. Part of Susan wants to finish her education and then get married. But another part of her wants to go on to build a career, to experience more of life before she settles down. Sometimes she feels torn in two.

OK, you say, so everyone's got problems.

That's life. Can anything be done about it?

Anyone who looks for quick, easy solutions is going to be disappointed. But over the last hundred years, specialists in human behavior known as psychologists have been searching for ways to help people live happier, more productive lives. Most psychologists are optimists. They believe that human beings can overcome the personal problems that fill too many lives with despair.

The following situations will give you some idea of what psychologists do.

At first glance, you might mistake the old stone building for an expensive resort hotel. If you look again, however, you'll see heavy steel mesh over the windows. A few solitary figures stroll across the lawn. In the distance you can hear the sounds of a spirited basketball game. Old movies to the contrary, in this mental hospital no one is wearing a straitjacket.

Stop for a moment outside a first-floor office. Through the window, you can see a white-coated doctor talking to a middle-aged woman.

The woman's eyes are smudged by recent tears. The doctor's voice reveals a warmth that you didn't expect.

Figure 1.1

Every child begins life with hundreds of thousands of possibilities. Some children grow up to find joy; others inherit only despair. The job of psychology is to help people find solutions to life's problems.

"Cindy," he says to the woman, "that's a real breakthrough. Do you know that those are your first tears since you came here?"

A hesitant smile brightens the woman's face. "That means I'm getting better, doesn't it? Dr. Browning, can I really start thinking about going home?"

The doctor leans over and pats her shoulder. "That's right, Cindy, you'll be going home soon. But we still have some work to do. Are you ready to talk about your husband and the time when . . . ?"

A thousand sharp-clawed feet scramble inside the banks of cages as you walk into the laboratory. Lights reflect from the white rats' watching eyes. You feel a little nervous. Where is Professor Peterson?

"Ah, you're right on time." As always, her voice is sharp and precise. "So you want to see what's going on in my lab, do you?"

You nod, wondering again what rats can possibly tell a researcher about human behavior.

Professor Peterson motions you over to a special cage. Inside, you can see a single rat. Just as you start to touch the cage, you stop. Something's different about this rat. It seems to have a piece of metal embedded in its head!

In one swift motion, Professor Peterson scoops up the rat and attaches electrical wires to the metal strip. She returns the rat to its cage, the wires trailing behind. At first, the animal seems confused, but Professor Peterson turns to a control panel and flips several switches. A motor hums, and a lever moves slowly in and out of the cage. Instantly, the rat runs to press the lever. Every time the lever emerges, the rat repeats this behavior.

Professor Peterson reads the question on your face. "That electrode is planted in a special part of the rat's brain. We call it the pleasure center," she goes on. "Every time the rat touches the lever, it receives a jolt of pure ecstasy."

You look thoughtful, your eyes following the rat's frantic behavior. You wonder what this experiment tells us about human beings. Perhaps we also have a pleasure center, and if it were stimulated . . .

You have an extra period with nothing special to do, so you drift into the counseling office. The file of college catalogs catches your eye, and you sit down and start leafing through one of them. The thin partition between you and Ms. Logan's office doesn't block out voices, however. Without really meaning to, you find yourself listening to the conversation going on inside.

"Sam," Ms. Logan is saying, "let's look at your choices. Your grandfather wants what he thinks is best for you, and he's willing to pay half your college expenses to prove it. You've got the grades for a prelaw program, and you've been accepted at the university."

Sam breaks in. "I know, but this last year has been a drag. I want to get away from school for a while and earn some money. Do you know what I mean?"

Ms. Logan's voice is calm. "I hear what you're saying, Sam. That job offer from the fast-food restaurant over in the valley sounds pretty good. To be an assistant manager at your age is quite a compliment."

"Well, why shouldn't I take it?" Sam's angry tone reflects the conflict going on inside his head. "Decisions! It was easier when I was younger!"

You can almost visualize the counselor's friendly gaze as she leans forward. "Maybe you'll find it easier to make a decision if you think about it this way, Sam. The restaurant will give you a quick payoff. Law school means postponing a lot of luxuries for seven or eight years. But what do you see yourself doing twenty years from now . . . ?"

Marge looks happier than you've ever seen her. In fact, when you think about it, you realize that she hasn't been laughing much lately. "Hey, what happened to you?" you greet her.

"Would you believe it?" she cries. "My mother and I are actually talking to each other! And it's not one of those one-way conversations, either. She's really listening to me."

"Tell me about it," you urge her.

Marge doesn't need much encouragement. "You know how it used to be. Every time I'd ask her for something, she'd automatically say 'no.' I'd get upset, and we'd scream at each other. Before long, we'd both be in tears. Finally, I heard in psychology class about a different way to handle conflicts. It was tough at first, but after a while I learned how to stay in control."

"What's this magic method for handling parents?" you ask.

"There's no magic—just a little insight into human nature. Once I understood that Mom was reacting to my childish behavior, I just acted as adult as I could. I told her how much I love her and appreciate the things she does for me. And then I tried to help her see that I'm eighteen now, not eight. Since I stayed calm and adult, she did, too. And before long we were *really* talking to each other. . . ."

Well, that gives you some brief glimpses of what psychology is all about. At one level, psychology is a science—the study of human behavior, whether it's trying out new drugs in a mental hospital or studying the behavior of white rats in a laboratory. But at another, more important level, it's one of the helping professions. Thanks to psychology, people like Bob, Susan, Cindy, Sam, and Marge can learn to cope with the frustrations of living in today's high-pressure world.

Perhaps this introduction has made psychology seem relatively simple. Unfortunately, that is not the case. Since human behavior is complicated, psychology cannot be reduced to a few easy theories. This chapter will help you learn something about the basic organization and methods of this relatively young science. More important, you'll also learn more about how psychology applies to your own life. The topics are as follows:

1.1 WHAT IS PSYCHOLOGY?

1.2 WHY SHOULD YOU STUDY PSYCHOLOGY?

1.3 HOW CAN PSYCHOLOGY HELP YOU ACHIEVE SELF-ACTUALIZATION?

1.4 HOW DO PSYCHOLOGISTS LEARN ABOUT HUMAN BEHAVIOR?

1.5 WHAT ARE THE BASIC AREAS OF STUDY IN PSYCHOLOGY?

1.6 WHAT CAREER OPPORTUNITIES DOES PSYCHOLOGY OFFER?

1.1 WHAT IS PSYCHOLOGY?

Sample a typical day's headlines: "Border War Breaks Out in Africa. Gunman Shoots Seven. New Scandal Rocks City Hall. Elderly Couple Beaten and Robbed."

Once in a while a note of hope creeps in: "Doctors Conquer Fatal Illness. Neighbors Aid Homeless Family. Hero Risks Life to Rescue Fire Victim."

People, apparently, are capable of both great cruelty and great compassion. If so, you might wonder why humanity so often chooses violence over caring. After all, poets and artists have created great art to remind us of the heights to which our species can aspire. A play by Shakespeare or a painting by Rembrandt (see Figure 1.2) speaks to the human potential within everyone. Shakespeare and Rembrandt, however, don't tell us *how* to achieve inner peace. That's the task the psychologist has taken on.

Psychology defined

The word *psychology* comes from the Greek *psyche*, which means "soul," and *logos*, which has come to mean "logic or science." In practice, however, this "science of the soul" has been given a modern definition: *Psychology is the study of human behavior.*

Psychologists use the scientific method to collect data about behavior. Using the insights gained through observation and experiment, they attempt to answer some of life's most important questions: Why do people act as they do? Can behavior be predicted or changed? Can people's lives be made happier and more productive? What

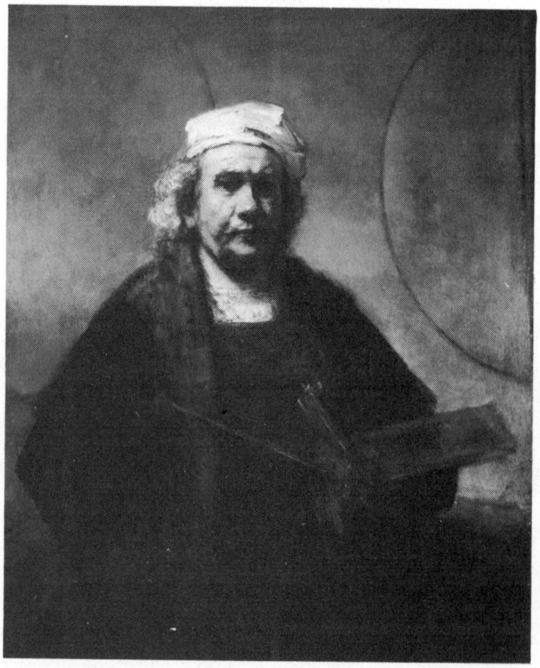

Figure 1.2

In this self-portrait, the great painter Rembrandt provides a glimpse of the dignity and self-awareness to which humanity can aspire. Psychology's goal is to help more people move toward that same peak of inner strength and insight.

can be done to help people who have lost touch with reality?

If human beings were simple creatures like dogs or horses, the answers to these questions would be relatively easy. But our species has escaped the control of instinct that dominates other forms of animal life. Human beings are uniquely gifted with the power of reason and language and the ability to create a complex culture. Psychologists, therefore, have their work cut out for them. The study of behavior yields few easy answers.

Psychology—a young science

In the beginning, no one thought too much about *why* people act the way they do.

SCENE 1: A cave, 500,000 B.C.
Obla: Why is Rad sitting there in the corner all by himself? It's nicer here by the fire with all the others.
Krik: I don't know. Forget him. I'm ready to eat.

Later, people blamed demons or spirits for behavior they couldn't explain any other way. If Rad acts strangely, the wise ones said, it is because an evil spirit has invaded his body.

It remained for the ancient Greeks to study behavior more carefully. Their gifted philosophers understood that emotional states can affect the way a person feels.

SCENE 2: Greece, Fourth century B.C.
Phipias: Plato, you're a philosopher. Do you think there's any connection between the mind and the body?
Plato: Whenever the soul within it is stronger than the body and is in a very passionate state, it shakes up the whole body from within and fills it with maladies.

Insights such as Plato's helped teach humanity that the mind can affect the behavior of the body. But until a little over a hundred years ago, psychology could not be called an organized science. A nineteenth-century

French-American doctor, Edouard Séguin, set the stage when he wrote, "I look upon psychology as . . . a science of observation, where things are to be observed and put in their places, and nothing is to be created or imagined."

In 1879, Wilhelm Wundt, a German professor, established the first psychological laboratory at the University of Leipzig. Wundt believed that he could discover the nature of the mind by studying behavior "from the inside."

SCENE 3: Leipzig, 1879
Student: Tell me again, Herr Professor, exactly what it is I should do.
Wundt: I call my method of self-observation *introspection.* While you take part in my experiments, you must keep careful records of your feelings, thoughts, emotions—everything that happens inside you. From these reports, we will learn about the structure of the mind and the nature of consciousness. We'll see how simple mental states are built up into complex experiences such as memory, creativity, and learning.

Wundt's methods put psychology on a firm footing as a science but gained little support in the United States. Americans were more interested in behavior that could be observed than in what the introspectionists claimed to feel. Philosophers such as William James and John Dewey studied the way individuals adjust to their environment. They emphasized the importance of experience and learning. Their followers made studies of mental illness, animal behavior, normal and retarded children, and ways of measuring intelligence.

So complex is human behavior, however, that other schools of psychology also developed. At the beginning of this century, Sigmund Freud developed his theory of *psychoanalysis*, a method of analyzing and treating mental disorders. Inspired by Freud's work, psychologists began to study the role of the unconscious in influencing our behavior.

SCENE 4: Vienna, 1900

Patient: But, Doctor Freud, what does my relationship with my father have to do with my problem?

Freud: Ah, everything. You must realize that the experiences of childhood, buried deep within your unconscious, still influence you. The child is father to the man.

But all psychologists weren't satisfied with Freud's emphasis on the role of the unconscious. Ivan Pavlov, a Russian physiologist who won the Nobel Prize in 1904 for his work on the digestive process, helped prepare the way for a new explanation for behavior. Pavlov discovered that dogs could be conditioned (trained) to salivate when they heard a musical tone. Normally, saliva is produced only when the animals see, smell, or taste food. Pavlov conditioned this automatic response by sounding the tone each time he fed the dogs a special meat powder. He repeated the process six to eight times. After that, the dogs salivated freely whenever they heard the tone, even when no food was present (see Figure 1.3).

John Watson, an American psychologist, saw the value of Pavlov's work. Soon after World War I, Watson announced that psychology should deal only with behavior that can be observed and measured. Watson was not interested in Freud's studies of the unconscious or in Wundt's introspection. The only task of psychology, Watson proclaimed, was to "predict and control

Figure 1.3

Ivan Pavlov performed one of psychology's most famous experiments with this apparatus. Pavlov began by sounding a musical tone whenever he presented food to the dog. In a short time, the dog salivated whenever it heard the tone.

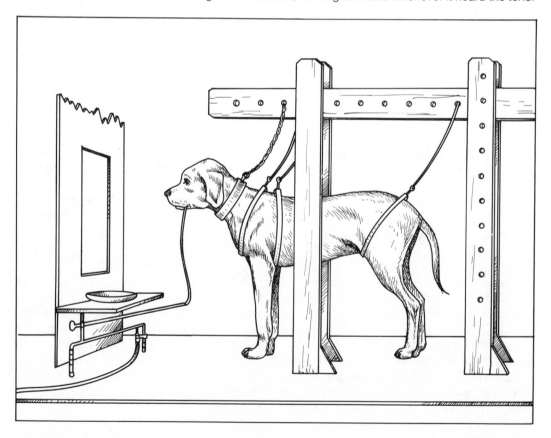

behavior." This approach, known as *behaviorism,* now ranks as one of modern psychology's most important concepts.

In the last quarter century, *humanist psychology* has emerged as a contrasting school of thought to both psychoanalytic and behaviorist theories. Humanist psychologists, who emphasize the study of healthy, productive emotions, believe that people can take responsibility for their own lives. Carl Rogers, a leading American psychologist, summed up the humanist philosophy when he said, "The aim is . . . to assist the individual to *grow,* so that he can cope with the present problem and with later problems in a better integrated fashion."

SECTION CHECKUP

1 Why has the study of human behavior attracted so much attention over the centuries?

2 How does Sigmund Freud's belief in the power of the unconscious differ from John Watson's behaviorist ideas?

3 What do the humanist psychologists see as the goal of psychology?

1.2 WHY SHOULD YOU STUDY PSYCHOLOGY?

In schools across the country, psychology ranks as one of the most popular of all courses. Can you think of a reason for this surge of interest? Perhaps the following comments by a high-school senior will help put your own answer into perspective:

> I first became aware of my own problems with identity when I started my psych class. I'd wondered who I was and what I'd do, but never really gave it a name. After I learned about identity problems, I realized that's what had been bothering me all along. I'm still working on my identity. I'm trying different ways to see which way I'm happiest and which relationships I'm most satisfied with.

Research in physics has provided the know-how that industries need to build space probes and pocket calculators. Similarly, a knowledge of psychology enables people to apply principles of behavior to their own lives. In this course, you can start learning to understand yourself, the people around you, and the society you live in.

Understanding yourself

As you master the basic teachings of psychology, you will find them useful in a number of ways.

1. Psychology can help you understand why you act the way you do. Seen in the light of psychological theory, the inner forces that drive you take on new meaning. Once you understand how important your need to be loved is, for example, you'll be in a better position both to give love and accept love from others.

2. You will learn to recognize the nature and causes of personal difficulties. If the problem is a minor one (such as a reluctance to speak in public), you may be able to deal with it yourself. But you will also learn that it's no disgrace to seek the help of a professional therapist for more serious problems.

3. As a student, you'll understand the nature of the lifelong learning process and your own boundless potential. You'll probably discover interests and abilities that you would otherwise have overlooked. Aptitude tests, for example, can help you choose a career fitted to your particular talents.

4. You will learn that only one person can be responsible for your life—you. Some people have physical or mental handicaps; others have had difficult and troubled childhoods. But no one has to remain a victim. Whatever your background, you have the

capacity to make a success of your life, if you choose to do so.

Understanding others

Like it or not, you must share your life with other people. Whether you're dealing with parents, friends, lovers, co-workers, teachers, or employers, psychology can help you develop better *interpersonal relation-ships*—productive, positive ways of dealing with people.

1. You will learn to recognize those emotional responses that keep people apart. As you break down the barriers to good relationships, you will get more done and experience more love in your life.

2. As a member of a particular age group, you will better understand what makes your friends and acquaintances tick. Once you realize why your friend Jason needs attention so badly, for example, you'll be in a position to help him resolve his inner insecurity.

3. At the same time, you'll be better equipped to cope with the different values and crises common to people both younger and older than yourself. Why, for example, do your parents find it so hard to let you grow up? Should you be worried about seven-year-old Tom's interest in violent war games? And as you grow older, you'll be better prepared to face each new challenge as it arrives.

Understanding society

Just as you wouldn't want to live apart from other people, you cannot divorce yourself from the larger society in which you live. You may not agree with every value or choice your culture makes. Nevertheless, psychology will help you understand how your personality has been affected by growing up in this particular country at this particular time.

1. You will appreciate how the freedom of choice guaranteed by American society affects each of us. As you learn more about your own aptitudes and interests, you will learn how to work within the system to find self-fulfillment.

2. You will understand why modern society has also bred such a terrible increase in crime, hostility, and rejection of traditional social values. With a better understanding of why these problems exist, you will become a more informed citizen and a potential force for helping solve these social ills.

SECTION CHECKUP

1 Why are so many more people interested in psychology nowadays?
2 How can psychology help you understand yourself better?
3 How can psychology help you enjoy better interpersonal relationships?

1.3 HOW CAN PSYCHOLOGY HELP YOU ACHIEVE SELF-ACTUALIZATION?

Many psychologists today look forward to a revolution that will alter the society we all live in. The revolution they describe has nothing to do with guns or violence, however. Using their insights into the workings of the human personality, psychologists propose nothing less than freeing all of us

from the chains of fear, anxiety, frustration, depression, and other self-defeating emotional states.

Let fifteen-year-old Patty explain their goal from her point of view:

A month ago, I had this big fight with my best friend. At first I cried about it, but after a while I began to realize what was happening. I began thinking, "What's wrong with me? What's wrong with my life? Where am I going? Who am I?" I felt so insecure. Then I realized that my friend was my crutch in life, that I liked her more than I liked myself. Well, I thank her very much for making me look at myself. Now I'm getting myself together. Oh, yes, our friendship now is better than ever.

A psychologist would describe Patty's insight as a step toward *self-actualization*, or *self-direction*. That means she's beginning to take responsibility for her own life and decisions, instead of leaning on others.

Many popular psychology books set self-actualization as an important goal. This idea comes from humanist psychology. The concept of self-actualization is based on the fact that the happiest, most productive people are those who have learned to satisfy their needs for personal esteem, accomplishment, and recognition. Like Patty, self-actualizing people understand their own psychological needs, and they take responsibility for their own mental health.

When you become a self-actualizing person, you gain realistic insights into what is possible. You don't frustrate yourself by working for impossible goals. You feel free to ask for help when it is needed, without feeling guilty or weak. You won't allow anyone or anything to dominate your life. Self-actualization frees you to start new projects, enter into new relationships, and seek new experiences. In fact, each experience becomes an opportunity for growth rather than a danger to be avoided.

Can you imagine a future in which self-actualization has become the rule instead of the exception? Problems won't disappear overnight, of course. Society will still suffer from poverty, crime, pollution, and unemployment. But when men and women are no longer burdened by negative emotions, they will be free to rebuild society in a new, more humane way.

SECTION CHECKUP

1 How would you define *self-actualization*?

2 Why do the humanist psychologists believe that self-actualization is a worthwhile goal?

1.4 HOW DO PSYCHOLOGISTS LEARN ABOUT HUMAN BEHAVIOR?

For most of this chapter, you have been reading about psychology as the *science* that studies human behavior. But can something as unpredictable as human behavior be studied scientifically? The answer is "yes." Despite the complexity and inconsistency of human behavior, psychologists have gathered together a large body of scientifically proven knowledge.

Using the scientific method

The basic technique for investigating an idea in psychology is the same scientific method used in physics or biology. In fact, whether you are a research psychologist studying learning theory or a student trying to solve a personal problem, the four steps of the *scientific method* will help you find answers to complex problems. The four steps are (1) defining the problem, (2) forming a hypothesis, (3) testing the hypothesis, and (4) drawing a conclusion.

Defining the problem. Research in psychology usually starts with a question. Why, for instance, do people in an elevator look everywhere except at one another? A psychologist interested in this problem would begin by gathering as much data about the subject as possible. Information about eye contact in close quarters might be found in studies published in psychology books and journals. Further information

Pro & Con: THE PSYCHOTHERAPIST RESPONDS TO CRITICISM

If you stopped the next ten persons you meet on the street, you'd find at least four who have negative feelings about psychotherapy. *Negative,* in fact, may be too soft a word. Many people would rather have a tooth pulled than visit a psychotherapist for help with an emotional problem.

   Like all arguments, however, that point of view has two sides. In this Pro & Con, you will see how psychotherapists defend their profession against the criticism they hear most often.

The criticism

1 Going to a "shrink" usually does more harm than good. People can get well without a psychiatrist filling them full of drugs or shocking their brains.

2 Psychotherapists are just in it for the money. Even if they could guarantee results, who can afford $50 an hour and up?

The response

1 No one claims that psychotherapy is perfect. Some patients get better without therapy, and others don't respond to treatment. Some therapists do prescribe drugs or electroshock, and that scares people. The real point, however, is that countless men and women live happy and productive lives today because a psychotherapist helped them put their lives back in order.

2 Like all professionals, psychotherapists expect to be paid for their long and expensive training. But no one need go without help. Free or low-cost therapy can be found in publicly supported mental health clinics and hospitals.

might be gained from interviews with elevator riders or from personal observation of people's reactions while riding in elevators.

   In time, the researcher can write a concise definition of the problem. This definition would include background data as well as the psychologist's own experiences, theories, and hunches. For example, the problem of avoiding eye contact in elevators might be defined as possibly relating to (1) social politeness, (2) fear of strangers, (3) a lack of interest in other people, or (4) a way of coping with enforced closeness.

Forming a hypothesis. Based on the definition of the problem, the psychologist can now form a *hypothesis*. Simply stated, a hypothesis is an educated guess about why certain things happen. In this case, the hypothesis would be a likely reason for the lack of eye contact in elevators. You may have already thought of a reason, but let's use this hypothesis: When people are forced to invade a stranger's private body space (the area around us that we don't want other people to enter without our permission), lack of eye contact makes the closeness bearable.

Testing the hypothesis. How would you test this hypothesis? Like a psychologist, you would probably end up using any or all of four basic methods: life histories,

3 For my money, most psychotherapists are just as mixed up as their patients.

3 Psychotherapists are people, just like everyone else. The profession has its share of poorly adjusted men and women—but so do medicine, education, and business. The majority of psychotherapists are concerned professionals who devote their lives to helping others.

4 Psychology calls itself a science, but few psychologists agree with one another. The whole field seems to be more a matter of opinion than of fact.

4 Psychologists use the scientific method to gather data and to test theories. But human behavior is complex and varied; people can't be put into a test tube to insure that they remain constant. Because disturbed people need help *now,* psychologists cannot afford the luxury of waiting until all proofs are in before trying to apply the results of their research.

5 Psychotherapists will mess up your head before you know what's happening. They can't be trusted with the power to control people's behavior.

5 Psychotherapists don't have any magic power to make people do things they don't want to do. The best psychotherapy can do is to show people *how* to change. No one can be forced to change who doesn't want to do so.

Have you heard any of these criticisms? If the responses make sense to you, perhaps some day you can help someone understand that psychology may not be perfect but that it can give people a chance to live better, happier lives. In this day and age, that has to be worth something.

surveys and questionnaires, observation, and experimentation. To test the eye-contact hypothesis, for example, one researcher might rely mostly upon interviews with people found riding on elevators. Another might set up a series of experiments to test the hypothesis under controlled conditions.

Drawing a conclusion. Finally, the psychologist concludes the study by evaluating the data that has been collected, hoping that clear-cut results will prove the hypothesis true or false. Often, however, the data will not clearly confirm or deny the hypothesis. In that case, the researcher may use statistical techniques to decide whether any useful conclusions have been obtained.

Even after a conclusion has been reached, it will be accepted as valid only if other researchers can duplicate the results. In the eye-contact study, the research verified the existence of private body space and the discomfort that comes when a stranger violates it. Check this out for yourself. Watch how uncomfortable other people become if you sit or stand too close to them.

The psychological experiment

Everyone conducts simple experiments. For example, people are always trying to improve their appearance.

Hypothesis: A tube of Smile-Brite toothpaste will give you more sex appeal. *Experiment:* You buy a tube and try out your new smile at a party. *Conclusion:* There's no magic shortcut to popularity.

Or faced by a family car that refuses to start, you try another *hypothesis:* It's out of gas. *Experiment:* Add a gallon of gas to the tank. *Conclusion:* It still won't start. So you try a new *hypothesis:* It's the ignition system. And so on, until you find the cause.

A scientist would call that the trial-and-error method of experimentation. Scientific experimentation differs in two ways. First, scientists attempt to control the *variables,* which are any aspects of an experimental situation that can change. Second, scientists keep careful records of everything that occurs during their experiments.

As an example, let's assume that a psychologist has come up with the following hypothesis: People are less likely to offer help to someone in trouble when others are present at the scene. How can this hypothesis be tested? One psychologist chose to have a young woman drop an armload of books while waiting in an office. (Figure 1.4 illustrates the variables in this experiment.)

Variables. Since the experimenter is looking for cause-and-effect relationships, all possible variables in the situation are kept constant except for the one being tested. The only factor allowed to change is called the *independent variable.* If the effect of the independent variable on the situation causes a measurable change, this result is known as the *dependent variable.* In the book-dropping experiment, a number of variables, called *controlled variables,* are kept constant: the location, the person who drops the books, the number of books, the reactions of the young woman who drops the books, and the absence of the receptionist. Only the independent variable—the number of people in the waiting room—is allowed to change. Will anyone offer to help the young woman? That is the *dependent variable* the researchers are waiting to measure.

In the actual experiment, the psychologists found that, when only one other person was present, that person almost always offered to help. Neither the age nor the sex of the helper seemed to matter. As the number of people in the waiting room increased, however, the offers of help decreased. Thus, the data supported the hypothesis. People in groups apparently look at one another and say, "I will if they will," and all too often, no one makes the first move.

Control groups. Not all experiments can be run as simply as the book-dropping study. In many types of experiments, the researcher must compare the presence of the independent variable on one group of subjects and the absence of the independent variable on another group. Groups of subjects who receive the independent variable are called *experimental groups.* Subjects who do not receive the independent variable are known as *control groups.*

For example, suppose that you hypothesize that learning how to meditate will improve a student's grade in a tough mathematics class. Since meditation is a rather simple technique for achieving relaxation, it can be taught to almost anyone. To conduct the experiment, divide your mathematics class into experimental and control groups. Each group should be matched to the other in as many factors as possible—age, sex, intelligence, previous mathematics experience, common interests, and the like.

Begin the experiment by teaching meditation techniques to the experimental group in addition to the standard work in mathematics. These students will be asked to meditate regularly for twenty minutes a day over a period of three weeks. At the same time, you will make sure that the control group receives identical mathematics instruction but no training in meditation. At the end of the three weeks, give all students the same exam. Since the two groups are matched, they would normally score about

Figure 1.4

THE VARIABLES INVOLVED IN A PSYCHOLOGICAL EXPERIMENT

Hypothesis: People are less likely to offer help to someone in trouble when others are present at the scene.

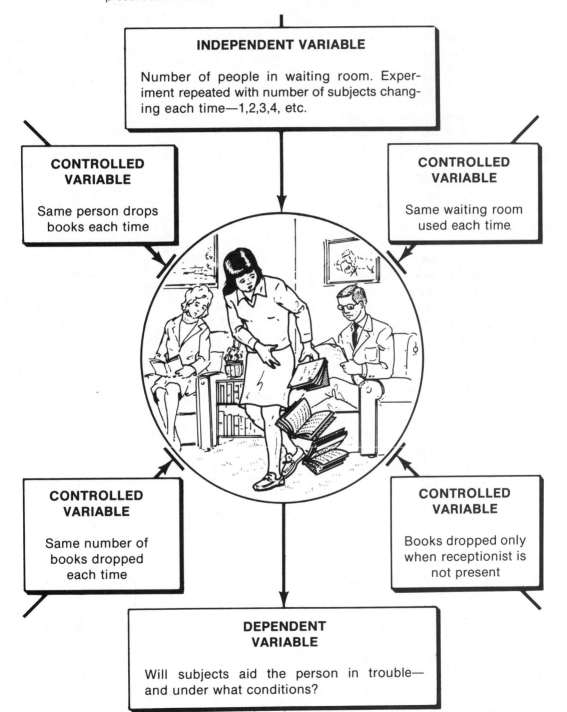

INDEPENDENT VARIABLE

Number of people in waiting room. Experiment repeated with number of subjects changing each time—1,2,3,4, etc.

CONTROLLED VARIABLE

Same person drops books each time

CONTROLLED VARIABLE

Same waiting room used each time.

CONTROLLED VARIABLE

Same number of books dropped each time

CONTROLLED VARIABLE

Books dropped only when receptionist is not present

DEPENDENT VARIABLE

Will subjects aid the person in trouble— and under what conditions?

the same. Any major improvement in the experimental group over the control group would verify your hypothesis.

Single-blind and double-blind experiments. Many experiments cannot succeed if the subjects know what is going on. If you try out a new drug for the common cold, for example, your subjects' reactions might be influenced by their excitement at being asked to try a new "miracle" drug. To combat this, the researcher might design a *single-blind experiment*. In such an experiment, both experimental and control groups receive apparently identical pills; neither group knows the purpose of the pills. The experimental group, of course, receives the new drug. The control group, however, is given a *placebo* (an innocuous substance, usually a sugar pill, that cannot affect the subject in any way). If the experimental group reports 40 percent fewer colds over a winter season, you can assume that the new drug did its job.

Medical researchers have discovered another complication in running such experiments, however. The attitude of the scientists who conduct the tests can influence the results. First, a researcher handing out the placebos might somehow project a different attitude than when giving out the actual drug. Second, observations and record-keeping might be influenced by "insider" knowledge. Studies show that researchers smile more encouragingly at members of the experimental group, for instance, or tend to overlook sniffles in the experimental group that would be recorded as full-fledged colds in the control group.

To avoid such problems, psychologists often turn to the *double-blind experiment*. In this procedure, a third party controls the distribution of the drugs and placebos. By adding this extra layer of control, neither researchers nor subjects can know who's in which group, or which pill is the drug and which the placebo. Such elaborate procedures add greatly to the cost of an experiment. But without them no scientist would accept the results as scientifically valid.

Using statistics

If you have a coin handy, flip it twenty times, counting the heads and tails. You can expect to get ten heads and ten tails. This ratio results from random chance. But suppose you obtained sixteen heads and only four tails. Have you violated the laws of chance? Twenty flips is too few to tell. But if you try ten thousand flips and you still get four times as many heads as tails (a ratio of 4:1), you'll have discovered a significant variation from chance.

Psychologists evaluate their experiments in a similar way. They keep their judgments objective by looking for *statistically significant* results based on standardized mathematical techniques. In order for results to be significant, comparison of the experimental and control groups must show a difference beyond what could be expected through random chance.

Remember the experiment on meditation as a way of improving mathematics grades (page 14)? If all members of the experimental group (Group *A*) improved their scores but none of the control group (Group *B*) did, chance could be ruled out. In actual practice, however, an overlap will probably be found. Some students in Group *A* will not be helped, and some Group *B* students will show improvement. In that case, just looking at the numbers won't prove or disprove the hypothesis. Instead, a mathematical formula must be applied to the data. The researcher can then tell if the results of the experiment are unlikely to occur on the basis of chance. If the experimental group showed a statistically significant improvement in their grades, the researcher would conclude that training in meditation helps improve mathematics scores.

Correlations

Another statistical measure often used to show relationships between two sets of data is called a *correlation*. After gathering data on two types of behavior, the researcher uses a formula to obtain a numerical value for the degree of relationship.

A correlation study. Most people would automatically agree that hours of study time and high grades are positively correlated; that is, increased study time leads to higher grades. But to find out for sure, you'd have to collect data on a large number of student subjects. Although a thousand would be a good number, adequate results can be obtained if you use at least thirty subjects, selected at random from the total school population. If you find that each hour of study time *always* produces a higher grade-point average (GPA), you'll have a perfect +1.00 *positive correlation*. If that result is reversed, so that more study time always results in lower grades, you'll have identified a −1.00 *negative correlation*. As a third alternative, you might find that no relationship exists at all—a *zero correlation*. (Figure 1.5 illustrates these three correlations in the form of easily constructed scatterplots. Each dot on the scatterplot stands for one student's study time shown in relation to that student's grade-point average.)

Misuse of correlations. Although a positive correlation may exist between two sets of data, this does not mean that one necessarily causes the other. For example, suppose that you surveyed students in your class and found that all the left-handed students made the honor roll last semester. Would you conclude from this evidence that left-handedness was the cause of their good grades? Probably not, just as you wouldn't conclude that all left-handers are certain to earn better grades than right-handed people.

Yet, in 1948, a group of scientists at Kalamazoo University (Michigan) thought they had discovered the cause of increased cancer among people in the developing countries. The people in these African and Asian nations, they found, not only had more cancer but also drank more milk. Using this apparent correlation, the scientists suggested that drinking milk might be the cause of cancer. More careful study later revealed, however, that the increased cancer was related to the pollution of the air, water, and soil that comes with industrialization.

Ethical considerations in gathering data

At what point do the rights of animal and human subjects take priority over the need to increase scientific knowledge? Generally, researchers agree that human subjects must not be placed in a situation where lasting emotional or physical harm could result. No such limits exist for the treatment of animal subjects, however.

Do animals have rights? A Rutgers University study estimated that eighty million mammals, reptiles, and birds were used for tests in 1971. The arguments over the use of these animals took on new importance in 1978 when a Michigan court saved the lives of six baboons scheduled to die in tests of auto safety equipment.

Supporters of experiments with animals point out that many people are alive today because of drug and surgical tests done with animals. Surgery for removal of brain tumors, for example, was perfected only after extensive experimentation on the brains of lower animals (see Figure 1.6). Many learning experiments could not be carried out if animal subjects couldn't be conditioned to pain, separated from their mothers, or otherwise treated in ways many people believe are inhumane. Experimenters feel that as long as the animals are well treated, except as required by the experiment, such tests must not stop just because some animals suffer.

Supporters of the rights of animals, however, feel differently. They believe that the human race's superior intelligence does not give it the right to exploit lower forms of life. Animal experiments that cause pain or mutilation, they believe, are not necessary. They point out that other procedures, such as the use of tissue cultures, often accomplish the same end. Instead of calling for a total end to animal studies, these animal-rights supporters ask that every new exper-

Figure 1.5

USING THE SCATTERPLOT: A WAY OF CHECKING CORRELATIONS BETWEEN TWO SETS OF DATA

If you collect data from thirty students on (1) the hours of study time they put in each week and (2) their grade-point averages (GPA), you can use a scatterplot to chart the degree of correlation. The three scatterplots on the right illustrate the possible extremes found in such a study. In reality, however, no scatterplot on human behavior ever turns out so exactly.

In these scatterplots, each dot equals one student's GPA (vertical axis) graphed against his or her hours of study per week (horizontal axis). Can you interpret each one? Scatterplot A tells us that hours of study correlates strongly with GPA—the longer you study, the better your grades. B says the opposite—the longer you study, the *lower* your grades. C reports no usable correlation—hours of study and GPA have no relationship.

Why not try your own scatterplot? Pick any two factors that might be related and that can be stated in numerical terms (ounces of orange juice consumed per week against number of colds in a year, for example). Use graph paper to construct a scatterplot similar to those shown here. If you survey a large number of people, you may discover some interesting relationships—not always what you would predict.

SCATTERPLOT A: STRONG POSITIVE CORRELATION

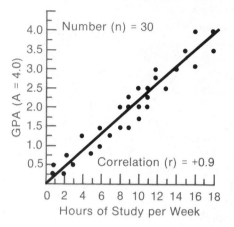

SCATTERPLOT B: STRONG NEGATIVE CORRELATION

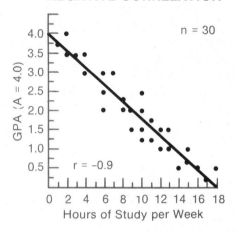

SCATTERPLOT C: ZERO CORRELATION

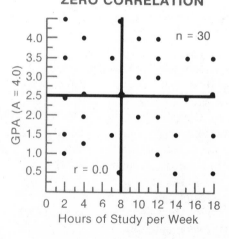

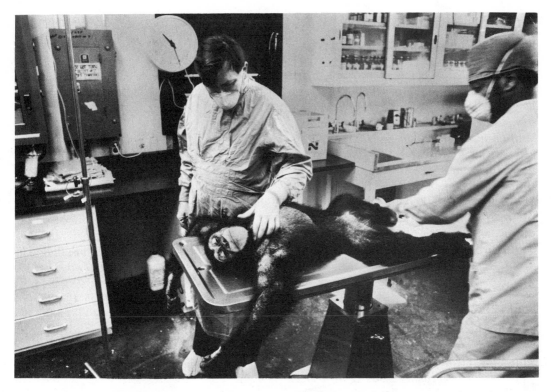

Figure 1.6

Should this healthy chimpanzee undergo experimental brain surgery, which will probably cause its death? Experimenters say that human lives can be saved through such procedures, but animal-rights supporters claim that most such experiments are needlessly cruel.

iment be judged by a single question: Will the death or suffering of this animal truly benefit humanity?

Misleading human subjects. Another debate centers on the degree to which a researcher should mislead human subjects about the true purpose of an experiment. Most studies, psychologists point out, could not obtain valid results if the subjects knew what behaviors were being observed. In the book-dropping experiment described earlier, for example, subjects who knew they were being watched would probably not react naturally when the young woman dropped her books.

In general, psychologists believe they are justified in misleading people during experiments as long as two conditions are met. First, the subjects must volunteer to participate in the experiment whenever possi-

ble. Some experiments, however, such as the book-dropping study, cannot be run if the subjects know they are part of an experiment. Second, the experimenters must do everything possible to protect the subjects from physical and emotional harm.

SECTION CHECKUP

1 What are the four steps in the scientific method as used by the psychologist?

2 Name the four methods a psychologist uses to gather data. Which method gives the most scientific results?

3 Describe the importance of the following terms used in a psychological experiment: (a) independent and dependent variables; (b) experimental and control groups; (c) single-blind and double-blind experiments.

4 Why does the psychologist use statistical methods to analyze experimental data?

1.5 WHAT ARE THE BASIC AREAS OF STUDY IN PSYCHOLOGY?

Psychology has become such a broad and complex field that the psychologist can no longer be expert in every area. If you someday decide upon a career in psychology, your graduate school will expect you to concentrate on a narrow specialty, such as abnormal psychology or learning psychology. But even as a beginning student, you should know how psychologists subdivide their subject. This section will introduce you to the major specialties (presented in alphabetical order).

Abnormal psychology

Public health experts estimate that 30 percent of the people in this country need therapy for emotional problems. Their problems range from mild depression to complete breaks with reality (see Figure 1.7). If you became a clinical psychologist, psychiatrist, or psychiatric social worker, you would identify, diagnose, and care for people with emotional problems. On a typical day, you might help a man who believes the devil has tapped his phone; a woman who cannot stop beating her child; a drug addict who wants to kick his habit; a girl who cannot get out of bed to go to school; and an elderly man who has tried to commit suicide. Successful therapy can help these people return to productive lives free from their overwhelming feelings of depression, guilt, rage, and fear. Many psychologists, both in *abnormal psychology* and in the eight other specialties that follow, also spend part of

their time teaching in colleges, clinics, and hospitals. (Chapters 8 and 9 take a closer look at the causes and treatment of emotional disturbances.)

Comparative psychology

A few years ago, psychologists set up a large, enclosed colony of rats. While the population was small, the rats lived an orderly, peaceful life. But as their numbers grew, the rat society began to break down. Even though the rats still had enough food, the animals apparently could not cope with the lack of adequate living space. Can experiments like this also give us insights into human behavior? *Comparative psychologists* believe that animal studies help us understand human problems such as those of our crowded cities.

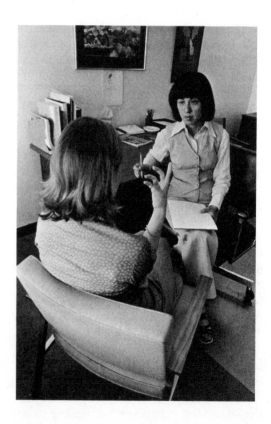

Figure 1.7

What goes on in a psychotherapist's office? Contrary to popular opinion, few psychotherapists use hypnosis, electroshock machines, or black-leather couches. Instead, you'd mostly hear two people talking about the problems of everyday living.

One group of comparative psychologists believes that animals are worth studying for their own sake. For instance, these psychologists would try to find out why salmon return to the river of their birth to spawn without trying to relate that behavior to humans. Other comparative psychologists say that animal studies are worthwhile only if they help us learn more about our own species.

Developmental psychology

If you were a *developmental psychologist*, your job would be to trace the behavior changes that occur as people grow and age. Since these changes take place most rapidly during the first years of life, children receive most of the developmental psychologist's attention. Along with other workers in this field, you would study specific behavior changes, such as how people acquire language, develop sex roles, and achieve a personal identity. Slow-motion photography of an infant, for example, reveals that language usage begins in the first few months of life. Such films clearly show the baby responding to its parents' speech patterns with similar movements of its head and mouth. (Chapters 4 and 5, which deal with child and adolescent development, show how such research pays off in better understanding of these age groups.)

Differential psychology

Differential psychology (often called *personality theory*) attempts to analyze and understand all the individual differences that make up the human personality. Differential psychologists have learned that personality is shaped by an enormous number of hereditary and environmental factors—from the physical size and hair color you receive from your parents to the effects of watching television and attending school. Sigmund Freud developed the first modern personality theory. Although a number of competing theories have been added since the early years of this century, no single theory has emerged that seems to satisfy all questions about behavior and personality. Differential psychologists believe that their studies will not only help us understand ourselves better but also point the way toward better systems of therapy for the emotionally disturbed. (Chapters 6 and 7 explore a number of important personality theories.)

Industrial psychology

In recent years, business and industry have hired more and more *industrial psychologists*. If you were president of General Motors, for instance, you'd expect the industrial psychologists on your staff to help design cars with high sales appeal and safety features that people will be willing to use. In addition, industrial psychologists would advise you on how to select and train your employees, maintain their morale, increase their loyalty to the company, and decrease accidents on the assembly lines. Psychologists who understand why consumers choose one product over another have also found important jobs in advertising and television.

Learning psychology

How do people and animals learn to cope with their environment? *Learning psychologists* try to answer that question by running experiments that measure the many factors affecting memory, creativity, and problem-solving ability. Researchers also study how learning is related to intelligence, motivation, and emotional states. Educational psychologists, meanwhile, focus on the special problems of learning found in schools. Perhaps you've noticed how worry and tension can interfere with your performance on a test. Advances in learning theory may teach you how to relax before a test—or help your teachers design less stressful test situations. (See Chapter 10 for further discussion of learning theory.)

Physiological psychology

The specialist in *physiological psychology* studies the way in which body processes relate to mental and emotional behavior. Many of the experiments in this field use animals because researchers cannot use human subjects for life-threatening experiments. A new surgical technique for treating epilepsy, for example, would first be tried out on monkeys.

Much of the work in physiological psychology concentrates on the brain and the central nervous system. Studies have begun to map the brain's control centers for body processes such as motor control, vision, pain, and sleep. Other researchers are probing the biological basis for learning and memory. Physiological psychologists also study the glandular system because hormones directly affect behavior. Testing is now well advanced, for example, on so-called "learning" drugs, which help people perform better on problem-solving exercises. (Chapters 2 and 3 provide an over-

view of the close relationship between mind and body.)

Research psychology

The role of the *research psychologist* overlaps all other work in psychology. Research psychologists design scientifically valid experiments to prove or disprove any new theories. You might wonder, does it make any sense to spend thousands of dollars to teach a rat to lower its heart rate on command? The researcher would point out that knowledge gained in such experiments has already been used to help people with high blood pressure control their problem without the use of drugs (see Figure 1.8).

Social psychology

The next time you walk down a busy street, take a minute to study the behaviors of the people who share the sidewalk with you. Each person is an individual, but each is also a member of several groups, including the large social group of contemporary American society. What would happen if you stopped a stranger and asked for help? Would you get assistance—or would the stranger brush on by, frightened or annoyed?

Such questions occupy the attention of *social psychologists*, who study the behavior of people in relation to their culture. They know that the society we live in exerts a powerful influence on both behavior and mental health. Typical research problems include changes in male and female roles; social pressures that force people to conform to group behavior; and causes of suicide. (Chapter 12 investigates the role of social pressures on behavior.)

Figure 1.8

Research psychologist Neal Miller trained rats to raise or lower their heart rate on command. Tiny jolts of electricity in the "pleasure center" of the brain rewarded the rats that responded by changing their heart rate.

SECTION CHECKUP

1 List the nine specialties in psychology. What work would a psychologist do in each specialty?

2 Which specialty (or specialties) would you look to for assistance if you were (a) a poli-

tician anxious to be elected, (b) a doctor who needs help in testing a new drug, (c) a parent whose child is having difficulty learning to read, (d) a patient in a mental hospital, (e) a high school student curious about the effect of sexual maturation on behavior, (f) a factory manager who wants to increase worker output?

1.6 WHAT CAREER OPPORTUNITIES DOES 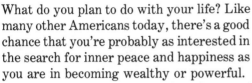 PSYCHOLOGY OFFER?

What do you plan to do with your life? Like many other Americans today, there's a good chance that you're probably as interested in the search for inner peace and happiness as you are in becoming wealthy or powerful.

No career can guarantee happiness, of course. But psychology does offer a wide variety of jobs with a number of positive benefits: (1) the chance of gaining insights that will improve your own life, (2) the opportunity of helping others, (3) the prestige of working at a useful and respected profession, and (4) the possibility of a better-than-average income.

Before you sign up for a career in psychology, however, you should also think about the possible disadvantages: (1) a long and demanding period of preparation (four years of college as a minimum, with as many as five or more additional years for a graduate degree); (2) the strain of working with people suffering from mild to serious emotional problems; (3) the prospect of a difficult job market, at least for the near future; and (4) the knowledge that being a psychologist doesn't automatically guarantee that you'll be successful in solving your own personal problems.

The scope of careers in psychology

As in most professions, prestige and income in psychology are based roughly on the amount of training completed and the value society places on the service you perform. The following chart (Figure 1.9) will give you a general outline of the most common

job titles, along with training requirements, possible income, and job responsibilities.

How psychologists spend their time

People who are thinking about careers in psychology usually assume they'll be working with severely disturbed people. As it turns out, only about three psychologists in ten do clinical work of that type. The others keep busy doing research, teaching, counseling, writing, and working in business or industry. A few move into administration and spend their time managing hospitals and clinics. The important point is that psychology is a growing, dynamic field with new opportunities opening up every year.

Getting started in psychology

If you had started a career in psychology in the 1960s, you'd have found three job openings waiting for every qualified psychologist. Since that time, membership in the American Psychological Association (APA) has more than doubled. Jobs have become scarce as more people have entered the field. The need for therapists, researchers, and counselors remains; but public and private budgets have not kept pace with the need. If you're very good at your work, you can still find a satisfactory job. The excess of trained psychologists, however, will probably not be absorbed into jobs for some years to come.

In order to begin practicing as a psychologist, you must meet state certification or

Figure 1.9

CAREERS IN PSYCHOLOGY

Title/average income*	Training	Job responsibilities
Psychoanalyst $40,000–$100,000	M.D. degree, psychiatric residency, special training in Freud's psychoanalytic technique, plus a personal psychoanalysis	Provides in-depth therapy for severely disturbed patients, using Freudian psychoanalytic techniques. Generally works in private practice. May also teach at a university or psychoanalytical institute.
Psychiatrist $30,000–$80,000	M.D. degree, psychiatric residency	Uses medical background as a basis for treating severely disturbed patients in public or private hospitals. Often opens a private practice or operates a clinic. May also teach at a college or university.
Clinical Psychologist $22,000–$60,000	Ph.D. in clinical psychology, plus internship	Works in a clinic, hospital, or private practice, diagnosing and treating disturbed patients. Frequently specializes in a particular type of practice—marriage counseling, children, elderly people, or group counseling. May teach at a college or university.
Educational or Industrial Psychologist $18,000–$45,000	M.A. or Ph.D. with specialization in a particular field	Applies psychological principles to problems of training, safety, efficiency, product design, testing, improvement of learning efficiency, and personal adjustment. Usually hired by public institutions and private businesses.
Counselor $12,000–$30,000	B.A. or M.A. in an academic field plus graduate work in psychology	Usually works in schools or clinics, assisting people who need help in making decisions about vocations, schooling, or personal problems.
Psychiatric Social Worker $14,000–$36,000	M.S.W. includes advanced training in psychology and social work. M.S.W. prepares holder to give therapy to disturbed patients	Helps people cope with economic, social, and marital problems. Often employed by public or charitable agencies to work with the poor or other people in need of assistance.
Paraprofessional $8,000–$24,000	Two years of college training in a special program. Often has previous experience that can be applied to the work. Some on-the-job training is usually required	Assists counselors, psychologists, and other professionals in treating and caring for patients. May conduct group therapy sessions, counsel the sick or dying, work with handicapped children, or give valuable assistance wherever fully trained psychologists are not available.
Lay Worker Income varies	Often college trained in own profession, but a degree is not required	Anyone (often a teacher, doctor, pastor, or nurse) who is called upon to counsel people about personal problems in the course of his or her daily work.

*Salary range for each job indicates an average figure only. Beginning wage scales may be lower than the first figure, and experienced, talented people will often exceed the top figure. Inflation will also affect these salaries.

licensing requirements. College catalogs usually list the course requirements for psychology majors. (See Figure 1.10 for a typical undergraduate program.) If you want general information on career opportunities, certification requirements, approved schools, and financial assistance, write to:

American Psychological Association
1200 17th Street N.W.
Washington, D.C. 20036

Your high-school or college counselor can also help you find additional information.

(Activity 5, page 29, will point you to a more immediate investigation of careers in psychology.)

SECTION CHECKUP

1 What would you say are the advantages and disadvantages of a career in psychology?

2 Name some of the typical jobs a psychologist would be responsible for.

3 Describe the training you would need if you wanted to become a clinical psychologist.

Figure 1.10

TYPICAL UNDERGRADUATE REQUIREMENTS FOR A MAJOR IN PSYCHOLOGY*

(University of California, Riverside)

Course	Semester Units	Quarter Units
English Composition	3	4
Biology	6	8
Physical Sciences	6	8
Social Sciences (Other than Psychology)	12	16
Humanities	6	8
Psychology (Lower Division)		
Introductory Psychology	6	8
Psychology (Upper Division)	30	40

    1. Psychological Methods: Statistical Procedures
    2. Psychological Methods: Research Procedures
    3. Physiological Psychology
    4. Fundamentals of Learning
    5. History of Psychology
    6. Social Psychology
    7. Personality Development
    8. Field Work in Psychology
    9. Seminars in Specialized Areas

*Students must take an additional 88 quarter units (66 semester units) in order to earn their college degree.

ing to analyze the motives that led to a baffling kidnapping. (*d*) A chemist develops a new form of plastic in the laboratory.

2 Wilhelm Wundt founded the first school of modern psychology, using a method he called (*a*) behaviorism (*b*) humanist psychology (*c*) introspection (*d*) comparative psychology.

3 The school of psychology that would be most concerned with the concept of self-actualization is (*a*) the humanist (*b*) the Freudian (*c*) the behaviorist (*d*) none of these.

4 Learning the principles of psychology will (*a*) guarantee that you will live a happy, productive life (*b*) give you control over the lives of others (*c*) lead to success in any career that you choose (*d*) help you understand your own behavior and how to change it if you want to do so.

5 Which example of behavior would you most likely find in a self-actualizing person? (*a*) When she's angry, Clara throws things at people. (*b*) When he's angry, Chester stays in his room and sulks. (*c*) When he has an argument with his wife, Clem goes out and gets drunk. (*d*) When Crissie received a grade on a paper she thought was unfair, she went directly to the teacher and asked for an explanation.

6 Which of the following data-gathering techniques used by the psychologist would have the greatest scientific validity? (*a*) collection of a life history (*b*) distribution and analysis of questionnaires (*c*) observation of people's behavior (*d*) controlled experimentation.

7 A social psychologist ran an experiment to find out which type of waiter receives the biggest tips—a smiling, friendly waiter or a less friendly waiter. The dependent variable in this experiment would be (*a*) whether the waiter smiled or not (*b*) the type of customer who eats in the restaurant (*c*) the amount of tips earned by each type of waiter (*d*) the quality and price of the food served to the customers.

8 A psychologist who is interested primarily in studying the changes that take place in children as they mature probably specializes in (*a*) physiological psychology (*b*) developmental psychology (*c*) social psychology (*d*) comparative psychology.

9 About three psychologists in ten are engaged in (*a*) research (*b*) educational psychol-

ogy (*c*) clinical work (psychotherapy) (*d*) counseling and guidance.

10 Psychologists estimate that the approximate percentage of the population needing therapy for emotional problems is (*a*) 20 percent (*b*) 25 percent (*c*) 30 percent (*d*) 50 percent.

Discussion questions

1 What are the basic goals of psychology? If these goals can be achieved, what effect might that have on the future of the society you live in?

2 How would you explain the concept of self-actualization to someone?

3 Why is it so important that experiments in psychology use proper scientific methods? What role do control groups play in maintaining objectivity and validity in experimentation?

4 History records several instances in which rulers ordered that babies be raised in isolation in order to see what language they would speak. What ethical considerations would be involved in setting up such an experiment today?

5 If a good friend asked for advice on a career in psychology, what would you say? Describe the different fields within psychology from which your friend could choose.

Activities

1 The odds are good that you know someone in your family or circle of friends who can be described as a "self-actualizing" person. Write a brief description of this person, concentrating on those traits, abilities, and ways of coping with problems that have impressed you. How does this person handle stress and the demands of school, job, and family? Do you spot any patterns of behavior that you could adopt for your own life?

2 Visit a local bookstore or library, and browse for a while in the psychology section. Many of the books will fall into the category that might be called applied psychology—the use of psychological principles and techniques to make a person's life happier. Read one or two of the books that appeal to you to see if they really can improve your life.

3 The yellow pages of your local phone book will list the names of practicing psychologists. In some cases, you will find that the local branch of the American Psychological Association maintains a speakers' bureau. Through that bureau, or through contacts with a local psychologist, invite someone to visit your class to discuss career opportunities in psychology. Ask the visitor to talk about training, job opportunities, personal experiences in the field, and the satisfactions he or she receives from helping people.

4 Pick up a recent copy of *Psychology Today*. This magazine brings news of what's going on in psychology to the general public. Survey the copy you've chosen. What do you think of its contents, artwork, special features, and advertising? Read an article or two that interests you. You'll find that the magazine will keep you current with interesting research and new insights into behavior. Perhaps even more important, you'll come across articles that relate to your own problems.

5 If you are seriously interested in a career in psychology, try the following plan. (*a*) Check academic requirements by studying a number of college catalogs. (*b*) Do some extra reading about the work of a psychologist or a psychiatrist. (David Viscott's book in the reading list that follows would be a good start.) (*c*) Make appointments to talk to as many people involved in the field as possible. Start with school counselors or the school psychologist; then interview local psychologists. (*d*) Check on future job prospects in your chosen specialty. (*e*) Finally, draw up a balance sheet of the pros and cons as you see them—your goals, your abilities, your financial position, and your determination.

For further reading

Karlins, Marvin and Lewis M. Andrews. *Psychology: What's in It for Us?* New York: Random House, 1973. An intriguing introduction to the new ideas in psychology—biofeedback, behavior modification, effects of overcrowding, and other positive applications of current research.

Keyes, Fenton. *Your Future in a Mental Health Career.* New York: Rosen, Richards Press, 1976. Fenton provides a useful guide to careers in the helping professions. Brief chapters discuss work in psychology, psychiatry, nursing, social work, and related fields.

Psychology Today. A monthly magazine produced by Ziff-Davis Publishing Co. This magazine is written and edited for the general public. Typical issues contain reports on current research, book reviews, articles drawn from all the behavioral sciences, and in-depth interviews with prominent psychologists.

Readings in Psychology, published each year. Guilford, Conn.: Dushkin Publishing Group. A well-indexed collection of articles of general interest drawn from popular and professional sources. A convenient way to review the latest research and to evaluate current interpretations of behavior.

Shapiro, Evelyn, ed. *PsychoSources: A Psychology Resource Catalog.* New York: Bantam, 1973. The editors of this large-format paperback call it "an access device for the field of psychology." They divide psychology into basic topics and then provide the reader with a survey of provocative books, articles, and ideas pertaining to each topic.

Viscott, David S. *The Making of a Psychiatrist.* New York: Arbor House, 1972. Viscott writes perceptively and honestly of the long years of training and growth that made him into a psychiatrist. Particularly recommended for anyone thinking of making a career in psychology.

2

CONSCIOUSNESS

Some people believe that they can take a guided tour of their past lives. That's right, their past *lives*, as they might have lived them in ancient Egypt, King Arthur's England, or even Kansas in the 1930s. Some subjects tell about living as far back as four thousand years ago. One white teacher "remembers" an earlier life as a black slave. His wife reports that she was once rescued from a Civil War battlefield.

How do these people get in touch with their past lives? Their trip begins with a visit to a hypnotist who specializes in *age regressions* (*regress* means "to go backward") (see Figure 2.1). Psychologists have long used hypnotism for similar regressions. In the late 1800s, Sigmund Freud used hypnosis to help people in therapy remember events from their childhoods. But Freud's patients, apparently, never relived an earlier existence.

Modern interest in age regression was stimulated by a book written in 1956 by Morey Bernstein. Bernstein, a business executive and amateur hypnotist, had a favorite subject named Ruth Simmons. Today, most people who know this story think of Ruth Simmons as Bridey Murphy. Listen

to Bernstein as he describes his "breakthrough":

I decided that I would use an ordinary hypnotic age regression to take my subject back to the age of one year. And then I would suggest that her memory could go even farther back. It seemed rather simple, but maybe it would do the job. . . .

This would be old stuff for Ruth Simmons; with me as hypnotist she had done the same thing twice before. On one occasion she had shown conclusively that she could, while hypnotized, recall events which had taken place when she was only one year old. But tonight I was going to attempt something more than an ordinary age regression. . . .

Farther and farther we went into memories stored deep, past the reach of the conscious mind, until Ruth remembered when she was only one year old. At the age of one year she had expressed her desire for water by saying, "Wa." But when she was asked to tell us how she had asked for a glass of milk, she replied, ". . . can't say that."

And now—now at last I was in a position to try something I had never before attempted. . . . In short, I was going to make an effort to determine whether human memory can be taken back to a period even before birth. . . .

Figure 2.1

Can the mind recall events of lives earlier than the one you're living now? Age-regression hypnotists believe that it can. But despite the claims made for this process, most serious scientists strongly doubt its validity.

I instructed the entranced Mrs. Simmons, who was now breathing very deeply, that she should try to go still farther back in her memory . . . "back, back, back, and back . . . until, oddly enough, you find yourself in some other scene, in some other place, in some other time, and when I talk to you again, you will tell me about it." I finished, and then waited anxiously for a few long moments. . . .

"Now you're going to tell me, . . ." I said. "What did you see? What did you see?"

". . . scratched the paint off all my bed!"

I didn't understand. I hesitated, and then asked the only question logical under the circumstances. "Why did you do that?"

Then we listened to that small, relaxed voice, so remote and so close, telling the logical touching story of a little girl who'd been spanked and who had taken her revenge against a grown-up world by picking the paint off her metal bed. She explained that they had just "painted it and made it pretty."

This little girl seemed part of another place, another time. And when I asked her name, the answer came from my subject: "Friday . . . Friday Murphy."*

Bernstein hadn't heard the name clearly. Ruth Simmons was telling the story of Bridey Murphy, a woman who lived in Cork, Ireland, in the early 1800s. Her detailed life history became a minor sensation when it was published by Bernstein as *The Search for Bridey Murphy*. Some people believed in Bridey Murphy because they thought that Ruth Simmons couldn't possibly have made up so much accurate detail about a time and

*Morey Bernstein, *The Search for Bridey Murphy* (Garden City, NY: Doubleday, 1956), pp. 7–10.

place far outside her own experience. Others believed in Bridey because the idea of multiple lives appealed to them on a philosophical or religious basis.

More skeptical observers pointed out, however, that Ruth Simmons could have been "remembering" a lifetime of information gathered through reading and listening to talk about Ireland. Other critics tried to find errors in Bridey Murphy's accounts of Irish life—not always successfully. Experts also pointed out that subjects under hypnotism often invent memories to please the hypnotist. Psychologist Martin Orne, for example, asked a group of college students to describe their sixth birthday while under hypnosis. His subjects responded with lengthy accounts of parties, presents, and other events. But Orne had researched each subject's actual sixth birthday—and the "memories" turned out to be largely inaccurate.

Thus, Pat M.'s age regression to a past life as a wealthy landowner in ancient China may be mostly wishful thinking. What do you believe? Whatever your answer, the power of the human mind to think, create, remember, analyze, and perform a thousand other feats of mental gymnastics cannot be argued.

This chapter will give you a chance to learn more about the behavior of the human mind, awake and asleep, while hypnotized or under the influence of drugs. The story of how you make contact with the world around you raises the following questions:

2.1 HOW DOES CONSCIOUSNESS HELP YOU DEAL WITH REALITY?

2.2 WHAT ROLE DO SENSORY EXPERIENCE AND PERCEPTION PLAY IN BRINGING ORDER TO A CONFUSING WORLD?

2.3 WHAT ROLE DO SLEEP AND DREAMS PLAY IN YOUR LIFE?

2.4 WHAT IS HYPNOSIS?

2.5 WHAT EFFECT DO PSYCHOACTIVE DRUGS HAVE ON BEHAVIOR?

2.1 HOW DOES CONSCIOUSNESS HELP YOU DEAL WITH REALITY?

When you're through studying, lay this book aside and walk outdoors. Open yourself up to the world around you. Perhaps it's a clear, bright day. Sunlight warms your skin and you see shadows across the sidewalk. You feel the cool touch of a breeze that also brings you the fumes of car exhaust. Rock music throbs from someone's radio. The smell of fried chicken cooking in a nearby kitchen makes your mouth water. You feel alive, alert to everything around you. It's a good feeling.

Yet none of these experiences registered on your senses in the way people normally assume they do. Your eyes did not "see" the shadows, nor did your ears "hear" the music. Instead, your eyes and ears sent information to your brain. There, a network of nerve cells converted that data into "seeing" and "hearing." In other words, your brain processed the incoming data so that you could make sense of what was happening around you.

Research into brain function

An amazing variety of thoughts and feelings takes place inside your head. Love, creativity, anger, sadness, memory—all occur within your brain. Even the most advanced computer can't begin to duplicate your ability to think and feel. But how can your brain—a complex of tissue, fluids, and electrochemical activity—produce human emotions and intellect? Centuries of research have only begun to unravel that mystery.

Early research. As early as the fourth century B.C., the Greek physician Hippocrates studied the effects of brain damage. He concluded, "From the brain only arise our pleasures, joys, laughter, and jests as well as our sorrows, pains, griefs, and tears." In the 1600s, researchers began to map the brain, based on the belief that specific parts of the brain could be matched up with specific behaviors. In the 1860s, a French surgeon, Paul Broca, located the region that controls speech. About the same time, two German doctors, Eduard Hitzig and Gustav Fritsch, proved that electrical stimulation of the brain can cause movement of various parts of the body.

Penfield's discovery. But muscle jerks and twitches are not the same as thought, feeling, and memory. It remained for a Canadian brain surgeon, Dr. Wilder Penfield, to prove that those processes also can be located within the brain. Penfield's discovery came out of a treatment for epilepsy that he developed in the 1930s. Penfield reasoned that if he could find the exact bit of brain tissue that triggers an epileptic seizure, he could destroy it and end his patients' problems. For a search tool, Penfield used an electric probe that could stimulate the brain without injuring it.

Penfield's patients received only a local anesthetic because the brain itself cannot feel pain. When the surgeon exposed the brain and began to probe its responses, the patients were awake and could report what they felt. Like Hitzig and Fritsch, Penfield found that stimulation of certain brain areas caused a variety of physical sensations. Patients reported tingling feelings in their fingers and toes, their arms and legs jerked, and they experienced brilliant flashes of light. During one operation in 1936, however, Penfield discovered a different response. As he probed a woman's brain, she suddenly cried out, "I hear my mother and my brother talking to each other." The patient reported that she felt as though she

had actually relived the long-forgotten experience. When Penfield stimulated the spot a second time, the identical memory repeated itself, like a videotape being replayed.

Penfield reported that when their brains were directly stimulated, other patients heard orchestras play, relived the birth of a child, and revisited the circus. They described these memories as "real," undimmed by time. Old feelings of sadness, joy, anger, and other emotions also accompanied the experiences. Penfield concluded that the brain files experiences away, ready to be recalled whenever they are needed.*

Modern brain researchers have gone well beyond these early discoveries. As Chapter 3 will show you, the various parts of the brain control a number of specific behaviors. But no single area of the brain has been pinpointed as the location of conscious thought and feeling.

The Process of Consciousness

Consciousness doesn't lend itself to easy definition. But if you're aware of what is going on around you right now and you're aware of yourself as a person, you're experiencing consciousness. Keep in mind, however, that consciousness is a process, not a "thing." So many individual events in the mind and body add up to consciousness that the best way to describe it is to experience it.

Imagine that you're out on the street, walking home from school. Suddenly, you hear a dog barking. Lips laid back, fangs gleaming, the brute runs directly toward you (see Figure 2.2). Your senses instantly send data to the brain about the sight, sound, and smell of the onrushing animal. Your brain interprets the incoming data and

---

*Based on Irwin Lausch, *Manipulation, Dangers and Benefits of Brain Research* (New York: Viking Press, 1974), pp. 59–61.

triggers a flurry of mental and physical responses.

1. Your *conscious mind* calculates the danger: How best can I handle the situation? Should I run or stay and fight? Past experiences with other dogs, your chances of picking up a weapon, your position relative to safety—the brain instantly evaluates all these. Within split seconds, you will make your decision.

2. At the same time, a part of your mind that lies outside your awareness, the *unconscious*, is also at work. Long-forgotten reactions to other dogs and other dangers remain in the unconscious and exert a powerful influence on the conscious mind. You won't be directly aware of these messages. Nevertheless, practically all human behaviors are affected in some way by the experiences stored away in the unconscious.

Figure 2.2

If you were faced with this unexpected danger, how would you react? Fortunately, you wouldn't have to spend a long time making up your mind. Your brain would take over and prepare your body to fight or flee.

3. Meanwhile, the brain has also alerted your *autonomic nervous system*. This network of nerves operates without your awareness. It regulates such vital activities as breathing, heart rate, blood pressure, digestion, and hormone production. When danger threatens, the autonomic nervous system prepares your body for the emergency by shutting down some systems and activating others. Digestion, for example, will stop, while your heartbeat will quicken and muscles will receive extra supplies of sugar. Once you've decided what to do, your body will be prepared to carry out your orders.

Luckily, your consciousness doesn't need to remain so intensely alert at all times. You've probably realized already that you can think about Friday's dance, chew gum, watch television, and pet your cat—all at the same time. For maximum efficiency, however, you must bring yourself to full alertness. This means that you concentrate your consciousness on the problem or activity at hand, whether it's pouring a glass of milk, reading a psychology book, or escaping from an angry dog.

SECTION CHECKUP

1 Imagine yourself walking through a forest. Just as you step over a log, you see a snake, coiled and ready to strike. Describe the reactions of your mind and body to this unexpected danger.

2 What is the basis for Wilder Penfield's conclusion that almost every life experience is filed away in the brain?

3 What does the psychologist mean by consciousness?

2.2 WHAT ROLE DO SENSORY EXPERIENCE AND PERCEPTION PLAY IN BRINGING ORDER TO A CONFUSING WORLD?

Imagine being bitten by a mosquito. Psychologists refer to the bite as a stimulus. The itching that follows is called a sensory experience. Thus, any event from the outside world that affects your mind and body is a *stimulus* (plural *stimuli*). The sensation created by a stimulus is a *sensory experience*. A particular stimulus does not always create the same sensory experience, however. The taste of your first bite of hamburger when you're hungry (the stimulus) would create a sensory experience far different from the taste of your tenth hamburger that same afternoon.

By now you've probably looked at Figure 2.3, the unusual stimulus printed on this page. What did you see when you first looked at it? Some people see two black faces. Others see a white vase. Even as you study the drawing, the faces may abruptly change into the vase—and vice versa. The process of making sense out of a stimulus and your sensory experience of it (in this case, deciding between the figure and its background) is called *perception*. Psychologists use this illusion to show how the brain depends upon visual clues to make sense out of confusing situations. But this drawing doesn't give you the clues you need to tell which is foreground and which is background. As a result, your perception of the figure varies.

Forming gestalts

When the brain makes a meaningful pattern out of many bits of sensation, the process is called a *gestalt* (from a German word that means "shape, figure"). If your brain "sees" a design made up of apparently random dots, for example, it immediately tries to organize the dots into a whole picture (see Figure 2.4). This need to make sense out of visual sensations probably explains why some people dislike abstract art. They look at the streaks, dribbles, and patches of color without finding a pattern they recognize. Their inability to perceive meaning upsets them; they prefer art that they can see and "understand."

Perceptual inference

By the time that you are a few years old, your brain has a good idea of how the world should look and act. For that reason, your brain tends to build its gestalts on the basis of past experience. Psychologists call this

Figure 2.3

Without clearcut clues as to which is figure and which is background, you see either the vase—or the two faces. Now look steadily at this figure-ground illusion for a moment or two. Watch the two figures switch back and forth as your perception changes.

Figure 2.4

Can you make a pattern out of these apparently random dots? From the moment you began looking at them, your brain started trying to organize them into a meaningful pattern—a *gestalt*. Now step back a distance from the page, and the picture will take shape.

reason, you don't feel surprised when a tiny dot on the horizon turns into a full-sized automobile as it speeds toward you. In fact, you don't even think of the car as growing in size. You know how large automobiles should be when seen at various distances.

By contrast, the Mbuti pygmies of Africa have not developed this form of perceptual inference. The Mbuti live in deep forest and may go a lifetime without seeing an open plain. A group of Mbuti hunters were once taken to a game preserve where they saw elephants grazing in the distance. "Elephants the size of ants!" they marveled. Only as they moved toward the animals did they realize how the unfamiliar perspective had fooled their perception.

Expectations affect what you "see"

Perception can also be influenced by what you expect to see. Look at the drawing of the old woman in Figure 2.5. Can you see her? Now look at the picture again, but this time find the old woman's daughter. She's really there! If you have trouble finding her, note that the eye, nose, and chin of the old

Figure 2.5

process *perceptual inference*. Imagine yourself walking into a room. You look around for a place to sit down. There's a chair, but you can see only three of its legs. Would you hesitate to sit on it? Probably not. Perceptual inference tells you that chairs have four legs and that the chair is probably safe to sit on. If you've ever mistaken a glass of buttermilk for regular milk, however, you know that perceptual inferences can't always be trusted.

Despite an occasional mishap, perceptual inference does help you handle situations that otherwise would confuse you. For example, you've learned that objects generally remain constant in size. For that

woman also form the ear, chin, and neck of the younger woman.

Did you see both women? If you tell your friends that they'll see the daughter first, they'll probably have trouble finding the old woman. Their expectations will affect what they see. Try this simple experiment and see what happens.

Now, see what tricks your expectations play on your perception when you look at the Roman arch in Figure 2.6. Is something wrong? Try to find the top of the middle column! You can see why this figure is called an "impossible figure" illusion. Your eye picks up information that conflicts with your expectations about the central column. As a result, your brain can't make any sense out of the data it receives.

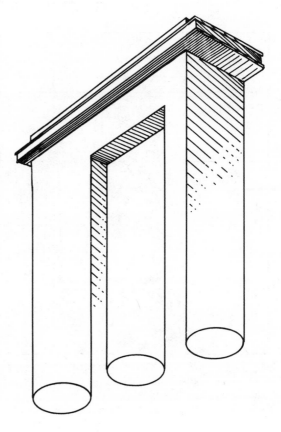

Figure 2.6

How can a Roman arch have three columns at the base and only two at the top? In reality it can't, of course. But in this drawing, the conflicting information given to the brain by the realistic perspective makes it seem possible—until you try to check it out!

SECTION CHECKUP

1 Name some of the stimuli of which you are aware at this moment. Why do some of them seem stronger or more important than others?

2 Define the term *perception*. Why would two people have different perceptions of the same event?

3 How does perceptual inference affect your ability to interpret objects and events in the world around you?

2.3 WHAT ROLE DO SLEEP AND DREAMS PLAY IN YOUR LIFE?

Consciousness exists in forms other than your normal waking state. *Altered states of consciousness* (called *ASC*s) take you into a world where sensations and perceptions are no longer restricted by everyday reality. During dreams, for example, you might fly with eagles, meet a long-dead friend, or struggle to escape the grasp of a monster. Hypnosis and the state induced by certain drugs are also altered states of consciousness that "turn off" your everyday waking consciousness.

Defining sleep and dreams

Sleep and dreams provide by far your most common ASC experiences. Although much mystery still surrounds the role of sleep and

THE FOUR STAGES OF SLEEP

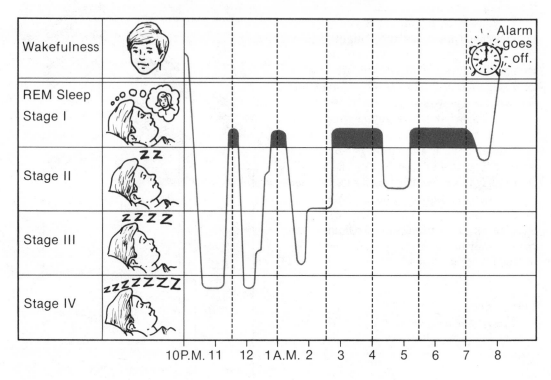

Figure 2.7

Each sleep cycle tends to last about ninety minutes. Dreaming, as shown by the shaded areas, takes place during stage-I sleep. Some REM (dreaming) sleep is possible during each cycle, but dream periods become longer during the early morning hours.

dreams in your life, both are now being studied in great depth. A special device called an *electroencephalograph (EEG) machine* helps scientists carry on this research. The EEG machine translates your brain waves into visible patterns that can be seen on a screen or printed on a piece of paper.

Sleep stages. When you fall asleep, your body shuts down some of its busy activities. You become less sensitive to outside stimuli, and your brain waves (measured in cycles per second) slow down from their usual 10–28 cps. Studies of the patterns of these brain waves on an EEG machine show that sleep is made up of four different levels, or stages (see Figure 2.7). About 75 percent

of your sleep time is spent in Stages II, III, and IV. During Stage IV sleep, brain waves are reduced to about three cps. Sleep-walking and talking, if they occur at all, usually happen during this deep sleep.

REM sleep and dreams. Stage I sleep, unlike the other three stages, is marked by brain-wave activity remarkably similar to normal consciousness. During Stage I sleep, your eyes dart back and forth beneath your closed eyelids as if they are following some interesting event. These *rapid eye movements* give Stage I its name: *REM sleep.* If someone wakes you up during a period of REM sleep, you'll probably remember that you've been dreaming, for dreams occur only during REM sleep. As Figure 2.7

shows, dream periods occur about every 90 minutes during the night but increase in length toward morning.

Dreams themselves are "stories" that your brain makes up during sleep. Like any good story, dreams include visual images, characters, and emotions. But like a badly edited film, dreams often ignore the rules of reality. They jump back and forth in time, invent new identities for old friends, and frequently defy common sense. Your body, however, moves very little during even the most active dreams. Hormone levels rise as if you were actually taking part in an emotional experience, but the brain "turns off" your muscles so that they won't act out those spectacular chase scenes.

Much of the data about dreams has come from special research laboratories. In these labs, volunteers sleep and dream while scientists observe and record their reactions. EEG machines record brain-wave patterns, and cameras record REM sleep and other physical movements. This research has enabled scientists to collect some useful information about dreams.

1. Everyone dreams, every night. You may not always remember your dreams, but dreams occupy about 18–33 percent of your total sleep time.

2. Most dreams run about the same length of time that the dreamed events would take in real life. This finding disproves an older belief that even long dreams take place in only a few seconds.

3. Most dreams deal with common, everyday events. Toward morning, your dreams tend to become more exciting and easier to remember.

4. Most people do dream in color, but only about one third of the time.

5. Dreams of anxiety or anger occur more frequently than those of love or contentment. This suggests that dreams may be your mind's way of working out problems or of calling problems to your attention.

6. Every dream has a meaning. You may find it difficult to interpret your dreams, but they have useful things to tell you if you make the effort to understand them.

Importance of sleep and dreams

Some years ago, a New York disc jockey sat in a window of a Times Square store and somehow kept himself awake for eight straight days. The stunt raised money for charity. But it also showed that lack of sleep can interfere with normal behavior. As the days went by, the disc jockey became irritable. His behavior grew increasingly confused, and he suffered memory lapses. Even after catching up on his sleep, the disc jockey went through a three-month period of depression.

In another experiment, subjects linked to EEG machines were awakened whenever they fell into REM sleep. On the first night, the subjects' attempts to dream jumped from the usual four or five to ten or more. By the fifth night, their dream attempts had skyrocketed to thirty or more. During the daytime, the subjects all showed increased irritability, anxiety, tension, and lack of concentration.

Sleep and dreams are essential to your physical and mental well-being because they perform the following functions.

1. Sleep provides a time for the body to do its own housekeeping. Cells are replaced or repaired. Waste materials are cleaned out. The brain apparently also uses the time to repair (but not replace) individual cells and the networks of nerve cells that make human behavior possible.

2. Dreams serve as a safety valve. Buried emotions can be bought to your consciousness—although the unconscious usually disguises these strong feelings. If you couldn't dream (as in the experiment mentioned earlier), these buried emotions would begin to intrude on your consciousness in the form of hallucinations and fantasies.

ANN FARADAY:

DREAMS CAN REVEAL HIDDEN TALENTS, BURIED BEAUTY

Ann Faraday (1935–), a British psychologist, has made dream analysis more than a favorite tool of psychotherapy. With two successful books, *Dream Power* and *The Dream Game,* she awoke public interest in the use of dreams for personal insight and problem solving.

Dr. Faraday explains that she became interested in dreams early in life:

> My night life as a child was full of excitement, drama, and terror, but I could never get my parents or teachers to take my nocturnal adventures seriously. Just dreams, they said. But I knew better, and decided to become a psychologist in order to explore the mysteries of the other world which manifests during sleep.

In time, Dr. Faraday began to form her own dream study groups. These groups adopted the American Indian motto, "Respect your brothers' dreams." Her interest in dreams has also made Dr. Faraday into something of a crusader. She writes, "In truth, dreams are even more powerful revealers of hidden talents, buried beauty, and unsuspected creative energy. They urge us to recognize that we are actually a lot nicer than we have hitherto realized. . . ."

Dr. Faraday says that she is amazed at the inconsistency of dream psychologists who insist that dreams reveal a person's true colors only when the insight is a negative one:

When the proverbial Plain Jane dreams of herself as beautiful and successful, her dreams are dismissed as mere wish fulfillment, attempts to compensate for the harsh realities of life. When George, the garage mechanic, dreams of winning the Grand Prix, he is told to come down to earth and stop indulging in Walter Mitty daydreams. But a dream is very different from a daydream . . . and my experience has shown time and time again that such dreams are actually *intimations* of what the dreamer might achieve if he made the effort in waking life. . . . Jane may never become a beauty queen, nor will George necessarily be a champion. But by enabling us to savor the sweet smell of success, as it were, dreams like these move us to realize our undeveloped potentialities.

Think of a recent dream of your own. Can you find any insights that might make your life healthier or happier, as Dr. Faraday suggests?

3. Both sleep and dreams give the brain time to sort out and store away the memories gathered during the day. In one study, researchers checked students taking an intensive language course. The students who were learning fastest showed an increase in REM sleep. The slower students didn't change their REM patterns. Perhaps the more you learn, the more you need dreams to lock the new information into long-term memory.

Freud's theory of dreams

Ancient people viewed dreams as messages from the gods. Tribal leaders often based important decisions on the interpretation of dreams offered by priests or tribal elders. Modern interpretation of dreams, however, began with Sigmund Freud. Dr. Freud called dreams "the royal road to a knowledge of the unconscious activities of the mind." He believed that during sleep the unconscious calls attention to your deepest needs. Dreams permit people to satisfy wishes and desires they may not consciously know they have. Freud spoke of this as "wish fulfillment." But the wishes of the unconscious are so powerful and disturbing, he went on, that they would interfere with your sleep if they were not disguised in symbols. These symbols must be interpreted before the true meaning of a dream can be discovered.

If you dream of getting a good report card, for example, Freud would probably say that it's because you unconsciously need the praise from your parents that goes with better grades. Many dreams are seen as being sexual in nature. Freud thought that childhood feelings of jealousy, self-love, and the desire to hold onto one's parents show clearly through the symbolism found in dreams.

Using dreams creatively

Today's dream experts do not deny Freud's ideas, but they have gone beyond his emphasis on wish fulfillment. Properly interpreted, they say, dreams can add insight, beauty, and creative energy to your life. As an example, Roy T.'s dream shows the here-and-now aspect of dreams:

Roy T., a high-school senior, dreamed that he was playing basketball. In real life, Roy plays basketball poorly, but in the dream he dribbled like a pro and threw in baskets from all over the court. Soon, however, every move he made drew a whistle from the referee. He looked to see who was calling these unfair fouls. To his surprise,

the referee was his mother. The game went on, but now every time he moved he heard the shrill blast of his mother's whistle.

Can you see any meaning in Roy's dream? At first glance, it doesn't make much sense. Roy doesn't play basketball very often, nor does his mother referee basketball games. So, on the surface, the dream seems empty of meaning. But as he thought about the dream, Roy remembered that his mother and he had been arguing about his plans for the summer. Roy planned to backpack through Canada with a friend, but his mother wanted him to stay home and work in the family business. As the dream illustrated so dramatically, she was "blowing the whistle" on his freedom to "hit a basket" with his summer plans. After analyzing the dream, Roy decided that the conflict had to be resolved. He sat down with his mother and told her how important the trip was to him. Together they worked out a compromise work schedule. When June came, Roy was able to leave on his backpacking adventure.

Manifest and latent dream content. Most dreams can be studied at two levels, as in Roy's basketball dream. The obvious, surface level is called the *manifest content*. The underlying, symbolic meanings are referred to as the *latent content* of the dream. In Roy's case, the latent content related to his conflict over the trip.

A second example will illustrate this point. Christie R. woke up from her dream feeling quite alarmed. In the dream, she had seen her garden flowers slowly wither and die from lack of water. She had rushed to water them, but it was too late.

To analyze that dream, Christie first looked at the manifest content. Were any of her plants dying because of lack of water, weeding, or fertilizer? If so, she could take the warning to heart and do whatever was necessary to save her flowers. But Christie's garden was doing fine. So she turned to the latent content. What could the garden symbolize? She decided that it must refer to some aspect of her life that she had been ignoring. As she looked over the possibilities, she realized that since she had started dating Bill, she had not been spending much time with her best friend, Gale. As the dream told her, the friendship would wither and die if she continued to neglect it. This analysis felt so right that Christie immediately picked up the phone and made plans to see Gale that afternoon.

Steps in analyzing your dreams. As valuable as your dreams can be, you must "catch" them first. That takes patience and sometimes requires that you rearrange your sleeping habits (see Figure 2.8). Next you must relate the dream to your own life. Dream dictionaries, which tell you that a gun equals power or a journey means a change in your life, simply can't substitute for your own insights. To analyze a dream, try the following five-step method. It should help you with all but the most difficult dreams.

1. *Check for warnings.* Begin by examining the manifest content. Is the dream telling you about something that needs immediate attention? A dream about your brakes failing while you're speeding downhill could be a signal from your unconscious that your brakes need fixing before they cause an accident.

2. *Relate the dream to recent events.* Most dreams are triggered by something that's going on in your life right now. If you can match your dreams to those current happenings, your analysis will begin to make sense. For example, Pat dreamed about seeing a beautiful city far away, splendid on its high hill. As she tried to get there, she found obstacles in her path, but the beauty of the city drew her onward. Since Pat was then trying to choose between college and a good job offer, she guessed that her dream related to that decision. When she suddenly realized that the "city" resembled the college campus she had visited a week earlier, she understood the dream. Her unconscious believed that college was the best choice for her, despite the financial hardships it would cause.

3. *Interpret the people and symbols.* When your unconscious creates a dream, it often conceals actual people and events in symbolic form. Your jealousy may become a green-eyed monster; your worry about grades may become a run-in with a traffic officer; guilt feelings about staying out too late can turn a parent into a prison warden. If the meaning of a person or object isn't obvious to you, think about possible symbolic meanings. A dream of falling, for example, could signify a feeling that you're "falling" in your personal life—falling in love, falling from grace, or whatever. Watch for puns as well. The unconscious apparently loves word games and riddles. If your dream shows you stuck in a giant honey jar, perhaps it means that your real-life "honey" is sticking too close to you.

4. *Examine the dream's feeling tone.* What feelings did the dream leave you with? Were you excited, depressed, uncaring, happy? This "feeling tone" can give you a useful clue in working out the dream's meaning. The heart-thumping fright that goes with a slow-motion chase in a typical nightmare, for example, suggests anxiety or fear about that unknown thing chasing you. A vivid dream of warfare, however, if accompanied by strong feelings of determination, may only reflect your decision to "fight through" some area of conflict in your life.

5. *Pull it all together.* Dreams don't come to waste your time. They bring fresh meanings, warnings, insights. You'll know that you've analyzed your dream properly when it makes sense in understanding or doing something constructive. Assume that in your dream you've been walking a dog on a leash. In your analysis, it becomes apparent that the dog is really a friend of yours. At the moment the symbol's meaning comes clear, you'll probably feel an "ah-so" reaction (as in, "Ah, so that's it"). Now the dream has done its work. It's up to you to decide whether you're going to stop treating

Figure 2.8

DREAM CATCHING: TEN WAYS TO HOLD ONTO YOUR DREAMS

Some people remember their dreams without effort, but others must try every trick in the book. Ann Faraday suggests ten steps to catching your dreams for later analysis:

1 Always keep by your bedside pen and paper or a tape recorder, if one's available. You can remember a dream clearly one minute, but if it's not written down, it will be gone the next.

2 Have a dim light or flashlight available that you can switch on without moving from your bed.

3 Tell yourself several times before falling asleep, "I will wake up from a dream tonight," or "I will remember one of my dreams tonight." The words aren't critical; the suggestion is.

4 If you're a heavy sleeper, arrange to be awakened several times during the night. A gentle alarm clock or a cooperative family member can do the job. Try this technique about every two hours, starting three or four hours after you've gone to sleep. You can't guarantee catching an REM period, but the odds are in your favor if you stick it out.

5 When you awaken with a dream in mind, sit up *very gently* and switch the dim light on. If you jolt yourself into wakefulness, you may lose the dream.

6 Write or record the dream immediately, in as much detail as possible. Try not to doze while you're doing this.

7 Also write down conscious associations that the dream triggers: events, feelings, insights as to the meaning of the dream symbols. These will be helpful when you begin analyzing the dream.

8 If you wake up in the morning with a dream in mind, write it down before you get out of bed. If you wait, you'll probably lose it.

9 As soon as possible, that day if you can, work on the analysis, using the five-step process described on pages 42–43.

10 Date your dreams along with your interpretations and keep them in a "dream diary" for later reference. As time goes by, this diary will provide useful data for working on new dreams and for clarifying your feelings about people and events in your life.

your friend like a dog. (Figure 2.9 illustrates six common dream symbols whose meanings tend to be alike for everyone.)

SECTION CHECKUP

1 Why are sleep and dreams necessary to physical and mental health? What happens if you don't get enough of either?

2 What does the psychologist mean by REM sleep?

3 How can dreams be used to enrich your life? Describe the five steps suggested for dream analysis?

Figure 2.9

COMMON DREAM SYMBOLS

Falling

People "fall" from grace or "fall" in the eyes of loved ones. Falling grades or a sense of falling out of touch with someone can trigger this type of dream.

Flying

The "feeling tone" of a flying dream is important. If you've sensed a feeling of power and freedom, the dream says you're "flying high" over some success in your life. Flying to escape something leaves you feeling upset and suggests a problem you can't "rise above."

Nudity

Dreams of nudity in public places often represent anxiety about a coming event where you might appear "naked" before others. If people don't notice your condition, your anxiety probably isn't necessary.

Examinations

Examination dreams in which you find yourself unprepared for the test can be warnings, particularly if you're in school. Otherwise, they tell you to get ready for the other "tests" that people face in everyday life.

Losing money

These are often warning dreams. Check your wallet, purse, or other valuables. Otherwise, think about what else you may be losing— a friend, a goal in life, a part of your identity. The loss may not be a bad thing but needs to be faced and resolved.

Finding money or valuables

Dreams of finding valuables usually mean that you should go ahead with some plan or purchase. Such dreams during a "down" period in your life can also be reassurance that you are really a person of value.

2.4 WHAT IS HYPNOSIS?

You've probably heard of the fakirs (magicians) of India who perform amazing tricks with a piece of rope. Andrija Puharich, a medical doctor and well-known researcher of psychic events, describes one such demonstration. According to the reports of several hundred onlookers, the fakir first threw a rope into the air, where it stayed, unsupported. Then a small boy climbed the rope and disappeared. Next, parts of the boy's cut-up body fell to the ground. The fakir put the pieces into a basket. Holding the basket, he climbed the rope. When he came down again, he had the boy with him, alive and well. The witnesses, including the scientists who arranged the demonstration, agreed with this description.

A motion picture of the event, however, showed that the fakir simply walked into the center of the crowd and threw his rope into the air. The rope dropped to the ground. The film then showed the magician and the boy standing quietly in the center of the crowd until the demonstration was over. Two hundred witnesses to the contrary, the rope did not stay in the air, nor did the boy climb it!*

Since nothing magical took place, the scientists looked to hypnosis for an explanation. They knew that under the altered state of consciousness created by the hypnotic effect, the mind accepts the impossible without question. Stage hypnotists can convince you that Elvis Presley is in the audience or that little green Martians have just landed on your shoulder. But hypnosis has uses far beyond entertainment.

Hypnotism defined

Hypnotism is an ASC in which the subject enters into a state of increased suggestibility. If you were hypnotized, you would focus your attention completely on

*Andrija Puharich, *Beyond Telepathy* (Garden City, NY: Doubleday, 1973), pp. 33–34.

the hypnotist. In this state you would accept almost any suggestion that the hypnotist gave you. In your condition of fixed attention, observers might think that you were asleep or in a trance. In actual fact, you would feel quite awake and in command of yourself. But if the hypnotist told you that you were playing baseball, you'd pick up an imaginary bat and swing lustily at an imaginary ball!

Achieving a hypnotic state is relatively simple. First, you must want to be hypnotized. Horror stories to the contrary, you normally cannot be hypnotized if you are not willing to cooperate with the hypnotist. If you agree to be hypnotized, the hypnotist will ask you to stare at an object (a swinging coin, perhaps) or a point in space. Then you will hear the hypnotist's soothing voice say over and over, "You are growing sleepy . . . you are feeling very relaxed. . . ." As your hypnotic state deepens, you will receive further instructions to obey the commands of the hypnotist. Even in a full hypnotic state, however, an EEG machine would not detect in your brain waves any great change from a normal state of consciousness.

Uses of hypnotism

Hypnotism is an ancient art that has recently gained new attention from both medical doctors and psychologists. The "tricks" performed by stage hypnotists have real-life applications that can improve both physical and mental health.

Medical uses of hypnotism. One of the first medical uses of hypnotism was to block off pain during surgery or illness. Today, doctors are using hypnosis to reduce or eliminate pain in dentistry and childbirth, especially in cases where the usual pain-killing drugs cannot be used. Hypnosis also seems to be helpful in treating problems that do not have a specific physical cause. Warts and allergies, for example, sometimes clear up "magically" when the patient is hypnotized and told that a simple medicine will make them disappear.

Psychological uses of hypnotism. Hypnosis gives psychologists an effective technique for helping people. Under hypnosis, for example, a patient can talk about a serious emotional problem that is normally too painful to discuss. Phobic fears, stammering, and insomnia have all been successfully treated with hypnosis. Age regression can also be achieved under hypnosis, allowing patients to remember childhood events that contribute to adult difficulties.

Posthypnotic suggestion. A hypnotist may plant an idea under hypnosis that stays with the subject afterward. This *posthypnotic suggestion* works well when subjects try to stop harmful habits such as overeating, drinking, or smoking. Smokers, for example, can be told under hypnosis that their cigarettes will have a bad taste. If that suggestion carries over into everyday life, the cigarettes really will taste bad. And if this posthypnotic suggestion is reinforced by a strong desire to quit, the smoking addiction can be broken.

Some psychologists also teach self-hypnosis as a means of improving performance in a given field. Subjects learn to relax, give themselves suggestions leading to greater self-confidence, and form a positive mental image of what they want to do. Baseball players, for example, have used self-hypnosis to raise their batting average by increasing self-confidence and concentration. You should remember, however, that hypnosis cannot give you abilities or skills you don't have. If you don't have the training, coordination, and experience, no amount of hypnosis will make you a .400 hitter. Self-hypnosis can also be used to relieve pain (see Figure 2.10).

A warning about hypnosis

Trained hypnotists know how to ensure the safety of their subjects. Amateur hypnotists, however, never know when they will stumble into some dark and painful area within their subject's mind. Such exploration can cause great harm to a person's emotional health. Hypnotists also must be careful not to pass on their own values and ideas to their highly suggestible subjects.

Another precaution should be noted. Many people believe that hypnotic subjects won't do anything that they wouldn't do in real life. That block does exist, but a clever hypnotist can get around it. Put mild-mannered Joe under hypnosis, for example, and tell him to shoot the next person who walks into the room. Normally, Joe will resist that suggestion to the point of ending his hypnotic state. But tell Joe that the person he's to shoot is a maniac who has just killed ten children—and Joe might very well pull the trigger.

Figure 2.10

Is fire walking a trick or a miracle? Neither, say scientists, who believe that fire walkers put themselves into a hypnotic state that prevents them from feeling the heat or pain.

Pro & Con: SETTING THE RECORD STRAIGHT ABOUT HYPNOSIS

Hypnosis seems to stand with one foot in its mysterious past and the other in modern science. Superstitions and misinformation about hypnotists and their seeming power to command people's minds alarm the uninformed. This Pro & Con matches up some of the most common false beliefs with the actual facts.

False beliefs

1 A hypnotist has special, mysterious powers that no one else can use. Hypnotism is probably a form of magic.

2 Only people with low intelligence or with little willpower can be hypnotized.

3 The majority of people cannot be hypnotized.

4 Being hypnotized means that the subject becomes unconscious or falls into a sleep-like trance.

5 Subjects always tell the truth while under hypnosis.

6 It is almost impossible to wake up someone who is in a hypnotic state.

7 Hypnotists can make their subjects do anything while under hypnosis, no matter how bizarre or dangerous the order.

Facts

1 Hypnotists do not possess any mystical powers. A hypnotist is merely someone who has learned to lead people into a state where they will accept almost any suggestion made by the hypnotist.

2 Creative people with high intelligence make the best subjects for hypnosis.

3 About nine out of ten people can be hypnotized. The best subjects are those who have a good reason to undergo hypnosis.

4 Even in a deep state of hypnosis, subjects remain aware of everything that goes on around them. What seems like a trance is their total concentration on the hypnotist.

5 People under hypnosis try to tell the truth. But they are so anxious to please the hypnotist that they will make up answers to fill in gaps in their memories.

6 Being hypnotized is similar to being totally absorbed in a book or movie. Either the hypnotist or the subject can end the hypnotic state at will.

7 Except in special circumstances, people cannot be made to do anything under hypnosis that violates their morals. Hypnotized subjects will usually refuse orders that could cause mental or physical harm to themselves or to others.

Would you have answered "false" to all seven statements listed under *False beliefs*?

From the book *Helping Yourself With Self-Hypnosis* by Frank S. Caprio, M.D. and Joseph R. Berger. © 1963 by Prentice-Hall, Inc. Published by Prentice-Hall, Inc., Englewood Cliffs, N.J. 07632.

2.5 WHAT EFFECT DO PSYCHOACTIVE DRUGS HAVE ON BEHAVIOR?

Is this the Space Age . . . or the Spaced-Out Age? Never before have so many people swallowed, snorted, shot, smoked, or otherwise turned on to so many *psychoactive (mind-altering) drugs.*

Many well-meaning adults have cried that all recreational drugs are evil, that all users are doomed. And too many others have proclaimed that psychoactive drugs are the only route to happiness in a crazy world. Obviously, neither extreme makes perfect sense. But psychologists believe that young people who examine the evidence will understand that experimenting with psychoactive drugs involves great psychological, medical, and legal risks.

That doesn't mean, of course, that you shouldn't take aspirin, penicillin, or other medical drugs designed to treat an illness. But what will you do the next time someone offers you a drink, pill, or joint "just for kicks"? The following questions and answers may help you make a healthy decision.

QUESTION: What effect do psychoactive drugs have on perception?

ANSWER: To a greater or lesser degree, all psychoactive drugs alter the user's perception of reality. Stimulants, for example, cause temporary feelings of alertness and well-being. That's why football players take "uppers" before a game. They believe the stimulant will improve their performance and reduce the pain of injuries. Hallucinogens such as LSD and PCP, however, lead users into a world beyond the reach of the ordinary senses. Tim G., for example, thought he'd achieved "a mystical sense of unity with the universe" the first time he tried LSD. A later "trip," however, ended in the hospital. While under the influence of the drug, Tim experienced the frightening illusion that his flesh was rotting off his bones. Even the artistic or religious insights gained through drug use fade as the drugs wear off. Artists often return from an ASC only to discover that their "great art" actually amounts to little more than scribbles.

QUESTION: Well, don't adults "turn on" with alcohol and nicotine, and "turn off" with sleeping pills and tranquilizers?

ANSWER: There's some truth to that. Public-health experts admit that alcohol and tobacco are the two biggest drug problems in the United States today. The real point is that *no recreational drug does your body any good!* The fact that adults use alcohol or sleeping pills doesn't make it logical for young people to try marijuana or PCP. Prolonged misuse of drugs can cause damage ranging from minor emotional problems to mental breakdowns and from addiction to incurable illness. In addition, possession of most recreational drugs can send you to jail. That gives you at least two practical replies to the argument that every generation should have its own choice of how it will "turn on" (see Figure 2.11).

Figure 2.11

QUESTION: Did you say that tobacco is a *drug* problem? I've heard about lung cancer, but that's a medical matter. Next you'll be telling me that coffee is a dangerous drug!

ANSWER: Surely you've seen coffee drinkers tremble while they're waiting for their first cup in the morning? The caffeine in coffee, tea, and cola drinks causes a dependency habit similar to an addiction. Overuse of caffeine can also cause nervousness, heart damage, and illnesses of the digestive system.

But nicotine is a more serious matter. In large doses, nicotine is a poison. In smaller amounts, it causes *psychological dependence*, that is, smokers become emotionally hooked on tobacco even though their bodies may not become physically addicted. People smoke because tobacco stimulates the central nervous system and helps distract their attention from their problems. Because of the life-threatening lung problems caused by excessive smoking, the U.S. government has ordered tobacco companies to print warnings on every package of cigarettes. Many public places have been declared "no smoking" areas. Even so, cigarette sales remain high. The lure of tobacco continues to tempt in particular young people, who see smoking as a sign of growing up.

Still, people don't lose their grip on reality when they drink coffee or smoke a cigarette.

QUESTION: Well, maybe so, but I've seen drunks who don't seem to be in touch with the real world. Are you going to say that it's worse to smoke a few joints than to have a couple of cocktails before dinner?

ANSWER: Honest psychologists would not say that. They do say that taking a drink is like playing Russian roulette. Statistics show that one out of every ten persons who take that first drink will go on to have a problem with alcohol. Six million Americans are alcoholics, powerless to stop drinking without assistance. Drinking helps kill 25,000 people and injures a million others on the highways each year. About 50 percent of the people in prison committed their crimes while drunk. And who can measure the suffering alcohol brings to the families of alcoholics, not to mention innocent bystanders?

QUESTION: I know a lot of people who drink. Are they in danger of becoming alcoholics?

ANSWER: There's a long road between social drinking and alcoholism. But as people continue drinking, their bodies require greater and greater amounts of alcohol to achieve the results they desire. That's called building up a tolerance to the drug. Alcohol is a depressant. It relaxes the brain centers that normally control social behavior. If people seem happier and more active when they're drinking, that's because their inhibitions have been lowered. Long-term heavy drinking causes damage to the liver and to the stomach. If alcoholics don't die in an accident, they usually die of medical problems brought on by their drinking.

QUESTION: On those terms, smoking marijuana is practically harmless, isn't it? So why do some people get so upset about a little grass?

ANSWER: If you mean, is marijuana as dangerous as excessive drinking, the answer is "no." But if you mean, can marijuana be abused, the answer is "yes." In moderate doses, marijuana (sometimes known by its scientific name, *cannabis*) can produce a feeling of inner peace, a distortion of time and space, a sense of hilarity, and free play of the imagination. But some users experience mild depression or feelings of persecution. Attempts to measure marijuana's effects have been frustrated by the unpredictable reactions of pot smokers. Some experiments using a substitute that smelled like marijuana, for example, produced the same reactions as did the real stuff.

QUESTION: What about all the claims that marijuana will ruin your life?

ANSWER: No studies thus far have shown marijuana to be addictive. Some people do develop a psychological dependence. Though many criminals use marijuana, there is no evidence that it causes crime—other than being in violation of laws against buying and selling it. Don't forget, however, that marijuana affects your sense of time and space relationships. People who are stoned shouldn't drive.

QUESTION: Does smoking pot lead to harder drugs?

ANSWER: The results of research are incomplete, but only a small percentage of marijuana users go on to narcotic drugs such as heroin. The catch is that many heroin users *have* used marijuana, although they're more likely to have started with alcohol than marijuana.

QUESTION: Does that mean that you're not against the moderate use of marijuana?

ANSWER: Not so fast! *No recreational drug is good for you.* Marijuana seems to be relatively safe, but doctors are still looking at the possibility that it can lower the body's ability to resist infection and to give birth to healthy children. Confirmed "pot heads" also tend to drift along without concern for anything except their immediate needs. Heavy users find it difficult to concentrate, to memorize, to solve problems. They may neglect their personal appearance. Formerly active, ambitious young people "kick back" and watch the world go by without them.

QUESTION: OK, I'll think about that. But you haven't even mentioned the other psychoactive drugs. Every time I turn around someone has come up with a new way of getting high. Is there any way to make sense out of all those different drugs?

ANSWER: Figure 2.12 on pages 52–53 gives basic data about the common psychoactive drugs. These drugs fall into four categories. The first class includes the *depressants* (downers), such as alcohol, tranquilizers, and the barbiturates. These drugs lower the level of activity in the brain. This creates a brief feeling of peacefulness and well-being.

Next come the *stimulants* (uppers), which create feelings of optimism and energy by triggering high levels of activity in the nervous system. Typical stimulants include caffeine, nicotine, cocaine, and the amphetamines.

The *hallucinogens*, or *psychedelics*, alter the user's perception of reality. Under the influence of one of these drugs, the senses play tricks, and emotions are also affected. The hallucinogens alter reality according to the amount of the drug taken, plus the user's expectations. A dose that gives one person a wild trip may leave someone else unaffected. Common hallucinogens include LSD, marijuana, peyote, and STP.

Finally, the *narcotics* lead directly to addiction. Opium, heroin, morphine, and codeine all reduce pain, depress the nervous system, and give users a temporary feeling of euphoria (intense feelings of well-being). As the user gains tolerance to a beginning dose, the body demands greater and greater amounts of the drug. Drug addicts may do any-

thing to get a "fix," including robbery and prostitution. Once addicted, a user must go through painful withdrawal symptoms before the habit can be broken. Narcotics users run the risk of arrest, as well as serious illnesses from dirty needles, impure drugs, and poor health habits. Overdoses can cause death.

QUESTION: With all that risk, why do people still use psychoactive drugs?

ANSWER: Some do it for a thrill. Others try them because they can't say "no" to their friends. To another group, it might be a way of saying, "Look at me. I'm grown up!" Far too many people use drugs as a way of escaping from problems that seem impossible to overcome. But no matter what the reason, people who use drugs regularly are gambling with their lives. As with any major decision, you must weigh the benefits against the risks. Everyone who works in the drug field agrees on this one fact: The drug scene isn't worth the cost.

A popular slogan of the 1970s said, "Get high on life!" That's not such a bad idea. But for those who still want to experience an ASC, drugless methods are available. Some people "get high" on yoga, meditation, or deeply felt religious beliefs. An isolation tank can also provide you with a drugless ASC (see Figure 2.13), as can various self-awareness exercises (see Activities 1, 2, and 3, page 57). The choice is up to you.

SECTION CHECKUP

1 What is a psychoactive drug?

2 Name the four categories of psychoactive drugs. Give one or two examples of each category.

3 Summarize the arguments against drug use that are based on medical and psychological reasons.

Figure 2.12

DRUG IDENTIFICATION GUIDE

Symptoms of abuse

Drug name (Street names)	Drowsiness	Excitability	Irritability/restlessness	Anxiety	Euphoria	Depression	Hallucinations	Panic	Irrational behavior	Confusion	Changed speech	Impaired coordination	Constricted pupils	Dilated pupils
DEPRESSANTS														
Alcohol (beer, wine, booze, liquor, juice, suds, etc.)	•			•		•			•	•	•	•		
Barbiturates (yellows, reds, pinks, nimbles, red devils, etc.)	•				•				•	•	•	•	•	
STIMULANTS														
Amphetamines (pep pills, bennies, peaches, eye openers, dexies, etc.)		•	•	•		•	•	•						•
Amyl nitrite, butyl nitrite (poppers, Locker Room, Rush, etc.)	•			•										
Caffeine (coffee, java, tea, cola, No-Doz, etc.)		•												
Cocaine (snow, coke, flake, C, dust, candy, etc.)		•	•	•						•	•			•
Methamphetamine (speed, meth, splash, crystal, etc.)	•	•	•	•		•	•	•		•	•			•

Dangers of abuse

Drug name (Street names)	Space/time distortion	Physical dependence	Psychological dependence	Tolerance	Unconsciousness	Hepatitis	Psychosis	Death from withdrawal	Death from overdose
DEPRESSANTS									
Alcohol (beer, wine, booze, liquor, juice, suds, etc.)	•	•	•	•					•
Barbiturates (yellows, reds, pinks, nimbles, red devils, etc.)	•	•	•	•			•		•
STIMULANTS									
Amphetamines (pep pills, bennies, peaches, eye openers, dexies, etc.)		•	•		•	•			•
Amyl nitrite, butyl nitrite (poppers, Locker Room, Rush, etc.)		•		•					
Caffeine (coffee, java, tea, cola, No-Doz, etc.)			•						
Cocaine (snow, coke, flake, C, dust, candy, etc.)	•	•	•		•				•
Methamphetamine (speed, meth, splash, crystal, etc.)		•	•		•	•			•

Nicotine (cigarettes, tobacco, snuff, chewing tobacco, etc.)

HALLUCINOGENS

LSD (acid, cubes, pearly gates, wedding bells, sugar, etc.)

Marijuana (grass, pot, Acapulco gold, smoke, splim, jive, etc.)

Hashish (concentrated form of marijuana—hash, kif, soles, etc.)

Peyote (buttons, beans, mescal, cactus, hikori, tops, etc.)

Phencyclidine (PCP, angel dust, peace pill, DOA, hog, etc.)

STP (serenity, tranquility, peace, Dom, etc.)

NARCOTICS

Codeine (schoolboy, fours, etc.)

Heroin (snow, junk, horse, H, joy powder, skag, smack, thing, etc.)

Meperidine (Demerol, Dolantol, Dethidine, Isonipecaine, etc.)

Methadone (X dollies, amidone, dolls, Dolophine, etc.)

Morphine (M, dreamer, white stuff, Miss Emma, monkey, morf, hocus, etc.)

Figure 2.13

JOHN LILLY'S ISOLATION TANKS: CREATING A DRUGLESS ASC EXPERIENCE

Dr. John Lilly, a scientist famous for his work with dolphins, has designed a special isolation tank. There, cut off from contact with the usual stimuli, subjects float in a 94° solution of Epsom salts. No light enters the tank, and the only sound is that of a quiet pump. Under these conditions, Lilly finds, the mind is free to rest, solve problems, or explore its outermost limits.

Lilly has collected firsthand reports of experiences in the isolation tank. This one is by Tom Wilkes, dated May 3, 1975:

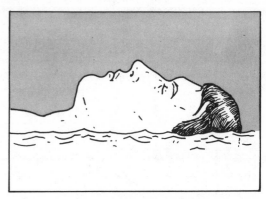

In the isolation tank, you are alone with your own mind.

> My first sensation was one of stuffiness, humid warm . . . floating. This soon changed to a cool secure feeling accompanied by the overwhelming rhythm of my heart beat; . . . I heard fragments of messages, voices saying things I could not decipher. This continued for an undetermined length of time until colored visual images would pass by me. These images were nonobjective and seemed to pulsate as they passed. The colors were generally magenta, blue or whitish.
>
> At some point, three female entities began questioning me. The feeling was warm and attracting. . . . I passed through them and there was a splash of golden light.

> At this point I became aware of three-dimensional spheres turning in several directions inside and outside of themselves, emitting a warm magenta glow. Their presence was awe-inspiring and produced a religious kind of emotional feeling. . . .

One woman, however, left after a few minutes, complaining of the "terrible noise" inside the tank. Lilly observed that the noise was inside her own head. Not everyone can take the tank. How do you think you would react?

John C. Lilly, *The Deep Self: Profound Relaxation and the Tank Isolation Technique* (New York: Simon & Schuster, 1977), pp. 252–253.

LOOKING BACK: A SUMMARY

1 Your eyes do not "see"; your ears do not "hear." Instead, the eyes and ears send data to the brain, where "seeing," "hearing," and other sensory experiences take place. Research shows that specific parts of the brain control specific behaviors. The brain, moreover, stores away all of your experiences, ready to be recalled when needed.

2 Consciousness is your normal waking state, when you're aware of yourself and the events around you. The unconscious contains stored experiences that you cannot readily remember, but it also exerts a powerful influence on your conscious behavior. When danger threatens, the autonomic nervous system prepares the body for emergency action. Consciousness operates during all your waking moments, but maximum efficiency comes only when you concentrate fully on the problem or activity at hand.

3 Physical events in the outside world that affect your mind or body are called *stimuli*. The feeling created by a stimulus is known as a *sensory experience*. The sense you make out of a stimulus and its accompanying sensory experience is called *perception*. Perceptual inference means that you interpret the world according to past experiences. Your expectations also affect your perception.

4 There are also altered states of consciousness, or ASCs. The most common ASC is sleep and dreams. Regular sleep and the dreams that come during sleep are apparently vital to your physical and emotional health. Sleep can be measured in four stages, according to the brain wave patterns typical of each stage. Stage I sleep, also called REM sleep because the eyes move rapidly under closed eyelids, coincides with dream periods.

5 Not only does everyone dream every night, but every dream also has a meaning. Freud thought of dreams as wish fulfillments, but many modern dream analysts believe that dreams bring useful messages from the unconscious about everyday problems. At the manifest level, a dream means exactly what it says. At the deeper, more complex latent level, the dream's meaning is concealed by symbols, puns, and disguises that make interpretation difficult.

6 Hypnosis is a state of heightened suggestibility in which a subject willingly accepts the direction of the hypnotist. Although the hypnotic state is considered an ASC, it does not involve sleep or a trance state. Once considered magical in nature, hypnosis today is used in medicine and in psychology. Doctors use it to block pain during medical procedures, and psychologists find it useful in helping people remember long-forgotten events or in overcoming fears and bad habits. Misuse of hypnosis can cause lasting harm to the subject.

7 Many people take psychoactive drugs to achieve an ASC. Doctors and psychologists agree that no behavior-altering drug does your body any good. While narcotics, marijuana, amphetamines, PCP, and other drugs receive most of the headlines, health experts agree that alcohol and tobacco are the country's biggest drug problems. Psychoactive drugs can be put into one of four categories: (*a*) depressants lower the level of activity in the brain; (*b*) stimulants raise the level of activity in the nervous system; (*c*) hallucinogens alter the user's perception of reality; and (*d*) narcotics cause a physical addiction to the drug.

8 A major controversy still rages over the use of marijuana. Studies have shown that marijuana is relatively safe and nonaddictive. Its long-range effects on the body, however, have still not been fully determined. Evidence shows that heavy use tends to interfere with people's ability to concentrate, memorize, and solve problems. For those young people who want to make something of themselves, marijuana probably works against high achievement in academics, athletics, and careers.

9 Despite the warnings against the use of psychoactive drugs, their use continues. Some people use them for thrills or as a means of rebellion. Others see in drugs a way of escaping from the problems of life. But one fact seems inescapable. No one uses drugs without taking the risk that the drug-induced ASC will become the most important thing in his or her life. Drugless ASC's can be obtained through meditation, religious experiences, and the use of isolation tanks.

PUTTING YOUR KNOWLEDGE TO WORK

Terms you should know

age regression

altered state of consciousness (ASC)

autonomic nervous system

conscious mind

consciousness

depressants

electroencephalograph (EEG) machine

gestalt

hallucinogens

hypnotism

latent content (of dreams)

manifest content (of dreams)

narcotics

perception

perceptual inference

posthypnotic suggestion

psychedelics

psychoactive drugs

psychological dependence

rapid eye movement (REM) sleep

sensory experience

stimulants

stimulus; stimuli

unconscious

Objective questions

1 You would be experiencing a state of normal consciousness if you were (*a*) drunk on beer (*b*) having a nightmare (*c*) hypnotized by a psychologist (*d*) frightened by the sudden sound of a car horn.

2 If you are chased by a barking dog, your reaction might very well be affected by long-forgotten childhood experiences. Those memories are stored in your (*a*) conscious mind (*b*) unconscious mind (*c*) autonomic nervous system (*d*) sensory experiences.

3 The process of making sense out of a stimulus and its sensory experience is called (*a*) consciousness (*b*) an ASC (*c*) perception (*d*) an optical illusion.

4 You don't feel surprised when a distant airplane increases in size as it comes toward you because (*a*) you've seen the effect of distance on the size of objects many times (*b*) perceptual inference allows you to accept the increase in size without conscious thought (*c*) your brain automatically interprets the size of objects in relation to their distance (*d*) all of these are explanations for this phenomenon.

5 The most common altered state of consciousness (ASC) that people experience is (*a*) the hypnotic state (*b*) the dream state (*c*) being under the influence of psychoactive drugs (*d*) daydreaming.

6 Which is *not* a true statement about dreams? (*a*) People need sleep, but they could get by very well without dreams. (*b*) Everyone dreams every night. (*c*) Dreams don't come to waste your time; they always have something to tell you. (*d*) A dream event lasts about as long as the same event would in real life.

7 If you have a dream in which you forget to take an important paper to school with you, what is the proper *first* step in interpreting the dream? (*a*) Try to interpret the symbolism represented by forgetting a homework paper. (*b*) Look for the wish-fulfillment aspects of the dream. (*c*) Check it out as a warning not to forget something you'll need at school that day. (*d*) Examine the dream's feeling tone.

8 Which of the following is a *true* statement about hypnotism? (*a*) A good hypnotist can turn you into an instant championship tennis player even if you've never picked up a racket before. (*b*) Since hypnotized subjects don't actually go to sleep, no harm can be done to them while they're in a hypnotic state. (*c*) Hypnotized subjects never remember anything that happened while they were under hypnosis. (*d*) Under hypnosis, you will accept as true any suggestion given to you by the hypnotist that doesn't run counter to your moral values.

9 As a drug, marijuana fits into the category of the (*a*) depressants (*b*) stimulants (*c*) hallucinogens (*d*) narcotics.

10 People who use psychoactive drugs (*a*) benefit their health (*b*) solve long-term problems (*c*) don't take psychological risks (*d*) pay a heavy price for their "kicks."

Discussion questions

1 How would you define the concept of "consciousness" to a ten-year-old? Since consciousness is so important, why is the psychologist also interested in the unconscious?

2 What is the difference between a stimulus and a sensory experience? Why would your perception of the taste of roast grasshopper be different from that of people who grow up eating grasshopper as a regular part of their diet?

3 Imagine that you've just had a dream in which you were looking frantically through hundreds of drawers for something you'd lost. Every drawer you opened was empty. Then, just as you were about to give up, you found the lost object in your own pocket. What steps would you go through to interpret this dream?

4 How would you explain hypnotism to a friend whose doctor has suggested its use for a painful tooth extraction? What would you say to another friend who wants to hypnotize you for fun?

5 Why has the use of psychoactive drugs become so common in today's society? What would you say to a twelve-year-old nephew who wants your advice on whether to experiment with drugs or not?

Activities

1 Have you wondered what lies hidden in your unconscious? A simple experiment may put you in touch with your unconscious. Begin by finding a quiet place some evening where you won't be disturbed. Place a single object on a table in front of you. A rock, a vase, or a figurine will do. Turn out all the lights except one that shines directly on the object. Sit comfortably and focus your attention on the object. Study it in its every detail. Shut your mind to distractions. In a little while, you may find that vivid, unexpected images will come to mind. These images are proba-

bly emerging from your unconscious, set free by your concentration on the object. Break off the experience anytime you feel yourself becoming anxious or too restless.

2 You can also expand your consciousness by making a deliberate effort to become more aware. If the weather permits, take off your shoes and walk outdoors. Forget about going anywhere. Now close your eyes. For a little while, just *be*. Listen for your heartbeat; study the rhythm of your breathing; sense the miracle of your body at work. Now expand your awareness to the world around you. Feel the texture of concrete, grass, wood, asphalt under your feet. Feel the air moving delicately around your body. Feel the warmth of the sunlight. Hear the little sounds of life. Smell a leaf, taste a stem of grass. If you really let yourself get into this experience, you may discover a renewed sense of the sheer joy of being alive.

3 An altered state of consciousness can be induced without the aid of drugs or hypnosis. You might want to take some friends on a fantasy trip via a technique called *guided imagery*. Begin by helping everyone relax. Ask them to lie on the floor, eyes closed. Describe the imaginary "bubble" that surrounds each person, keeping its occupant safe, warm, and comfortable. Use these bubbles to transport everyone to a peaceful, natural spot of your choice. It could be a mountain meadow, a deserted beach, a quiet lake. Take everyone for a walk around your hidden place. Let them feel the breeze, listen to the sounds of wind or surf, sniff the flowers. In short, recreate all the lovely sensory experiences that the place has to offer. Take your time. Keep your voice low and calm. When it's time to return, bring everyone back gently to the room where you started. You'll find that most people can make the trip with you and that they'll report a pleasant and relaxing experience.

4 Keep a dream diary for several weeks. That means writing down as much of each night's dreams as you can remember. The suggestions in Figure 2.8, page 43, should help. As you collect your dreams, analyze them according to the five-step procedure outlined on pages 42–43. By having a number of dreams to work with, you will probably find that interpretations are easier.

5 You probably have a pretty good idea of what law-enforcement agencies say about drug abuse. But what about other concerned professionals?

With your teacher's help, arrange for a speaker to talk to your class about the drug situation in your own community. Sources of speakers include free clinics, drug abuse clinics, public health offices, psychologists in private practice, a representative from Alcoholics Anonymous or Nar-Anon, or any other qualified person familiar with drugs and drug abuse.

For further reading

Faraday, Ann. *Dream Power*. New York: Coward, McCann & Geoghegan, 1972. Faraday takes the mystery out of dream interpretation. Her book emphasizes the use of dreams in improving your ability to solve problems and to make decisions.

Gregory, Richard L. *The Intelligent Eye*. New York: McGraw-Hill, 1970. Gregory's book is somewhat technical, but it presents a complete discussion of visual perception. The book comes complete with three-dimensional glasses, gestalt diagrams, and many interesting experiments.

Hyde, Margaret O., ed. *Mind Drugs*. New York: McGraw-Hill, 1974. Leading authorities on drugs discuss the use and abuse of psychoactive drugs in calm, logical tones. Of particular value is Allan Cohen's chapter on alternatives to drug abuse.

Ornstein, Robert. *The Psychology of Consciousness*. New York: Viking Press, 1973. This important work examines consciousness from all angles. Ornstein explains biofeedback, meditation, and the different types of consciousness that originate in each half of the brain.

Smith, Adam. *Powers of Mind*. New York: Random House, 1975. Consciousness and ASCs in all their variety are explored in this interesting book. Smith personally investigated the many routes to awareness he writes about. The style is light and funny.

3

THE BRAIN AND BEHAVIOR

Psychologists have long known that the mind and the body affect each other far more than most people think. Perhaps you've noticed how a flare-up of acne can depress one of your friends. Or maybe you know a busy executive whose job tensions have caused a case of ulcers. In short, what happens to the body affects the mind; and what happens in the mind affects the body.

That principle has been put to work in the revolutionary cancer treatments pioneered by Dr. O. Carl Simonton and his wife, Stephanie Matthews-Simonton. Over the strong objections of most cancer specialists, Dr. Simonton has enlisted his patients' minds in the battle against their cancers. Of course, Simonton still uses traditional radiation and drug therapies. But he also asks his patients to use a special visualization technique to stimulate the body's natural defenses against the invading cancer:

"Force yourself to mentally picture the cancer," says the doctor's voice on a fifteen-minute cassette that summarizes his revolutionary cancer therapy. "Picture your body's own white blood cells—a vast army that was put there to eliminate the abnormal cells . . . see the white blood cells attacking the cancer cells and carrying them off . . . see the cancer shrinking . . . see yourself becoming more in tune with life."*

The Simontons encourage their patients to use the visual images that work best for them. A retired army general, for instance, saw his cancer as an invading army that had established a beachhead in his body. His white blood cells became his defending troops. In the "battle" that followed, his army gradually forced the invaders to retreat. Eventually, the general "killed" the last enemy soldier—and at the same time lab tests reported that the cancer was gone.

Other patients visualize the cancer cells as crabs, rats, or evil trolls. In turn, the defending white cells become sharks, polar bears, or knights. Even the radiation and drug treatments become a part of the mental warfare. Some patients have visualized cobalt rays as a powerful laser beam and pills as boulders that crush the invaders.

Does such visualization work? A number of cancer patients say they are alive today because it does. The Simontons present some impressive survival figures. Between

*Quoted in Jonathan Kirsch, "Can Your Mind Cure Cancer?" *New West* (January 3, 1977). Copyright © 1977 by NYM Corp. Reprinted with the permission of New West Magazine.

1972 and 1977, they treated 134 patients. Of these, 100 were still alive. The normal survival rate for their advanced cancers would be only about 5 percent, or 7 patients out of the 134!

Despite such success, opposition to Dr. Simonton's therapy is not hard to find. Many doctors, especially cancer specialists, fear that patients will ignore traditional treatments in favor of "thinking bad thoughts about cancer." They do not believe that Simonton has any real evidence that the mind can influence the body's white cells to repel cancer. Only when Simonton presents proof collected under proper controls, they say, can medical science accept visualization technique.

Faced with this criticism, Simonton admits that he isn't sure why his methods work. But his patients do get better, he says, and he's determined to continue his visualization therapy. Simonton declares:

> I *believe* we can use our emotional resources to control our bodies, but I don't *know* we can—that comes with proof and the testing of time . . . We've been deeply involved for five years, but I feel like an infant in the area of manipulating emotional tools to improve health.*

Whatever the final decision on the Simon-

tons' work, doctors have learned not to ignore the role of the mind when they treat the illnesses of the body. Just as important, psychologists realize that the mind itself is a product of the complex and fascinating organ called the brain. But before the brain can be put to work—whether the problem is curing cancer or tying a shoelace—it must receive data about the outside world through the eyes, ears, nose, skin, and other senses.

This chapter will provide you with a brief introduction to the study of physiological psychology. When you finish the sections that follow, you will have a better understanding of the body you inhabit—and the marvelous brain that controls it.

3.1 WHAT ROLES DO THE BRAIN AND GLANDS PLAY IN BEHAVIOR?

3.2 WHAT EFFECT DOES VISION HAVE ON BEHAVIOR?

3.3 HOW DOES YOUR SENSE OF HEARING AFFECT BEHAVIOR?

3.4 HOW DO YOUR SENSES OF SMELL AND TASTE WORK?

3.5 WHAT EFFECT DO THE SKIN SENSES HAVE ON BEHAVIOR?

3.6 DO YOU HAVE ANY SENSES BEYOND THE BASIC FIVE?

3.1 WHAT ROLES DO THE BRAIN AND GLANDS PLAY IN BEHAVIOR?

Just as a great airliner cannot fly without proper commands from its pilot, your body cannot function without its own command center, the brain. If you could look inside your skull, you'd see a mass of gray-colored tissue that is shaped somewhat like an oversized walnut. Under a microscope you would see that the tissue is composed of individual nerve cells, called *neurons*. Don't try to count them—the human brain contains approximately 10 billion neurons.

In size, your brain is the largest in propor-

tion to body weight of any animal species. The extinct stegosaurus weighed almost 2 tons, but its brain weighed only 2½ ounces (compared to your 3½-pound human brain).

Brain size alone, however, does not correlate directly with intelligence. Some highly intelligent people have relatively small brains. Instead of size, a better measure of intelligence might be the individual brain's ability to store and retrieve data for later use and to make connections between apparently unrelated events or objects. Thus, to most people a falling apple is something to eat. But, to a genius like the English scien-

*Quoted in Kirsch.

tist Sir Isaac Newton, a falling apple was a clue to the universal law of gravitation.

Research shows that brain activity is both electrical and chemical in nature. This electrochemical activity is fueled by oxygen and sugar from the bloodstream. Twenty-five percent of the oxygen pumped by the heart is used by the brain. If that supply should be cut off for as little as four minutes, permanent damage results. Once lost, brain cells cannot be replaced. A stroke victim, for example, may be paralyzed if the blockage of blood vessels cuts off oxygen to brain cells in the area that controls the leg muscles. But

therapy can sometimes help the brain learn to transfer the function of walking to other, undamaged brain cells.

Even as you read these words, a tornado of activity is taking place in your brain. One part, the forebrain, is actively engaged in translating letter symbols into ideas. This is the "new brain," where conscious thought takes place. But another part of the brain, the hindbrain, is also at work, taking care of essential body functions. Without it, you'd be dead within a few minutes. (A diagram that maps the basic parts of the brain can be seen in Figure 3.1.)

Figure 3.1

In this diagram, the brain has been split down the middle to show its basic internal parts. Hindbrain structures are shown in gray; the forebrain appears in white. Both halves of the brain contain the same structures even though the left brain and the right brain control different behaviors.

BASIC PARTS OF THE HUMAN BRAIN

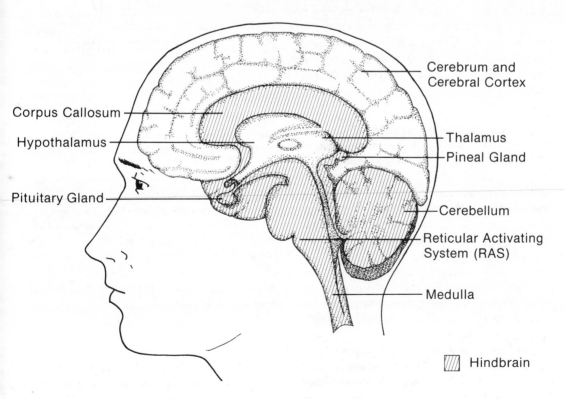

Interior of the Brain When Split on Midline

The hindbrain

Have you ever forgotten to tell your heart to beat? Of course not, you say—that vital function happens automatically. But it's not fully automatic. The *hindbrain* regulates many of the basic body activities, including heartbeat, breathing, balance, the physical appetites, and sleep. Three of the hindbrain's most important parts are the medulla, the cerebellum, and the reticular activating system (RAS).

Medulla. The *medulla* provides a connection between your brain and spinal cord. It helps regulate breathing, heartbeat, and blood pressure. Even if you deliberately stopped breathing, the medulla would take over within four minutes and resume breathing for you. At the same time, your conscious mind "blacks out" and no longer interferes with this vital activity.

Cerebellum. The *cerebellum* helps maintain the body's balance and plays an important role in coordinating fine-muscle activity. When you thread a needle or repair a watch, your cerebellum makes sure your fingers follow the orders of your conscious mind.

Reticular activating system (RAS). Are you sleepy right now or wide awake? Whichever state you find yourself in, the signals that control wakefulness and sleep, as well as arousal and alertness, originate in the *reticular activating system (the RAS)*. Chemicals created within the brain stimulate or depress the RAS—and you wake up or fall asleep. The RAS also helps sort out important messages from the constant flow of trivia reported by your sensory receptors. Thus, you can ignore normal traffic noises—until the screech of brakes alerts you to possible danger.

The hindbrain also connects directly to the *spinal cord*, a vital bundle of nerves that runs through the backbone. From the spinal cord, long cables of sensory and motor

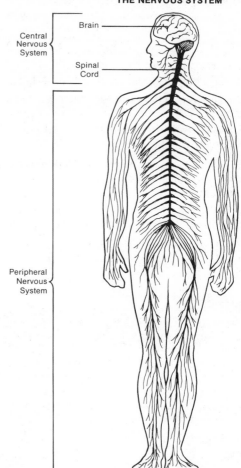

Figure 3.2

Your brain receives information and sends orders via two nerve networks. The central nervous system is made up of the brain and spinal cord. When this system is connected to the peripheral nervous system, it ties the body into a unified system under direct control of the brain.

nerves connect the *central nervous system* (the brain and spinal cord) to the *peripheral nervous system* (the nerve pathways that stretch to all outlying parts of the body, including the muscles). But even with all of these structures, you'd still be little more than a jellyfish. It is the forebrain that makes you a human being.

The forebrain

Your highly developed *forebrain* makes it possible for you to experience the pleasures and pains of existence. Whether you're smelling a rose or solving a tricky math problem, the conscious thought that directs your activity takes place in the forebrain. Three of the most important parts of the forebrain are the thalamus, the hypothalamus, and the cerebrum.

Thalamus. The *thalamus* connects the forebrain with the rest of the body. All incoming messages from the sense organs (except for smell) pass through the thalamus. Like a high-speed switchboard, the thalamus sorts out the signals and passes them on to the proper groups of neurons in the forebrain.

Hypothalamus. The *hypothalamus* plays an important role in controlling instinctive behavior, particularly when you are in danger. If you were threatened by a mugger, for example, your hypothalamus would order the hormones that prepare your body to protect itself. The hypothalamus also directs the body's responses to hunger and thirst, sexual feelings, and stress. The "pleasure center" is located in the hypothalamus. Imagine a future in which every member of society was "hooked up" at birth with a radio-controlled pleasure-center stimulator. Whoever controlled the transmitter would probably receive unquestioning obedience from everyone, so great would be the desire to receive regular jolts of pleasure!

Cerebrum. The *cerebrum*, the great dome of tissue that lies atop the brain, allows you to experience consciousness. This area forms 60 percent of your brain's mass. By far the most important part of the cerebrum is the *cerebral cortex*, which contains most of the specific areas that affect muscle coordination, memory, concentration, problem solving, and decision making. This outermost layer represents a marvel of engineering, for the one-eighth-inch thick cortex would fill an area of over six square feet if it were laid flat. In order to fit inside the skull, the cerebral cortex is folded many

times. This folding gives the brain its wrinkled appearance.

The cortex is divided into four regions called *lobes* (see Figure 3.3). The *occipital lobe* is located at the back of the head. Here the brain interprets the signals transmitted by the eyes and creates the mental image that allows you to "see."

At the side of the head lies the *temporal lobe*. This area allows you to hear and understand the noises around you, from the tick of a clock to a conversation with your best friend.

The *parietal lobe* is found at the top of the head. This region governs your sense of touch and also keeps track of the different parts of the body. If the parietal lobe were damaged, for example, you wouldn't be aware of what your feet were doing.

Finally, the *frontal lobe*, located behind the forehead, handles your sense of smell, controls body movement, and allows you to speak. Its motor-control area provides the coordination that keeps your feet, legs, arms, hands, and other body parts working together. A large portion of this area is devoted to the control of two small parts of your body, the hands and mouth. Because tool use and spoken language are the major developments separating humans from the lower animals, this unequal development makes biological sense. Even the simple act of saying "hello" to a friend requires that you coordinate hundreds of muscles with high precision.

Left brain vs. right brain

The left and right sides of your brain look much alike, but their functions differ greatly. Research shows, for example, that your left brain controls movements on the right side of your body, and vice versa. Take a moment and scratch your nose with your right hand. It was the motor cortex on the left side of your brain that controlled your arm and finger movements.

One side of the brain always takes a dominant role. Left-brain dominance leads to right-handedness. Since more than 90 per-

THE FOREBRAIN: WHERE THOUGHTS BECOME ACTION

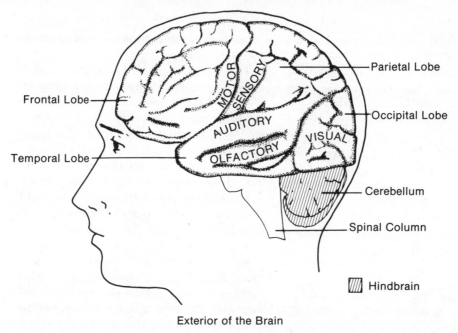

Exterior of the Brain

Figure 3.3

Exploration of the brain has enabled researchers to map the major parts of the forebrain. "Seeing," for example, takes place in the visual cortex at the back of the brain. Can you locate the control centers for the other senses?

cent of the people in the world are right-handed, you can conclude that most people are left-brain dominant. If you happen to be left-handed, you already know that you're in the minority. You may also have noticed that many left-handers use their right hands for everyday activities, such as throwing a ball or opening a jar. British scientist Oliver Zangwill believes that these left-handers are still left-brain dominant. He estimates that less than one half of all left-handed people are right-brain dominant.

Even more interesting to researchers has been the discovery that the left and right brains control different abilities. The dominant left brain takes charge of logical thought (solving mathematical problems, for example) and verbal abilities (talking to a friend or writing a poem). As a consequence, damage to the language areas of the left brain would leave you unable to speak or write. The right brain handles artistic, musical, athletic, and other nonverbal activities. When you want to dance, paint a picture, or play a set of tennis, the right brain takes over.

A band of nerve fibers called the *corpus callosum* connects the two halves of the brain. This connection enables the brain to work as a single unit. But something interesting happens when the corpus callosum is cut or damaged. Since the two halves of the brain can no longer communicate freely, the two sides of the body no longer coordinate their skills. Mary O., for example, had split-brain surgery to relieve the effect of severe epileptic seizures. Since she was left-brain dominant, she could still write with her right hand. Her right hand, however, could no longer draw pictures or work jigsaw puzzles—which are right-brain, nonverbal activities! When she switched to her left hand, she was quickly able to finish a puzzle. Figure 3.4 further demonstrates the effect of split-brain surgery on drawing ability.

Transmittal of messages

One of the marvels of your body is the speed and efficiency with which messages move to and from the brain. Message impulses move along a network of nerve cells called a *neural pathway*. Each neuron (see Figure 3.5) is composed of three major parts: (1) a *cell body*, where the nucleus and other equipment vital to the work of the cell are located; (2) a number of branching fibers called *dendrites*, which carry the incoming signals to the cell body; and (3) the *axon*, a single arm that branches out at the end and carries impulses from the cell body to the dendrites of nearby neurons.

Basic action of the neurons. The basic nerve impulse is electrochemical in nature. When a dendrite of one of your neurons receives a stimulus, a change takes place in the end of the dendrite. This change is like a signal that says "stop" or "go." If the signal is "go," the neuron fires. This means that a wave of electrochemical activity travels from the receiving dendrite to the cell body and onward through the axon to other neurons in the neural pathway. When the impulses reach the proper neurons in your brain, a thought, image, word, or emotion takes shape in your mind. Once a neuron has fired, it takes about a thousandth of a second to "recharge" and get ready for the next impulse to arrive.

Impulses can pass from one neuron to another only by jumping a tiny space between pods at the end of the axon and its neighboring dendrite. This space, only seven millionths (.000007) of an inch wide, is called the *synaptic gap*. You can see the pods at the end of the axon and the synaptic gap in Figure 3.5. When an impulse reaches one of these pods, it releases a chemical called a *neurotransmitter*. The chemical crosses the synaptic gap and sets up an impulse in the next cell. In this way, the impulse passes from one neuron to the next in the neural pathway until it reaches its destination. Despite the complexity of this process, impulses speed through the body as fast as two hundred miles per hour.

	RIGHT HAND	LEFT HAND
"This is a pretty day."	*This is a pretty day*	
"Your name"	*nancy*	*Nancy*

Figure 3.4a

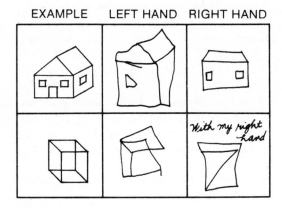

EXAMPLE   LEFT HAND   RIGHT HAND

Figure 3.4b

Experiments with patients who have had split-brain surgery for severe epilepsy reveal the different functions of the two halves of the brain. In Figure 3.4a, a right-handed patient has been given spoken instructions. The left brain (right hand) follows the directions, but the right brain (left hand) cannot do so. As you can see, the problem is not simply an inability to write with the left hand. In Figure 3.4b, the patient has been asked to copy the two drawings. In this case, the right brain (left hand) shows its superior ability in nonverbal skills, such as drawing three-dimensional objects.

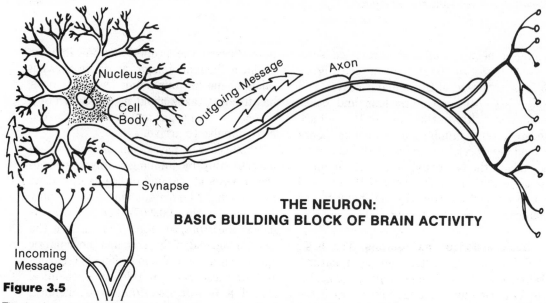

THE NEURON:
BASIC BUILDING BLOCK OF BRAIN ACTIVITY

Figure 3.5

The brain contains some ten billion nerve cells. Each neuron (shown here in simplified form) interconnects with hundreds of other similar cells. A hundred million neurons would fit into a cubic inch.

ENDOCRINE GLANDS ALSO AFFECT BEHAVIOR

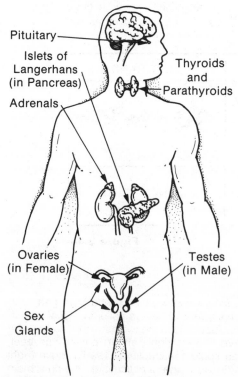

Figure 3.6

The *endocrine glands* regulate many important human behaviors. Too large or too small a quantity of the hormones secreted by these glands can lead to physical and emotional problems.

Breakdowns in transmission. Any breakdown in the transmission of nerve impulses can cause serious problems. When multiple sclerosis damages the insulation that covers many axons, paralysis and loss of muscular control result. Epileptic seizures result when damaged neurons fire wildly. Mild epileptic seizures cause only a brief blackout, but more severe seizures can result in unconsciousness and convulsions. While multiple sclerosis still resists therapy, drug or surgical treatments enable most epileptics to lead productive lives.

Role of the endocrine glands

As important as the central nervous system is, your behavior is also affected by busy chemical factories called *glands*. Ducted glands pipe saliva, sweat, tears, and digestive juices to where they are needed. But some of your most important glands pump powerful chemicals called *hormones* directly into the bloodstream. These ductless glands regulate everything from physical growth to sexual functioning. The most important of the hormone-producing glands, or the *endocrine glands*, are the pituitary, the adrenal, the thyroid, and the sex glands (see Figure 3.6).

Pro & Con: IS PSYCHOSURGERY A PROPER TREATMENT FOR MENTAL PROBLEMS?

In 1891, a Swiss surgeon performed brain surgery designed to change the abnormal behavior of mental patients. Although these first experiments were not successful, a new method of dealing with the mentally ill had been created. *Psychosurgery,* as it is called today, involves the use of precise surgical techniques to destroy the brain tissue thought to be causing the abnormal behavior. Violently aggressive people, for example, can return to normal life, no longer dangerous to themselves or to others. The usefulness and ethics of such surgery, now being used on hundreds of patients each year, have become a major issue in psychology. The main arguments on each side of the issue are summarized below:

Pro

1 Psychosurgery offers the only real hope for returning many severely disturbed mental patients to any type of normal life. Advanced techniques have made the procedures relatively foolproof.

2 The cost of keeping disturbed patients in jails or mental hospitals is immense. For a few thousand dollars, many such people can be returned to society as productive citizens.

3 Although psychosurgery sometimes causes changes in the patient's personality, the price should be considered minor. Modern surgical techniques remove only the brain tissue responsible for the offending behavior.

4 Fears that psychosurgery will lead to loss of freedom are overstated. Every scientific advance carries with it the possibility for evil as well as good. Some people fear that psychosurgery can be used to hook up citizens to mind-control computers. But this process can happen only in science fiction.

Con

1 Psychosurgery's record is one of poor legal and scientific controls. Published studies often suffer from a lack of follow-up that makes it difficult to evaluate accurately the success of the surgery.

2 Psychosurgery is an unacceptable violation of individual rights. In most cases, psychosurgery is performed on those patients least able to object—the residents of mental hospitals and prisons.

3 Despite improved techniques, the surgeon cannot guarantee that severe personality changes won't occur. Drug treatments can be stopped and hospital gates opened—but brain surgery cannot be reversed.

4 Reliance on psychosurgery could easily lead to even greater use of similar techniques for changing behavior. Today, the surgeon treats the mentally disturbed; tomorrow, psychosurgery might be performed on anyone who disagrees with those in power.

Do you think psychosurgery should be allowed to continue? If so, what circumstances do you think should exist before a doctor is allowed to do this type of surgery? Compare your answers with those of others who have read this Pro & Con.

JOSÉ DELGADO:
PROPHET FOR A BRAVE NEW WORLD OF ESB

The fighting bull charged straight at the apparently helpless José Delgado. The speeding animal was only twenty feet away when Delgado pressed the button on a transmitter in his hand. The bull skidded to an abrupt stop. It looked blankly at Delgado, then wandered off.

What happened in that bullring? Before the demonstration, Delgado had implanted a tiny radio receiver called a *stimoceiver* in the bull's brain. When he activated his transmitter, the stimoceiver delivered tiny jolts of electricity to an area in the bull's brain that inhibits aggression. In effect, the stimoceiver "turned off" the bull's desire to attack.

The man who performed this demonstration was born in Spain in 1915 and trained in medicine at the University of Madrid. He came to Yale University in 1950 to carry on his research. Delgado states his goals by saying, "I would like to cure epilepsy, cure mental disorders, and construct a better world. That's all." What makes these goals seem possible to Delgado is his faith in research that uses the mind to influence its own behavior. He believes that the exploration of "inner space" should be established as a first-level national goal.

Delgado's special interests center on electronic stimulation of the brain (ESB). Through electrodes implanted in the brain, he believes, two-way radio communication between the brain and computers can be arranged. In this way, scientists could send information, instructions, and directions for planned behaviors to a subject's brain. Delgado claims that this method would allow an infant to be trained and educated to reach the highest possible levels of development. Such a person would be freed from the chains of blind emotion. No longer will the accident of birth, which gives one child loving parents and another an abusive mother or father, cripple humankind.

To those critics who claim that the stimoceiver would lead to enslavement of people by ruthless dictators, Delgado replies that ESB cannot make robots of people. Behavior can be influenced, he says, but not controlled. From a practical standpoint, ESB has limits that can be overcome only in the pages of a novel. In reality, it can be used to help people shape their minds, train their thinking power, and direct their emotions more rationally.

In any event, Delgado concludes, society already has developed powerful drugs that are nearly as effective as ESB and far simpler to use. The stimoceiver has been used effectively to locate lesions in the brain that cause violent, uncontrolled rages. Why not go the next step, Delgado wonders, and apply this new technology to making the human personality more truly "human"?

Do you agree with Dr. Delgado that this country should promote the exploration of "inner space"? Do you see any dangers in research on the use of the stimoceiver and ESB?

Pituitary gland. The *pituitary gland* produces many hormones that regulate a wide range of body activities. A properly working pituitary produces a growth hormone that ensures normal growth. Too much or too little of this hormone can cause giantism or dwarfism.

Different pituitary hormones act as chemical messengers that turn other glands off and on. The sex glands, for example, would not turn a child into a sexually mature adult if they were not stimulated by the pituitary at the proper time. In 1978, Russian women gymnasts were accused of taking drugs to slow down sexual maturation. Slimmer, smaller bodies, it was thought, would give them a better chance of winning world meets. Whether the charge was true or not, researchers can bring about seeming miracles with the use of pituitary hormones. One tiny six-year-old girl with an underactive pituitary grew over twenty inches in eighteen months after doctors had treated her with growth hormones.

Adrenal glands. The *adrenal glands* produce a variety of hormones. Adrenalin, one of the most important products of the adrenals, prepares the body to cope with emergencies. Next time you're under stress, check for these changes as the adrenalin begins to flow: You feel stronger, more energetic as extra sugar is released into the blood. Your blood pressure rises and your pulse rate increases. You breathe more easily as air passages in the lungs are enlarged. You see better as your pupils admit more light into the eyes. Your skin temperature rises, and your palms begin to sweat. In a few seconds, you'll be ready for anything (see Figure 3.7).

The adrenals also work behind the scenes to regulate the chemical balance of the body. More obviously, at puberty the adrenals cooperate with the sex glands to produce the physical changes that occur during early adolescence. Adult body hair sprouts, boys' voices lower, and girls' breasts develop.

Adolescent acne, unfortunately, also seems related to the action of the adrenals and the sex glands during this period of rapid physical change.

Thyroid gland. The hormones produced by the *thyroid gland* help determine the body's energy level. If you have an overactive thyroid, you will lose weight, have trouble sleeping, and be full of nervous energy. Too little thyroid production leads to sluggish behavior and weight gain. Severe thyroid deficiency in early childhood can also affect intellectual development. This condition, known as *cretinism*, results in low intelligence and poor physical development. Early hormone therapy for children born with this condition can sometimes prevent mental retardation by restoring normal growth in the nervous system.

Sex glands. The *sex glands*, properly called the *gonads*, are the ovaries in women and the testes in men. These glands produce the hormones that regulate the development of the sex organs and prepare the body for reproduction. In most animals, the production of sex hormones leads to instinctive mating behavior. The sexual life of human beings, however, is so complex that the work of these potent glands should not be thought of only in biological terms. Humans have developed sexual behaviors that are influenced by psychological factors as well as by cultural rules and customs.

SECTION CHECKUP

1 What are the basic differences between the hindbrain and the forebrain?

2 Why is the cerebral cortex so important to your behavior as a human being?

3 How are nerve impulses transmitted from one neuron to another?

4 Why are the endocrine glands considered so important to your growth and development?

Figure 3.7

SPY vs. SPY: THE STRUGGLE FOR SELF-PRESERVATION

Novelist Adam Hall has created a superspy named Quiller, who appears in such books as *The Mandarin Cypher* and *The Quiller Memorandum.* Quiller is unusual, however, in that his frequent close scrapes with death are described in vivid physiological detail. Readers step inside Quiller's skin and experience all the brain-mind reactions that they might feel themselves in a similar struggle. In *The Mandarin Cypher,* for example, Quiller enters a Hong Kong snake shop only to be instantly attacked from behind by a hired killer. Their fighting smashes some jars of poisonous snakes. Quiller fights off a snake and then thinks about the assassin.

> . . . I blocked my mind and tried to concentrate totally on the need to survive.
> Forebrain processing was taking over the gross elements of the task while the primitive creature conditioned itself, the nerve signals triggering the medulla and pouring adrenalin into the bloodstream, the pulse rate and blood pressure rising as sugar flowed in to feed the muscles, the senses increasing in their refinement so that the input of data should receive almost instantaneous assessment by the cortex. . . .
> Forebrain. The youth was coming back in a rebound from the shelf and I could take him with a single bracket throw if I waited long enough: it would need a tenth of a second. . . . his shoulder had smashed fairly hard into the edge of the shelf and the muscle would be in trauma. . . .

Quiller now hits the assassin with a partially successful karate blow, but the man responds with a throw that almost topples Quiller into the writhing mass of snakes.

> He could have done it then because my spine was exposed and he still had the strength in one hand but what he didn't realize was that he was throwing me back into that bloody snakepit *and I wasn't going to have it.*
> The forebrain shut off almost completely and the organism took over and I was vaguely aware of the action being triggered by the emotional syndrome: horror, desperation, fury—each emotion contributing to the next and powering the physical body with speed and strength otherwise unavailable. No science, no cerebration, no technique. Blind rage. In this way murder is often done, and the well-known statement is heard later in court: *I don't know what happened. Something just came over me.* . . .
> I wasn't on the floor any more because that was the place where the organism had been determined not to go: It had been quite adamant about this because it had known that if it fell down there among those things again [the snakes] it would go mad.

In a less violent way, the same reactions take over in your own body every time you are faced with danger. Where does the strength come from that permits Quiller to save himself from the snakes or for you to jump out of the path of an oncoming truck?

Adam Hall, *The Mandarin Cypher* (Garden City, NY: Doubleday, 1975), pp. 95–96.

3.2 WHAT EFFECT DOES VISION HAVE ON BEHAVIOR?

Close your eyes. Instantly, you will lose much of your contact with the world around you. Even though you can still hear, smell, taste, and touch, you'll probably feel rather helpless. With care, you can still move around your house or find objects on your desk. But just try pouring a glass of milk! It won't take long to verify that about 75 percent of your information about the world comes to you through your eyes.

Thanks to your eyes, you have a number of important abilities. These include (1) depth perception, which enables you to judge fast-moving traffic while you're driving; (2) color discrimination, so you can pick out the ripe banana from the green ones; (3) rapid focus (from short-range to long-range and back again), which lets you catch a hard-thrown baseball; and (4) the ability to adjust quickly to differences in brightness, so that walking out of the shade into the sunlight doesn't leave you blinded.

Technically, *vision* refers to your eye's ability to respond to light. The human eye is sensitive to only certain types of light. Bees, for example, can see ultraviolet light, but normally you cannot. Similarly, you could be photographed in a dark room "lighted" only by infrared light. Since your eye cannot see infrared light, you wouldn't know the picture had been taken until someone showed you the print.

Mechanism of the human eye

One way to understand the working of the eye is to think of it as a television camera. Like the camera, your eye continuously gathers reflected light from whatever scene lies in front of its lens. As the light varies, your eye adjusts automatically for changes in brightness. Then, just as the camera transmits pictures to a receiver, your eye converts the image focused by the lens into electrical impulses and sends them to the brain. As shown in Figure 3.8, the mechanism of the eye has six major parts.

1. The *cornea* is the transparent outer covering found at the front surface of the eye. The curved surface of the cornea enables it to gather light from a much wider field of vision than would be possible if the eye's opening were flat.

2. The *iris* is a circular arrangement of

MECHANISM OF THE HUMAN EYE

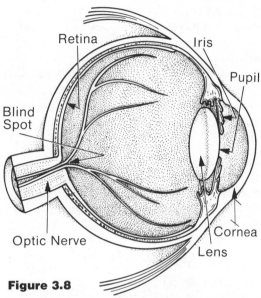

Figure 3.8

The human eye is your personal "TV camera." It provides you with 75 percent of the sensory data you gather from the world around you. But the eye only collects and transmits visual data. "Seeing" actually takes place in the visual cortex of the brain.

muscles that regulates the amount of light admitted into the eye. When people tell you, "Oh, you have such beautiful eyes," they're talking about the color of the iris. The iris can be blue, green, or brown, with additional flecks of other colors. Brown is the most common color, however, probably because the darker shade gives the most protection from bright sunlight.

3. The *pupil* is the dark opening in the center of the iris through which light passes on its way to the retina. The size of the pupil is regulated by the contraction and relaxation of the iris. Pupil size normally varies with the amount of light reflected from the scene you're observing. Your pupil gets bigger in dim light and contracts to its smallest size in bright sunlight. You can test this size change for yourself with a mirror.

Researchers have found that pupil size is also affected by emotions. When you look at something you find exciting or interesting, your pupil size enlarges. When you look at something unpleasant, however, your pupils contract. This change in pupil size is entirely unconscious and cannot be controlled. In experiments to test this finding, groups of men and women were shown pictures of babies. All of the women—whether or not they had children—showed an increase in pupil size. Only those men who were fathers, however, had a similar reaction.

4. The *lens* is a focusing device whose job is to deliver a sharp image to the retina. Special muscles adjust the shape of the lens so that you can see objects close up or far away with equal clarity.

5. The *retina*, the area at the back of the eye, is lined with about 125 million light-sensitive cells. These cells convert light into electrical impulses for transmission to the brain. Ninety-five percent of the cells are *rods* (named because of their long, narrow shape). The rods are sensitive to low levels of light but "see" everything in shades of gray. The remaining cells in the retina, the *cones*, provide you with color vision. Cones are concentrated near the center of the retina, where your vision is sharpest. Since the cones do not respond to low light levels, your night vision tends to lack color perception.

6. The *optic nerve* is a bundle of nerve fibers that serves as a transmission line to the brain. The optic nerve is composed of over a million fibers, each of which carries impulses from many rods and cones at once. Because there are no rods or cones at the spot where the optic nerve leaves the retina, you have a "blind spot" in your vision (see Figure 3.9). You aren't normally aware of the blind spot, however. Psychologists believe that the brain "fills in" the "hole" by constructing a logical extension of the surrounding area.

Color blindness

Color perception depends upon which type of cone receives the stimulation. Some cones are sensitive to red, others to yellow and green, and the rest to blue and violet. When one type of cone or another is missing or does not work properly, color blindness results. About seven men out of a hundred have this condition, but only one woman in a thousand is color blind. Red-green is the most common color blindness, followed by blue-yellow. Because Ronnie L. is red-green color blind, he cannot tell a red apple from a green one. Ronnie can see that the apples are different, but both appear gray to him. Blue skies and yellow tulips look normal to Ronnie, but not to Sue N., who is blue-yellow color blind. Even so, Ronnie

Figure 3.9

You can prove the existence of this blind spot by holding the diagram at arm's length. Close your left eye and focus the right eye on the X. Now move the book slowly toward you. Somewhere along the way, the black spot will disappear. If you keep moving the book toward you, it will reappear.

YOUR REALITY HAS A HOLE IN IT

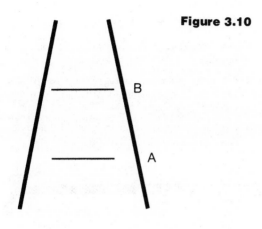

Figure 3.10

Figure 3.11

and Sue are better off than the one person in 40,000 who is totally color blind. With no working cones on their retinas, these people see only a black, white, and gray world.

Vision adaptation

Remember the last time you walked into a darkened theater? At first you felt blinded, and you may have stumbled into someone standing in the aisle. But gradually your eyes adjusted to the darkness. Gray shapes emerged, and finally you spotted an empty seat. Full adjustment to near-total darkness would have taken almost an hour. By that time, your eyes would have become a hundred thousand times more sensitive to light than they are outside on a sunny day.

Vision also adjusts for objects of various sizes. You can work up close or spot details at remarkable distances. If you have normal eyesight, you can probably see a ¼-inch-thick wire at a distance of 440 yards—al-

most the length of four football fields! Many people, however, cannot see clearly because of defects in the eye. If the lens does not focus an image clearly on the retina, for example, vision becomes fuzzy. Most problems of this kind can be corrected with eyeglasses, properly designed to compensate for the faults in the lens or cornea.

Fooling the eye

Visual illusions work because the clues that you normally use to identify size or shape of objects have been changed. Look at the illusion in Figure 3.10, for example. Which line, A or B, is longer? Your perception will probably tell you that B is longer than A, but your ruler will show you that they're the same length. The illusion created by the converging "railroad tracks" tells your brain that B is farther away; in order to look as long as A, it must be longer than A! Psychologists call this concept *size constancy*. To test the concept, hold one hand at arm's length, the other at half that distance. The two hands will look the same size, yet the image size of the far hand on your retina will be exactly one half that of the near hand. Only when you overlap the far hand with the near hand will the size difference become apparent.

An *after-image* occurs when you stare steadily at an image for some time. As the retina's cells tire, the image becomes "fixed." Then, when you look away, an after-image appears. You can test this illusion by using the target circle printed here (see Figure 3.11). After staring at the target for sixty seconds, look at a white wall. The target will now appear on the wall, but it will be many times larger than the original. That's size constancy at work again; the brain now sees it as being farther away. The after-image will also reverse colors. You should see it as white instead of black, a result of continued firing of the retina cells and optic nerve after stimulation.

The after-image also makes motion pictures possible. Film is actually a series of still pictures, each of which appears on the screen for about $1/24$th of a second. Your own retina provides the illusion of motion by holding on to an after-image of each frame. This allows the next frame to blend smoothly into the last, creating the illusion of motion.

SECTION CHECKUP

1 How would your life be changed if you could not see?

2 Name the six major parts of the eye. What is the role of each part in providing you with vision?

3 Explain how size constancy and after-image work to create visual illusions.

3.3 HOW DOES YOUR SENSE OF HEARING AFFECT BEHAVIOR?

A door slams in a distant part of the house. You turn your head, waiting for footsteps. Automatically, a series of ear mechanisms have gone into action, converting the sound into impulses that speed to the brain. Was it the wind? Or an intruder? In the dark of night, your eyes won't help you find the answer. This time, you'll have to depend upon your ears for help.

Physicists define *sound* as a form of energy consisting of air waves of changing pressure. These waves are measured in cycles per second (cps). *Frequency*, which is the number of vibrations per second, is expressed in cps. For example, middle C on the musical scale has a frequency of 256 cps. The human ear can detect sounds ranging from about 20 cps up to approximately 20,000 cps. At the low end of the scale, you hear the sound as deep, rumbling bass notes, while high-frequency sounds are heard as high-pitched squeals. But technical terms hardly account for the wonderful world of sound that surrounds you. From the creepy noises outside your window at night to the soaring beauty of a great orchestra, your ears add an important dimension to your knowledge of the world around you.

Mechanism of the ear

The working parts of your hearing mechanism cannot be seen. The *outer ear* merely collects sound waves and funnels them through the *auditory canal*. At that point,

the ear really begins to go to work (see Figure 3.12).

1. The *eardrum* is a thin, flexible layer of tissue that stretches across the end of the auditory canal. Sound waves that strike the eardrum cause it to vibrate.

2. Three tiny bones, each hinged to the next, magnify the vibrations transmitted by the eardrum. These vibrations are increased by a ratio of 30 to 1 before they are passed on to the cochlea.

Figure 3.12

The human ear converts sound waves into electrical impulses for transmission to the brain. The semicircular canals control your balance and are not involved in hearing (see pages 82–83).

MECHANISM OF THE HUMAN EAR

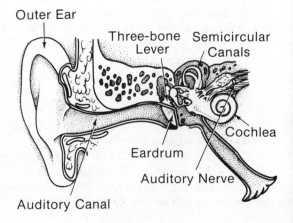

Outer Ear

Three-bone Lever

Semicircular Canals

Cochlea

Eardrum

Auditory Nerve

Auditory Canal

3. The *cochlea* converts sound energy into electrical impulses for transmission to the brain. The snail-shaped cochlea is filled with fluid and sensitive hair cells. When vibrations enter the cochlea, the fluid moves back and forth, stimulating the hair cells. In turn, the hair cells convert the movement into impulses that can be delivered to the auditory nerve.

4. The *auditory nerve* carries the impulses from the cochlea to the part of the brain responsible for hearing, the auditory cortex. Now your brain can decide about those strange noises. Perhaps this time they were only made by your cat jumping around on the back porch.

The art of hearing

Each ear operates independently of the other. Because sound waves usually strike one of your ears a fraction of a second sooner than the other, you can locate the source of a sound with good success. Confusion results when competing noises or echoes conceal the true source of a particular sound. Drivers on city streets, for example, often have difficulty pinpointing the location of a siren because of traffic noise and the echo of the siren from nearby buildings. In addition, the ear does not respond equally to all types of sound. Sound waves between 2,000 and 4,000 cps, for example, will give you few clues as to their source. Perhaps it is no coincidence that many smaller animals such as mice, birds, and insects give their warning cries in that frequency. That way, you and other larger animals will be less likely to find their location—and maybe they'll escape to live another day.

Some sounds are pleasant and other sounds are just "noise." Music creates a good feeling because the sound waves come in regular patterns, with each instrument adding its own set of pleasing tones. When chalk screeches on a blackboard, however, it creates irregular waves with unrelated frequencies. That's why you cover up your ears and complain about such an unpleasant

noise. The quality of a musical tone is also determined by the number of weaker vibrations (called overtones) which are added to the primary tone. Your ear can detect an amazing number of overtones. For instance, think of the difference between a note played on the piano and the same note struck on a glass jar.

Noise pollution

Each year, American cities and towns become a little noisier. Is that really so bad? Some recent research suggests that too much noise can do more than keep you awake.

Scientists use a measure known as the *decibel scale* for measuring the range of sound to which the ear can respond (see Figure 3.13). Since the ratio (from the softest to the loudest noise you can hear) is something like 1 to 5 million, the scale has been simplified. It starts at zero (the point at which sound becomes audible) and moves upward to the 150 range (the incredible roar of a wind tunnel). Each 10-decibel (db) increase in noise actually means that the pressure on your eardrum increases 10 times. A typical residential street measures 50 db, but heavy rush-hour traffic might hit 90 db. The 40-decibel difference actually means a ten-thousand-times ($10 \times 10 \times 10 \times 10$) increase in noise level!

But loud, sustained noise can do more than drown out your phone conversation or wake a baby. Prolonged exposure to sounds at 90 db or above can cause permanent hearing loss. At 130 db, most people find that the noise causes actual physical pain. This fact takes on particular importance when you realize that discos often amplify their music to an average of 110 db. Some hard-rock groups have been measured at 125 db. Hearing experts warn that hearing damage begins after 30 minutes exposure to a decibel level of 110; at 125, the damage would begin within 5 minutes. Tests show that some twenty-year-olds who have listened to a lot of high-decibel music have paid for their enjoyment with a hearing loss in the high

Figure 3.13

Sounds above 80 decibels (shaded area) cause physical discomfort to the listener. Above 110 db, your ears will hurt from the additional pressure. Prolonged exposure to high decibel levels has been found to cause permanent hearing loss.

THE DECIBEL SCALE: HOW LOUD IS LOUD?

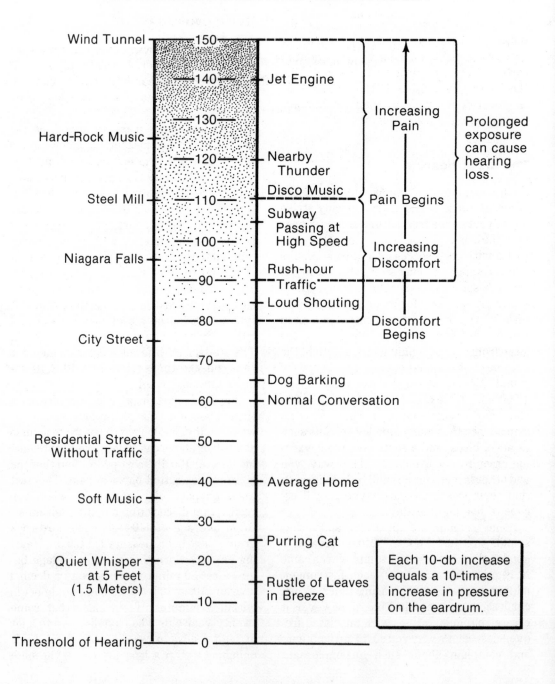

frequency tones. These young people now hear with sixty-five-year-old ears.

Living with loud noise day and night can cause even more serious problems. In 1978, Dr. William Meecham of UCLA ran a study of death rates near Los Angeles International airport. He discovered that death rates among residents living within three miles of the airport were 19 percent higher than among people living six miles away. In matched neighborhoods, the researchers found that 890 people died in the high-noise area, compared to 670 in the low-noise community.

Along with warnings about cigarettes, alcohol, and drugs, government may soon be telling you, "Too much noise is dangerous to your health."

SECTION CHECKUP

1 Trace the path of a sound from the time it enters the outer ear until it reaches the auditory cortex.

2 How do you locate the direction from which you hear a dog barking?

3 What are the dangers of excessive noise in the environment?

3.4 HOW DO YOUR SENSES OF SMELL AND TASTE WORK?

"The taste of your bread," an ancient Persian poet once said, "depends on whether you are hungry or not."

Perhaps more than any of your other senses, smell and taste are conditioned by your emotional state at any given moment. Imagine the delightful, mouth-watering smell of a bakery. Fresh bread, tangy tarts, and cinnamon rolls perfume the air. But what if you work there, and you don't like the job? Those same smells, so pleasant to your customers, will become distasteful reminders of your unhappy situation.

As the example also shows, the senses of smell and taste are closely related. Both smell and taste are "chemical senses." Sensory receptor cells in the nose and mouth react to chemical substances carried in the air or dissolved in liquids. Lower forms of life use smell and taste to help find food, select a mate, and avoid danger. These senses enrich your life as a human being with some of the most delightful sensations known to our species.

The sense of smell

In comparison with dogs, bears, deer, and other animals, you do not have a highly developed sense of smell. Birds, on the other hand, apparently cannot detect odors at all.

Insects may be the champion among "smellers." Some male moths, for example, can detect the tiny amounts of sex-attracting chemicals released by females of the species at distances of up to fifteen miles. One unhappy researcher proved this fact conclusively when he spilled a tiny amount of the chemical on his skin. For days afterward, he attracted love-struck male moths from miles around.

How the sense of smell works. When an odor enters your nose, it excites two small areas at the roof of the nasal passage. These *olfactory patches*, one on each side of the nose, connect directly to the *olfactory bulbs* of the brain (see Figure 3.3). As with the other senses, you don't actually "smell" an odor until the brain analyzes and interprets the incoming messages. Your limited sense of smell grows out of two related factors. First, the olfactory patches are relatively small in human beings. Second, only 5 percent of the cerebral cortex processes data regarding odors, compared to 33 percent in dogs. A dog can be trained to sniff out heroin or cocaine no matter how carefully the drugs are sealed in their containers. A number of drug smugglers now in prison can testify to this fact.

WHY DO YOU LICK AN ICE CREAM CONE?

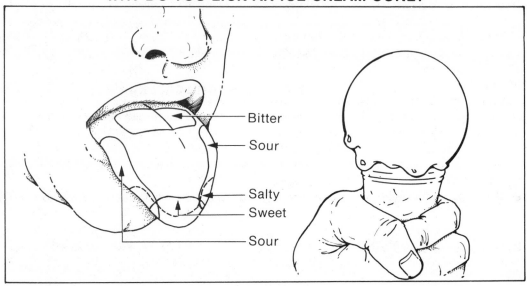

Figure 3.14

Taste buds sensitive to the four basic flavors can be mapped as shown above. Since sweet and salty flavors signal that a food is probably safe to eat, those taste buds are located at the tip of your tongue. Thus, you can best enjoy the sweet-salty taste of ice cream by licking it.

Categories of smells. No exact scale has been worked out for putting smells into categories. One system suggests that only six classes of smells exist—spicy, flowery, fruity, resinous, putrid, and burnt. Few smells, however, would fall into a single category. A perfume may be flowery and fruity; a cake may be spicy, fruity, and flowery—and burnt, if it's left in the oven too long.

The sense of taste

Take a bite of a juicy apple. What a lovely sensation! But imagine for a moment that you have a cold. That same apple will taste like so much straw, because you can't smell its fruity odor! Your sense of taste, then, begins in the mouth but also involves smell and touch. Scent, texture, and shape all combine to create this complex sense.

How the sense of taste works. What happens when you bite into an apple? Taste begins with the sight of the apple; saliva begins to flow as your mouth prepares for the first bite. Waiting inside your mouth are about ten thousand complex cell structures called *taste buds*. The saliva dissolves the apple into a solution to which the taste buds can react. Taste buds are located in each of the many bumps that cover the tongue, but they can also be found at the back of the mouth and in the throat.

As the taste buds react, other receptors join in. Your mouth and tongue report on whether the apple is cold or warm, firm or mushy, and whether the skin is tough or tender. When you chew, odors reach the nose and enable it to add its own judgment. As a simple experiment, cut up identical chunks of raw potato and apple. Ask your subjects to sample both, closing their eyes and holding their noses. Most people won't be able to tell the difference!

The cells of your taste buds do not live very long. They are constantly dying out, to be replaced by new cells. As you grow older, however, fewer and fewer of the worn-out cells will be replaced. As a consequence, older people often complain that their food has lost its flavor. Actually, their ability to taste it has broken down.

Categories of tastes. Research shows that taste buds respond to only four flavors: sweet, sour, salty, and bitter. Taste buds that respond to these flavors are grouped in fairly well defined areas on the tongue (see Figure 3.14). When you bite into a well-cooked piece of steak, for example, your tongue can report only its dominant flavor—a salty savor. The color, texture, and odor of the steak as reported by your eyes, mouth, and nose add the critical elements that make it so enjoyable.

SECTION CHECKUP

1 Why are smell and taste considered to be chemical senses?

2 How does the sense of smell contribute to your sense of taste?

3 What are the basic odors? The basic flavors?

3.5 WHAT EFFECT DO THE SKIN SENSES HAVE ON BEHAVIOR?

Popular wisdom refers to your fifth sense as the "sense of touch." In a psychological sense, that's a good name, because touching (hugs, handshakes, pats, and other direct contact between you and another person) is such an important means of communicating feelings. From a physiological viewpoint, however, a more accurate name would be the *skin senses*. What is commonly called touch actually involves four distinct types of sense receptors: pressure, pain, heat, and cold.

How the skin senses work

Hidden beneath the surface of the skin lie countless specialized nerve endings and other types of receptors. When these receptors are stimulated, as by touch of your finger on a jellyfish, they send signals to the brain. In turn, the brain interprets the signals (soft, squishy, cold) and decides on appropriate action (ugh! move away!). Most skin sensations, such as tickling, itching, burning, and the like, result from the mixing of several skin sensations at the same time.

Like the other senses, your skin senses are often fooled. You can experiment with a sharp pencil pressed lightly on the back of your hand. In certain spots, you'll feel a cold sensation rather than pressure or pain. This means that you've activated cold-sensitive receptors, and your brain perceives these impulses as the touch of something cold.

Pressure receptors

Sensitivity to pressure varies over different parts of the body. Your tool-using hands contain about 135 pressure receptors per square centimeter, but your upper arm has only 1/10th as many. Another area of your body that is richly supplied with pressure receptors is the lips. Perhaps that explains why kissing is such a pleasant activity: The pleasure center of the brain receives a flood of impulses whenever you press your lips against those of someone you love.

Pressure receptors also demonstrate the principle of *sensory adaptation*. After the receptors have responded to a stimulus for a short time, they become adapted to the stimulus and no longer respond. The sensation disappears. Without sensory adaptation, your sense of touch would keep you constantly aware of anything in contact with your skin: clothes, air currents, the change in your pocket, and so on. After a few hours of such annoyance, you'd be ready to tell your brain, "Enough already!"

Pain receptors

The next time you have a headache, think of those rare newborn babies who cannot feel pain. These children seldom live long. Without the early-warning system of danger that pain receptors provide, the children quickly run up high rates of bruises, scrapes, and bumps. Even eating a hotdog can become dangerous when there's nothing to tell you that you're also biting your own tongue.

The simple receptor cells that signal painful stimuli to the brain spread their dendrites out like the branches of a tree just beneath your skin. These *free nerve endings,* as they're called, respond to a number of intense stimuli: cutting or pricking, twisting, heat or cold, damage to tissue, or pressure severe enough to cause injury. Pain receptors vary in number on different parts of the body. The bottom of your foot has only about 50 pain receptors per square centimeter, for example. But you have 230 in the same-sized area of your neck.

Your body also has different ways of responding to painful stimuli. For example, suppose that you're running water into the sink to wash the dishes. You dip your hand into the water and find that it's too cool. As you turn up the hot water, you keep your hand in the sink. That way, you'll know when the water's the right temperature. At the same time, the radio starts playing your favorite song. While you're listening, you suddenly realize the water's now too hot. You pull your hand out. In this case, the hand's pain receptors sent warning messages to the brain. Your brain then reacted to the danger and told your hand to move.

Now assume a second case. What happens if you accidentally put your hand on an iron that you think is cold but that is heated to 300° F (149° C)? If you left your hand on the iron until your brain took action, your skin could be badly burned. In this case, a special reflex action (called the "hot-stove reflex") will cause you to pull your hand away instantly. Only after your hand is safe will your brain scold you: "That was a hot iron, dummy!"

Not everyone feels pain in the same way. Even your state of mind can affect the intensity of the pain. Soldiers in wartime sometimes refuse morphine, for example, even though they have been severely wounded. Civilian patients, by comparison, demand painkillers for minor surgery far less painful than the soldiers' wounds. Psychologists who studied this contrast during World War II soon realized that the soldiers were *happy* to be wounded! Their injuries meant that they could escape the terrors of the battlefield, and the relief overwhelmed the pain. In a similar way, football players often play with injuries that would put most people in bed. The excitement of the game blanks out the pain impulses.

Heat and cold receptors

Skin receptors for heat and cold measure temperature changes above or below normal skin temperature, about 90° F (32° C). Touch your heat receptors with a metal rod heated to 110° F (43° C), and the receptors will send impulses that the brain will perceive as warmth. A cold rod that is used to excite separate cold receptors will give you the opposite response. Cold receptors outnumber heat receptors by over three to one. This probably is related to your lack of insulating body hair. Unlike a furry bear or wolf, cold presents a greater threat to your survival than does heat.

Your body adapts quickly to temperatures within a range of 60° to 106° F. After spending a few minutes in 62° ocean water, for example, the initial shock of the cold water disappears, and you feel fairly comfortable. In fact, if you run into a current of 68° water, it will feel quite warm. If both heat and cold receptors are stimulated at the same time, however, a strange thing happens. Lay your arm on a row of tubes filled alternately with cold and warm water, for instance. Your first impression will be one of intense heat! Psychologists explain that, when both heat and cold receptors are stimulated at the same time, the brain interprets this as great heat—but no one understands exactly why.

Figure 3.15

It's no wonder a hug feels so good! For most people, the touching stops when they become adults. But the need continues, a reminder of the security and love they knew as babies.

Importance of touching

Can you remember what it was like to be a baby? Probably not. But the memory of those important months lies buried in your unconscious. Like most babies, you were probably held, carried, patted, rocked, kissed, tickled, stroked, and touched in a thousand loving, tender ways. You felt loved and protected.

But now you're grown up. Do you still need the touching that made your early days of life so happy? Psychologists are unanimous in their answer: Yes, you do. Physical contact with other people seems to be a lifelong need. The problem is, of course, that social custom restricts the amount of touching that you're allowed to have. What was OK for a child becomes taboo for the adult

(see Figure 3.15). As a result, many people in our society are "touch-starved."

A university library demonstrated this human need in a simple experiment. Librarians were instructed to casually touch on the hand or arm each person who checked out a book. These people were later interviewed about their attitude toward the library. Unlike library users who weren't touched, these subjects reported highly positive feelings about the library and its personnel. Apparently even a casual human contact is enough to change negative or neutral feelings into positive responses.

A popular bumper sticker asks, "Have you hugged your child lately?" Perhaps it should be revised to read, "Have you touched your friends today?"

1 What are the four types of receptors that make up the skin senses?

2 What does sensory adaptation refer to? Why

do your pain receptors not show sensory adaptation?

3 Why do psychologists believe that touching is so important to emotional health and happiness?

3.6 DO YOU HAVE ANY SENSES BEYOND THE BASIC FIVE?

Quick, how many senses do you have? If you're like most people, you'll answer, "Five: vision, hearing, taste, smell, and touch (the skin senses)." Or perhaps you'll add a "sixth sense" of psychic powers. But most scientists do not accept telepathy, clairvoyance, or the other ESP powers as proven fact (see Chapter 14).

Modern science, however, does accept the existence of three additional senses: (1) kinesthesis, the sense that reports the position and movement of your body; (2) equilibratory senses, your sense of balance; and (3) circadian rhythms, the sense of time.

Kinesthesis

Wiggle your fingers. Raise your arm. *Kinesthesis* is the muscle, tendon, and joint sense that enables you to make these seemingly simple movements. Because of sensory receptors located in the joints, you know the position of your arms and legs and can keep track of their movements. Additional receptors in the muscles and tendons enable you to know whether a muscle is relaxed or contracted.

This kinesthetic sense enables you to carry on all your physical activities, from walking and climbing to threading a needle or catching a frisbee. The importance of this sense will quickly be evident the next time your foot "goes to sleep." If circulation is cut off for a few moments, the normal flow of sensory data is severely reduced. Try to walk. Without the usual kinesthetic information, you can't tell what your foot is doing!

Equilibratory senses

The orientation of your body in relation to the earth and the space around you is controlled by the *equilibratory senses*. Until you become dizzy, seasick, or disoriented after a whirl on a spinning carnival ride, you probably take this sense for granted. But with it, your body can respond and adjust automatically to changes from upright to not-so-upright. Bend over and touch your

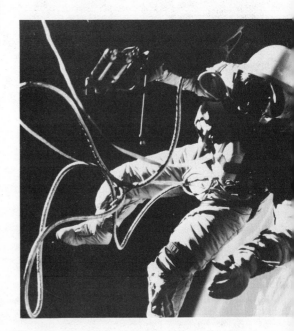

Figure 3.16

The equilibratory sense helps you stay oriented with respect to the earth. But take away gravity, as in space flight, and untrained astronauts would experience extreme dizziness. One Soviet cosmonaut, in fact, had to return to earth early because he could not overcome this problem.

toes, for example. Even with your eyes closed, you don't become confused about where you are. Similarly, you'll know when an elevator starts and stops, even though you cannot see any motion.

The receptors of your equilibratory senses are located in the inner ear in organs called the *semicircular canals* (see Figure 3.12). As your body turns, a fluid inside the canal moves tiny hairlike filaments, which convert the movement into impulses to be relayed to the brain. Dizziness results when the brain receives an overload of messages from the semicircular canals. To make it worse, these "motion detectors" are also connected directly to the parts of the brain that control your vomiting reflex. People who have trouble with car or air sickness know all about this unpleasant reaction (see Figure 3.16).

Circadian rhythms

Plants and animals feed and reproduce according to natural rhythms based on subtle changes in light, air pressure, and the pull of gravity. Human beings sometimes forget that they are also governed by internal body clocks. The pattern of your days seems so natural that you probably ignore the changes in body temperature, blood pressure, pulse, and mood that coincide with the passage from day to night. This natural cycle is called a *circadian rhythm* (from the Latin words *circa,* "around," and *dies,* "day").

Even when isolated from the outside world in a submarine or cavern, people keep their natural cycles of sleep and wakefulness. These human "body clocks" don't keep totally accurate time, however. Subjects in such experiments tend to gain one or two hours a day. Thus in ten days, a normal ten o'clock bedtime may have advanced to eight A.M.!

Jet airplane travel can also disrupt your body clock. After flying across several time zones, you will find your eating and sleeping patterns upset. For the first few days, you'll feel sleepy at the wrong time and you'll wake up in the middle of the night. Sports teams and business executives know that this "jet lag" leaves people sluggish and mildly depressed.

Evidence gathered in animal experiments points to the pineal gland, located near the center of the brain, as the source of your body's circadian rhythms. Although the main rhythm is twenty-four hours long, shorter subcycles have also been spotted. About every ninety minutes, for example, your brain relaxes its attentiveness. That's the time you're likely to get up from your desk to look for a snack. During the night, dreams appear in ninety-minute cycles. Finally, life and death also seem tuned in on circadian rhythms. More babies are born and more people die between the hours of midnight and six A.M than at any other time of the day.

SECTION CHECKUP

1 Describe the roles of (a) kinesthesis, (b) the equilibratory senses, and (c) circadian rhythms.

2 Why would astronauts need artificial gravity to live normally on long space voyages?

3 Explain the problem of "jet lag" as it relates to circadian rhythms.

LOOKING BACK: A SUMMARY

1 The human brain functions as the command center for all mental and physical activity. The hindbrain contains those brain structures primarily concerned with basic life functions: breathing, balance, digestion, heartbeat, and sleep. The forebrain handles most of those conscious activities associated with the pleasures and pains of existence. Of particular importance are the cerebrum and the cerebral cortex. These centers control the muscles, interpret sensory data, and regulate higher mental processes such as decision making, abstract thought, and language.

2 Each side of the brain takes charge of different abilities. Most people are left-brain dominant. In such people, the left

brain takes responsibility for logical thought and verbal abilities. The right brain deals in artistic, musical, athletic, and other non-verbal activities.

3 Impulses travel quickly through the nervous system via neural pathways made up of individual nerve cells called *neurons.* Nerve impulses enter a neuron via the branching arms known as *dendrites.* The impulses then travel as a wave of electro-chemical activity to the cell body before moving along the axon to the next neuron in the network. Since the axon does not actually touch the nearby dendrites, chemicals called *neurotransmitters* carry the message across the synaptic gap.

4 The endocrine glands also play an important role in controlling growth and behavior. The pituitary gland regulates physical growth; too much or too little activity can cause giantism or dwarfism. The pituitary also acts to turn on other glands at the proper time. The adrenal glands produce adrenalin, which prepares the body to cope with emergencies. They also regulate the body's chemical balance and help produce hormones that are necessary for sexual maturation. The thyroid gland helps control the body's energy level and also plays a role in ensuring proper intellectual development. The sex glands, or gonads, regulate the development of the sex organs and prepare the body for reproduction.

5 Humans receive about 75 percent of their sensory data through their eyes. Like the other sensory receptors, the eye itself does not "see." Rather, it converts light waves into electrical impulses by means of specialized cells called *rods* and *cones* located in the retina. These impulses travel via the optic nerve to the brain, where "seeing" actually takes place. Color blindness results when the color-sensitive cone cells are missing or do not work properly. The eye is capable of adjusting to extreme ranges of light and dark, but it can also be tricked. When the image projected on the retina cannot be properly interpreted by the brain, an optical illusion often results.

6 Hearing plays a key role in communication among people. The ear picks up sound waves, which are converted into electrical impulses in the cochlea. The auditory nerve carries these impulses to the brain, where the sound is "heard." Whether a sound is pleasant or not depends upon the pattern of sound waves it creates. Overexposure to noises over 80 db can cause hearing loss, deafness, and higher death rates.

7 The senses of smell and taste are called *chemical senses* because both react to chemicals carried in the air or dissolved in liquids. The sense of smell is located in receptors at the roof of the nasal passage. These receptors convert the stimulus into electrical impulses, which the brain analyzes and interprets. Taste depends upon clusters of cells located on the tongue and in the mouth and throat. Taste cells respond to four basic flavors: sweet, sour, salty, and bitter. The sensations of taste and smell are strongly affected by a person's past experiences and present emotional state.

8 The skin senses respond to four distinct types of stimuli: pressure, pain, heat, and cold. Different parts of the body vary greatly in the number of receptors for collecting these stimuli. Within limits, pressure and temperature receptors adapt to the touch of clothing or the warmth of bath water, a process called *sensory adaptation.* The brain is sometimes "fooled" by conflicting reports from the sensory receptors in the skin.

9 In addition to the familiar five senses, three other senses have been identified. Kinesthesis refers to the brain's ability to detect and control the position of the body and to monitor its movements. The equilibratory senses provide the sense of balance needed to keep the body properly oriented in relation to the earth. Circadian rhythms enable the body to stay in time with the environment, living in a regular rhythm of sleeping and waking.

PUTTING YOUR KNOWLEDGE TO WORK

Terms you should know

adrenal glands	equilibratory senses	parietal lobe
after-image	forebrain	peripheral nervous system
auditory canal	frequency	pituitary gland
auditory nerve	frontal lobe	psychosurgery
axon	glands	pupil
cell body	gonads	reticular activating
central nervous system	hindbrain	system (RAS)
cerebellum	hypothalamus	retina
cerebral cortex	iris	rods
cerebrum	kinesthesis	semicircular canals
circadian rhythms	lens	sensory adaptation
cochlea	medulla	sex glands
cones	neural pathway	skin senses
cornea	neuron	spinal cord
corpus callosum	neurotransmitter	synaptic gap
decibel scale	occipital lobe	taste buds
dendrite	olfactory bulbs	temporal lobe
eardrum	olfactory patches	thalamus
endocrine glands	optic nerve	thyroid gland

Objective questions

1 Which of these is a *true* statement about the human brain? (*a*) Nerve impulses travel from neuron to neuron at the speed of light. (*b*) Human beings no longer need the hindbrain, which is left over from an earlier stage of development. (*c*) Like all cells in the body, brain cells are replaced when they die. (*d*) The size of a person's brain does not correlate directly with his or her intelligence.

2 If Jerry is left-brain dominant, he'll use his right brain when he (*a*) translates English into Spanish (*b*) asks Karen for a date (*c*) picks a new color scheme for his room (*d*) counts his change at the auto-parts store.

3 When a mother hears her baby's cry and instantly wakes from a deep sleep, the part of the brain that controls waking and sleeping is the (*a*) cerebral cortex (*b*) RAS (*c*) pituitary glands (*d*) peripheral nervous system.

4 Conscious thought processes take place in the (*a*) hindbrain (*b*) medulla (*c*) thalamus (*d*) cerebrum.

5 Messages travel to and from the brain via a network of nerve cells that operate on the basis of (*a*) electrical impulses (*b*) chemical impulses (*c*) electrochemical impulses (*d*) mechanical impulses.

6 Three quarters of the sensory impulses received by the brain originate in the (*a*) eyes (*b*) ears (*c*) skin senses (*d*) kinesthetic sensory receptors.

7 Permanent damage to the ear may be caused by prolonged exposure to sounds starting at decibel levels of (*a*) 60 db (*b*) 90 db (*c*) 110 db (*d*) 130 db.

8 The senses that operate primarily through chemical stimuli are (*a*) the skin senses (*b*) circadian rhythms (*c*) smell and taste (*d*) kinesthetic and equilibratory senses.

9 Sensory adaptation is the process by which (a) sensory receptors in the skin no longer respond to a stimulus (b) you assume that the world is consistent—chairs have four legs, knives cut, and so on (c) you maintain your balance on a carnival ride or a skateboard (d) you set your body clock for the time zone you live in.

10 The endocrine gland that prepares the body to cope with emergency situations is the (a) adrenal gland (b) thyroid gland (c) pituitary gland (d) sexual glands.

Discussion questions

1 Why is the brain called the "command center" of the body? What makes the human brain superior to that of the lower animals?

2 Imagine yourself in a Spanish bullring, facing the charge of a rampaging bull with only a bullfighter's cape in your hand. Describe what takes place in your mind and body from the moment you see the animal move toward you until you decide whether to face the bull or to run for your life.

3 List several activities that would be primarily controlled by the hindbrain. Now list several forebrain activities. What is the basic difference between the two lists?

4 Describe the activity of a single neuron from the moment a message is received from a neighboring nerve cell. What are some of the dangers that result when breakdowns occur in the transmission of impulses along the neural pathways?

5 Which of your eight senses would you be most willing to do without if you had to give up one of them? Explain why.

Activities

1 Prepare a poster collage in which you illustrate basic brain functions. For each major part of the brain, find a magazine picture that demonstrates its function. For example, the sensory-motor cortex might be illustrated by a picture of a violinist, the medulla by an exhausted runner gasping for breath. Draw a line from your drawing of the brain to the picture and label the picture with the proper identification.

2 A number of books are available that explore the interesting topic of sensory illusions. Richard Held's compilation of readings from *Scientific American*, called *Image, Object, and Illusion*, is an excellent example. Obtain a book about illusions and copy a number of simple illusions to show to your family and friends. Keep a record of their reactions to each illusion. Do you find any consistency in the way people interpret such illusions?

3 How far has American society moved toward mind control through the use of drugs and psychosurgery? Do some research to find out, and report your results to your psychology class. Your local school or public library would be a good starting place. But you might also want to visit a nearby hospital or mental health clinic to interview the staff members. In your conclusion, try to answer this question: At what point should individual rights give way to society's right to protect itself from dangerous or abnormal behavior?

4 A simple experiment conducted with cold, lukewarm, and hot water in three pans will convince you of the confusing nature of temperature perception. Begin by half-filling pan A with cold water from the tap. Then half-fill pan B with lukewarm water (90° F or so) and pan C with hot water (but not so hot as to cause pain). Now ask your subject to place his or her left hand in pan A and report on the temperature. Do the same with pan C for the right hand. The subject will almost certainly report accurately that A is cold and C is hot. Now tell the subject to place both hands at once into pan B. What report do you get this time? The reports from hand A ("warm") and from hand C ("cold") demonstrate that each hand had adapted to its earlier bath—and now pan B seems to have two water temperatures at the same time.

5 If you've ever tasted a diet drink made with saccharin, you may have noticed that the immediate sweet taste was followed by a sensation of bitterness. The placement of taste buds, which respond to each of the basic tastes, can explain that unexpected sequence. You can "map" the location of the four basic taste areas on your own tongue by touching a toothpick dipped in a "pure" taste to various places on the tongue. For the four pure tastes, use lemon juice (sour), salted water (salty), sugar water (sweet), and a solution of baking soda, one teaspoon to two ounces of water (bitter).

For further reading

Bailey, Ronald H. *The Role of the Brain.* Alexandria, VA: Time-Life Books, 1975. Part of the Time-Life series on Human Behavior, this beautifully illustrated book provides a concise, understandable introduction to basic brain-mind processes. Photo essays on how people cope with abnormalities of the central nervous system dramatize the more technical material.

Crichton, Michael. *The Terminal Man.* New York: Knopf, 1972. Crichton uses his medical background to dramatize the issue of psychosurgery and mind control. This fast-paced novel convincingly argues that medical techniques are far ahead of society's ability to control their effects, particularly where the brain is concerned.

Keller, Helen. *The Story of My Life.* Garden City, NY: Doubleday, 1902 (available in many modern editions). The inspiring story of Helen Keller's escape from the dark and soundless world of her childhood has lost none of its power. She also provides an honest and useful look at what it means to lose both sight and hearing.

Mueller, Conrad G. and Mae Rudolph. *Light and Vision.* Alexandria, VA: Time-Life Books, 1966. This book provides an informative, well-illustrated examination of the physiological and psychological processes of seeing. Its companion volume is *Sound and Hearing* by Pied Warshofsky and S. Smith Stevens (1969).

Scientific American. *Image, Object, and Illusion.* Introductions by Richard Held. San Francisco: W. H. Freeman, 1971. This attractive book provides useful explanations as to why common visual illusions fool the mind so completely.

Scientific American. *Progress in Psychobiology.* Introductions by Richard F. Thompson. San Francisco: W. H. Freeman, 1976. This is a highly technical, but fascinating look at the latest research in such areas as evolution, brain activity, brain chemistry, the sensory processes, and perception.

UNIT II

HOW PEOPLE GROW

4

THE CHILD GROWS UP

Like most people, you're probably looking forward to life's great adventures. Maybe you plan to dive for sunken treasure, write a novel, compete in the Olympics, run for president. Or maybe you've thought about becoming a parent.

What's that! Is parenthood such a great adventure? Yes, say psychologists. To be responsible for the growth and development of a child will challenge your capacity for love and discipline as nothing else in life will. In fact, when parents do not provide adequate love and care for their children, the results can be disastrous. Consider the case of Joey.

Psychologist Bruno Bettelheim called Joey "a mechanical boy" because Joey could exist only by imitating machines. Reality had become too painful for Joey. He was forced to escape into a world of illusion. So remarkable was Joey's "mechanical" behavior that his observers were almost convinced that they were watching a human machine at work.

When Joey arrived at Bettelheim's Orthogenic School in Chicago, he was nine years old. His behavior at mealtimes was typical. When he entered the dining room, he would string an imaginary wire from an imaginary electrical outlet. This provided him with his "energy source." When he sat down, Joey "insulated" himself with paper napkins, then "plugged" himself in. Only then could he eat, for Joey believed that his body could not absorb food without electrical energy. Joey's pantomime was so well done that hospital workers stepped carefully so as not to "trip" over the imaginary wires!

During the rest of the day, Joey led an equally unusual existence. Most of the time, he would sit quietly, his "machinery" at rest. Then he would suddenly "turn on." Like a wind-up toy, he would "run" faster and faster, yelling louder and louder, until he "exploded." Screaming "Crash, crash!" he would smash items from his collection of radio tubes, light bulbs, and other breakable objects. Afterward, he would slip once again into his speechless, motionless nonexistence.

What caused Joey's behavior? Bettelheim checked back into Joey's childhood for the answer. Some children become mentally ill because they are abused or because they are alternately loved and then rejected. Joey, however, had been completely ignored.

Joey's mother stated, "I never knew I was pregnant. I had no feeling of actual dislike—I simply didn't want to take care of him." She kept Joey on a rigid feeding schedule. She never cuddled the baby, nor did she play with him. Left alone most of the day, Joey was punished by his father if he cried at night.

When he began to talk, Joey spoke only to himself. He played with machines at an early age and quickly learned how to take an old fan apart and put it together again. When he reached school age, Joey's withdrawn behavior made it impossible for him to stay in a regular classroom. Time after time, he found that human feelings led only to pain and rejection.

By the time Joey came under Bettelheim's care, his ability to imitate his beloved machines was almost total (see Figure 4-1). For weeks, his only answer when someone spoke to him was "Bam!" His "explosions" served to keep people at a distance, for he feared contact with others. Machines, he told himself, were strong and tough. If he could be a machine, he reasoned, he couldn't be hurt.

Slowly, the loving care he received at the Orthogenic School began to break down Joey's defenses. Each day, gentle hands bathed and cared for him. Nurses, doctors, and teachers worked long and patiently to help him accept himself as a living, feeling person. Gradually, Joey's machinelike existence ceased to dominate his behavior. He began to draw trucks and cars with human operators. Joey even learned to make friends with other children.

By the time he was twelve, Joey had rejoined the human race. The journey was a painful one for him, but Joey never considered retreating into his old prison. As he announced to Dr. Bettelheim, "Feelings are more important than anything under the sun."*

Most children never experience the neglect that robbed Joey of his humanity. More often than not, children move along predictable pathways of physical, emotional, and intellectual growth. In this chap-

*Bruno Bettelheim, "Joey: A 'Mechanical Boy,'" *Scientific American*, Vol. 200 (March 1959), pp. 116–127.

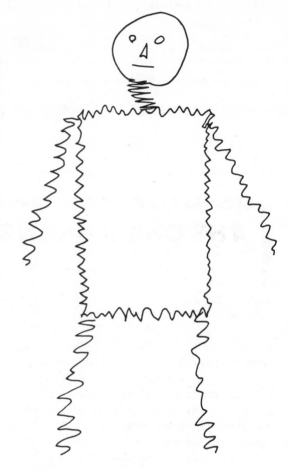

Figure 4.1

Joey, the mechanical boy, drew this self-portrait soon after coming under the care of Dr. Bruno Bettelheim. Joey hid from human feelings by imitating the behavior of machines.

ter, you will learn about those first years of life, when many lifelong personality patterns begin to take shape. The questions discussed in this chapter include the following:

4.1 WHY IS THE PSYCHOLOGIST INTERESTED IN CHILD GROWTH AND DEVELOPMENT?

4.2 WHAT EFFECT DOES HEREDITY HAVE ON HUMAN DEVELOPMENT?

4.3 WHAT FACTORS INFLUENCE THE PHYSICAL DEVELOPMENT OF THE CHILD?

4.4 WHAT ARE THE STAGES OF INTELLECTUAL DEVELOPMENT?

4.5 HOW DOES A CHILD DEVELOP EMOTIONALLY?

4.6 WHAT CAN PARENTS DO TO ENSURE THAT THEIR CHILDREN DEVELOP PHYSICALLY, INTELLECTUALLY, AND EMOTIONALLY?

4.1 WHY IS THE PSYCHOLOGIST INTERESTED IN CHILD GROWTH AND DEVELOPMENT?

Perhaps you've heard the old saying, "As the twig is bent, so grows the tree." Sigmund Freud translated that bit of folk wisdom into psychoanalytic terms by stating, "The child is father of the man."

However you say it, the earliest years of life play a major role in determining the emotional, intellectual, and physical qualities of the mature adult. Locked within the mind and body of the infant, developmental psychologists believe, lie the basic blueprints for later growth and development (see Figure 4.2).

Strangely enough, human societies have not always recognized childhood as a distinct phase of the life cycle. In the 1700s, eight-year-old children worked in mines and factories. The modern child's years of play and education would have seemed wasteful, or perhaps even sinful, not too long ago. As society allows children more and more time for "growing up," the importance of childhood as a critical period of development has been increasingly recognized.

Human infants remain dependent upon their parents longer than the young of any other species. Newborn turtles must fend for themselves immediately upon hatching from their eggs. Even young chimps receive only a few years of care from their mothers. And while a newborn chimp can grasp its mother's fur as she swings from tree to tree, humans have been forced to invent strollers and cradleboards to carry their helpless babies.

Can you imagine leaving two-year-old Perry to take care of himself in a wilderness? Birds don't need to be taught how to build nests, and a young lion instinctively knows how to stalk game. But Perry has none of these built-in survival instincts to help him. Left alone, he would soon die. Human children need long-term care and training during all of their early growth stages.

Stages of growth

The work of developmental psychology centers on two types of research. First, the psychologist is interested in describing the physical, intellectual, and emotional activities that can be expected during each stage of growth. And second, the psychologist tries to explain why certain behaviors occur. Six stages of growth have been identified.

1. *Prenatal Phase* (conception to birth). The Chinese long ago recognized the importance of the prenatal phase by saying that a baby's day of birth is also its first birthday. The importance of the nine months of life before birth is also accepted by medical doctors and psychologists. They know that

Figure 4.2

At this stage of development, the infant chimpanzee is far ahead of the human baby in most physical and intellectual skills. But their heredity will take them on widely separate paths through life. The chimp's intellectual growth will soon end, while the baby may go on to become a poet, politician, or physicist.

Figure 4.3

REDUCING THE TRAUMA OF BIRTH: CAN—OR SHOULD—ANYTHING BE DONE?

As far back as 1923, Otto Rank, an Austrian psychoanalyst, described the theory of birth trauma. Rank claimed that after nine months of warm security in a protected womb (uterus), where all needs are met, the newborn experiences being born as a severe shock. Suddenly, without warning, the newborn is exposed to bright lights, cold air, and contact with hard, unyielding objects. Rank believed that this trauma of separation from the mother lasts throughout our lives.

Frederick Leboyer, a French baby doctor, has devoted his life to relieving this birth trauma. Leboyer likens birth to finding oneself suddenly transported to the moon:

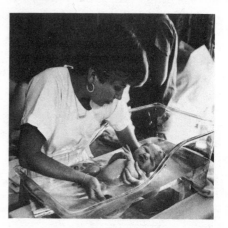

> Out of the uterus, the body has a different weight and density. Its surroundings are vast and unfamiliar. The sounds it hears are tremendous and the air it breathes is different in substance. . . . I sought to make the transition from internal to external life a gradual development by prolonging some of the sensations felt in the uterus, and by slowly introducing the baby to the new ones.

The Leboyer method is still controversial, but other doctors are gradually accepting it. In the delivery room, the Leboyer method requires that the following steps be followed.

1 *Light and sound.* The baby is delivered in dim, indirect light to protect the eyes after the darkness of the womb. Silence is maintained in the delivery room to protect the baby's ears, for the world of the womb was hushed and quiet.

2 *Breathing and the spine.* Breathing air is a brand-new experience. The umbilical cord is not cut immediately, so that the baby has two ways of obtaining oxygen. To protect the spine, the baby is handled gently and massaged. The doctor never dangles the child upside down to promote breathing.

3 *Touch.* Because even the softest cloth will feel painfully harsh to the baby's skin, the infant is left naked. The doctor places it gently on the mother's abdomen. Nothing is hurried. The newborn is left to uncurl slowly from the fetal position, supported by the mother's hands.

4 *The bath.* The baby is bathed in water a little above body temperature. At this time, a real smile often appears on the baby's face. Leboyer believes that the infant is now at peace with the world.

Does Dr. Leboyer's method make sense to you? Some doctors feel that these methods are unnecessary and hinder the doctor's ability to deliver babies properly. If you're interested, look up some of the follow-up studies of Leboyer infants. If his theory is correct, they should turn out to be calm, happy, healthy babies.

Caterine Milinaire, *Birth: Facts and Legends* (New York: Harmony Books, 1974).

the mother's physical and emotional health directly affect the baby. For example, the baby of a heroin addict is born sharing her addiction. Even the birth process itself has been given renewed attention by doctors who believe that the baby's entry into this world should be as painless as possible (see Figure 4-3).

2. *Newborn phase* (birth to one month). During this period, the baby makes its first contacts with the outside world. It must learn to breathe, cry, take food through its mouth, sleep under new conditions, and begin to relate to other people. It's a big job. But the newborn is more capable of adjusting to these demands than most people realize. Experiments show that a baby's ability to respond to adults is well advanced during these early days of life. In one study, one-month-old infants learned to control the spin of a colorful mobile by sucking on a special nipple. Previously, psychologists would not have believed the babies capable of such learned behavior. (Figure 4.4 describes a similar experiment.)

3. *Infant phase* (one month to two years). During these months, the baby shows enormous growth in every aspect of life. At two months, the infant can respond to stimuli but is largely helpless. No longer passive, the baby adds new interests and abilities each month. Curiosity about the world outside the crib or playpen grows quickly. At six months, blocks are mostly good for putting in the mouth. A year later, the same baby will find a dozen uses for the same blocks, including throwing them for the sheer pleasure of seeing someone pick them up. At two years, most children can walk and have begun to develop language skills.

4. *Childhood phase* (age two to about twelve). Childhood is often divided into preschool (two to five years) and the middle years (five to twelve). During the childhood phase, the child learns to cope with the world outside the home. Most five-year-olds begin school, where they must learn new

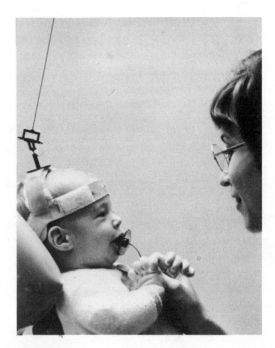

Figure 4.4

In this experiment by Harvard Professor Jerome Bruner, a nipple is hooked up to a brightly colored light box. When the infant sucks hard enough on the nipple, the film in the box comes into focus. The baby's repeated efforts to make this happen seem to prove that even month-old infants will work to make their environment more interesting.

and difficult intellectual skills. They face the hard tasks of sitting still and learning how to relate to classmates, teachers, and other people. Perhaps you can remember your own experience in the early elementary grades. Your world was fresh and exciting, but scary, too. You gained new knowledge and made new friends. But you probably also discovered how painful the ridicule of others could be.

5. *Adolescence* (age twelve to eighteen). The challenge of building a personal identity occupies the adolescent. You will learn more about this challenging and often confusing period in Chapter 5.

6. *Adulthood*. No clear-cut age defines the passage from adolescence to adulthood. Most teenagers are accepted as adults when

they take on adult economic and social roles. Thus, when you begin to support yourself and you move away from home, most people will consider you an adult.

Theories of behavior development

Imagine a group of first-graders at play. Watch them run, jump, and scream their way around the playground. You'll soon spot individual differences among the children. Some will be large and strong. Others will be quick at solving problems. A few will dominate by sheer force of personality. Still others will stand alone, cut off from their classmates because somehow they don't fit in.

How do these strongly individual behavior patterns develop? Despite all their research (see Figure 4.5), psychologists have not been able to agree on a single theory to explain why individual differences occur. Instead, they have developed three major ideas: the behavior-learning theory, the evolved-primate theory, and the psychodynamic theory.

Behavior-learning theory. According to the *behavior-learning theory*, children learn each new behavior mostly because they receive rewards for doing so. The development of language, social behavior, and other complex skills takes place because children's needs for security, love, approval, and shelter cannot be met in any other way.

In this way, behaviors that bring rewards are continued. But behaviors that are punished or ignored tend to disappear. Behaviorists such as B. F. Skinner (see Chapter 7) admit that certain skills (using a spoon, for example) cannot be learned before the child is physically ready to learn them. But behaviorists also point out that a child who is never encouraged to use a spoon will probably not do so. Even newborn infants can learn to turn their heads to receive milk at the sound of a bell. Behaviorists believe that even complex behaviors, such as truthfulness or a love of music, can also be conditioned.

Evolved-primate theory. A second important way of explaining development is the *evolved-primate theory*. This theory is named for its belief that human behavior begins with the individual's biological inheritance. Sarah, for example, may be genetically programmed with the potential to be an Olympic volleyball player. But if she is raised in an environment that doesn't meet her growth needs, she may never achieve her full physical and emotional potential. Social forces, therefore, are the second crucial factor in Sarah's development.

Figure 4.5

The psychologist can observe human children but cannot run experiments on them that might cause physical or emotional harm. Such studies, therefore, are done with monkeys, whose behavior is often similar to that of humans. Psychologist Harry Harlow first separated young monkeys from their mothers. He then found that the young monkeys preferred the warmth of a "cloth mother" to a "wire mother," even though they received their food from the "wire mother." What conclusion about the role of a mother's nurturing can you draw from this experiment?

Unlike the behaviorists, psychologists who accept the evolved-primate theory believe that children take an active role in their own development.

Jean Piaget, a Swiss zoologist and child psychologist (see BioBox, pages 110–111), adds that children pass through critical stages during which behaviors must be learned. If Sarah does not learn to catch a ball at the critical time, Piaget says, she may never completely catch up with other children in that particular skill. There are also critical periods for the development of language skills. An American couple living in Mexico City, for instance, might find it difficult to learn Spanish. But their five-year-old child will probably learn to speak and understand Spanish within a few months. In this case, the five-year-old is still within the critical period for developing language skills—while the parents have long since passed through that stage.

Psychodynamic theory. Psychologists who believe in the *psychodynamic theory* of development emphasize the social aspects of a child's life. They do not overlook the realities of biological inheritance, but they believe that personality develops out of the interaction between one's inner needs and the demands of the environment. They see this as an active, dynamic process. Each child develops a "self" that tries to achieve identity and self-fulfillment within the framework of the culture. In this view, children grow and develop because their needs for love, security, and the like are met by

the realities of life in their own society.

Every child, for example, is born with a capacity for violence. Left totally on their own, children would probably behave like savages (as British novelist William Golding predicted in *Lord of the Flies*, a novel about children alone on an island after a plane crash). In the Yanömamo Indian culture of South America, for example, boys learn early that aggression pays off. The child who kicks his mother or pokes another child with a spear is applauded. But culture usually limits the ways children express their aggressions. In American society, most children are taught to repress their aggressive tendencies. An argument over stolen food that would lead to bloodshed among the Yanömamo will usually be resolved by arguing out the conflict in our culture.

SECTION CHECKUP

1 Describe the phases that Pat will go through before being graduated from high school. Why does Pat need a longer period of parental care than all the lower animals?

2 How would a psychologist who believes in the behavior-learning theory explain Pat's learning to talk? Contrast that view with the explanations given by those who believe in the evolved-primate theory and the psychodynamic theory.

3 Why would motherless monkeys prefer a cloth "mother" to a wire "mother"? Would you expect human babies to show the same behavior in a similar situation?

4.2 WHAT EFFECT DOES HEREDITY HAVE ON HUMAN DEVELOPMENT?

One of the oldest debates in psychology centers on the question of *nature versus nurture*. In that conflict, *nature* stands for the individual's biological inheritance, or *heredity*. Your parents contributed the genes that determine many of your physical, mental, and emotional characteristics. *Nur-*

ture stands for the experiences and environment that have shaped your body, mind, and personality since you were born. Your height, for example, is determined largely by heredity. But whether you're happy or unhappy with your height is determined largely by your environment.

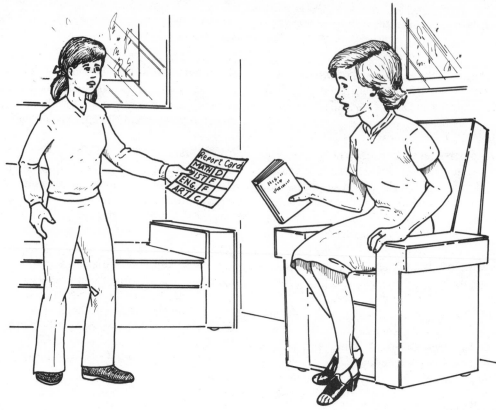

Figure 4.6

"Well, based on the evidence, Mom, do you still think heredity is more important than environment?"

Today, psychologists realize that heredity and environment cannot be separated. In order to study child growth and development, researchers must look at both influences. Scientists who study heredity, for example, know that a boy's height may be programmed by nature to end at 5′9″—and no amount of diet, exercise, or desire will give him the extra inches he needs to play professional basketball. Environmental factors, moreover, may prevent that same boy from reaching his growth potential. A poor diet during early childhood, for instance, could prevent him from growing to his full potential. Similarly, he may never develop the emotional "growth" needed for tough basketball competition if his parents don't give him enough love, affection, and discipline.

Environmental variables

The environmental factors that affect a child's development can be classified as either physical or social. Physical factors include diet, pure air and water, and proper medical care. The child's physical environment also plays an important role. If Kitty grows up in a big city, she'll experience life differently from her cousin, Robyn, born on a Minnesota farm. Kitty may be quite good at finding her way around the city on buses and subways, while Robyn might be terrified by the traffic. But when it comes to saddling a horse, she will be far ahead of Kitty, who may have seen horses only on TV.

Social factors in the environment include children's families, the schools they attend, the television shows they watch, the books they read, and the friends they play with. A community that provides good schools and recreation for children makes an important contribution to proper development. Well-adjusted children can be found in any environment. But they are most likely to be found where families and community combine to provide the emotional support children need.

Heredity

Each new human being has a unique set of physical characteristics. When the male sperm combines with the female ovum (see following section), millions of years of human development ensure that the child will look and act like other members of the species *Homo sapiens*.

At the same time, the child's parents, grandparents, and great-grandparents have each contributed genes that will determine skin color, general body shape and size, hair and eye color, and a thousand other specifics. Experiments with laboratory animals, moreover, show that children can inherit other characteristics as well. Positive correlations have been established between a child's intelligence and that of the parents, for example.

Unfortunately, a connection also seems to exist between mental illness in parents and their children. Although the serious mental illness of schizophrenia occurs in less than 1 percent of the general public, psychologists have found that the figures rise to 16 percent for children with a schizophrenic parent. In families where both parents are schizophrenic, 68 percent of the children are affected. Researchers do not yet know if this finding means that schizophrenia can be inherited. The emotional strain of growing up in a disturbed family might "teach" children to adopt schizophrenic behavior as a defense against a chaotic, unpredictable environment.

Role of the genes in heredity

Nature locks in a child's heredity at the moment of conception. As the female ovum (egg) moves down the fallopian tube, a swarm of male sperm fight their way toward it. Each ovum and each sperm carry twenty-three threadlike bits of genetic material known as *chromosomes* (see Figure 4.7). Once the ovum has been fertilized by a single sperm, it contains a total of forty-six chromosomes, twenty-three from each parent. Every chromosome contains at least three thousand *genes*, which are the

actual carriers of heredity. A baby's genetic blueprint, therefore, comes from both parents.

Even though they have the same parents, brothers and sisters seldom look exactly alike. The twenty-three chromosomes contributed by a single parent can occur in over eight million combinations. Add the second parent, with eight million different combinations, and the total possible number of combinations is now 150 trillion. The combination for each child is, of course, the result of random selection. Only when a single fertilized ovum splits and creates two identical twins do two human beings ever have an identical genetic blueprint. Unless you're an identical twin, therefore, you are truly a unique person. No one exactly like you exists anywhere in this universe!

Genetic complications

Genes and chromosomes usually combine to produce healthy children. But the complications possible in genetic inheritance begin only when an ovum and sperm meet. The

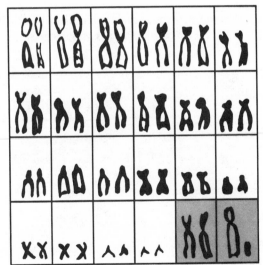

Female or Male

Figure 4.7

Under the electron microscope, human chromosomes look like this. Of the twenty-three pairs, only the last two are different (gray areas). XX is the female chromosome, XY the male.

THE ROLE OF DOMINANT AND RECESSIVE GENES

Pete and Millie have brown eyes. Genetically, however, each has one dominant gene for brown eyes (Br) and one recessive gene for blue eyes (bl).

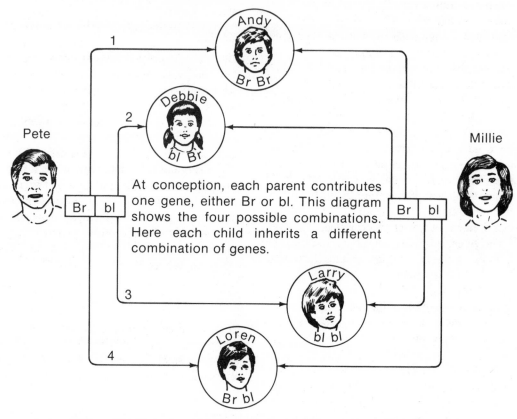

At conception, each parent contributes one gene, either Br or bl. This diagram shows the four possible combinations. Here each child inherits a different combination of genes.

When the Br gene appears, the child will always be brown-eyed. Only when two bl genes match up will the child have blue eyes. Which child has blue eyes in this family?

Figure 4.8

If the mathematical odds hold true, two brown-eyed parents who each carry the recessive gene for blue eyes can expect to have one blue-eyed child out of four. In actual practice, of course, they might have all brown-eyed children, all blue-eyed children, or some other combination.

random effect of dominant and recessive genes and the effect of chromosomal abnormalities can have enormous consequences for the newly conceived child.

Dominant and recessive genes. The genes that determine individual traits are either *dominant* or *recessive*. A dominant gene always wins out over a recessive gene when a child's characteristics are being determined. If the genes that determine eye color are isolated, for example, scientists know that the gene for brown eyes is dominant. Genes for blue eyes are recessive.

Other typical dominant genes are those for curly hair and dark skin.

Now let's see what color eyes baby Larry will have. Remember that he has two genes for eye color, one from each parent. If he receives a dominant gene for brown eyes from either parent, he'll have brown eyes. Only if he receives two recessive genes for blue eyes, one from each parent, will he have blue eyes. If Larry's parents each carry one dominant gene for brown eyes and one recessive gene for blue eyes, Larry's chances of having blue eyes are one in four (see Figure 4.8).

Eye color, of course, is actually of little importance in your life. But a number of serious illnesses and physical conditions are caused by recessive genes. When both parents carry a recessive gene, the odds are always one in four that each child they have will receive two recessive genes and therefore be affected by disease. Hemophilia, Tay-Sachs disease, sickle-cell anemia, some forms of mental retardation, and dwarfism occur when a child has two recessive genes for these conditions. Fortunately, screening tests have been developed that warn would-be parents about possible genetic risks if they decide to have children (see Pro & Con, pages 106–107).

Chromosomal abnormalities. Breakdowns in the transmission of chromosomal information can also cause serious physical or mental defects. Severely retarded children born with the condition known as *Down's syndrome* (formerly called *mongolism*), for example, carry an extra chromosome. Scientists believe that this extra bit of genetic information causes Down's syndrome.

More controversial is the effect of the so-called XYY chromosome. Although most males are XY (females are XX—see Figure 4.9), some men carry an XYY abnormality. Evidence suggests that these men (about one in two thousand) are inclined toward violent, antisocial behavior. They have difficulty resisting temptation. Like small children, XYY males tend to take what they want, when they want it. Hospitals for the criminally insane house a much larger percentage of XYY males than are found in the general population.

What should be done, therefore, with XYY males? Psychologists know that if you expect a child to misbehave, it probably will. If parents are alerted to children who have the XYY abnormality, will the children receive proper training and love—or will they be seen as potential criminals with little to offer to the family or to society? As scientists learn more and more about behavior, questions such as these will appear more

often. What would you do if you had an XYY child?

Disease and drug use during pregnancy

Infectious diseases that strike a woman just before or during pregnancy can seriously harm an unborn child. The greatest danger occurs during the first few months of the prenatal period. A pregnant woman who comes down with German measles may give birth to a blind, deaf, or brain-damaged baby. The crippling effects of venereal diseases can also be passed on to the baby, as can anemia and jaundice.

Equally dangerous to the unborn child are the drugs the mother takes during pregnancy. The tranquilizer thalidomide, for example, caused an epidemic of severely deformed babies during the early 1960s. Even mild tranquilizers such as Miltown and Librium can cause deformities. Drug use by pregnant women, particularly narcotics, has led to the birth of infants who are addicted to heroin or codeine. These babies, victims of their mothers' habits, suffer severe withdrawal symptoms at birth. Other research has cited LSD as a contributor to chromosomal abnormalities. Some researchers also worry about evidence that points to marijuana as a possible cause of birth defects.

Smoking cigarettes and drinking alcoholic beverages can also harm the unborn. Pregnant women who smoke generally give birth to smaller babies and have a higher rate of premature births than nonsmoking mothers. British doctors report that physical and mental retardation occur more frequently in children whose mothers smoke during pregnancy. A mother's drinking during pregnancy can also cause severe problems for the unborn. Alcohol builds up in the baby's body, causing retarded growth and subnormal development. Even two drinks a day may cause brain damage to the unborn child. Such research leads to only one conclusion: Mothers who drink or smoke during pregnancy are gambling with the health of their children.

Figure 4.9

HOW SEX IS DETERMINED

Female Body Cell—two X-chromosomes, twenty-two other pairs

Male Body Cell—one X-chromosome and one Y-chromosome, twenty-two other pairs

During the creation of a sex cell, the body cell divides into a new cell with only one half the usual number of chromosomes (twenty-three instead of forty-six).

When a sex cell is created, the female sex cell (the ova) always contains one X-chromosome. Male sex cells (the sperm) carry either an X-chromosome or a Y-chromosome.

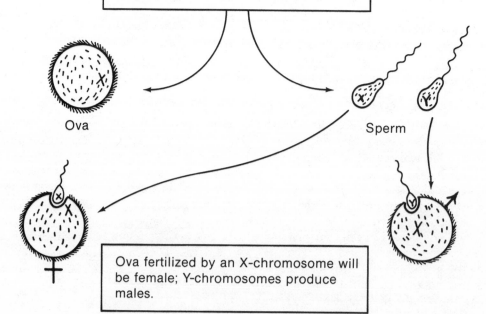

Ova

Sperm

Ova fertilized by an X-chromosome will be female; Y-chromosomes produce males.

SECTION CHECKUP

1 What is meant by the debate over "nature versus nurture"? Which do you think is more important to the development of a healthy child? Explain your answer.

2 What role do chromosomes and genes play in determining a child's heredity? What is meant by a chromosomal abnormality?

3 What advice would you give to a pregnant woman who wants to do everything she can to give birth to a healthy baby?

4.3 WHAT FACTORS INFLUENCE THE PHYSICAL DEVELOPMENT OF THE CHILD?

During infancy and childhood, children grow and develop at a rapid pace. This development seems to follow a predetermined course. Premature infants, for example, even though born a month or two early, develop at approximately the same rate as infants who spend a full nine months in the womb. Physical development can be slowed down but not speeded up. A poor diet can retard children's growth, and inadequate care can harm them emotionally—but neither care nor calories can speed up their development.

Many behaviors follow an orderly sequence that is not greatly influenced by the child's environment. American Indian babies, for instance, are sometimes tied into a cradleboard that restricts their arm and leg movements. Despite this apparent handicap, studies showed that these children learn to walk at about the same age as children who grow up in playpens and strollers. Similar studies looked at infants in an orphanage who were left alone on their backs or stomachs for long hours at a time. These children developed simple hand-eye skills, such as putting their fingers in their mouths, on schedule. Although they did show a slight lag in other motor skills, such as standing and walking, researchers found that the delay wasn't permanent. The children ran, jumped, and climbed as well as children raised in more normal conditions. Lack of loving treatment during the first nine months of life, however, can leave deep emotional scars.

Role of maturation

The process of growing to adulthood is called *maturation*. Psychologists find it useful to study maturation in infants because so many changes occur during the first years of life. Also, because babies cannot do much on their own, researchers can easily measure the effect of environmental factors on behavior. Studies show, for example, that babies tend to master most motor skills in sequence. About 95 percent of all children learn to walk according to schedule (see Figure 4.10).

Some infants will reach each stage ahead of others, and some infants will be slower than most. Such differences fall into the range of normal behavior for babies. In fact, as generations of parents have learned, neither reward nor punishment can hurry the maturation process. One-year-old children cannot be toilet-trained, for example, because they have not gained control of the necessary muscles. During the second year of life, however, toilet training can proceed efficiently. By that time, maturation has prepared the baby's body to do what its brain wants to do—please its parents by using the toilet.

Consider young Maria for a moment. As she grows, her ability to control her own body increases. When she was a few months old, she often aimed her rattle for her mouth but ended up jabbing it into her eye. By six months, however, she can easily stick almost anything into her mouth, much to her

THE CHILD'S DEVELOPMENTAL CALENDAR

at birth
fetal posture

1 month
chin up

2 months
chest up

3 months
reach and miss

4 months
sit with support

5 months
sit on lap
grasp object

6 months
sit on high chair
grasp dangling object

7 months
sit alone

8 months
stand with help

9 months
stand holding
furniture

10 months
creep

11 months
walk when led

12 months
pull to stand
by furniture

13 months
climb stair steps

14 months
stand alone

15 months
walk alone

Figure 4.10

Although babies do not develop at the same rate, they tend to develop their
motor skills in the sequence described in the chart above.

parents' dismay. Meanwhile, Maria has also been busy putting together individual movements into complex actions. Just to roll over requires that she coordinate arm, neck, stomach, and leg movements. No wonder she looks so pleased when she finally makes it!

Effect of the emotional environment

Frederick II, ruler of Sicily in the 1200s, believed that all babies came into this world with an inborn language. Curious to find out what this language was, he gathered a group of newborn infants for an "experiment." He turned the babies over to foster mothers with orders to raise the children in strict silence. Frederick never heard the children speak their "natural" language, however. Deprived of the love, encouragement, and stimulation normally given by parents to their children, all the babies died.

Indeed, as recently as the early years of this century, 90 percent of all newborn babies placed in Baltimore orphanages died within a year. They received adequate physical care, but no one had time to cuddle or hold them. When babies raised under these conditions don't die, they often suffer mental or emotional damage. Loving parents seem to have always known this, even though psychologists have only recently proved it: Babies cannot develop normally unless they receive proper emotional nurturing.

Effect of physical defects

Some children start life with a handicap. Faulty genetics, illness, or accident can leave a child with more than the usual difficulties in growing up. Unless such children receive proper care and counseling, they may feel themselves "different" from others, unworthy, and rejected. At the same time, if they are treated with pity rather than encouragement, they may not learn how to take responsibility for their own lives.

Psychologists believe that the most important gift you can give handicapped people is to treat them with dignity and respect. Perhaps you know someone who is handicapped—blind, deaf, or crippled. If so, you may have had the same experience seventeen-year-old Kathy C. had.

Over several months, Kathy developed a phone friendship with Nelson, a friend of her older brother. She knew that Nelson had been a victim of cerebral palsy since birth. Over the phone, his handicap didn't show. She learned to relate to him as a warm, intelligent person. But when she met Nelson for the first time, the full extent of his physical defect became apparent. He was confined to a wheelchair, and his face and hands were crippled. Kathy broke down and cried. She couldn't face him. It took several meetings before she learned to see Nelson as a real person who happened to be handicapped.

Now, when they meet, Kathy sees only her good friend Nelson. It hasn't been easy, but she's learned not to feel sorry for him. She lets him take care of his own needs when he can, instead of jumping to help him every time he moves. She's also learned that he isn't perfect. Like everyone else, he can be annoying or overly demanding. But Kathy and Nelson agree that their friendship has enriched them both.

SECTION CHECKUP

1 What is meant by the term *maturation*? Describe the steps a typical child goes through before learning to walk.

2 What would you say to reassure a worried parent whose baby is slow to begin walking?

3 How important are love and affection to the proper growth of a child?

Pro & Con: SHOULD GENETIC SCREENING BE MADE COMPULSORY FOR COUPLES WHO PLAN TO MARRY?

A number of serious illnesses and physical deformities can result from inherited genetic traits (see pages 99–101). In recent years, medical science has developed a *genetic screening* procedure that can identify the carriers of hereditary illnesses. Carriers are people who do not suffer from the illness themselves but can pass the condition on to their children. A proposal has been made that would require genetic screening for everyone before issuing a marriage license. Would you agree to such a law? The following arguments might help you make up your mind.

Pro

1 Most states already require that couples planning to marry take a blood test to screen for venereal disease. Since a simple procedure also exists that can predict who might give birth to a genetically defective child, society cannot morally refuse to use it.

2 The social costs of caring for defective children can be counted in dollars, time, and emotional harm to otherwise healthy families. Any measure that will prevent such births should be taken.

Con

1 Further limits on personal freedom of choice by government cannot be allowed. Genetic screening should be available for those who want it. But the decision should be a purely voluntary one.

2 Couples who truly desire to be parents will accept and care for their children, handicapped or not. Society should not interfere with the basic human right to have children.

4.4 WHAT ARE THE STAGES OF INTELLECTUAL DEVELOPMENT?

What goes on in the mind of a baby? No one knows for sure. Studies show, however, that even unborn infants respond to a variety of stimuli. The steady rhythm of the mother's heartbeat, for example, can be both heard and felt by the infant. A month-old infant gives every indication of conscious thought as it reacts to its father's voice or the sight of a colorful ball. Undoubtedly, infants do not think in the same way you do, but their *cognitive processes* (thinking processes) begin very early.

Step by step, infants must learn to cope with the puzzling stimuli reported by their limited senses. "What happens to objects when they disappear from sight? Will Mommy come when I cry? What was that loud noise?" Gradually, infants develop cog-

nitive skills that allow them to make sense out of questions such as these. But these processes do not develop in a vacuum. Motivation, emotional responses, and even birth order in the family (see Figure 4.11) play important roles in the maturation of a child's thinking skills.

Piaget's four stages of cognitive development

The work of Jean Piaget has greatly influenced modern research on the cognitive development of children (see BioBox, pages 110–111). Piaget believes that the child's thinking processes move through four orderly stages. Progress from one stage to another depends upon maturation as well as

3 Genetic counseling can provide couples with the information they need to make good decisions about their future. Before they are married, couples who are carriers can think through the possibility that their children might be born crippled or retarded.

3 Experience shows that many couples react badly to the knowledge that they are carriers of genetic defects. Instead of leading to positive decisions about the future, screening can lead to feelings of guilt, depression, and a sense of having lost control of their own lives.

4 Once conceived, a genetically defective child must either be aborted or allowed to be born. Neither option presents a fair choice for the child or for the parents.

4 Other options exist besides giving birth to defective children or having abortions. Couples who cannot face the possibility of having a crippled or retarded child can choose not to marry, not to have children, or even to adopt children.

5 Society owes each child the best possible start in life. Modern existence is tough enough without adding the difficulty of a genetically linked handicap to that struggle.

5 Except for those genetically linked conditions that result in an early death, handicapped children can, and do, contribute a great deal to both their families and to society. They should not be denied that opportunity.

If you were about to be married and your doctor offered you a genetic screening test, would you take it? How would you react if the test showed that you and your spouse-to-be were carriers of a genetically linked disease?

favorable environmental factors. Even a bright three-year old cannot grasp the same concepts that almost all seven-year-olds handle easily.

Sensory-motor stage. The sensory-motor stage begins at birth and generally lasts for two years. During this period, children learn to distinguish themselves from the objects around them. Curiosity develops, and the baby attempts to make interesting events last longer. Infants learn to coordinate sensory experiences with sucking, reaching, or grasping movements. Language use begins toward the end of this stage.

Another development during the sensory-motor stage is called *object constancy*. From the point of view of six-month-old Curt, for example, objects no longer exist when they disappear from sight. It makes sense, therefore, to cry when Mom leaves. He believes that she may no longer exist and may never return! At two years, however, Curt will search for a concealed toy, certain that it is only hidden from view. He has developed the cognitive concept of object constancy.

Preoperational stage. Piaget's second phase lasts from age two to age seven. During this stage, children focus on their own desires, pleasures, and pains, usually without thought for the needs of others. Children at this age are learning to use language as a tool for understanding and controlling the world around them. But their thought processes still do not conform to adult standards of realism or logic. Four-year-old Melissa may tell you, for example, that a flower grows because the ants are pushing it up from underneath.

Figure 4.11

THE EFFECT OF BIRTH ORDER AND FAMILY SIZE ON INTELLIGENCE

A child's intelligence—its ability to solve problems and to learn new information—is derived from a number of related factors. These include heredity, family life, quality of education, even diet. But research also reveals that Linus (in the *Peanuts* cartoon) knew what he was talking about. Firstborn children, particularly in a family where the children are born close together, tend to score higher on intelligence tests than their younger brothers and sisters. Summed up, the evidence seems to show that (1) intelligence declines with family size; (2) the fewer children in your family, the smarter you are likely to be; and (3) the firstborn child will likely be the brightest.

These circumstances can probably be charged to environmental influences, not heredity. Psychologists Robert Zajonc and Greg Markus worked out the problem via a mathematical model. They believe that each new child lowers the intellectual environment of the family. Thus, if the mother and father together produce an intellectual environment rated at 100, each new child (whose adult intellect begins at zero) lowers the total intelligence level in the household proportionately. The first child reduces the rating to 67; the second child born two years later lowers the rating to 51. (These figures do not refer to IQ but to the total quantity of intellect—wisdom, skills, and experience—at the family's disposal.) With each new child, the rating falls again because a child's cognitive growth is heavily influenced by the intellectual level of the other people in the household.

If you're a second, third, or fourth child, are you doomed to be a dumbbell? Not really. The differences created by birth order don't amount to much—about ten points on an IQ test. Even so, loving parents will want to make sure their younger children receive the extra nurturing they need to make up for their lower positions in the family's birth order.

Source: Robert B. Zajonc, "Dumber by the Dozen," *Psychology Today,* vol. 8 (January 1975), pp. 37–43.

In the early years of this phase, from about two to four, children believe that if two objects share a feature in common, then all features must be shared in common. Thus two-year-old Celia believes that if her favorite ball is red, round, and bounces, then a round, red Christmas-tree ornament should also bounce. By the time she's four or five, however, Celia will understand that such

logic doesn't work. She'll no longer expect all round, red objects to bounce.

Even with greater maturity, however, Celia won't be working with adult logic. Her thought processes will lead her to jump to conclusions, bypassing the usual rules of reason. During this period, children also learn to apply past experiences to new situations. They no longer are content simply to

| Three Years | Four Years | Five Years | Six Years |

Figure 4.12

Arnold Gesell, one of the major figures in the study of child growth and development, collected these drawings from children of different ages. When told to "draw a man," the youngsters responded with their own unique ideas of what a "man" looks like. You can see how the children's cognitive development improved year by year in their ability to "see" and draw faces, arms, legs, and clothing.

imitate what they see others doing. Figure 4.12 provides an example of how developing cognitive skills can be seen in children's drawings.

Concrete operations stage. Between the ages of seven and eleven, children begin to think in more mature concepts. They understand and use a number of specific skills, including what Piaget describes as *grouping* and *conservation*. In grouping, children learn to form systems of classification that allow them to place similar objects into logical classes. For example, Patricia, who is eight, can now classify dogs, turtles, fish, and hamsters by their common identity. "They're all pets," she'll tell you.

When children learn the concept of conservation, they can no longer be fooled into thinking that two half-doughnuts are "bigger" than one whole doughnut. They understand that changing the shape or distribution of an object does not change its mass or volume. Before he understood this concept, young Tim insisted that milk poured from a shallow bowl into a tall pitcher had actually increased in volume.

Formal operations stage. As early adolescence begins, so does Piaget's period of formal operations. Eleven- and twelve-year-olds begin to understand how political, moral, religious, and scientific ideas work in the abstract. Children can now construct and test their own hypotheses. Within a few more years, Piaget believes, the average adolescent will have mastered all of the basic cognitive skills that he or she will ever need. What remains is learning to put those skills to use. Young people must finish school, make a living, and relate to family, friends, and lovers. Chapter 5 will explore these challenging problems in greater depth.

Mastery of language

Language specialists believe that an infant vocalizes every basic sound needed to speak any language. Out of a babble of squeals, coos, clicks, and grunts, growing children slowly put together the sounds that allow them to master their native language. While putting thoughts into words may not seem very difficult to you, language remains one of humanity's greatest achievements.

When you began to talk (see Figure 4.14), you had to cope with three problems common to everyone who learns a language. First, you had to learn the basic speech sounds used in the language. English vowels and consonants require that you master forty-five different sounds. Second, you had to learn a vocabulary, the words that allow you to speak about concrete things (such as jeans, movies, and swimming pools) and abstract things (fun, holidays, and the shock

BioBox

JEAN PIAGET:
A THEORY THAT GIVES MEANING TO THE TIMETABLE OF INTELLECTUAL DEVELOPMENT

For Jean Piaget (1896–1980) all human understanding grows out of the interaction between children and the people and objects they come in contact with. When a baby grasps, throws, sucks, bangs, or strokes a teddy bear, a chain of learned behaviors is started that eventually will lead the child toward control of its environment. This seemingly simple concept has become one of the most influential in modern developmental psychology.

Born in Neuchâtel, Switzerland, Piaget became interested in both zoology and psychology at an early age. He published his first scientific paper at the age of ten! His revolutionary theories of intellectual development were drawn from his own observations. Many were based on experiments he and his wife conducted on their two daughters. During his lifetime, Piaget was called "the greatest living psychologist."

Piaget's basic theory is that a child cannot master a new intellectual concept before he or she has reached the correct stage of maturation. Thus, Piaget said, knowledge cannot be separated from biology. His observations convinced him that children adapt to their environment only as fast as their biological development permits.

Piaget described how he first discovered what he calls the concept of *conservation*. Adults know that changing the shape of an object does not alter its volume. A ball of clay weighs the same, whether rolled into a ball or smashed into a pancake. But children under the age of seven or eight do not recognize this apparently basic fact.

Piaget had been trying to find some easy way of identifying children whose epilepsy hadn't been discovered. For a while he thought he'd found the method. He would place four coins and four beads

---

of diving into cold water). And third, you had to learn grammar, the way the English language puts words together to convey meaning.

Social interaction with older people is crucial to the development of language. Children who spend their earliest years in total isolation may remain permanently mute or mentally retarded (see Figure 4.15). Psy-

chologists also believe that the way you perceive reality changes according to the language you happen to speak as you grew up. That's why the authors of this book are careful not to use words such as *man, he,* or *his* when referring to both men and women. Many people believe that using male-oriented language promotes a belief in male superiority. If women are to gain equality, in front of the subject (Figure 4.13a). Then he would hide one of the coins. If at the same time he stretched the remaining three coins out into a longer line, the epileptic child said there were more coins than beads (Figure 4.13b). Piaget thought that this simple test would separate epileptic children from other children. But when he tried the test on nonepileptics, he found that all children of this age lack the concept of conservation.

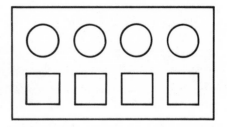

Figure 4.13a

Now, Piaget wondered, do children lack this concept because the principle has never been taught to them? He had some children taught the same language as that used by children who did understand the concept of conservation. These nonconservation children quite readily learned to use the words *long* and *short* and *wide* and *narrow* in a consistent way. But learning the language didn't teach the concept. When the instructor rolled a ball of clay into a snakelike shape, the children could describe it as "long" and "thin." But they also thought that the new shape contained a greater quantity of clay than the original ball.

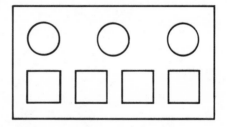

Figure 4.13b

Piaget believed that his principles hold true no matter how different children might be in intelligence, size, or emotional stability. Children, he said, can learn "tricks" to make their parents happy. But true understanding of the logic behind these concepts must wait until they reach the proper developmental stage.

You can try out some of Piaget's insights by testing them on a young child. Perhaps you have a younger brother or sister or a young neighbor or live near a nursery school. Test these children on their understanding of the concept of conservation, for example. Along with Jean Piaget, you'll probably discover that "cognition follows biology."

our language can help condition children to recognize and use expressions that reflect a nonsexist society.

Formation of concepts

Another major step in the cognitive process requires that children learn to form concepts. Simply stated, *concept formation* is the ability to recognize the common features of situations or objects you encounter in the outside world. Children must learn to overlook unimportant features in order to determine which features are important. Cars and trucks are both motor vehicles, for example, even though they come in various sizes and shapes. But is an airplane a motor vehicle? It is. Like a car, it carries passengers and cargo, has an engine, and goes from

Figure 4.14

THE MASTERY OF LANGUAGE:
A DEVELOPMENTAL TIMETABLE

The range of normal language development is quite wide. Some children say their first word at seven months; others wait past twelve months. These ages are average.

Birth to nine months	One year
Baby hears and reacts to sounds after the fourth day.	First words appear: mama dada bye-bye
Baby's heart rate speeds up when listening to regular speech patterns.	
Extensive babbling develops at six months. Infant produces all sounds needed to reproduce any language spoken by humans.	Beginning words are almost always nouns that refer to a person or an object.
Range of babbled sounds narrows at nine months as baby begins practicing syllables needed for first words.	Words are seldom reproduced with total accuracy, for the baby will avoid difficult consonant sounds. *Milk* becomes "mi" and *water* is "wa-wa."

Eighteen months	Two years
At eighteen months, the child begins to put words together. Although he or she still uses gestures and tone of voice to convey meaning, the use of language is becoming much more flexible.	Full sentences with phrases and complex structures develop at twenty-four months. Grammar is used correctly more often than not.
Sample sentences: See that. Bad girl. Drink of water. I do it. Pretty dress. I see doggy. Gimme cracker.	Sample sentences: Cup all gone. Where's Mommy gone? You get it for me. I don't want to go to bed. Don't forget the 'nanas. Baby sat in my lap. I see Daddy go bye-bye car.

place to place. But most children who can form concepts wouldn't classify an airplane as a motor vehicle because airplanes don't operate on land as cars and trucks do.

By the age of six, most children have also mastered the basic concept of categories. They can define almost any type of relationship in words. The two-year-old says, "A ball is to throw." But at six, the same child will categorize balls by size, features, or similarities to objects that are not balls. In this way, children learn to react to the constant bombardment of stimuli in a practical way. When faced with a new situation, they can reduce the complex to simple terms and make an appropriate response. Thus, at age four, young Adam may be frightened by a ride on a roller coaster. But three years later, he'll understand that amusement-park rides are meant to frighten in a "safe" way and will probably want to go on the roller coaster again and again.

Figure 4.15

THE WILD BOY OF AVEYRON

Late in 1799, the Department of Aveyron in central France buzzed with gossip touched off by an unusual event. Hunters and farmers told of seeing a boy about fourteen years old, who lived alone in the woods of the region. The reports described the boy as wild and uncivilized. They said he scavenged for food by digging roots and bulbs, drank from streams, and ran on all fours.

When he was finally captured, the Wild Boy came under the care of Jean-Marc Itard, a physician at the National Institute of Deaf-Mutes. Itard believed that he could civilize the child, but many people disagreed. The debate touched off by Itard's efforts centered on the question, "Was Victor (as the boy came to be called) abandoned because he was an idiot, or was he an idiot because he was abandoned?"

Itard stubbornly maintained that Victor could be helped. After all, he pointed out, the boy had managed to exist in the woods, living by his wits, for an unknown length of time. Victor, he believed, possessed a normal intelligence stunted by lack of contact with loving parents and the social interaction of everyday family life.

Despite Itard's five-year training program, Victor did not learn to speak more than a few words. He was never fully comfortable in clothing or sleeping in a bed, although he would do both to please the people who cared for him. Victor died in 1828, still "fearful, half-wild, and unable to learn to speak, despite all the efforts that were made."

Jean-Marc Itard, however, had opened new doors for the education of children, normal and retarded. His work with Victor, for example, inspired Maria Montessori, the famous Italian educator. Her approach to teaching children, revolutionary when she opened her first school in the early years of this century, emphasizes that children should be free to develop their own capacities for physical and intellectual development. Montessori children choose their own activities. They learn carpentry, household tasks, and other how-to jobs in addition to art, music, and the traditional subjects. Victor, the Wild Boy of Aveyron, would have enjoyed some of those same activities.

SECTION CHECKUP

1 Describe Piaget's four stages of cognitive development.

2 What is meant by object constancy? How can you test a baby to see if it has developed this concept?

3 Why is language development so important to the growth of a child's cognitive skills?

4 What is meant by concept formation? How does this cognitive skill help children make sense of the world around them?

4.5 HOW DOES A CHILD DEVELOP EMOTIONALLY?

Physical and intellectual growth represent only part of a child's development, for human beings also live in an emotional dimension. Your own catalog of emotions is a long one: you love, laugh, cry, and grieve; you feel joy, jealousy, anger, and disgust. Most people call themselves logical, thinking beings, but they are also creatures of emotion. And what a dull world it would be if that weren't so!

Defining emotions

Imagine two-year-old Mary playing in her backyard. Watch her for a little while. Right now, she's the picture of sunny contentment. But her mother just called her to come inside. Her face clouds up, the joy wiped away. Now she's sulking, her lower lip pushed out, her body sagging as she drags herself toward the door. Inside, Mary is told to take a nap. Displeasure turns into anger. She cries, holds her breath, and kicks at the rug as she's dragged off to bed.

What was going on in Mary's head? A psychologist would describe her behavior as the expression of *emotions*, the feelings that swept her along from joy to resentment to anger. Was Mary born with these feelings? Or did she learn them from other people? Researchers believe that emotions occur as a result of the body's reaction to events in the outside world. But they also know that the mind receives and interprets a stimulus according to past experience and that the mind, in turn, tells the body how to act.

To prove this relationship, try a simple experiment. Clench your fists, hunch your shoulders, and tighten your neck muscles. This is the body posture most people take when they're angry. And now, by deliberately copying the muscular tension of anger, chances are you'll actually begin to *feel* tense and angry.

The mind and body interact to determine the emotions that you feel. An instinctive fear reaction might occur when you're faced with the prospect of climbing down a cliff. The sight of the sheer drop to the rocks below sends a cold shiver through your body. But if your best friend is trapped and needs help, your mind can probably overcome that fear. Slowly, adrenalin pumping, you make the descent. You've proved that emotion is a matter of learning and conscious decision making, as well as instinct.

Emotional behavior in infants

Psychologists disagree over the number of basic emotions that infants feel. One viewpoint holds that there are only two basic emotions: delight, which results in behavior designed to hold on to a stimulus; and distress, which results in attempts to evade or lessen the stimulus. An approximate schedule for the appearance of specific emotions in babies through the second year can be seen in Figure 4.16.

Figure 4.16

The complex nature of emotional development can be traced in this "tree of feelings." Note that by age two the child expresses almost all of the basic emotions normally associated with adulthood.

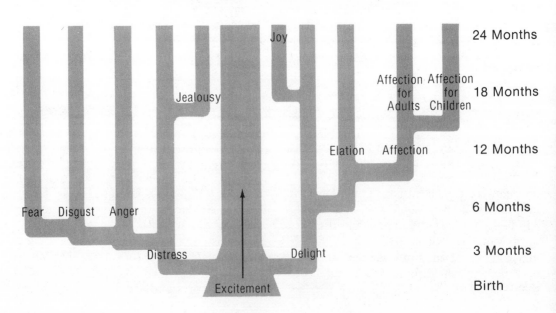

THE TREE OF FEELINGS: EMOTIONAL DEVELOPMENT FROM BIRTH TO TWO YEARS

Joy — 24 Months

Affection Affection for for — 18 Months
Adults Children

Jealousy

Elation   Affection — 12 Months

6 Months

Fear   Disgust   Anger

Distress   Delight — 3 Months

Excitement — Birth

Are emotions instinctive or learned? No one can give a final answer to that question, but research shows that learning does modify the way children display their feelings. Thus, at age three, Diane may express anger by kicking and screaming at her mother. But a few years later, she'll know how to control that anger. Instead of throwing a tantrum, Diane may now silently pout or take a swing at her younger brother when her mother isn't looking.

This process of taming children's self-centered behavior so that they can become accepted members of society is known as *socialization.* Three basic forces work to help children develop these emotional controls. First, children learn that certain behaviors bring them affection and acceptance. Children will do almost anything for rewards such as ice-cream cones and affectionate hugs. Second, by adopting socially acceptable behavior, children avoid rejection and punishment. No child wants to be ignored or spanked. And finally, children naturally model their behavior on the people around them. If they have parents who behave in socially acceptable ways, they will learn to do likewise.

Development of morality

One of the most important requirements of socialization is that children learn a system of morality. Society is changing rapidly, and social standards seem to turn upside down almost overnight. But each child must develop consistent standards of right and wrong, a sense of responsibility, and a basis for judging individual behavior.

The moral concepts of a child differ from those of adults. As a young adult, you understand that values can change. For example, most people agree that killing another human being is wrong. But if you were a police officer protecting school children from a sniper, *not* to kill might be equally wrong. Children, however, tend to see morality in absolute terms. Five-year-old Tommy, for example, has learned that it's wrong to cross the street. He'll probably not cross the street under any circumstances until told by his parents that it's OK to do so.

As children grow up, their ability to deal with moral questions improves. At first, they simply memorize the moral principles their parents teach them. Later, their thinking process permits them to understand and evaluate the rules of behavior. Piaget thinks this process develops with maturity, just as other thinking skills develop when the child's mind is ready to handle them. Sigmund Freud, however, believed that moral behavior depends upon the development of the conscience. He said that experience and training provide each of us with an inner "voice" that knows the difference between right and wrong. Without such inner controls, children would simply give in to their impulses. No one minds when a year-old baby does that. But such behavior in a six-year-old is difficult to tolerate—and unthinkable in an adult.

Development of sex roles

Being male or female doesn't mean that a child will automatically learn masculine or feminine *sex roles.* By their third birthday, however, most children have adopted appropriate behavior based on the models provided by their parents or other key adults in their lives. If every adult presented a perfect model for such behavior, children would have few problems. But most American parents and guardians tend to carry on the stereotyped sex roles they learned from their own parents. Many fathers tell their sons, "Don't cry, that's sissy stuff," and boys learn not to express their feelings. Some mothers teach their daughters to use "feminine" wiles and charms in dealing with men. These girls learn to avoid honesty in their relationships.

This type of sex-role modeling has created rather fixed ideas about men and women. Writing about his insights after taking a psychology course, Sam K. said:

I learned that girls have the same feelings I do. I used to think they were some sort of different species, that they didn't think like us guys. I can talk to them a lot better now. I just treat them like people!

Changes of attitude such as Sam experienced are only beginning to spread throughout American society. Most men would still say that women are more emotional than men, but also warmer, softer, and less aggressive. Women, on the other hand, tend to stereotype men as rugged, dominant, and resistant to expressing emotion.

Today's feminist movement strongly challenges these stereotypes. Not only does such sex-role stereotyping limit the full de-velopment of the personality, the feminists point out, but they don't even reflect the reality of life in this country today. (Chapter 13 discusses sex roles at greater length.)

SECTION CHECKUP

1 What two emotions does the newborn start life with, according to psychologists?

2 Why do children accept the process of *socialization,* even though it requires that they control their emotions?

3 How do children learn masculine and feminine sex roles?

4.6 WHAT CAN PARENTS DO TO ENSURE THAT THEIR CHILDREN DEVELOP PHYSICALLY, INTELLECTUALLY, AND EMOTIONALLY?

When their needs for love, approval, security, food, and shelter are met, most children develop into vigorous, healthy adults. But the same new parents who take skiing lessons or who hire an expert mechanic to fix their car somehow assume that parenting comes naturally. Too late, they discover that caring for a baby requires training and experience. All of a sudden they find themselves changing diapers, mixing formulas, caring for rashes and sniffles, and wondering what to do about toilet training. And even when they've mastered those skills, they still must face the moment when their six-year-old asks where babies come from.

Fortunately, no one has to start from scratch when it comes to raising children. There is help available to parents from doctors, relatives, friends, and books on child raising. There's no way to guarantee that a child will have a happy life, but the following guidelines will help make success more likely.

Love and affection

The need for *nurturing*—warm, affectionate parent-child relationships—cannot be stressed too greatly. For the infant, this means cuddling, kissing, much skin-to-skin touching, and many loving words. As the child grows, these needs for simple, physical displays of affection do not diminish (see Figure 4.17). But older children also need verbal encouragement and approval. Watch thirteen-month-old Sharon take her first, hesitant steps. It's hard work, and the falls can hurt. But her parents' cheers and inviting arms more than make up for temporary setbacks.

The child's entire world lies within the home. How can children develop a sense of self-worth unless the parents—those all-powerful and all-important givers of love and favors—provide support and love and interest? A well-known child psychologist, Urie Bronfenbrenner, summed up the need for love by writing, "The child should spend a substantial amount of time with somebody who's crazy about him."

Adequate diet

A child's nutritional needs begin at the time of conception. If the mother eats a diet rich in protein and essential vitamins and min-

Figure 4.17

If you touch me soft and
*   gentle*
If you look at me and
*   smile at me*

If you listen to me talk
*   sometimes before you talk*
I will grow, really grow.

—BRADLEY (age 9)

Reprinted from *Born to Win* by Muriel James and Dorothy Jongeward. Copyright © 1971, by permission of Addison-Wesley Publishing Co., Reading, Mass.

erals, her unborn child will develop normally. Studies have demonstrated that IQ scores of poorly nourished children can be raised about ten points when they are fed a proper diet. Countless children in underdeveloped countries will never reach their full physical and mental potential because their parents cannot afford to feed them properly. Sadly, growth losses suffered in the early childhood years cannot ever be fully made up.

Adequate diet does not require expensive cuts of meat or rich desserts. In fact, some well-to-do families suffer from "hidden hunger" because they rely too heavily on junk foods that are heavy in sugar and chemical additives. Many less wealthy families eat well because they understand the basic principles of food choice and preparation. Family doctors, health clinics, home-economics courses, and libraries can provide valuable assistance in planning menus for growing children.

Sensory stimulation

As a perceptive psychologist once noted, "Play is a child's work." Even when left in a crib or playpen, babies need exciting, colorful objects to look at. During the first year, a collection of simple, brightly colored toys gives babies a chance to find out how the world works. Sturdy, safe toys that match the child's developmental level can be used for banging, throwing, pushing, building, balancing, teething, and a hundred other useful activities. This type of rich, active environment, when coupled with proper nurturing, stimulates the development of the baby's cognitive and motor skills (see Figure 4.18).

The importance of sensory stimulation and proper nurturing was demonstrated in a recent study at Harvard University. Psychologists there became interested in why some children grow up better prepared to cope with life than other children. When they visited a kindergarten, for example, researchers could quickly distinguish between two kinds of children. Both groups were similar in motor and intellectual skills, but there the similarities ended. Group *A* children, as they were called, adjusted easily to change. *A* children were more outgoing, welcomed new experiences, and seldom seemed restless, bored, or upset. Group *C* children, on the contrary, cried easily and resisted change. They did not find school exciting and would cling to their parents when delivered to the classroom.

Since the parents were matched for economic and intellectual background, the researchers thought that the differences probably would be found in the children's

Figure 4.18

Why are some children emotionally more mature and intellectually more vigorous than others? One study shows that such children received high-quality love, encouragement, and stimulation during the critical developmental period between ten and eighteen months.

environmental background. Eventually, the study showed that the contrasting child-raising behavior provided by *A* and *C* families between the ages of ten and eighteen months apparently made the difference. Before this age, the differences were not apparent; later, changes in nurturing did not seem to change the behavior.

What happened during those critical months? *A* parents provided a rich variety of toys and allowed their children to roam freely around their living area. *C* parents, however, were overly protective and often left their children in playpens and high-chairs for long periods. *A* parents often stopped to talk to their children for a few moments. They challenged their curiosity, refused to help with problems until the children had made their own attempts, and reinforced the idea that adults can be used as a resource. *C* parents seldom encouraged their children to explore their world in order to make sense of it. Just as a *C* child started to look into the mysteries of the vacuum cleaner or the dog's water dish, a *C* parent came running to scold and snatch the child back to confinement. *A* children fell down

and were encouraged to pick themselves up; *C* children were smothered with sympathy when they fell. In short, *C* parents failed to provide the stimulating environment that would have brought out the best in their children just when such stimulation was most important.

Consistent discipline

Have you ever met a spoiled, undisciplined child? If so, you probably agree that it wasn't a pretty picture. Children need discipline for their own protection. Proper discipline protects youngsters from obvious physical dangers, such as hot stoves and heavy traffic. But discipline also creates a balance between the child's desires and the desires of others. Children who expect everyone else to give in to their wishes usually end up in painful battles with those who won't give in.

The task for parents lies in achieving a proper balance between lax permissiveness and harsh repression. Too little discipline leaves children without proper guidelines for their conduct; but too much discipline keeps them from growing up free and independent. At its best, discipline comes from within. Self-disciplined children know how to act even when adults aren't around. But children also must learn to accept reasonable controls imposed by others. You may not agree with some of your school's rules, for example, but you probably understand the chaos that would result if everyone ignored them.

Child psychologists suggest six basic rules of good discipline.

1. Fit the discipline to the child's maturity level. There's no sense in lecturing a two-year-old on philosophic concepts of right and wrong. Simply insist that two-year-old Hank stop pulling the dog's tail.

2. Discipline should be firm and consistent. Children feel much more secure when they know what the limits are. Throw out rules you're not willing to enforce.

3. Use physical punishment only when truly necessary and always in moderation. Punishment should be swift, reasonable, and related to the offense. Old-fashioned "whippings," often given in anger, do little to increase a child's self-discipline and may build great resentment.

4. Help the child understand the reason for the discipline. The old line, "Do what I say and not what I do!" leaves the child more determined than ever to try the forbidden behavior.

5. Reward *good* behavior with your attention and praise. Too many parents ignore their children when they're playing quietly—but give them lots of attention when they're noisy or mischievous. This pattern just tells children that the way to get attention is to *be* noisy and mischievous.

6. Responsibility for discipline should be shared equally among all adults responsible for raising the child. The classic threat, "Just wait 'til your father gets home!" only sets Dad up as a fearful figure more to be avoided than loved. And most children are quick to learn how to manipulate parents who can't agree on how or when to discipline.

Motivation

There's fifteen-year-old Luanne, changing the washer on the kitchen faucet. Dad's watching, offering advice. But Luanne's not quite fast enough. Pretty soon, Dad says, "Here, let me do that. You're too slow." Luanne steps aside. She'll soon be convinced that she can't handle anything mechanical.

Or join the dinner table conversation at the Simpsons. Jimmy has just shown his report card to the family. "Well," says Mom, "that's pretty good. But in this family we expect all *A*'s. So you'll just have to work harder from now on." You can see from Jimmy's face that he feels doomed. How can he ever meet that standard of achievement?

Without knowing it, too many parents constantly tell children that they're dumb,

slow, stupid, lazy, or bad. Eventually, those messages get through, and the children start acting dumb, slow, stupid, lazy, or bad. Psychologists call this a *self-fulfilling prophecy*.

But parents can also give their children positive self-fulfilling prophecies. In general, psychologists find that well-motivated children come from homes where parents provide four positive messages. First, they believe that learning is important, and they communicate that belief through their own actions. Second, they encourage their children to talk freely about their experiences and feelings. Third, they frequently express a warm interest in their children's accomplishments. When the childish voice cries, "Mom and Dad, look at me!" Mom and Dad take time to look and praise. Finally, they expect their children to achieve only up to each one's capacities (see Figure 4.19).

Adults tend to forget how important their responses can be to a child. Silence or inattention, for example, can devastate a child's sensitive feelings. Positive reinforcement,

Figure 4.19

How important is it for parents to take part in their children's activities? Psychologists agree that unconditional parental support (not pushing or demanding perfection) is necessary for children to develop positive self-images.

moreover, doesn't cost much. It means merely being present when needed, giving an extra smile or touch, and rewarding even small achievements with a hug, kiss, and extra attention. This simple principle can give every child the motivation he or she needs to succeed. And isn't that what parenting is all about?

SECTION CHECKUP

1 Why should every child spend as much time as possible with "somebody who's crazy about him or her"?

2 What's wrong with parenting that protects a child from all danger and that prevents frustration by solving problems for the child?

3 Describe some of the rules for proper discipline.

4 What is meant by a *self-fulfilling prophecy*? How would you advise eight-year-old Pat's parents to act when she is clumsily trying to build a doghouse?

LOOKING BACK: A SUMMARY

1 Psychologists emphasize that the experiences of early infancy and childhood play a critical role in determining future personality and behavior. The forces that shape the child's development include the biological limitations of heredity as well as the environmental conditions imposed by home, community, and the wider society. Behaviors not developed at the proper stage of life—prenatal, newborn, infant, childhood, or adolescence—may never be fully learned.

2 Individual differences in behavior develop as a child grows through the life stages. Psychologists have three major theories to explain these differences. (a) Behavior-learning theory states that children learn new behaviors because they are rewarded for doing so. (b) Evolved-primate theory holds that behavior results from the interaction between the biological develop-

ment of the human species and the social environment into which the child is born. (c) Psychodynamic theory believes that personality develops out of children's search for satisfaction of their needs, conditioned by the demands of the culture.

3 Heredity and environmental influences cannot be separated when evaluating the forces that shape a child's life. Environmental influences include physical factors such as diet, medical care, and clean air; social factors include the family, schools, friends, and the community. Heredity is a gift of the child's parents, who pass on a random selection of traits through the twenty-three chromosomes and thousands of genes each contributes to the fertilized ovum. Some traits, such as physical features, height, and hair color, are clearly controlled by heredity. Other traits, such as intelligence, are influenced by both heredity and environment.

4 Genes are either dominant or recessive. Some physical defects can be traced to combinations of recessive genes or to chromosomal abnormalities. Disease or careless use of drugs during pregnancy can also damage the developing fetus.

5 Most children develop motor skills on a schedule set by the maturation of the nervous system. This schedule can be slowed down by injury, illness, or poor diet, but it cannot be speeded up. Most infants learn to roll over, sit up, and walk within a month or two of babies their own age. Handicapped children often need special care and counseling so that they can learn to take responsibility for their own lives.

6 Intellectual (cognitive) development also advances in stages. Jean Piaget described four such periods. (a) The sensory-motor stage, birth to age two, is when infants learn how to respond to sensory experiences in the environment. (b) The preoperational stage, age two to seven, is when children focus on their own needs without thought for others. Language and more logical thought processes also develop during this period. (c) The concrete operations stage, age seven to eleven, is when children learn to use concrete cognitive skills such as grouping and conservation. (d) The formal operations stage, age eleven through adolescence, is when children learn to test their ideas against reality and to use advanced abstract reasoning.

7 Mastery of language is a major cognitive development. In order to communicate with others, the child must learn the complex mix of sounds, vocabulary, and grammar that makes up spoken speech. Another essential cognitive skill involves the ability to form concepts. This process allows the child to solve more difficult problems by organizing data into logical patterns.

8 When the mind and body interact and respond to stimuli from the environment, the resulting sensation is called an emotion. Psychologists disagree over the number of emotions that infants can feel. At a minimum, the newborn shows clear evidence of delight and distress. Emotional responses become more complex as children develop and learn to adjust their basic needs

to the demands of the world around them. This process is known as *socialization*.

9 Before age seven or eight, most children accept moral values (such as whether or not they should lie, steal, or obey orders) only when forced to do so. A more mature sense of morality develops when children learn to accept the needs and rights of others. Learning sex roles also places a heavy burden on a child's emotional growth. Parents and other adults in the family play a major part in determining sex-role behavior because children tend to model themselves on adults of the same sex. Old, stereotyped sex roles are beginning to change, but the change is nowhere near completion.

10 The most important contribution parents can make to their young children is to provide an environment rich in nurturing and sensory stimulation. A balanced diet helps children grow strong and healthy. Firm, consistent discipline teaches children how to control their behavior. Praise and attention, as well as patience, help children develop the kind of motivation that can ensure later success in school, at work, and in building close personal relationships.

PUTTING YOUR KNOWLEDGE TO WORK

Terms you should know

behavior-learning theory	formal operations stage	object constancy
childhood phase	genes	prenatal phase
chromosomes	genetic screening	preoperational stage
cognitive processes	grouping	psychodynamic theory
concept formation	heredity	recessive genes
concrete operations stage	infant phase	self-fulfilling prophecy
conservation	maturation	sensory-motor stage
dominant genes	nature versus nurture	sex roles
emotions	newborn phase	socialization
evolved-primate theory	nurturing	

Objective questions

1 The childhood schizophrenia demonstrated so vividly by Joey the Mechanical Boy almost certainly resulted from (a) a chromosomal abnormality (b) injuries suffered during the birth process (c) lack of nurturing on the part of the parents (d) inadequate diet during infancy.

2 Present-day psychologists agree that the most important factor in the development of personality is (a) heredity (b) the environment (c) the socialization process (d) heredity and environment, which cannot be separated.

3 The first period of life during which the actions of the mother have any influence on the child is the (a) prenatal phase (b) newborn phase (c) infant phase (d) childhood phase.

4 Which of the following is a *true* statement about children whose parents are both mentally ill with schizophrenia? (a) The children have almost a 70 percent chance of also developing this serious mental illness. (b) The children of schizophrenics never develop this mental illness. (c) Only the younger children of schizophrenics develop this mental illness. (d) Children of schizophrenics show the same incidence of the illness as the general population—about 1 percent.

5 If each parent carries one dominant gene for black hair and one recessive gene for blond hair, the odds of their giving birth to a blond-haired baby are (a) zero (b) one in two (c) one in four (d) impossible to predict because the inheritance of physical features occurs at random.

6 Babies who are confined in a restricted environment during the first months of life (a) never catch up with other children (b) develop motor skills faster than other children (c) develop language skills faster than normal (d) follow much the same timetable for developing motor skills as other children.

7 According to Piaget, a child who understands the concept of conservation will be able to (a) recognize that changing the size or shape of a mass does not change its volume (b) solve a problem by using a new approach when the old one fails (c) make categories of objects with similar features (d) solve abstract problems involving social issues.

8 A child's cognitive processes first include the ability to understand fully abstract political or scientific concepts at about (a) age six (b) age eight (c) age twelve (d) any age from two to twenty; all children develop at their own speed.

9 Children learn basic masculine and feminine behavior (a) instinctively (b) from playmates (c) from watching television (d) from using parents as role models.

10 The most critical period for determining whether children will develop the intellectual and social competencies to succeed in our society occurs at (a) birth to two months (b) ten to eighteen months (c) eighteen to thirty-six months (d) age four to six.

Discussion questions

1 What does the psychologist mean by the statement, "The child is father to the man"? What does it tell us about the importance of early childhood?

2 Name some of the various hereditary and environmental forces that determine four-year-old Jamie's behavior. What would you say to Jamie's parents, who are worried that he's been slow to develop the same running and throwing skills as his friends?

3 Is there anyone else in the world exactly like you? Discuss the genetic and environmental reasons for your answer.

4 Name some physical and mental problems caused by (a) heredity, and (b) environmental forces. Discuss ways in which each of these problems can be prevented.

5 Imagine identical twins (brothers or sisters who developed from a single ovum that split) who were separated at birth and raised apart—one in a large city in the United States and the other on a Russian farming commune. What physical differences, if any, do you think they'd display at age eighteen? What cognitive and emotional differences would you expect?

Activities

1 Do you know an infant or a child under three years of age? If so, arrange to spend some time in careful observation. Keep a record of the baby's play activities, television viewing, language skills, motor skills, and eating habits. Does the child seem to fit the developmental schedule for his or her age?

2 If your parents kept a baby book for you, read through it. How did your own developmental stages match up with the norms? Do you see patterns of behavior that still exist today? As a further insight, check your height at eighteen months if you're a girl, twenty-four months if you're a boy. Studies show that at those ages most children are one half their adult height. Does it appear as though the prediction will work out for you?

3 Volunteer to spend some time helping out in a day-care center or play school. Pay particular attention to the teaching methods used and the amount of nurturing given to the children. Discuss your experience with your psychology class. What does the school do well? Are there any areas that need improvement?

4 Organize your class to survey a sampling of the television shows that children watch. Categorize the number and variety of violent acts committed during these programs. Can you draw any conclusions as to the possible effect this exposure will have on young children?

5 Write down a list of your basic values and beliefs concerning money, morality, sex, ways of expressing emotion, and the like. How many of your values are the same as those of your parents? How many are different? How do you account for the similarities and differences? When you look at the way you have been raised, would you change anything with your own children?

For further reading

Axline, Virginia. *Dibs: In Search of Self*. Boston: Houghton Mifflin, 1965. A dramatic true account of the gradual recovery of a severely disturbed young boy under the guidance of a compassionate psychotherapist who is also a pioneer in the use of "play" therapy.

Bronfenbrenner, Urie. *Two Worlds of Childhood: U.S. and U.S.S.R.* New York: Russell Sage Foundation, 1970. This story vividly contrasts American child-raising practices with those of the Soviet Union. Bronfenbrenner gives you excellent insights into the methods chosen to bring about the type of socialization each country desires.

Developmental Psychology Today. New York: Random House/CRM, 1975. A readable, thorough examination of this interesting field. The book is well organized and beautifully illustrated.

Dodson, Fitzhugh. *How to Parent*. New York: Nash, 1970. Out of a wealth of how-to books on the art of raising children, Dodson's book is notable for its commonsense approach and lively sense of humor.

Ginott, Haim. *Between Parent and Child*. New York: Macmillan, 1965. In this popular approach to parent-child communication problems, Ginott tells parents how to help children cope with their feelings. He teaches techniques that stress listening and nonjudgmental responses.

Harris, Bobie H. and Elizabeth Levy. *Before You Were Three*. New York: Delacorte Press, 1977. In clear, simple language and in numerous photographs, the authors recreate the first three years of life. If you can't remember what it was like to take your first step or to have your first temper tantrum, here's your chance to relive those moments.

5

THE ADOLESCENT SEARCHES FOR IDENTITY

Every adult has passed through adolescence. Despite their eight years of "on-the-job training," however, not every adult understands the emotional riptides that mark the transition from childhood to young adulthood.

Even when adults try to help, adolescents do not always respond in a predictable way. Perhaps you can sense some of the confusion Owen Harding is feeling as he talks to his homeroom teacher about his failing grades:

I wasn't even too worried about seeing Mr. Harris, but when I walked back to my home room at three-thirty I stood outside for a long time before I walked in. I wasn't too crazy about seeing Mr. Harris all of a sudden. . . .

Finally I just barged in, and Mr. Harris looked up from a whole bunch of papers he was leafing through.

"Be with you in a minute, Owen."

I just stood there like a dunce.

Then I asked him if he wanted the door closed and he said yes, so I closed it. I almost asked him if he wanted it locked too, but he didn't seem to be in a very happy mood.

"Have a seat," he said. . . . "I would like to help you, Owen," he said.

"What d'you mean, Mr. Harris?"

"You must realize that you're doing very badly. For instance in Geometry and Bi-

ology"—he looked through some stupid records that must have been mine—"if you don't pass those examinations, you could be kept back a year." . . .

Mr. Harris drummed his fingers on the desk and looked at me in a funny way, like I was a stranger who'd just barged in on him. . . . He seemed very nervous the way he kept drumming his fingers. . . . He made me nervous doing that! . . .

He gave me the old X-ray eye treatment —one of those I-can-see-right-through-you looks. Sometimes he talked like he wasn't a teacher, when there was something wrong and he felt he had to know you. He did that sometimes, because he was a pretty good guy. But it always made me uncomfortable, because he really was a teacher and he didn't know very much about you at all. . . .

"All right. We'll get down to the facts." . . . He fiddled around with some yellow sheets that were probably my stupid records; it looked like he had a whole pile of them on his desk. . . .

"In junior high school you made the honor roll five times. Your total average through junior high school was eighty-nine percent. *Eighty-nine percent!*" he said. The way he looked at me I thought he was going to ask me if I'd paid off the teachers. He took out his handkerchief and blew his nose again. "I hate to tell you what your average is now. It's not

Figure 5.1

THUMBPRINT

In the heel of my thumb
are whorls, whirls, wheels
in a unique design:
mine alone.
What a treasure to own!
My own flesh, my own feelings.
No other, however grand or base,
can ever contain the same.
My signature,
thumbing the pages of my time.
My universe key,
my singularity.
Impress, implant,
I am myself,
of all my atom parts I am the sum.
And out of my blood and my brain
I make my own interior weather,
my own sun and rain.
Imprint my mark upon the world,
whatever I shall become.

—EVE MERRIAM

good—I'll tell you that. You're doing very badly."

I stared at this half-rotten apple on his desk. I wondered if one of the hundred percenters had given it to him.

"I didn't do very well in the ninth grade, though," I said. "It's not only in high school I've done bad."

"Bad*ly*, Owen. Bad*ly*."

"*Bad*ly," I said. He was always correcting you instead of listening to what you said. "I did very badly in the ninth grade. Almost as badly as I'm doing now." . . .

"And since you've been in high school," he said, picking up one of the yellow sheets and squinting at it, "you've barely maintained a passing seventy-five." . . .

"The only reason is, I haven't studied."

"Yes, but why haven't you studied?" he asked me.

"I don't know. I don't like to study, I guess."

"Well, do you know why you don't like to study?"

"No," I said. "I don't know. The work doesn't seem to interest me." . . .

"What d'you suppose the answer is?" he asked me.

"Well," I said, "maybe I've gotten too smart for school." Boy, that was the biggest mistake going! He stuck the chewed-up pencil in his mouth again and almost bit it in two.

"Owen—I'm not going to become personal. . . . But if you'll permit me, I'd like to make a personal observation."

"I don't mind," I said. "Say anything you want."

"Well," he said, "after talking to some of your teachers, I've come to a conclusion. I think that you're unreasonable. You're very unreasonable."

Are adolescents unreasonable? Or does Owen have good cause to mistrust Mr. Harris? Whatever the answer, it's clear that for most young people, growing up involves a long and sometimes painful journey of self-discovery.

Psychologists have long been aware of the importance of adolescence. In this chapter you'll learn about the changes that occur during these years. Some of these changes are physical; others are emotional. Both go together in a way that challenges every adolescent. The questions to be discussed include:

5.1 WHAT IS ADOLESCENCE?

5.2 WHAT PHYSICAL CHANGES TAKE PLACE DURING ADOLESCENCE?

5.3 WHAT EMOTIONAL CHALLENGES DOES THE ADOLESCENT FACE?

5.4 WHAT ARE THE DEVELOPMENTAL TASKS OF ADOLESCENCE THAT RELATE TO THE SELF?

5.5 WHAT ARE THE DEVELOPMENTAL TASKS OF ADOLESCENCE THAT RELATE TO OTHERS?

5.6 WHAT SPECIAL PROBLEMS DO ADOLESCENTS FACE TODAY?

5.1 WHAT IS ADOLESCENCE?

Psychologists agree that adolescence is a state of mind as well as a physical reality. For some young people, it's a time of rapid and exciting growth. After all, the term adolescence comes from the Latin verb *adolescere*, "to grow up." That's how sixteen-year-old Maria K. sees it:

I can hardly wait to start each day. There's always something exciting to do, something new to learn. My parents give me a lot more freedom, and my boyfriend and I get along great. Also, since I decided to be a paramedic, school makes a lot more sense. Sure, it bugs me that some adults still treat me like a little kid. But I'm not in any rush to grow up. I'm having a good time right now.

Other adolescents find it difficult to make sense out of their new physical maturity. Suddenly, the world seems to close in on them. As Hammond A. says,

I wasn't prepared for all the crazy feelings that go through my mind. Sometimes I feel OK, but other times I feel like dying. Girls scare me, and I can't seem to talk to my folks any more. It's like having a bomb inside me that might go off any minute. I wish people would get off my back and just leave me alone.

Why do some people seem to coast through adolescence, while others find it a constant struggle just to keep their heads above water? In truth, the years between twelve and eighteen (as our society usually defines adolescence) are a period of tremendous physical, intellectual, and emotional growth. To make matters even more complicated, this is also the time when young people often come into direct conflict with their parents regarding life-style, authority, and values. But knowing something about the process of growing up may make it a little easier for you.

The stages of adolescence

No one would suggest that the values and experiences of a twelve-year-old seventh-grader are the same as those of an eighteen-year-old high-school senior. Social scientists, therefore, have divided adolescence into three stages: preadolescence, adolescence, and young adulthood.

Preadolescence. Childhood ends with a period of rapid physical growth, including the first signs of sexual maturation. *Preadolescence* can begin as early as eight or nine, but the typical ages are ten to fourteen

Figure 5.2

THE ADOLESCENT CHALLENGE

STRANGE, DEEP YEARNINGS FOR . . . SOMETHING
as interpreted by Thomas Wolfe

During these years, Eugene would go away from Pulpit Hill, by night and by day, when April was a young green blur, or when the spring was deep and ripe. . . .

He was devoured by a vast strange hunger for life. At night, he listened to the million-noted ululation [howling] of little night things, the great brooding symphony of dark, the ringing of remote churchbells across the country. And his vision widened out in circles over moon-drenched meadows, dreaming woods, mighty rivers going along in darkness, and ten thousand sleeping towns. He believed in the infinite rich variety of all the towns and faces: behind any of a million shabby houses he believed there was strange buried life, subtle and shattered romance, something dark and unknown. At the moment of passing any house, he thought, some one therein might be at the gate of death, . . . murder might be doing.

He felt a desperate frustration, as if he were being shut out from the rich banquet of life. And against all caution, he determined to break the pattern of custom, and look within.

Thomas Wolfe, *Look Homeward, Angel* (New York: Scribner's, 1929), pp. 596–597.

for girls and twelve to fifteen for boys. The behavioral changes typical of adolescence begin during these years. Parents may notice that once happy-go-lucky children now seem moody, withdrawn, and rebellious. These emotional changes are a normal part of growing up. They may even intensify after the adolescent has completed *puberty*, the physical development that signals the beginning of adult sexual maturity.

Adolescence. During the years between fifteen and eighteen, teenagers must complete what psychologists call the developmental tasks of *adolescence* (described in detail later in this chapter). Adolescents need to work toward emotional and economic independence, for example. They must also come to terms with their own physical development. And they must find their own individual identity.

Young adulthood. The passage from adolescence to adulthood begins at eighteen or nineteen and extends through the early twenties. By this time, the majority of teenagers have completed their adolescent development. As young adults, they are ready to accept their new responsibilities for career building, development of long-term love relationships, and making a life outside their family homes.

If you lived in a simpler, tribal society, you'd have become an adult shortly after puberty (see Figure 5.3). To mark the occasion, you'd have undergone certain ceremonies that social scientists call *rites of passage.* If you are male, you'd have been required to demonstrate your strength, endurance, and courage. Tribal elders would have taught you special chants and dances. You might have been sent to hunt dangerous game, such as an elephant or lion. If you are female, you'd have had your own rites of passage. As a woman, you would have learned special dances, and you might be tattooed to enhance your beauty. Older women would also introduce you to the mysteries of sex and motherhood in order to prepare you for marriage.

Figure 5.3

Formal ceremonies known as *rites of passage* mark the passage from childhood to adulthood in most cultures. Whether the ceremony requires a display of courage on the hunt or completion of the high-school course of study, such ceremonies tell everyone that the adolescent is now an adult.

To an American adolescent, however, adulthood comes in bits and pieces. You may have reached puberty at twelve, but in most states you can't drive a car until you're fifteen or sixteen. You probably started paying adult prices at the movies when you were thirteen, but you're not allowed to see X-rated films until you're seventeen. You can vote at eighteen, but insurance companies charge you "young-driver" premiums until you're twenty-five. It's no wonder young people often feel confused as to what their status really is.

Contrasting views of adolescents

To a degree, adolescence is a modern invention. Only in the 1800s did society begin to set aside a period between childhood and adulthood in which young people would have time to develop their adult personalities. As adolescence became a reality, social scientists began to look for theories to explain adolescent behavior. Out of those studies, two significant ideas emerged.

The "storm-and-stress" theory. In 1904, psychologist G. Stanley Hall described adolescence as a stormy passage from childhood to adult maturity. Hall saw this period of "storm and stress" as a natural expression of physical and emotional growth. Extremes of mood, in which the adolescent swings from joy to gloom, were seen as necessary to growth. Hall's theory claims that the teenager's rebellious behavior, idealism, and self-interest are normal. Many social scientists still accept this concept as the best explanation for adolescent behavior.

Adolescence as a self-fulfilling prophecy. Other experts maintain that adolescence need not be a time of "storm and stress." Anthropologist Margaret Mead points out that adolescence in the traditional Samoan culture is a happy and peaceful time. She believes that Western technological societies cause problems for adolescents by cutting them off from full participation in adult life. For example, well-meaning parents often try to "protect" their teenagers by excluding them from important family business, as when a father hides the fact of his wife's fatal illness from their children.

Other psychologists agree with Dr. Mead. Their research shows that most adolescents pass through the teen years without great difficulty. These psychologists say that problems develop when society tells adolescents that they are expected to become rebellious, wild, or mixed-up. This expectation can become a self-fulfilling prophecy, they say, which creates the very behavior the adult society predicted.

SECTION CHECKUP

1 How would you define adolescence? Why do psychologists believe that it is an important time of life?

2 What are rites of passage? Why are they important?

3 Contrast the "storm and stress" theory of adolescence with that of adolescence as a self-fulfilling prophecy.

5.2 WHAT PHYSICAL CHANGES TAKE PLACE DURING ADOLESCENCE?

Have you noticed how small many of the ninth-grade boys are these days? What high-school senior has not stopped to marvel at the tiny people who appear on campus each September. "They're no bigger than third-graders!" the six-foot seniors laugh, forgetting that two or three years ago most of the seniors were also that height.

The growth spurt that marks preadolescence is the most obvious signal that childhood has ended. But emotional development may not keep up with physical development. Imagine that you have learned to ride a 50-cc moped. But suddenly you're given a giant 750-cc motorcycle. Learning to handle that powerful cycle is something like the job preadolescents face when their bodies suddenly take on adult dimensions and develop adult sexual drives.

External changes

"What happened to my babies?" Mom says sadly. Her smooth-cheeked son has abruptly sprouted a mustache. He seems to have grown six inches taller overnight. His sister, meanwhile, has developed some distinctly feminine curves. And both of them are fighting a troubling case of acne.

This adolescent growth spurt, known as *puberty*, originates in the brain's hypothalamus. As the key control center for many body processes, the hypothalamus stimulates the pituitary gland. The pitui-

tary, in turn, triggers the production of growth hormones in the thyroid, the adrenal, and the sex glands. This flurry of chemical activity brings almost immediate results. Typically, girls grow three to four inches and gain twenty-two pounds. Boys average increases of four to six inches and forty pounds (see Figure 5.4).

During childhood, twins George and Patty looked much alike in their jeans and T-shirts. But as they reach puberty, their body proportions and contours will begin to show significant differences. Patty will probably reach physical maturity first. Her slender, straight lines will give way to the rounded shape of her breasts, hips, and legs. Patty's feminine curves result from a buildup of underskin fat, along with changes in the bone structure, particularly in the pelvic area.

George, meanwhile, will develop a masculine body line, with broadened shoulders, slender hips, and straight legs. As he spurts past Patty in height and weight, his nose and jaw will become much more prominent. George's voice will take on deeper tones as his larynx (the "Adam's apple") enlarges. Patty's voice will also deepen, but not as much. George will probably suffer a period when his voice alternates treacherously between baritone and squeaky soprano. Finally, both George and Patty will grow additional body hair, nature's final signal that they have reached sexual maturity.

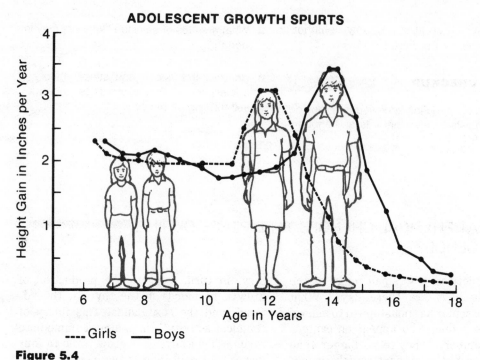

ADOLESCENT GROWTH SPURTS

---- Girls ⎯⎯ Boys

Figure 5.4

Girls reach their adolescent growth spurt approximately two years earlier than boys, but boys catch up quickly. The growth period for girls is twelve to thirteen, for boys fourteen to fifteen.

Internal changes

George's and Patty's rapid physical growth will also be matched by major internal changes. Neural tissue grows most rapidly between birth and age six. During adolescence, however, lymphoid tissue (intestines, lymph nodes, thymus, and tonsils) expand greatly, followed closely by the growth of genital tissue. Neither George nor Patty will be much aware of these internal changes, but another profound signal awaits each of them. As puberty begins, Patty will experience her first menstrual cycle. For girls who have not been given clear, understandable information about the meaning of menstruation, this can be a frightening experience. A year or two later, George's body will begin producing sperm, which means that he is then physically capable of fathering a child.

Although George and Patty are now approaching physical maturity, they will need a number of years of further psychological maturation before they can adjust to their new bodies. Their sex drives, however, will not wait. The internal and external changes described above will lead them into a new world of sexual feelings, all of which carry emotional consequences. These feelings are discussed at greater length in section 5.3 (page 133).

Coping with physical problems

The physical growth that goes with adolescence doesn't always take place smoothly. As Harrison M. put it, "Here I am, trying to cope with all kinds of emotional changes—and my own body refuses to cooperate!" In Harrison's case, he's talking about an outbreak of acne. For other teenagers, the problems involve the effect of rapid growth or the consequences of physical maturation that comes early or late.

Acne. Few adolescents escape the torments of acne. The eruptions of pimples and

Figure 5.5

THE ADOLESCENT CHALLENGE

COPING WITH THE "AWKWARD AGE"
as remembered by authors looking back

I feel self-conscious. I don't want to be handsome, but I hate my present appearance. Weak, pale, small ears, big nose, 'peach fuzz,' weak chin. Now my mouth is out of shape and I cannot smile, for Dr. Singer put my brace back yesterday.

DAVID S. KOGAN

When I think of what I shall be when I am twenty, I am filled with delight. At thirteen I was too fat and was taken for sixteen. Now I am slender, well-formed, and remarkably curved, perhaps too much so.

MARIE BASHKIRTSEFF

My hands and feet grew farther and farther away from my body and set up on their own, reminding me of their distant connection by getting in the way and declining generally to do what they were told. I would have been glad to get rid of them and go handless and footless through life and did not realize that they were as unhappy as I, hiding themselves under chairs and tables.

JOHN A. RICE

If there's one thing I desire in life, it's not to be as hungry as I am. I'm disgracefully hungry. I never had a day in my life when I didn't want to eat a lot.

HELENA MORLEY

When I was in about the tenth grade, I didn't consider myself to be especially popular. I was not particularly good-looking, I was ashamed of having acne, I wasn't a star athlete . . . and I didn't get especially good grades. . . . You can imagine how surprised I was, then, when I was elected president of my class at the beginning of my junior year.

JAMES L. COLLIER

A little later I attended the wedding of a cousin in the north; . . . During the long, boring ceremony . . . I was sadly conscious of what the wedding photographs later confirmed: badly dressed, ungainly, I was hovering shamefacedly between girlhood and womanhood.

SIMONE DE BEAUVOIR

blackheads on face, chest, and back cause new heartache every time they appear. Dermatologists (skin doctors) consider mild cases of acne normal. They explain that acne results when certain hormone secretions that occur during adolescence cause a disturbance in the glandular functions of the skin. Frequent bathing with soap and wa-ter, mild medication, and exposure to sunlight generally produce marked improvement. Scarring can be kept to a minimum if the acne sufferer resists the temptation to squeeze the eruptions. More severe cases should be referred to a dermatologist, who can provide proper medical care.

The psychological impact of acne is harder

to treat. Just when they want most desperately to be physically attractive, acne sufferers find their skin marked by angry-looking pimples. Well-meaning friends and parents will tell these unhappy young people that "no one really notices," but kind words cannot erase the reality revealed by the mirror. Nor does the knowledge that most acne disappears with the end of adolescence help very much. Perhaps the best advice that psychologists can give to people like Harrison is to say, "Take good care of your skin. Practice proper skin hygiene, and see a doctor if the acne gets out of control. Meanwhile, work to develop such an outgoing, self-confident personality that no one will pay attention to a few blemishes on your face."

Rapid growth. Adolescence has often been called "the awkward age." During early adolescence, many young people do seem to spend a lot of time tripping on stairs or knocking over glasses at the dinner table. Psychologists explain that their sudden growth spurt outdistances the muscle coordination needed to handle longer arms and legs. Muscle strength also increases dramatically, almost doubling between preadolescence and late adolescence. The time lag between developing full body size and strength and achieving full neuromuscular control may last as long as twelve months. Boys usually run into greater problems with awkwardness, probably because their height and weight increases are almost double those of girls.

Like acne, awkwardness often arrives just when the adolescent wants to make the best possible impression on others. But while no one laughs at acne, most people seem to find great amusement in watching a teenager misjudge distance and spill peas all over a restaurant table. The laughter and jokes may not be meant to hurt, but they do. Psychologists offer no cure for the problem except to recommend that adolescents develop a sense of humor—and patience. At least, in this case, practice does make perfect.

"HI, FELLAS,,, WANTA GO DOWN TO THE PARK AN' KNOCK THE OL' BALL AROUND ?"

Figure 5.6

Early or late maturation. In the seventh grade, Greg was a well-adjusted, happy youngster. Although a few of his classmates had begun to show signs of physical maturation, he still fit in with most of his friends. But when he reached the tenth grade and still looked like a little kid, Greg began to feel desperate. Taller, stronger boys teased him, and the girls either ignored him or laughed at him. Like many other boys going through the same problem, Greg defended himself by becoming more aggressive. He became a discipline problem at school and at home. He seemed to be always in trouble.

Saralee, on the other hand, reached puberty earlier than the rest of her classmates. She began menstruating at ten, and the changes in her body frightened her. To make matters worse, the other children were aware of her new figure. No matter what she wore, or how carefully she slouched to avoid being the tallest person in her class, Saralee couldn't escape their curious glances and cutting remarks.

Adolescents find it difficult to cope with being "different" from their friends. Yet nature's schedule of physical growth always leaves some people outside the "normal" age range for beginning puberty. Greg and Saralee would find their growth patterns easier to bear if they could talk to a trusted adult honestly and openly about their feelings. In turn, they would be assured that both early and late starters end up exactly where their own genetic blueprints specified they would. In the long run, the age of maturation matters far less than the individual adolescent's ability to handle the emotional challenges that go with growing up.

SECTION CHECKUP

1 Describe the basic physical changes that take place when Patty and George reach the age of puberty.

2 How can physical maturation during adolescence contribute to the emotional problems of this time period?

3 What advice would you offer to a younger friend who is late in reaching his or her adolescent growth spurt?

5.3 WHAT EMOTIONAL CHALLENGES DOES THE ADOLESCENT FACE?

Perhaps you've heard adults say, "I wouldn't be sixteen again for all the gold in Fort Knox." Actually, that's not really a put-down. What they mean is that they vividly remember their own adolescence, and they sympathize with those who are still coping with the emotional challenges of growing up. These challenges include learning to deal with sexual maturation, coping with restlessness and anxiety, and handling shifting emotional ties.

Responding to sexual maturation.

Think for a moment about the last time you were with a group of your friends. You probably talked about a dozen or more topics, from football to music, and from religion to career plans. It's possible you didn't talk about sex. But you can be sure it was on just about everybody's mind.

Sexual maturation begins during preadolescence and remains a powerful influence over behavior during the teenage years. All adolescents find that their developing self-image is tied closely to their success in dealing with sexual feelings. Because today's society permits people to express their sexuality more freely, more adolescents than ever before have become sexually active.

Parental attitudes. Adolescent sexual experimentation arouses resistance on the part of most parents, who expect their sons and daughters to remain virgins until they marry. Some of this fear grows out of the belief that sexual permissiveness is harmful to young people. Parents know that adolescent sex only seems carefree and romantic. The reality often includes unwanted pregnancies and early marriages that interrupt school and career plans. Other parents communicate negative or mixed messages to their children. In the minds of some parents, for example, sex and drugs may be always linked together. Thus, both are seen as evil. Or these parents may promote a double standard of behavior in which sex is OK for boys but taboo for girls. In the final analysis, almost all parents would prefer that their children bury their sexual feelings in school, sports, music, scouting, and other energy-consuming activities (see Figure 5.7).

Despite parental hopes and fears, young people do seek out sexual experiences. Recognizing this reality, many skillful and loving parents provide information and reassurance about the physical and emotional "facts of life." In addition, sex-education classes help teenagers learn about sex in a nonjudgmental atmosphere. Perhaps the most important outcome of such classes is that many young people begin to lose their doubts and fears of being "different." Far too many adolescents, however, still rely upon half-truths gathered from friends, the media, and hit-and-miss experimentation that can lead to unhappy, even tragic consequences.

Problems of being sexually active. Faced with rising divorce statistics, many young adults choose to live together before marriage. In this way, they hope to bypass the mistakes they see their elders making. The most mature of these young men and women see sex as a natural part of a larger love relationship. They believe that sex is not an end in itself but a means of deepening their feelings of affection and shared experience.

At the same time, the statistics show that increased sexual activity has led to more pregnancies, more venereal disease, and increased emotional pressure on young people. Teenage pregnancies seldom work out well. All too often they place severe emotional and financial burdens on the young couple. Whether the young couple marries or not, life plans often collapse. The odds against the success of such a marriage are high. Although venereal disease can be cured with early treatment, it has the potential to cause long-term physical disabilities. In addition, the embarrassment that goes with a case of VD sometimes makes it difficult for people to seek medical help.

Finally, greater sexual freedom puts pressure on adolescents who are not emotionally ready for intimate relationships. No one would think of asking a thirteen-year-old to drive an Indianapolis 500 racing car. But at times the overload of sexually oriented messages received by young people seems to be pushing them into sexual activities they're equally unprepared to handle.

Figure 5.7

Psychologists believe that rock concerts give young people an outlet for the excess emotional energy of adolescence.

Restlessness and anxiety

Life sometimes seems full of contradictions. Consider Josie. At fifteen, Josie's moods swing swiftly and unpredictably from sweet cooperation to angry aggressiveness. She demands more responsibility, then ignores everyday chores and misses her deadlines for getting home at night. Fiercely independent in some things, she wouldn't dream of dressing differently from the other girls in her group. Josie worries a lot about her looks, her boyfriends, her relations with her parents. In short, she's caught up in typical adolescent feelings of restlessness and anxiety.

Restlessness. Adolescents often find it difficult to achieve inner peace. Boys and girls are driven by a general *restlessness*—a need to be in motion, to be doing several things at the same time. Nervous habits such as foot tapping, gum chewing, or fingernail biting may grow into long-term habits. Like Josie, mood swings pull some

Figure 5.8

THE ADOLESCENT CHALLENGE

THE DILEMMA OF EMOTIONAL GROWTH
as interpreted by Anne Frank

Tuesday, 1 August, 1944

Dear Kitty,

"Little bundle of contradictions." That's how I ended my last letter and that's how I'm going to begin this one. . . .

I've already told you before that I have, as it were, a dual personality. One half embodies my exuberant cheerfulness, making fun of everything, my high-spiritedness, and above all, the way I take everything lightly. This includes not taking offense at a flirtation, a kiss, an embrace, a dirty joke. This side is usually lying in wait and pushes away the other, which is much better, deeper and purer. You must realize that no one knows Anne's better side and that's why most people find me so insufferable.

Certainly I'm a giddy clown for one afternoon, but then everyone's had enough of me for another month. Really, it's just the same as a love film is for deep-thinking people, simply a diversion, amusing just for once, something which is soon forgotten, . . . My lighter superficial side will always be too quick for the deeper side of me and that's why it will always win. You can't imagine how often I've already tried to push this Anne away, to cripple her, to hide her, because after all, she's only half of what's called Anne; but it doesn't work. . . .

adolescents from wild optimism one minute to dark-hued depression the next.

Gradually, as Josie grows in maturity and self-awareness, her restlessness and mood changes will lessen. Ask her high-school teachers, who yearly see the difference between the noisy restlessness of the ninth-graders and the more controlled behavior of the seniors. Like so much in adolescence, time usually eases the difficulties brought on by rapid physical and emotional growth.

Anxiety. Psychologists define *anxieties* as vague fears that a person cannot pin down to a specific cause. Adolescents who fear failure in school, rejection, or loss of status may react to their anxieties by adopting hostile behaviors. By directing their built-up feelings against parents, school, or other teenagers, they may find temporary relief from inner pressures. Anxious about her ability to attract a boyfriend, Josie may become a truant or turn to drug use. Other adolescents may take refuge in daydreaming, or they may put on a swaggering, tough-guy mask to hide their inner worries. A few may become physically ill, their symptoms caused by psychological stress rather than disease.

If Josie talked to a counselor, she might gain enough self-understanding to overcome her problem. With professional help, she would learn that most girls share her doubts. Her anxieties wouldn't disappear overnight; but if she is basically healthy, she will be able to work out a productive solution in time. Often enough, as soon as she stops worrying about boys and turns to other interests, her new inner peace will attract new friends—of both sexes!

CATHY   by Cathy Guisewite

Figure 5.9

Shifting emotional ties

"What's wrong with adults is that they knew us as children!" This statement by a teenage girl summarizes the dilemma of many young people. They see themselves as "new" people, unfairly tied by their families to a childhood long since outgrown. Because parents represent a constant reminder of those early years, some adolescents delight in challenging, shocking, or ignoring their parents. In this way, they hope to prove their newly found independence.

Carl, for example, joined his gang as a way of putting distance between himself and his family. Secure within his circle of friends, Carl can act according to what he thinks are his own values and beliefs. Ironically, Carl will probably accept without question the dress styles and values of his friends. Parents, in fact, often feel that their teenage children embrace any new idea, from a dance craze to career plans, simply as a way of expressing contempt for adult values. This disagreement is often referred to as the *generation gap*—the difference of viewpoint that separates parents from their children (see Figure 5.9).

Adolescents also feel frustrated by another set of conflicting statements: "You're too young to do *this*," they're told. But the next minute someone says, "Grow up! You're too old for *that*." Young people rightfully resent such a muddled definition

of their status. Wise parents recognize that their teenage children need gradually increasing amounts of trust and responsibility. Family councils can meet to decide such matters as curfew hours, television viewing versus homework obligations, rules for the use of the family car, and other matters.

What can Carl do, for example, when his father vetoes his decision to take an after-school job? He can get angry, or he can beg. But that isn't very adult, is it? If Carl wants to be treated as an adult, his first job is to behave like one. Instead of giving way to anger or tears, he might try bargaining. "Let me try the job for a month," he could say quietly, in an adult voice. "You be the judge of whether I'm keeping up my responsibilities at school and here at home. If it doesn't work, I'll take responsibility for my failure."

Who knows? Carl might win with that sort of approach.

SECTION CHECKUP

1 Describe some of the emotional challenges faced by a typical adolescent.

2 Why is sexual maturation so difficult for most adolescents to handle?

3 What do you think parents can do to help their teenage children overcome the anxieties that go with adolescence?

5.4 WHAT ARE THE DEVELOPMENTAL TASKS OF ADOLESCENCE THAT RELATE TO THE SELF?

Have you ever tried out for an athletic team or a part in a school play? If you were serious about your effort, you probably asked yourself a few questions: Am I physically ready to do this? Am I mentally prepared to cope with this challenge? Can I handle the emotional involvement? If you answered "yes" to all of those questions, you probably went ahead with the tryout. In a very real sense, you had developed in mind and body to the point where you were ready for a new challenge.

Before you can "try out" for adulthood, you must complete a number of what psychologists call *developmental tasks*. These tasks, completed successfully, are signs of your continuing maturation. Some developmental tasks involve the way you relate to yourself; others involve the way you relate to other people. In this section, you will find out about the developmental tasks that relate to the self.

To accept the reality of your physical appearance

Adolescents often hear people say that "looks aren't all that important." But they look around them at the idealized body image promoted by the media, and they know that's not true. As children, they could still believe in the legend of the ugly duckling who turned into a beautiful swan. By middle adolescence, however, most young people realize that they will never be models or movie stars.

Some young people overcome their own negative feelings about their looks by achieving success in school, sports, or work. Others, however, try too hard to compensate for their feelings of inadequacy. They may overdress or become loudly aggressive. People who cannot come to terms with their body image may close themselves off from normal social contacts. Shy and uncertain of their desirability, they sometimes fall into long periods of depression.

Plastic surgery may be helpful in remedying serious defects such as severe scars, but most adolescents discover that heroic measures really aren't necessary. Sixteen-year-old Kim, for example, wasn't happy with her appearance. She hated her glasses, her chubby figure, and her straight black hair. She was a good student, but that didn't satisfy her desire for a more active social life. Finally, with her mother's help, she started a program of self-improvement. A new, shorter hairstyle complimented her facial features. She went on a diet and took up jogging. When she had lost some weight, she bought some new, more stylish clothes. Then, with greater confidence in herself, Kim set out to make some new friends. As you might guess, her social life improved dramatically.

Was there any miracle in what Kim did? Of course not. If she hadn't been a basically likable person, the changes she made in her appearance wouldn't have accomplished very much. But by coming to terms with the reality of her looks, she was able to develop the self-confidence she needed to take chances in her relationships with others. In the long run, it was the attractive personality inside that really counted.

To achieve impulse control

Do you get up when the alarm clock rings instead of grabbing another hour of delicious sleep? Do you clean up your room when you are supposed to instead of watching just one more TV show? No matter what the incident, when you did what you thought you should do, you accepted the reality of life as it is.

In American society, adolescence is the time for young people to complete the task of socialization. As you approach adulthood, you are expected to develop what psychologists call *impulse control*. This means that you give up the childish insistence on having your needs and desires gratified instantly.

Figure 5.10

THE ADOLESCENT CHALLENGE

THE STRUGGLE TO ACHIEVE INNER CONTROL
as interpreted by Marjorie Kinnan Rawlings

"Boy, life goes back on you."

Jody looked at his father. He nodded.

Penny said, "You've seed how things goes in the world o' men. You've knowed men to be low-down and mean. You've seed ol' Death at his tricks. You've messed around with ol' Starvation. Ever' man wants life to be a fine thing, and a easy. 'Tis fine, boy, powerful fine, but 'tain't easy. Life knocks a man down and he gits up and it knocks him down again. . . .

"I've wanted life to be easy for you. Easier'n 'twas for me. . . . I wanted to spare you, long as I could. I wanted you to frolic with your yearlin'. I knowed the lonesomeness he eased for you. But ever' man's lonesome. What's he to do then? What's he to do when he gits knocked down? Why, take it for his share and go on." . . .

[Jody] went to his room and closed the door. . . . He must be up early in the morning, to milk the cow and bring in wood and work the crops. When he worked them, Flag would not be there to play about with him. His father would no longer take the heavy part of the burden. It did not matter. He could manage alone.

He found himself listening for something. It was the sound of the yearling for which he listened, . . . Flag—He did not believe he should ever again love anything, man or woman or his own child, as he had loved the yearling. He would be lonely all his life. But a man took it for his share and went on.

You must learn to defer the immediate pleasure of staying in bed for the longer-range pleasure of good marks in school or the paycheck that comes with your early-morning job.

Learning impulse control isn't easy. Many adolescents become impatient when the world does not respond to their wishes. They feel locked into an artificial world of school and family that seems far removed from "real" life. In time, however, most young people learn to exercise control over the impulse to strike out at what they don't like or to grab what pleases them. Those who don't learn this lesson as adolescents will find that the adult world has little patience with people who can't wait for their pleasures.

To prepare for economic independence

Not too many generations ago, children usually followed in their parents' footsteps when they selected a vocation. Most boys became businessmen, machinists, butchers, or farmers; most girls became wives and mothers. In the second half of this century, a number of factors have changed that limiting choice of careers.

1. Many parents no longer demand that their children follow in the family tradition. Today's young people tend to choose occupations that meet their own interests and needs, rather than those that meet family expectations.

2. Rapid technological change puts a premium on specialized training. Fewer and fewer low-skill, manual-labor jobs are available. Even trained workers must be ready to adjust to a changing job market. Economists warn that at least half the jobs people will be working at ten years from now do not exist at the present time.

3. With more time to grow up and study the world of work, many young people feel confused as to the vocation they want to pursue. On the one hand, they want a job that pays well enough to support a comfortable way of life. On the other hand, they also demand a job that gives them a feeling of inner satisfaction. Unfortunately, the majority of jobs available do not meet both of those objectives.

4. The old certainty that a college degree will automatically open the door to a well-paid, satisfying career no longer holds true. Magazines, newspapers, and television often report on Ph.D.'s who tend bar or work in heavy construction. As a result, people have begun to demand that high schools and colleges teach skills that can be converted into jobs upon graduation.

5. The civil rights and feminist movements have opened up new career opportunities to minorities and women. Equal opportunity and equal pay for equal work have been added to the legal and social foundations of American society. Teenage girls, for example, can now aspire to be astronauts and engineers. The goal of previous generations to marry "Mr. Right" and live in an ivy-covered cottage no longer has the attraction it once had.

School and community agencies provide vocational counseling that can help young people connect the three corners of the career triangle: abilities, training, and job opportunities. You might have friends, however, who took the first opening that came along. The lure of a quick paycheck that could be turned into a car, apartment, or expensive stereo often leads to boring, dead-end jobs. If you're willing to wait, you can use the insight provided by vocational counselors to make plans that will lead to responsible, satisfying—and financially rewarding—jobs in the future.

To develop a new concept of self

Psychologist Erik Erikson believes that the single most important task any human being must face is that of achieving a clear sense of personal identity. He stresses that success in the tasks of adult life, such as building a career and achieving intimacy with friends, depend in large part upon completing the search for identity during adolescence.

To achieve *self-identity* means to adopt goals and values that will allow you to make good decisions about your life. You'll make some of these decisions consciously, others unconsciously. Your age, sex, ethnic background, religious training, school experiences, family goals, and personal values will all play a part in your choices (see Figure 5.11). Developing a sense of pride and confidence in yourself is also part of self-identity. That feeling—what psychologists call self-worth—is a measure of your success in reaching the goals you set for yourself. People who lack self-worth tend to let others make their life decisions for them.

Another difficulty in achieving self-identity comes, surprisingly enough, from the "freedom to be" that most Americans enjoy. You can go practically anywhere and do practically anything. If you wish, you can join the Navy, learn karate, or apply to law school. Faced with so many choices, some young people become paralyzed. They fear that a single wrong decision will destroy their chances for future happiness. Psychologists are quick to point out, however, that life is made up of many choices. Some matter more than others. Life-shaping decisions should be made only after you've carefully evaluated all the factors involved. But if you do make a mistake, you can always correct it. The only person who can truly lock you into a bad choice . . . is *you*.

SECTION CHECKUP

1 What does the psychologist mean by "developmental tasks"? Discuss the importance of the four developmental tasks that apply to the self.

2 Why would it be a mistake for a parent to tell a child, "Don't worry, dear. When you grow up you'll be even better looking than a movie star."?

3 Explain what Erikson means by "achieving a clear sense of personal identity." Why is it so hard to do?

WHO AM I?

Figure 5.11

Self-identity is composed of all the influences that shape a person's life. Can you pick out the people and ideas that affect your life and identity?

5.5 WHAT ARE THE DEVELOPMENTAL TASKS OF ADOLESCENCE THAT RELATE TO OTHERS?

Most adolescents must grow and find their self-identity within the borders of their own communities. To do so requires that they add developmental tasks related to the people around them to those related to the self.

To achieve emotional independence from the family

True emotional independence comes only when adolescents and their families work together to untie the bonds that have held

Figure 5.12

YOU CAN'T MAKE ANYONE LOVE YOU

Psychologist-author Sheldon Kopp sat down one day to write a letter to a friend. What came out, he says, was "a visionary list of the truths that at my best shape my life." These are some of the things he wrote:

1 There is no way of getting all you want.

2 You can't have anything unless you let go of it.

3 You can't make anyone love you.

4 Everyone lies, cheats, pretends (yes, you too, and most certainly I myself).

5 Love is not enough, but it sure helps.

6 You are free to do whatever you like. You need only face the consequences.

7 We have only ourselves, and one another. That may not be much, but that's all there is.

Do any of Kopp's ideas match up with your own experiences? Can you use any of them to help shape your own sense of who you are and what you want out of life?

Reprinted by permission of the author and the publisher from *No Hidden Meanings,* by Sheldon Kopp. Palo Alto, California. Science & Behavior Books Inc., 1975.

them together. Because many stressful parent-adolescent relationships make good communication almost impossible, this mutual cooperation may not come easily. But even if Neal R. packs his bags and runs a thousand miles away, the old emotional ties will remain. Growing up in his family left Neal with a great deal of unfinished business. Before he can be truly free, he must take care of old debts and guilts, speak openly about his feelings, and listen to what his parents have to say. Some families make a ceremony of this, clearing the air by exchanging feelings in open, honest exchanges. When the sons and daughters leave home, they receive a house key as a symbol of their right to return at any time, no questions asked.

The process by which young people achieve emotional independence from their families is not a smooth one, however. What complicates this process is that young people and their parents approach the task with different views.

Adolescent views. For most adolescents, the struggle with parents can be summed up in a single word: *independence!* Issues that are minor in themselves may lead to major battles when parental orders run counter to the young person's wishes. You've probably gone through debates over clothes, curfew hours, choice of friends, use of alcohol or drugs, tastes in music, or driving the family car. As adolescents mature, parents should give them progressively greater freedom and responsibility to make their own choices. A parent who exercises overly strict control in such matters runs the risk of touching off a rebellion. Parents who keep few limits, however, often leave their children convinced that Mom and Dad don't really care what happens to them.

More complex emotions also enter into parent-adolescent relations. Young people may also experience vague guilt feelings about leaving the family circle. Rhonda may know, for example, that her parents want her to celebrate the Fourth of July at home in the traditional way. But the party at her friend's house promises to be really great. This dilemma pulls teenagers in two directions. To get rid of the conflict, they may attack the family's values, magnifying their faults as a means of justifying their own decisions. Thus, Rhonda will justify going to her friend's party by saying to her parents, "These family picnics are really dull! You just want me to stay around home so I won't have fun with my friends."

In time, adolescents will learn to see their parents in a more objective light. This may not happen until they reach adulthood. With maturity will come an appreciation for the positive contributions the family made to their growth. Even the parental faults that in adolescence created such fury will be seen as forgivable. Mark Twain, creator of Tom Sawyer and Huckleberry Finn, summed it up when he wrote, "When I was fourteen, I wondered how a man like my father could be so dumb and still live. When I was twenty-one, I was amazed at how much the man had learned in seven years!"

Parents' views. Many parents see adolescence as a long period of obnoxious behavior by the same children who only a few years earlier were sleeping in their arms. Even though they sincerely want to help their children achieve adult independence, they also want to protect them from pain and disappointment. Mr. Rose, for example, remembers the trouble he got into when he smashed up the family car. So it's little wonder that he holds back on giving his son Bob permission to use the family car for a Saturday night date.

Many parents also experience unconscious emotions that keep them from giving independence to their children, even where the independence has been earned. Some nonworking mothers, for example, unconsciously fear the "empty-nest syndrome," that sense of uselessness that follows when the last child has left home. Parents whose lives are filled with hard work and worries may also unconsciously envy the fresh start and apparently carefree existence of their adolescent children. Finally, growing children signal to parents that they are growing older themselves. Middle-aged men and women can no longer pass for "almost thirty" when a son or daughter is claiming adult privileges.

To cope with group pressures

"Everyone else is doing it, Sammy."

"Come on, Sue, don't be chicken!"

How many times have you heard similar statements from your friends? Or how do you feel if your *A* on the test results in sarcastic comments from the rest of the class?

This type of peer pressure makes the search for self-identity even more difficult. Despite such conflicts, many courageous young people hold fast to the values they have gained from family, church, and their own personal philosophy. In keeping with the teachings of her church, Nadia would never take a drink of liquor, for example. But Sophia, whose own religion has equally clear rules, may "go along" with the group in order to save face. Her feelings of guilt, however, will make it difficult for her to enjoy her hard-won popularity. That Sophia would continue to give in to peer pressure despite her bad feelings demonstrates the powerful need adolescents have for peer-group approval.

If you want to avoid being caught in this type of bind, take a careful look at the peer groups you join. Groups such as Explorer Scouts, church youth groups, community orchestras, and the like, generally are predictable. You know ahead of time exactly what you're getting into. But choosing a group of friends opens up other possibilities. Delinquency, for example, frequently grows out of peer group associations. In a study of two matched groups from inner city neighborhoods, researchers discovered that 98.4 percent of the delinquents ran around with other delinquents. Only 7.4 percent of

Figure 5.13

THE ADOLESCENT CHALLENGE

THE CONSEQUENCES OF EMOTIONAL DEPENDENCE ON PARENTS
as interpreted by Sherwood Anderson

You are always hearing it said that fathers want their sons to be what they feel they cannot themselves be but I tell you it also works the other way. . . . I wanted him to be a proud, silent, dignified one [father]. When I was with other boys and he passed along the street, I wanted to feel in my breast the glow of pride.

"There he is. That is my father."

But he wasn't such a one. He couldn't be. It seemed to me then that he was always showing off. Let's say someone in our town had got up a show. . . . He had managed to get the chief comedy part. . . . He had to do the most absurd things. They thought he was funny, but I didn't think so.

He couldn't ride for shucks. He fell off the horse, and everyone hooted with laughter but he did not care. He even seemed to like it. I remember one such occasion when he had done something ridiculous, . . . I was with some other boys and they were laughing and shouting at him and he was shouting back to them and having as good a time as they were. I ran away. There was an alleyway back of the stores on main street and I ran down that. There were some sheds, back of the Presbyterian church, where country people stabled horses during church on Sundays and I went in there. I had a good long cry.

Sherwood Anderson, *Memoirs* (New York: Harcourt Brace Jovanovich, 1942), pp. 78–79.

---

the nondelinquents who lived in the same neighborhood had friends among the trouble-prone youths.

Nevertheless, psychologists encourage you to spend time with your peers. Growing up, after all, requires that you spend more time with your friends and less with your family. The trick is to find those true friends with whom you can share your deepest thoughts and feelings. These are the people who accept you for the person you are. They don't try to change you, nor do they measure friendship in money or willingness to go along with the "gang." When you do find that sort of friendship, it will lead to some of the most rewarding experiences of your life. Sharing good times and helping each other

through the bad can build the trust and intimacy it takes to bridge the years.

SECTION CHECKUP

1. What are the developmental tasks of adolescence that relate to others?

2. Why do psychologists say that you can achieve emotional independence from your family only when you all cooperate to untie the bonds that hold you together?

3. What are some of the unconscious feelings that cause parents to hold on too tightly to their children?

4. Despite the possible dangers of giving in to peer pressures, why would it be unwise for sixteen-year-old Bill to refuse to join any peer group?

Pro & Con: DO MANY OF THE PROBLEMS OF ADOLESCENCE RESULT FROM THE BREAKUP OF THE TRADITIONAL AMERICAN FAMILY?

Since the turn of the century, some psychologists have described adolescence as a natural time of "storm and stress." Others, however, believe that the problems of adolescence reflect changing social conditions. Many of the stresses of adolescence, they charge, lie in the breakup of the traditional American family. The following arguments will give you a chance to make up your own mind about this debate.

Pro

1 Divorce today threatens the stability of one out of three American marriages. These divorces always disrupt home life when children are involved.

2 Children raised in one-parent families, by guardians or relatives, or in families where both parents work seldom receive sufficient nurturing. During adolescence this neglect often shows up in antisocial behavior. This behavior can almost always be seen as a demand for parental attention.

3 Juvenile delinquency statistics show alarming increases. Some experts believe that this epidemic of teenage crime can be related to family breakup. Society cannot afford to ignore this connection.

4 Lack of parental guidance often leaves adolescents exposed to antisocial values. Reliance on negative values often leads, in turn, to drug use, gang membership, and crime.

5 A mobile, restless society has turned many homes into places where people merely eat and sleep. Americans have been segregated into age groups, thus releasing adolescents from family contacts and encouraging a "do-your-own-thing" mentality.

Con

1 Family life goes on, regardless of statistics. Most kids still grow up in intact families. When divorce or separation do occur, emotionally healthy children seem to handle the disruption quite well.

2 Being raised by two biological parents does not guarantee proper nurturing. Moreover, the economics of survival often require that both parents work. Children, it turns out, can grow up healthy in one-, two-, or multi-parent families. Quality of care, not quantity, determines adolescent stability.

3 The media play up the sensational aspects of adolescent crime. Kids do get into trouble, but people seldom remember that the "pranks" of yesterday are often defined as crimes today.

4 Adolescents naturally seek out involvement with friends who share their values. This is a normal part of the growing-up process. Poverty, unemployment, and inadequate schools are far more likely than family breakups to lead to juvenile problems.

5 Age segregation, if it does exist, is neither good nor bad. Social change happens; societies accept it or reject it. America's emerging life-style has many positive values, and a back-to-the-family movement has already begun.

What evidence have you seen in your own family or neighborhood to confirm or deny these arguments? What advice would you offer to the parents of an eleven-year-old about guiding their child through the adolescent years?

5.6 WHAT SPECIAL PROBLEMS DO ADOLESCENTS FACE TODAY?

Apparently, adolescence has never been an easy period for either parents or young people. A clay tablet from the four-thousand-year-old Fertile-Crescent civilization of Sumer records the words of a father: "Why do you idle about? Perverse one with whom I am furious . . . Night and day am I tortured because of you. Night and day you waste in pleasures."

The possibilities for mistakes and self-destructive behavior, however, seem greater now than ever before. Today's adolescent faces problems that make growing up both difficult and challenging. Some of the most critical of these problems are early marriage, unwanted pregnancy, use of drugs or alcohol, and delinquency.

Early marriage

With all the experiments in living together that have marked America's changing sexual patterns, you might wonder if anyone is getting married these days. In fact, large numbers of young people still fall in love and decide to marry (see Figure 5.14). But al-

---

Figure 5.14

ERICH FROMM ON "THE ART OF LOVING"

Erich Fromm (1900–1980), one of this century's most respected psychologists, believes that love is an art. Like all worthwhile achievements, people will experience true love relationships only when they learn how to love, Fromm tells us. First, one must master the theory; later, one can gain mastery through practice—much as an artist learns to paint or a woodworker to build beautiful furniture.

Why do so few people learn this art? Fromm suggests that we don't believe that love is important enough:

Susan Lapides 1981, Design Conceptions.

> In spite of the deep-seated craving for love, almost everything else is considered to be more important than love: success, prestige, money, power—almost all our energy is used for the learning of how to achieve these aims, and almost none to learn the art of loving.

How do we know when we are truly and rightly in love? Listen to these words:

If I truly love one person I love all persons, I love the world, I love life. If I can say to somebody else, "I love you," I must be able to say, "I love in you everybody, I love through you the world, I love in you also myself."*

*Erich Fromm, *The Art of Loving* (New York: Harper & Row, 1956).

Figure 5.15

THE ADOLESCENT CHALLENGE

THE DAY THAT CHILDHOOD ENDED
as interpreted by Ann Head

I gave BoJo the bad news the next day in the same booth in the same drugstore where all those million trillion years ago we had promised not to let things get out of hand again.

He didn't faint, and he didn't swear, and he didn't actually break down and cry . . .

"Have you told your family?"

"No."

. . . "I think maybe you should, don't you?" . . .

I said, "I think you're trying to tell me something, . . . I think you're trying to tell me that this is *my* little red wagon. *All* mine. I think—"

"Aw no, kid!" He reached under the table and grabbed my hand. "I'm just scared like you. And studying the angles . . . You don't really think I'd run out on you, do you?"

"I just don't know," I blubbered. . . . "Actually, I guess there are a lot of things I don't know about you." . . .

"If it's marriage you want, we'll do it."

"Of course I don't *want* it!" I said. "Not any more than you do. But what else?" . . .

"You got me there," he said. "When and where do we wrap it up?"

We wrapped it up three days later on a Saturday in a town over the line in Georgia, where we'd heard they'd marry anybody sober enough to stand up and lie about their age.

Ann Head, *Mr. and Mrs. BoJo Jones* (New York: G.P. Putnam Sons, 1967), pp. 33–35. By permission.

though few such couples would admit that the low odds apply to them, studies show that teenage marriages do not often succeed.

Even when a teenage marriage does not end in divorce, young couples face problems that include (1) interrupted or incomplete educations; (2) financial hardships caused by low salaries and soaring costs; (3) limited recreational opportunities, for there never seems to be enough time or money for having fun; and (4) the likelihood that the husband and wife will grow apart as their adult personalities develop.

Unwanted pregnancies

Strangely enough, at a time when sex education and contraceptives are more available than ever before, more unmarried teenage girls than ever are becoming preg-

nant. Experts number such pregnancies at over a million each year. Those figures suggest that many adolescents have not been learning the "facts of life" as thoroughly as they should. The mistaken idea that sex can be enjoyable only if it is done on the spur of the moment—which usually means without contraception—also contributes to the problem. As a result, psychologists strongly urge adolescents to learn about sex and its possible consequences. Only then, they counsel, can young people make mature decisions.

Unwanted pregnancies always create emotional complications, for another life must now be considered in the decision making. Young people are usually ill-equipped, emotionally and financially, to take on the responsibility of raising a child. Family strains can also make their lives more difficult. Whether the young mother decides on an abortion, gives the baby up for adoption, or raises the baby herself, the emotional stress can greatly affect the lives of everyone involved.

Drugs and alcohol

Americans are hooked on drugs. They live in what has been called a *drug culture.*

You don't believe it? Remember that many drugs are substances that change behavior or create an altered state of consciousness. Then take a look around your own house. You'll probably find at least several of the following drugs: diet pills, cold medications, tonics, pep pills, tranquilizers, sleeping pills, aspirin, liquor, beer, caffeine, and nicotine. Perhaps it's no wonder that many adolescents find the road to drug and alcohol use so easy to take.

Many drugs have helpful effects, of course. But the benefits of using any reality-altering substance for recreational purposes must be weighed against the possible harm it can do. The use of narcotics and alcohol can lead to physical addiction. But many young people who would never experiment with heroin will casually run the risk of psychological addiction.

People rarely become physically addicted to drinking beer. But long-term dependence on beer—or marijuana, or any other "soft" drug—can create a psychological addiction. The world may look better through a drug-induced high, but a temporary escape from reality only postpones life's problems. A few of the costs of such addiction are easy to spot: auto accidents, unwanted pregnancies, senseless crimes. Less easy to see, however, is the loss to society of people whose psychological dependence on drugs or alcohol leads them to "drop out" of school and careers. These people seem content to accept a limited, nonproductive life. A further negative attitude often develops among adolescents, for whom even the purchase of alcohol and tobacco is illegal. These young people may develop a disrespect for

the law that can lead to more serious delinquency.

Psychologists look on the use of drugs and alcohol as psychological "crutches." They believe that dependence on any reality-altering substance denies the individual the chance to live fully and productively. Emotionally healthy people of any age, they insist, find satisfaction in life without hiding behind the blurred perceptions and relaxed inhibitions of stimulants, depressants, or hallucinogens.

Delinquency

Almost every day you see a headline featuring juvenile crime or violence. Youthful lawbreakers are often called *delinquents:* those who violate laws, disobey authority, or behave in ways that endanger the safety or morals of themselves or others. Juvenile delinquency is nothing new, however. Aristotle, the philosopher of ancient times, complained that Greek youth "are in character prone to desire and ready to carry any desire they may have formed into action."

Psychologists believe that much delinquency grows out of the adolescent need to rebel against the restrictions of the adult world. Such rebellion in earlier times usually took the form of pranks, such as tipping over outhouses or hoisting a cow to the courthouse roof. Then, as now, some young people simply ran away from home. But the increase in more serious teenage crimes such as muggings, burglaries, rape, car theft, vandalism, and assault is alarming. Many adults now feel that the courts should punish youthful criminals with the same sentences given adult offenders.

Causes of delinquency. Delinquency is not restricted to the United States, nor is it to be found only in large cities. Studies of the problem have identified a number of possible causes for increased juvenile crime.

1. Parents no longer exercise the same supervision and control of their children

that they once did. Working or divorced parents have less time to spend with their children, who sometimes turn delinquent as a way of saying, "Hey! Pay attention to me!"

2. For many inner-city youth, inadequate schools and high unemployment rates cause anger and despair. Without hope for the future, they turn to delinquency as a release for their frustrations.

3. Similarly, many communities provide few recreational facilities for youth. Left with nothing to do, teenagers may turn to delinquency just for "kicks."

4. The police and courts have not been able to develop effective antidelinquency programs. Moreover, all delinquents are not treated equally. In one state, a twelve-year-old may be sent to prison for the same offense that ends in probation in another state.

5. The drug culture breeds its own delinquency. Hooked on expensive drugs, young people may turn to theft, prostitution, and other crimes to support their habits.

6. World problems such as inflation, the threat of war, distrust of politicians, and worry about the environment cause many young people to "turn off." Without hope for the future, they find it easy to distrust the adult world. Some of these "turned-off" young people put their energy into changing the society, at times through radical or violent means. Others let their self-contempt, pessimism, and distrust of adult institutions lead them to drugs, vandalism, or crime.

Treatment for delinquency. Most treatments for delinquency have had only limited success. The law generally treats juveniles with greater leniency than it does adults. This "soft" approach has frequently returned young criminals to the streets without effectively changing their behavior. Fifteen-year-old Rod, for example, has been to court seven times for various juvenile offenses. Each time, he has received probation and has been returned to the custody of

his parents. But the forces that make Rod a potentially dangerous criminal never change. Rod's father is still unemployed, and Rod still finds school totally alien to his needs.

Would a detention home, reform school, or an adult prison change Rod's behavior? These costly, harsher punishments do not seem to work much better than Rod's merry-go-round on probation. The only thing that had an effect on Rod was his visit to a local prison. There, he and some of his friends listened to the inmates tell about prison life. Their language was so tough and graphic that Rod has stayed out of trouble ever since (see Figure 5.16).

Another hopeful experiment has taken place in Sweden. There, delinquents and their families gather on a remote island for a period of intensive counseling. The Swedish psychologists believe that delinquent behavior is a family responsibility. Until the

Figure 5.16

Potential delinquents find out firsthand about the realities of prison life in a program started by prisoners at the Rahway, New Jersey, penitentiary. The harsh reality of this encounter usually leaves the adolescent audiences ready to change their antisocial behavior.

entire family works together on the problem, they say, the delinquent's behavior will probably not change.

In the long run, adolescents will always have extra energy to invest. Perhaps one cure for delinquency will be programs that focus on positive uses for this energy and idealism. Summer work programs that "get the kids off the streets" have been helpful in cooling off the inner cities. Political parties, environmental action groups, YMCA and YWCA, scouting programs, community recreation activities, and other positive-action groups may be society's best bet for curing the costly ill called juvenile delinquency.

SECTION CHECKUP

1 Why do psychologists believe that a teenage marriage has a poor chance for success?

2 Explain what is meant by a "psychological addiction."

3 How would you explain the high rate of juvenile crime in the United States today? What can be done to change this pattern?

LOOKING BACK: A SUMMARY

1 Adolescence is the period of growth and maturation that modern Western societies have defined as the years from about twelve to nineteen. During three stages—preadolescence (10–14 for girls and 12–15 for boys), adolescence (15–18), and young adulthood (18–25), young people are expected to gain emotional maturity, achieve independence from parental control, choose and prepare for a career, and achieve self-identity.

2 Psychologists hold two contrasting views of adolescence. The "storm and stress" theory sees the mood swings and rebellion of adolescence as necessary to emotional growth. Others believe that adolescence is stressful only when the adult society tells young people it will be so. Many teenagers, in fact, do live through the adolescent years without significant difficulty.

3 Physically, adolescents grow from children into adults within four to six years. Their height and weight change dramatically, and so do bodily proportions. Perhaps most notable of all, boys and girls develop the sexual characteristics of men and women. Physical appearance becomes critically important to adolescents, who must also cope with problems of acne, rapid growth, and the possibility of maturing earlier or later than their friends.

4 Emotionally, adolescents face the problem of coping with sexual maturation. Even though society permits young people to express their sexuality more freely than ever, unwanted pregnancies, venereal disease, and the difficulty of coping with powerful sex drives still make this adjustment difficult. Adolescents must also cope with feelings of restlessness and anxiety. So many changes take place so rapidly that the teenager often feels nervous, surrounded by vague worries related to popularity, career choice, and relations with parents. Sometimes confused over their status, treated one day as children and the next as adults, adolescents must also begin the process of gaining greater independence from parental control. This process often intensifies what some have called "the generation gap."

5 Psychologists often speak of the developmental tasks the adolescent must complete. These are the ways teenagers must grow in mind and body before they can be called mature adults. Tasks that relate to the emotional and mental makeup of young people include (a) the need to accept the realities of physical appearance and to make the best of what nature has provided; (b) the building of inner controls that allow the individual to postpone instant gratification of needs and to work for longer-range goals; (c) the need to make career choices that will provide economic independence as well as a satisfying way of life; and (d) the need to achieve a clear sense of personal identity,

with values and goals that will guide young people through the tough decisions of adult life.

6 Developmental tasks that relate to other people include (*a*) the need to achieve emotional independence from the family, a step that requires both adolescents and parents to respect each other's feelings; and (*b*) the need to act maturely when group pressures run counter to the individual's own values. These tasks become much more complex when each person's perception of the adolescent's needs comes from a different angle. Parents, for example, see questions of independence differently from the way their children do.

7 Life in today's rapidly changing society creates new opportunities for the adolescent, but new problems as well. Relaxed sexual standards may bring the pressures of unwanted pregnancy and early marriages that too often fail. A drug-oriented culture tempts pleasure-seeking young people to experiment with drugs and alcohol as escapes from reality. Delinquency among adolescents may be seen as a sign of growing social unrest. Normal adolescent feelings of restlessness and rebellion may be compounded by lack of jobs or recreation and despair over social ills. The best cures for delinquency are close-knit families and social-action groups that direct youthful energy and idealism into positive channels.

PUTTING YOUR KNOWLEDGE TO WORK

Terms you should know

adolescence	drug culture	preadolescence	rites of passage
anxiety	generation gap	puberty	self-identity
delinquency	impulse control	restlessness	young adulthood
developmental tasks			

Objective questions

1 Which of the following is a *true* statement about adolescence? (*a*) In every culture ever studied, adolescence is a time of rebellion and gradual development toward adulthood. (*b*) Since a thirteen-year-old and an eighteen-year-old are both adolescents, both are going through the same physical and emotional changes. (*c*) Because boys generally grow to be larger than girls, their adolescent growth spurt starts earlier. (*d*) The majority of young people pass through adolescence without becoming wildly rebellious or deeply disturbed.

2 Adolescents who have completed puberty generally (*a*) undergo rites of passage at home and in school (*b*) show little change from childish behavior (*c*) experience some emotional problems in learning to cope with their physical growth and development (*d*) take on full adult responsibilities.

3 Which statement is *true* about adolescents who mature later than their classmates? (*a*) Delayed growth can never be made up. (*b*) Professional counseling is always needed. (*c*) Many boys who mature later tend to work out their frustrations by being aggressive and rebellious. (*d*) Late maturation only affects boys.

4 The best way to treat acne is to (*a*) ignore it completely (*b*) look for a miracle cure at the drugstore (*c*) hide until it goes away (*d*) keep the skin clean, use a mild medication, and develop a positive outlook on life.

5 Adolescents often shock their parents with rebellious behavior as a way of (*a*) proving that all adolescents are delinquents (*b*) providing their own rites of passage (*c*) demonstrating that they're not children any longer (*d*) making up for the spankings and punishments of childhood.

6 An example of a decision that shows impulse control instead of instant gratification of desires is to (*a*) quit the tennis squad when you're not made captain (*b*) take a job to pay for car insurance instead of taking the science class you need for graduation (*c*) tell the boss where to get off when she doesn't accept your idea for changing the restaurant's menu (*d*) hold your tongue and get the job done when Granddad fusses at you for not raking the leaves.

7 The search for self-identity by typical adolescents (*a*) can be achieved only when they learn who they are and what they want to do with their lives (*b*) will take care of itself (*c*) requires many years of study (*d*) requires that they cut off contact with their families as soon as possible.

8 Ernest can achieve emotional independence from his parents by (*a*) leaving home (*b*) working toward a mutual acceptance of his growing ability to handle adult responsibilities (*c*) demanding his rights and forcing his parents to admit he's an adult (*d*) staying at home as long as his parents need him.

9 An adolescent with a good sense of personal worth will (*a*) never enjoy peer group activities (*b*) accept parental direction without question (*c*) engage in delinquent behavior, since it's part of growing up (*d*) not violate personal values in order to gain group approval.

10 Teenage marriages often fail because (*a*) the couple cannot cope with financial problems (*b*) one partner or the other feels tied down by the marriage and rebels (*c*) career opportunities are limited by the need to support the family (*d*) all of these reasons help explain the failure of many teenage marriages.

Discussion questions

1 Imagine yourself as the parent of ten-year-old twins who are nearing puberty. What would you say to your son and daughter about the physical changes that lie ahead of them?

2 Why do some adolescents find it difficult to talk to their parents? Can you suggest any methods to make communication more open and more effective?

3 Your friend Newt is really worried about his looks. Why is his physical appearance so important to him at sixteen? Does psychology have any insights that can help young people like Newt who are worried about their lack of model-perfect looks?

4 List some of the changes in our culture that make it more difficult today to choose a vocation. What are some of the dangers in choosing the first job that comes along?

5 Explain some of the social and psychological forces that lead to an increase in juvenile crime. Do you think this problem can be solved with stricter laws and harsher penalties? Why or why not?

Activities

1 Do you have an ongoing disagreement with your parents over an issue such as curfew, choice of friends, or use of the car? A useful technique for dealing with such problems is to hold an imaginary dialogue with the adult involved—mother, father, guardian, whomever. In this dialogue, you take both roles. First, give your reasons. Then switch roles and imagine how the other person would respond. What are his or her reasons? It will be difficult at first, but as you get into it, the dialogue will begin to flow. By speaking for the other person, you may gain some valuable insights into why he or she takes the position you have found so disagreeable.

2 As noted in the chapter, this culture does not provide rites of passage for every adolescent. We do have a few occasions to mark movement toward adulthood—the Jewish *bar mitzvah* and *bat mitzvah*, the granting of driving privileges, high-school graduation. Try designing a special ceremony that marks a person's becoming an adult in this society. You might want to include qualifications of age and achievement, testing of newly acquired adult skills, a formal ceremony, and a really great party. Share your ideas with your family and your psychology class.

3 Urie Bronfenbrenner, noted specialist in child development, points to age segregation as a major contributor to adolescent alienation. Read what he has to say:

Look, here's an example of how cultures differ in the ways they deal with children. I was working in the U.S.S.R. and my family was with me. One day we were walking along a street in Moscow with our young son, who was then about four years old, when I looked up and saw a bunch of teenage boys running toward us. . . . As they got closer, one shouted, "hey, little one," in Russian. One of them swept him up and gently threw him to the next one. They tossed him around that way, went into a little dance, and had a great time with him.

They knew how to handle him, and our son felt that; he had no problems at all with their tossing him around because they did it well. Then they told us, "Thank you very much for your son," and handed him back.

Our society is a bit different. Here, kids are segregated by age, and they just don't learn how to handle younger kids. You can live through the first 16 or 17 years and rarely know another human being of an age different from your own. You won't know many older people, either.*

Stage a class debate over this issue. After both sides have presented their views, the class can decide on whether Bronfenbrenner's criticism applies to your community. If it does, can anything be done about age segregation where you live?

4 Psychologists like to challenge people to think about their values—what's important in their lives. Try this exercise yourself and share it with your friends. It's fun to do—and the insights you gain will be worth thinking about.

DESIGN YOUR OWN T-SHIRT
Use any design of words and/or pictures that tells the world what you want to say about yourself right this minute.

Your Message Goes Here!

5 Do you feel as though your life has been settling into a rut? Try a "new experience" experiment for a month. The procedure is simple. Every week, take time to try two new activities that you've never done before. What can you do? The list is endless, but here are some examples: fly a kite, go fishing, take up meditation, eat Japanese food, make a new friend, try a new

*"The Erosion of the American Family," *Psychology Today*, vol. 10 (May 1977), p. 45.

hairstyle, go blindfolded for a day. Use your own ingenuity. After each experience, write a short description of how you felt about it. At the end of the month, you'll have eight new experiences to add to your list of things you like or don't like (after all, you may not like raw fish!). But more important, you'll have given yourself permission to take chances that can open up your life and give you renewed zest for living.

For further reading

Freed, Alvyn M. *TA for Teens (and Other Important People)*. Sacramento, CA: Jalmar Press, 1976. TA (Transactional Analysis) teaches you how to use this powerful concept as a way of coping with the daily dilemmas of living. Freed's book gives it to you in straightforward, no-nonsense terms, with lots of exercises and activities to make TA both useful and practical.

Ginott, Haim G. *Between Parent and Teenager*. New York: Macmillan, 1969. A companion volume to Ginott's *Between Parent and Child*, this easy-to-read discussion of adolescent-parent relationships works as well for young people as it does for parents.

Konopka, Gisela. *The Adolescent Girl in Conflict*. Englewood Cliffs, N.J.: Prentice-Hall, 1966. Many books have been written *about* adolescent problems. This well-researched book stops often to allow the girls to speak for themselves—which they do most effectively.

Parks, Gordon. *The Learning Tree*. Greenwich, Conn.: Fawcett, 1963. The famous black photographer writes about growing up in a small Kansas town. A beautifully written book that crosses over from the black experience to speak to all people, everywhere.

Shepherd, Jean. *Wanda Hickey's Night of Golden Memories and Other Disasters*. Garden City, N.Y.: Doubleday, 1971. Shepherd's antic imagination recreates his disaster-prone adolescence with perception and comic style.

Simon, Sidney, et al. *Values Clarification: A Handbook of Practical Strategies for Teachers and Students*. New York: Hart Publishing Co., 1972. A book full of exercises to help you clarify your feelings about yourself, your family, and your society. Strictly nonjudgmental, the activities are a simple and enjoyable way of getting in touch with your own developing values.

PERSONALITY DEVELOPMENT

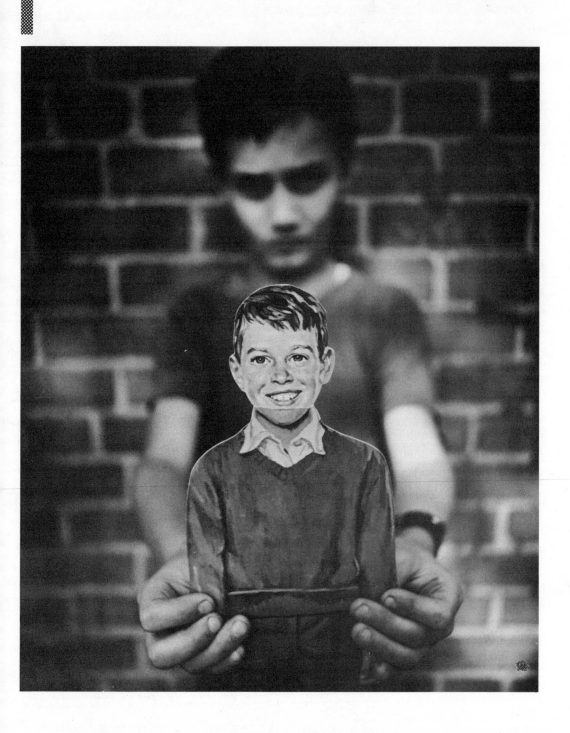

6

FREUD'S THEORY OF PERSONALITY

If any single topic can be said to represent a beginning point in psychology, it is the study of personality.

The mysteries of human behavior have fascinated philosophers and scientists since men and women first walked the face of the planet. A lonely girl, for instance, starts out for the supermarket. But without being aware of what she's doing, she drives a mile out of her way and ends up at her best friend's house. Or Rob, who really meant it last night when he said he'd never cut psych class again. . . . Today's he's already left campus, unable to hold to his promise.

Why do people act in ways that don't seem to make sense? Why do they keep on doing things that harm themselves and others? Until Sigmund Freud made his landmark discoveries at the turn of the century, no one had a satisfactory answer to these questions. The workings of the personality seemed as mysterious as the far side of the moon.

Freud was a Viennese doctor who specialized in illnesses of the nervous system. As he worked with his patients, he gradually realized that some emotional force they weren't aware of and couldn't control was influencing their behavior. A woman named Anna O., whom Freud never met, helped him find that hidden force.

Freud learned about Anna O. from his friend, Dr. Joseph Breuer. Anna's mother had called Dr. Breuer to treat the twenty-one-year-old woman, who was ill and refused to leave her bed. Before her breakdown, Anna had spent six months nursing her dying father. Her symptoms, Breuer discovered, included partial paralysis of her arms and legs, poor vision, some loss of speech and hearing, and a painful cough. Anna also suffered hallucinations in which her father's face appeared to her as a death's-head. Over and over, Anna insisted that something was tormenting her.

Breuer was interested in the case of this beautiful, intelligent woman. As was his custom, he tried hypnosis as a means of treating her. Under hypnosis, Anna talked about her passionate fondness for her father. When she spoke of the difficult months of nursing him, she burst into tears, laughed wildly, and flew into terrible rages.

But these emotional sessions also led to a remarkable change. Afterward, Anna's mind would be perfectly clear. She would leave her bed and spend hours writing letters to her friends. As Breuer wrote, "It

Figure 6.1

Sigmund Freud opened a new chapter in our understanding of the human personality. He discovered that the emotional illnesses suffered by his patients began in the unconscious.

was truly a remarkable contrast: in the daytime the irresponsible patient, pursued by hallucinations, and at night, the girl with her mind completely clear." At the same time, he found that her physical symptoms were also disappearing. Breuer concluded that by revealing her feelings, she was "talking away" the buried emotions that she had been unable to face during the long nights of caring for her father.

One by one, Anna's symptoms faded as their cause became clear. For example, her vision improved after she described a night when she had been sitting by her father's bed. As she thought about his dying, her eyes filled with tears. Just at that moment, he asked her to tell him what time it was. Not wanting him to know that she was crying, she ignored her tears. But in order to see her watch, she had to bring it close to her face, squinting as she did so. Ever since, Anna had squinted, which caused her poor vision.

Her hearing loss began when her brother caught her listening outside her father's bedroom. Angry, he grabbed and shook her. Anna wanted to hit him back, but she was afraid of making a scene. Her partial deafness started that night. Similarly, her cough began the night she heard dance music while

on duty beside her father's bed. The music reminded her of the fun she was missing. Briefly, she dreamed about going to a party. But the wish made her feel guilty, for it seemed to mean that she wanted to desert her father.

Unfortunately, Anna also transferred her affection for her father to Dr. Breuer. This led to his breaking off her treatment, for his wife was jealous of the time he spent with Anna. His abrupt withdrawal from the case led to a relapse, and Anna had to be put into a sanitarium. She later recovered and went to live in Germany. There she became one of Germany's first social workers, devoting her life to helping unwed mothers and their babies.

Freud remembered the case of Anna O. when he began treating his emotionally disturbed patients. He found that longforgotten events usually lay at the root of their problems. In time, he traced these buried memories to a part of the mind he called the unconscious. The unconscious serves as a storehouse for powerful feelings, Freud decided. It also has the power to affect behavior according to those hidden drives. Anna O.'s physical symptoms, Freud concluded, grew out of her conflict over her father's illness. One part of her wanted to love and care for him, but another part of her wanted to be free of the sickroom and the fear that he would die.

Freud used his theory to help his later patients. Freed of their unconscious conflicts, many of them recovered and returned to normal life. In time, he also developed a consistent theory of personality and behavior based on psychoanalysis. Today, psychologists and psychiatrists trained in Freudian techniques still follow in the footsteps of this man who "shook the sleep of the world." Even though modern psychology does not accept all of Freud's ideas, any study of personality must at least consider the insights he pioneered.

Your study of personality will take you through Chapters 6 and 7. This chapter will begin the investigation by looking at the following questions:

6.1 HOW DO PSYCHOLOGISTS DEFINE PERSONAL-ITY?

6.2 HOW HAVE PHILOSOPHERS AND SCIENTISTS TRIED TO EXPLAIN PERSONALITY?

6.3 WHAT BASIC CONTRIBUTIONS DID SIGMUND FREUD MAKE TO THE UNDERSTANDING OF PERSONALITY?

6.4 HOW DOES FREUD EXPLAIN THE DEFENSE MECHANISMS THAT THE EGO USES TO PRO-TECT THE PERSONALITY?

6.5 WHY DID FREUD'S THEORY OF PSYCHO-SEXUAL DEVELOPMENT AROUSE SO MUCH CONTROVERSY?

6.6 WHAT HAPPENS DURING PSYCHOANALYSIS?

6.1 HOW DO PSYCHOLOGISTS DEFINE PERSONALITY?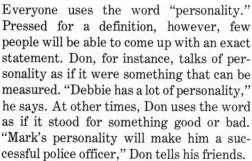

Everyone uses the word "personality." Pressed for a definition, however, few people will be able to come up with an exact statement. Don, for instance, talks of personality as if it were something that can be measured. "Debbie has a lot of personality," he says. At other times, Don uses the word as if it stood for something good or bad. "Mark's personality will make him a successful police officer," Don tells his friends.

Psychologists, however, can't let such an important idea be defined so vaguely. They believe that a good definition must apply to all people and all behavior.

Defining personality

Can any general truths about human personality be found? In a field notable for its disagreements, most psychologists would agree on three basic observations about a normal personality.

1. Each person generally behaves in a consistent way from one situation to another. Thus, if Anne is usually aggressive in her relationships, you can count on her to come on strong in most social situations.

2. This consistent pattern of behavior comes from a complex system of conscious thought and unconscious drives that re-flect an individual's personal values and goals. These value decisions help you set priorities from day to day. Thus, Anne may decide, "I'm tired of being behind in my biology class. From now on I'll finish my homework before I turn on the television."

3. Every person possesses a unique personality. No two persons will behave in exactly the same way, even when faced with similar circumstances. Both Don and Anne might have aggressive personalities, for example. But faced with an angry traffic officer, Don might become frightened and passive, while Anne flares up, angry and upset. A careful study of their childhood experiences with authority figures would probably help explain the differences.

By putting these observations together, psychologists can arrive at the following definition: *Personality is the unique pattern of thought, feeling, and behavior by which each person reacts to the external world.* How can you possibly understand something as complex as Anne's and Don's personalities? You'll have to rely upon your own observations, coupled with their limited ability to express their inner thoughts and feelings. Because of these variables, theories about how personalities develop and function vary widely.

Contributions of heredity and environment

Many individual differences begin with a person's genetic inheritance. To some extent, genes determine such factors as your physical strength and coordination, your ability to resist sickness, and your physical appearance. Such physical traits obviously influence your behavior. Most psychologists, nevertheless, conclude that a person's environment affects personality more than heredity does.

The environmental factors that influence your physical and mental growth include such basics as a good diet, adequate health care, and freedom from worry. More important than other environmental factors, however, are your interpersonal relationships. The feelings you share with family and friends, it turns out, have more to do with your personality than anything else (see Figure 6.2). In experimental situations, for example, monkeys have been isolated from the rest of the pack. Although they received proper food and health care, these lonely monkeys developed into neurotic (disturbed) adults. Under stress, they became withdrawn and depressed. In test situa-

tions, they solved problems poorly. Meanwhile, their brothers and sisters, raised in a normal environment, developed into well-adjusted adults.

What do such experiments prove? For one thing, they show the importance of proper nurturing of growing children. For another, they reinforce the idea that no child is born either "good" or "bad." Both good citizens and mass murderers are made, not born.

Importance of personality theory

Psychologists continue to search for a systematic theory of personality to help them explain the behavior of healthy and unhealthy individuals everywhere. Such a theory would explain why Eskimos react one way to change and Swedes another. It would help scientists predict how Americans in general will react to an energy crisis and how Mr. and Mrs. Juarez in particular will feel when faced with a mile-long gas line. A valid personality theory will help explain human values, motivations, emotions, and abilities.

Finally, once a solid theory of personality

Figure 6.2

The importance of affectionate nurturing during childhood has been demonstrated by raising monkeys in isolation. What if these children were treated the same way? Would they grow up as withdrawn and unhappy as the young monkey shown here?

has been established, it can be used as the basis for inquiry into specific problems. Such conditions as mental illness, depression, adolescent suicide, and antisocial behavior can all be attacked more successfully. In time, an answer might even be found for the question heard from people of every age: "Why can't I have more happiness in my life?"

SECTION CHECKUP

1 Define *personality* in terms that your nine-year-old neighbor would understand.

2 Which is more important to the development of personality, genetic inheritance or environmental influences? Why?

3 Why do psychologists believe that developing a workable theory of personality is so important?

6.2 HOW HAVE PHILOSOPHERS AND SCIENTISTS TRIED TO EXPLAIN PERSONALITY?

The search for a universal theory of personality isn't new. For thousands of years, philosophers and scientists have tried to find a consistent system that can be applied to all people and all cultures. Albert Einstein was able to sum up the energy potential of the atom in a single equation: $E = mc^2$. No such breakthrough formula seems likely for personality. In this section you will learn about four of the theories that have been used to explain personality. Some are ancient, while others belong to this century.

Supernatural forces and personality

For most of history, people have believed that personality was under the direct influence of the supernatural. Surrounded by gods, demons, and spirits, humans were forced to balance their own needs against the demands of these unseen forces. The Incas of Peru went so far as to treat mental illness by opening the patient's skull to allow the demons trapped inside to escape. The ancient Greeks, on the other hand, sometimes challenged their gods and dared their wrath. Odysseus, the hero of Homer's *Odyssey*, angered Poseidon, the god of the sea. As a result, Poseidon sent a great storm that wrecked Odysseus' ship. Only the Greek's fierce pride and determination allowed him to overcome the god's anger and find his way home again.

Few Americans today believe in demons, spirits, or sea gods. But about one out of five people still thinks that the position of the sun, stars, and planets helps determine the human personality. This ancient art, known as astrology, assigns personality traits according to the position of the sun and planets at the time of birth. People born under the sign of Aquarius (January 20–February 18), for example, are said to be spiritual, loving, and life-giving. Pisces people, born a month later (February 19–March 20), are destined to be compassionate, tolerant, and long-suffering. Experience shows that these predictions sometimes seem to come true. Careful study shows, however, that astrological predictions have about the same ratio of success to failure as would any random measure. It might make as much sense to predict your personality by the birthdate of the doctor who delivered you.

Physical attributes and personality

As scientific viewpoints began to compete with supernatural beliefs, early peoples found measures of the personality in the body itself. Ancient Hebrews, Egyptians, and Greeks often described organs other than the brain as the center of behavior. Some writers pointed to the liver or stomach as the key to understanding personality. In the fourth century B.C., the Greek philosopher Aristotle described the heart as the organ of understanding. Aristotle thought that the brain was an inert organ whose main function was to absorb the heart's excessive heat.

Phrenology. In the Middle Ages, Albertus Magnus, a German writer and teacher, revived the concept that the brain was the supreme organ. Albertus Magnus went so far as to locate various aspects of personality in different parts of the brain. In the early 1800s, another German, a doctor named Franz Joseph Gall, picked up the concept and founded a short-lived science he called *phrenology*. Gall claimed that he could read a person's character and abilities by studying the shape of the skull, along with its bumps and depressions. Taken over by con artists and frauds, phrenology quickly became a popular fad. Speaking abilities, for example, were said to be located behind the eyes, while parental love could be measured at the back of the skull (see Figure 6.3). Research soon disproved the claims of the phrenologists. The part of the brain that controls speech turned out to be in another part of the brain entirely. Today, scientists know that the shape of your head has no more to do with personality than do the bumps in the sidewalk outside your home.

Sociobiology. A new theory to explain behavior, based on genetic attributes, appeared in 1975. In that year, Harvard zoologist Edmund Wilson launched a controversial concept called *sociobiology*. According to this theory, behavior and personality are genetically based, the result of evolutionary processes dating back two to four million years. Genes, the sociobiologist claims, program the behavior of all organisms, whether housefly or human being, in order to protect their continued existence.

Sociobiologists believe that this basic drive to survive explains the most complex social behaviors. Ethnic pride, for example, is explained as the human preference for a mate who will produce children with facial features, hair, and skin color similar to your own. Also, maternal love may be seen as an investment by the mother to ensure that her genes will be carried on in the next generation. Sociobiology is still too new to have been applied directly to personality theory. That step is likely to come in the future. For the present, the sociobiologist still has trouble explaining individuals who sacrifice their own lives for those of strangers. Perhaps something more than genes is involved when someone runs into a burning building to rescue an older person.

Typologies as a way to explain personality

The humors. As early as 400 B.C., the Greek physician Hippocrates took a step toward placing the study of personality on a scientific basis. In his writings, he created a *typology* (a system in which people are classified into a limited number of categories)

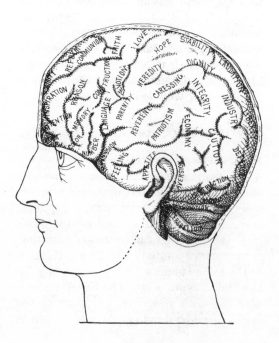

Figure 6.3

Phrenologists claimed to have scientifically charted the location of individual character traits, as shown in the diagram above. In the nineteenth century, people used this fake science as a way of choosing careers or hiring people for jobs.

based on the "humors" of the body. Hippocrates thought that one of four humors, or body fluids, is dominant in every person. This dominant humor, he believed, determines both physical health and individual character. Hippocrates identified the four humors and the character traits each controlled as follows:

Body humor	Character traits
Phlegm	Passive, careful, slow-moving
Black bile	Melancholic, anxious
Yellow bile	Irritable, angry
Blood	Easygoing, optimistic

Fourteen centuries later, the people of the Middle Ages still accepted the ideas of bodily humors. And even today, you may have heard someone described as "melancholy" or "phlegmatic." A modern translation of the four humors into their related character traits is illustrated in Figure 6.4.

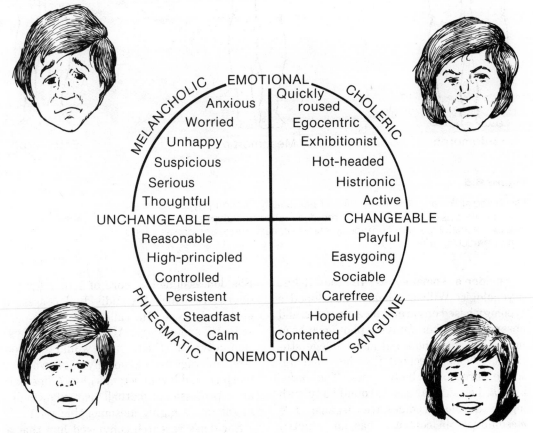

Figure 6.4

British psychologist H.J. Eysenck drew upon both ancient and modern theories of personality to design this representation of the structure of personality. Can you locate yourself in this chart of character traits? [From H.J. Eysenck, *The Biological Basis of Personality,* copyright © 1967 Charles C. Thomas, Publisher. Courtesy of Charles C. Thomas, Publisher, Springfield, Illinois.]

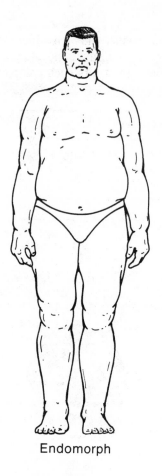
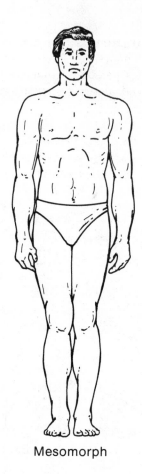
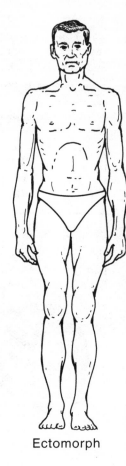

Endomorph   Mesomorph   Ectomorph

Figure 6.5

Psychologist William Sheldon explained personality through physical characteristics. He classified people into three dominant somatotypes. Can you find your own somatotype here? Are your interests similar to those Sheldon assigned to that particular somatotype?

Sheldon's somatotypes. In the 1940s, psychologist William Sheldon developed a typology based on careful measurement and observation. After studying photographs of more than four thousand male college students, Sheldon decided that he could describe three basic body types. The *endomorph,* he said, has a soft, round body with highly developed digestive organs. The *mesomorph,* in contrast, has an athletic, well-muscled body. And finally, the *ectomorph* can be recognized by a tall, thin, fragile body (see Figure 6.5).

Since few people can be classified as pure endomorphs, mesomorphs, or ectomorphs,

Sheldon assigned a score of 1 to 7 for the degree to which the individual possesses each body type. He called this three-part score the *somatotype.* According to this system, a typical athletic build would be rated 3-6-2: average in endomorphy, high in mesomorphy, and low in ectomorphy. A lineman for a professional football team, however, might rate a highly mesomorphic 1-7-1.

Sheldon's research convinced him that a high correlation exists between character traits and somatotypes. An endomorph, he believed, is comfort-loving, social, gluttonous, slow to react, and even-tempered. Mesomorphs, he went on, are aggressive, courageous, love vigorous activities, and tend to dominate others. Ectomorphs, Sheldon concluded, seem to be introverted, self-conscious, poorly coordinated, and interested in intellectual activities.

Psychologists admit that Sheldon's typology holds up fairly well when tested against actual personalities. They are not certain, however, that body type actually influences behavior. One pro-Sheldon theory suggests that a particular body type pushes its owner toward certain kinds of activities. Thus, endomorphs feel best when they are eating and relaxing—so that's what they do. But Sheldon's correlation might also grow out of a self-fulfilling prophecy. If society demands that fat, muscular, or skinny people behave in certain ways, they probably will behave as expected. In any event, you need not feel that you're captive to your own somatotype. Your body shape may influence your interests, but it probably won't determine them. Only you can do that.

Personality defined by traits

Psychologists define *traits* as the tendency to respond to most situations or people in a particular way. If you usually act independently of what others think, you possess the trait of independence. Psychologist

Raymond Cattell, a pioneer in mental testing, used a trait-rating scale to divide people into specific personality types. On his scale, twelve pairs of traits are tested to provide a measure of how an individual relates to his or her environment.

In the rating scale shown in Figure 6.6, each pair of traits represents the end points of a range of behavior. Where would you place yourself on Cattell's scale for each pair of traits? Does your trait "score" give you any insights about strengths or weaknesses in your personality?

Psychosocial theory of personality

What would happen if identical twins were separated at birth and raised in two different cultures? Imagine that one twin grew up in England, her sister in Cuba. The girls would still look alike, except for their haircuts and tans. But their personalities—their values, feelings, likes and dislikes, and reactions to stress—would vary greatly.

The example illustrates what psychologists call the *psychosocial theory* of personality. The theory states that heredity and environment interact to shape each person's unique pattern of behavior. As children grow, their family, friends, and community all join to reward some behaviors and punish

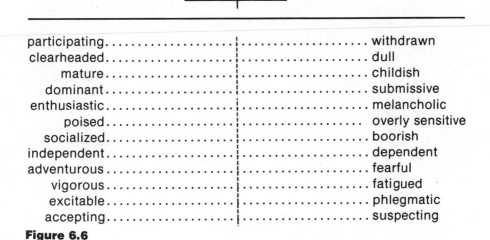

CATTELL'S RATING SCALE FOR PERSONALITY TRAITS

Trait ◄—┼—┼—┼—┼— | Average | —┼—┼—┼—► Trait

participating.............................	.... withdrawn
clearheaded..............................	.... dull
mature..................................	.... childish
dominant................................	.... submissive
enthusiastic.............................	.... melancholic
poised.................................	.... overly sensitive
socialized...............................	.... boorish
independent.............................	.... dependent
adventurous.............................	.... fearful
vigorous................................	.... fatigued
excitable................................	.... phlegmatic
accepting...............................	.... suspecting

Figure 6.6

SIGMUND FREUD:
PIONEER EXPLORER OF THE UNCONSCIOUS

Sigmund Freud (1856–1939) was born in Freiberg, Moravia (now a part of Czechoslovakia), but his family moved to Vienna when he was four. A bright, ambitious student, Freud studied at the University of Vienna. In 1886 he set up practice as a neurologist, a specialist in diseases of the nervous system. That same year, Freud married Martha Bernays, and the marriage produced six children. The youngest, Anna Freud, later became a world-renowned psychoanalyst in her own right.

The Freuds lived and worked at Berggasse 19, an address that has become famous as the birthplace of psychoanalytic theory. In 1938 the Nazi takeover of Austria forced the family, which was Jewish, to leave its home and take refuge in England. Freud was already suffering from the cancer of the jaw that eventually killed him, but he was determined to "die in freedom."

Freud's theories grew out of the discoveries he made while treating his emotionally disturbed patients. At first, he tried the traditional treatments: hot baths, electrotherapy, and rest cures. But as he became aware of the powerful influence of the unconscious, he turned to his new "talking out" therapy. Psychoanalysis seemed the only way of uncovering the forgotten events that were causing his patients' emotional problems.

But Freud's work did not go smoothly. In order to help his patients, he felt that he must first overcome his own neurotic fears. It was during this period, in 1897, that he wrote about his self-analysis:

> Business is hopelessly bad, it is so in general, right up to the very top of the tree, so I am living only for "inner" work. . . . Some sad secrets of life are being traced back to their first roots, the humble origins of much pride and precedence are being laid bare. I am now experiencing myself all the things that as a third party I have witnessed going on in my patients—days when I slink about depressed because I have understood nothing of the day's dreams . . . and other days when a flash of lightning brings coherence into the picture, and what has gone before is revealed as preparation for the present.

At one time, Freud was so full of anxiety and fear that he couldn't bring himself to leave his house. But gradually he worked through his own analysis so that he could open doors for the proper treatment of the mentally ill. Before Freud, emotionally disturbed people were shunned like lepers or locked up like criminals.

Essentially a modest man, Freud at times refused to take full credit for his accomplishments. In his autobiography, he wrote:

> Looking back, then, over the patchwork of my life's labors, I can say that I have made many beginnings and thrown out many suggestions. Something will come of them in the future, though I cannot myself tell whether it will be much or little. I can, however, express a hope that I have opened up a pathway for an important advance in our knowledge.

Did Freud "open up a pathway" for new advances in psychology? The following sections will help you make up your mind.

others. In this way, the Cuban girl would be punished for the same spirit of independence for which her English sister would be rewarded. This socializing process teaches children how to function as members of their particular culture. The psychosocial theory, therefore, does a better job than other theories in explaining the differences in behavior found in varying cultures.

Not only did Sigmund Freud devise the first major psychosocial theory of personality, but his work also marked the beginning of psychology's interest in the influence of the unconscious on behavior. Before Freud, psychologists had been content to explain personality on the basis of observable conscious behavior. After Freud, psychologists never again believed that human actions derive totally from the exercise of conscious will.

SECTION CHECKUP

1 Why have astrology and phrenology been rejected by psychologists as explanations for human behavior?

2 How does William Sheldon's theory of somatotypes explain human personality? Contrast the three somatotypes he describes—endomorph, mesomorph, and ectomorph.

3 Why is the psychosocial theory thought to be a better way of explaining personality than typologies or trait theory?

6.3 WHAT BASIC CONTRIBUTIONS DID SIGMUND FREUD MAKE TO THE UNDERSTANDING OF PERSONALITY?

Imagine for a moment that an earthquake has struck your community. As the earth rumbles and sways beneath your feet, you'd probably feel a surge of unreasoning terror. If you can't trust the stability of the ground beneath your feet, what can you trust?

In the late 1800s the writings of an unknown Viennese doctor created the same sort of shattering reaction. The existence of childhood sexual feelings, the influence of the unconscious, the enormous power of the mind—all of Sigmund Freud's ideas seemed to challenge the stability of nineteenth-century society. Disturbed and angry, psychologists joined the public in accusing Freud of trying to tear down the foundations of society. Many objected particularly to Freud's theory that childhood almost totally determines the adult personality. Even today, this apparent denial of free will bothers people who otherwise would accept Freudian ideas more readily. As Freud wrote in *An Autobiographical Study*, ". . . I had no followers. I was completely isolated. In Vienna I was shunned; abroad no notice was taken of me. My *Interpretation of Dreams*, published in 1900, was scarcely re-

viewed in the technical journals." From this beginning, recognition of the importance of Freud's work came slowly. But by the 1920s his theories had gained widespread acceptance.

What were the basic principles of Freud's theory? In this and the following sections, you will have a chance to examine the key concepts of Freud's psychoanalytic theory.

Power of the unconscious

Sigmund Freud described the human mind as an iceberg with the great bulk of its mass hidden beneath the dark surface of the sea. The tip of the iceberg he called the *conscious mind*, where everyday thought processes take place. At the water line, he identified a crossover zone called the *preconscious*. Here you store memories that can be called back to consciousness when you need them. You're using the preconscious when you hesitate, then say, "Just a minute. I've got it on the tip of my tongue."

Finally, submerged and closed off from direct contact with the conscious mind lies the *unconscious* (see Figure 6.7). This great

WHAT'S GOING ON INSIDE YOUR HEAD:
THE THREE LEVELS OF CONSCIOUSNESS

Conscious mind
Everyday thought processes take place here: decision making, problem solving, daydreaming, reactions to events in the environment.

Preconscious
A crossover zone between the conscious and unconscious. Material not being used at the moment but not repressed can be found here.

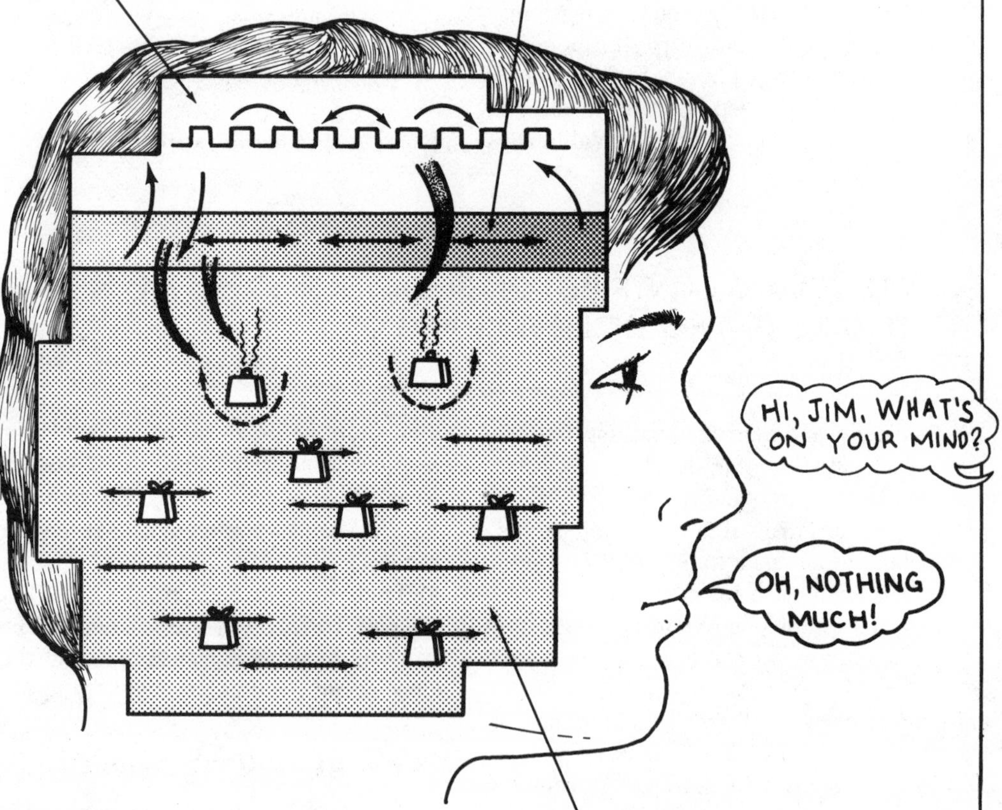

HI, JIM, WHAT'S ON YOUR MIND?

OH, NOTHING MUCH!

LEGEND
ᴨᴨ Organized thought
⌒ Random, nonfocused thought
↔ Stored material
⬛ Repressed material
⬛ Repressed material released during dreams and free association
⊢⊣ Material moving from one level of consciousness to another
⟋ Experience so painful it is repressed immediately

Unconscious
The great storehouse of our basic drives, sexual desires, more savage emotions, and most painful memories. Even while repressed, these "forgotten" feelings can greatly influence our everyday conscious thought and behavior.

Figure 6.7

Figure 6.8

Works of art like Salvador Dali's surrealistic *Persistence of Memory* seem to confirm Freud's theory of the unconscious. The strange, dreamlike images in this impossible landscape may represent repressed material that has been stored away, out of sight but not out of mind. What do the limp clocks and insects suggest to you? [Dali, Salvador, *The Persistence of Memory (Persistance de la mémoire)*. 1931. Oil on canvas, 9½ x 13″. Collection, The Museum of Modern Art, New York. Given anonymously.]

storehouse contains all your life experiences, particularly the harsher, more savage emotions—your secret hates, fierce loves, uncivilized passions. These memories, feelings, and desires are buried (*repressed*, the psychologist would say) because they are too powerful to be handled easily by the conscious mind. But out of sight doesn't mean out of mind. These hidden memories and emotions influence almost everything you think, feel, and do (see Figure 6.8).

If you aren't convinced that you really do have an unconscious, Freud would ask you to keep careful track of your speech and everyday actions. If you're like most people, every once in a while you "slip" and say or do something you didn't mean to. Perhaps you have agreed to go someplace with your family that you really don't want to go. Is it any surprise that you're late getting ready and everyone has to wait for you? Or have you ever been making polite conversation and had something embarrassing slip out? After class one morning, a student tried to impress his teacher by telling her how "really interesting" her lectures were. "All of them," the student assured her, "are rarely interesting." Freud would have smiled at this "Freudian slip" and said, "Yes, young man, we know what you are actually thinking."

Psychoanalysis, Freud's method of treating mentally ill patients, grew out of his research into the unconscious. As his friend Dr. Breuer had discovered with Anna O., repressed memories seemed to lose their power to harm Freud's patients once they talked freely about these "forgotten" experiences. The unconscious does not give up its treasures easily, however. This psychoanalytic method requires a long-term commitment to therapy between the patient and the analyst (see Section 6.6, pages 177–179).

Life and death forces

According to Freud, all behavior ultimately can be reduced to two fundamental drives: eros and thanatos. *Eros* (derived from the name of the Greek god of love) stands for the life drive—the satisfaction of hunger, thirst, sex, and self-preservation. Freud said that energy was needed to keep the life drive in motion. He found this psychic energy in the *libido*. The libido includes all of the different kinds of love experienced by human beings. Not only does it energize your sexual drives, but it also provides the energy for love of self, parents, friends, country, even works of art.

Thanatos (derived from the Greek word for death), in contrast, stands for the death drive. Freud believed that all people carry this death wish inside them. When the death drive becomes overwhelming, it can lead to suicide. More often, thanatos leads people into aggressive behavior toward others, even into crime. Psychoanalysts believe that war is the ultimate expression of this death wish turned against other human beings.

Role of the id, ego, and superego

As Freud studied human behavior, he came to believe that the raw energy of the life force, the libido, derives from and is modified by other powerful forces in the mind. Human beings, he said, are caught between their own needs and those of society. Three forces within the mind, however, help people resolve this conflict. He called these forces the id, ego, and superego (see Figure 6.9).

The id. Buried within the unconscious is the *id*, a storehouse for all your instincts and passions and the source of many of your habits. Like a great savage infant, the id constantly demands satisfaction of your needs. If your body is hungry, the id says, "Eat! Now!" If you're angry, the id says, "Hit back! Now!" The id not only wants pleasure but also wants to avoid pain. Freud named this desire of the id to reduce tension and to gain immediate satisfaction without counting the cost the *pleasure principle*. Although the id's untamed appetites can cause you trouble, you couldn't do without it. From the id comes the energy that allows you to enjoy life and solve problems.

The ego. Computerlike, almost always in control, the *ego* acts as a moderating force between the demands of the id and the reality of the world around you. Without the ego to exercise control, the id would send you bolting for the cafeteria at your first hunger pangs. Instead, the ego measures the risk such action requires. If it's unacceptable, the ego tells the id, "Wait twenty minutes till lunchtime, and we'll get a hamburger." This process of analyzing the consequences of possible actions, in order to provide pleasure with the least amount of pain, Freud named the *reality principle*.

The ego also serves to repress desires that conflict too strongly with reality. You might want that new Mercedes in the worst way, but the ego will help you deal with the id's impulsive urge to get in and drive it away. Note, however, that the ego serves primarily to satisfy the id, not to frustrate it. The ego doesn't know right from wrong; that role is filled by the superego.

The superego. Freud believed that the *superego* absorbs the social values you learned from your parents and other adults. These were enforced during your childhood by rewards, punishments, and restrictions. The superego demands that you practice a perfect morality, a goal that often brings it into conflict with the id's desire for pleasure.

Imagine that you're walking through a department store. Your id spots an expensive calculator and immediately wants it, even though you don't have any money. The ego quickly evaluates your chances of stealing it. When the clerk's back is turned, it signals "go." But the superego overrides the ego with its own "stop" command. Fearing punishment and unwilling to face the guilt feelings the superego would give you, you

Figure 6.9

The conflicting demands of the id, ego, and superego are represented here. The id demands immediate satisfaction but must work through the ego to achieve it. The superego upholds standards of morality taught during childhood. The ego, meanwhile, must reconcile these conflicting demands with the reality of the external world.

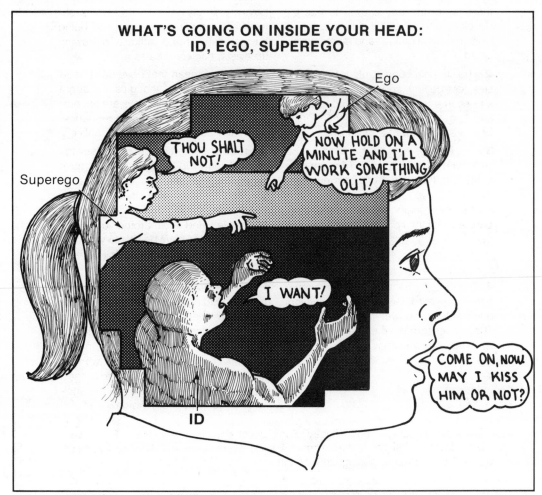

PRO & CON: HOW WOULD TODAY'S WOMEN DEBATE SIGMUND FREUD?

For all his genius, Sigmund Freud was a man of his time and culture. In the late 1800s, Victorian society expected women to take a passive, submissive role in relation to men. Women who spoke out for equality or who did not repress their sexuality were put down as traitors to their sex. Given this repressive condition, it is no wonder that Freud saw many female patients. Most suffered from hysteria, a mental illness caused by repression of natural feelings.

If Freud were alive today, many women would want to argue with him about his attitudes toward their sex. With that in mind, a "debate" has been arranged between Dr. Freud and a modern feminist. After you "listen" to both sides, you can make up your own mind as to whether times have changed or not. Freud's words, by the way, are taken directly from his own books.

Dr. Freud

1 A comparison with what happens in the case of the boy shows us that the development of the little girl into a normal woman is more difficult and more complicated.

2 The little girl is as a rule less aggressive, less defiant, and less self-sufficient; she seems to have a greater need for affection to be shown her and therefore to be more dependent and docile.

3 . . . for women to be loved is a stronger need than to love. Their vanity is partly a further effect of penis envy, for they are driven to rate their physical charms more highly as a belated compensation for their original sexual inferiority.

4 The great question that has never been answered, and which I have not been able to answer despite my thirty years of research into the feminine soul, is: What does a woman want?

Feminist

1 No such difficulty exists. Girls and boys are simply people, with all the problems and potentials that go with being human. If any greater difficulty in growing up exists, society creates it.

2 Does this mean that boys don't need affection? The fact is that girls are taught to need attention, while boys are encouraged to develop greater independence. Why can't both sexes be treated alike?

3 Freud projected his own male feelings of superiority upon women. Men have been exaggerating the importance of genital differences ever since. Of course little girls notice the differences between themselves and their brother or father. But do they also have beard envy or muscle envy? The answer is obvious: Freud was flat-out wrong on this one.

4 Women want to share equally with men in building a decent, peaceful society. They want equal opportunity and equal pay when they work outside the home. They want men to join them in raising their children. In brief, they want to see a world in which people are judged by who they are rather than by the accidents of sex, race, or religion.

Times have changed, haven't they? Some psychologists believe that, if Freud were alive today, his attitudes toward women would be quite different. What do you think? Would Freud admit to "losing" this debate?

walk on by the temptation. These feelings of guilt derive from the *conscience*, a part of the superego. The superego also contains the *ego ideal*, which rewards you with approval when you act according to the superego's moral code. In this way, the superego not only makes you feel guilty and unhappy when you violate a rule but also rewards you with a feeling of satisfaction when you do the right thing.

SECTION CHECKUP

1 Describe the roles of the conscious, the preconscious, and the unconscious.

2 Describe some human activities that would derive from eros, the life drive; from thanatos, the death drive.

3 Imagine that you're standing by the teacher's desk with the test answers in plain sight. What messages will the id, ego, and superego give you at that point?

6.4 HOW DOES FREUD EXPLAIN THE DEFENSE MECHANISMS THAT THE EGO USES TO PROTECT THE PERSONALITY?

Sometimes the demands of the id and superego trap the hardworking ego into a no-win position. Imagine yourself caught between two such conflicting pressures. You've just backed Dad's car into a neighbor's new Porsche. The id says, "No one saw us! Get out of here fast before we get caught!" But superego jumps in with its stern, moralistic tone: "It would be wrong to run away. You caused the accident with your careless driving. Stay and accept the consequences."

Both drives are too strong to be ignored, yet you can't act until the ego makes a decision. Caught in such a bind, the ego often chooses a response that disguises or compromises the id's socially unacceptable desires. In this case, the ego might choose to stay with the damaged car, thus obeying the law. But it might also decide to rationalize (alibi) the accident: "It was either hit your car, Mr. Krukow, or run over the little kid who ran in back of me."

Freud's description of a number of these *defense mechanisms* used by the ego make up one of his most enduring contributions to psychology. Perhaps you can see your own behavior in a number of these techniques for converting taboo feelings into acceptable behavior.

Repression

When she was seven years old, Rachel was attacked by a large watchdog. She escaped without serious injuries. Today she does not remember that incident, but she is terrified of dogs. If even the most gentle toy poodle runs toward her, Rachel feels almost suffocated by fear.

Repression protects you from disturbing memories, forbidden desires, or painful feelings by burying such material in the unconscious. Repressed feelings remain "alive," however, capable of influencing behavior without the person's being aware of it. Part of Rachel wants to like dogs, but, whenever she gets close to one, the old repressed fear takes over. Similar repressed material can also affect normal physical drives such as hunger or sex. At times, the repressed material can be so powerful that it can cause actual physical illness. A constant need to clear one's throat, for example, may be the physical signal of a repressed need for attention from others. As you might guess, doctors often find it difficult to diagnose such *psychosomatic illnesses*, which some experts estimate make up 40 percent of a physician's caseload.

Since you cannot "remember" what you have repressed, it sometimes takes a lengthy period of therapy before the hidden material can be uncovered. Even when unearthed, you must still accept and deal with what you've repressed. In Rachel's case, that would not be too difficult, for her fear of dogs gives an obvious clue as to where to look. But repression also acts to conceal those drives and feelings that people cannot admit having. In such cases, the patient often vigorously resists discovery of the repressed material.

Displacement

Harry had a bad day. He forgot his math homework, his girl friend broke a date, and he missed the bus after school. Seething with the injustice of it all, he walked into the house just in time to hear his mother say, "Harry, did you get a haircut as I asked you?" Just then his baby brother ran up to be hugged, and Harry released all his built-up aggressions by pushing Huey away with a violent shove.

When you can't focus your feelings on the person or thing that caused them, you often strike out at other, generally less threatening people or objects. Freud called this *displacement*. Harry couldn't strike out at his girl friend or his mother, so baby Huey became the substitute. If Huey hadn't come by just then, Harry's door, dog, or dresser drawer might have caught the built-up energy of his anger.

Anger isn't the only emotion that can be displaced, but it is the most common. People sometimes displace nervousness or fear by chewing gum or picking at their fingernails. Some psychologists have described prejudice as displaced aggression, as when an unemployed worker blames all of his troubles on a minority group. Psychologists believe that, if you learn to recognize your displacement behavior, you can channel it into useful, less harmful ways of releasing tension. If Harry had put in some time running, chopping wood, or punching a bag, he would have felt better. And baby Huey wouldn't be crying.

Sublimation

Susan thought her world was going to end when her parents told her they couldn't afford to send her to college. After a period of depression, she took a job at a local law office. The work proved interesting, and she was soon putting in extra hours. At night she took extra training at the local junior college. Within a year, her boss promoted her to the level of executive secretary and gave her increased responsibility as well as a raise.

Without knowing it, Susan was practicing *sublimation*, the defense mechanism that detours powerful, frustrated drives into socially useful behavior. Freud believed that civilization could not exist without sublimation, for it allows people to contribute to society while also achieving their own inner peace (see Figure 6.10). In this way, a rock-throwing youngster in trouble with the law might find release from his inner tensions on the baseball field. Or people who have just ended a love affair might feel better if they put all their energies into creating beautiful ceramic figures. A childless couple that befriends stray cats and dogs may also be sublimating the desire to have children of its own. Sublimation does not always absorb all the energy created by frustration, however. The aggressive youngster described above may find success in baseball—but the chances are that he'll often lose his temper when an umpire's decision goes against him.

Projection

Jimmy secretly wishes he had as much money to spend on clothes as some of the other kids in school. On campus, however, he goes out of his way to put down other teenagers who wear expensive outfits. "Look, there comes Vernon," he yells, "and he's wearing that crummy Dior jacket again. What's the matter, Vernie, can't you afford anything better?"

Your ego can cope more easily with tension if it originates in the external world. Stress that actually comes out of the conflict between the id and the superego, therefore,

Figure 6.10

Sublimation provides a release from inner stress and frustration by directing energy into socially useful activities. Can any of your own interests in sports, art, music, or volunteer work be considered sublimation?

is often projected by the ego upon an outside target. Jimmy is using *projection* to cope with his inner feelings. In short, he uses a scapegoat in order to conceal the desires he cannot fulfill within himself. Similarly, a husband who frequently accuses his wife of not loving him may really be saying, "I don't love you (but I can't admit it to myself)." You might suspect projection almost anytime someone, in Shakespeare's phrase, "doth protest too much." Thus, those who loudly criticize young people and their music may secretly wish they could be young again.

Regression

Overheard in the teachers' lounge: "I don't know what to make of my ninth-graders this year. Usually they're great—alert, interested, cooperative. But just mention extra work or toss them a tough problem, and they come unglued! They pout, stamp their feet, practically throw temper tantrums. I can't figure them out."

A psychologist would instantly identify the students' antics as *regression*, a return to an infantile stage of behavior. When faced with frustration or stress, some people fall back on anxiety-releasing techniques that worked when they were young. Regression is not limited to young people. Under stress, adults often revert to childlike behavior—chewing their fingers, eating or drinking to excess, or throwing temper tantrums. Caught in the pressures of an unhappy marriage, husbands and wives have been known to stomp out of the house, perhaps to "go home to mamma." Finding refuge from reality in alcohol or drugs is also considered regressive behavior.

Since regression usually means a refusal to face reality, overuse of this defense mechanism can lock a person into a nonproductive life situation. As for those unruly ninth-graders, give them a few years. Most of them will leave that regressive behavior behind as they mature.

Reaction formation

The neighbors marvel over John's devotion to his aging mother. After all, he's thirty-eight years old and gave up his marriage plans to take care of her. Despite Mrs. R.'s cranky disposition, he plays the role of dutiful son with a smile and a cheery willingness to do whatever's necessary. "And what's so marvelous about it all," says old Mrs. Johnson next door, "is that she never gave him much love or attention when he was little."

Maybe John really enjoys his limited role in life, but the odds are good that he's using *reaction formation* to deal with inner feelings of bitterness and rage. In reaction formation, the unconscious converts a forbidden feeling into its opposite. John has good reason to dislike his mother, but he's also been taught to honor and respect her. Unable to deal with his anger, he has converted it into love and devotion, feelings he can live with. In much the same way, kidnapping victims sometimes become willing defenders of the people who held them captive.

You may have run into reaction formation around school without being aware of it. Think of someone like Margaret, for example. No one works harder or is more serious about her studies, right? But if you could see inside her head, you'd find out that Margaret unconsciously detests the routine of schoolwork forced on her by her ambitious parents. But to rebel would be unthinkable. Instead, she turns that urge to give up on school into supercareful study habits.

Rationalization

"Anne, did you call your editor? He'll want to know about the problem you ran into researching that story."

"No, his line is always tied up. And besides,

I was really busy this morning. I practiced piano for an hour and worked on my new dress, and then Tom called . . ."

No one likes to be criticized. All people have an ideal image of themselves built up in their minds, and when they don't live up to that ideal, they feel guilty about it. *Rationalization* is the process of finding reasons or excuses for thoughts, feelings, or actions that don't measure up to your expectations of yourself. In this way, you "get off the hook," as when you look Dad in the eye and say, "I know it's late, but Ivan's car ran out of gas. We couldn't help it."

Anne didn't want to admit her difficulty, so she postponed her confrontation with her editor by inventing reasonable excuses for her inaction. Similarly, a salesclerk who takes merchandise from the store might say, "Sure I took a few things, but so does everybody else. The company can afford it." Rationalization makes living easier (who hasn't used it?), but a psychologist would be concerned about Ben, for example, who constantly rationalizes his every action. Ben's behavior is unhealthy, the psychologist would conclude, because he never seems to take responsibility for anything he does.

SECTION CHECKUP

1 What purpose do the defense mechanisms serve in human behavior?

2 Define and give an example of each of the following defense mechanisms: repression, displacement, sublimation, projection, regression, reaction formation, and rationalization.

6.5 WHY DID FREUD'S THEORY OF PSYCHOSEXUAL DEVELOPMENT AROUSE SO MUCH CONTROVERSY?

To your great-grandparents, children represented one of life's great puzzles. The popular literature of the Victorian period described boys and girls as "pure, innocent, and unspoiled," terms usually reserved for

angels. In fact, then as now, children seldom lived up to that unrealistic image. Even so, few people stopped to wonder about the gulf that separated the ideal child from the flesh-and-blood one.

Figure 6.11

THE INFLUENCE OF SEXUAL DRIVES: A THUMBNAIL SUMMARY OF FREUDIAN THEORY

1 Sex, in the broad Freudian interpretation, is the single most powerful force in determining our feelings, thoughts, and actions.

2 Sexual feelings (again in the broad meaning of that term) can be traced as far back as infancy. Anyone who has watched a baby at play has noticed the enjoyment it receives from its own body.

3 Emotional problems are caused by the repressing influence of individual and group taboos on our sexual feelings. These taboos begin in the nursery when our parents first scold us for doing or saying what otherwise would be natural behavior.

4 All people carry within themselves a hidden reservoir of sexual desires, memories, and tendencies. Society would label some of these tendencies "abnormal." Thus, these feelings are repressed into the unconscious.

5 Repressed sexual feelings fight their way to the surface of our lives in disguised but socially acceptable forms. They do so in many ways—dreams, myths, art, literature, slips of the tongue, clothing styles, and even jokes and wisecracks.

In 1900, Sigmund Freud's statement that all children lived an unconscious but passionate sex life shocked people everywhere. The reaction to Freud's idea of *childhood sexuality* was as great as the shock that had greeted Darwin's theory of evolution just fifty years earlier. As one critic noted, "Freud has murdered childhood." In some ways, that storm of controversy has never completely disappeared. Many people still reject the concept of childhood sexuality on religious or philosophical grounds. In addition, most psychologists today believe that Freud overemphasized the importance of sexual forces in shaping the personality. (Figure 6.11 summarizes Freud's views on this subject.)

Basically, Freud believed that personality is shaped when children are forced to learn new methods of reducing tensions. Each stage of life, he said, brings new physical and emotional pressures for which old solutions no longer work. Of the five stages Freud described, three occur during the first six years of life. To followers of psycho-analytic theory, this fact seems proof enough that the ages from birth to six are the most decisive period in shaping personality.

Oral stage

For the first year of life, the infant's pleasures and frustrations center on the mouth. In this *oral stage*, pleasure grows mostly out of stimulation of the lips and mouth, either through sucking, eating, drinking, or licking. Babies reject unpleasant sensations by literally spitting them out, as anyone who has ever tried to feed a baby strained liver can testify.

Freud explained that many adult character traits have their origins in this stage of life. A baby who doesn't have enough food during the oral stage may become a possessive adult who can never get enough of anything. Likewise, a baby who is allowed to bite people without being disciplined may mature into a destructive grown-up. Freud guessed that many later behavior patterns such as gum chewing or pipe smoking may be substitutes for the simple pleasures enjoyed during the oral stage.

Psychoanalysts also believe that because of unresolved conflicts during this or later stages, people may become *fixated* (locked into infantile behavior patterns). Physically, they continue to grow, of course. But emotionally, they remain dependent on behaviors that worked for them during that crucial stage. Many compulsive eaters, who use food as a compensation for a lack of love in their lives, may be acting out a fixation from the oral stage of development.

Anal stage

Freud placed great emphasis on the behaviors learned during the second and third years of life. He called this the *anal stage*, for the child finds pleasure during these years in the daily bowel movement. Toilet training, which usually begins in the second year, gives the child a first experience with the need to regulate an instinctive, impulsive behavior.

Freud believed that harsh, overly strict toilet training may cause development of one of two extreme personalities. Some children may develop a retentive personality, becoming stingy and stubborn. Other children may grow into expulsive personalities—rebellious, destructive, and disorderly. Freud also explained that adults who find all their security in making money may be resolving the sense of loss they experienced during the anal stage. Parents can help their children through this stage by making toilet training a low-pressure, natural development that takes place only when the child is ready for it.

Phallic stage

Between ages four and six, children go through the *phallic stage*. The search for pleasure now centers on the genitals, and boys and girls often engage in sex play during this time. Freud observed that the most important challenge of this period is the working out of the *Oedipus complex*.* Boys and girls in the phallic stage feel an unconscious sexual attraction to the parent of the opposite sex. A boy wants to "marry" his mother, so that he can have all her affection. Similarly, a girl fantasizes about having her father all to herself. These unconscious drives bring the child into competition with the parent of the same sex. It's not unusual, for example, to see a boy of four or five deliberately place himself between his parents, as if trying to keep his father away from his mother. Girls and boys may have vivid dreams involving the death of their "rival."

Freud explains that these Oedipal feelings must be resolved if the child is to grow into a sexually normal adult. Children have little power to control their lives, however. Complications arise when the boy begins to fear that his father will punish him for his feelings by cutting off his penis. Freud called this fear the *castration complex*. He claimed that girls develop penis envy, which he defined as a jealousy of males, who own something important that they lack. Torn by guilt over their secret desires and fearful of punishment, children eventually repress their Oedipal feelings in favor of identifying with the same-sex parent. The rapid development of the superego during the phallic stage helps resolve the Oedipus conflict by building into the child's personality social and moral values related to sex roles.

Latency period

After the stormy years of the phallic stage, the child enters the relative calm of the *latency period*. Between the ages of six and the onset of puberty, most sexual feelings

---

*The name derives from the classic Greek tragedy by the playwright Sophocles. The play tells the story of Oedipus, doomed by the fates to kill his father and marry his own mother. Oedipus unknowingly fulfills his destiny. When he's confronted with the terrible knowledge of his incestuous marriage, he gouges out his own eyes.

are repressed. Children prefer the company of their own sex and invest enormous amounts of energy in school, sports, hobbies, and play activities. You may remember your own involvement in Scouting, Y groups, Little League, model-building clubs, street games, school, and similar activities during those years.

Genital stage

Following puberty, adolescents enter the *genital stage*, the period of adult sexual growth. Previously, children were mostly interested in their own bodies. Now, as young adults, teenagers begin to explore the pleasures of genuine love relationships. Individuals develop interests in career plans, join peer groups, and debate the desirability of marriage and having their own children.

Normal development during the early years now provides a firm foundation for achieving productive, satisfying personal relationships. For people who were fixated at an earlier stage, or who didn't work out the Oedipus complex, however, the genital stage may represent a difficult ordeal. Driven by unconscious forces they can only vaguely sense, these people often need the help of a counselor or therapist before they can unravel the tangled threads of their personality problems.

SECTION CHECKUP

1 Why did the theory of childhood sexuality alarm the Victorian world?

2 Name the five life stages that Freud described. What is the key growth pattern of each stage?

3 Why does psychoanalysis put so much emphasis on the Oedipus complex? What exactly did Freud mean by it?

6.6 WHAT HAPPENS DURING PSYCHOANALYSIS?

None of Sigmund Freud's twenty-four volumes of writings would be of more than theoretical value if his insights could not be applied to real people with real problems. Whatever else psychoanalysis teaches about personality, it is essentially a system of therapy.

How does psychoanalysis work? You may remember that almost all psychoanalysts are psychiatrists who have taken special advanced work in Freudian analytic methods. Psychoanalysts, therefore, use Freud's own techniques to help their patients unscramble the forgotten events of the past that influence today's behavior. Armed with insights about their past, patients can then overcome the barriers that prevent them from living happy, productive lives. Psychoanalysis works best with patients whose emotional problems, however painful and limiting, are relatively mild. Since the therapy involves a lengthy period of talking out of the patient's past life, those who cannot communicate freely will probably not benefit from analysis.

Each analysis is individual, of course, but the pattern that Freud started still dominates. Since you may never talk directly to an analyst (short for psychoanalyst) yourself, here are some of the questions and answers you might hear if you could listen to a new patient beginning therapy.

Patient: What do you mean by the psychoanalytic contract?

Analyst: Before you start therapy, you and I must agree upon certain basic principles. You will promise to visit my office two or more times a week. You will agree to speak freely, without feelings of shame, guilt, or embarrassment. I call this technique *free association*. That's a Freudian way of saying that you'll be encouraged to talk about anything that comes into your mind.

For my part, I will listen carefully to everything you say. I won't give advice, criticize, or make decisions for you. My job is to interpret, not to take over. I'll also refuse to make snap judgments about your illness, for each new insight that emerges from your free association will probably modify my diagnosis.

Patient: Why do patients lie on a couch during analysis?

Analyst: Actually, many analysts no longer use a couch. It has become a rather unfortunate stereotype. But a couch does have its purposes. First, you must be relaxed in order to free-associate. Second, you can't see my face while you're lying on the couch. That way, you can't try to guess from my expressions what I think of your remarks. If you could, you might try to impress me, or you might turn away from embarrassing material. Finally, I can see you, and often your face will give away what your words try to hide.

Patient: Why will I do so much of the talking? Will you always remain silent?

Analyst: I'll speak, when it's time. But Freud taught that the analyst's silence is an important part of therapy. I want to maintain a tension in our relationship. If we talk freely back and forth, that's only conversation. But if I remain silent, you will be forced to fill the spaces with your own words. And eventually those words will lead to repressed material that lies at the heart of your problem.

Patient: What do analysts mean by transference?

Analyst: Freud considered *transference* the key discovery in the analytic process. He believed that it shows you are beginning to make real progress. You see, as our relationship develops, you will begin to transfer your feelings about important people in your life to me. What you feel about your father, mother, brother, or whomever, will become part of our relationship. You will rely on me more and more, but you'll also hate me at times. These feelings will be powerful and upsetting. But transference means that you're asking yourself what you want from me—and from your life. When you love me, I will understand. And when you hate me, I will also understand. In the emotional storms that rage in this office, I will remain neutral and objective. You cannot upset me. You cannot make me think less of you. And nothing you say will ever leave this office.

Patient: Do you mean that I will feel free to tell you everything?

Analyst: By no means! As we approach more painful episodes in your life, you will set up *resistances.* Your unconscious won't give up its secrets without a struggle. You will "forget" your appointments. You will tell me you can't remember your dreams. Days will go by in which you will lie silent for our entire hour, unable to find a single word to speak. You may even talk about ending the analysis. But your resistance means that we are approaching the most important stage of the analysis! That is the time to redouble our efforts, for it means a breakthrough is possible.

Patient: When do you do your job? Won't you ever give me an interpretation of what's been happening?

Analyst: That's a fair question. Remember, it isn't always easy for the analyst to remain silent. But the time does come when all the elements of your problems have been opened up. Then it's my job to point out the connections and meanings that you might otherwise miss. I will confront you with omissions, contradictions, and inconsistencies. Perhaps your relations with older people trouble you. I'll help you clarify those feelings and lead you back through the childhood experiences that caused them. If my insights are correct, you will begin to adopt new and more mature behavior patterns. Your old, self-defeating hang-ups will be left behind.

Patient: I've heard that analysis sometimes goes on for years. Won't the time ever come when I can end my therapy?

Analyst: No analysis is ever complete. The childhood experiences that lie at the root of your problem won't go away; they're part of you. We'll both know, however, when you're ready to end your treatment. You'll be satisfied with the progress you've made and impatient at the lack of further insights. You'll feel much better about yourself, and you'll be able to handle your relationships with other people. Your life will never be all smooth sailing—but you'll be able to handle any storms that blow your way.

Patient: Ummm, as you know, analysis is the most expensive type of therapy around. Why is that?

Analyst: I could make a joke out of that, as when the yacht salesperson says, "If you have to ask how much it costs, you can't afford it." But you've asked a fair question. First, it took me twelve years of university study to learn my profession. While I was in training at the Psychoanalytic Institute, I went through an analysis myself. So I had invested a lot of my life and a lot of money before I was ready to take my first patient through analysis. Second, I can see only a handful of patients each week. I need time to write up my notes, do my study and research, and run my office. I'm sorry, but that fee we agreed to is what my services are worth. And if analysis works for you, I think you'll agree that it was worth every penny.

Patient: That brings up one last question. Is psychoanalysis the only effective therapy? What about the other therapies?

Analyst: Many of my fellow psychologists and psychiatrists report excellent success with other therapies. But as I told you, my training has been in psychiatric medicine and in psychoanalysis. I know I don't have all the answers, but I believe that Freud came closer to truly understanding the complexities of the human personality than anyone else.

SECTION CHECKUP

1 Define the psychoanalytic terms *free association, transference,* and *resistance.*

2 What is the purpose of the analyst's silence? At what point does the analyst begin to add interpretations and commentary?

3 Why does psychoanalysis take so long?

LOOKING BACK: A SUMMARY

1 *Personality* can be defined as the unique pattern of thought and behavior by which each person reacts to the outside world. Both heredity and environment play key roles in shaping personality, but environment is the more important factor. Psychologists are interested in personality theory as a way of explaining human behavior for all people, everywhere.

2 For centuries philosophers and scientists have searched for a workable theory of personality. The earliest theories said that behavior resulted from the action of super-

natural forces. Various parts of the body, such as bodily fluids, have also been described as controlling the emotions. Later research tried to define personality through systems of categories, or typologies. One such typology is Sheldon's somatotypes, which use three basic body types to predict individual behavior. Other efforts centered on the measurement of individual traits, such as dependent-independent or dominant-submissive. Finally, modern psychosocial theory sets forth the idea that behavior results from the interaction of genetic inheritance and the socialization process. Of all the theories, the psychosocial approach does the best job of explaining cultural differences in behavior.

3 When Sigmund Freud announced that personality derives from psychological forces rather than hereditary influences, few people accepted his revolutionary theories. Starting with the concept of the unconscious, Freud showed that every human being is driven by two basic forces: eros (the life force) and thanatos (the urge to self-destruction). The life force is energized by the libido, which includes love in all its forms: sexual love, friendship, love of family, patriotism, and love of beauty.

4 Freud divided the mind into three parts. The conscious mind carries on everyday thought processes. The preconscious stores material not currently in use. The unconscious serves as the storehouse of all repressed feelings and memories: loves and hates, painful experiences, and primitive passions. Freud believed that neurotic fears and irrational behavior can usually be traced to events hidden in the unconscious.

5 Three powerful forces modify and use the raw energy of the libido: the id, the ego, and the superego. The id represents instincts, passions, and habits. It seeks tirelessly to gratify its needs, a process Freud called the *pleasure principle.* The ego acts as a moderating force between the id and the external world. Like a computer, the ego processes the id's demands and attempts to satisfy them within the limitations of reality. Freud thought of this process as the *reality principle*. Moral behavior derives from the superego, which contains the conscience and the ego ideal. When people violate the values they have learned from their parents and other adults, the conscience makes them feel guilty. When they act according to the superego's moral code, the ego ideal allows them to feel pride in their "good" behavior.

6 The ego sometimes denies or distorts reality when caught between the demands of the id and the superego. This process is known as a defense mechanism. Freud identified seven such mechanisms: (a) Repression—"forgetting" painful experiences by burying the memory in the unconscious. (b) Displacement—the transfer of a strong emotion from the person or situation that caused it to another, generally less threatening person or object. (c) Sublimation—the conversion of powerful, frustrated drives into socially useful behavior. (d) Projection—the concealing of one's inner fears and needs by "finding" them in the behavior of others. (e) Regression—a return to childish behavior when under stress. (f) Reaction formation—the unconscious conversion of a stress-causing impulse or drive into its opposite emotion. (g) Rationalization—the tendency people have to use excuses as a means of protecting the idealized image they have of themselves.

7 Freud alarmed Victorian parents when he asserted that children pass through five sexually oriented stages of development. During the first year, an infant is in the oral stage, when all pleasure and displeasure center on the mouth. The anal stage, ages two to three, shifts the child's attention to the daily bowel movement. Improper methods of toilet training can fixate a child at this stage, creating a number of undesirable adult personality traits. During the third stage, ages four to six, the child enters the phallic period. At this time the Oedipus complex (the child's attachment to the parent of the opposite sex) must be worked out if the child is to achieve a normal adult sex life. Following a period of latency in which sexual feelings are repressed, puberty marks the beginning of the genital stage. As they become sexually mature, adolescents end the self-involvement of childhood and begin to take an active interest in developing more mature love relationships.

8 During Freudian therapy, usually known as *psychoanalysis*, the patient slowly works through the layers of the unconscious to the underlying causes of disturbed behavior. The analyst remains mostly silent, allowing the patient to talk about whatever comes to mind. This is called *free association*. In time, the patient experiences transference, the shifting of strong feelings about parents and other significant people to the analyst. Points of resistance appear, signaling the presence of important feelings that must be opened up. Finally, the analyst helps interpret the accumulated insights gathered over the preceding weeks and months. Analysis ends when patients feel good about themselves and accept responsibility for handling future problems on their own.

PUTTING YOUR KNOWLEDGE TO WORK

Terms you should know

anal stage	conscious mind	ectomorph	endomorph
childhood sexuality	defense mechanism	ego	eros
conscience	displacement	ego ideal	free association

genital stage	phallic stage	reality principle	sublimation
id	phrenology	regression	superego
latency period	pleasure principle	repressed feelings	thanatos
libido	preconscious	repression	traits
mesomorph	projection	resistance	transference
Oedipus complex	psychosocial theory	sociobiology	typology
oral stage	rationalization	somatotype	unconscious
personality	reaction formation		

Objective questions

1 Which of the following is *not* a true statement about Freud's psychoanalytic theory? (*a*) Children go through a period during which they love and desire the parent of the opposite sex. (*b*) Once sexual feelings have been repressed, they have no further power to influence people's lives. (*c*) The repressed memories contained in the unconscious can dramatically influence the thinking of the conscious mind. (*d*) Disturbed or unhealthy behavior can be resolved only when the patient understands the underlying causes of the problem.

2 The attempt to develop a workable personality theory (*a*) is useful because such a theory would provide a way to understand all aspects of human behavior (*b*) will fail because the influence of supernatural forces on personality makes it impossible to understand what shapes human behavior (*c*) is useless because human behavior is so unpredictable it can never be summed up in a workable personality theory (*d*) ended with the Greeks, whose personality theory is still the basis for modern psychology.

3 A personality theory that is based on a typology is (*a*) phrenology (*b*) Freud's psychoanalytic theory (*c*) Cattell's trait theory (*d*) Sheldon's somatotypes.

4 Philosophers tend to be tall, thin, self-conscious, and mostly interested in intellectual pursuits. According to somatotype theory, they should be classified as (*a*) endomorphs (*b*) mesomorphs (*c*) ectomorphs (*d*) fixated personalities.

5 During a baseball game, Steve has been "brushed back" by a pitch that almost hits him. He rushes toward the mound, ready to swing his bat at the pitcher. The part of Steve's personality that seems to be in control at that moment is the (*a*) id (*b*) ego (*c*) superego (*d*) libido.

6 Which of the following statements about the id is *true?* (*a*) Human beings would be much happier if the id could be removed at birth. (*b*) The id is the source of the energy that drives the personality. Without it, there would be no creativity, love, or strong emotion. (*c*) The id is the only element in the personality that keeps people from behaving like wild beasts. (*d*) The id provides the energy and intellect needed to solve complex problems.

7 Depressed because her SAT scores were too low to get her into a well-known university, Sally goes to a party and drinks too much. She is using the defense mechanism of (*a*) repression (*b*) reaction formation (*c*) regression (*d*) sublimation.

8 Recovered from her hangover, Sally tells her friends that she didn't really want to go away to college anyway. "Besides, my lousy high school didn't prepare me properly for the SAT," she says. Now Sally's using (*a*) repression (*b*) rationalization (*c*) regression (*d*) projection.

9 Probably the most critical of the psychosexual stages, because it is the time when the Oedipus complex must be resolved, is the (*a*) oral stage (*b*) anal stage (*c*) phallic stage (*d*) genital stage.

10 During his psychoanalysis, Stanley began to forget his appointments even though he had been seeing Dr. Murdock on Monday afternoons for nine months. Dr. Murdock suspects that Stanley has reached a point of (*a*) transference (*b*) resistance (*c*) free association (*d*) regression.

Discussion questions

1 How would you define personality? Why are psychologists so interested in developing a workable personality theory?

2 Can you spot examples of Sheldon's somatotypes among the people around you? Do their personality characteristics seem to match their physical attributes?

3 Describe the roles of the id, the ego, and the superego. What kind of behavior would result if the superego failed to develop properly? Can you detect the influence of these forces in your own behavior?

4 Some critics charge Freud with saying that the adult personality is shaped during childhood, and that it can never be changed. How would a Freudian answer that charge?

5 Name the psychosexual stages of development. What behaviors would you expect from a child as he or she passes through each of these stages?

6 Give a real-life example of someone using each of the seven defense mechanisms. Which ones seem potentially most harmful? Which ones seem least harmful (when not used to excess)?

Activities

1 Does astrology give any real insights into personality? You can run an interesting test that may give you at least a partial answer to this question. First, consult an astrology book and list the personality traits associated with each sign of the zodiac. Next, draw up a list of ten notable figures from history, such as Madame Curie, John Kennedy, Julius Caesar, Susan B. Anthony, Michelangelo, and the like. Look up these people in encyclopedias, biographies, and other sources. List their actual personality traits along with their birthdays. Do they correlate with the astrological predictions? Adolf Hitler, for example, was a Taurus. Did he have the predicted Taurus qualities of generosity and caring for others?

2 Do the psychosexual stages actually exist? After carefully defining the behaviors that would be expected at each stage, observe children and infants of differing ages to see if you can spot oral, anal, phallic, or latent activity. It might help to consult with the child's mother or father, since they see the youngster on an intimate, daily basis. Present your findings in a paper or oral report to your class.

3 Free association is one of the key techniques of Freudian psychoanalysis. You can see a similar method for getting in touch with your own unconscious. First, choose a time and place where your privacy is assured. Sit down with paper and pen. Begin writing about anything that seems important or interesting—your feelings, recent experiences, personal problems. Don't make a conscious effort to direct the writing in any way. Forget about grammar and style. Just keep on writing. After a while, your thoughts should begin to flow. Let them go, one idea picking up from another. You may come up with some useful insights into repressed emotions, or you may come across solutions to what seemed like unsolvable problems.

4 Try making a poster or collage representing the roles the id, the ego, and the superego play in your behavior. The id, for example, might be represented by pictures that represent basic drives, creativity, open expression of love, satisfaction of hunger, and the like. The ego can be shown as people *doing* things, such as driving, playing, working, and studying. The superego represents morality and authority. Show it with pictures of a house of worship, parents scolding a child, a police officer or judge, and so on. A few old magazines will probably provide all the material you need for making an artistic poster.

5 Keep a "defense mechanism" diary for a few days. This diary will serve two purposes. First, it will help you get in touch with your own behavior patterns, a useful goal under any circumstances. Second, you will gain a greater appreciation of the role defense mechanisms play in protecting the ego. You may not find yourself using all of the defense mechanisms described on pages 171–174, but almost everybody resorts to rationalization, displacement, and regression on a fairly regular basis.

For further reading

Freud, Sigmund. *The Interpretation of Dreams.* New York: Avon, 1954. For those interested in investigating Freud's own writings, this work (first published in 1900) contains his first comprehensive explanation of the role of the unconscious. Many psychologists consider this book Freud's greatest single contribution to psychoanalytic theory.

Kardiner, A. *My Analysis with Freud: Reminiscences.* New York: Norton, 1977. Kardiner, himself a psychoanalyst, writes with interest and good humor about his own months of analysis with Sigmund Freud.

Miller, Jonathan, ed. *Freud: The Man, His World, His Influence*. Boston: Little, Brown, 1972. This collection of essays takes a critical look at Freud and his work. The essays are a useful counterbalance to both the "Freud could do no wrong" approach and the "Freud, who needs him?" attitude of some modern schools of personality theory.

Rosner, Joseph. *All About Psychoanalysis—In Questions and Answers*. New York: Collier, 1962. A readable source of basic material on the psychoanalytic theory and on psychoanalysis as a treatment for mental illness. The question-and-answer format makes it easy to zero in on specific topics.

Stone, Irving. *The Passions of the Mind*. Garden City, N.Y.: Doubleday, 1971. As an alternative to Ernest Jones's massive three-volume biography, this fictionalized account of Freud's life and work provides a humanized approach to the great pioneer of the psychoanalytic theory.

7

PERSONALITY THEORY SINCE FREUD

The revolution launched by Sigmund Freud at the turn of the century turned psychology in new directions. Many young psychologists became firm supporters of Freud and his psychoanalytic theories. Other psychologists followed Freud for a time but then broke away to establish their own schools of thought. And still others never accepted Freud's interpretation of personality at all.

As a result, psychology today seems a little like the automobile market. You can "shop around" for a system that matches your own insights about human behavior. If you want to find out which system is "best," however, that's a little like trying to choose between a Ford and a Chevrolet. Like any good salesperson, each school of psychology believes that its own theories best explain human personality.

Since you already know something about Freudian theory, you're ready now to sample some different ideas. Behavioral psychologists, for example, have little use for Freudian ideas about the unconscious or the Oedipus complex. They believe that almost all behavior is a reaction to stimuli from the world around you. Control the stimuli, they say, and you can control behavior.

How does *behavioral psychology* work? Step into the behaviorist's lab for a moment. Meet B. F. Skinner, Harvard psychologist and world-famous behaviorist. Dr. Skinner

startled the country in the mid-1940s when he raised his baby daughter in an enclosed crib. Skinner called the crib a "baby tender," but critics labeled Deborah Skinner "the baby in the box."

Skinner designed the baby tender because he wanted Deborah to have the best possible environment. The baby tender was actually a glassed-in, temperature-controlled crib (see Figure 7.1). Skinner

Figure 7.1

Behaviorist B.F. Skinner raised his daughter in this baby tender. The experiment was part of his effort to design an environment that develops healthy, stable adult personalities. Why didn't the baby tender become popular? Would you raise your child in one?

thought that if his invention worked for Deborah it would change the way all babies were raised. As a behaviorist, he was certain that baby tenders would produce healthy, happy children.

Skinner had observed that babies in tropical climates need little clothing. In colder climates, however, parents must bundle their babies in several layers of clothing and blankets. The clothing restricts movement and can cause rashes. When they're freed of confining clothing, babies seem more content. Skinner also noted that someone has to change and wash all those diapers, shirts, and sheets.

Skinner designed the baby tender so that Deborah didn't need to wear any clothing, except a diaper. Temperature and humidity controls kept her warm and comfortable. She never developed a rash or caught a cold. "She has never shown any sign of not wanting to be put back and simply does not cry," Skinner wrote in his autobiography. "The only times she has cried in the past four months . . . have been when she had diphtheria shots . . ., when I nipped the tip of her finger while trimming her nails, and once or twice when we have taken her bottle away to adjust the nipple!"

As a bonus, the baby tender was so efficient that the Skinners had to bathe Deborah only twice a week. Skinner installed a single ten-yard-long sheet so that a clean section of the sheet could easily be cranked into place. The glass sides of the air crib also kept out noise, and a shade protected Deborah from light when she was sleeping.

Not everyone admired Skinner's invention. Many people looked on the baby tender as a "human goldfish bowl" that cut Deborah off from normal human contacts. Rumors started in later years that Deborah became psychotic because of her stay in the baby tender. In fact, however, she was graduated from college, married happily, and earned an international reputation as an artist.

Skinner defended his invention. He told his critics, "The baby is not at all isolated socially. She is taken up for feeding, of course, and at six months spends about one and one-half hours per day in a play pen or teeter-chair. . . . She . . . greets us with a big smile when we look at her though the window."* As Skinner noted years later, many hundreds of babies have been reared in similar devices.

OK, you're probably saying at this point, "Hold on a minute. Would Freud agree with Skinner that raising a baby 'in a box' is a good thing?" Probably not. So how can anyone have faith in psychologists if they're always so far apart? Don't psychologists ever agree about anything?

Most critics of psychology forget that modern psychology barely predates the airplane. Wilhelm Wundt opened the first psychology lab in 1879, just over a hundred years ago. And no matter how hard Wundt and later researchers tried to put their field on a strictly scientific basis, human nature refuses to fit neatly into a test tube. As a result, psychologists have seldom agreed upon the meaning of the huge amounts of data they gather. Given this basic handicap, perhaps a young science like psychology should be applauded for its successes rather than blamed for its lack of consistency.

In this chapter you'll learn about four major schools of psychology to go with your understanding of Freud: the behaviorists, the neo-Freudians, the humanists, and the existentialists. And if you're still wondering what Skinner was trying to prove when he put Deborah in her "box," it seems only fair to begin with the behaviorists.

7.1 HOW DO THE BEHAVIORISTS DESCRIBE THE DEVELOPMENT OF HUMAN PERSONALITY?

7.2 WHAT HAVE THE NEO-FREUDIANS CONTRIBUTED TO PERSONALITY THEORY?

7.3 WHAT CONTRIBUTIONS DID CARL JUNG MAKE TO PERSONALITY THEORY?

7.4 HOW DO THE HUMANIST PSYCHOLOGISTS APPROACH PERSONALITY THEORY?

7.5 WHAT NEW IDEAS HAVE THE EXISTENTIALISTS ADDED TO PERSONALITY THEORY?

*From B. F. Skinner, *The Shaping of a Behaviorist* (Knopf, 1979), pp. 275–305.

7.1 HOW DO THE BEHAVIORISTS DESCRIBE THE DEVELOPMENT OF HUMAN PERSONALITY?

Throughout the history of psychology, researchers have been faced with a curious paradox: They must study the workings of the mind without ever knowing exactly what goes on inside the brain. John B. Watson (1878–1958) tried to cut through that problem in 1913 by announcing that psychology should no longer deal with the mind. Only behavior is observable and verifiable, he said. Therefore, behavior is the only proper subject for the psychologist.

Watson's theories were greatly influenced by the historic work on classical conditioning by Ivan Pavlov, a Russian physiologist (see page 8). Pavlov conditioned (that is, trained) dogs to salivate when they heard a musical tone. Pavlov sounded the tone whenever he fed a meat powder to the dogs. After six to eight trials, the dogs began to salivate at the sound of the tone whether food was present or not. What particularly interested Watson was the fact that salivation in dogs is a reflex action. Pavlov had trained his dogs to do something over which they had no conscious control.

Watson went on to describe behavior as a system of *stimulus-response* units. In behaviorist terms, any behavior can be represented as S→R (stimulus causes response). When an infant sees its mother, for example, the sight of the mother is the stimulus, S. The stimulus activates certain circuits in the nervous system (signified by the arrow) that are conditioned to interpret that particular stimulus as signifying food, warmth, and love. The baby's response, R, is determined by the strength of the stimulus. With most babies, the response would include a smile, cooing noises, and perhaps some enthusiastic arm waving.

B. F. Skinner (1904 –   ), Watson's successor as the leading American behaviorist, also dismissed the psychoanalytic approach. Freud, Skinner says, "loves the superego, the ego, and the id, and the various geographies of the mind and all that

stuff. I say we can get along without that. In fact, we can get along better without it."

Skinner also believes that the development of the personality is too important to leave to parents and the random learning that goes with growing up. In his novel *Walden Two*, Skinner invents a self-sufficient community run on behaviorist principles. Professional nurses raise the children, shaping their personalities to the type of behavior needed to maintain a stable and productive society. When Skinner applied these same principles to all of American society in *Beyond Freedom and Dignity*, the reaction was loud and angry. Critics accused him of wanting to sacrifice freedom and individual responsibility in favor of a controlled, robotlike population. (The Pro & Con on page 190 debates this issue at greater length.)

Behaviorist theory: How responses are learned

Behaviorists believe that infants are born with only three instinctive responses: fear, rage, and love. All other behaviors, they reason, develop through learning. Skinner classifies all behavior as either respondent or operant.

Respondent behavior. When a stimulus causes a reflexive, automatic, or involuntary response, it is termed *respondent behavior*. For example, if someone directs a puff of air at your eye, you will blink. The air puff is the stimulus: the reflexive blink is the response (puff → blink). But that same eye blink can be conditioned, just like the salivation of Pavlov's dogs. Suppose that the experimenter sounds a clicker at the same instant the air puff hits your eye. Now the S→R is $\frac{puff}{click}$ → blink. If that stimulus is repeated a number of times, your eye blink will eventually be conditioned to respond to the click, even when no air puff is used. Now the S→R has become click → blink.

Figure 7.2

Skinner's ping-pong-playing pigeons learned their "sport" through operant conditioning. Do you see any similar conditioning in the behavior of these human "pigeons" working at their slot machines?

Operant behavior. Behaviors that act on the environment in order to gain a reward are called *operant behaviors*. Most human activities, from eating a grape to flying a 747, fall into this category. Behaviorists believe that operant behaviors can be conditioned by *reinforcement* (any event that increases or decreases the probability that the behaviors take place). For example, when her parents praise Rosa for taking good care of her pets, they're using *positive reinforcement*. Rewards, such as praise, money, grades, and other desirable things make people feel better. Positive reinforcement, therefore, increases a desired behavior.

Rosa's parents also have other choices. For example, they might choose *negative reinforcement* instead of positive reinforcement. In this case, Rosa's mother starts yelling at Rosa to do her chores every day at 4:30. Not until Rosa does her jobs will the yelling stop. Thus, Rosa learns the de-

sired behavior (feeding her pets) as a way of avoiding something she doesn't like (her mother's yelling).

Finally, Rosa's parents might try *punishment* as a way of getting Rosa to do her work. Punishment means to penalize a person after an undesirable behavior takes place. To punish Rosa, her parents might take away a privilege, such as watching TV, every time she forgets to feed the pets. To avoid the punishment, Rosa will probably start caring for her pets on time.

As a way of dramatizing his theories, Skinner has used positive reinforcement to teach pigeons a number of remarkable behaviors. Pigeons make good subjects because they seem to enjoy their work! They will put in long hours doing a task over and over for a small number of food pellets. By using the shaping process described in the next paragraph, it took Skinner only a few hours to teach his pigeons to bowl, play ping-pong, and peck out a tune on a piano (see Figure 7.2). During World War II, in fact, Skinner trained pigeons to guide missiles to their targets. Even though his pigeon navigators were more accurate than the electronic gear then in use, no one in Washington took Skinner very seriously.

Shaping behavior. You may not want to train pigeons to blow up battleships, but you can train both people and animals to perform complex operant behaviors through a process known as *shaping*. The desired behavior must first be broken down into small steps. When the subject performs the first step, you provide reinforcement. Your dog might respond to a biscuit, your little brother to a smile and praise. Step by step, you build up the more complex behavior by reinforcing each step in the chain. If your subject shows undesirable behaviors, you ignore them.

If you're teaching little Mark to swim, for example, you'd start by breaking swimming down into its individual movements. Perhaps you'd start by introducing him to the water. Then he would learn to put his head underwater. Each bit of progress

Figure 7.3

WILL THIS BE THE SHAPE OF THE FUTURE?

English novelist Aldous Huxley looked at the future and found it terrifying. In his novel *Brave New World,* Huxley describes a society totally dedicated to conditioning human behavior according to a preplanned blueprint.

In Huxley's world, free choice has disappeared, along with most human emotions. To achieve this, the all-powerful state has created totally obedient human beings. The training process begins soon after birth in the "Neo-Pavlovian Conditioning Room." The nurses set out large bowls of roses and a row of brightly colored pictures of animals.

> "Now bring in the children," [said the Director].
> They hurried out of the room and returned in a minute or two, each pushing a kind of tall dumb-waiter laden, on all its four wire-netted shelves, with eight-month-old babies, all exactly alike (a Bokanovsky Group, it was evident) and all (since their caste was Delta) dressed in khaki.
> "Put them down on the floor."
> The infants were unloaded.
> "Now turn them so that they can see the flowers and books."
> Turned, the babies at once fell silent, then began to crawl towards those clusters of sleek colours, those shapes so gay and brilliant on the white pages. As they approached, the sun came out of a momentary eclipse behind a cloud. The roses flamed up as though with a sudden passion from within; a new and profound significance seemed to suffuse the shining pages of the books. From the ranks of the crawling babies came little squeals of excitement, gurgles and twitterings of pleasure.
> The Director rubbed his hands. "Excellent!" he said. "It might almost have been done on purpose."
> The swiftest crawlers were already at their goal. Small hands reached out uncertainly, touched, grasped, unpetaling the transfigured roses, crumpling the illuminated pages of the books. The Director waited until all were happily busy. Then, "Watch carefully," he said. And, lifting his hand, he gave the signal.
> The Head Nurse, who was standing by a switchboard at the other end of the room, pressed down a little lever.

---

earns him your praise and encouragement. Gradually, you add the movements of arms and legs that will all come together in a complete swimming stroke. You don't have to be a psychologist to see that this approach is much more effective than the old "sink-or-swim" method of throwing Mark off the dock to learn on his own. (Activity 3, page 214, gives you a chance to experiment with shaping behavior.)

Behaviorism applied to the personality

Behaviorists believe that they can also explain the underlying causes of neurotic be-havior. Even though they reject concepts such as the unconscious, they recognize that early life experiences can condition adult behavior.

In an experiment carried out in 1920, Watson introduced eleven-month-old Albert to a tame white rat. At first, Albert played happily with his new pet. But one day, just as the baby reached for the rat, Watson sounded a sharp, startling noise just behind Albert's head. Albert withdrew his hand and began to cry. After several repetitions, Albert cried whenever the rat was brought in, even after the noise was stopped. In behaviorist terms, Albert had been *conditioned* to fear the rat because he

There was a violent explosion. Shriller and even shriller, a siren shrieked. Alarm bells maddeningly sounded.

The children started, screamed; their faces were distorted with terror.

"And now," the Director shouted (for the noise was deafening), "now we proceed to rub in the lesson with a mild electric shock."

He waved his hand again, and the Head Nurse pressed a second lever. The screaming of the babies suddenly changed its tone. There was something desperate, almost insane, about the sharp spasmodic yelps to which they now gave utterance. Their little bodies twitched and stiffened; their limbs moved jerkily as if to the tug of unseen wires.

"We can electrify that whole strip of floor," bawled the Director in explanation. "But that's enough," he signalled to the nurse.

The explosions ceased, the bells stopped ringing, the shriek of the siren died down from tone to tone into silence. The stiffly twitching bodies relaxed, and what had become the sob and yelp of infant maniacs broadened out once more into a normal howl of ordinary terror.

"Offer them the flowers and the books again."

The nurses obeyed; but at the approach of the roses, at the mere sight of those gaily-coloured images of pussy and cock-a-doodle-doo and baa-baa black sheep, the infants shrank away in horror; the volume of their howling suddenly increased.

"Observe," said the Director triumphantly, "observe."

Books and loud noises, flowers and electric shocks—already in the infant mind these couples were compromisingly linked; and after two hundred repetitions of the same or a similar lesson would be wedded indissolubly. What man has joined, nature is powerless to put asunder.

"They'll grow up with what the psychologists used to call an 'instinctive' hatred of books and flowers. Reflexes unalterably conditioned. They'll be safe from books and botany all their lives." The Director turned to his nurses. "Take them away again."

Few people would vote for such a cruel system of training children to their task in life. But what if such techniques could end crime, end unhappiness, end violence? Would you then accept such a solution to social problems?

connected it with the fear-producing noise $\left(\begin{smallmatrix} \text{rat} \\ \text{noise} \end{smallmatrix}\right| \rightarrow \text{fear})$. More important, Albert generalized his fear to other furry animals and even to inanimate objects such as a fur coat and a Santa Claus mask. (See Figure 7.3 for a look at this principle carried to its frightening extreme.)

Behaviorists, therefore, classify neurotic behaviors as poorly chosen responses to stimuli. Underlying these responses (an unreasoning fear of high places, for example) is a general anxiety that makes it impossible for the individual to cope with the symptoms. In therapy, a behavioral psychologist might learn that Eunice's fear of heights began when she was trapped in a tree overnight by playmates who took away the ladder. A behaviorist, however, would largely ignore this childhood event and concentrate on ending Eunice's specific disability.

One common technique is called *systematic desensitization*. Over several meetings, Eunice will first be taught to relax. Then she will gradually be led to think about being in high places. When she can think about heights without disabling fear, she might be taken to a second-story window. With that conquered, she can then go up to the third story. Eventually, she'll "graduate" by walking freely around the observation deck of the tallest building in town.

Pro & Con: IS BEHAVIOR MODIFICATION THE ANSWER TO SOCIAL PROBLEMS?

Most psychologists prefer to treat individual patients. But one group of behaviorists, led by B. F. Skinner, have more ambitious ideas. In *Beyond Freedom and Dignity,* Skinner says that social problems such as crime, violence, role confusion, and other disturbed behavior can be eliminated from this culture if the society adopts behaviorist conditioning techniques. But the debate over the behaviorist approach arouses considerable controversy. Listen to the two sides argue their case; then see how you would vote on this issue.

Pro

1 Since all behavior is learned, society can guarantee that people act in socially desirable ways only if it uses behaviorist conditioning techniques to shape the behaviors it wants.

2 What actually goes on inside the human mind cannot be studied scientifically. Psychologists, therefore, must limit their work to behavior that can be observed and verified.

3 The belief that behaviorist techniques will lead to a *1984*-type dictatorship is groundless. The fact that conditioning techniques have been misused in the past, such as in the brainwashing of war prisoners, should not count against their use in a free society.

4 Traditional methods of dealing with social problems have been tried for centuries—with incredibly bad results. Isn't it time society tried a scientifically proven method of curing social problems? Why wait until humanity destroys itself?

5 Behaviorism offers the only experimentally validated method of coping with emotionally disturbed people in today's mixed-up society. Other schools of psychology depend upon "insights" and observations that cannot be proved or disproved experimentally.

Con

1 Behaviorism ignores almost everything that psychology has learned about personality since Freud opened the doors to the unconscious. Conditioning can alter behavior, but it cannot erase the powerful influence of the unconscious.

2 Behaviorists seem to believe that humans are little more than "complicated" animals. But treating people as animals that can be easily and safely conditioned ignores the hidden complexity of the human mind.

3 Who will design the behaviorist "blueprint" for people's future behavior? History provides little assurance that any form of government can be trusted with that much power. In fact, many people are already alarmed by the growing tendency of big government to invade the private lives of its citizens.

4 The present system by which people run their society isn't perfect, but neither is it a total failure. People now enjoy freedom of choice and freedom to grow and become what they will. Social peace bought at the cost of turning everyone into a programmed robot is too expensive.

5 Behaviorist techniques can be useful for modifying simple habits such as smoking or overeating. But the behaviorist dream of changing an entire society has never been attempted. The behaviorists cannot be turned loose to "experiment" on an unsuspecting population.

Do you think the opponents of behaviorist techniques win the debate? Or do you believe that the problems facing humanity today are so pressing that behaviorist techniques must be adopted to preserve civilization?

In brief, behaviorists believe that if people behave "normally" they probably are healthy human beings. Unlike Freud, the behaviorists have no desire to backtrack through the dark maze of the mind to discover some distant childhood trauma. By concentrating on relieving the symptoms of disturbed behavior, they feel that they can benefit the greatest number of people. Time is too short and the pressures of modern living too great, they believe, to do anything else.

SECTION CHECKUP

1 How does the behaviorist use stimulus-response theory to explain human behavior and personality?

2 Contrast respondent and operant behaviors. Give an example of each.

3 Explain the concept of conditioning. How could you use positive reinforcement to train a dog to jump through a hoop?

4 Use the little-Albert experiment to explain the behaviorist's concept of neurotic behavior. How could you use systematic desensitization to end Albert's fear of furry objects and animals?

7.2 WHAT HAVE THE NEO-FREUDIANS CONTRIBUTED TO PERSONALITY THEORY?

As revolutionary as Sigmund Freud's theories were, they were not completely supported by the research of twentieth-century sociologists and anthropologists. These new studies described human beings as highly adaptable to changes in the environment. In keeping with these newer insights, a number of psychoanalysts began to modify Freud's ideas. Among these *neo-Freudians*, as they are often called, are such important names as Alfred Adler, Karen Horney, and Erik Erikson. (The work of another great neo-Freudian, Erich Fromm, is discussed in Chapter 5, page 145. The neo-Freudians see personality as more a product of social influences than of heredity and early childhood experiences (see Figure 7.4).

Alfred Adler

Alfred Adler (1870–1937), a Viennese psychiatrist, broke with Freud in 1911 to form a new school he called "individual psychology." Adler believed that Freud put too much emphasis on the role of sexuality in personality development. Instead, Adler placed social needs on an equal basis with Freud's sex drives. He claimed that personality develops through expression of inborn *social urges*. Each society modifies these social urges according to its own values.

The creative self. The *creative self* was Adler's name for the inner system that guides the individual toward a fulfilling style of life. In a sense the creative self *is* the person, for it makes you the unique person you are. Each person chooses a particular role because society seems to reward that choice. Your creative self may emerge as happy-go-lucky, intellectual, romantic, or melancholy. If choosing a melancholy role seems strange, remember that the melancholy person receives rewards of sympathy, attention, and the "right" to blame others for misfortune.

All of your drives to be a superior person grow out of this creative self. Unlike Freud, Adler believed that the individual consciously chooses the kind of person he or she will become. Freud gave that role to the unconscious and seemed to put it out of reach of individual freedom of choice.

Other key concepts. Although Adler is not as important a personality theorist as

Figure 7.4

FREUD VERSUS THE NEO-FREUDIANS: MAJOR AREAS OF AGREEMENT AND DISAGREEMENT

Freud and the neo-Freudians agree:

1 Unconscious motivation is a powerful force in human behavior.

2 Repression is an important method for coping with anxiety.

3 The defense mechanisms play a key role in protecting the ego.

4 Early childhood is the time when the basic personality is formed.

Freud says:	**The neo-Freudians say:**
1 Sex is the basic human drive and the greatest single influence on behavior.	**1** Social and cultural forces, not sex, are the most important influences on behavior.
2 Childhood sexuality must be understood for its critical effect on development of the personality. This process often requires psychoanalysis.	**2** The personality can fully develop if people learn to handle personal relationships in their adult life successfully.
3 Resolution of the conflicts caused by the Oedipus complex is basic to proper emotional growth. This process is common to all peoples, everywhere.	**3** Resolution of conflicts that grow out of the clash between individual needs and the demands of the environment is basic to proper emotional growth.
4 Women are an inferior sex.	**4** Neither sex can be considered superior to the other.
5 The id, the ego, and the superego actually exist as part of the human mind.	**5** Concepts such as the id, the ego, and the superego should not be thought to have an actual existence.

Freud and Carl Jung (see following section), a number of his ideas have gained widespread acceptance.

1. *Feelings of inferiority.* Adler believed that *feelings of inferiority* (the belief that other people are better than you are) greatly influence behavior. Basic inferiority begins during childhood, when adults have almost total control of your life. To the child, everyone else seems bigger, stronger, and more powerful. Most people gradually overcome these feelings as they grow up. But mental disabilities, lack of social skills, or not being part of the mainstream society can also cause painful feelings of inferiority (see Figure 7.5).

Healthy people try to overcome their feelings of inferiority. Nonreaders will work hard to master basic reading skills. The classic "ninety-pound-weakling" will take up weight lifting. Adler called this *compensation,* the attempt to deal with the specific causes of inferiority. History records

Figure 7.5

Nobody knows better than Charlie Brown what it means to struggle with feelings of inferiority. How could Charlie compensate for his lack of social standing?

many examples of such compensation. Napoleon, for example, overcame his self-consciousness about his height and Corsican background to become a great French military and political leader. President Theodore Roosevelt refused to let his weak body and poor eyesight keep him from achieving success as a boxer, horseman, soldier, writer, and politician.

Adler also warns against over-compensation, however. An individual may become so determined to compensate that he or she goes too far. Overweight adolescents, for example, sometimes go on diets so severe that they endanger their health.

2. *Fictional finalism.* Adler thought that people are sometimes motivated by ideals that may be pure fiction but that they pursue with great determination. Common fictions include "Honesty is the best policy," and "If I'm good, everyone will love me." Healthy people can see beyond these overly simple rules, but neurotic personalities often try to live rigidly according to such slogans. Honesty *is* a good policy. But can you imagine the strain of being totally honest, in word and deed, at all times?

3. *Social interest.* Most people want to make their communities better places in which to live. Adler believed that this feeling is an inborn characteristic. He showed that *social interest* explains why people will risk their lives to rescue a stranger or will give generously to a charity. In too many communities, however, fears for personal safety have begun to override social in-

terest. A subway passenger may be attacked and robbed in full sight of twenty other people, all of whom will turn the other way.

Karen Horney

Karen Horney, a German psychiatrist (see BioBox), has been called "the gentle rebel of psychoanalysis." Although trained in Freudian methods, she saw that instinctive urges and childhood sexuality were not enough to explain all neurotic behavior. In addition, Horney also objected strenuously to Freud's labeling women as the inferior sex. In *The Neurotic Personality of Our Time*, she described the importance of social forces in shaping personality. She believed that the root of the individual's ability to cope with life begins with the way children learn to deal with anything that disturbs their security. The adult personality, Horney goes on, grows out of the child's success or failure in coping with this basic anxiety.

Basic anxiety. Unable to control its environment, the infant feels helpless and insecure. This *basic anxiety* is often increased by negative parental behaviors, such as indifference, harsh criticism, lack of guidance, overprotection, and erratic discipline. Unless children overcome this basic anxiety during childhood, they will often show neurotic behaviors during adolescence and adulthood. Horney defines neurotic behaviors as poorly chosen strategies for solving problems. For example, Jason, a basi-

KAREN HORNEY:
THE GENTLE REBEL OF PSYCHOANALYSIS

If a computer could be programmed to duplicate the perfect psychologist, the model could well be based on Karen Horney (1885–1952). This German-born psychoanalyst brought a warmth, dedication and joy of living to her work that touched all who knew her.

Karen Horney was born into a world that did not accept women as the equals of men. In order to become a psychiatrist, she had to overcome centuries of built-up prejudice. But she was strong-minded and intelligent. By the time she finished medical school and was ready to take the state exams, her professors had learned to respect her abilities. As a result, they let her space out her tests so that she could continue nursing her infant daughter.

That same determination served her well when she began to rebel against Freudian teachings. The more she worked with neurotic patients, the more she came to believe that psychosexual drives could not explain all disturbed behavior. Even though her new ideas cost her a teaching position, she refused to back down. Today, Horney's insistence on the role of cultural factors in causing basic anxiety have been largely accepted by most psychologists.

One of Horney's useful insights relates to what she called "the tyranny of the *should*." She described how people contribute to their own emotional distress in these words:

> Let us consider another demand: I should always be understanding, sympathetic, and helpful. . . . I had a patient [who felt as though she should be as forgiving as a priest]. But she did not . . . have any of the attitudes or qualities which enabled

the priest to act as he did toward the criminal. She could act charitably at times because she felt that she *should* be charitable, but she did not feel charitable. As a matter of fact, she did not feel much of anything for anybody. . . . Without being aware of it, her neurosis had made her egocentric and bent on her own advantage—all of which was covered up by a layer of compulsive humility and goodness.

Where do such conflicts come from? Horney believed that the problem begins in childhood with "a lack of genuine warmth and affection. A child can stand a great deal of what is often regarded as traumatic—such as sudden weaning, occasional beating, sex experiences—as long as inwardly he feels wanted and loved. Needless to say, a child feels keenly whether love is genuine and cannot be fooled by any faked demonstrations."

Along with such insights, Horney also believed that human beings can change, grow, and escape their neuroses. She herself remained a growing, vibrant person all her life. A therapist, writer, and teacher, she also liked to sing, eat good food, and drink good wine. As her friend Paul Tillich said of her, "Few people were so strong in the affirmation of their being, so full of the joy of living, . . . She wrote books but loved human beings."

Can you see why Karen Horney was so highly regarded by all who knew her? How would you summarize her insights into the causes of the troubled personality?

cally healthy person, feels angry when he's denied a raise for which he's worked hard. But he understands the real world. He resolves his anger by asking the boss for an explanation or by looking for another job. But Roger, who has never resolved his basic anxiety, cannot control his anger in the same situation. He curses at the boss and quits his job on the spot.

Neurotic needs. Karen Horney made a major contribution to personality theory by identifying the basic neurotic needs. These needs, she believes, grow out of the strategies people use to combat anxiety. She considers them neurotic because they often force people to make unrealistic demands on themselves or on others.

1. *Neurotic needs that move an individual toward people.* (a) The neurotic need for affection and approval: The individual must please others and live up to their expectations. (b) The neurotic need for a "partner" who will take over one's life: Afraid to be alone, the individual gives all control of his or her life to someone else. (c) The neurotic need for prestige: Self-confidence and personal identity rest totally on receiving recognition from others. (d) The neurotic need for personal admiration: The individual expects to be admired on the basis of a false self-image.

2. *Neurotic needs that move an individual away from people.* (a) The neurotic need to restrict one's life within narrow borders: To be noticed is frightening or painful, so the individual withdraws into as narrow a corner of life as possible. (b) The neurotic need for self-sufficiency and independence: The individual has suffered from attempts to build relationships with others, so refuses to accept love or friendship. (c) The neurotic need for perfection: To make a mistake is to admit weakness, so the individual tries to be infallible in everything.

3. *Neurotic needs that move an individual against people.* (a) The neurotic need for power: Power and control are so important that the individual will do anything to attain them. (b) The neurotic need to exploit others: Taking advantage of other people serves as a way of relieving feelings of helplessness and insecurity. (c) The neurotic need for personal achievement: The individual tries desperately to achieve ever more splendid successes at the expense of others.

Can these neurotic tendencies be eliminated from people's lives? Horney believed that the best solution would be to raise all children in an atmosphere of warmth, security, love, and respect. Adults who find their lives controlled by these self-defeating needs often require the assistance of a therapist. In therapy, Karen Horney's insights often provide a powerful healing power.

Erik H. Erikson

Erik Erikson (1902–   ) ranks as one of the key names in modern psychology. He began his career while teaching art in Vienna at a school founded by Anna Freud. With her encouragement, he turned to the study of psychoanalysis. In 1933, he moved to the United States, where he became an eminent therapist and teacher. Erikson first came to public attention in 1958, when he published a biography called *Young Man Luther.* In this book he interpreted Martin Luther's religious career in psychoanalytic terms. This new approach to interpreting history, now called *psychohistory,* has since become an accepted—but controversial—part of the field of historical research.

The theory of psychosocial development. Erikson's ideas can be summarized as follows:

1. At the same time that people pass through the Freudian stages of psychosexual development, they must also move through a series of *psychosocial stages* of

ego development. At each stage, people must achieve a new way of seeing themselves in relation to society and to other people. In other words, eighteen-year-old Jeanne can no longer deal with life in the same way she did when she was eight years old.

2. Personality development continues through each person's entire life cycle. In popular terms, Erikson is saying that no one "has it made" at any age.

3. During each stage of life, a conflict develops between positive and negative ego qualities. These conflicts are present at every age, but each life stage requires that you focus on a particular crisis. Failure to resolve that particular crisis will result in damage to the ego. This damage makes the next stage that much harder to cope with.

Stages of psychosocial development. In Erikson's concept, the eight stages of personality development make up your total life cycle. During each stage a particular crisis must be resolved.

1. *Trust vs. Mistrust* (infancy, birth to one year). Babies learn to trust or fear the world depending upon their experiences with other people, particularly their parents. They need to feel that the world is orderly and predictable. Without the ability to trust, the infant will face the second stage handicapped by anxiety and personal fears.

2. *Autonomy vs. Doubt* (early childhood, ages two and three). During this stage, children must develop confidence and independence. Typically, this means that they learn to dress themselves, help out around the house, and do things "all by myself." Children who do not receive this freedom to explore new skills and develop self-confidence will be left full of shame and doubt about their abilities.

3. *Initiative vs. Guilt* (play age, ages four and five). Active and curious, children of the play age should be encouraged to develop their intellectual resources and their indi-

vidual interests. They should be free to run, play, fantasize, and question everything. Guilt feelings result when parents clamp down too hard on the vigorous, self-motivated activities of this age. Instead of saying, "Look at me!" the child is forced to whisper, "I hope they don't see me doing this."

4. *Industry vs. Inferiority* (school age, ages six to eleven). Most children enter school eager to learn and to demonstrate their growing intellectual skills. They want to learn about new things and love trying to make things with their hands. Group games give them a chance to explore their relationships with others. Teachers and parents who push too hard, however, can cut off their children's feelings of industry. This pressure may cause feelings of inferiority, for children *feel* inferior when asked to complete tasks beyond their abilities.

5. *Identity vs. Role Confusion* (adolescence, ages twelve to eighteen). This critical period requires that adolescents find their own identity. This crisis is made more difficult by the other challenges of adolescence: dealing with sexual maturity, choosing a career, and working out relationships with parents. Erikson himself spent two years, from ages eighteen to twenty, wandering aimlessly through Germany and Italy, trying to resolve his own identity crisis. In time, he achieved a sense of identity, as his later career reveals. Young people who do not achieve their own identities enter adulthood confused about their goals, values, and vocational possibilities.

6. *Intimacy vs. Isolation* (young adulthood, ages nineteen to thirty-five). Young adulthood usually finds people looking for a partner with whom they can share their lives. Erikson warns, however, that young adults will also find their values and identity challenged by new friends and lovers. This stage of life requires that young adults develop the strength to stick to commitments, even when they call for sacrifice or compromise.

Figure 7.6

From infancy to old age, each stage of the life cycle brings its own crisis and requires its own solution. Can you identify the five life stages illustrated here? What crisis does each of these persons face?

Figure 7.7

HOW MANY AGES ARE THERE, ANYWAY?

Are there three, five, seven, or eight ages along the way to our Biblical "three score and ten"? The question has challenged humanity from the ancient Greeks to modern psychologists.

The Riddle of the Sphinx (an ancient Greek myth)

One day, while Oedipus was on his way to the city of Thebes, a terrible Sphinx stopped him. This winged monster, which had the body of a lion and the head of a woman, asked all who passed a riddle. The penalty for not guessing the answer was to be killed and eaten. The terrified Thebans had offered the throne and the hand of Queen Jocasta to whoever should answer the riddle and overcome the monster.

"What animal," the Sphinx asked Oedipus, "walks on four legs in the morning, two at noon, and on three at night?"

Oedipus quickly replied, "Man, for in the morning, the infancy of his life, he creeps on all four. At noon, in his prime, he walks on two feet. And when the darkness of old age comes over him, he uses a stick for better support as a third foot."

Thereupon the Sphinx threw herself over the rocky precipice and perished. Oedipus became King of Thebes and married (unknowingly) his mother, Jocasta, thus sealing the fate that had been prophesied for him at his birth.

Freud's Psychosexual Stages

Oral Stage . . . First year

Anal Stage . . . Second and third years

Phallic Stage . . . Fourth and fifth years

Latent Period . . . Sixth to twelfth years

Genital Stage . . . Thereafter

Shakespeare's Seven Ages of Man

> All the world's a stage,
> And all the men and women merely players.
> They have their exits and their entrances,
> And one man in his time plays many parts,
> His acts being seven ages. At first the infant,
> Mewling and puking in the nurse's arms.
> Then the whining schoolboy, with his satchel
> And shining morning face, creeping like snail
> Unwillingly to school. And then the lover,
> Sighing like a furnace, with a woeful ballad
> Made to his mistress' eyebrow. Then, a soldier,
> Full of strange oaths, and bearded like
>   the pard,
> Jealous in honor, sudden and quick in quarrel,
> Seeking the bubble reputation
> Even in the cannon's mouth. And then,
>   the justice,
> In fair round belly with good capon lined,
> With eyes severe, and beard of formal cut,
> Full of wise saws and modern instances,
> And so he plays his part. The sixth age shifts

> Into the lean and slippered pantaloon,
> With spectacles on nose, and pouch on side,
> His youthful hose, well saved, a world too wide
> For his shrunk shank, and his big manly voice,
> Turning again toward childish treble pipes
> And whistles in his sound. Last scene of all,
> That ends this strange eventful history,
> Is second childishness and mere oblivion,
> Sans teeth, sans eyes, sans taste,
>   sans everything.

As You Like It, by William Shakespeare,
Act II, Scene vii

Erikson's Eight Stages of Development

Infancy (Trust vs. Mistrust) . . . First year
Early Childhood (Autonomy vs. Doubt) . . . Second and third years
Play age (Initiative vs. Guilt) . . . Fourth and fifth years
School age (Industry vs. Inferiority) . . . Sixth to eleventh years

Adolescence (Identity vs. Role Confusion) . . . Twelfth to eighteenth years
Young adulthood (Intimacy vs. Isolation) . . . Nineteenth to thirty-fifth years
Adulthood (Generativity vs. Stagnation) . . . Thirty-sixth to sixtieth years
Old age (Ego Integrity vs. Despair) . . . Over sixty

Which sequence makes the most sense to you? Why did you make that choice?

7. *Generativity vs. Stagnation* (adulthood, ages thirty-six to sixty). Mature adults begin to plan for future generations, either through their children or through their contributions to community and society. Such "generativity" adds greatly to the quality of life in any society. Examples of such activities include volunteer work in hospitals and at city hall, coaching youth athletic teams, going without a new car to pay for a child's college tuition, or joining a crusade to clean up the local water system. Erikson labeled "stagnant" those adults who are concerned only with themselves. They try to deny the aging process by concentrating solely on material pleasures.

8. *Ego Integrity vs. Despair* (old age, sixty and over). You may know some well-integrated elderly people. You recognize them because they know they have accomplished what they could with their lives. They remain active and interested right to the end, like the eighty-year-old man who returns to college to "find out what's going on in the world." Elderly people who fill their conversations with, "I wish I'd had a chance to . . ." and, "It's not fair!" have not achieved ego integrity. Such people often fear death and wake up each morning with a sense of despair that robs them of any joy in life.

Importance of Erikson's work. Erikson's life-cycle theory allows psychologists to treat adult emotional crises as genuinely adult. By contrast, the Freudian analyst must always search back for infantile traumas. In a generally gloomy world, Erikson's teachings provide hope that early failures can be offset by later developments. A child who does not resolve the crisis of industry vs. inferiority at age seven, for example, can still overcome feelings of doubt and inadequacy later on. Often, added maturity enables people to develop on their own. In other cases, the help of a therapist may be needed. With Erikson's insights to draw on, however, you may have a better idea of what lies ahead in your next life stage. And recognizing the crisis may be halfway to resolving it.

SECTION CHECKUP

1 What is meant by the term *neo-Freudian*? What basic differences lie between Freud and the neo-Freudians?

2 What did Adler mean by the creative self? What have feelings of inferiority to do with mental health?

3 How would Karen Horney define *basic anxiety*? How does she relate anxiety to neurotic behavior?

4 What does Erik Erikson mean by the crises of the life stages? What is the crisis of your particular life stage?

7.3 WHAT CONTRIBUTIONS DID CARL JUNG MAKE TO PERSONALITY THEORY?

For seven years, from 1906 to 1913, it appeared that Carl Jung (1875–1961), a Swiss psychiatrist, would follow Freud as leader of the psychoanalytic movement. Their friendship ended, however, when Jung refused to accept Freud's emphasis on sex as a primary force in personality development. Where Freud thought primarily of primitive drives, Jung came to place equal emphasis on the spiritual and moral aspects of life. Jung's ideas were so original and his influence so great that he cannot be classified as a neo-Freudian. His concept of the personality, known as *analytic psychology*, stands on its own.

A jovial, vigorous man, Jung possessed a keen, active intellect. His investigations carried him far beyond the boundaries of psychology. During his busy life, he studied such varied fields as the occult, extrasensory perception, yoga, religion, mythology, and art. He even got involved in the study of flying saucers! But Jung's passion remained the study of the *psyche*, his name for the human personality. Although he accepted many Freudian concepts, Jung added several totally new ideas of his own relating to the unconscious.

The Jungian unconscious

Jung divided the unconscious into two parts, the personal unconscious and the collective unconscious.

The personal unconscious. The *personal unconscious*, Jung believed, contains an individual's experiences that were once conscious but have since been forgotten, ignored, or repressed. Like Freud, Jung thought that these memories could influence an individual's conscious behavior. In this way, Jung's personal unconscious is quite similar to the Freudian unconscious.

Jung went on, however, to describe a number of organized groups of feelings, thoughts, and perceptions within the personal unconscious. He called each of these a *complex*. Jungian analysts often speak of a

"mother complex" or a "power complex." Since a strong complex usually dominates the personality, it can be harmful if it prevents the person from establishing a realistic, freely chosen identity. A "money complex," for example, may lead Neal to sacrifice family and friends in his quest for financial gain. He may not be aware of this central theme in his behavior; he knows only that he must have money in order to feel at peace with himself.

The collective unconscious. During his studies of art and literature, Jung found evidence of what he identified as universal instincts, drives, and memories. This *collective unconscious*, as he named it, forms a "racial memory" shared by all members of the human race. Jung believed that these collective memories cross all boundaries of time, skin color, and geography (see Figure 7.8).

If you're wondering why you can't remember back to the Stone Age, Jung would say that no one can recall such ancient memories. They do exist, however, as un-

Figure 7.8

Carl Jung believed that art and literature provide clues to the existence of universal symbols that derive from our collective unconscious. What common archetypes do you see in these two scenes, even though the dragon has been replaced by a locomotive? [*Saint George and the Dragon;* Raphael; National Gallery of Art, Washington; Andrew W. Mellon Collection.]

seen forces behind your thoughts, feelings, and perceptions. The fact that many people love to hunt and fish wouldn't surprise Jung. He would say that hunting and fishing are examples of influences from the collective unconscious translated into conscious behaviors.

Many psychologists refuse to accept the idea of the collective unconscious. Jung, however, insisted that two million years of evolutionary experience must have left their mark on the human brain. He pointed to the work of anthropologists, who have described apparently universal behaviors among widely separated peoples. What is a smile, a blush, a handshake, Jung asked, but an automatic physical response to the common fund of behavior found in the collective unconscious?

Archetypes. Jung was fascinated by the reappearance of common themes and symbols in dreams, literature, mythology, and art. Throughout history and in widely varied cultures, he found images of birth and rebirth, death, magic, God, the devil, the hero, the wise old man, and the earth mother. He called these universal thought patterns *archetypes*. These ideas come out of the collective unconscious, he believed. Unlike complexes, which can dominate the personality, individual archetypes create images on which you base your understanding of the world around you. From them comes your sense of wholeness and completeness. Thus, your hero archetype gives you a sense of what it means to protect those you love and to fight for what is right. Your earth-mother archetype, meanwhile, helps you understand the miracle of life and the nurturing of children.

Four of Jung's archetypes have evolved to the point where they are treated as separate systems within the personality. These are the persona, the anima and animus, the shadow, and the self.

1. *Persona.* All people wear masks in public, Jung believed, behind which they hide their true natures. He called this mask the *persona*. Each individual forms his or her persona in response to social pressures,

traditions, and the need to be accepted by others. Heidi's persona, for example, is that of the "good girl." She judges the "rightness" of everything she does according to her rigid concept of behavior. At times, Heidi would like to "break loose" from her self-created restrictions, but her persona is so important to her that she cannot admit to having such "bad" feelings. That's not to say that it's wrong for Heidi to use the "good girl" persona. A Jungian analyst would become alarmed only if she allows the persona to dominate her life.

2. *Anima and animus.* Jung believed that all people have elements of the opposite sex within them. The *anima* is the feminine side of men, and the *animus* is the male side of women. These archetypes provide shading and balance to the personality. Each enables one sex to understand and respond to the other. Some people have so idealized these archetypes, however, that no one can live up to their expectations. Joe's anima, for example, doesn't allow the women in his life to have a single blemish. With that impossible standard, it's little wonder that Joe is still looking for someone perfect enough for him to love.

3. *Shadow.* The *shadow* represents the animal side of the personality. Perhaps you can see some elements of the Freudian id in the shadow, but the parallel is not exact. Socially unacceptable thoughts and desires that come from the shadow are usually repressed into the personal unconscious. Most people hide the shadow behind their persona. How could you love me, they seem to be saying, if you caught a glimpse of the terrible passions contained in my shadow?

4. *Self.* Analytic psychology places great emphasis on the concept of the *self*. Jung regarded the self as a life goal, a striving for unity and completeness. Few people reach this point, however, for all other elements of the personality must be fully developed first. Perhaps only a few great religious leaders and philosophers have attained the joining of the conscious and unconscious minds that is necessary for emergence of the completed self.

USING FREE ASSOCIATION TO TRAP A SUSPECTED "CRIMINAL"

The Jungian free-association test is based on a simple principle: As the subject responds to a list of prepared words, repressed or concealed material will slip past the mind's censors and enter into speech. This experiment makes use of Jung's technique to expose a criminal suspect, much as the polygraph (lie detector) does, but without the elaborate equipment.

Step 1 On a slip of paper, write a description of a fictional crime. Include details of time, place, the identity of the victim, the amount of money stolen, the colors of the victim's clothing, and the like.

Begin the description, "You have committed a serious crime. Last night, you. . . ." Make up several other slips of paper that simply state, "You are a subject in a psychological experiment. Thank you for your help."

Step 2 Extract from the scenario of the crime a list of ten key words. For the stickup of an armored car, these words might include *diamond, note, guard, shotgun, car,* and the like. Don't use too-obvious words such as *stickup, robbery,* or *getaway*. Now add to the list fifteen general words that have no connection to the crime: *flower, breakfast, football,* and the like. Complete this step by adding the ten key words at random to the second list of fifteen.

Step 3 Select three or four subjects. Set up a grand jury to judge the guilt or innocence of the suspects.

Step 4 The subjects should be kept isolated from one another and from the jury. Give each subject a slip of paper. One person will receive the description of the crime, while the others will receive the meaningless second statement. Distribute the slips at random—it's best if the experimenter doesn't know the identity of the criminal. Give each jury member a copy of the word list.

Step 5 Bring the suspects one at a time before the grand jury. Instruct them to say nothing except in response to the list of words you are going to read to them. Tell them to reply to each word with whatever second word comes to mind. Do not give any further explanation. Now read the list of words to each suspect, pausing after each word for the subject's response. The jury should write down the suspect's replies, as well as any physical reaction—long pauses, laughs, nervous mannerisms, and the like.

Step 6 After all suspects have been "questioned," ask the jury to identify the criminal. If your word list has been properly keyed to the crime, the guilty person's responses to the key words will usually give him or her away.

Jung's other contributions

The popular terms that refer to shy and outgoing personalities, *introversion* and *extroversion,* were introduced in Jung's work. Introverts look inward and take pleasure pursuing their own thoughts and feelings. They are happiest when they're alone, for people tend to make them nervous. Extroverts, on the other hand, invest their psychic energy outside of themselves. They need company, excitement, and activity. Successful salespeople are usually extroverts. You've probably already discovered that you have both elements within your own personality. Jung said that one or the other usually dominates and that most people are aware of which one it is.

The word association test (see Figure 7.9)

also derives from Jung's analytic techniques. The test is widely used as a tool for revealing repressed or concealed personal data.

Carl Jung also brought a new compassion and openness to psychoanalytic theory. Despite the complexity of his ideas, people could relate to his outgoing personality. Unlike Freud, for example, the Jungian analyst sits facing the patient and takes an active role in the therapy. Overall, Jung's approach to therapy has been described as warmer and less mechanical than Freud's.

Analysts who use this Jungian technique can be found in cities around the globe.

SECTION CHECKUP

1 What are some of the basic differences between Jung's analytic psychology and Freud's psychoanalytic theory?

2 Distinguish between the personal unconscious and the collective unconscious.

3 What did Jung mean by a complex?

4 What is an archetype? How do archetypes affect behavior?

7.4 HOW DO THE HUMANIST PSYCHOLOGISTS APPROACH PERSONALITY THEORY?

Humanist psychology is based on the research and influence of Abraham Maslow (1908–1970). An American psychologist, Maslow told his fellow psychologists to stop defining personality in light of their disturbed patients. Instead, he said, psychology should concentrate on studying healthy people.

Along with Carl Rogers, the other guiding spirit of the humanist movement, Maslow believed that all members of society should be given the chance to realize their full potential as human beings. This goal is achievable, he thought, because people are basically good. His beliefs contrast with those of Freud, who seemed to define human beings as victims of their biological and psychological past. Not so, Maslow claimed, for if their basic needs are met, most men and women naturally live happy, productive lives.

Maslow's definition of human nature

Maslow criticized the older schools of psychology for what he saw as their negative attitudes toward human nature. He attempted to paint a brighter, more optimistic picture of emotional life. In doing so, Maslow defined five basic concepts concerning human nature.

1. Humanity's essential nature is made up of needs, capacities, and tendencies that are good (or natural) rather than harmful.

2. Full, healthy personality development comes when people develop their basic natures and fulfill their potential. People must grow from within rather than be shaped from without. Unless they do, they can never reach true maturity.

3. Mental illness results when people's basic needs are not satisfied, frustrating or twisting their inner nature. The role of the psychotherapist is to restore the patient to the path of growth and self-knowledge along the lines dictated by the patient's inner nature.

4. People's inner nature is weak, delicate, and subtle, unlike the overpowering instincts of animals. Although a person's inner nature can grow tall and strong, it begins as a tiny seed. At that stage it can be easily overcome by cultural pressures, the failure to satisfy basic needs, or unhealthy habits. No one's basic goodness ever disappears, even though it may be submerged for a while under self-defeating behaviors.

Figure 7.10

Abraham Maslow wouldn't agree with Lucy's opinion. According to Maslow, how could Charlie Brown achieve self-actualization?

5. As people mature, their potential goodness shows itself even more clearly. The *self-actualizing* person, as the humanist psychologists describe the fully mature personality, stands out in any environment (see Figure 7.10). Perhaps only a few people reach full self-actualization. But even those who are making progress toward that level of maturity are recognized and sought after by others.

Basic needs and metaneeds

Maslow recognized that people must satisfy their *basic needs* for health, safety, and love before they are free to fulfill their higher growth needs. He defined the basic needs as:

1. Physiological needs: satisfaction of the body's requirements for food, drink, air, sex, sleep, and relaxation.

2. Safety needs: feeling secure and safe from danger in an orderly, predictable world.

3. Love needs: satisfaction of the need to belong to groups, to receive and give affection, and to maintain friendships.

4. Esteem needs: attainment of acceptable levels of recognition, achievement and competence.

Maslow called these basic needs *deficiency needs* because they must be met be-

fore people can bring beauty, goodness, and justice into their lives. Striving to attain these higher growth needs, called *metaneeds*, is just as much a part of human nature as is working to satisfy basic needs. Maslow defined the metaneeds as:

1. Cognitive needs: satisfaction of the mind's need to know, understand, and explore.

2. Aesthetic needs: the desire to bring beauty and order into one's life.

3. Self-actualization needs: the desire for self-fulfillment; the realization of individual potential.

You can see how deficiency needs and metaneeds work by looking at the career of Gilda G., an actress. When Gilda was young, she was forced to take any job she could get. With rent to pay and food to buy, satisfying her deficiency needs took all her time and energy. She did commercials, worked at trade shows, and took roles that did little more than pay the bills. In time, she got better parts, and finally landed a leading role in a Broadway hit. Today, wealthy and sought after, Gilda chooses roles that allow her to express her creativity and dramatic abilities. She takes time off from her career to raise her child. Happy and self-fulfilled, her deficiency needs satisfied, she now concentrates on satisfying her metaneeds.

Self-actualization

As part of his research for his influential book *Toward a Psychology of Being*, Maslow studied the lives of a number of successful people. If he could find the common qualities that made these men and women successful, he reasoned, he would have defined the concept of *self-actualization*. Among the figures that Maslow counted as self-actualizing were Thomas Jefferson, Albert Einstein, Eleanor Roosevelt, George Washington Carver, and Jane Addams. He also included personal friends, people he thought demonstrated the qualities of health and creativity that go with self-actualization.

Self-actualizing people, Maslow discovered, can satisfy both their basic needs and their metaneeds. They tend to be outgoing, creative, self-reliant, nonconforming, and democratic. You probably know several people who fit this description (see Figure 7.11). Just look for people who live their lives to the fullest, yet always seem to have

Figure 7.11

HOW DO YOU RECOGNIZE A SELF-ACTUALIZING PERSON?

Abraham Maslow described the healthiest of all personalities as belonging to the self-actualizing person. Based on his research, he identified a list of characteristics that describe the self-actualizing personality. You might want to rate yourself on these qualities.

Self-actualizing people:

- Perceive reality better than most individuals.
- Accept themselves, others, and the natural world without worrying about what they cannot control.
- Are spontaneous in their thought and behavior but seldom do bizarre or unusual things.
- Focus on problems outside themselves, rather than being self-centered.
- Stay independent of the social pressures that rule most people's lives.
- Find fresh enjoyment in activities that they have experienced many times before.
- Are open to profound spiritual or mystic experiences, although they are not necessarily religious.
- Identify with the rest of humanity in a positive way.
- Maintain deep emotional relationships with a limited number of people.
- Are democratic in their values and attitudes and free of prejudice.
- Enjoy the process of reaching a goal as much as the achievement itself.
- Enjoy a funny situation without turning the humor into hostility.
- Are capable of great creativity, often in a number of different fields.
- Are part of their culture but do not blindly conform to its standards.

time to help others. They have problems as everyone else does, but somehow they never let those problems dominate their lives.

Perhaps most interesting of all, self-actualizing people have frequent *peak experiences*. Humanist psychologists define peak experiences as those moments of intense awareness when you feel totally alive; in tune with the universe; and fully aware of the beauty, naturalness, and rightness of the moment. For some people, that moment may come as part of a religious experience, during prayer or a solemn ceremony. For others, it develops out of their passionate commitment to the activity of the moment. A former professional football quarterback, for example, described a peak experience that came during a game. He told of fading back to pass and suddenly feeling totally alive, with every sense heightened. Time seemed to stand still. He could "see" every player and knew exactly what he would do next. The football fitted his hand perfectly, and he knew that when he threw the pass it would go for a touchdown. When his end

took the pass in for a score, the moment passed. But no one who experiences such high points forgets them.

Sadly enough, some people try to find shortcuts to peak experiences. They use drugs or alcohol to create an artificial environment that they hope will give them the insights and sense of well-being that self-actualizing people create for themselves. But true peak experiences cannot be ordered up or created with drugs. Maslow believed that anything that subtracts from the "will of health" moves people away from the path toward self-actualization.

SECTION CHECKUP

1 Why does Abraham Maslow suggest that psychologists study healthy people instead of disturbed people?

2 What are basic needs? What are metaneeds? Why must the basic needs be satisfied before the metaneeds can be met?

3 Define the concept of self-actualization. How would you recognize a self-actualizing person?

7.5 WHAT NEW IDEAS HAVE THE EXISTENTIALISTS ADDED TO PERSONALITY THEORY?

A patient once asked psychologist Victor Frankl (1905–) to tell him the true meaning of life. Frankl answered the question with another question: "What is the best move in a game of chess?"

Frankl wasn't trying to be difficult. As an existentialist, he was using the question to say that there is no universal *best* move. You always have a choice, depending upon the circumstances of a particular game. In a sense, that defines *existential psychology:* Human beings are free agents; they determine their behavior by choice. They are not controlled by unconscious forces over which they have no control. According to existential psychologists such as Rollo May (see BioBox, page 208), no one is bound to the past.

The existential approach to personality

Existentialism grew out of the chaos that descended on Europe during World War II. The cruelties of war, magnified by the Nazi concentration camps, convinced many people that a universal meaning of life does not exist. To help fill that vacuum, existential psychology came into being. Even today, it does not offer a unified body of personality theory. But it does provide a set of attitudes toward such uniquely personal qualities as love, appreciation of beauty, and the full development of the human potential. For many people, the belief in the human spirit of existential psychology gives meaning to their lives.

BioBox

ROLLO MAY:
LIFE IS MORE THAN A SENTENCE IMPOSED BY THE PAST

As a young man, Rollo May (1909–   ) became ill with tuberculosis. Already interested in the study of human behavior, he "lived in a state of constant anxiety, like a horse running wild. I accepted it and recovered through the sheer exertion of my will. . . . I learned along the way to tune in on my being, my existence in the *now,* because that was all there was—that and my tubercular body. It was a valuable experience to face death, for in the experience I learned to face life."

Today, Rollo May lives in San Francisco, a handsome, gray-haired man who practices psychotherapy. Most people know him better, however, as the best-selling author of such books as *The Meaning of Anxiety* and *Man's Search for Himself.* May sees a few patients but spends most of his time writing and lecturing on his existential theories.

In his first book, *Love and Will,* May declared that awareness is not opposed to but essential to life. He also disagrees with the Freudians by suggesting that people need not be held prisoner by their past. He believes that people are prisoners only if they choose to be. As an existentialist, May also encourages people to take responsibility for their own lives. He believes that personality problems result from contact with society but that most of these problems can be corrected.

When he was asked the value of psychotherapy, May replied:

Before you begin psychotherapy, you might feel completely alienated, without anyone who believes in you. But when you establish a relationship with a therapist, you have found someone who is listening. The therapist might be the first person who has ever really listened, the first person who believes in you. This then builds courage in you. You feel like you are worth something, and you can venture forth into the world, because a strong person has confidence in you.

May feels strongly that some people won't make the commitment needed to make therapy worthwhile. He refuses to work with anyone who is "looking for kicks" or who thinks it's fashionable to be in analysis. The patient he does want is similar to the woman who gave up a job in the Midwest and moved to the San Francisco area just because she wanted to talk regularly with May. Since she thought it was so important, and because she committed herself to the therapy, he took her on.

What do you think May means by "taking responsibility for your own life"? As an existentialist, why is commitment in his patients so important to May?

Key existential beliefs

1. The central concept of life is *being*. Human beings live in a world made up of the physical environment, other people, and one's own consciousness. All you can know is what you perceive of that world. The existentialist sums this idea up: You are part of the world, and the world is part of you.

2. Being also means becoming. Unlike a rock or a mathematical formula, you have potential. You can grow, change, commit yourself to projects—or you can give in to frustration and a sense of futility. To realize your potential requires that you explore your own being.

3. Each person must take responsibility for his or her own life. This means that you must make choices, even though that means taking a risk. Even if you make a poor choice, you are still free to make a better choice in the future. No one has the right to say, "That's the way I am. My parents hit me when I was little and I can't change." You not only can change but have an obligation to do so.

4. Happiness results when you make a commitment to what you have chosen. In a sense, you should make each choice in your life as if you were making it for all of humanity. Anxiety and existential despair result when you refuse to take responsibility for making decisions about your own life or give in to the knowledge that you are alone.

Perhaps you've been tempted at times to say, "That isn't fair!" when you didn't get something you wanted. The existentialist would nod and add, "You're right. Life *isn't* fair. The world is full of unfairness. Look at the senseless death, disease, and other forms of inhumanity that happen every minute. But once you know that life is unfair, you are free! You no longer need wait for good things to happen. Instead, you can begin living your life as fully and as richly as is humanly possible."

The existential view of neurotic behavior

The existentialist believes that anxiety and despair are inescapable parts of the human condition. Every time you make a choice, you're taking a risk. If you decide to ask someone for a date, you may be turned down. You can apply for a job, but the employer may not like your looks. And so it goes. Each new choice brings a new anxiety. If you cave in under the pressure of anxiety, you will probably begin to behave in a neurotic way. Some people react by withdrawing from most contacts with other people. Others launch upon a desperate search for pleasure, using whatever means are available. Far too many let themselves be frozen into conformity, allowing others to determine what they will say, do, and think.

Existential despair results when people's inborn "will to meaning" is frustrated. Frankl called this the "existential vacuum." Here's how eighteen-year-old Gary B. described his own existential vacuum:

> All at once I knew that life didn't have any meaning. Like, you know, everyone else was faking it. I just felt hollow, all emptied out inside. Everything I tried to do fell apart. My job, my girl friend, my family, nothing seemed worthwhile.

Most people experience this feeling at one time or another. Frankl saw it often in the World War II concentration camp to which he was sent. He found that those who survived were the men and women who had a task in life to complete. When someone else or some cause is dependent upon you, you can rise above human limitations and overcome despair.

Rollo May adds that anxiety, in small doses, can be constructive. He believes that it sharpens your sensitivity and sparks your creativity. Both Frankl and he would also agree that living up to your responsibilities will strengthen you. You can take risks when you're a healthy person because you have your own resources to fall back on. In freedom and commitment, the existentialists believe, you will find the happiness that seems to elude so many people today.

SECTION CHECKUP

1 Why would the existentialist say that "there's no best choice in life"?

2 What brings happiness to the individual, according to existential theory?

3 Describe the existential concept of anxiety and despair. How can they be overcome?

LOOKING BACK: A SUMMARY

1 Psychologists have not found—and may never find—a single, all-purpose theory to explain how the personality develops. Different theories place different values on biological, psychological, and environmental influences. Six major schools that provide a wide range of contrasting opinions about personality theory are the psychoanalytic (Freudian), the behaviorist, the neo-Freudian, the analytic (Jungian), the humanist, and the existentialist.

2 Behavioral psychologists John Watson and B. F. Skinner dismiss the study of mental processes, which cannot be seen or measured. They believe that psychologists must study behavior, which can be observed, measured, and identified. Behaviorists claim that behavior is a system of stimulus-response units (S→R). When the stimulus is modified, the response will change. Responses that are reflexive or involuntary are called *respondent behaviors*. Responses that act on the environment are called *operant behaviors*. Desirable operant behaviors can be strengthened by positive reinforcement. Undesirable behaviors can be eliminated by applying either negative reinforcement or punishment.

3 Behaviorists view neurotic behavior as inappropriate responses to stimuli. Therapy, therefore, consists of helping pa-

Figure 7.12
KEY PERSONALITY THEORIES: HOW DO THEY COMPARE?

School	Important figures
Psychoanalytic	SIGMUND FREUD
The neo-Freudians	ALFRED ADLER KAREN HORNEY ERIK ERIKSON
Analytic Psychology	CARL JUNG
Behaviorism	JOHN WATSON B. F. SKINNER
Humanist Psychology	ABRAHAM MASLOW CARL ROGERS
Existential Psychology	ROLLO MAY VICTOR FRANKL

Basic personality theory	Origin of neurotic behavior
Human personality is formed by working out the conflict between the desire of the individual to seek pleasure and the demands of the outside world. Much behavior results from the influence of the unconscious, where the repressed experiences of childhood are stored.	Neurotic behavior develops when the ego cannot cope with the conflicting demands of the id and the superego. Unresolved traumas from the past can also cause the individual to act neurotically.
Social and cultural forces combine to shape the personality. The healthy person has learned to cope with the conflict caused by individual needs and the demands of the environment.	Anxiety growing out of an inability to develop good personal relationships causes neurotic behavior. Inability to resolve the periodic crises of life also contributes to neurotic behavior.
The human personality, or psyche, develops out of the interrelationship of the personal unconscious with its complexes, the collective unconscious with its archetypes, and the conscious mind, or ego.	Failure to cope with a complex that forces unrealistic behavior can cause neurotic behavior. Forces from the collective unconscious can also overwhelm the ego and cause neurotic behavior.
All behavior grows out of the individual's response to stimuli from the environment. Any desired behavior can be developed by using proper conditioning techniques.	Neurotic behaviors are poorly chosen responses to stimuli. Many such behaviors were learned in the past and later became generalized to an entire series of responses.
Human beings are essentially good and have a will to health. They grow by meeting basic needs and metaneeds, thus building a self-actualizing personality.	Neurotic behavior results when an individual's basic needs are not met. Cultural pressures or unhealthy habits can also submerge a person's basic goodness.
Every human being is free to make choices concerning behavior. People are free to grow and change, or they can choose not to develop their full potential. Happiness comes from commitment and acceptance of responsibility.	Anxiety and despair result from the sense of aloneness and risk that go with being responsible for making choices about life. Faced with that sense of hopelessness, people may make poor choices or decide to make none at all.

tients "unlearn" the unhealthy behavior through conditioning techniques. Society can also be improved by applying the same conditioning principles to shape "desirable" behaviors. This view has been hotly contested by humanist psychologists.

4 The neo-Freudian school of psychology rejects Freud's emphasis on sexual drives and his mechanistic view of adult life. Instead, neo-Freudians give greater emphasis to the influence of social forces. Alfred Adler stressed people's needs to find positive expression for their inborn social urges. He also wrote of overcoming natural feelings of inferiority through compensation. Karen Horney described the neurotic personality, which she thought developed out of basic anxieties unresolved in childhood. She also listed the neurotic needs that grow out of people's attempts to combat anxiety. Erik Erikson identified eight psychosocial stages of development that all people must pass through during their lifetimes. Each stage brings a new crisis, which must be mastered if a person is to move on freely to the next stage. The crisis of adolescence, for example, is that of identity vs. role confusion.

5 Carl Jung made important contributions to personality theory. Of particular interest is his concept of the collective unconscious, which he said contains the ancient memories and experiences of the human race. Within the collective unconscious, Jung identified universal thought patterns he called *archetypes*. Some archetypes, which help people understand the world around them, include the earth mother, the hero, the wise old man, and death and rebirth. Four archetypes have become separate systems within the personality. These are (a) the persona (the public mask people wear to conceal the secret person underneath); (b) the anima and animus (elements of the opposite sex found in every person); (c) the shadow (the repressed, animal side of the personality

that is kept hidden from others), and (d) the self (the goal of wholeness and fulfillment sought by healthy personalities). Another part of the mind, the personal unconscious, contains organized groups of feelings, thoughts, and perceptions called *complexes*. Complexes have the power to dominate a personality if the individual is not able to deal with the influence of a "mother complex" or a "power complex."

6 The humanist psychologist believes that people are essentially good. Given the opportunity, they can become self-actualizing, a state in which they reach their full potential within the social environment. Abraham Maslow, the outstanding humanist psychologist, described a series of human needs he termed *basic needs* and *metaneeds*. Both types of needs must be met, but the metaneeds (the desire for knowledge, beauty, and self-actualization) cannot be achieved until the basic needs (physical, safety, love, and esteem needs) are taken care of. Maslow described the self-actualizing person as one who is outgoing, creative, democratic, and independent. Self-actualizing people have more peak experiences (emotional high points) in their lives than other people do.

7 Existential psychologists believe that human beings are free agents; that is, all men and women must determine their own behavior by making choices. They are not controlled by unconscious forces. Existentialism teaches that the central concept of life is being. People can grow, change, and commit themselves, or they can give in to anxiety and despair. People must take responsibility for their own lives. Happiness results when they make a commitment to what they believe in. Making choices involves risk, however, and the anxiety that arises from fear of making poor choices can cause neurotic behavior. Those people who survive and grow are those who have something in life to live for, such as another person, a family, or a cause.

PUTTING YOUR KNOWLEDGE TO WORK

Terms you should know

analytic psychology	creative self	neurotic needs	respondent behavior
anima	deficiency needs	operant behavior	self (Jungian)
animus	existential psychology	peak experience	self-actualization
archetypes	extroversion	persona	shadow
basic anxiety	fictional finalism	personal unconscious	shaping
basic needs	humanist psychology	positive reinforcement	social interest
behavioral psychology	inferiority (feelings of)	psyche	social urges
collective unconscious	introversion	psychosocial stages of development	stimulus-response (S→R)
compensation	metaneeds	punishment	systematic desensitization
complex	negative reinforcement	reinforcement	
conditioning	neo-Freudians		

Objective questions

1 The experiment in which B. F. Skinner raised his daughter in an enclosed, temperature-controlled crib demonstrates the behaviorist belief that (*a*) infants should be isolated from human contact (*b*) infants have no defense against infection at birth and must be protected from the outside environment (*c*) society can create a race of strong, mentally healthy children only if their environment is carefully controlled (*d*) infants must be protected from traumatic childhood experiences until they have control of their unconscious minds.

2 The personality theory *furthest* removed from Freudian psychoanalysis is (*a*) neo-Freudian (*b*) Jungian (*c*) humanist (*d*) behaviorist.

3 Which of the following is a *true* statement about Jung's theory of the collective unconscious? (*a*) The collective unconscious is of little interest, since Jung believed that it has little influence on behavior. (*b*) Jung believed that the archetypes located in the collective unconscious represent some of the most powerful forces in the human mind. (*c*) Jung borrowed the idea of the collective unconscious from Freud. (*d*) Jung said that the collective unconscious determines the degree of introversion or extroversion in personality.

4 The feelings of inferiority that Alfred Adler believed all people are born with must be overcome through (*a*) compensation (*b*) positive reinforcement (*c*) self-actualization (*d*) persona and shadow.

5 Karen Horney believes that the basic anxiety felt by infant Carole may later be expressed as (*a*) neurotic needs that move her away from or against other people (*b*) an unresolved Electra complex (*c*) a feeling of emptiness and despair known as the existential vacuum (*d*) an inability to solve the crises brought by each of the eight stages of psychosocial development.

6 According to Erikson, the crisis that must be overcome during adolescence is that of (*a*) Trust vs. Mistrust (*b*) Industry vs. Inferiority (*c*) Identity vs. Role Confusion (*d*) Intimacy vs. Isolation.

7 The basic concept of existential psychology can be summarized as the belief that all people must (*a*) overcome feelings of inferiority (*b*) maintain ego integrity (*c*) have numerous peak experiences (*d*) take responsibility for the choices that affect their lives.

8 A school of psychology that focuses its attention on the healthy, "normal" personality is the (*a*) neo-Freudian (*b*) existential (*c*) behaviorist (*d*) humanist.

9 Saul isn't a self-actualizing person. Which description best describes him? (*a*) He is content with satisfying basic needs. (b) He maintains deep emotional relationships with a small number of other people. (c) He enjoys many peak experiences. (d) He stays in touch with reality better than most people.

10 A parent who wanted to improve little Tony's table manners would probably have the most success with (a) punishment (b) psychoanalytic techniques (c) hypnotism (to get in touch with Tony's "food complex") (d) positive reinforcement.

Discussion questions

1 Why do psychologists find it so difficult to agree on a single personality theory?

2 Imagine that Sigmund Freud and B. F. Skinner have just met for a debate. What would Freud criticize about Skinner's behaviorist ideas? How would Skinner, in turn, criticize Freud's psychoanalytic theory?

3 Do Erikson's psychosocial stages of development accurately describe the people you know? How well do you think they are coping with the crises Erikson assigns to each life stage?

4 Define the concept of self-actualization as used by Maslow. What do you think keeps people from achieving this level of development as often as the humanist psychologists think they should?

5 Would you like living in a society where everyone is self-actualizing? Why or why not?

6 Discuss how behaviorist theories could be applied to training a chimpanzee to eat with a fork instead of its fingers.

7 Imagine that everyone could be hooked up to a computer-controlled mind probe at birth. Socially desirable behaviors could be rewarded with a jolt of pure pleasure, while harmful behaviors could be punished by unendurable pain. Would you be for or against such a plan? Why?

Activities

1 After reading about the various personality theories in the last two chapters, you may have found one that appealed most strongly to you. Others in your class may have picked a different theory. This difference of opinion could be the basis for an interesting round-table discussion

with your class as the audience. Select the panel members and allow them time to prepare statements telling why they think the theory they have chosen is the most successful in explaining human behavior. On the day of the round table, allow each speaker five minutes for a formal presentation. Then allow time for other class members to question the panel on the theories and goals of the schools they represent.

2 How well do you know your own personality? You can gain some useful insights by making a "self-box" to represent your values, goals, and past experiences. Begin by finding an empty box. Decorate it with pictures from magazines or with your own photographs. Now, rummage through your past—baby book, closets, junk drawers, everywhere you keep mementos. Place in the box only those items that have meaning to you. Your future can be represented by symbols—a college catalog, a doll dressed for a wedding or hoped-for job, a map of Europe. Some people organize their boxes quite carefully; others drop things in helter-skelter. However you organize it, your self-box will end up being important to you—because in a way, it will *be* you.

3 Ask a group of friends to join you in this experiment in shaping behavior. Choose a subject. Send the subject out of hearing while the rest of your group selects a specific action to which you will shape your subject's behavior. For example, you may choose to have your subject sit backward on a certain chair or open and close a window. Don't make the behavior too complicated. Select one person to be the controller. When the subject returns, no one is permitted to speak. The subject is told only that some form of behavior is expected and that when the subject performs any movement that is part of the desired activity or moves to the proper location, the controller will "reward" the action by clapping three times. The controller ignores actions that are not part of the desired behavior. Because most human subjects are smarter than laboratory rats, they usually can be shaped to the desired behavior in ten minutes or less.

4 Do you know someone who you think is self-actualizing? Write a short paper about that person in which you identify those specific personality traits that make him or her a self-actualizing person. Later, tell that person how important he or she is to you. That may be hard to do, but the results will probably be quite rewarding.

5 One of the symbols that Jung identified as growing out of the collective unconscious is the *mandala*—a circular symbol of wholeness, completion, and renewal. Examples of mandalas can be seen in the Oriental yin-yang symbol, the sun-disk symbol, the ruins of ancient Stone Age forts, etc. Make up a collection of mandalas to display on a poster along with an explanation of the significance of this eternal symbol. See Jung's *Man and His Symbols* for background reading on the mandala and other archetypes.

6 As a class project, assign a different culture to each group of three students. Ask them to research the myths, legends, and folk tales of the culture to find archetypal figures (wise old man, hero or heroine, earth mother, trickster, witch, and the like). Then compare the archetypes and the plots to see if Jung's prediction of similarities is true or not. One group might examine modern movies and television programs to see if the archetypes still appear today.

For further reading

Burgess, Anthony. *A Clockwork Orange.* London: Heinemann, 1962. Burgess looks into the future and finds it filled with teenage violence. Desperate to end the senseless bloodshed, behavioral scientists decide to use behavior-modification techniques to end the protagonist's violent tendencies. Horrifying, and yet thought-provoking, the novel vividly examines both sides of the issue regarding behaviorist theories of social control.

Huxley, Aldous. *Brave New World* and *Brave New World Revisited.* New York: Harper & Row, 1932/1958. *Brave New World* is a classic anti-utopian novel that has gained in stature over the years. Modern science now seems capable of fulfilling Huxley's vision of a totally drug-controlled future society in which individuality has disappeared along with freedom of choice.

Jung, Carl G. *Man and His Symbols.* Garden City, N.Y.: Doubleday, 1964. In this book, completed just before his death, Jung tried to convey his ideas to the general public. The book offers a fascinating exploration of symbols, the unconscious, and Jungian dream interpretation.

Nordby, Vernon J. and Calvin S. Hall. *A Guide to Psychologists and Their Concepts.* New York: Scribner's, 1974. This guide contains biographical sketches and a rather technical summary of the important contributions of forty-two leading psychologists.

Rogers, Carl R. *On Becoming a Person.* Boston: Houghton Mifflin, 1961. This comprehensive description of humanist psychology was written by one of the movement's founders.

Skinner, B. F. *Walden Two.* New York: Macmillan, 1948. Behaviorism takes on a more human dimension in Skinner's novel about a commune where behavior is scientifically "engineered."

UNIT IV

WHEN PERSONALITY IS DISTURBED

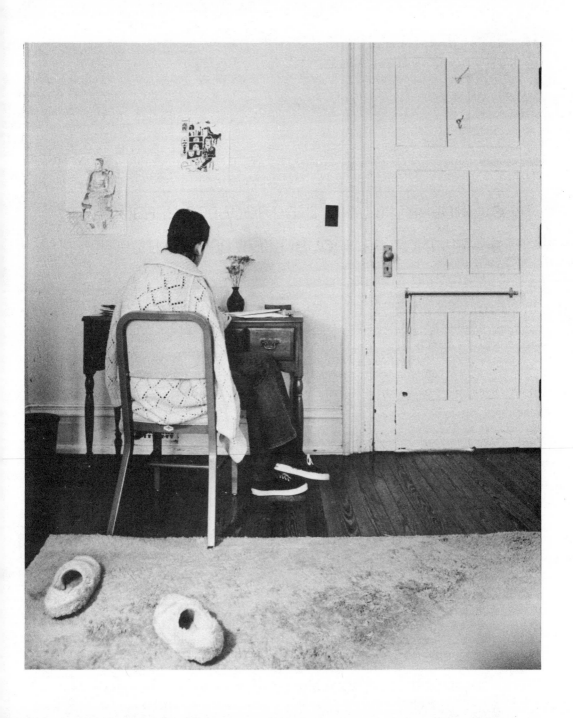

8 UNDERSTANDING THE TROUBLED PERSONALITY

9 HELPING THE TROUBLED PERSONALITY

8

UNDERSTANDING THE TROUBLED PERSONALITY

You're not the only one whose life doesn't always go smoothly. History tells you that. The newspaper tells you that. And life itself tells you that.

What happens to people when they can't cope with the pressure in their lives any longer? Psychologists say that they adopt confused, irrational behavior because the more usual behaviors don't seem to work any more. Troubled personalities take up new defenses when the old ones stop working.

The problem is that the new defenses are almost always worse than the old ones. That's how the American poet Sylvia Plath describes it in her autobiographical novel *The Bell Jar:*

I was still wearing Betsy's white blouse and dirndl skirt. They drooped a bit now, as I hadn't washed them in my three weeks at home. The sweaty cotton gave off a sour but friendly smell.

I hadn't washed my hair for three weeks, either.

I hadn't slept for seven nights.

My mother told me I must have slept, it was impossible not to sleep in all that time, but if I slept, it was with my eyes wide open, for I had followed the green, luminous course of the second hand and the minute hand and the hour hand of the bedside clock through their circles and semi-circles, every night for seven nights, without missing a second, or a minute or an hour.

The reason I hadn't washed my clothes or my hair was because it seemed so silly.

I saw the days of the year stretching ahead like a series of bright, white boxes, and separating one box from another was sleep, like a black shade. Only for me, the long perspective of shades that set off one box from the next had suddenly snapped up, and I could see day after day after day glaring ahead of me like a white, broad, infinitely desolate avenue.

It seemed silly to wash one day when I would only have to wash again the next.

It made me tired just to think of it.

I wanted to do everything once and for all and be through with it.

As you can see, Esther, the narrator of *The Bell Jar*, retains some insight into her problems. But the troubled teenagers in Theodore Isaac Rubin's *Jordi, Lisa and David* have crossed over the boundary. In the following excerpt, Rubin, a well-known psychologist, introduces Lisa. She's in the dayroom of a private hospital, talking to John, one of her therapists.

"John, John, begone begone—enough, enough of this stuffy stuff."

219

Figure 8.1

When people feel overwhelmed by the problems in their lives, they may adopt behavior that itself becomes a problem. How well do these inmates of a mental institution appear to be dealing with the pressures in their lives?

"Are you angry with me, Lisa?"

"Angry, angry—bangry, wangry,—be gone, John; John, be gone."

"I guess you are angry. What is it that makes you so angry?"

"You foo, you foo—it's you, it's you—it's you, you foo; foo you, foo you.". . .

She looked up at the big man and grinned—an inane, foolish kind of grin. Her mood changed suddenly. . . . She faced the wall and talked to herself in a barely audible whisper.

"He won't give me anything. He's big and fat and mean and why won't he give Lisa the crayons? He would give them to Muriel [Lisa's other personality] . He likes the Muriel me—but today I'm Lisa me, Lisa me."

In his coldly superior way, Lisa's friend David, who is also a patient, diagnoses Lisa's behavior. He explains that her "rhyming serves as a decoy or camouflage for what she actually feels." John reaches out and pats David on the shoulder as he leaves the room. But that innocent touch causes a violent break in David's rigid control.

The boy lurched away and screamed, "You touched me, you boor, you unmitigated fool—you touched me! Do you want to kill me? A touch can kill. . . ." His face was contorted with rage. He turned and left them, muttering to himself, "The touch that kills, the touch that kills."

The power of the mind to alter the logic that most people live under can also be seen in *Mania*, L. M. Jayson's account of his own troubles with a voice that started talking to him from nowhere.

The sounds were so clear and so loud, I knew that pretty soon the people next to me would hear them. So I got up, and started walking slowly away, down the stairs of the boardwalk to the stretch of sand below. . . . I waited until the voice came back, the words pounding in this time, not the way you hear any words, but deeper, as though all parts of me had become ears, with my fingers hearing the words, and my legs, and my head, too.

"You're no good," the voice said slowly, in the same deep tones. "You've never been any good or use on earth. There is the ocean. You might just as well drown yourself. Just walk in, and keep walking." As soon as the voice was through, I knew, by its cold command, I had to obey it.

Jayson listened so well to his "voice" that it took the combined efforts of lifeguards and police officers to keep him from committing suicide that day.

Esther, Lisa, David, L. M. Jayson—all are troubled, unhappy people, whose lives have slipped out of control. What causes mental illness and other disturbances that change behavior? Psychology and medical science have come a long way since the days when people blamed devils and demons for all emotional distress. In this chapter, the problems of troubled personalities will be explored in response to the following questions:

8.1 WHAT IS A TROUBLED PERSONALITY?

Look carefully at the next ten people you pass on the street. Mental health experts estimate that three of them at some time in their lives will need help for an emotional disturbance.

Does having a troubled personality mean that these people are "crazy"? Should they be locked up, drugged with tranquilizers, given shock treatments, or undergo psychotherapy?

The answer isn't either "yes" or "no." Most troubled people manage to cope with their lives. They hold down jobs, raise families, go to church, attend school, jog, garden, and do just about everything that other people do. But somewhere along the way, something interferes with their ability to manage their lives fully.

Sometimes a troubled personality results from emotional stress. Mrs. S., for example, can't handle the day-to-day demands of raising three active children. She screams at them more than she wants to, and she cries a lot. Carey A., another example, has spells of depression brought on by a biochemical imbalance in his body. It's not unusual, moreover, for the two factors—stress and physical disorders—to occur together, one triggering the other.

Defining normal behavior

Where would you draw the line between normal and abnormal behavior? Most cultures have different definitions. Arabs compliment their hosts by belching loudly after a good meal. But just try belching loudly at your own dinner table. Your family and friends will think you've taken leave of your senses. Some things that are normal in an Arab country are definitely abnormal in this country.

Psychologists, therefore, define *normal behavior* as the range of actions that are socially acceptable in a given culture. People who usually exhibit normal behavior are considered *well adjusted*. Those who consistently act in a socially unacceptable way are labeled *maladjusted* or *troubled personalities*. Psychologists assume that well-

Figure 8.2

Mental-health experts estimate that three out of every ten Americans will need help in dealing with emotional problems at some time during their lives. Unfortunately, many of them will never visit a psychologist or a mental-health clinic. Why do you think so many people hesitate to ask for help?

Figure 8.3

THE CONTRAST BETWEEN WELL-ADJUSTED AND TROUBLED PERSONALITIES

Well-adjusted people:

- Can see others as they really are.
- Accept others as they are and do not try to change them.
- Can express warm, intense feelings.
- Have the ability to respond to life's pleasures and challenges.
- Maintain a serenity and calmness in most situations.
- Treat other people fairly and show good impulse control.

Troubled people:

- See others as they wish them to be.
- Demand that others meet their standards, no matter how unrealistic.
- Have difficulty coping with feelings and emotions.
- Are defeated by the realities of life.
- Exhibit inappropriate extremes of emotion.
- Adopt a self-centered and demanding life position.

adjusted people will enjoy stable, productive, and relatively happy lives. Troubled people, however, often suffer feelings of depression, guilt, rage, and general unhappiness. The contrast between the two can be seen in Figure 8.3.

Degrees of abnormal behavior

In Figure 8.4a, the black circle A represents society's definition of normal behavior. The white circle B represents behaviors judged to be abnormal; that is, they lie outside the range of normal behavior. Spanking a child for painting the cat would fall into A. But breaking the child's arm for the same prank would fall into B. In theory, a normal person remains safely within the boundaries of A, never straying into B. In reality, however, most people cross that boundary at times, as shown in the second figure, 8.4b. Here the individual stays mostly inside the center area A but occasionally moves out into B. By definition, *abnormal behavior* (the time

spent in B) is a psychologically unhealthy choice of responses to life situations.

Most people who show some abnormal behavior can still function at an acceptable

Figure 8.4a

Figure 8.4b

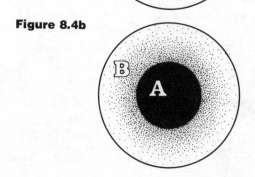

BioBox

KARL A. MENNINGER:
EVERYONE IS SUBJECT
TO THE PRESSURES
THAT LEAD TO
MENTAL ILLNESS

The name of Menninger has been linked with mental-health care in the United States ever since 1919. In that year, Karl Menninger (1893–) and his father, Charles Menninger, opened the Menninger Clinic in Topeka, Kansas. The Menningers used their clinic to help the public accept the need for humane treatment of mental illness.

Educated at Harvard University, Karl Menninger has spent a lifetime in the mental-health field. He views mental health and disease as opposite ends of a continuous line. At one end lie health and happiness; at the other wait depression, anxiety, and delusion. Menninger believes that mental health varies according to people's stage of life and the stresses they encounter. When individuals cannot obtain satisfaction with a simple defense technique, they resort to more extreme measures. They may burst into tears or take a few drinks. But if the problem continues, they may move on to more desperate behaviors—fainting, use of drugs, or violence against others.

Dr. Menninger's deep concern for his patients and his understanding of their needs comes through in these words:

> We have even begun to speak earnestly of prevention—not only to speak of it, which has often been done before, but to relate it to sociological and educational and recreational programs. . . .

What we cannot prevent we must deal with, especially the extreme and disabling attacks of mental illness which are so costly to the individual and those around him. For these we should provide first of all accurate diagnosis . . . of the factors which have combined to produce it, the internal factors and the external factors. . . .

Being realistic, we know that in spite of the best diagnosis and the best treatment some patients will not recover. This is a minority, but of all people we psychiatrists should be the last to ignore a minority. And there are some who in spite of everything will continue to need our sympathy, our patience, and our help in the hope that some vestige of inner strength will sustain them. . . .

Dr. Menninger doesn't promise any miracles. But the helping hand he and other therapists hold out to troubled people can be the difference between emotional health and mental illness.

level of efficiency. But as more and more behaviors fall into B, these people find that the everyday problems of living become increasingly harder to handle. The resulting behaviors are often called neurotic or psychotic, depending on their seriousness.

Mental-health problems in American society

In an old story, one farmer says to another, "Everyone's crazy but you and me—and sometimes I worry about you."

The farmer's estimate that 99.9 percent of the population has emotional problems turns out to be somewhat high. But a 1978 study by the President's Commission on Mental Health estimates that 25 percent of all Americans—some 55 million people—suffer from depression, anxiety, psychosomatic disorders, insomnia, loneliness, and other emotional troubles. This commission broadened the definition of mental health problems to include emotional distress and neurotic behavior; problems caused by physical handicaps; alcohol and drug abuse; social isolation of the chronically disabled and the elderly; and the anxiety, depression, and anger caused by poverty and discrimination.

This broad-scale definition of mental health problems has angered some psychologists. They fear that the public will begin to reject everyone who has a mental health problem, no matter what the cause. Fears are created when a few seriously disturbed people commit terrible crimes. But to see all troubled people as potential murderers or sex offenders is both unfair and inaccurate.

Perhaps the best approach would be to apply the same judgments to emotional problems as you do to medical problems. If you break your leg or catch pneumonia, you go to a doctor. Why shouldn't emotional problems receive the same immediate, unquestioning treatment? One useful step would be to educate the public to the causes, symptoms, and treatment of troubled personalities. After all, most mental problems are short-lived. Almost everyone returns to everyday, productive activities after an episode of emotional disturbance. Another step forward would be to make treatment available to all without regard to how much money they have.

You can also help at a more personal level. Hold out a supporting hand to anyone you know who suffers from an emotional problem. In many cases, the knowledge that you care may help that person take a major step back toward mental health.

SECTION CHECKUP

1 How would you distinguish between normal and abnormal behavior? Why is it unfair to label people's behavior abnormal just because you disagree with it?

2 Contrast the behavior of well-adjusted and troubled people.

3 What percentage of the population has a mental-health problem? Why do these people often fail to seek the help they need?

8.2 WHAT ARE THE CAUSES OF MENTAL ILLNESS?

When does abnormal behavior slip across into the area where the medical term *illness* should be used? No hard lines can be drawn to divide a "life scale" that ranges from self-actualization to Menninger's fifth level of mental illness. But a graphic indication of that scale would look like Figure 8.5, with each level of adjustment, from self-actualization to total mental breakdown, fading gradually into the next.

Why do people move from one area to another on the scale? If you pressed mental health experts for an answer, they would say that no single factor can be blamed. In-

MENTAL HEALTH-ILLNESS SCALE: FROM SELF-ACTUALIZATION TO TOTAL MENTAL BREAKDOWN

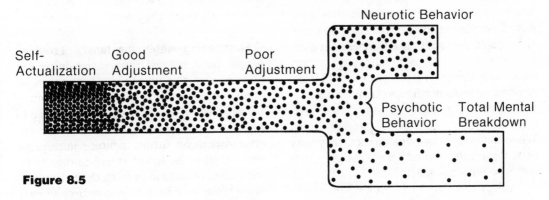

Figure 8.5

stead, they believe that a combination of environmental and physical conditions usually causes mental illness.

Environmental causes of mental illness

Everyone experiences difficulty in adjusting to the demands of the outside world. You've probably felt some of that difficulty when your needs run headlong into the reality of parental rules, limited spending money, or the desires of your friends. Well-adjusted people learn to cope with such problems. They argue, compromise, or give in. By contrast, the poorly adjusted person often can't find a way to handle everyday problems.

Research and common sense have combined to point out the specific forces in the environment that cause the greatest problems. These areas include (1) dealing with stress, (2) handling frustrations, (3) coping with anxieties, (4) functioning within the family, (5) functioning on the job, and (6) functioning in society.

Dealing with stress. In a psychological sense, *stress* results when pressures upset the body's emotional balance. Stress may grow out of unmet personal needs, work pressures, poor personal relationships, or inner drives that push people past their

capabilities. When stress becomes unbearable, the poorly adjusted person unconsciously chooses a behavior that seems to promise an escape from tension. For example, Mary feels greatly pressured by her guardian's demands that she excel in school. Faced with that kind of stress, Mary often "forgets" test dates and "misplaces" her notes and essays.

Handling frustration. *Frustration* results when people cannot satisfy a personal need or desire. Everyone suffers frustrations, such as the traffic signals that slow your ride home or the summer job that doesn't come through. A common symptom of the mentally ill, however, is their inability to put off gratification of their needs. When frustrated, they often behave in illogical or bizarre ways. Some become excessively angry, while others withdraw from contact with the frustrating situation. Pete, for example, was under stress trying to keep up the payments on his new van. When an older man accidentally scraped the van's fender, Pete blew up and punched him. Fortunately, the judge who heard the case recognized Pete's problem and saw to it that he received psychotherapy. Otherwise he could have ended up in jail.

Coping with anxieties. Psychologists define *anxiety* as vague worries about something that might happen in the future. Some people worry more than others and experience greater anxiety. Mentally healthy people know how to put such anxiety in proper perspective. By contrast, poorly adjusted people cannot control their anxiety. If the radio reports that a hurricane is coming, everyone in its path will rightly worry about the danger. Most people will take reasonable precautions and then wait it out. But others will continue to worry, their anxiety mounting with each passing hour. When the real danger does strike, they may be so depressed and fatigued that they cannot cope with the storm.

Anxiety can also lead troubled people to fasten onto a single thought pattern or be-

havior. This may be a nonsense rhyme or an overwhelming urge to step on all the cracks in the sidewalk. When their heads are filled with such trivial concerns, they don't have to face the thing they fear.

Functioning within the family. Troubled people have a hard time maintaining the close relationships demanded by family life. Some have grown up in families where emotional stress is a daily fact of life. Trying to cope with a chaotic home life can lay the groundwork for future mental health problems. Under the stress of day-to-day living with another person or with their own children, troubled adults may have breakdowns in mental health.

Figure 8.6

When asked to draw his family, seventeen-year-old Mike, an underachiever at school and socially withdrawn, produced these pictures. Does Mike feel close to his parents? Why does he show himself opening the refrigerator?

When Don and Joy were married, for example, everything seemed perfect. They loved each other and their families encouraged them. But Don soon developed a taste for going out "with the guys." Left alone too often with no close friends nearby, Joy began behaving strangely. Sometimes she felt on top of the world with energy to spare. But more often she sank into periods of depression. Her moods upset Don, who reacted by staying out more often.

The day Joy discovered that she was pregnant was not a happy one. She couldn't handle the thought of taking care of a child. That night Don came home to find Joy had locked herself in the bathroom. She screamed that she wanted to die. It took the paramedics and several months of therapy before Joy could again cope with her life.

What could Don have done? First, marriage requires a mutual sharing of experiences. It's OK for him to see his friends, but not to the exclusion of his wife. Second, when he saw her wild mood swings, he should have gone with her to a counselor. Even if they didn't know how to find a psychologist, they could have talked to their family doctor, a counselor at a free clinic, or their clergyman. Finally, he should have been aware of his own withdrawal from Joy at a time when she needed him most. A liberal dose of TLC (tender, loving care) might have prevented Joy's later explosion.

In fairness, Joy also shares the responsibility. Instead of tackling the issue of Don's nights out, she remained quiet. She could have also made an effort to make friends on her own or to get involved in school or charity work. Unfortunately, Joy waited for Don to take care of her, and he wasn't mature enough to do so.

Functioning on the job. American society looks on success at work as a sign of personal achievement. Many people, therefore, see their jobs as more than a way of making a living. Their salaries, promotions, titles, and other measures of progress up the ladder give these men and women their basic identity. But even though work can provide personal satisfaction, it also puts people in competition with each other. Many poorly adjusted people already feel insecure and unworthy. When their jobs force them into stress-causing situations, their anxieties and fears increase greatly.

The complicated nature of individual reactions to job stress can be seen in the cases of Jill and Andrew. Jill drifts from job to job. She can't seem to hold down a position for very long, even though she has excellent clerical skills. Responsibility makes her feel anxious, and as soon as the boss begins to depend on her she starts calling in sick. Before long, she resigns or gets fired. Andrew, meanwhile, *wants* to work. But every time he takes a job he breaks out in a rash. Even though he knows the rash is probably psychosomatic, he can't work when his body is covered by red, itchy welts.

You might guess that Jill and Andrew are "allergic" to work. A psychologist, however, would first have them checked to make sure no medical condition lies at the root of their problems. If the tests turn out negative, the psychologist would then conclude that their problems relate to basic personality troubles. Work simply triggers the mechanism that protects them. Both would profit from counseling. If they don't receive help, the odds are good that their poor adjustment may become even more serious.

Functioning in society. In any society, freedom of action is always limited by the rights of others. Perhaps you'd dearly love to race the family car on the nearby highway. You know, however, that, if you drive too fast, you would endanger other drivers and risk getting a speeding ticket; so you stick to the 55-mph limit. Emotionally disturbed people, however, find it hard to accept limits when their own desires and needs seem to be so overwhelming. Society's pressures to conform often cause them to behave in ever more abnormal ways (see Figure 8.7).

Society seems to tell young men, for example, that their masculinity is measured by their success with girls. At seventeen, Ray's shyness made it difficult for him to talk to girls, much less to ask them for dates. To make it worse, his friends teased him about his problem. His insecurity increased, and he withdrew even further into himself. Almost without realizing what was happening, Ray started prowling the neighborhood at night, peeking into bedroom windows. Fortunately, he was caught by a neighbor and his parents were alerted. With the help of a counselor, Ray will probably be able to overcome his poor adjustment. Otherwise, his inner drives will continue to create even greater anxieties.

Physical factors that cause mental illness

If you've ever had a high fever, you know that changes in your body's internal chemistry can affect your mental state. A rise in body temperature of only a few degrees can cause you to sink into a depression, lose concentration, and even see and hear things that aren't there. Psychologists have identified four physical factors that can cause

Figure 8.7

The social pressures to conform to peer-group standards of behavior can be particularly high during adolescence. Why would such pressures sometimes lead an individual into abnormal behavior?

abnormal behavior: (1) accidents of heredity, (2) biochemical imbalances, (3) disease, and (4) accident trauma.

Accidents of heredity. Evidence seems to indicate that a tendency toward some forms of mental illness can be inherited. A severe mental illness, schizophrenia, affects about 1 percent of the population. But anyone who has a schizophrenic grandparent has a 4 percent risk factor, and someone who has a schizophrenic parent carries a 16 percent chance of also becoming schizophrenic. On the other hand, it has been argued that environment rather than heredity is the crucial factor in schizophrenic families. Children who grow up in a household torn by the emotional chaos of schizophrenia tend to learn faulty ways of coping with the world. Given this environmental handicap, perhaps it's no wonder that schizophrenic parents often produce schizophrenic children.

Biochemical imbalances. Scientists have long known that an excess or deficiency of many otherwise useful chemicals can upset the nervous system. Some people create this *biochemical imbalance* on their own. Percy O., an alcoholic, has built up enough toxic substances in his body to cause memory loss, feelings of persecution, and visions of nonexistent snakes. Some schizophrenics show excessive blood levels of a protein called leu-endorphin. Scientists who are researching this recent discovery suggest that the protein excites the brain into behaving erratically. Long-term depression has also been treated with a trace element called lithium. In some cases, when the lithium brings the body's sodium level into balance, depression disappears.

Researchers caution, however, that correcting biochemical imbalances may not provide the simple solution to mental illness that some people hope for. Schizophrenics have been helped by blood dialysis, which "strains" the leu-endorphin from their systems. But a critical question remains. Does the chemical imbalance cause the schizophrenia? Or does the schizophrenia cause the imbalance? Perhaps the best that can be said is that a hopeful avenue of research has been opened up.

Disease. Physical diseases, particularly those that affect the nervous system, can lead to abnormal behaviors characteristic of some forms of mental illness. Memory loss, loss of speech, hearing "voices," and outbursts of violent behavior may result from a purely physical cause. Inflammation of the brain and tumors that put pressure on certain parts of the brain can cause these symptoms. Strokes that interrupt blood flow to the brain may also result in loss of memory and speech. Venereal diseases and other infections may cause the breakdown of brain tissue.

Accident trauma. In medical terms, a trauma is an injury or shock to the body. Any blow to the head that causes damage to the brain can also lead to personality changes. Trauma can also occur during birth, when brain tissues may be destroyed by lack of oxygen or by severe pressure on the skull. Symptoms resulting from such accidents include memory loss, speech impairment, inappropriate emotional responses, and partial paralysis. When damage occurs in only a small area, proper therapy can often restore all or partial function to mental and physical processes. Severe brain damage cannot be reversed, however, because brain tissue cannot grow back once it has been destroyed.

Depression—a cause and a symptom

You probably recognize the symptoms. Something unpleasant has happened and you feel "down." You don't have much energy, food tastes like straw, and no idea sounds worth pursuing. People try to cheer you up, but you push them away. You'd rather be left alone to brood and feel miserable. Those feelings of sadness and hopelessness are part of what psychologists call *depression.* Everyone has depressions, but a good night's sleep or a heart-to-heart talk with a friend is usually enough to snap most people out of them.

Psychologists do worry, however, when otherwise healthy people remain depressed for weeks or months. This type of depression often begins when people feel they cannot control their own lives. Personal problems, such as divorce, a death in the family, or loneliness can bring on depression. Social ills such as poverty, discrimination, and unemployment also can trigger a depressed state. Whatever the cause, if depression is left untreated, it can lead to suicide. About 7 percent of the population will require medical treatment for severe depression sometime during their lifetimes.

As one woman said, "I felt desolate and abandoned. My brain was telling me that I was not abandoned, but the feeling was that I was bereft even by God. It was as if the earth had opened at my feet, and I was standing at the edge." In these severe cases, doctors sometimes recommend antidepressant drugs or electroconvulsive therapy (ECT) as well as talk therapy. ECT has many critics (see Pro & Con, page 242), for it works by using an electric current to produce a convulsion in the patient. But depressed patients agree that something must be done.

SECTION CHECKUP

1 List some of the environmental forces that can cause abnormal behavior or mental illness. Why are stress, frustration, and anxiety considered so important in evaluating the causes of poor adjustment?

2 Describe some of the physical factors that can cause abnormal behavior or mental illness.

3 Why are psychologists reluctant to point to any single factor as a cause of mental illness?

8.3 WHAT SPECIFIC ABNORMAL BEHAVIORS DOES THE PSYCHOLOGIST LABEL AS NEUROTIC?

You'd enjoy meeting Nick S. He's a pleasant, middle-aged man, soft of speech and an expert on trivia questions. Nick is shy, but generous to his friends. He's not a remarkable person but anxious to please. There's just one thing. If you want to meet Nick, you'll have to visit him at his house. You see, Nick lives in a single windowless room, and he almost never leaves it. He'd like to, but he can't. He suffers from agoraphobia, an unreasoning fear of open spaces, crowds, traffic, and the other hallmarks of city life.

In psychological terms, Nick suffers from a *neurosis*—a repeated, inappropriate, and involuntary response to stress or a fear-provoking situation. Like most neurotic behaviors, Nick's fear of going outdoors started with some unpleasant experiences. He was mugged twice within ten days, and soon afterward he got lost in a strange part of town. He began to stay closer to home, and gradually the area he felt safe in became smaller and smaller. His inability to meet his basic needs for personal safety led to full-scale neurotic behavior.

All fears and feelings of nervousness shouldn't be labeled as neuroses, however. A lot of people's worries are based in reality. You can recognize the signs of neurotic behavior. They include (1) excessive tension or nervousness; (2) an inability to work at a level in keeping with one's abilities; (3) an overwhelming need for love and approval; (4) an inability to relate to other people; (5) rigid, repetitive behaviors; (6) overreacting to what others say or do; and (7) an inability to make decisions. The following sections describe five of the most common neuroses.

Obsessions and compulsions

Mrs. G. dresses all in white. She wears spotless linen, and her hands are always super-clean. They're also badly chapped and cracked. That's because Mrs. G. washes them over fifty times a day.

When Mrs. G. washes her hands over and over, she is demonstrating what psychologists call obsessive-compulsive behavior. People with such a neurosis can be recognized by their endless attention to detail and the performance of ritual (repetitive) acts. *Obsessions* are thoughts, impulses, or feelings that are repeated continuously and that the individual cannot control. When the person translates these thoughts or impulses into repeated, involuntary actions, the resulting behavior pattern is called a *compulsion*.

You've probably had a song or a jingle go around and around inside your head. After an hour or a day, it goes away. But troubled people sometimes find that their thoughts or actions threaten to take over their lives. Most psychologists believe that obsessive-compulsive behaviors develop because the individual fears that "unacceptable" impulses originating in the unconscious may "break loose." In order to control these impulses, the neurotic works out a behavior that will suppress the unacceptable thoughts. Mrs. G.'s obsession with cleanliness may be intended to keep her from giving in to an impulse to wallow in mud and filth. Freud, in fact, described obsessive-compulsive behavior as a personal religion that acts to ward off evil.

Phobias

When Carole was four years old, she hid in a closet during a game of hide-and-seek. The door locked behind her, and she couldn't get out. No one heard her cries, and she was trapped in the dark, almost airless closet for several hours. Today, Carole cannot bear to be in any small, enclosed space. Once she had to cancel a cruise to the Bahamas because she discovered that just stepping into the small stateroom made her feel panicky.

When fears become irrational, intense, and uncontrollable, they are called *phobias*.

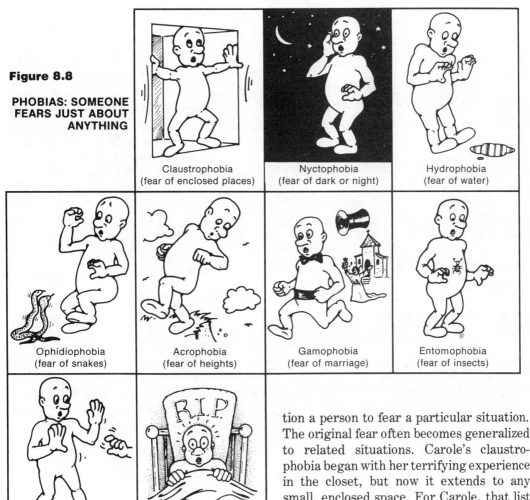

Figure 8.8

PHOBIAS: SOMEONE FEARS JUST ABOUT ANYTHING

Claustrophobia
(fear of enclosed places)

Nyctophobia
(fear of dark or night)

Hydrophobia
(fear of water)

Ophidiophobia
(fear of snakes)

Acrophobia
(fear of heights)

Gamophobia
(fear of marriage)

Entomophobia
(fear of insects)

Haphephobia
(fear of being touched)

Thanatophobia
(fear of death)

Everyone experiences such fears, but most people learn to handle them. You may have a slight fear of heights, for instance, but it doesn't keep you from flying in an airplane or enjoying the view from the top of a building. Occasionally, however, a phobia becomes strong enough to dominate a person's life. These phobic fears (see Figure 8.8) include almost every life situation you can imagine.

Psychologists explain phobias as the result of frightening experiences that condi-tion a person to fear a particular situation. The original fear often becomes generalized to related situations. Carole's claustro-phobia began with her terrifying experience in the closet, but now it extends to any small, enclosed space. For Carole, that list includes elevators, tents, and tunnels, as well as a cruise-ship stateroom.

Conversion hysteria

On the eve of an important concert, guitarist Rudy S. woke up to find that he couldn't move his left hand. He seemed quite calm despite the apparent tragedy. When ques-tioned, he shrugged and said, "Well, I guess the concert will have to be canceled."

If Rudy had been totally honest, he would have admitted to feeling extremely fearful about that concert. His paralysis resulted when those inner fears became so great that he couldn't cope with them any longer. His condition is known as *conversion hysteria*, a neurotic behavior in which repressed emotions appear as physical disabilities. Symptoms vary from patient to patient, but range from paralysis in some part of the body to deafness, blindness, or fainting spells.

In many cases, the physical symptoms relate in some way to the fears that underlie them. A dancer would be more likely to experience paralysis of her legs. One new father, overwhelmed by the sense of responsibility he saw in raising a child, promptly "lost" his eyesight.

Victims of conversion hysteria usually seek medical attention. The condition causes doctors great difficulty, for the paralysis or other physical symptom is all too real. Once physical causes have been eliminated and the proper diagnosis has been made, the patient must be helped to recognize the underlying fear that caused the symptoms. At that point, the paralysis or other problem often disappears like magic (see Figure 8.9). In cases where the hysterical disability has lasted for a long time, prolonged therapy may be necessary.

Dissociative reactions

Most of his neighbors would agree that Jack W. is the gentlest of men. He loves birds, takes good care of his family, and supports every charity that knocks on his door. But several nights a year, Jack slips out of his house and creeps silently through the nearby streets. Along the way, he feeds poisoned meat to the neighborhood cats. When morning comes and the news of the dead animals spreads, Jack is as amazed as anyone else about the crime. If he were to take a lie-detector test, he'd swear to his innocence and pass with flying colors.

Neurotic responses to fear or stress in which parts of the personality or memory dissociate (split off) are known as *dissociative reactions*. Like most people, you probably integrate several different "people" within your personality. You may be a fierce competitor at school or at work, but then you relax into an easygoing way of life at home. Some people, however, reach a point where their conflicting personalities can no longer cope with the stress caused by the different needs of the "people" who live inside them. In Jack W.'s case, he has seen cats hunt and kill his beloved birds. His own personality would never let him harm a cat. But his unconscious desire to gain revenge breaks out in a separate personality, who calls himself Rocky. Rocky can—and does—punish the cats for killing his birds. Under a similar strain, someone else might develop amnesia instead of a multiple personality.

Amnesia. *Amnesia* is a state in which people literally "forget" all or part of their identity and past life. Amnesia may result from a blow on the head or other brain injury. Patients almost always recover from this type of amnesia. Memory loss may also occur when the mind literally "blacks out" a painful life situation. To treat this type of amnesia, therapists try to find the conflict that caused the loss of memory.

Evelyn I., for example, lost her memory when a chain of events put her under unendurable stress. A widow, she had to give up her apartment because of a rent increase. She traveled to California to stay with a friend, only to find that the friend had become ill and had been moved to New York. At that point, Evelyn blanked out, leaving her purse and her identity behind. The police later found her wandering aimlessly around town, unable to identify herself. Rest and therapy eventually ended the amnesia and helped her recover her memory.

Multiple personalities. This most dramatic form of dissociative reaction was made famous by Robert Louis Stevenson's fictional account of *The Strange Case of Dr. Jekyll and Mr. Hyde*. In the story, the kindly and upright Dr. Jekyll swallows a mysterious liquid that changes him into the evil Mr. Hyde. In true-life cases of *multiple per-*

Figure 8.9

SMALL MIRACLE IN THE EMERGENCY ROOM: COPING WITH CONVERSION HYSTERIA

In *The Making of a Psychiatrist,* David Viscott takes us inside the emergency room of a large New York City hospital. There he finds a young woman named Charlotte waiting for him. Charlotte's legs are paralyzed. The man who's with her tells Viscott that they've just come to New York from North Carolina. Charlotte, he says, was fine when she left home. After talking to her mother on the phone, however, she became upset. By the time they reached New York, she couldn't walk.

Viscott knows that another doctor couldn't find any obvious physical cause for Charlotte's paralysis. After mentally diagnosing acute conversion hysteria, Viscott says:

> "Charlotte, what's wrong?"
> "It's my feet, doc. I can't move my feet." Charlotte looked very calm. She stared at the ceiling. "I have to be at work tomorrow. . . ."
> "You don't seem very worried about your feet," I said.
> "Why should I, doc? You're the doctor. It's your problem. I don't know nothing about no feet. You know about feet." This detached attitude of a hysteric toward her symptoms is typical . . .
> "What did your mother have to say about your coming north?"
> "That's my business," said Charlotte, moving one leg.
> "It's important."
> "It may be important, but it ain't none of your business."
> "Mothers sometimes see situations very differently from their daughters." . . .
> "We sure do." Charlotte looked angry. "She thinks just because I'm going north with a man means I'm a tramp. She says I should marry Warren first, but I say I don't have to. I'm gonna live with him . . ."
> "If you could say what you wanted, what would you have said? Go on, pretend I'm your mother. What would you say to me? Go ahead, let me have it, I can take it."
> Charlotte . . . got right into it. "You have no right telling me what to do with my life. I went to high school. I didn't get pregnant like half my girlfriends did. You can't tell me I got to spend my life in this place."
> "But, Charlotte, your father and I have plans for you—"
> "You're always talking about you and your plans," she yelled at me. "You keep telling me I gotta do this and I gotta do that because Jesus is watching me. Well, I'm watching me too and I don't like what I see. I'm sick and tired of North Carolina and I got plans of my own."
> "You're going to stay right here if I have anything to say about it," I said, . . .
> "You shut your big fat . . . mouth," she said, and stood up. "I'm old enough to do what I want and go where I want, and I don't need to ask your permission."
> Charlotte was standing in front of me, glaring and making a fist.
> "You sure sound like you've got a lot of good reasons to be angry," I said.
> "Yes, I do," she snapped.
> "I think maybe you were afraid of getting angry and weren't as sure of yourself as you sounded. Your mother obviously made you angry and you seem to have felt guilty about something."

With that seemingly miraculous cure, Charlotte is ready to leave the hospital and pick up her life again. After making an appointment for a further checkup, she turns to Viscott.

> "Too bad [I won't see you at the clinic] ," she said as she left. "You sure know how to fix a girl's legs."

sonality, the individual develops one or more separate identities in addition to the original personality. These new personalities are usually born out of desperate childhood circumstances.

In Flora Schreiber's case history, *Sybil,* young Sybil's strict religious training required that she love and honor her mother. Sybil's mother, however, was a severely disturbed woman, who alternately loved and tortured her child. In self-defense, Sybil's personality dissociated into sixteen separate personalities. Each personality represented a different aspect of Sybil's character. Vickie, for example, was calm and worldly, dressed well, and liked to speak with a French accent. By contrast, Martha was depressed and suicidal.

Can you imagine the shattering impact of such dissociation on the personality? Imagine waking up and finding your room painted a different color. Or imagine meeting someone who seems to know you quite well—but whom you don't remember at all! Like most multiple personalities, Sybil didn't suspect the existence of her other selves. It took years of therapy and great patience on the part of Sybil's therapist to bring all her personalities together again. Fortunately, such multiple personalities are rare. Psychologists estimate that hysteric conversions and dissociative personalities make up less than 5 percent of all neurotics who seek help from a therapist.

Anxiety reactions

When the alarm goes off, Perry stays in bed for a while, thinking, "I've got to get moving." But as his mind focuses on the day that lies ahead, he feels the first signs of panic. His head hurts, his hands sweat, and his stomach ties up into one big knot. When questioned, Perry admits that school really isn't too bad. His teachers treat him well and none of the other students picks on him. Some days, in fact, he manages to get himself off to school. But on other days he stays

in bed, a victim of his neurotic feelings of anxiety.

Doctors estimate that half of the people in the United States will receive treatment for *anxiety reactions* similar to Perry's at some time in their lives. Abnormal states of anxiety make a person thoroughly miserable. The anxiety often borders on the edge of panic. Physical symptoms can include a general feeling of ill health, stomach disturbances, fatigue, and diarrhea. Certain periods of life (early childhood, adolescence, and the onset of middle age) seem to trigger more anxiety attacks. Most doctors prescribe tranquilizers for anxiety. But if the underlying cause of the anxiety is not dealt with, the anxiety may return later or take another form.

If a patient describes feelings of general nervousness, fatigue, and insomnia, psychologists refer to the condition as *neurasthenia* (literally, "nervous weakness"). Most neurasthenics complain of chronic fatigue, the feeling of being worn out and unable to carry on regular activities. Many of their anxieties are "free floating." That is, the individual has no specific idea as to what is causing the worn-out, nervous condition. Typically, such anxiety reactions grow out of repressed conflicts over the individual's inability to satisfy basic needs: sex, security, achievement, and self-esteem.

SECTION CHECKUP

1 What is the difference between being afraid to pet a tiger and being afraid to pet a house cat? At what point does a behavior stop being normal and become neurotic?

2 Describe the behavior you would expect from someone suffering from each of these neurotic reactions: obsessive-compulsive behavior; a phobic fear; conversion hysteria; a dissociative reaction; an anxiety reaction.

3 Why do many psychologists say that the underlying cause of a neurotic reaction must be uncovered before the condition can be fully overcome?

8.4 HOW DOES THE PSYCHOLOGIST CLASSIFY DIFFERENT TYPES OF PSYCHOTIC BEHAVIOR?

Somewhere in the United States there's probably a man who compulsively buries bones in his backyard. His mild neurosis doesn't harm anyone, and his neighbors probably kid him about his unusual behavior. But what if that same man began kidnapping and burying the neighborhood children "to save them from the devil"? The diagnosis would abruptly shift from neurosis to *psychosis*.

Most neurotics can carry on their lives fairly well, but psychotics are frequently dangerous to themselves or to others. In legal terms, they may be judged insane and committed to a mental hospital. Psychologists generally avoid the use of emotion-laden words such as *insane* (or crazy, mad, daffy, touched, and similar colorful but inaccurate descriptions). Psychoses are not simply more extreme forms of neurotic behaviors, however. The neurotic personality rarely becomes psychotic, even in the face of increased frustration or failure.

Psychoses may be divided into two major types, organic and functional. Organic psychoses begin with disease, accident trauma, a breakdown of nervous tissue, or a biochemical imbalance that affects the mind. Functional psychoses originate primarily in painful emotional experiences.

Major symptoms of psychotic behavior

Psychotic behavior usually develops rather suddenly, even though the underlying causes of the psychosis have existed for a long time. Almost overnight, the psychotic person loses contact with reality, becomes highly defensive and withdrawn, or begins to exhibit bizarre behaviors. In many cases, the speech of psychotics breaks down. Unable to explain their feelings, they may become highly agitated, or they may give up trying to speak. Two other major symptoms of a psychotic condition are hallucinations and delusions.

Hallucinations. The psychotic who sees snakes or angels or long-dead relatives is suffering from a *hallucination*, a false perception not based on reality. Psychotic individuals may see and talk to nonexistent people. Frequently, they claim that these phantom figures are threatening them (see Figure 8.10). Other psychotics assert that they feel weird vibrations, experience atomic radiation, or see the walls closing in on them.

Delusions. A patient who "sees" Tarzan of the Apes is hallucinating. But if he says he *is* Tarzan, he's experiencing a *delusion*, a false belief not based on reality. Delusions often lead psychotics to announce that they are the living Buddha, Mary Queen of Scots, the President, or other powerful authority figures. Other delusions involve persecution, the feeling that outside forces are threatening the individual's safety.

Figure 8.10

The schizophrenic girl who drew this hallucination saw herself "threatened on all sides by hideously grimacing heads of monsters . . . who wanted to tear her to bits." Can you sense some of the terror she must have experienced?

If one of your friends began hallucinating, your natural reaction would be to assure him that there really aren't any spiders on his ceiling. But logic and physical evidence cannot convince psychotics that their hallucinations or delusions are false. To your friend, those spiders do exist. He can see them, feel them, sense them. People who treat psychotics must remember that psychotic behavior grows out of unconscious needs that the patients generally cannot describe or understand. Faced with some overwhelming fear or need, their minds take refuge in the illogic of psychotic thinking and behavior.

Organic psychoses

Any psychosis that can be traced to damage to the central nervous system is known as an *organic psychosis*. The organic psychoses result from disease, accident trauma, damage to the nervous system, or a biochemical imbalance that affects behavior. Symptoms of organic psychoses may include any or all of the typical psychotic behaviors, including bizarre actions, loss of memory, hallucinations, and the like. Three typical organic psychoses are described in this section.

Paresis. If left untreated, syphilis bacteria make their way through the bloodstream and into the brain. This deadly process may take years. Patients suffering from the advanced stages of syphilis show a breakdown of intellectual and behavioral functions known as *paresis*. Symptoms include delusions, episodes of extreme excitement, and deep depression. The combination of modern antibiotics and early diagnosis of venereal diseases have made paresis a relatively rare disorder.

Delirium tremens (D.T.'s). Mental-health authorities consider alcoholism a serious illness. Not only does long-term excessive drinking cause alcoholics and their families emotional and financial harm, but the psychotic reactions that appear after a long period of alcohol abuse are severe and frightening. This reaction, known as *delirium tremens*, or the *D.T.'s*, occurs when the chronic alcoholic's blood-alcohol level drops suddenly. The psychotic reactions include hallucinations, delusions, trembling, sweating, and confusion. The vitamin deficiencies associated with alcoholism may also cause severe loss of memory. The D.T.'s often last for several days, during which alcoholics may think that they are being attacked by rats, snakes, bats, and other terrifying creatures. Therapy for an alcoholic must include treatment of both the physical condition and the emotional problems that led to the alcohol abuse.

Senility. One of life's saddest experiences is to visit a much-loved grandfather, only to discover that *senility* has robbed him of his capacity to relate to you. Senility is the psychosis of old age. Its symptoms include disorientation (inability to recognize time or place), memory lapses, and delusions. With people living longer than ever, senility has become an increasing problem. Studies of senile patients reveal that their brains have deteriorated, a condition often accompanied by a restricted blood flow to the brain.

Far from being an inevitable part of the aging process, however, senility can apparently be avoided or slowed. The best prescription comes from the example set by numerous elderly people: Stay healthy and active, and you'll have a good chance of remaining vigorous and alert right to the end. Your own community probably has numerous men and women in their seventies, eighties, and older, who jog, play golf, do volunteer work, attend adult classes, and take care of their homes and apartments (see Figure 8.11). Even some apparently hopelessly senile patients have recovered at least part of their vitality when therapists put them on good diets and give them the affection and attention so often missing in the lives of America's elderly.

Figure 8.11

Artur Rubinstein was giving marvelous concerts while in his eighties, but many older people end up "warehoused" in rest homes. What can be done to keep the elderly healthy and active?

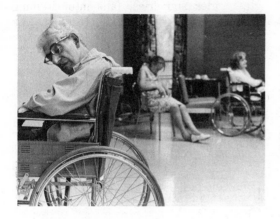

Functional psychoses

Unlike organic psychoses, *functional psychoses* are believed to originate in painful emotional experiences. The influence of heredity and biochemical imbalances cannot be ignored in diagnosing and treating such illnesses, however. So varied are the symptoms of the common functional psychoses that psychologists often disagree on how to categorize them. One relatively simple system uses three main headings: (1) schizophrenia (psychoses marked by thought disorders), (2) affective reactions (psychoses marked by mood disorders), and (3) paranoid reactions (psychoses marked by systematic delusions involving persecution). To make matters more complicated, individual patients may display symptoms from more than one of these categories.

Schizophrenia. About one half of all patients in mental hospitals are diagnosed as schizophrenics. In fact, schizophrenia has become so common that some psychotherapists accuse other therapists of lumping all difficult psychotic cases under this label. Schizophrenics display five general disturbances of their thought processes: bizarre, erratic personal behavior; delusions and/or hallucinations; loss of contact with reality; breakdowns in communication; and the display of inappropriate emotions. If you were to follow a staff member through the wards of any mental hospital, you'd probably see the four most common forms of schizophrenia.

1. *Simple schizophrenia.* That's Barbara, sitting so quietly over there. She's lost interest in the outside world, and she probably won't talk to you. If she does, her speech may break down into a "word salad," with nouns and verbs and adjectives thrown in at random. She looks terrible, since she hasn't combed her hair or cared about her appearance for a long time.

2. *Catatonic schizophrenia.* Peter has been sitting in that contorted position with arms outspread since early this morning. It's as if he's been frozen in place. Occasionally he'll break into wildly aggressive behaviors; that's why he's locked up in his padded room. Doctor Thorn says it's as if Peter withdrew into the deepest reaches of his mind and slammed the door shut. When he does talk to people, he's terribly negative about everything. Last week he said someone was putting poison in his food.

3. *Paranoid schizophrenia.* Watch out, Mrs. L. knows you're new here. She'll want to show you her scars and plead for you to take a message to the bishop. She's certain that she's being held here because of her religious beliefs and that she's being denied sainthood. Some days she changes roles and says that she's God. It's hard to keep up with her shifts in attitude and behavior, but they mostly involve persecution of one type or another.

4. *Hebephrenic schizophrenia.* Every mental hospital has its Napoleons and Florence Nightingales, right? This is Quintin—or, according to him, Julius Caesar. Quintin also regresses to childish behavior at times. He giggles and cries, falls into rhyming speech, and forgets his toilet training. In a way, he combines a lot of the behaviors associated with the other forms of schizophrenia. Listen, he's trying to tell you something.

Figure 8.12

BREAKDOWNS IN COMMUNICATION: WHAT IS THE SCHIZOPHRENIC TRYING TO SAY?

To most of us, the shattered speech of a schizophrenic would be beyond understanding. But careful study of this highly "personal" language reveals an inner logic based on word associations and breakdowns in attention. In the following example, Brendan Maher analyzes a typical schizophrenic sentence:

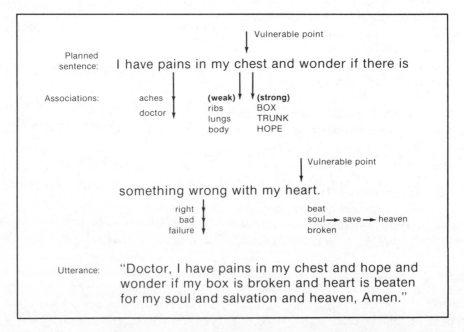

Source: Quoted in *PsychoSources*, Evelyn Shapiro, ed. (CRM, printed by Bantam, New York, 1973), p. 114, *from* Brendan Maher, "The Shattered Language of Schizophrenia," *Readings in Psychology Today* (CRM Books, 1972).

I'm Julius Caesar, old geezer just squeez 'er, why don't you? The noblest Roman of them all, a dandy randy fandy sandy silence on the wing on the sling on the cling. Thank you, fank you, I Caesar rank you.

Schizophrenics tend to stay in the hospital a long time. The severity of their symptoms often defies the best efforts of the hospital therapists to reach them. Traditional talk therapies have had only limited success. Some better results have been achieved with other treatments, including antipsychotic drugs, strict diet, massive doses of vitamins, and blood dialysis. Thus far, however, no certain therapy has been devised, because no one knows exactly what causes schizophrenia.

Affective reactions. Psychoses that cause extreme variations in mood are known as *affective reactions*. A *manic-depressive psychosis*, for example, causes cyclical mood swings that carry the individual from the heights of elation (the manic phase) to the depths of despair (the depressive phase). Patients may also get "stuck" in recurrent cycles of either manic or depressive behavior.

Annette M. flew into a large Midwestern city just after two deaths in her family and the breakup of her marriage. She was taken to a hospital after a series of outbursts that totally disrupted the hotel where she was staying. She broke windows, argued profanely over her bill, flirted with every man she saw, and capped her performance by taking off her clothes in the hotel restaurant. At the hospital, her manic phase continued. She played practical jokes, sang bawdy songs in the hallways, and broke some more windows. Then, without warning, she withdrew into a deep depression. She announced that her soul was damned to hell and that her only solution was suicide. She became totally inactive and refused to eat. Her behavior was described in the hospital records as that of a classic manic-depressive.

Long-term depressive psychosis has become an increasingly common problem. As you can see from the example of Annette's depressive phase, the simple depression most people occasionally experience is as unlike Annette M.'s depressive phase as a cold is to double pneumonia. Therapists have begun to zero in on the biochemical causes for some long-term depression. Carefully controlled dosages of lithium and norepinephrine have worked well with some patients, while others respond well to electroconvulsive therapy (ECT). With treatment that combined talk therapy, an antipsychotic drug, and proper diet, Annette was able to leave the hospital after four months. Her life is now under control, and she doesn't expect to return.

Paranoid reactions. People who suffer from *paranoid reactions* have delusions that center on feelings of persecution and overblown feelings of self-importance. For many paranoids, the delusions take the form of imaginary plots directed against them by powerful groups such as the FBI, the Mafia, or the Soviet Secret Service. Unlike the confused and contradictory delusions reported by paranoid schizophrenics, true paranoids often have good contact with reality except for their highly convincing tales of persecution.

Just listen to Roland N.'s story of his persecution by the big oil companies, for example. Roland's speech is quick and precise. He looks people in the eye when he tells them about the tap on his phone, the interception of his mail, and the mysterious agents who follow him everywhere. When asked why the oil companies are after him, Roland talks vaguely about having perfected a secret, cheaply made fuel. But if you ask too many questions, he'll begin to get suspicious of *your* motives. When you leave him, you won't be positive that he *doesn't* have an invention. Roland can be quite convincing.

Like Roland, paranoids often believe themselves gifted with superpowers. They

Figure 8.13

THE PSYCHOTIC EXPERIENCE: FIRST-HAND ACCOUNTS

Many former mental patients have described their experiences while locked in the grip of their psychosis. These short excerpts express the painful reality of mental illness from a very personal point of view.

Delirium tremens

I . . . sprang in among the hissing serpents. They leaped at me and entwined themselves around my legs and arms. They . . . tore and lacerated my flesh. . . . Seizing a large heavy one, I pulled off its head and used its body for a weapon. . . . I had only one more monster between me and safety. . . . "Too late! Too late!" said the boatman, and as I flung the serpent behind me the boat moved off [to safety].

Delusion of personal power

My radar beam was a source of delight to me. . . . I could repel attendants or patients at will. All that was necessary was to recognize the central source of heat in my solar plexus and move it into my eyes, stare angrily at my enemy and he would become pale, frightened and usually leave. Since the source of the power was definitely located inside me, in my chest, it must obviously come from the sun. Solar power, solar plexus. For this reason . . . I gazed at the sun, absorbing its light and warmth.

Paranoid schizophrenia

During the paranoid period I thought I was being persecuted for my beliefs, that my enemies were actively trying to interfere with my activities, were trying to harm me, and at times even to kill me. . . . In order to carry through the task which had been imposed upon me, and to defend myself . . . I was endowed in my imagination with truly cosmic powers. . . . I felt that I had power to determine the weather which responded to my inner moods, and even to control the movement of the sun in relation to other astronomical bodies.

may take the identity of a famous person, complete with elaborate details to confirm their delusion. These delusions often center on religious figures, such as the Virgin Mary, or political leaders, such as the President. Paranoid patients show up more often in fiction than in fact, however. Only one percent of the patients who enter therapy are diagnosed as having a true paranoid reaction.

SECTION CHECKUP

1 How would you define the difference between a neurosis and a psychosis?

2 Contrast the specific symptoms commonly found in schizophrenia, affective reactions, and paranoia.

3 Distinguish between an organic psychosis and a functional psychosis. Why is it difficult to place schizophrenia, for example, strictly in the category of functional psychoses?

Obsessions and compulsions

I am forced to remember everything; I hear something on the radio and then I have to know all about the words of that song; when I look at the window I have to keep counting all the windows and try to remember them; when I go to bed at night I have to keep repeating the names of the patient on my left and the one on my right for fear I won't remember them in the morning and this keeps me from sleeping; I know I am incurable; this drives me mad.

Depression

That night, the creeping tide of depression washed away the sand of self-esteem. I was a fool to think I could win. There was no victory for such as me. I was a crippled puppy running by the road, dust on a cathedral floor, a blind lion, for me there was no hope. Was there anyone at all? There was no one at all. My wife had betrayed me to my enemies. I was separated from my family, afraid for my children. . . . All was depression.

Schizophrenia

I felt so light that I was certain I should have risen off the ground if I had not had hold of his [the attendant's] arm. . . . and as I got lighter and lighter, I got quite frightened, and clutched hold of him, saying I had not the slightest idea where I was going to if I "went up." Instantly I felt as heavy as lead, and could hardly lift my feet off the ground. . . . I had a strong suspicion that he was "willing" me to feel these sensations; indeed, I felt somewhat afraid, and went off by myself . . .

Pleas for help

Being crazy is like one of those nightmares where you try to call for help and no sound comes out. Or if you can call, no one hears or understands. You can't wake up from the nightmare unless someone does hear you and helps you to wake up.

All this other raving and howling going on around me—will not someone come and awaken me—so that I may go free?

From Carney Landis, *Varieties of Psychopathological Experience* (New York: Holt, Rinehart and Winston, Inc., 1964). By permission.

8.5 WHAT ABNORMAL BEHAVIORS HAVE BEEN IDENTIFIED AS PERSONALITY DISORDERS?

What can you do about people who show none of the common symptoms of neurotic or psychotic behavior but who consistently violate society's standards of normal behavior? Psychologists find it difficult to help such people because they seldom recognize their need for therapy. They rarely lose contact with reality, and they often appear to be charming and intelligent. But people with personality disorders exploit those around them. Three major categories of personality disorders include the psychopathic personality, the hysterical personality, and the passive-aggressive personality.

Pro & Con: SHOULD DEPRESSED PATIENTS BE GIVEN ELECTROCONVULSIVE THERAPY?

Electroconvulsive therapy (ECT) was first introduced for the treatment of mental illness in 1938. The therapist attaches electrodes to the patient's skull and administers an electric shock of 70 to 150 volts. The patient then experiences a severe convulsion. In order to prevent pain or injury during the convulsion, therapists give muscle relaxants and sleep drugs before the ECT. Most patients receive a series of ECT's at a rate of three a week. Costs average $150 a treatment.

Despite its widespread use, ECT remains something of a mystery. No one knows exactly why it helps some severely depressed patients who have not responded to other forms of therapy. A heated debate has arisen over the use of ECT, as the following arguments demonstrate.

Pro

1 ECT benefits patients who would otherwise remain mentally ill. Forty to ninety percent of depressed patients who receive ECT show marked improvement in their ability to cope with their problems.

2 Despite the scare stories, ECT is safe and painless. The memory loss that sometimes results from ECT is only temporary. A number of well-known psychotherapists consider ECT "safer than aspirin."

3 Following ECT therapy, many potential suicides discard their plans for self-destruction and respond to therapy. Unfortunately, some patients have used ECT as a scapegoat for their own failure to deal with their mental problems.

4 State and federal agencies have approved ECT as a proven and successful treatment when administered by qualified psychotherapists under proper conditions.

5 Therapists have learned to restrict ECT to those patients who are most likely to benefit from it. Its success makes it a reasonable choice when nothing else seems to work.

Con

1 Depressed patients often show improvement even when no therapy is given. ECT has not been successful with schizophrenic patients, but it is still being used to treat them.

2 ECT results in the death of one patient in every thousand. Memory losses caused by ECT often last for four weeks or more, and some patients have a permanent memory loss.

3 No statistics exist to prove or disprove the argument that ECT prevents suicides. Many depressed patients talk about suicide but never attempt it. Ernest Hemingway, in fact, blamed ECT for destroying his ability to write. He committed suicide one month after his second series of ECT treatments.

4 Studies of ECT effectiveness suffer from lack of adequate controls. Government agencies have approved many procedures that later proved useless or even dangerous.

5 Estimates suggest that about one hundred thousand Americans receive an average of five ECT treatments every year. This high volume probably means that some psychotherapists use ECT when they don't know what else to do.

Critics of ECT describe its continued use as little better than burning incense over the patient. Its supporters say that it works, so why quarrel with success? If you were suffering from a serious depression, with no hope of quick improvement, would you accept a series of ECTs? Tell why or why not.

The psychopathic personality

Some of society's most dangerous men and women fall into the category known as the *psychopathic personality*. Mental-health experts also refer to them as *sociopaths* or *antisocial personalities*. Some psychopaths attain material success rather easily, for they impress others with their quick minds and creative abilities. If these faculties don't work, they will lie, cheat, and steal to reach their goals. Their aggressive, exploitive behavior, however, usually prevents them from establishing satisfying social, sexual, or work relationships.

When Gwen T. didn't get the grades she wanted in school, she skillfully revised her report card to turn the *D*'s and *F*'s into *B*'s and *A*'s. Too lazy to learn the routines, she talked her way into the Pep Club by charming the sponsor. When she was thrown off the squad for missing too many games, she retaliated by pouring sugar into the gas tank of the sponsor's car. Gwen left school early and altered her sister's diploma so that she could get a job. Her looks and ready smile couldn't make up for her poor work habits, however, and she was fired three times in a month. She started hanging out in bars and soon married an older man with two children. The marriage ended when Gwen disappeared one day, "tired" of taking care of the house and children. She then served some time in a state prison, having been caught writing bad checks. Although Gwen is full of promises about changing her life, her probation officer doesn't have much hope. Gwen has been drinking heavily, and she lasted only three weeks on her latest job.

Gwen can be termed an *inadequate psychopath*, for she cannot cope with the demands of a normal life-style. Like Gwen, inadequate psychopaths often respond to stress by lying, swindling, resorting to petty crime, or deserting their families. Even more troubling is the *aggressive psychopath*, whose outbursts of violent behavior occur suddenly and with no apparent cause. Aggressive psychopaths frequently choose a life of crime as the easiest way of meeting their needs. Because they see others as objects to be exploited, some won't hesitate to murder if that will give them what they want. Abuse of alcohol or drugs often contributes to this pattern of violence.

Studies of brain-wave activity in psychopaths reveal a pattern more typical of children than of adults. Other research adds the possibility of linking psychopathic behavior with abnormal sex chromosomes (see Chapter 4, page 101). Most psychologists, however, still believe that the psychopathic personality grows out of an unhealthy environment during childhood and adolescence (see Figure 8.14). Psychopaths often reveal a past that includes desertion by one or both parents, life in an orphanage or foster home, poor school records, delinquency, an unstable work record, and dependence on drugs or alcohol. Group therapy, in which strong social pressures can be placed on people like Gwen, usually works better with antisocial personalities than does individual psychotherapy.

The hysterical personality

Have you ever met someone like Roger? Any happening, large or small, sends Roger into a highly emotional state. He dramatizes every injury and expects his friends to take care of his needs. Whatever he doesn't like, he represses. Most of his friends think he's terribly immature.

A psychologist would define Roger as a *hysterical personality*. His tendency to repress information about the world, his overly emotional reactions, and his dependence on others mark this type of personality disorder. Like most hysterical personalities, Roger can change abruptly from wild laughter to childlike tears.

The passive-aggressive personality

It's late afternoon, and Mrs. Yates asks, "What would you like for dinner?" Mr. Yates replies, "Oh, I don't know. Just fix something simple." So Mrs. Yates cooks a

Figure 8.14

The aggressive psychopath often turns to crime or other antisocial activities as an "easy" way of satisfying basic needs.

noodle casserole and calls the family to the table. Mr. Yates takes one look and starts to pout. He makes sure his wife sees that he's eating only a few bites of the casserole. When she asks him what's wrong, he sighs loudly and says in a whiny voice, "I'm just not very hungry. You know I don't like casseroles very much."

Can you see Mr. Yates' technique for getting his way? He never speaks up for what he wants. It's up to others to guess, and when they guess wrong he lets them know about it. That's the tip-off to the *passive-aggressive personality*. Such people cannot show their normal aggressions in the usual way. Instead, they arrange situations in which the other person cannot possibly succeed. Since passive-aggressive people are

quite immature, they also throw frequent temper tantrums. Beneath their quiet, passive exteriors, they carry a great deal of hostility for others. They don't know how to deal with this anger, however, and can only let it out in ways that do not attack the other person directly.

SECTION CHECKUP

1 What is meant by *personality disorders?*

2 Why is the aggressive psychopath considered a possible danger to society?

3 Describe the behavior patterns of the hysterical and passive-aggressive personalities.

8.6 WHAT PERSONALITY PROBLEMS CAN BE TRACED TO BRAIN DAMAGE OR DYSFUNCTION?

Mental retardation may result from brain damage during birth or from a chromosomal abnormality. Would it be fair to call a retarded person neurotic or psychotic? Psychologists don't think so. But they do believe that people whose behavior problems or troubled personalities result from brain damage or dysfunction need special attention. In many cases, they can be helped to develop healthy personalities far beyond what once was considered possible.

Improper brain development

When the brain does not develop properly, infants are born profoundly retarded. In aplasia, for example, the child's cerebral cortex never develops, leaving the brain's thinking mechanism badly crippled. In microcephaly, the upper skull does not grow to full size. Caught within a constricted space, the brain cannot develop to its full potential. Children born with these conditions may learn to feed and toilet themselves, but they will probably never learn to walk or carry on a conversation.

Down's syndrome (formerly known as *mongolism*) is caused by a genetic defect. Down's syndrome children carry an extra chromosome that apparently prevents their brains from developing past a mental age of three to seven years. About one in every seven hundred births is a Down's syndrome child, but the odds increase as a woman ages. At 29 or under, a woman's chances of having a Down's syndrome child are about 1 in 3,000; by age 45, the chances are 1 in 40.

At one time, because they often develop serious heart or lung problems, Down's syndrome children rarely lived past childhood. Today, with better medical care, many live into adulthood. Although they are severely retarded, these individuals can learn to speak and take care of themselves. Some can perform simple tasks in sheltered workshops and can live at home with their families rather than being placed in an institution.

Brain trauma

Any injury to brain tissue is termed a *trauma*. In difficult births, the infant's head may be compressed so severely that brain damage results. Fortunately, such birth traumas have become quite rare. Later in life, any severe blow to the head can cause swelling and bleeding, with possible injury to brain tissue. This condition is sometimes seen in boxers who have taken too many punches in the face and head. Accident trauma, in which bone fragments or a foreign object damages the brain, can cause the growth of scar tissue or the death of brain cells. In all three cases, the trauma can interfere with normal physical and mental behavior. Accident trauma may also lead to unexpected personality changes (see Figure 8.15).

Trauma sometimes results from conditions inside the body itself. The slow growth of brain tumors will eventually interfere with normal brain functioning. Strokes are cerebral "accidents" in which a segment of the brain loses its blood supply. Strokes often cause paralysis, speech difficulties, and personality changes.

Endocrine and metabolic disorders

Changes in the internal chemistry of the brain can also affect the personality. The most common disorders involve the thyroid and adrenal glands. An overactive thyroid, for example, can cause a number of symptoms often associated with extreme anxiety states. These symptoms include excessive physical activity, hallucinations, and feelings of great apprehension. A deficient thyroid, by contrast, leaves the individual feeling depressed and lacking in energy.

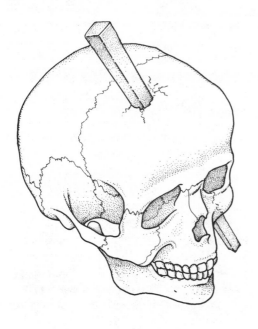

Figure 8.15

A railroad construction accident in the 1880s left Phineas Gage alive—but with a tamping iron driven through his skull. Incredibly enough, Gage lived through the ordeal. Doctors removed the iron bar, but the trauma to the frontal lobe of his brain changed his personality. Once a popular, easygoing man, he became moody, stubborn, and profane.

Brain dysfunction

Some people must live with conditions that originate in a disorder of the nervous system itself. These dysfunctions can result in abnormal behavior, both physical and emotional. Although these individuals should not be considered mentally ill, their conditions often do result in troubled personalities. Three relatively common examples of brain dysfunction include epilepsy, hyperkinesis (hyperactivity), and autism.

An underactive adrenal gland can lead to depression, anxiety, and withdrawal symptoms. A rare condition caused by an overactive adrenal gland leads to obesity and extreme shifts in mood, ranging from total indifference to angry violence. Fortunately, all of these conditions can be controlled by medical therapy. President John F. Kennedy, for example, had Addison's disease, an underactive adrenal gland. But proper medication enabled him to carry on his political career.

Other related disorders are caused by inflammation of brain tissue and higher-than-normal body temperatures. A group of illnesses known as encephalitis (sleeping sickness), for example, can lead to prolonged periods of lethargy and sleep, convulsions, disorientation, and hallucinations. Some children also exhibit personality changes following their recovery from such illnesses. They may develop antisocial personalities, their behavior marked by aggressiveness and cruelty. High fevers interfere with normal brain activity and can lead to a state of delirium. In a delirium, the patient experiences delusions, anxiety, confusion, and periods of unconsciousness.

Epilepsy. *Epilepsy* (also known as *convulsive disorder*) has been recognized for centuries. Julius Caesar and Vincent van Gogh were both epileptics, for example (see Figure 8.16). The condition may be caused by a variety of factors, such as heredity, brain injury, tumors, or infection. Just as frequently, no known organic cause can be isolated.

The typical epileptic seizure involves a second or two of unconsciousness and an almost invisible convulsion. This is a petit-mal seizure, and it generally causes little interruption in normal activities. Grand-mal seizures, which occur in a small percentage of epileptics, cause general convulsions and a longer loss of consciousness.

Oscar D.'s parents suspected his epilepsy early, and their doctor confirmed it with an EEG. With medication, Oscar's seizures are well controlled, and he carries on a normal, productive life. One of his friends had a more serious condition that required surgery before the seizures could be brought under control. But like many other epileptics, Oscar finds that the idea of epilepsy bothers people who don't know much about it. He laughs about that, a little grimly:

You know, they expect me to fall down in a roaring fit at any moment. And the parents of the girls I date! All they can imagine is a family of epileptic grandchildren. Don't they know that heredity is only one of the possible causes of epilepsy? My condition started with measles when I was a baby. As long as I'm taking my medicine, I can even drive a car safely. After all the campaigns against prejudice we've had in this country, it's about time people stopped being prejudiced against people like me. Almost all epileptics have normal intelligence and can do just about everything anyone else can do. It would make as much sense to discriminate against diabetics or people who wear glasses.

Hyperkinesis. "Bobby can't you sit still even for a minute?" The chances are good that Bobby can't sit still if he's one of the 4 to 10 percent of the elementary-school population that suffers from *hyperkinesis* (more commonly called *hyperactivity*). Bobby's symptoms include restlessness, constant movement, a short attention span, and aggressive outbursts of temper. Even if his parents have learned to cope with his demanding, explosive behavior, it's unlikely that the schools will be that patient. Hyperkinetic children such as Bobby frequently become discipline problems because of their inability to concentrate, work quietly in their seats, and get on with other children. Although the ceaseless motor activity tends to end during adolescence, the behavioral problems that go with hyperkinesis do not always disappear.

Hyperkinetic behavior has been described as a group of symptoms rather than a disease. Its causes have not been pinpointed, but may include brain injury, biochemical imbalance, or allergies to something in the diet. Most doctors prescribe drug therapy, using an amphetamine such as Ritalin. Usually a stimulant, Ritalin serves as a tranquilizer for hyperkinetic

Figure 8.16

The haunting gaze of Vincent van Gogh conveys the same power and anguish we find in his paintings. In 1889, when these works were painted, van Gogh was depressed over his recurring mental illness. He committed suicide in 1890.

Figure 8.17

The forces that lock autistic children into their own private worlds make therapy difficult and time-consuming. Would you have the love and patience needed to work with these autistic children?

youngsters. Under proper dosage, they begin to function more normally at home and in school. Many psychologists fear, however, that too many difficult, nonhyperkinetic children are being put on drugs simply as a shortcut to controlling them. Such therapy may cover up their real problems and may also create a long-term drug dependency. Some hyperkinetic behavior has been reversed by putting children on special diets free of chemical additives.

Autism. To look at Avis, you wouldn't think anything's wrong. She is four years old, slender, and attractive. But try to talk to her, and she won't seem to hear you. Avis isn't deaf or mute, but she lives in her own inner world, from which she emerges only occasionally. Today she's playing with her favorite toy, a wooden hammer. She uses the hammer to bang on a special spot on the floor. Over and over, hour after hour, Avis bangs her hammer. Last month, when she had a sore throat, she couldn't explain the problem to her parents. Frustrated, she had one of her tantrums. Her father still has scars where Avis scratched him when he tried to calm her down.

Avis is the one child in 2,500 who suffers from *autism*. Unlike childhood schizophrenia, autism is present at birth. The autistic child ignores the outer world and responds primarily to inner drives and needs. Self-stimulating behavior, such as rocking back and forth, flapping the arms, or banging the head against the wall, are common. Unable to communicate their needs, autistic children often have violent, destructive tantrums. The causes of autism still puzzle researchers. Most studies suggest a possible organic brain defect, perhaps biochemical in nature.

Considerable effort has been made at breaking through to self-isolated children such as Avis (see Figure 8.17). Patient, repetitive "shaping" techniques, combined with love and affection, seem to work best. As taught by behaviorists, each task is broken down into tiny steps and repeated over and over. Rewards of small treats or hugs and praise are given when the child responds to the training. A variation on this procedure uses physical punishment to break through to the children. As you might guess, such negative reinforcement techniques arouse great controversy. Whatever training methods are used, only a small percentage of autistic children presently escape from their isolation. Many eventually end up in institutions when their families can no longer cope with their uncontrollable temper tantrums.

SECTION CHECKUP

1 Define what is meant by *brain dysfunction*.

2 Contrast the behavior of a hyperactive child and an autistic child if they were put in a first-grade classroom.

3 How would you explain to some friends that they shouldn't be fearful of, or prejudiced against, someone who has epilepsy?

LOOKING BACK: A SUMMARY

1 Every culture defines normal and abnormal behavior according to its own standards. When people consistently behave abnormally, they are termed *maladjusted*. As the abnormal behavior increases in severity, the individual is often spoken of as being neurotic or psychotic. People with troubled personalities tend to have difficulty coping with the realities of life and often exhibit inappropriate emotions.

2 Psychologists today see mental illness as a temporary breakdown in the individual's ability to handle the problems of work and personal relationships. Mental-health experts believe that as many as 30 percent of the population will need help with an emotional problem some time during their lifetimes. Improved mental-health care and changing attitudes have made it possible for many people to seek help for emotional problems that formerly would have been kept hidden.

3 No single factor can be pointed out as the cause of all mental illness. Instead, environmental and physical factors frequently combine to cause neurotic or psychotic behavior. Environmental factors that affect behavior include dealing with stress, handling frustration, coping with anxieties, functioning within the family, adjusting to job pressures, and finding a place in society. Physical factors at the root of some troubled personalities include heredity, chemical imbalances, disease, and accident trauma. The most common symptom of emotional distress today is depression, a feeling of hopelessness and sadness that affects almost everyone at some time or another. Troubled personalities, however, often find it difficult to escape from their depressions.

4 Almost everyone occasionally shows mildly neurotic behaviors. Neurotic personalities respond to stress or fear-causing situations with repeated, involuntary, and inappropriate behaviors. Common neuroses include obsessions and compulsions, which are continuously repeated, involuntary thoughts or actions. Phobias are irrational, uncontrollable fears, and anxiety reactions are feelings of general nervousness, fatigue, and physical upset. Less common types of neuroses include conversion hysteria, in which inner conflicts surface in the form of paralysis or other physical disability, and dissociative reactions, which cause parts of the personality to "split off," as in amnesia or multiple personalities.

5 Psychotic behavior, popularly and legally termed *insanity*, involves a loss of contact with reality. Because psychotics live in an unreal world, they can be dangerous to themselves or to others. Hallucinations (false perceptions) and delusions (false beliefs) are common symptoms of psychotic behavior. Organic psychoses begin with damage to the central nervous system. Three types of organic psychoses are paresis, an advanced stage of syphilitic infection; delirium tremens, the hallucinations and confusion that accompany advanced stages of alcoholism; and senility, the disorientation and memory loss caused by old age.

6 Functional psychoses originate in painful emotional experiences. The symptoms of schizophrenia include breakdowns in communication, disorientation, delusions, and bizarre behaviors. Affective reactions, another type of functional psychosis, put the individual through wild mood swings from mania to deep depression. Paranoid reactions involve delusions of persecution and self-importance.

7 Some personality disorders do not involve loss of contact with reality. Psychopathic personalities exploit other people in order to achieve material success. Inadequate psychopaths cannot cope with life's demands and often react by turning to petty crime, lying, or running away from responsibilities. Aggressive psychopaths often use violence to achieve their goals. The hysterical personality represses information that sounds unpleasant, and reacts emotionally to whatever happens. The passive-aggressive personality takes out his or her angers indirectly, often by arranging situations so that the other person cannot succeed.

8 Abnormal behavior can also result from brain damage or dysfunction, which are primarily medical problems. Incomplete brain development can cause profound retardation, as in aplasia and microcephaly. Down's syndrome results from a genetic defect and also causes retardation. Brain trauma that damages brain tissue can result from difficult births, blows to the head, tumors, or a loss of blood supply to a part of the brain. Severe trauma may cause paralysis, loss of speech, or personality changes. Symptoms of endocrine disorders, which are caused by malfunctions of the thyroid or adrenal glands, include hallucinations, depression, and mood changes. Memory loss, personality changes, and delirium may follow a high fever or an attack of encephalitis.

9 Brain dysfunction, a breakdown of normal brain activity, can cause abnormal physical and emotional behavior. People with brain dysfunction should not be considered mentally ill, but they need medical treatment and often psychotherapy to help them handle their problem. Three disorders associated with brain dysfunction are epilepsy, hyperkinesis, and autism. Epileptics and hyperkinetics who receive prompt treatment can live normal lives, but autistic children are often trapped within their self-isolation despite every effort to free them.

PUTTING YOUR KNOWLEDGE TO WORK

Terms you should know

affective reactions

aggressive psychopath

amnesia

anxiety

anxiety reaction

autism

biochemical imbalance

catatonic schizophrenia

compulsions

conversion hysteria

delirium tremens (D.T.'s)

delusions

depression

dissociative reaction

Down's syndrome

electroconvulsive therapy (ECT)

epilepsy

frustration

functional psychoses

hallucinations

hebephrenic schizophrenia

hyperkinesis (hyperactivity)

hysterical personality

inadequate psychopath

manic-depressive psychosis

multiple personalities

neurasthenia

neurosis

obsessions

organic psychoses

paranoid reaction

paranoid schizophrenia

paresis

passive-aggressive personality

phobias

psychopathic personality

psychosis

schizophrenia

senility

simple schizophrenia

stress

trauma

Objective questions

1 Lisa's compulsive, rhyming speech (see pages 219–220) is a symptom of (a) conversion hysteria (b) paranoia (c) manic-depressive reaction (d) schizophrenia.

2 A mentally healthy person will (a) never show signs of maladjustment or abnormal behavior (b) occasionally behave in self-defeating or unhealthy ways (c) eliminate all stress from his or her life (d) probably experience some sort of brain dysfunction once or twice during a lifetime.

3 Imagine a typical classroom of thirty-six students. The number that will need psychological help for a severe emotional problem sometime during their lifetime is approximately (a) six (b) eleven (c) sixteen (d) eighteen.

4 Percy has a tendency to worry about future events, whether he can control them or not. This causes an emotional state known as (a) anxiety (b) frustration (c) stress (d) hyperkinesis.

5 Sam T. feels faint whenever he drives through a tunnel or rides in an elevator. His condition would best be called (a) a phobia (b) a manic-depressive reaction (c) a dissociative reaction (d) a hysteric conversion.

6 Tammy K. has periods in which a separate personality emerges who is different from Tammy in many ways. This neurotic behavior is properly described as (a) a dissociative reaction (b) schizophrenia (c) conversion hysteria (d) free-floating anxiety.

7 Wilson B. believes that the FBI has tapped his phone and has been opening his mail in an attempt to steal his plans for an antigravity machine. This psychotic behavior is properly described as (a) an affective reaction (b) a manic-depressive reaction (c) psychopathic (d) a paranoid reaction.

8 Toni O. exhibits symptoms that include disorientation, hallucinations, and bizarre behavior. This psychotic condition is properly described as (a) an affective reaction (b) schizophrenia (c) a paranoid reaction (d) senility.

9 During a bank robbery, a man kills a guard without apparent reason. When questioned, he shows no guilt over his action. In all other respects, he has perfect contact with reality. His personality disorder can be described as that of a (a) schizophrenic (b) psychopathic personality (c) manic-depressive (d) neurasthenic.

10 Damage to the brain, whether caused by trauma, lack of oxygen, endocrine imbalance, or other condition, is of great concern because (a) it always causes insanity (b) it leads to paresis (c) it causes genetic damage (d) it can result in depression, hallucinations, and disorientation.

Discussion questions

1 List five behaviors you would consider normal in this culture and five behaviors you would label as abnormal. Would everybody in your culture agree with your choices? Why or why not?

2 Whitney E. is presently being treated for schizophrenia in a mental hospital. His three brothers show no sign of mental illness, nor do his parents. List a number of possible causes of Whitney's mental illness, both environmental and physiological. Why do you think that he became mentally ill while the rest of his family remains healthy?

3 Explain the difference between neurotic and psychotic behavior in regard to (a) contact with reality (b) orientation in time and place and (c) chances for recovery.

4 Describe briefly the behaviors you would expect from a person who has been diagnosed as (a) schizophrenic (b) manic-depressive (c) paranoid and (d) psychopathic.

5 How does the average person react when faced with the unpredictable behavior of the mentally ill? What do you think can be done to overcome this reaction, so that people can learn to treat a person suffering from mental illness as compassionately as they treat someone with a physical illness?

6 How do you think American society might be changed to reduce the incidence of mental illness? Why would such changes be a good investment for the future?

Activities

1 Prepare a collage that demonstrates the contrast between mental health and mental illness. Use cut-out pictures, your own original artwork, and copies of the artwork produced by the mentally ill. (You'll find samples of such artwork in most books on abnormal psychology.) Discuss the meaning of the images you chose for your collage with your class.

2 If you're like most people, you probably follow a regular routine as you get up in the morning and get ready for the day. Get up on the opposite side of the bed (if possible), eat breakfast before combing your hair, put your shoes on in the opposite order, take a different route to work or school, and so on. Do you find it difficult or easy to vary the routine? This experience will give you some insight into compulsive behaviors. A truly compulsive person, however, wouldn't be able to change his or her routine at all.

3 If there is a school for exceptional children in your area, try to arrange a visit. Such a school may teach autistic, retarded, and cerebral-palsied children. Observe the procedures that have been developed to help these children. If your career plans include the possibility of working with disturbed or exceptional children, you might want to volunteer to work at the school.

4 All people have some fears that have become so much a part of their lives that they seldom notice them—until the fear-causing situation arises. Make an inventory of your own fears. Then survey your friends and relatives in order to find out what fears are most common. Can you figure out how your own fears became part of your personality?

5 Ask the members of your class to join in examining the theme of mental illness in current literature, films, and television. Each person can report on one such work or program. Is mental illness being fairly treated in the media, or is it being exploited? After the general discussion, try to pull together an evaluation of current attitudes toward troubled personalities.

For further reading

Calhoun, James, editor. *Abnormal Psychology: Current Perspectives*. New York: CRM/Random House, 1972. This is a well-illustrated and readable textbook on abnormal psychology.

Capote, Truman. *In Cold Blood*. New York: Random House, 1966. Capote has written a thorough, insightful study of the murder of a Kansas family and the two troubled men found guilty of the crime.

Grant, Vernon W. *Great Abnormals: The Pathological Genius of Kafka, van Gogh, Strindberg, and Poe*. New York: Hawthorn Books, 1968. Grant's book is an interesting exploration of the relationship between the art they created and the troubled minds that tortured these men of genius.

Green, Hannah. *I Never Promised You a Rose Garden*. New York: Holt, Rinehart & Winston, 1964. This powerful, well-written novel focuses on a sixteen-year-old girl and her long struggle with schizophrenia. It provides good insights into the therapy process as well as the inner world of mental illness.

Greenfeld, Josh. *A Child Called Noah*. New York: Holt, Rinehart & Winston, 1972. Greenfeld writes honestly and lovingly about his autistic son Noah. You share his family's hopes and despairs as they try to help Noah break out of his silent, self-involved world.

Schreiber, Flora Rheta. *Sybil*. New York: Warner, 1974. Sybil's story will help you understand the puzzling complexity of multiple personalities and the terrible forces that create them.

9

HELPING THE TROUBLED PERSONALITY

Dr. David Viscott makes his living helping people. That's not unusual for a doctor, but the patients Dr. Viscott works with suffer from anxiety reactions, phobias, depression, and other emotional problems. Like most modern psychotherapists, Dr. Viscott doesn't pretend that he can bring about "miracle" cures for anxiety reactions, phobias, paranoia, or other problems. Instead, he uses his skills to help his patients help themselves.

In the following excerpt from *The Making of a Psychiatrist*, Dr. Viscott is working with Roberta Goldman, who has made a great deal of progress since their first therapy sessions together. But today, something has gone wrong . . .

Roberta was in the OPD [Outpatient Department] waiting room. She was twenty minutes early and looked uncomfortable, restless. There was no sense making her wait since I had free time.

We walked down the hall toward my office. What could have happened to upset her? . . . the divorce had been an anxious struggle for her. Many times she'd thought she'd made a mistake and wanted to go back to Gary. . . . Law school, though, had been a breeze for her and she had received an offer with an excellent law firm in town. She had even learned to cope with her mother by being firm and saying no when her mother infringed on her rights. She had also been dating, but . . . why did Roberta look so terrible?

"I think I'm going crazy," Roberta said, near tears, collapsing in her chair. "Yesterday was the worst day of my life. Everything seemed unreal. Floors seemed to be rising and falling, and the perspective of rooms kept changing. I felt I was losing my mind. . . . I couldn't stand being with people, and yet I wanted someone to help me." . . .

"When did all this start, Roberta?"

"I'm not sure. I think I woke up with it."

"Did you have a dream that night?" I asked, playing a hunch.

"Oh, God, yes, a horrible dream." . . . "I dreamt I went back to Gary. Oh, yes, there was a bizarre religious ceremony! . . . I . . . had to crawl down the aisle on my hands and knees, begging forgiveness from all the relatives for leaving him. I wanted to turn around and run, but I couldn't. I just went on crawling. . . . Please, tell me what's *happening!*"

"I think, Roberta, that you reacted to your dream as if it were real, even though you couldn't remember it. The feelings you had during the day were mostly fear. The feeling in the dream was the fear of being caught again in the trap of your marriage. I think they were both the same fear but you didn't know it."

Roberta suddenly seemed more relaxed. "That feels very true," she said.

"I had a similar thing happen to me once," I said. "I had a dream I couldn't remember. I had a horrible day. The way I felt was the way I would have felt if the events in my dream had actually happened."

Figure 9.1

Psychotherapists work at helping people whenever and wherever they're needed. No matter what type of therapy they use, their goal is to help their patients regain control of their lives.

"You had the same thing happen to you and you didn't crack up?"

"And neither did you. The feelings you had were real, but the event that caused them, your dream, was only a dream."

"It's really strange," said Roberta, "the things that happened in the dream were like losing everything I've worked so hard for in here. I mean my independence, my ability to stand on my own two feet."

"Sometimes," I said, "a dream reveals a part of yourself that you find very hard to face.". . .

Finally she said, "I guess I'm still afraid of being alone, and I guess I'm afraid of being better. If I'm better, it means I don't have you anymore and I'm *really* on my own. I know I can make it but I guess there always are some doubts." . . .

It suddenly struck me how many of my patients, like Roberta, spent their lives reacting to a feeling from a forgotten event, a feeling whose source was obscure but would be felt whether they wanted to feel it or not. And unless they found out where the disconnected feeling came from and measured it, it would make them distort the world around and inside themselves and they would begin to lose their sense of what was real.

Roberta Goldman's story demonstrates that psychotherapy *can* help people regain control of their lives. This chapter will help you focus on some of the different ways of treating the troubled personality by answering these questions:

9.1 WHAT IS PSYCHOTHERAPY?

9.2 WHAT TYPES OF INDIVIDUAL PSYCHOTHERAPY ARE AVAILABLE?

9.3 HOW DO DIFFERENT GROUP THERAPIES WORK?

9.4 WHERE CAN TROUBLED PEOPLE GO FOR HELP?

9.1 WHAT IS PSYCHOTHERAPY?

Although some people might argue the point, psychologists do have a sense of humor. For instance, they enjoy a joke on themselves that goes like this:

What is the difference between a neurotic, a psychotic, and a psychologist?

The neurotic builds castles in the air, . . . the psychotic lives in them, . . . and the psychologist collects the rent.

The psychologist who treats troubled people earns that "rent" fairly. In the same way that your family doctor might set a broken arm or heal an infection, specially trained *psychotherapists* help their patients regain their mental health.

Historical approaches to psychotherapy

The term "mental illness" probably suggests to you that people can be mentally as well as physically ill. At different times in human history, however, there were other ways of thinking about those who had mental problems.

Supernatural explanations. Humanity's oldest explanation for disturbed behavior is known as the *demonological model*. When primitive cave dwellers had spells of screaming, manic behavior, the tribal elders nodded wisely. They "knew" that demons or devils had invaded their friend's body and were causing the strange actions. Perhaps the elders prescribed rest, special herbs, or fasting. Or they may have called in the tribal shaman (healer) to perform ritual dances and chants. The ancient Incas of Peru sometimes "released" the demons by drilling a hole in the disturbed person's skull. Surprisingly enough, these treatments sometimes worked. And most primitive peoples still believe that the demonological model fully explains the mysteries of abnormal behavior.

In a society organized by priests and based on religious values, mental illnesses were diagnosed differently. According to the *religious model*, mental illness comes from violating the will of God. The sufferers were thought to have sinned so terribly that they were punished in this way. Only the priests could help them. First, the individual had to confess his or her sins and pray for forgiveness. Next came an assigned penance in the form of fasting, making gifts to the church, or punishing one's own body. In cases where the devil was thought to have taken possession of the person's body, the individual was put through an exorcism. In this ceremony, the priest or other religious figure performed special prayers and chants to drive out the evil spirit. Some religions still perform exorcisms when normal therapies don't seem to help.

Figure 9.2

Traditional and modern cultures treat troubled personalities in their own ways. How do methods of psychotherapy differ in these two societies? In what ways are they the same?

Figure 9.3

THE CAUSES OF MENTAL ILLNESS: CHANGING VIEWPOINTS SUGGEST A COMPLEX INTERACTION OF PHYSICAL AND SOCIAL FACTORS

	Model	Cause	Treatment	Therapist	Current status
Supernatural explanations	Demonological	Demons invade the body.	Rituals, prayer, herbal medicines, and fasting.	Shaman or priest.	No longer believed except among primitive peoples.
	Religious	Individual has committed a mortal sin.	Confession and penance; exorcism.	Priest or minister.	No longer believed except by fundamentalist religions.
Medical explanations	Neuropathological	Breakdown in brain function.	Surgery, massage, hydrotherapy.	Surgeon, physical therapist.	Certain organic mental illnesses still treated in this way.
	Toxin	Poisonous toxins prevent brain from working properly.	Surgery to remove organ causing the problem, changes in diet, treatment with specific drugs.	Surgeon or other medical practitioner.	New research confirms connection between biochemical imbalances in the body and certain mental illnesses.
Psychosocial explanations	Psychoanalytic	Painful emotional experiences in childhood.	Help patient come to terms with repressed memories.	Therapist trained in Freudian techniques.	High prestige among those who can afford it. Most "talk" therapies derive from psychoanalysis but place less emphasis on sexual causes.
	Behaviorist	Learned behaviors interfere with normal life adjustment.	Behavior modification (reward "good" behaviors and punish or ignore "bad" behaviors).	Psychologist trained in behaviorist techniques.	Widely used because of emphasis on changing behavior; useful with neurotic conditions.
	Radical	A sick society generates sick behavior.	Uses existential concept that patient must take responsibility for behavior.	Radical or existential psychiatrist.	Strong influence on other forms of therapy.

Medical explanations. Over 2,500 years ago, the Greek physician Hippocrates refused to treat abnormal behavior as an invasion by demons. Instead, he thought of it as an illness to be treated like other illnesses. When dealing with a mentally ill person, Hippocrates prescribed rest, avoidance of stress, special exercises, and a vegetarian diet. Under this type of care, many troubled people improved greatly. But without the humane treatment practiced by Greek doctors, these simple therapies would have been less successful.

Despite the insights gained by the ancient Greeks, during the Middle Ages the demonological model was revived, often mixed with religious beliefs. It was not until the 1800s that a more scientific approach to mental problems developed. Many doctors of that time came to believe that disturbed behavior was caused by a breakdown in brain function. This *neuropathological model*, as it was known, relied on surgery, massage, and other physical therapies to relieve symptoms. If the patients' behavioral problems originated in organic dysfunctions such as brain tumors, infection, or other medical conditions, the treatment had a good chance of helping them. Functional illnesses with roots in emotional stress, however, did not respond well to such treatment.

Other doctors, meanwhile, decided that mental illnesses such as depression were caused by poisonous substances in the body. This *toxin model* sometimes led them to remove the spleen, which was thought to be the source of the behavior-altering toxins. Changes in diet and doses of various drugs were also tried. Renewed attention is being paid today to this theory. Evidence has been gathered that shows a connection between biochemical imbalances in the body and some forms of mental illness.

Psychosocial explanations. The medical approach to treating mental illness achieved some success in treating organically caused problems. But not all emotional problems could be blamed on infections or biochemical imbalances. Beginning with the theories of Sigmund Freud (see Chapter 6), a *psychosocial model* for abnormal behavior began to take shape. According to this model, abnormal behavior is the end result of harmful environmental (social) forces acting on the personality of the individual. As a result of that process, some people adopt abnormal behaviors as a way of coping with their unendurable problems.

According to Freud's *psychoanalytic model*, for example, mental illness is the result of painful childhood experiences. The influence of the child's environment, he said, affects the individual's ability to cope with personal relationships. Thus, mental illness is seen as a condition based on past experiences, rather than as a battle with demons or a breakdown in brain function. When patients lay down on Freud's couch, they were encouraged to come to terms with repressed memories. In time, they gradually uncovered long-forgotten experiences that lay at the heart of their troubled personalities.

Freud's model was not the only psychosocial explanation. In the *behaviorist model*, mental illness results from learned responses to stimuli. Using a program of behavior modification, patients change harmful habits and feel better for having gained a greater degree of control over their daily lives. By contrast, the *radical model* locates the cause of mental illness in society. A *radical psychiatrist* attempts to cure mental illness by showing patients that they don't need to feel guilty for being disturbed. If society is sick, according to the radical model, it is no wonder that people also become disturbed.

Treatment of the mentally ill

The introduction of better explanations for mental illness did not save the mentally ill from cruel and inhumane treatment. Mental hospitals from the 1600s onward were grim prisons, where patients could be isolated from the rest of society. London's St. Mary of Bethlehem asylum stands out as a terrifying example. Londoners soon shortened the

Figure 9.4

London's St. Mary of Bethlehem hospital clearly deserved its name of "Bedlam." In this scene, one man is being chained to prevent him from committing suicide, while others act out their sad states of delusion and melancholy. What effect do you think the visit of the two curious society ladies had on the inmates?

hospital's name to "Bedlam," a term that has come to mean any place of wild confusion (see Figure 9.4). For a penny, visitors could come to watch the inmates "perform." Therapy at Bedlam consisted of chains, whips, straitjackets, and other restraints. The patients mostly cared for one another, for medical care was sadly lacking. Even when other mental hospitals were opened, improvements in patient care came slowly. In one early hospital, a favorite therapy was dousing the patients with buckets of ice water.

In the late 1700s, a French physician took a new and revolutionary position. Philippe Pinel believed that the mentally ill were no different from anyone else, except for their severe personal problems. Pinel walked into his asylum one day and ordered that the inmates be freed from their chains and dungeons. He had them moved to sunny, well-furnished rooms, where they ate well and were no longer mistreated. Pinel sat down with each one, listened to individual problems, and began to compile case histories. For the first time, large numbers of patients began to recover and return home.

In the United States, similar reforms began. Dr. Benjamin Rush, a signer of the Declaration of Independence, took the first steps toward providing humane treatment of the mentally ill. But much remained to be done. In 1842, Dorothea Dix, a Bos-

ton schoolteacher, began to campaign for proper hospital facilities for the mentally ill. Dix discovered that most emotionally disturbed people were being held in prisons and poorhouses. They were often whipped and confined in cages, closets, cellars, and pens. Thanks to Dix's effective publicity, the public voted to pay for properly equipped mental hospitals. Even today, the struggle to maintain good hospitals has not yet ended, as you will learn in Section 9.4.

Choosing a type of therapy

Imagine that for some time you have been feeling increasingly anxious. You wake up each morning with a strong feeling of dread, yet you know there's no real reason for your anxiety. Finally, you decide to get some help.

But there are so many types of therapy. Should you try a psychoanalyst? A behaviorist? Should it be individual or group therapy? The choices seem endless.

Everyone going into psychotherapy faces these decisions. One point in a patient's favor is that almost any therapy may be helpful, provided two factors are present. First, the individual must want to be helped. Second, the therapist must inspire trust and open communication. Even so, therapists can't give guarantees. Many troubled people get better, but others stay the same or get worse. Still, all good therapists follow a similar process in treating the troubled personality.

A good therapist provides support in time of crisis. Therapy provides an emotional safety net for troubled people. Good therapists care deeply about their patients. They believe that every person has a right to noncritical support, no matter what he or she may have done in the past. In turn, patients know that the therapist will be available whenever they feel themselves losing control.

A good therapist screens patients for medical problems. Just as some physical ailments are psychological in origin, some abnormal behavior is caused by organic conditions. A careful psychotherapist will always have patients checked for possible chemical imbalances, infections, brain tumors, and other medical problems that can cause disturbed behavior.

A good therapist develops catharsis. *Catharsis* (from the Greek for "to purge or clean out") is the release of tension through talking or otherwise working out painful memories or repressed feelings. When patients air out long-buried emotions, they often feel a release from anxiety. At the same time, both the patient and the therapist receive valuable insights into the causes of the unhealthy behavior.

A good therapist helps people change disturbed behavior. Once the emotional problems have been identified, the therapist helps patients learn to cope with their problems. In time, most people learn how to satisfy their needs in healthy, productive ways. Comedian Bob Newhart went into therapy because he wasn't satisfied with the way his life was going. He summed up his feelings about the experience in these words: "I think the whole experience of therapy was painful at first but, . . . I like where I am now and I didn't like where I was before. The shrink helped me get to the point where I am today. It's made my life better: I've gotten to know myself better, and I like myself a little more."

SECTION CHECKUP

1 Contrast the causes of mental illness as described by the three major theories—the supernatural, medical, and psychosocial.

2 Why was Philippe Pinel's approach to therapy for the patients of his asylum so revolutionary?

3 List several of the services that good psychotherapists will provide for their patients.

Figure 9.5

SHAKESPEARE KNEW IT ALL THE TIME: THE PATIENT IS THE KEY TO SUCCESSFUL THERAPY

Writing four hundred years ago, William Shakespeare summed up the entire modern concept of successful psychotherapy in these lines from *Macbeth* (Act V, Scene iii). Here Macbeth is asking the doctor to cure his wife's strange behavior.

Macbeth: Canst thou not minister to a mind diseased,
Pluck from the memory a rooted sorrow,
Raze out the written troubles of the brain
And with some sweet oblivious antidote
Cleanse the stuffed bosom of that perilous stuff
Which weighs upon the heart?

Doctor: Therein the patient
Must minister to himself.

9.2 WHAT TYPES OF INDIVIDUAL PSYCHOTHERAPY ARE AVAILABLE?

Take one therapist. Add one troubled patient. Encourage the patient to start talking. The therapist listens, counsels, and occasionally controls the discussion. The patient gradually gains in self-understanding and recovers control of his or her life. That's *individual therapy*.

Ever since Freud, this one-to-one relationship has been the heart of psychotherapy. Even today, despite the growing popularity of group therapies, individual therapy remains the first choice of most troubled people when they seek help. Choosing a type of therapy, however, presents a further difficulty. Since no single psychotherapy can be rated as "most effective" or "least effective," a sampling of the more commonly available therapies might help you understand what goes on in the therapist's office.

Psychoanalysis

Although Chapter 6 describes a typical Freudian analysis (pages 177–179), a brief review should be useful. After all, most modern systems of therapy depend to one degree or another upon the insights and techniques developed by Sigmund Freud.

Basic concepts. Psychoanalysts believe that emotional disorders have their origins in childhood. That is when the demands of the id first come into conflict with the superego. Caught between the "I want" drives of the id and the "Thou shalt not" commands of the superego, the ego must work desperately to moderate sexual drives in light of reality. When this struggle leads to painful conflicts, the individual represses those experiences into the unconscious. Freud believed, for example, that Oedipal conflicts are always repressed in this way.

These repressed experiences can lead to feelings of depression and other emotional problems. Repressed experiences, however, do not cause everyone to become emotionally disturbed. Most people manage to live normal lives despite their repression of the terrifying conflicts of childhood. Psychoanalysts would agree with that point. But they'd also say that people's lives could be even more productive if they had the chance to go through analysis.

What is it like to lie on an analyst's couch? Martin Shepard, himself a psychiatrist, describes his own experience in psychoanalysis.

> It was not the lying on a couch four times a week that "cured" me. Nor was it my analyst's interpretative skills that made me realize the absurdity of my self-contemptuous, vicious cycle. That that was a blind-alley way of thinking emerged gradually as I listened to all of the claptrap I was free associating. . . .
>
> Another thing that helped was my daring to go beyond my fears and old ways of dealing with myself and others. . . . Last, and perhaps most significant, was the fact that I felt fully accepted by this woman analyst of mine.
>
> I could tell her about my "worst self"—both historically (stealing money from my mother and lying about it) and in the present (passing by an auto accident at a roadside and not stopping to see if I could help)—and I felt she still was interested in me. I dared to ask her if she liked me, and she said that she did. I dared to insult her by sneering at her "superkindness," and yet she remained kindly disposed. I risked being thought "disgusting" because of my sexual interest in her. Yet she found this flattering.
>
> It was this acceptance by her of all these parts of me that I felt also led to my accepting myself.

Three stages of analysis. An analysis such as the one that Shepard went through takes place in three stages. Because each person brings different problems to the therapy sessions, no one can determine in advance how long each stage will take.

First, in order to uncover the roots of

Figure 9.6

STRENGTHS AND WEAKNESSES OF INDIVIDUAL THERAPY

Strengths

1 Therapists and patients can develop a close, safe, and rewarding relationship in which to work out difficult emotional problems.

2 Individual therapists are free to use whatever techniques they think will best help their patients.

3 Many patients prefer the privacy of individual therapy and make progress faster in such a situation.

4 Strict licensing requirements for individual therapists generally ensure that patients receive competent care.

Weaknesses

1 Individual therapy is too expensive for most people. Few therapists charge less than $40–50 an hour. Public health agencies, free clinics, and similar organizations do provide some low-cost or free individual therapy, but such services are not always available to those who need them most.

2 Because of the expense, many patients drop out of therapy before the benefits of the treatment become evident. A typical course of therapy may take six months to a year, with psychoanalysis lasting even longer.

3 Because of the personal relationship that develops between therapist and patient, people may be reluctant to end therapy or change therapists even when the treatment is not working.

---

their troubled behavior, patients learn to *free-associate*. They lie on the analyst's couch and say anything that comes to mind, particularly as it relates to their past lives. During this stage, the patient meets *resistances*, those locked doors of the unconscious where the most troubling memories lie waiting. Patients also begin to experience *transference* during this period. All the love/hate emotions they feel about parents, marriage partners, lovers, or other important people in their lives become part of their feelings toward the therapist.

In stage two, *catharsis* begins to take place. Tensions disappear as patients talk more freely about experiences dating back to early childhood. After months of near silence, the analyst begins to offer evaluation and interpretation.

Finally, in stage three, the patients are ready to *work through* the final resistances. They must replace the last self-defeating attitudes and feelings with increased control over their emotions. Therapy ends when the patients achieve greater independence and healthier ways of coping with their tensions.

The neo-Freudian approach to therapy

Even during Freud's lifetime, a number of psychoanalysts disagreed with his insistence that sexual drives are the most important forces in shaping the personality. The neo-Freudians shifted their emphasis to the psychosocial forces, both cultural and environmental, that influence behavior. The neo-Freudians also insisted on a more active dialogue between the therapist and patient.

Among the important analytical therapies that emphasize psychosocial causes of disturbed behavior are those developed by Alfred Adler (1870–1937) and Harry Stack Sullivan (1892–1942).

Alfred Adler: Individual psychology. Adlerian analysts see themselves in a role similar to that of a parent. As a parent interprets social customs and rules to a child, so the analysts help their patients understand the nature of their neurotic behaviors. Adler particularly looked for behaviors linked to his patients' feelings of inferiority, which he believed all people experience in one degree or another.

According to Adler, abnormal behavior results from misguided attempts to compensate for these feelings of inferiority. Seventeen-year-old Oliver, for example, tries to compensate for his poor performance in the classroom by playing the role of class clown. His jokes and pranks gain him some of the recognition he needs. But clowning around doesn't resolve the basic problem, as a sympathetic analyst would point out to Oliver. In therapy, Oliver would learn how to develop the social skills that he could use to increase his feelings of self-worth. Once mastered, he would then be free to discard his clownish behavior as an overcompensation he no longer needs.

Harry Stack Sullivan: Interpersonal therapy. The American psychiatrist Harry Stack Sullivan emphasized the role of culture in causing disturbed behavior. The individual can be defined only in light of his or her relationships with other people, Sullivan insisted. Children learn love, responsibility, and generosity from their parents and other adults. But they also learn loneliness, despair, guilt, and anxiety.

Sullivan believed that it was a waste of time for the therapist to try to free patients from the causes of their unhealthy behavior. For example, if a young woman named Betty has learned to see her parents as cold

and rejecting people, she will tend to transfer that image to all the authority figures in her life. In this way, her relationships with teachers, bosses, and even her husband will be colored by her early experiences. The analyst's job, as Sullivan saw it, is to help Betty "see" others as they really are. She can then discard the false images and begin relating to people honestly and fully.

The existential approach to therapy

The unconscious, childhood sexuality, and other psychoanalytic concepts have little meaning for existential therapists. In their view, only the present moment matters. Each person stands alone. You cannot blame other people for what you feel, nor can you explore repressed desires as a means of freeing yourself from unhealthy behaviors. Anxiety arises, the existentialist will tell you, from being unable to face what you already are. The only route out of that terrible feeling of existential despair, out of the emptiness of life, is to face the fact that you must take responsibility for your own choices. In taking that responsibility, you can tap your potential for growth toward the highest human qualities—love, commitment to a cause, appreciation of beauty.

No two existential therapists follow the same rules. But out of the insights of therapists Victor Frankl and R. D. Laing have come some interesting approaches to helping the troubled personality.

Victor Frankl: Logotherapy. In his therapy, Victor Frankl emphasizes the search for meaning (logos). He believes that all people begin with a primary motivation to find meaning in their lives. The troubled personality results when this "will to meaning" is frustrated. To a sixteen-year-old named Maura, who comes in complaining of an obsessive-compulsive condition, the logotherapist would say, "You may not be able to control the circumstances of your life. But you can control your attitudes toward those

Figure 9.7

"NOW TELL ME ALL YOUR TROUBLES . . ."

Therapists know that there are a lot of people around who need to talk to a psychotherapist but who are afraid to get started or don't know where to go for help. Researchers Charles and Warner Slack tried to solve this problem by programming a computer to take over the therapist's job.

Let's follow Jenny D., a twenty-year-old college student, as she sits down in front of the computer. What Jenny sees is a TV screen with a typewriter keyboard attached. She looks around, rather nervous. She wants to talk to someone, but the impersonal appearance of the computer puts her off. Still, she decides she might as well go ahead. She punches a button to start the program.

The computer begins by asking her name, address, sex, and other basic information. Jenny enters her responses via the keyboard. Next, the computer asks her a series of thirteen questions. These rather probing queries include, "Have you been feeling sad or down in the dumps?" and "Do you have trouble expressing yourself?" If Jenny answers "yes" to any of these questions, the computer asks if she would like to talk about the problem.

Jenny has now been caught up in the action. She pushes the "yes" button, and the screen responds, "OK, the tape recorder is now running. You may talk about your feelings." Jenny starts right in, and the screen tells her, "Good! We are listening to you talk about . . ." and it names the problem area. If Jenny has trouble deciding what to say and too much time passes, the computer says kindly, "Are you having trouble getting started?" Jenny's "yes" brings another bit of encouragement: "Begin by saying, 'Well, if you really want to know the way I feel . . .' "

The computer doesn't really understand what Jenny is saying, but it is a well-informed listener. It has all of Jenny's keyed-in responses to draw upon.

One experiment with the computer involved thirty-two young adult male volunteers, none of whom were in therapy. Twenty-nine of these subjects answered "yes" to at least one of the thirteen diagnostic questions, and twenty-two went on to talk with the computer. Like Jenny, the majority of the subjects said that they would have preferred talking to a human. But six stated they liked talking to the computer better than to a doctor. Four said they felt better after their conversation with the computer, and seven weren't sure.

circumstances. You have the freedom to take a stand."

In therapy sessions with Maura, the logotherapist would help her explore the underlying causes of her obsessive-compulsive behavior. Perhaps she comes to realize that the compulsion that requires her to keep her desk, locker, and room perfectly neat at all times stems from an underlying fear of disorder. Maura now remembers a chaotic period in her life when her parents were divorcing and the house, as well as her life, seemed to be in constant turmoil. The logotherapist becomes her partner in exploring these feelings.

Gradually, Maura will understand that in order to overcome her obsessive-compulsive behavior, she must do exactly what she most fears. First, she will learn to be disorderly in her personal habits. In small, "baby steps," she will leave clothes lying around her room or jumble her books in her locker. As she discovers that she *can* endure this amount of disorder, she can then

leave her bed unmade, the dishes un-
washed, and so on. At the same time, Maura
will be asked to redirect her attention from
her compulsive behavior to more positive
aspects of living. She might join the local
swim team or begin volunteer work at a
nursing home. As Frankl would tell her,
"The cue to your cure is not self-concern, but
self-commitment." Maura will probably always be rather tidy in her personal habits,
but she will now do so through choice, not
compulsion.

R. D. Laing: Radical psychiatry. British
psychiatrist R. D. Laing (1927–) says that
the insane are perhaps the only truly sane
people in a world gone crazy. As an illustra-
tion of this antipsychiatric view, he asks
you to imagine two people. One is a girl who
believes that an atom bomb is ticking away
inside her, ready to explode. The other is
a bomber pilot ready at any moment to deliver his load of nuclear bombs. Most psychologists would label the girl as crazy, says
Laing, perhaps schizophrenic. Most would
call the pilot normal. So, who's crazy, asks
Laing: a girl who admits that her world may
blow up at any moment or a man who stands
ready to kill millions of people?

Laing uses this type of argument to reinforce his belief that society uses mental illness as a way of coping with people who
make the rest of society uncomfortable.
Once patients are labeled schizophrenic, for
example, they can be confined to a hospital,
drugged into tranquility, shocked into
forgetfulness, and even have odd bits of
their brains removed. After a while, they'll
stop saying, seeing, hearing, feeling, and
doing whatever it is that's so queer (see
Figure 9.8). Laing and the other radical
psychiatrists think that this type of treat-

Figure 9.8

THE DOUBLE BIND OF THE TROUBLED PERSONALITY

Radical psychiatrist R. D. Laing believes that mental illness grows out of the impossible demands society places on the individual. In the short poems he calls "Knots," he
tries to put that concept into simple, abstract terms that can speak to the heart as well
as the mind.

In this "Knot," Laing asks you to think about how pressures to conform affect the
disturbed individual.

There must be something the matter with him
    because he would not be acting as he does
        unless there was
    therefore he is acting as he is
    because there is something the matter with him

He does not think there is anything the matter with him
    because one of the things that is
    the matter with him
    is that he does not think that there is anything
    the matter with him
therefore
    we have to help him realize that,
    the fact that he does not think there is anything
    the matter with him
    is one of the things that is
    the matter with him

Source: R. D. Laing, *Knots* (New York: Pantheon, 1970), p. 5.

ment is often used to quiet rebellious, non-conformist personalities. Laing, in fact, claims that 95 percent of the professors of psychiatric medicine in America regard him as schizophrenic.

Given this philosophy, how would Laing treat a schizophrenic? First, Laing says that schizophrenics need a life-support system that will nurture them while they find their way down into madness and then up again to health and control. At Kingsley Hall, a residential center Laing established for psychotic patients, people were given the chance to work with and through their crises in living. Those who were "up" took care of those who were "down." The doctors dressed like everyone else and served as "guides" rather than therapists. In this atmosphere of acceptance, love, and support, the psychotic patients did improve. For example, forty-one of the Kingsley Hall residents had previously been hospitalized. After their stay, only twelve went back into mental hospitals. No one who had not already been in a hospital was later hospitalized.

In describing her experience at Kingsley Hall, Mary Barnes writes about her madness:

> My fear of love was even greater than my fear of anger. All twisted up and matted together in my mess state, I didn't know much what was happening.
>
> Joe [Dr. Joseph Berke, Mary's doctor] assured me it was all right to paint. . . .
>
> Paint I did. Gradually, it seemed to *me*, perfectly right again, to paint. Painting, when I wasn't too "bad" to do it, got me together, my body and soul. All my insides came out, through my hands and my eyes and all the colour. It was free and moving, loving and creative.

Client-centered therapy

Unlike psychoanalysis and existential therapies, with their European background, *client-centered therapy* carries a made-in-America label. Psychologist Carl

Rogers (1902–) developed this humanistic form of therapy. Rogers defined neurotic behavior as the result of life experiences that make people defensive, prevent them from communicating freely and openly with others, and keep them from full self-actualization.

As the name suggests, client-centered therapy spotlights the client as a person capable of directing his or her own therapy. Rogers believes that the word *patient* automatically puts the person seeking help in an inferior position. *Client*, in contrast, implies that the therapist and client are equally interested and involved. In this relationship, the therapist's job is to provide understanding, warmth, and acceptance. Client-centered therapists do not attempt to find out what is "wrong" with their clients. Instead, they use a method called *nondirective therapy*. Rogers described this as creating a sympathetic setting in which clients can find their own path to self-awareness. In the following excerpt, Rogers describes his discovery of this method:

> An intelligent mother brought her very seriously misbehaving boy to the clinic. . . . We decided in conference that the central problem was the mother's rejection of her son. . . . In interview after interview I tried . . . to help the mother see the pattern of her rejection and its results in the boy. To no avail. After about a dozen interviews I told her I thought we both had tried but were getting nowhere, and we should probably call it quits. She agreed. Then as she was leaving the room, she turned and asked, "Do you ever take adults for counseling here?" Puzzled, I replied that sometimes we did. Whereupon she returned to the chair she had just left and began to pour out a story of the deep difficulties between herself and her husband and her great desire for some kind of help. I was bowled over. What she was telling me bore no resemblance to the neat history I had drawn from her. I scarcely knew what to do, but mostly I listened. Eventually, after many more interviews, not only did her marital relationship improve, but her son's problem behavior dropped away as she became a more real and free person. . . . This was a vital

learning for me. I had followed *her* lead rather than mine. I had just *listened* instead of trying to nudge her toward a diagnostic understanding I had already reached. It was a far more personal relationship, and not nearly so "professional." Yet the results spoke for themselves.*

The client-centered therapist follows Rogers' three basic principles.

1. All clients receive the therapist's *unconditional positive regard*. With sympathy, understanding, and personal involvement, the therapist assures clients that they are valued as people, no matter what they have done in the past. This security frees clients to express their feelings without risking the loss of the therapist's respect.

2. Client-centered therapists do not hide behind their professional masks. They appear to the clients as genuine, warm, well-adjusted, and caring human beings.

3. Client-centered therapists do not judge their clients, nor do they prescribe solutions to their problems. The therapist's job is to reflect back the client's feelings for evaluation and exploration.

Thus, if twelve-year-old Gordon says, "I hate my father!" Dr. Gonzales doesn't look shocked, nor does she begin probing for an unresolved Oedipal complex. Instead, Dr. Gonzales replies, "Oh, you do have strong feelings about your father, don't you?" That gives Gordon a chance to reflect on what he's said. Now he continues, "Well, he does make me terribly angry. Just last week I wanted to buy a new camera and he wouldn't let me, even though I worked for the money!" To which Dr. Gonzales replies, "You must want that camera quite badly to become so angry about not getting it."

In time, this dialogue will enable Gordon to understand what is causing his emotional problems. Once he realizes what is missing

*Carl R. Rogers, "My Philosophy of Interpersonal Relationships and How It Grew," address at Association for Humanistic Psychology, Honolulu, Hawaii, September 1972.

from his life, he can learn new behaviors to replace the old, self-defeating ones. This type of therapy works best with mildly troubled people who have enough insight to be able to respond to the challenge of self-discovery. Rogers' nondirective ideas have found widespread use among counselors, social workers, ministers, and other people in the helping professions.

Behavior therapy

Behavior therapy (sometimes called *behavior modification*) departs totally from the techniques used by psychoanalytic and client-centered therapists. Behaviorists believe that all behaviors are learned responses to the environment. Behavior therapists, therefore, pay little attention to the causes of abnormal behavior or to increased self-awareness. Instead, they try to change the behavior itself, using techniques that replace unproductive behaviors with healthier ones.

Most behavior therapists today use the *operant conditioning theories* of B. F. Skinner (see Chapter 7, page 187, and Chapter 10, pages 295–297). Skinner believes that people learn at an early age to "operate" on the environment in particular ways. These learned behaviors are either rewarded or punished by parents and other adults. Typically, a child learns to use a specific behavior because it works. For example, if saying she's ill earns Monica extra sympathy and a chance to avoid work, she'll probably continue to use illness as a way of coping with stress when she's an adult. In time, Monica's "colds" or "fainting spells" will become automatic responses to any situation in which she feels threatened.

In the following case study, behavior therapy was used to treat a case of school phobia. At age fourteen, Lance literally could not stay in school. After fifteen minutes in the classroom, he would become dizzy and nauseated. Then, palms sweating and pulse rate rising, he would run out of the room. After a few weeks of this, Lance's parents took him to a hospital for therapy.

Pro & Con: DOES PSYCHOTHERAPY WORK?

At first glance, you might think that's a dumb question. Of course psychotherapy works! If it didn't, why would so many people pay so much for therapy sessions, drug treatments, ECT's, and other ways of resolving their emotional problems? Surprisingly enough, a number of serious questions have been raised about that very issue.

Pro

1 Psychotherapy produces positive changes in the behavior of troubled people. If someone starts therapy with a particular problem and completes the therapy no longer locked into that unhealthy behavior, the improvement must be credited to the course of therapy.

2 Qualified therapists bring two essential ingredients to therapy. One ingredient is professional training and experience. The other is the warmth, intelligence, and insight of a caring human being. Without them, their patients would remain locked into their self-destructive behaviors.

3 Trained and experienced therapists can make accurate diagnoses of their patients' problems. Otherwise, useful therapy cannot take place.

4 Without psychotherapy, countless people would be sentenced to lives of misery and despair. Although it's not perfect, psychotherapy is still the best answer yet found for helping emotionally troubled people.

Con

1 Positive changes in patients' lives can take place whether they go into therapy or not. One major study showed that one third of the people in therapy improve, one third stay the same, and one third get worse. Troubled people who don't go into therapy get better or worse in about the same ratio.

2 Almost any sympathetic person who is willing to listen can provide as much help as most trained therapists. The key factor in therapy is a motivated patient who wants to get better. If that ingredient is there and if the patient believes in the therapy being used, improvement is almost certain.

3 Therapists seldom agree on a diagnosis. The definitions of the various mental illnesses are so inexact that the same symptoms may be classified in several ways by different psychotherapists.

4 Statistics show that more severe mental illnesses are the least likely to respond to treatment. This means that the benefits of psychotherapy are granted primarily to those who need them the least.

Do you think that psychotherapy is a giant con game? Or do you think that therapists provide an invaluable service to troubled people? You might want to talk to some people who have been in therapy before you decide on your answer.

At the hospital, Lance was put on a behavior-modification program. After talking with the psychologist, Lance agreed that he could handle five minutes a day in the special classroom run by the hospital. When the five minutes were up, Lance was given permission to leave the room and carry his completed assignment to the psychologist's office. Then he could do anything he wanted for the rest of the day.

When Lance brought his work to the office, the psychologist entered his progress on a large chart. After praising Lance for his accomplishment that day, the psychologist would ask Lance to set his target for the next class period. Challenged by the chart and pleased by the praise, Lance steadily increased his time in the classroom. By the fifth day he had reached thirty minutes, and on the sixth day he stayed for forty minutes. At the end of the month, Lance was attending class full-time. Soon afterward he was discharged from the hospital.

A follow-up showed that Lance kept up his good attendance and improved his grades. What made this turnaround possible? The positive reinforcement Lance received from the psychologist for each day's improvement kept him motivated to overcome his phobia. Behavior-modification therapy thus accomplished in a few weeks what traditional psychotherapy might have taken months to achieve. You will note that the psychologist focused on changing Lance's behavior. The cause of Lance's school phobia never became a subject of the therapy.

Once the patient has "unlearned" the inappropriate behavior, the behaviorist feels that the therapy is complete. Other types of therapists claim that eliminating one neurotic behavior in this way often leads the patient to substitute another, equally unhealthy behavior. They point to former smokers who stop smoking only to start overeating. Behaviorists respond by saying that symptom substitution doesn't happen often enough to be a cause for concern. The former smoker who is overeating, they add, should now receive therapy for that new symptom.

Behavior therapy works quite well for phobias, bedwetting, compulsive behaviors, and other specific personality problems. Its critics point out, however, that it has less success with more complex disorders. Schizophrenia, alcoholism, anxiety reactions, and feelings of existential despair do not respond well to behavior modification.

SECTION CHECKUP

1 Contrast the Freudian psychoanalytic approach to therapy with the psychosocial theories of Adler and Sullivan.

2 Why would the various types of therapists described in this section (psychoanalytic, existential, client-centered, and behaviorist) all have difficulty treating a schizophrenic?

3 Ed is now twenty-three, and he still can't cope with his fear of airplanes. He's about to lose a good job if he can't fly to sales meetings. What type of therapy would you recommend for Ed? Why?

9.3 HOW DO DIFFERENT GROUP THERAPIES WORK?

Have you ever taken part in a *group-therapy* session? No? But surely you've attended a football game, gone to a movie, or joined your friends for a picnic. These group experiences, while not technically a form of therapy, did give you something, didn't they? Afterward, you probably felt different. Happy, perhaps, or excited. The interaction of people in social situations creates these feelings. And that's what group therapy is all about.

Group therapy brings a number of people, usually eight to ten, together with a therapist. The group-therapy situation acts as a miniature society. The interpersonal relationships that develop within the group become an important part of the treatment. Group members learn to share their personal problems, feelings, and insights. Within the safe and supportive environment of the group, the therapist can then help the members discard their unhealthy behaviors and develop a more productive way of life.

The number of types of group therapy available would fill a good-sized directory. A few of the most important group therapies will be discussed here: conventional group therapy, psychodrama, encounter groups,

Figure 9.9

STRENGTHS AND WEAKNESSES OF GROUP THERAPY

Strengths

1 Psychotherapists can reach a greater number of people by using group techniques.

2 Costs of therapy are reduced as each patient pays a smaller share of the therapist's fee.

3 Patients learn that their problems are not unique but that other people suffer from the same (or similar) painful feelings.

4 The support, advice, and criticism of other group members play an important role in advancing the course of therapy.

5 Group members learn to help one another and in doing so are often helped themselves.

Weaknesses

1 Each group member receives only a small fraction of the therapist's time and attention.

2 The success of the group depends almost entirely on the skill of the therapist, who must provide each patient with proper insights and direction.

3 Many group therapists are not properly trained. In some states, anyone with a desire to do group therapy can open a "clinic" and start group sessions.

4 New group therapies appear regularly. Not all are backed up by valid research.

5 Not everyone can handle the free give-and-take of the typical group session. It is not unusual for people to leave their groups in worse condition than when they started.

Gestalt therapy, and addiction group therapies.

Conventional group therapies

Most individual psychotherapists also conduct conventional group therapies, using their own approach to therapy. In some cases, therapists recommend group therapy because they believe that the social interaction of the group will contribute to the patient's recovery. In other cases, group therapy permits patients to remain in treatment when they cannot afford individual therapy.

One common rule applies to all of the conventional group therapies: enforced participation. Group members must talk about their feelings, hang-ups, and life experiences. If the therapist doesn't draw a member out, the other group members will. The group also joins the therapist in discussing, judging, attacking, and supporting everyone else's statements. Through this process, according to theory, group members will be led to see themselves as others see them. This self-knowledge often serves as the first step toward achieving more positive attitudes and behaviors in everyday life.

Psychodrama

For more than thirty years, *psychodrama* has ranked as one of the most popular and effective of group therapies. Psychiatrist

Figure 9.10

PSYCHOPOETRY: FINDING YOURSELF THROUGH VERSE

Therapy groups that use poetry as a way of opening up communication between therapists and clients have achieved some success. Psychologist Gilbert Schloss, of Manhattan College, one of the pioneers in this field, believes that poetry can serve as a bridge between a person's past experiences and present feelings.

In psychopoetry groups, members read their own poetry or the poems of others that have special meaning to them. Through the poetry they come to know one another and themselves. Schloss cautions, however, that poetry therapy is a technique, not a magic cure for emotional problems. He does believe that it can be a useful tool with any conventional therapy system.

Psychopoetry group members mark their progress through the poems they write. M.B. is a twenty-year-old teacher whose first poems touched upon the hurt and anger she was feeling:

My World

My world's a world of
darkness
Groping
I do not see
That's how I want
it—In my world
is nothing
only brain gray
grinding out the circles
that enclose
me.

J. L. Moreno developed psychodrama as a means of exploring and analyzing the real-life roles that cause some people to develop neurotic behavior. In a typical psychodrama session, group members take turns acting out roles or fantasies related to their problems. The therapist acts as "director," with other members joining the "protagonist" in dramatizing the relationships that are causing his or her emotional difficulties.

Thirty-year-old Bobby M., for example, is still neurotically dependent upon his mother. He has never learned to separate himself from her control, even though he says he wants badly to be free. In his psychodrama, Bobby will play himself. Alice, another group member, will play Bobby's mother, and Smitty will take the role of Bobby's *alter ego*—the angry person inside Bobby. The alter ego wants independence and despises Bobby for not being able to achieve it. The director will control the action, keeping it on track and protecting the actors from becoming so emotionally involved that they might be harmed.

Psychodrama sometimes uses trained actors experienced in therapy to get the scene started. The therapist-director usually limits the patients to roles they have experienced personally or to those they would normally fear or avoid. Patients might start a scene playing themselves and then be asked to "reverse" roles and play the other person in the same scene. You can see the psychodrama at work in this scene. Suzy is the protagonist, free for once to talk openly

After many sessions with her psychopoetry group, M.B. was able to express her new sense of awareness and confidence:

At the Beauty Parlor

Inside there is something stilled
I am quiet
after many sleepless
days.
I've bought a gown of blood red.
I know what jewels I want to wear.
I am performing in one single line of
black.
What is this quiet?
Is it all right to stop?
To grasp this piece of me?
May I parade it for a night?
My hair dries quietly.
Soon I shall be
crowned.

Another group member wrote about her feeling of renewal and growth:

I like blue, green
blue-green, new-green
soft hard, light dark
in the park
woods trees, spring breeze
first snow
I'm going to grow.

Why not try putting your own feelings into a poem? You don't have to worry about rhyme or meter. Just write what you feel inside.

to her husband, played by another group member.

Suzy [*speaking to her husband about their children*]: I've been having difficulty with John again. I wish you would talk to him about picking on Marie. He will not leave her alone. I find it is all becoming too much to handle by myself.

Husband: They will work it out themselves. I'll talk to them tomorrow [*yawning*].

Director: Is that the way it was?

Suzy: No, not exactly.

Director [*to Suzy and "husband"*]: Reverse roles.

Suzy [*as husband: Looks up impatiently from newspaper "he" has been reading*]: You make too much out of it. They are just like all kids. You are as capable as I am in dealing with these little arguments. [*"He" continues reading.*]

Director: Reverse roles.

Suzy [*as herself*]: You seem more concerned about your paper and the TV than about me. I'm left on my own to deal with all the dirty work. . . . [*Her emotions rise to the surface.*] I guess I'm trying to say I feel lonely. Somehow we don't communicate. I feel I'm losing you, and I can't handle the children without your support. I feel myself isolated from them as well. . . .

Director: How do you feel?

Suzy: All right—not nearly as tense.

Director [*to "husband"*]: Could you share with Suzy as her husband?

Husband [*to Suzy*]: You made me feel guilty. I could feel your anger. Then later I suddenly felt very warm toward you.

Suzy: That makes me feel better because I really love you.*

When psychodrama works well, the patient-actors gain the same kinds of insight into the causes of their behavior as occur in psychoanalysis. The other group members tend to identify with the protagonist and often gain insight into their own feelings. After the role playing is over, the therapist leads the group in a discussion of the day's session, thus giving the members a chance to relate their new insights to the real world outside.

Encounter groups

Encounter groups come in all shapes and sizes. At different times they have been called *confrontation groups, sensitivity groups, human-relations groups, personal-growth groups, human-potential groups,* and so on.

Unlike more traditional therapies, encounter groups appeal mostly to people who want more joy, warmth, and growth in their lives. Other encounter members join because they sense that they have lost contact

*Jacob L. Moreno and Dean G. Elefthery, "An Introduction to Group Psychodrama," in George M. Gazda, ed., *Basic Approaches to Group Psychotherapy and Group Counseling* (Springfield, IL: Charles C. Thomas, 1968), pp. 82–86.

with themselves and the world around them. For these people, the group experience promises honest interpersonal relations, self-discovery, and an escape from isolation. This aspect of the encounter movement grew out of humanist psychology's emphasis on self-awareness and growth. Although encounter-type groups can be found in almost every large and small community in the country, the original groups began at Esalen in Big Sur, California. There psychologists such as Abraham Maslow, Fritz Perls, and Carl Rogers pioneered the movement.

Most encounter groups range in size from eight to twenty members, plus a therapist or leader. Many groups meet for a limited number of hours or days, then disband. During the sessions, the groups generally focus on the "here and now." They discard the usual social manners and deliberately set out to strip away the polite masks that people hide behind. The leader's job is to zero in on the "unfinished business" in each person's life. If you are in a group, you are not permitted to evade responsibility for your feelings. Everything you say must be open and honest, with nothing held back.

Encounter groups depend heavily upon *sensory-awareness games* as a way of pushing people toward self-awareness. These "games for grown-ups" require group members to "be" or do any number of exercises or activities (see Figure 9.11). Some games are fun, others are challenging, and a few can embarrass the shy members of the group. In *Own Your Own Life*, Richard Abell describes his experiences during a sensory-awareness exercise at an encounter workshop:

> "Each of you take a sheet," Gloria said. "You are to be born under the sheet; feel what

Figure 9.11

Encounter groups provide activities designed to help people develop a richer, more satisfying outlook on life. What do you think these workshop members are learning about themselves in this awareness exercise?

it's like just to be born; begin to move around and explore the environment and gradually grow up." . . .

I got under my sheet. "Now imagine that you are being born." I curled up in the fetal position and made little whimpering noises and felt completely helpless. It was a good feeling, feeling helpless and not feeling afraid.

"Now begin to move around with your sheet over you, just a little at a time, and explore the environment." I began to move my body, my hands, my feet, still lying down. Then I began slowly crawling around. . . . I tried to take the point of view of a baby toward the end of the first year, for whom the world is new, unexplored.

"Now move more, until you bump into something or someone. Then explore that," Gloria said. . . . I bumped into a big irregular object, very muscular and solid. A man. . . I kept on bumping for about fifteen minutes until I was beginning to feel pretty grownup. Just before the exercise ended, I had the impulse to grab the last girl I bumped into and roll over and over again in the deep grass, down the slight hill that we were on. I did, and we laughed. I was still under my sheet and couldn't see her.

Later, as group members discuss their feelings, insights emerge. People begin to express their emotions more openly. If a man says, "My wife left me and I feel lonely," several women may go to him and hug him. A woman who believes she's homely will be reassured that she has many attractive qualities. Encounter language often becomes vivid and unrestrained, but as long as the leader thinks it's honest, nothing is censored. After several sessions of such open expression of feelings, many participants say that for the first time in their lives they understand the inner forces that keep them from being truly happy.

Does encounter work? Not all psychologists applaud the encounter movement, however. One complaint centers on the old question that applies to all therapies: Is it useful? A study at Stanford University yielded mixed results. Of 170 students who joined one or another of 18 encounter groups headed by well-trained leaders, almost 60 percent of the participants judged themselves as having changed. But 52 percent of the control group reported the same thing, even though they did not take part in an encounter activity.

Since no therapy helps everyone who tries it, that mixed result might be rated as consistent with other therapies. But the same study showed that 10 percent of the participants had been hurt by the encounter process. These casualties ranged from damaged self-esteem to mental breakdowns. Most of the casualties resulted from verbal "attacks" on the individuals by group leaders. One student reported, "The leader dismissed me and my whole life." Another said sadly, "The leader said I was on the verge of schizophrenia." Other surveys have uncovered instances where group members have been physically abused during encounter sessions. In short, encounter is no magic road to mental health. (See Figure 9.12 for some rules to follow when you're thinking about joining a group.)

Typical encounter groups. Among the hundreds of exotic encounter groups meeting today, three represent the range and vitality of this approach to psychotherapy: T-groups, Gestalt groups, and marathon groups.

1. *T-groups.* The *T* in *T-groups* stands for *training*. Psychologist Kurt Lewin designed T-groups as a way of training people to do a better job of coping with their job or life situation. A group of new college students, for example, might form a T-group as a way of preparing for the demands of academic and dormitory life. The T-group leader organizes the group and provides the information and exercises, which focus on human relations skills. The group members share their personal feelings, fears, and insights. This shared experience often provides each member with a new self-confidence in his or her ability to face the challenge ahead.

2. *Gestalt therapy groups.* Frederick "Fritz" Perls (see BioBox, page 275) almost

Figure 9.12

HOW TO CHOOSE A GROUP EXPERIENCE: LOOK BEFORE YOU LEAP

A successful group experience can change your life—or it can leave you more unhappy than when you started. The following rules will help protect you from bad experiences.

1 Never respond to a newspaper ad. The best groups, run by trained professionals, do not advertise in newspapers.

2 Never take part in a group of less than six members, nor of more than sixteen. Small groups do not develop the necessary group interactions, and large groups cannot be properly controlled.

3 Never join an encounter group on impulse. Important decisions deserve careful thought. If you suspect that you may be on the edge of a breakdown, seek regular psychotherapy instead.

4 Never join a group with close friends, schoolmates, or business associates. Insist that everything said in the group remain confidential.

5 Never stay with a group that insists that everyone *be* something—whether that identity is political, artistic, or intellectual. You deserve the chance to follow your own goals and to seek your own self-expression.

6 Never join a group whose leader does not possess proper credentials or training. Far too many well-meaning but poorly prepared amateurs have been attracted to the encounter movement.

single-handedly made Gestalt therapy one of the most popular of all group therapies. Perls took from traditional Gestalt psychology the idea that any unsatisfied need creates tension. Just as you automatically tend to fill in the gap left in the circle shown here, you probably feel compelled to complete a task or fulfill a need that you haven't attended to.

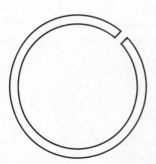

In a healthy person, needs emerge, are satisfied, and disappear. This process, Gestalt psychologists say, is continuous. Each need is met in turn. For example, young Derrick may be watching television. The screen absorbs his attention. But his gestalt (sense of completeness) does not last. His back starts itching. At first he ignores it, but the itching continues. An incomplete gestalt—the need to remove the discomfort—now becomes the center of his attention. Once he finds a backscratcher and removes the itch, he can go back to his program—until another need emerges that must be taken care of, such as his mother calling him to dinner.

Gestalt therapists define neurotic behavior as confusion over how to respond to each new need. They say that this confusion

BioBox
FRITZ PERLS:
"I AM NOT IN THIS WORLD TO LIVE UP TO OTHER PEOPLE'S EXPECTATIONS"

When Frederick S. Perls (1893–1970) arrived in the United States from Europe in 1946, he looked very much like what he was—a psychoanalyst well trained in Freudian theory. He sported a carefully tended mustache, white spats, and cane. Twenty years later, Perls wore a full beard, love beads, and a jump suit. He had become the "guru" of a new and influential nonanalytic therapy called Gestalt. To his group sessions at Esalen in California came twenty-five thousand people a year to undergo an intense emotional experience.

If Fritz Perls demanded openness, honesty, and cooperation from his group members, he worked hard at applying the same standards to himself. But he was not a simple person. He could be wise and earthy, loving and spiteful, wildly outgoing and intensely personal. His wife, after their separation, referred to him as "half prophet and half bum." Perls rather liked the description, and perhaps it helps explain the enormous appeal of his therapy.

Perls wrote colorfully and well about his theories. For example, he saw the parent-child relationship differently from most other psychologists:

> Possibly the most difficult mental feat for any patient is to forgive his parents. Parents are never right. They are either too stern or too soft, too strong or too weak. There is always something wrong with parents. And the balance between guilt feelings (that he owes them something) and resentment (that they owe him something) is achieved by a very peculiar phenomenon — gratefulness. Gratefulness leads to closure. Neither party owes the other anything. . . .

Responsibility also plays a major role in Perls' thinking. He described the need to take responsibility for yourself in these words:

> Full identification with yourself can take place if you are willing to take full responsibility — response-ability — for yourself, for your actions, feelings, thoughts; and if you stop mixing up responsibility with obligation. . . . You are responsible only for yourself. *I* am responsible only for *myself*. This is what I tell a patient right away. If he wants to commit suicide, that's his business. If he wants to go crazy, that's his business. . . . But I am not in this world to live up to other people's expectations, nor do I feel that the world must live up to mine.

Fritz Perls loved a good argument. If you disagree with his ideas, do you think he'd be upset? What would you say to him if he were standing beside you right now?

Reprinted by permission of the authors and publisher from Joen Fagan & Irma Lee Shepherd's *Gestalt Therapy Now* (Science and Behavior Books Inc. Palo Alto, CA 1970).

Figure 9.13

THE GESTALT PRAYER

I do my thing, and you do your thing.
I am not in this world to live up to your expectations
And you are not in this world to live up to mine.
You are you and I am I,
And if by chance we find each other, it's beautiful.
If not, it can't be helped.

Source: Frederick S. Perls, *Gestalt Therapy Verbatim* (© Real People Press, 1969. All rights reserved).

takes three forms. Some people have poor perception of their own bodies. Such people will literally not "see" what troubles them. Other individuals are unable to express their needs openly. Lillian may need love, for example, but not know how to ask for it. Still others repress feelings through muscular tension. These people often contract their facial muscles and tense their hands, arms, and shoulders to prevent themselves from speaking angrily to those around them.

Perls geared his therapy to put people in touch with these blocked emotions. He combined elements of psychoanalysis, Gestalt concepts of treating the "whole person," and existential ideas of "here-and-now" reality. Perls strongly believed that too many people live in the past ("Oh, I wish I'd done that") or in the future ("Someday I'll be able to do that"). In his therapy sessions, he insisted on getting in touch with the real needs that must be met before a person can feel whole again. The Gestalt prayer (Figure 9.13) sums up this aspect of Perls' philosophy.

The Gestalt therapist pays close attention to posture, movements, gestures, and involuntary sounds. The "why's" of behaviors are of little concern. Exercises in awareness help the group members regain contact with their blocked feelings. The therapist might ask a woman to complete the sentence, "At this time I'm aware that. . . ." Or a man might be told to conduct a dialogue between the opposing sides of his personality. Perls said that everyone has these warring voices—the *topdog* and the *underdog*. Topdog is the stern voice of conscience and duty. By contrast, the tricky, submissive underdog tries to explain away the failures that fill everyone's life.

In a typical Gestalt session, someone like June will take the center stage. The therapist will suggest a subject for a dialogue. Then June will sit on a stool and start by having her topdog say, "Get to work, dummy." After topdog has spoken, she will shift stools and respond to topdog's complaints. "I can't, I've been sick," her underdog might reply. The therapist will guide her dialogue, alternately babying her, threatening her, and scolding her. The aim is to push June through the blocks that keep her from expressing her honest feelings. If she fights back, the therapist may ask her to play the role of therapist in order to better voice the criticism she feels.

Figure 9.14

The Daytop Village "hot seat" provides a tough encounter approach to treating drug addiction. While on the hot seat, addicts are stripped of all defenses so that they can begin to accept responsibility for their actions. Why does this "pressure-cooker" method work with addicts when conventional therapies fail?

3. *Marathon groups.* During the mid-1960s, some encounter-group leaders decided that faster breakthroughs to self-awareness could be made if the encounter experiences were lengthened. As a result, *marathon groups* meet for prolonged sessions of up to forty-eight hours. Participants remain together for the entire marathon. No time for sleep is provided, and meals are taken as part of the group's ongoing activity. Under the stress caused by lack of sleep and constant group interaction, weary participants forget their usual social roles and speak freely of their feelings. In this emotional confrontation, old barriers to interaction break down. People weep, laugh, hug, fight, scream, and lash out at each other.

At the end of the marathon, many participants report feeling a great sense of catharsis, as if they had finally been able to release years of built-up emotions. Follow-up studies, however, show that the insights gained during marathons tend to disappear when people return to their regular lives. Critics also caution against the intensity of the marathon experience. People who seem otherwise under control may be tipped over into neurotic or psychotic behavior by emotional experiences too strong for them to handle.

Addiction group therapies

No individual- or group-therapy system has had much success with the treatment of addicts. Whether the individual is addicted to drugs, alcohol, or food, something more than psychoanalysis or encounters is needed. To fill this need, several *addiction group therapies* have been developed. Two of the

best known are Daytop Village and Alcoholics Anonymous.

Daytop Village. Conventional methods of treating drug addicts have been largely ineffective. Over 90 percent of the patients released from U.S. Public Health Service hospitals fall back into their habits within two or three years. At Daytop Village, a live-in treatment facility on New York's Staten Island, 75 percent of the addicts who stay more than three months never return to drugs. The Daytop philosophy works because it was developed by ex-addicts. Everyone on the staff is a former junkie, so new residents can't get away with the well-polished lies that they have always used to excuse their addiction.

Therapy at Daytop centers on a group-therapy technique known as the "pressure cooker" (see Figure 9.14). Three times a week, residents take a turn on the "hot seat." Let's say it's Alan's turn today. As a new resident, Alan might begin by explaining why he turned to drugs. He explains about his abusive parents, the poor neighborhood he grew up in, and—but Sylvia breaks in. "Alan, we know why you're a junkie! It's because you're *stupid!*" she shouts at him. Others join in. Alan has no choice but to submit to these attacks. He withers under criticism of his former life, his personal habits, his excuses. But Alan will soon learn that the violent criticism is offered out of love, in the hope that his life can be saved. He also knows that no one escapes the "hot seat," not even the manager of the facility.

Daytop people estimate that it takes a year and a half to two years to transform a drug addict into a responsible human being. For many former junkies, Daytop represents the first time in their lives that they have accepted responsibility for their own actions. Surrounded by caring people, working at useful tasks within the house, addicts begin to grow out of their immature, empty ways. Not everyone who enters can take the pressure. Within a month, 8 percent leave, and another 17 percent drop out before the 90-day mark. But those who stay have a chance to rebuild their lives and move on to normal lives on the outside.

Alcoholics Anonymous. Every member of Alcoholics Anonymous is a reformed alcoholic, including the leaders. Like Daytop Village, AA does not seek out its members. Instead, alcoholics must want help badly enough to attend their first meeting. At that first session, as at all AA meetings, alcoholics tell about the misery that liquor caused them and their families. Often with tears in their eyes, they tell how they found a fresh life through AA. This testimony gives hope to new members, who are encouraged to concentrate on remaining sober, one day at a time. Alcoholics must admit that they are powerless over alcohol and that they must give themselves up to a power greater than themselves.

The American singer Lillian Roth overcame her alcoholism with the help of AA. Here she describes her first testimony at an AA meeting:

> I stood up. I had faced many audiences without qualms. This was the toughest appearance I had to make. I couldn't act. . . . This was the real me on display for the first time in my life.
>
> Stammeringly I tried to tell about myself. These are all my blood brothers in the audi-

ence, I thought. We all suffer from the same illness, and these talks we give are our blood transfusions to one another. We all have an incurable disease—alcoholism.

> "I can't get up here and tell you I'm a happy person," I said. "But I am sober. I am trying to contact God as I understand Him. I don't yet have the peace of mind I know many of you have, but I'm told that if I hold on, it will come. . . ."
>
> I was limp when I sat down. "What a beautiful talk," one woman said. A girl approached me. "This is my first meeting," she confided. "You don't know how you've encouraged me. I have such a terrible alcoholic problem. I looked at you and I thought, 'If she can do it, after what she's gone through, I can do it, too.' "
>
> Her words left me with a warm glow. Was this what they meant when they said I would be happy again? Because I had helped someone?

AA also promotes the "buddy system." Members need only pick up a phone and ask for help, and nearby AA'ers will soon arrive to support them during a difficult time. This mutual support has helped create an international network of AA chapters. Nor have the families of alcoholics been forgotten. Al-Anon provides support for the wives and husbands of alcoholics, and Alateens gives special attention to the needs of adolescents who live with alcoholic parents or guardians.

Not every alcoholic who joins AA remains with the program. Some find the emphasis on religious faith difficult to accept. Others are not ready to face the problems that alcohol helps them hide from. But of every hundred alcoholics who attend at least seven AA meetings, seventy-five will never take another drink.

SECTION CHECKUP

1 Summarize some of the strengths and weaknesses of group therapies.

2 Describe what happens at a psychodrama session. Why would psychodrama probably not work for a drug addict or an alcoholic?

3 Who would be better suited for an encounter group: a man with a phobia about snakes or a woman who is having difficulty relating to her family?

4 What do Gestalt therapists mean when they say, "I am not in this world to live up to your expectations"?

9.4 WHERE CAN TROUBLED PEOPLE GO FOR HELP?

Let's say it's four in the morning and your phone rings. Your friend Ginny is on the other end. She sounds upset, frightened about something. You know she's been having trouble with her personal life. Out of her confused story of growing nervousness, sleeplessness, and general depression, you finally figure out what she's saying. Ginny feels as though she can't cope with her problems any more, that she may be having a "nervous breakdown." Her parents are out of town and she's turned to you for advice on where to go for help.

What can you tell her? You vaguely know that your community has resources for people with emotional problems. But where? Is there anyone Ginny can turn to at four o'clock in the morning? Your first task is to help Ginny regain control. You might be able to do this on the phone, or you may have to go and stay with her for a while. Just knowing that someone cares will probably help her get through the night.

Next, you can help Ginny and her parents choose a place to go for counseling or for therapy. The following section describes the most typical mental health services.

Community resources

Most mental-health problems can be taken care of close to home without hospitalization or lengthy therapy. Some agencies are publicly funded and provide their services without charge. Private doctors and clinics charge the "going rate," although some may offer their services on an ability-to-pay basis. With the help of your telephone directory, the area Mental Health Association, a community referral service, a local minister or doctor, or through friends, you can locate an appropriate place for Ginny.

Crisis intervention. If Ginny were threatening suicide, or if her condition seemed desperate, you would want immediate help. Most towns and cities today have one or more *hot lines*, some of which operate around the clock. These telephone services are staffed by trained volunteers, who can give advice and a sympathetic ear to anyone who calls. Most hot lines also make referrals, that is, they direct the caller to an appropriate agency for more in-depth counseling. Some hot lines specialize in particular problems, such as suicide prevention or helping rape victims.

A few hospitals provide emergency mental health services along with their regular medical care. If the hospital doesn't have a mental health unit, however, it may not

Figure 9.15

Ginny has decided that she can no longer cope with her feelings of anxiety and depression. If she asked you for help, what would you tell her?

have qualified doctors on duty. Call ahead, and make sure the staff can handle Ginny's needs. In addition, *community mental-health centers* often offer emergency services. Most are connected with a general hospital and serve a specific geographic area. Because they are funded by state and federal money, their services are usually free or low-cost. But they also tend to be busy and impersonal. Ginny may have to wait several hours before a doctor is available to see her.

Most family doctors and clergymen are trained today in crisis intervention. It helps if they know Ginny personally, but their skills and knowledge of other mental-health resources can be invaluable during an emergency situation.

Counseling services. If Ginny's problems do not need emergency attention, you might help her find a counseling service where she can talk to a trained mental-health worker. Counseling services have become much more available in recent years as the need for them has grown. If Ginny is in school, a school counselor will be available to talk with her about her problems. Most school counselors specialize in educational counseling, however, and may not be trained to handle complex emotional problems. Free clinics often offer personal counseling in addition to their medical services. Doctors and clergymen can also provide counseling services.

If Ginny has talked of suicide, a suicide prevention center may be available to work with her in dealing with her feelings. Similarly, rape crisis centers work with rape victims to support them through the emotional shock and legal proceedings that usually follow that crime of violence against women.

No exact line can be drawn between where counseling stops and therapy begins. In general, counseling is geared to short-term emotional problems and emergencies. Skilled counselors recognize the point at which their clients need referral to a psychotherapist. By the same token, counseling

services tend to be less expensive and more easily available than individual or group therapies. Vocational, marriage, and family counseling are also available in most communities.

Private psychotherapists and clinics. If Ginny wants to get into more intensive therapy, she will have to choose between a private psychotherapist and a clinic. Private therapists work alone or in groups. They are in business for themselves and usually do not accept patients who cannot afford their fees. Clinics, on the other hand, are organizations that employ therapists, social workers, and counselors for the purpose of providing mental-health care. Some operate on a private basis with a regular schedule of fees. Other clinics receive support from public funds or charities and can offer their services on an ability-to-pay basis. Most people prefer private therapists to clinics, but excellent care can be found in both situations. Ginny will have to make up her mind on the basis of cost, availability of treatment, and the type of therapy with which she feels most comfortable.

Mental hospitals

Ginny may not need to enter a mental hospital for her problems, but one American in ten will spend time in a mental hospital during his or her lifetime. What will these troubled people find when they get to the hospital? Some will find pleasant, well-managed facilities. Professional staffs of doctors, nurses, and orderlies will provide individual and group therapy sessions, medical care, occupational therapy, recreation and social events, home visits, and frequent contact with the outside world. The best hospitals clearly project a sense of being part of a healing community.

Not all hospitals match that bright picture. For every quality facility, another stands as a living monument to society's ability to ignore the needs of the mentally ill. Kenneth Donaldson found that out in 1957 when he was sent to a state hospital for "observation." It took Donaldson fifteen years to obtain his release after being diagnosed as a paranoid schizophrenic. During that time he was kept in a locked ward, denied the right to go outside, and refused occupational therapy. Donaldson's doctors apparently believed that his attempts to obtain a release from the hospital marked him as mentally ill! Donaldson later sued the state, and his $38,500 award was upheld by the U.S. Supreme Court. The Court ordered that no one may be confined against his or her will unless it is for the purpose of treatment. Only in cases where patients are dangerous or unable to care for themselves may they be kept in the hospital.

But the Donaldson case has not ended neglect in many state and private hospitals. Costs per patient now average over $20,000 a year, and mental patients have a low priority when tax dollars are distributed. As a result, overworked doctors and nurses may depend too heavily on tranquilizing drugs to keep patients quiet. Hospital workers, particularly the orderlies who clean the wards and care for the patients on a daily basis, are often poorly paid and undertrained. As a consequence, those who do remain to work under these conditions may be careless at best and sadistic at worst. Newspapers sometimes publicize such scandals (see Figure 9.16), but efforts at reform too often die for want of adequate funding.

Hospital treatment. Once admitted, patients receive a wide variety of treatment, depending on the type of hospital. At the bottom of the scale, they may receive little more than the basics of food, clothing, and a bed. In these hospitals, described so vividly in Ken Kesey's novel *One Flew Over the Cuckoo's Nest* people are treated as objects rather than human beings. The nurses and orderlies have little time to spend in personal contact with patients beyond handing out medication and maintaining order. Visits from the staff psychologist are brief and infrequent. Most recreation comes from a television set. Organized sports, games, outings, and occupational therapy are

THE NIGHT NURSE

Figure 9.16

largely ignored. All too often, moderately disturbed patients become worse under these conditions. Boredom, loneliness, anxiety, and adverse reactions to medications all contribute to the decay of people warehoused in such hospitals.

At better hospitals, however, pleasant physical surroundings, a dedicated staff, and individually prescribed therapy all play a role in shortening the time patients spend there. A good hospital may be public or private, large or small. What seems to count most is an enlightened attitude toward patient care and an adequate budget to run the facility. In such hospitals, the following treatment techniques will be used.

1. *Psychotherapy.* Staff psychologists provide individual- and group-therapy sessions for the patients. The type of therapy may range from analytic techniques to behavior modification, depending on the needs of the patients and the philosophy of the hospital administration. Typically, patients see their therapists two or three times a week and may also be involved in group sessions. Many hospitals emphasize *milieu therapy*, which means that the hospital envi-

ronment itself becomes part of the therapy. Good milieu therapy involves the patients in organizing and administering the social activities within the hospital. This approach keeps patients active who might otherwise become withdrawn when faced by the boredom of hospital routine.

2. *ECT and psychosurgery*. Electroconvulsive therapy (ECT) and psychosurgery (brain surgery) are both used in the hospital setting. Electric shock remains a popular treatment for severely depressed patients despite its possible side effects (see Pro & Con, page 242). But if ECT only occasionally does permanent harm, psychosurgery almost always changes the patient's personality. Psychosurgery was once a common treatment for conditions of abnormal excitement or uncontrolled outbursts of anger. The use of surgery to change behavior has been drastically reduced, however, since a 1977 study of psychosurgery by a national commission alerted both government and public to its dangers. This type of surgery should not be confused with necessary procedures for the removal of diseased or injured brain tissue, as in the case of tumors or head injuries.

3. *Drug therapy*. The introduction of tranquilizers and other *psychoactive* (behavior-changing) *drugs* in the 1950s changed the course of modern psychotherapy. Between 1969 and 1974, for example, the number of patients in American mental hospitals dropped by 50 percent—from 500,000 to 250,000. With the help of properly prescribed drugs, many of these patients were able to resume their normal lives.

Today, drug therapy has become a standard part of psychotherapy in and out of hospitals. Most therapists use drugs in combination with more traditional therapies. Unfortunately, these powerful drugs can also be abused. Budget-starved hospitals sometimes overdose their patients to keep them quiet. Such patients don't make much trouble for the staff, but neither do they get well.

The most commonly used drugs fall into two types: calming (tranquilizing) drugs and antidepressant drugs. Agitated or violent patients who once would have been restrained in padded cells or wrapped in wet sheets can now be treated effectively with tranquilizers. The major tranquilizers include such drugs as chlorpromazine (Thorazine) and haloperidol (Haldol). These powerful drugs are used only for severe emotional problems. The major tranquilizers relieve panic, delusions, and other types of disturbed thinking. Side effects include drowsiness, dizziness, weight gain, and restlessness. Proper dosage usually controls these problems.

Minor tranquilizers include chlordiazepoxide (Librium) and diazepam (Valium). These tranquilizers relieve anxiety quite effectively and do not reduce mental alertness when taken in proper dosages. Side effects from minor tranquilizers are rare, but many people have developed a drug dependency habit following prolonged usage. These "Valium addicts" suffer withdrawal symptoms when they try to end their dependency.

Antidepressant drugs have mushroomed in number and popularity. Originally, the amphetamines were used to treat depression, but their potential for abuse made them a poor choice. Today, the preferred antidepressants include such drugs as imipramine (Tofranil and Imavate) and amitriptyline (Elavil). These drugs relieve depression in many people, although some depressed patients do not respond to them. Side effects are generally mild. Lithium carbonate (Eskalith) has sometimes proved successful for manic-depressive conditions and cases of repeated, long-term depression.

4. *Occupational and recreational activities*. Well-run hospitals provide a number of additional activities for patients as part of milieu therapy. Workshops and training programs in fine arts, homemaking, and crafts encourage self-expression and build

self-esteem. Dances, field trips, sports activities, and frequent contact with the outside world keep patients alert and encourage social interaction. Some hospitals also offer educational programs to enable patients to earn high-school or college credits. Family members are encouraged to visit often, and home visits for qualified patients often mark the first step toward a return to life outside the hospital.

The halfway house. In 1955, only one in four mental patients could be treated on an outpatient basis. By the mid-1970s, two out of three were able to live at home and continue working while undergoing therapy. In many cities, halfway houses have been established to help patients make the transition from the hospital to life at home. Like mental hospitals, not all halfway houses receive proper funding. Many are little better than skid-row hotels. The best, however, provide a much-needed service.

Twenty-eight-year old Chester W.'s experiences illustrate how a well-run facility can help. When Chester realized that he could no longer cope with his overwhelming feelings of anxiety, he voluntarily signed himself into a state mental hospital. After two months of rest and therapy, he felt much more in control. The tranquilizer he was taking controlled his anxiety, and his weekly therapy sessions put him in better touch with his feelings.

Anxious to return to work but still not ready to live on his own, Chester next moved to a halfway house run by the county mental-health clinic. There he lived in a private apartment but received therapy and support from a specially trained staff. He made new friends in the well-equipped lounge and crafts shop. He returned to his old job, but without the pressure of taking complete care of himself. Gradually, his doctor decreased the dosage of his tranquilizer.

Six months after his initial breakdown, Chester was ready to return to his own home. For the first time in years, he was free of his crippling anxieties.

SECTION CHECKUP

1 If a friend asked you for help in finding a source of mental-health care in your community, where would you send that person?

2 Contrast the treatment given in a good mental hospital with that found in a poor one.

3 Why have drug therapies become such an important part of modern psychotherapy? Why do mental-health experts worry about the widespread use of minor tranquilizers to treat "everyday" anxiety?

LOOKING BACK: A SUMMARY

1 Throughout history, many different explanations have been advanced to explain disturbed behavior. According to the demonological model, mental illness was caused by evil spirits that invaded the body. In the religious model, emotional problems were viewed as punishment for sins against God. Later, more scientific explanations centered on the medical and the toxin model, according to which mental illnesses were believed to start with organic brain dysfunctions or with poisonous substances in the body. Finally, believers in the psychosocial model point to environmental forces that cause conflicts between individuals and their surroundings as the primary cause of most mental illness.

2 Only in modern times have the emotionally disturbed been treated with sympathy and understanding. Early treatments were painful and largely useless attempts at therapy. In the late 1700s Philippe Pinel began the movement to free mental patients from the chains and dungeons that had formerly been their lot. Dorothea Dix did the same for America's emotionally disturbed in the 1840s, when the first modern mental hospitals in this country were established.

3 Psychotherapy is the process of helping patients replace neurotic behaviors with more healthy responses to stress, anxiety, depression, and other symptoms. All established psychotherapies have certain qualities in common. Each provides support in time of crisis, screens patients for medical problems, develops catharsis (the release of tension), and attempts to resolve disturbed behavior.

4 Freudian psychoanalysis began the tradition of individual therapy, with its one-to-one relationship between therapists and patients. According to Freud, adult neurotic behavior begins when the sexual drives of the id come into conflict with the superego during childhood. Psychoanalysis tries to resolve this conflict through free association, transference, catharsis, and overcoming resistances. During the lengthy period of analysis, patient and analyst work together to overcome resistances that conceal the patient's deepest, most painful memories.

5 Later psychoanalysts placed less emphasis on sexual conflicts and more on cultural influences as the causes of disturbed behavior. Alfred Adler believed that therapy must help the patient recover lost feelings of self-worth as a way of overcoming feelings of inferiority. Harry Stack Sullivan pointed to interpersonal relationships as the cause of mental problems and tried to help his patients "see" people as they really are. Existential therapist Victor Frankl says that human beings develop neurotic behavior out of the frustration of not finding meaning in their lives. Only when people take responsibility for their decisions and make a commitment to something outside themselves can they return to mental health.

6 Another existential therapist, R. D. Laing, believes that only the insane are truly sane in what he sees as a crazy world. Laing believes that society uses mental illness as an excuse for locking up people who make the "normal" population uncomfortable. His therapy involves giving schizophrenics and other seriously disturbed people a life-support system that enables them to find their way down into madness and back again.

7 Client-centered therapy, as developed by Carl Rogers, concentrates on helping clients find their own path to self-awareness. Therapists use unconditional positive regard to assure their clients that they are valued human beings no matter what they have done in the past. Rogers also believes in a nondirective relationship between clients and therapists, so that clients will take the primary responsibility for changing their own self-defeating behaviors.

8 Behavior therapy is based on the theory that all behaviors, healthy and unhealthy, are learned responses to the environment. Behaviorist therapists pay little attention to unconscious motivation. They usually use operant conditioning techniques to cure specific phobias, compulsive behaviors, and the like.

9 Group therapies have grown in popularity in recent years. Each group acts as a miniature society, in which the interaction of therapist and patients brings about the needed changes in behavior. Most individual therapies also run group sessions using the basic techniques of that therapy system. All group therapies require that each member participate. This leads to self-knowledge that can become the first step toward more positive behaviors and attitudes.

10 A psychodrama group casts its members in roles and scenes taken directly from their own lives. The therapist directs the action and assigns the roles to be played. By acting out the scenes, participants gain insight into their feelings. This insight can lead to meaningful change under the guidance of the psychodrama leader.

11 Encounter groups challenge their members to grow and change through direct confrontation. They emphasize the here-and-now aspects of life and often use tough-minded techniques to force people to discard their defenses. T-groups are a type of encounter group designed to train people to deal with the challenges of new or changed life situations. Gestalt groups, developed by Frederick Perls, emphasize "how" over "why" and put group members in touch with their blocked-off feelings. Marathon groups are speeded-up encounters of twenty-four to forty-eight hours, during which group members work through their current life problems under the stress of enforced participation and fatigue.

12 Addiction group therapies deal with the difficult problems of drug and alcohol addiction. Daytop Village uses the stress of confrontation with other ex-addicts to force drug addicts to take responsibility for their own lives. This process of mutual caring also works at Alcoholics Anonymous, where ex-alcoholics testify about their past lives and provide one another with the support an alcoholic needs to stop drinking.

13 Most communities provide a number of places where troubled people can go for help. Crisis-intervention services are provided by hot lines in suicide-prevention centers, emergency facilities in hospitals and community mental-health centers, family doctors, and members of the clergy. Counseling for less immediate problems can be found in schools, clinics, and the like. Psychotherapy can be obtained from either private or public therapists and clinics, depending on need and the ability to pay.

14 Modern mental hospitals have come a long way from the grim asylums of the past. Physical conditions have been improved, patients stay for shorter times, and release rates are higher. Not all hospitals meet these standards, however. Low budgets and public apathy leave some state hospitals with overcrowded wards and overworked staffs. Patient care in the better hospitals includes traditional individual and group therapies, along with occupational and recreational activities. ECT and psychosurgery are still found in mental hospitals, although little psychosurgery is being done today. Drug therapy with tranquilizers and other psychoactive drugs has enabled many patients to return home with their behavior problems under control. Many drugs have side effects, however, and the temptation remains to overdose patients in order to keep them quiet. The halfway house has allowed many former mental patients to work their way back into every day life, by giving them support and therapy during the critical period when they first leave the mental hospital.

PUTTING YOUR KNOWLEDGE TO WORK

Terms you should know

addiction group therapies

behaviorist model

catharsis

client-centered therapy

demonological model

encounter groups

Gestalt therapy groups

group therapy

halfway house

hot lines

individual therapy

marathon groups

milieu therapy

neuropathological model

nondirective therapy

psychoactive drugs

psychoanalytic model

psychodrama

psychotherapist

psychotherapy

radical psychiatry

religious model

sensory-awareness games

T-groups

toxin model

unconditional positive regard

Objective questions

1 The first modern psychotherapist was (*a*) Ivan Pavlov (*b*) Sigmund Freud (*c*) Carl Rogers (*d*) B. F. Skinner.

2 Catharsis plays an important role in therapy because it allows the patient to (*a*) release tension (*b*) end phobic fears (*c*) get through therapy without the help of a therapist (*d*) overcome neurotic behaviors related to brain dysfunction.

3 A good therapist will (*a*) refuse to treat any patient who has committed a crime (*b*) help patients learn to solve their own emotional problems (*c*) never use psychoactive drugs (*d*) know that medical problems have nothing to do with disturbed behavior.

4 Which therapy system believes that patients can find meaning in their lives only if they take responsibility for their life choices? (*a*) Freudian psychoanalysis (*b*) behavior therapy (*c*) Frankl's existential therapy (*d*) Rogerian client-centered therapy.

5 A key requirement for client-centered therapists is that they give their clients (*a*) group encounter experiences (*b*) unconditional positive regard (*c*) time for free association (*d*) treatment for inferiority complexes.

6 The most rapid treatment for overcoming Nick's phobia about snakes would probably be (*a*) psychoanalysis (*b*) client-centered therapy (*c*) behavior modification (*d*) an encounter group.

7 A group therapy that would ask Lydia to act out a role based on her actual life problems is (*a*) a marathon encounter group (*b*) a psychodrama group (*c*) an Alcoholics Anonymous group (*d*) a T-group for young actors.

8 The type of therapy *least* concerned with an adult patient's childhood experiences would be (*a*) existential therapy (*b*) psychoanalysis (*c*) client-centered therapy (*d*) behavior modification.

9 Overcrowded, poorly staffed mental hospitals (*a*) never existed except in novels and films (*b*) no longer exist because mental patients are now cared for in halfway houses (*c*) exist only in underdeveloped countries where money is scarce (*d*) exist wherever the public turns its back on the mentally ill and refuses to provide adequate budgets for therapy.

10 The major danger Chet faces from prolonged use of a minor tranquilizer such as Valium is that he will (*a*) become dependent on the drug (*b*) suffer serious side effects (*c*) never be allowed to leave the hospital (*d*) lose all desire to carry on a normal life.

Discussion questions

1 Contrast the different approaches to psychotherapy based on the theories of Sigmund Freud and Carl Rogers. Which would you prefer if you were to undergo therapy? Why?

2 List the different explanations people have offered as to the cause of mental illness over the centuries. What type of therapy was developed for each of these models?

3 How does the idea of encounter groups fit the attitudes of today's society? What are some of the advantages and disadvantages to such groups?

4 Why do the Daytop Village and Alcoholics Anonymous approaches to addiction group therapy work where other therapies frequently do not?

5 Suppose you were on a state board investigating mental hospitals. What would you look for when you visited a hospital? What questions would you ask the hospital administrator? The staff? The patients?

6 Which of the therapies discussed in this chapter would be most effective in dealing with schizophrenia? Which would be least effective? Give reasons for your answers.

7 Many people have said that the Gestalt prayer (page 276) helps them by stating that they are not responsible for changing other people. But some critics point out that the last three lines seem to say that no one is responsible to anyone else. How do you feel about the Gestalt prayer? Does it lead to mental health or to greater selfishness?

Activities

1 If possible, arrange for a class visit to a mental-health facility in your area. Most hospitals provide guided tours of the wards, recreation rooms, and offices. Ask for a chance to talk to some of the patients. In many hospitals you will be encouraged to join in their games, read to them, or simply visit. Observe the care provided by the staff. Perhaps you can arrange in advance to talk with one of the staff psychologists about the therapy programs provided. Write a report of your experience. If you discover seriously deficient conditions, you should communicate your findings to your state mental-health commission and to your state legislator.

2 Alcoholics Anonymous meetings are held in almost every city of any size in the United States. Visitors are usually welcome, though you might want to check ahead of time. Try to discover what makes AA so effective. Listen to the testimonials, and talk to the members. What impressions do you come away with? A similar visit to a meeting of Overeaters Anonymous can also be interesting and instructive. Note the similarities and differences between the two organizations.

3 Find a friend or relative who is both a good listener and someone you respect. Tell that person that you want to talk about a personal problem. Pick a situation that is honestly bothering you. Share your feelings as openly as you can. Afterward, analyze the experience. Were you able to express your emotions clearly and honestly? How well did your partner listen? Were his or her remarks directive or nondirective? How could the situation be improved next time?

4 Work with your psychology teacher to invite a local psychiatrist or clinical psychologist to speak to your class. If the therapists in private practice are too busy, ask the school psychologist to come in. Suggest to your guest that he or she answer the following questions: "What type of training have you had? What kind of psychotherapy do you specialize in? Tell us about some typical patients you've worked with. What would you recommend as good mental-health advice?"

5 As an alternative to Activity 4, ask your psychology teacher about writing to Recovery, Inc., 116 S. Michigan Avenue, Chicago, IL 60603, to arrange for a demonstration panel. The panel will be made up of former mental patients. They will speak to your class on their therapy experiences and on Recovery, a self-help organization. You might also ask them to talk about their experiences since their illnesses. Do they feel discriminated against in social or work situations? Why are they willing to speak in public about their problems?

6 Do some research on the expanding use of psychoactive drugs in psychotherapy. Compare the advantages of such treatment with its possible dangers. Report to the class on your findings.

7 With the help of your psychology teacher, organize your class to survey the mental health facilities available in your community. Resources might include hospitals, mental-health clinics, community service organizations, hot lines, and special counseling programs provided by schools and churches. As a community service, your class can write up data on locations, hours, costs, and telephone numbers to mimeograph or print for distribution through school counselors, churches, city hall, and libraries. You'll probably be amazed at just how many resources are available to those who need help.

For further reading

Ehrenberg, Otto and Miriam Ehrenberg. *The Psychotherapy Maze: A Consumer's Guide to the Ins and Outs of Therapy.* New York: Holt, Rinehart & Winston, 1977. In this clearly written guide to getting the most out of a therapy situation, the problems and pitfalls of therapy are discussed, along with the values of each major type of therapy, individual and group.

Kesey, Ken. *One Flew Over the Cuckoo's Nest.* New York: Viking Press, 1962. This explosive novel hinges on the conflict between one man and a mental hospital that would rather keep patients sick than make them well. Tough-minded and profane, the novel's insights into hospital life are unforgettable, as is the Academy-award-winning film based on the novel.

Linder, Robert. *The Fifty-Minute Hour.* New York: Bantam, 1954. Lindner's fascinating case histories read more like fiction than fact. The role of the therapist comes through clearly in these dramatic accounts of five deeply disturbed patients.

Mishara, Brian and Robert Patterson. *Consumer's Handbook of Mental Health.* New York: New American Library, 1977. This guidebook tells you everything you need to know about finding help for emotional problems. It is factual, up-to-date, and written to protect the people who pay the bills for mental health services.

Rubin, Theodore I. *Jordi, Lisa and David.* New York: Ballantine Books, Inc., a Division of Random House, Inc., 1975. These are powerful accounts of three cases of mental illness treated in a hospital setting. *Lisa and David* was made into a popular film. Watch for it to be rerun on your local TV stations.

Szasz, Thomas, ed. *The Age of Madness*. Garden City, NY: Doubleday, 1973. Szasz, a well-known critic of the psychiatric "establishment," attacks the commitment and treatment of the mentally ill in this collection of essays, first-hand accounts by patients, bits of fiction, and other interesting material. A typical Szasz comment: "When a man says he is Jesus or Napoleon, or that the Martians are after him, or claims something else that seems outrageous to common sense, he is labeled psychotic and locked up in the madhouse. Freedom of speech is only for normal people."

UNIT V

HOW PEOPLE LEARN

10

LEARNING, THINKING, AND DEVELOPING CREATIVITY

At age two, Mandy and Glenn spoke only a handful of words. They couldn't tie their shoes, write their names, or count past four.

Today, less than twenty years later, Mandy and Glenn have mastered language, shoe tying, arithmetic, and a thousand other complex skills. What happened in those in-between years isn't much of a mystery. With the help of their parents, teachers, and friends, they learned to cope with the world around them.

Psychologists have long been interested in the learning process. Much of their research is done with animals. Rats find their way through mazes, dolphins retrieve objects on command, cats escape from puzzle boxes, and dogs have their brain waves scanned. The psychologists' favorite animal for learning experiments, however, is the one closest in intelligence and physical abilities to Mandy and Glenn—the chimpanzee.

One line of research has centered on teaching chimps to talk. If chimps can learn to communicate, learning psychologists reason, the experiments will have accomplished two useful tasks. Science will know more about language development in human beings, and the barrier to communication between humans and animals might finally be overcome. Early experiments, however, proved that chimps can't duplicate human speech. Only when they were introduced to sign language did the chimps build up usable vocabularies.

But is this "chimp talk" the equal of human speech? Skeptics point out that dogs can be taught to "count" on command and parrots can mimic dozens of words and phrases. They want proof that the sign messages between chimpanzees and their trainers are more than a clever trick.

Psychologist Maurice Temerlin thinks his "daughter" Lucy will help answer that question. Temerlin and his wife, Jane, adopted Lucy as a four-day-old baby in 1966 and raised her as their own daughter. The family lived, played, ate, and studied together in the Temerlins' Oklahoma home. Lucy learned her language lessons with surprising speed, and she could tell people what she wanted quite clearly. What's unusual about that? Nothing, but most people seemed quite surprised when they met Lucy for the first time. Lucy Temerlin, you see, is a chimpanzee. Maurice Temerlin loves to talk about his adopted "daughter."

> I want to describe her typical day. . . . Lucy awakened at 7 A.M. after eight hours' sleep in a king-sized bed. . . . Still sleepy, she walked into the living room and sat on a Danish modern sofa while I fixed coffee for the three of us. Jane slept until the coffee was ready.
>
> Perked-up by the coffee, Lucy made a circular nest of sofa cushions on the floor and sat in it for half an hour, looking at *Time*, *Newsweek*, and the *National Geographic*. We keep them on the coffee table because they seem to be her favorites, . . . About the time she finished reading, Jane had her breakfast ready—a bowl of oatmeal to which raisins and

Figure 10.1

Lucy, raised by Maurice and Jane Temerlin as their "daughter," enjoys looking at magazines. Does Lucy's capacity for learning make her "human"?

beef protein powder had been added, and a glass of grape Tang.

After breakfast she went to her room and played alone for about an hour and a half. Then she was visited by [her teachers]. . . . After a half hour of language lessons they stopped for tea when Lucy went into the kitchen and started filling the teakettle with water. Lucy drank a cup of tea sweetened with honey. . . .

Jane came home about 5:00 and I saw my last client at 6:00. Then the three of us had a gin and tonic together sitting in the living room. Then Lucy [using sign language] invited Jane and me to chase her. I didn't feel like it and was grateful to see Steve and Nanuq [the Temerlins' son and his dog] drive up. So Nanuq and Lucy played chase; they took turns chasing one another about the house. . . .

Lucy . . . went to the refrigerator and helped herself to a carton of raspberry yogurt, a few bites of left-over pot roast, a carrot, half a carton of partially defrosted frozen strawberries, and took three or four bites out of a head of lettuce. Then she went back to the sofa, covered herself with her blanket, and fell asleep. . . .

From the time she was two years old it was clear to us—though we could not prove it at the time—that Lucy understood many of the words Jane or I uttered. . . . For example, Jane might fix bowls of ice cream covered with fruit for dessert. Lucy might then ignore hers and try to get a spoonful of Jane's or mine— even though they were all alike. If one of us said, "Eat your own," she then would do so.

Or, if she clearly was thirsty, I could say, "Get a cup and I'll fix you some tea," and she would open the right cabinet door, get a cup, and often bring me a tea bag from the pantry. . . .

Although Temerlin spent many hours with Lucy, her language training was left to psychologist Roger Fouts. Fouts is an expert in American Sign Language (ASL) and one of the pioneers in the chimpanzee language program. After teaching Lucy a new word, Fouts watched to see if she would apply that word to new situations.

For example, on three different occasions she learned a sign for *cry, food,* and *hurt.* Then, sometime later, she was shown a radish. When she bit into it she signed, "Cry hurt food." After that moment . . . when shown a radish she always signed either "Cry food" or "Hurt food" or "Cry hurt food." . . .

Shortly before a language lesson, when no one was looking, Lucy defecated [moved her bowels] in the middle of the living room floor. When Roger noticed the crime had occurred he turned to Lucy. Here is their verbatim conversation in ASL.

ROGER: "What's that?"
LUCY: "Lucy not know."
ROGER: "You do know. What's that?"
LUCY: "Dirty, dirty."
ROGER: "Whose dirty, dirty?"
LUCY: "Sue's." [Sue was another of Lucy's teachers.]
ROGER: "It's not Sue's. Whose is it?"
LUCY: "Roger's!"
ROGER: "No! It's not Roger's. Whose is it?"
LUCY: "Lucy dirty, dirty. Sorry Lucy."

This incident excited my imagination. Given the conceptual tool of language Lucy had told her first lie to avoid personal responsibility. She must have had a primitive concept of "good" and "bad" or she would not have lied; has Lucy taught us that "morality" is the mother of deceit?*

Along with the fun and excitement of watching chimps learn to "talk," psychologists are finding out about human learning as well. Most of the classic learning experiments, such as Pavlov's work with conditioned reflexes, start with animals. In time, new data about the process of thinking, memory, problem solving, and creativity find their way into psychology's ever-widening knowledge of human behavior. This chapter will introduce you to some of the important concepts in learning psychology.

10.1 HOW DO PEOPLE LEARN?

10.2 HOW DOES MEMORY WORK?

10.3 HOW DO PEOPLE THINK?

10.4 HOW CAN YOU IMPROVE YOUR LEARNING AND PROBLEM-SOLVING ABILITIES?

10.5 HOW CAN YOU IMPROVE YOUR CREATIVITY?

10.1 HOW DO PEOPLE LEARN?

Every summer, the American Field Service and Youth for Understanding send high-school students overseas to live with foreign families. Would you accept this once-in-a-lifetime opportunity to visit a different culture? A little hesitation would be understandable.

What if you were sent to Japan, for example? You'd want to learn at least a few words of the language. And you'd want to know about the social customs, the unusual foods, and novel ways of bathing and sleeping. That's a lot of learning to cram into a few weeks. Yet people cope with similar challenges all the time. Human beings, *Homo sapiens*, learn quickly.

Defining learning

Psychologists have long been interested in the learning process. *Learning*, by definition, is the lasting change in a person's behavior brought about by study, training, or experience. Temporary changes in behavior due to fatigue, drug use, or instinctive reactions don't count as learning. Nor is learning restricted to gaining new knowledge and skills. You also learn to grow as a person. This type of learning includes new ways of relating to other people; new insights into your goals and values; and new attitudes toward people, issues, and problems. On your trip to Japan, for example, your learning would be of three basic types.

1. You would learn new *information*. Before you came home again, you'd know something about vocabulary, geography, weather conditions, transportation, farming, and many other aspects of Japanese life and customs.

2. You would learn new *skills*. After some awkward fumbling, you'd learn how to use chopsticks. You might learn how to write your name in Japanese characters and how to wear the kimono. After a while, with your new skills, you'd begin to feel more comfortable in your Japanese surroundings.

3. Finally, you'd learn new *social behaviors*. Some of these would involve politeness and respect for tradition. You'd learn how to greet your Japanese family and how to act during the tea ceremony. But you'd also gain insights into your own ability to cope with change and newness. You'd learn to adjust to the different dating customs in Japan, for example, and you'd discover what it's like to be far from home without your family around you.

You don't have to travel to Japan to continue learning. Every day you have a chance

*Reprinted by permission of the author and the publisher from *Lucy: Growing Up Human*, by Maurice K. Temerlin. Palo Alto, CA. Science and Behavior Books Inc. 1972.

Figure 10.2

The challenge of mastering tennis calls on all the learning ability these young people can bring to their new sport. What skills, information, and social behaviors will be required before they learn to play well?

to grow as a person, to adjust to changes in your environment, to gather new information, to modify old skills and learn new ones. Not everyone learns at the same speed, however. Elliot may be a whiz at learning to play the drums, but he barely scrapes through in biology. Nettie picks up math quickly, but she's all thumbs around the kitchen.

Psychologists also know that children cannot learn certain skills or concepts before they are intellectually ready. Try as you might, you won't be able to teach five-year-old Bertie the concept of historical time. To Bertie, last week is about as long ago as 1066.

Even though psychologists know a lot about what and when people learn, they haven't reached any agreement yet on *how* learning takes place. There are two basic learning theories. One approach is called stimulus-response theory; the other is known as cognitive theory. Neither theory totally excludes the other, but each emphasizes different factors in a learning situation.

Stimulus-response theory

American learning psychologist Edward L. Thorndike published his first descriptions of the *stimulus-response (S→R) theory* of learning in 1898. Thorndike described learning as the relationship between a *stimulus* (any event or impulse) and a *response* (the

resulting behavior). He called the connection between stimulus and response a *bond*. When bonds are strengthened by repetition, they become habits or behavior patterns.

Thus, as a child you may have watched everyone else eating with forks while you had to make do with a spoon. In that case, the stimulus was the desire to feed yourself as everyone else did; the response was to eat with a fork. At first you probably had trouble picking up the food and putting each forkful safely in your mouth. But you kept at it, and soon you could stab peas and carrots with the best. Through repetition, you established a habit.

But, Thorndike adds, successful responses become habits. Unsuccessful responses will be extinguished (fade out). Think of the S → R learning that many children go through when they first pull a dog's tail. The tail is the stimulus; grabbing and pulling it is the response. But tail pulling doesn't become a habit because parents scold and dogs bite. After a few unsuccessful tries, the response fades out even though the stimulus remains.

Trial-and-error learning. Thorndike believed that most learning takes place through *trial and error*. When faced with a problem, he explained, people try different solutions until they find one that works. If a response works often enough, they make that response part of their permanent behavior.

Thorndike ran a series of experiments to prove this idea. He collected stray cats and put them inside puzzle boxes, which could be opened only when the cat pulled on a latch-string. Tempted by food placed outside the box, the cats mewed, scratched, and poked about until they accidentally released the latch. One cat, for example, took 230 seconds on the first trial. By the sixth trial, its time had improved, but only to 170 seconds. Then, on the seventh trial, it apparently learned the routine, for it escaped in 30 seconds. Thorndike concluded that the cat had learned from its earlier trial-and-error efforts. Later experiments with both animals and humans seemed to verify these results, at least for simple tasks.

Operant conditioning. E. L. Thorndike's theories dominated learning psychology through the 1930s, when B. F. Skinner's ideas about operant conditioning added an important new concept. (See also Chapter 7, pages 186–187.) Skinner identified two types of behavior: respondent and operant. *Respondent behavior* takes place, he said, when a specific stimulus causes an involuntary response in the subject. Respondent behavior is also known as *classical conditioning* and can be related back to Pavlov's landmark experiments (see Chapter 1, page 8). Pavlov's dogs salivated automatically at the smell of the meat powder. Their conditioned response to the sound of the bell was an automatic one, that is, they salivated when the bell rang whether they wanted to or not. In the same way, the pupil of your eye contracts in bright light. If someone hit C# on the piano every time a bright light was flashed in front of you, a respondent behavior would be established after six to ten repetitions. For some days afterward, your pupils would contract automatically whenever you heard a C#. Respondent behavior, therefore, is passive and mechanical. The appropriate stimulus will always cause the related response.

Skinner was much more interested in *operant behaviors.* Operant behaviors, he noted, are active. The individual must decide which behavior will gain the desired reward. A rat, for example, will learn to press a lever to gain a reward of food. Let's say that five levers are available, each a different color. Only the red lever will pro-

duce a food pellet. The rat now has a choice. It can press none of the levers, it can press them all, or it can press only the food-producing lever. As you might guess, the rat will choose to press the red lever and enjoy the reward. Skinner would say that it has voluntarily learned an operant behavior.

Most human behavior is operant, Skinner goes on, whether it is reading a book, playing a piano, or running for President. The important point, he says, is that human operant behaviors can be conditioned, just as the rat's choice of levers was conditioned by the lure of a reward. To understand just how that conditioning works, however, several additional principles of operant behaviors must be considered.

1. *Reinforcement.* According to behaviorist theory, operant behaviors depend upon rewards and punishments. *Rewards*, or *positive reinforcement*, tend to increase the chances that a particular behavior will be repeated, as you can see in a number

Figure 10.3

This rat is learning how to get food by pressing a lever in a special research cage known as a Skinner box. If the rat learns to press the lever whenever a light flashes, would you call that a respondent or an operant behavior? Why?

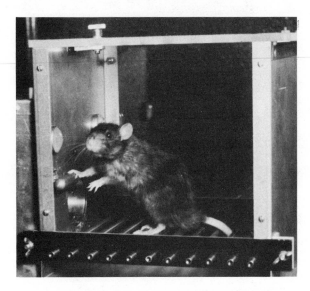

Figure 10.4

Different societies have always produced different kinds of people. What rewards and punishments do you think were used to train a generation of German youth to absolute obedience to Adolf Hitler? Could mass conditioning ever happen in the United States?

of ways. Teaching a dog to do a trick involves giving rewards for the desired behavior. Out of the thousands of movements a dog can make, it will learn to select those specific moves that you are rewarding. In this way, step by step, you can teach Prince to sit up, beg, roll over—or jump through a fiery hoop. The same principle works with people. Reward four-year-old Sophia for straightening up her room, and she'll be likely to do it again. In time, if the rewards continue, keeping her room neat will become a habit.

Punishment tends to extinguish operant behaviors. If you hit Prince every time he sits up, he'll soon stop sitting up. Training Prince with punishment instead of reward, however, will probably backfire. If he learns at all, it will probably be at the expense of developing several undesirable behaviors, such as barking, biting, or running away. Similarly, comparing Sophia unfavorably with her older sister's neater habits may cause her to stop taking care of her room entirely.

Even when rewards stop, operant behaviors don't extinguish immediately. Prince will still sit up every now and again, hoping for one more dog biscuit. That's one reason people hold on to nonproductive behaviors longer than they should. Unconsciously, they keep hoping that the rewards they once enjoyed will return.

2. *Signals.* Have you ever crossed a street against the red light? Even if you have, you probably hesitated for a moment, because the red light acted as a stimulus for a particular operant behavior—waiting until it's safe to cross. Many stimuli serve as signals for particular behaviors. Your alarm going off in the morning signals that it's time

to start the day. A bit of theme music on the television signals that your favorite program is about to start. In each case, the signal tells you that reinforcement is likely to follow. if you do the right thing.

Signals can also become generalized. You learned about red lights, perhaps, when you first began crossing streets. But now any red light tends to be generalized to mean, "Stop, avoid danger." Green lights give you the go-ahead to proceed, whether on the street or while you're operating a computer.

3. *Schedules of reinforcement.* Surprisingly enough, you can achieve more stable operant responses if you don't reward the behavior every time. Let's say that, after training Prince, you now reward him every fifth time he sits up. He'll soon learn that schedule and will work happily for reinforcement that comes only one time in five. Now, try an experiment. Stop the rewards completely. Prince will still sit up, certain that the reward is bound to come soon. The behavior will extinguish in time, but Prince will keep on working at it for quite a while. If he's used to being rewarded every time, however, the behavior will extinguish much more quickly when rewards stop.

The most effective schedule of reinforcement seems to be a *variable-interval reinforcement*, meaning that the rewards come at unpredictable times. If you've ever watched people feeding money into a slot machine, you've seen an excellent demonstration of variable-interval reinforcement. Think about it. Would you play the slot machine if you knew that it paid off only every tenth time? But the casino sets it to pay off at irregular intervals, so people hang on, hoping for that big jackpot.

Cognitive theory

Many modern psychologists do not believe that stimulus-response theory gives proper weight to the mind's higher mental processes. Human beings, they observe, carry on a number of complex intellectual activities called *cognition*, such as reasoning, abstract thinking, and problem solving. These high-level mental processes, they believe, amount to more than S → R behavior. According to *cognitive theory*, therefore, learning is putting pieces together to create a new understanding. It is an active process that involves the "whole" person.

A psychologist at the University of California at Berkeley, E. C. Tolman, described this process as building up experiences based on what you already know about the environment. Tolman's experiments seemed to show that rats were capable of insights that cut across laborious trial-and-error learning. In a typical experiment, rats were turned loose in mazes containing a network of alleys and dead ends. Many paths led through the maze to a reward of food, but one path was always shortest. The rats clearly preferred the shortest path. But when it was blocked, they immediately shifted to the next shortest route. Apparently, Tolman concluded, they had built up a mental map of the entire maze and could quickly move from one path to another without trial and error. In this way, the cognitive theory makes the rats— and people—active, thinking participants in the learning process.

You can see cognitive learning at work if you watch Libby learning to ride her first two-wheel bicycle. First, you might notice that some S → R learning is taking place.

Libby quickly discovers what happens if she runs into a curb or loses her balance. She also responds positively to the praise of her parents. These responses could all be explained as operant responses. But watch closely. You'll see Libby take time to plan each new step, using past experiences as a guide. This response is cognitive learning at work. If she can't straddle the seat easily, she'll figure out how to use the curb to get started. If her shoes slip off the pedals, she'll change them for sneakers that won't slip. Libby will also watch older children riding their bikes, and she'll apply those insights to her own learning. She may ask her father to give her a boost by holding the bike steady while she gets started.

To see Libby learning to ride her bike is to see *all* of Libby actively involved in learning something that's important to her. Simple conditioning doesn't fully explain that type of learning. Libby will certainly enjoy the rewards of learning to ride. But the inner satisfaction that comes from using all her mental and physical resources to master a difficult skill will be her most important reward.

Factors that influence learning

How well a person learns skills, attitudes, and values is influenced by a number of factors. Here are some of the most important.

1. *The self.* Learning takes place more readily when what you learn matches your self-concept. If you think of yourself as athletic, for example, you'll learn a new sport faster than someone who doubts his or her athletic ability. Personality traits, such as laziness or restlessness, can also interfere with learning.

2. *Past experience.* You tend to relate what you see and hear and feel to past experiences. If the new material doesn't match up to past learning, you'll be more likely to reject it. That's why it's often so hard to talk someone into trying an unusual food or accepting a new hairstyle.

3. *Intelligence.* Intelligence is the ability to solve problems and to absorb new information quickly. Scores on intelligence tests tend to give the impression that intelligence is a single quantity, something like the amount of money you have in a bank account. But intelligence is really the sum of a number of specific abilities. Mechanical skills, verbal skills, artistic skills, athletic skills, and dozens of other skills all make up individual intelligence. Your ability to learn depends to some degree on which of these abilities you can apply to what you're learning.

4. *Motivation.* Anything that makes you want to learn is called a *motivation.* When you *want* to learn a new skill, such as typing, you'll make more rapid progress than you would if you lacked interest and involvement. That's probably why you do better in some classes than in others. If you see the reason for learning a body of material, you'll probably do the work more readily and get greater satisfaction from it.

5. *Emotions.* Your emotions can either help or hinder learning. Enthusiasm is a positive factor, while anxiety generally gets in the way of learning. For example, you might have had the experience of reading a textbook and then realizing that you didn't absorb anything that you read. Your mind may have been preoccupied with worry about money or a problem with a friend. The anxiety got in the way of your ability to concentrate and remember what you were studying.

6. *Rewards and punishments.* Rewards are important stimuli to learning. Money, food, and grades are obvious rewards, but praise and affection often create an even greater incentive to learn. Punishment doesn't help people learn as well as rewards do. Punishments, when used, should be immediate so that the learner connects the punishment with the incorrect behavior. On an adult level, punishment works only if it is coupled with rewards. If your employer criticizes you for poor work but never re-wards you for a good performance, you'll lose interest in learning how to improve.

7. *Feedback.* You'll learn more rapidly if you know right away whether your response was correct or not. When you're learning to shoot pool, the feedback is immediate: The ball either goes into the pocket or it doesn't. Schools often delay feedback, as when a teacher doesn't return a test until two weeks later. Programmed textbooks try to overcome that problem by providing immediate feedback (see Figure 10.5).

8. *Guidance.* When you receive guidance from a more experienced person, you can often shortcut errors and move quickly to the correct solution. Think of trying to teach yourself how to perform surgery by reading a textbook! Experienced teachers who give positive feedback can make learning both efficient and enjoyable.

9. *Novelty.* Dull routine interferes with learning. You'll learn better when new and unexpected factors are occasionally added to the learning situation. Skilled teachers provide this novelty by varying classroom routine with films, guest speakers, debates, and other techniques. Overuse of novelty, however, can detract from learning. A teacher who entertains too much may interfere with the class's concentration. The students may enjoy the class, but they won't learn as much as they would with a more serious presentation of material.

SECTION CHECKUP

1 Define learning. List some of the things you've learned in the past months: new information, new skills, and new social behaviors.

2 Your friend Nathan wants to teach his pet cockatoo to pull a little wagon with its beak. How would you use stimulus-response theory to explain to Nathan how he should go about this training?

PROGRAMMED TEXTBOOKS: USING FEEDBACK
TO SPEED UP LEARNING

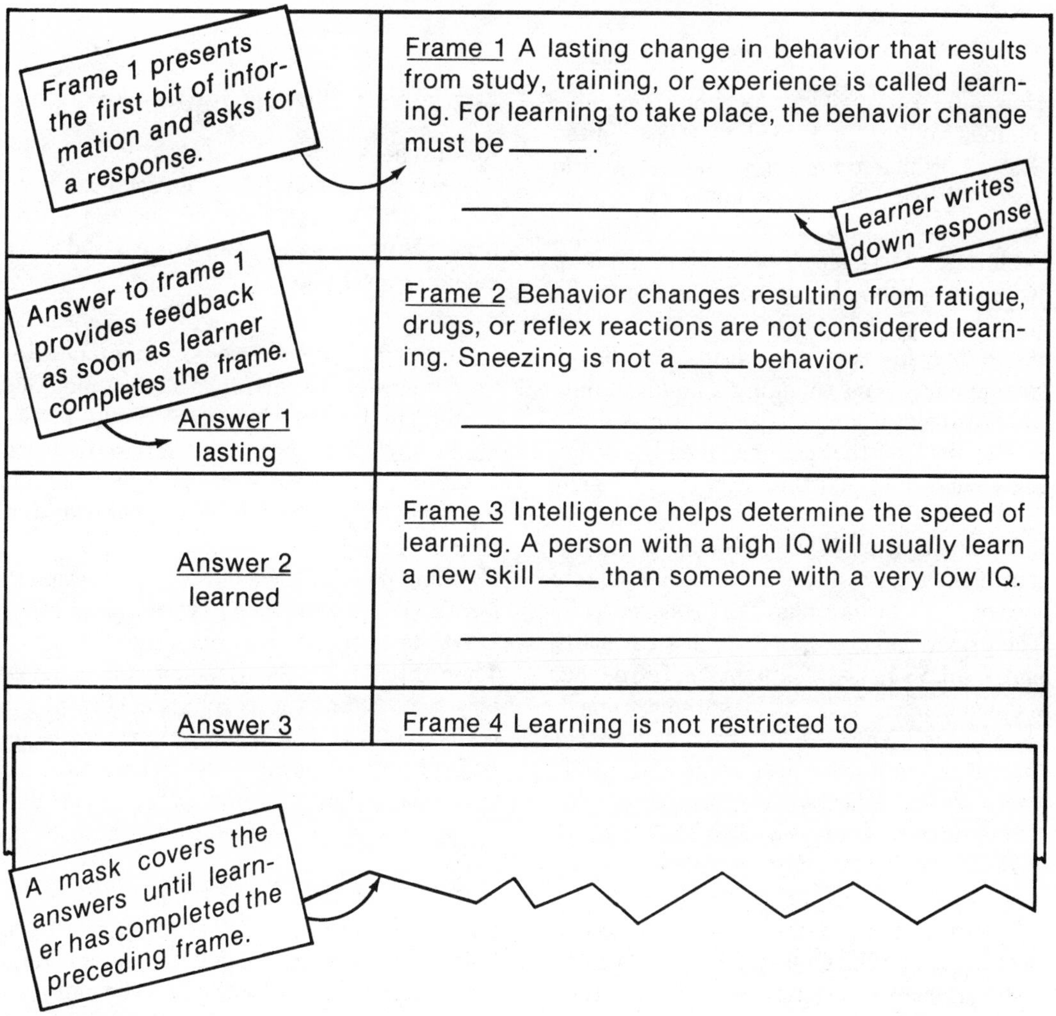

Frame 1 presents the first bit of information and asks for a response.

Frame 1 A lasting change in behavior that results from study, training, or experience is called learning. For learning to take place, the behavior change must be _____ .

Learner writes down response

Answer to frame 1 provides feedback as soon as learner completes the frame.

Answer 1
lasting

Frame 2 Behavior changes resulting from fatigue, drugs, or reflex reactions are not considered learning. Sneezing is not a _____ behavior.

Answer 2
learned

Frame 3 Intelligence helps determine the speed of learning. A person with a high IQ will usually learn a new skill _____ than someone with a very low IQ.

Answer 3

Frame 4 Learning is not restricted to

A mask covers the answers until learner has completed the preceding frame.

Figure 10.5

In a programmed textbook, the learner proceeds one frame at a time. At every step, the book provides immediate feedback to ensure that each part of a concept is learned before the next new idea is presented. Students work at their own pace, using the feedback as reinforcement.

3 Why wouldn't cognitive theory be of any value to Nathan in training his bird? Describe a situation where you've seen cognitive learning taking place.

4 Think of two types of learning, one that is easy for you and one that is difficult for you. What factors influence your learning in each case? How could you improve your performance in the types of learning that you have trouble with?

10.2 HOW DOES MEMORY WORK?

How old are you? What's your telephone number? Who's the President of the United States? Which team won the last World Series? What did you eat for lunch yesterday?

Simple questions? Yes, if your memory works properly. A psychologist would define *memory* as the process of storing and retrieving information within the brain. People carry an astounding amount of data around inside their heads. The answers to questions like these come quickly, seemingly without effort. But not if you're Henry M.

Henry M. doesn't have a memory. He lost it in 1953, when a surgeon cut too deeply into a part of his brain called the *hippocampus*. The psychosurgery was done in an effort to cure Henry's massive epileptic seizures, but today he lives in a world without a past, except for memories left from before the operation. Henry's motor skills and intelligence weren't affected. He earns a living by doing light assembly work. At home, he rakes leaves and shovels snow.

If you were to meet Henry, you'd find him pleasant and easy to talk to, but vague about details. Experience slips through his mind like water from a leaky pail. Henry does recognize John F. Kennedy's picture on a coin and connects it with the assassination of the former President in 1963. Apparently, the emotional impact of that event impressed itself on Henry's quicksand memory, just as it did for millions of other people. But for the most part, Henry is truly a "child of the moment," unable to retrieve recent memories. Talk to him one day and he won't remember meeting you the next. He can read the same magazine every day, and it's new to him each time. No one can give Henry his memory back, but researchers have begun to put together a fairly complete picture of how normal memory works.

The physical basis for memory

Researchers have concentrated on two questions regarding the physical basis of memory. Where is memory located in the brain? How does the brain process and store incoming data to create memory?

The search for a "memory center." Researchers now believe that a true "memory center" may never be found. Parts of the hindbrain, which regulates automatic body functions, are necessary to memory, but memory itself apparently isn't located there. Karl Lashley (1890–1958), an outstanding physiological psychologist, tried to locate the elusive memory center in rats. First, he trained the animals to run a maze. Then, little by little, Lashley cut out ever larger pieces of the cerebral cortex of his trained rats. Even when he'd removed 90 percent of the visual cortex, the rats were still able to limp, hop, or stagger through the mazes they'd learned to run before the surgery.

Related studies on human patients, in which large amounts of brain tissue have been removed for medical reasons, yield similar results. Even though the surgery produces changes in personality and some loss of learning ability, most memory functions of the brain are not affected. As Henry M. demonstrates so tragically, the hippocampus may be directly concerned with laying down or retrieving new memories. Lashley and other researchers have concluded, however, that memory storage itself seems to be spread throughout the cerebral cortex.

Memory as an electrochemical process. A way of explaining memory starts by saying, "Look at the capital *A* that opens this paragraph. As that image is picked up on the retina of your eye, electrochemical impulses carry a message about its size, shape, and color to the brain. This sets off a burst of activity in the visual cortex. Circuits of neurons fire or don't fire according to the impulses delivered by their neighbors.

If you had never seen an *A* before, a new pattern of neurons would be activated. The RNA molecules in that chain of neurons would be coded (rearranged) to store the new information. You can think of it as similar to the programming of a computer. New data is coded into the memory bank and kept for future use.

In order to recall that capital *A*, the coded neurons are somehow stimulated to respond to a "search" signal. The response is returned to the processing center of the brain, where you "remember" the letter. When you think of 10 billion neurons handling over 100 million electrical impulses each second, you can begin to appreciate the enormous complexity of the brain's task.

The role of RNA possibly becomes clearer when you look at the research of University of Michigan psychologist James McConnell. McConnell's work apparently demonstrates that RNA-stored memory can be transferred from one animal to another. Experiments have been carried out using such animals as flatworms, rats, and goldfish. Let's say that a flatworm is taught to run a T-maze. That is, the flatworm learns to turn right each time it is put into the maze. Now, McConnell cuts the flatworm into small pieces and feeds them to an untrained flatworm. After the new flatworm has digested the old one, it is introduced into the maze. The new flatworm now runs the maze beautifully! Other experimenters have extracted brain matter from trained donor rats and injected it into untrained animals. Once again, the untrained injected rats "learned" skills that the trained donor rats had previously mastered.

Although these studies show considerable statistical validity, no one can yet explain how the transfer of training takes place. Some scientists, including McConnell, believe that RNA molecules carry the message. If true, memory exists as a physical change in the brain's electrochemical makeup.

Three types of memory

Has the following happened to you? You look up a phone number, close the phone book, and then as you start dialing you realize you've already forgotten the number.

Memory researchers have learned that just looking at something doesn't move information into permanent memory. Before that happens, you have to work at retaining the phone number or whatever else you want to remember. Psychologists recognize three types of memory, each serving a different purpose.

Sensory memory. As you read, your body and brain are monitoring temperature, drafts, the feel of your chair, the intensity of the light, and a thousand other sensory impressions. This continuous stream of data registers on the *sensory memory*. Sensory memory fades almost as quickly as it registers. No one's brain could cope with that overwhelming flood of mostly useless data. But when something important happens, as when the room suddenly goes dark, that information is immediately called to your attention. You can think of sensory memory as an early-alert system. It monitors your environment at all times but only sounds the alarm when your attention is needed to deal with some new event.

Short-term memory. Psychologists describe *short-term memory* as a type of "holding tank." It holds five to nine items (words, sounds, faces, and so on) for about twenty seconds. After that, unimportant items are discarded. Thus, short-term memory is perfect for remembering a phone number—but only if you rehearse the number while you dial. By *rehearsal*, psychologists mean the process of concentrating on the item you want to remember,

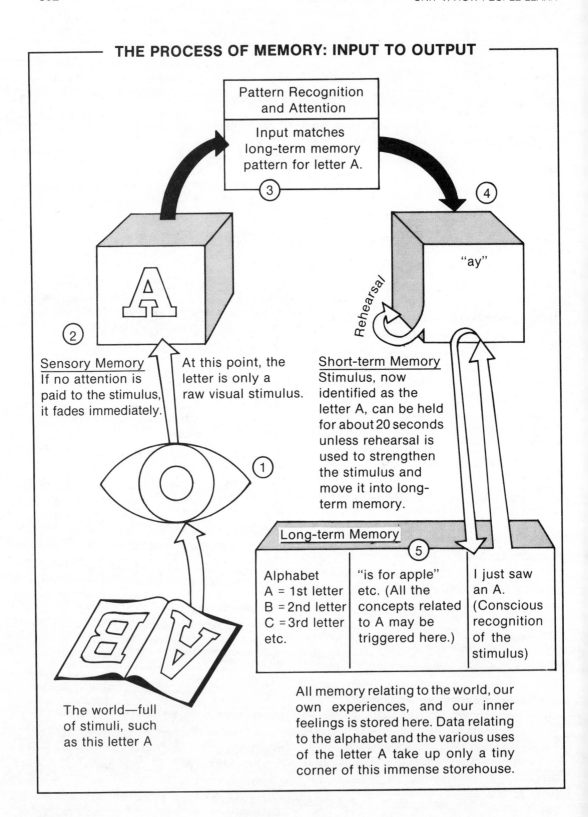

THE PROCESS OF MEMORY: INPUT TO OUTPUT

Pattern Recognition and Attention

Input matches long-term memory pattern for letter A.

③

④

"ay"

Rehearsal

② Sensory Memory
If no attention is paid to the stimulus, it fades immediately.

At this point, the letter is only a raw visual stimulus.

Short-term Memory
Stimulus, now identified as the letter A, can be held for about 20 seconds unless rehearsal is used to strengthen the stimulus and move it into long-term memory.

①

Long-term Memory
⑤

Alphabet	"is for apple"	I just saw
A = 1st letter	etc. (All the	an A.
B = 2nd letter	concepts related	(Conscious
C = 3rd letter	to A may be	recognition
etc.	triggered here.)	of the
		stimulus)

All memory relating to the world, our own experiences, and our inner feelings is stored here. Data relating to the alphabet and the various uses of the letter A take up only a tiny corner of this immense storehouse.

The world—full of stimuli, such as this letter A

Figure 10.6

perhaps by repeating it several times. Since you're often distracted while going to the phone and dialing, you tend to lose the number unless you do something to hold it. Short-term memory also explains the common experience that begins when someone asks you a question. You weren't paying attention, so you ask, "What did you say?" Even as you say it, however, you realize you do know what the original question was. It was held in short-term memory, waiting to be noticed.

Long-term memory. Everything you know about the world is stored away in *long-term memory*. That includes more than just names and dates and spelling words. Landscapes, plots of old movies, birthday parties, childhood friendships—all are kept in long-term memory. To move data from short-term to long-term memory requires some exercise of attention. One experiment on remembering words, for example, found that people can move only about twelve unrelated words into long-term memory in a two-minute period. (This type of learning experiment is usually done with nonsense "words"; a typical list might include *toron, briop, slarl,* and so on.) But if you're highly motivated or emotional about the material, greater chunks can be transferred. Just watch your concentration when a teacher says that the next bit of information will be on tomorrow's test!

Remembering and forgetting

Wilder Penfield's experiments (described more fully in Chapter 2, page 33) confirmed the existence of long-term memory. Penfield triggered specific recollections of long-ago events with an electric probe during brain surgery. Except for the loss of brain cells during the aging process or through accidental injury, long-term memories are never completely lost. But the process by which the brain stores information has not been fully understood. Apparently, your mind works constantly to organize its memories. Like an inefficient filing system, however, it doesn't always work. It's one thing to put something into long-term memory; it may be quite another to retrieve it.

Remembering. To *remember* is to respond to a stimulus by retrieving one or more of the memories you've stored away. Psychologists speak of *recollection* or *recall* when they refer to the process of using word cues, stimuli, or "reminders" to remember something you've learned. If someone asked you, "Who invented the telephone?" you probably wouldn't have to search your memory for a long list of inventors' names. The cue word *telephone* would quickly recall the proper name: Alexander Graham Bell.

Recognition. By contrast, *recognition* depends on visual stimuli to retrieve a particular memory. Familiar shapes, patterns, or combinations of letters trigger a memory of what similar images meant at an earlier time. Bird watchers who can quickly tell a meadowlark from a thrush are demonstrating this type of remembering.

Some people have almost total recall, an ability known as *photographic memory* (technically, *eidetic recall*). Most adults can say the alphabet quickly and automatically. In their memory process, *A* triggers *B*, which triggers *C*, and so on, but that's far different from eidetic recall. Ask those average people to recite the alphabet backward, and they'll probably stumble badly. An eidetic recall, however, provides a visual image of what has been seen. Thus, people with this special type of memory recite the alphabet backward, by simply calling off the letters as they see them! One study showed that about four percent of elementary school children have eidetic recall, but most of them lose the ability during puberty. Apparently, adult thought processes interfere with the visual images necessary to eidetic recall.

Forgetting. If little is ever lost from long-term memory, why can't people remember whatever they want to remember?

Figure 10.7

MNEMONIC DEVICES: WAYS TO IMPROVE YOUR MEMORY

Memory experts promise that you can improve your memory through the use of techniques they call *mnemonic* (pronounced ne-MON-ik) *devices.* The following devices will improve your memory almost overnight if you're willing to practice them and use them consistently.

MNEMONIC DEVICE	TECHNIQUE	EXAMPLE
First-letter code (list of related items)	Make a sentence out of the first letter from each word in the list.	Memorize the notes on the lines of the musical staff: E-G-B-D-F. Mnemonic sentence: Every Good Boy Does Fine.
Association (names and faces)	When meeting people, first concentrate on the name. Then form a visual image from the name. Couple this with an impression of the person—a strong facial feature of some type. Rehearse this coupled image several times, and you'll have it.	 Mr. Page / Mrs. Robinson 
Pegwords (shopping lists, errands, dates of historical events —anything that can be visualized as an object)	Begin by memorizing a simple list of rhymes for one to five. A typical list: one/gun; two/shoe; three/tree; four/door; five/hive. When you have a list to remember, hook each word to the rhyme word with a vivid mental picture—the more bizarre, the better. For example, when you need the items, say "one/gun..." and a mental picture will pop immediately to mind.	Try this shopping list: bread, milk, apples, butter, steak. 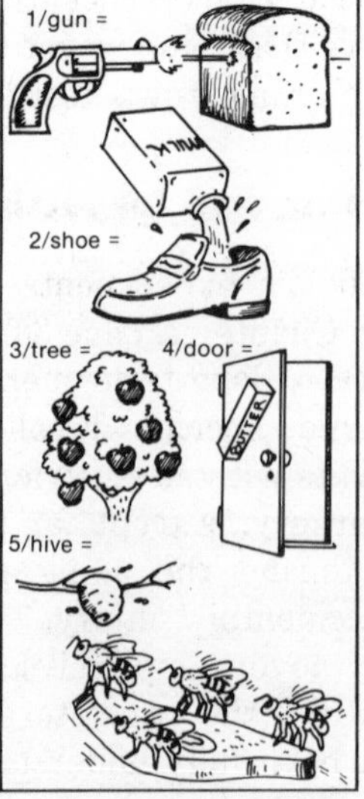 1/gun = 2/shoe = 3/tree = 4/door = 5/hive =

Figure 10.8

How good an eyewitness would you make? Study the accident scene for sixty seconds. Then cover the picture and write down all the details you can remember. Afterward, check your notes against the actual scene. What did you leave out? Did you add any new details? How do you explain any errors you made?

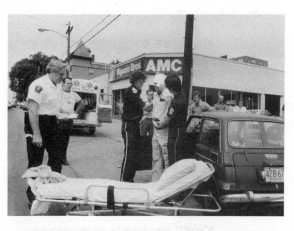

This inability to retrieve material when you want it is called *forgetting*. No single theory accounts for everything you forget. Most likely, each of the following explanations plays a part.

1. *Interference* occurs when newly learned material blocks retrieval of data you learned earlier. Learn your new phone number, for example, and you'll very likely lose your old one. Another kind of interference occurs when an old memory, such as a strong prejudice, blocks retention of new learning. An older man who dislikes children, for instance, may find it difficult to remember how hard the neighborhood kids worked to raise money for the local hospital.

2. *Distortion of memory patterns* is a polite way of saying that people's memories change and distort reality. Ask five different eyewitnesses to describe the same robbery, and you'll probably get five different reports. This type of distortion happens in several ways. The most common type of distortion is *leveling*. The eyewitnesses see what happens but remember only the general events. They may remember that the holdup men came into the store and emptied the cash register, but may not agree on what was said, whether the men were armed, or what type of car they used for their escape. *Sharpening* also distorts memory by focusing on a few unusual details. The witnesses may remember the money that was scattered on the floor but forget more important details, such as the physical description of the criminals. Finally, *assimilation* distorts memory by altering events to fit people's expectations or stereotypes. If the eyewitnesses were prejudiced against a particular ethnic group, they might very well report that the masked crooks were "obviously" members of that group.

3. *Repressed material* is forgotten because to remember it would be too painful. If Nelda witnesses a violent crime, for example, her mind may quickly repress that memory as too disturbing for her to handle. The unconscious stands guard over such memories and permits disclosure only under special conditions—during dreams, hypnosis, or free association.

4. *Decay through disuse* suggests that memories fade when you don't rehearse them. But walk through your childhood neighborhood some day, and apparently forgotten memories will spring back to vivid life. The actual role of decay in the forgetting process remains unclear.

Drugs to improve memory and learning

"I've got a psychology test tomorrow. What have you got for me?"

"Psych, is it? Then you won't want the creativity pills. Here's one that will increase your attention span and improve visual memory."

"Thanks doc. How much do I owe you?"

That conversation hasn't taken place yet, but in years to come it could be commonplace. Experiments with drugs that aid learning and memory or alter moods have excited the imaginations of scientists every-

Figure 10.9

WHAT ARE YOU MOST LIKELY TO REMEMBER . . . AND FORGET?

In *Techniques for Efficient Remembering,* Eleanor and Donald Laird summarize a number of interesting findings relating to the way people's memories work. Based on their research, they can predict what you're most likely to remember and what you'll probably forget.

You'll probably remember:

- Pleasant experiences
- Whatever you review before you go to bed
- Things you feel are worth remembering
- Whatever you let sink in before going on to new material
- Things you talk about often
- Difficult material you have to work hard at to learn
- Material you think about often or rehearse frequently
- Your successes
- Things that make sense to you
- Memories tied in with motor (muscle) skills
- What you use frequently
- Material you had a reason to remember for a long time when you first learned it

You'll probably forget:

- Names of things and people
- Numbers and dates
- Unpleasant things
- Material you learn barely well enough to remember for a test
- Facts that don't fit with your beliefs and prejudices
- Anything you learn by cramming
- Your failures
- Whatever you pick up casually without trying to remember
- Things you think of only once or twice after remembering them
- Material you don't understand
- Anything you try to remember when embarrassed, frustrated, in poor health, or fatigued

Adapted from *Techniques for Efficient Remembering,* by Eleanor C. Laird and Donald A. Laird. Copyright © 1960 McGraw-Hill Book Company. Used with the permission of McGraw-Hill Book Company.

where. The hormone ACTH (adrenocorticotrophic hormone), for example, helps rats —and humans—remember what they've learned. Mentally retarded subjects who take ACTH complete their tests in half the usual time. Another hormone, MSH (melanocyte-stimulating hormone) also im-proves attention and memory in the retarded. Controlled experiments show that both ACTH and MSH work on normal subjects as well.

To be sure, these and other drugs now being developed do not turn slow thinkers into math wizards or poor writers into

Hemingways. They simply help people use their abilities more fully. But work in the United States and in Holland has also pointed to the possibility of isolating drugs that will affect the brain in very specific ways. Vasopressin, a hormone, improves memory storage, thus increasing learning ability. Another hormone called oxytocin erases and represses information. With such a drug, psychologists may one day be able to treat people who are haunted by painful experiences, such as survivors of concentration camps.

ACTH, MSH, vasopressin, and the hundreds of other experimental drugs raise important ethical questions. How far should society go in modifying behavior through treatment with drugs? For example, what if the government owned an obedience-producing drug? You can see the potential danger of such a compound. To ignore new drugs, however, would be to turn away from drugs that can possibly help countless people. Just helping the retarded and senile to lead more productive lives would justify the research in drugs of this type.

Only one conclusion is certain. In the years to come, you will be asked to take a position in the debate over drugs that change the way people think and learn.

SECTION CHECKUP

1 Describe the general process by which a memory is stored in the brain. Why have researchers never been able to discover a "memory center"?

2 Distinguish among sensory memory, short-term memory, and long-term memory. What is the purpose of each type of memory?

3 What are some of the reasons you forget things you really thought you would remember?

10.3 HOW DO PEOPLE THINK?

Have you noticed how people tend to classify everything that goes on around them? When anything happens, they study it, label it, file it. When someone else asks, "What happened?" they retrieve it and find words to describe their experience. They may even say something new and original about it.

This complicated behavior is *thinking:* the active, conscious process that enables people to reorganize their memory so that they can develop ideas, establish relationships, and ask questions. Thinking consists of images, symbols, concepts, and rules.

1. An *image* is the pictorial recall of a specific object or event. Most images lack specific detail, as if only the highlights remained in your memory. When you visualize your grandmother's house, the ice cream you made last summer, or the look of the park in winter, you're using images.

2. *Symbols* allow people to label objects and events so that they can deal with them when the objects themselves aren't around. The words you're reading right now are symbols, the most common symbols of all. With words, you don't need to have an elephant in the room to think or talk about elephants. Words also enable you to deal with abstract ideas. How could you ever talk about love, freedom, and justice without words? Commonly accepted pictures also serve as useful symbols. People the world over recognize the symbolic meaning of the Red Cross and of their national flags.

3. *Concepts* allow you to put things into categories and to establish relationships. *Dog* is a word, but the concept of "dog" stands for a class of four-footed animals that bark, chase sticks, wag their tails, and shed hair on the sofa. When someone says *sports,* an entire family of relationships comes immediately to mind. Without concepts, you'd have a difficult time organizing your thinking.

Figure 10.10

PITFALLS IN THE PATHWAY OF LOGICAL THINKING

The wonderful mechanism called the human mind is capable of towering achievements . . . and of silly errors that should never be made. See if you're ever guilty of these common pitfalls in logical thinking.

Pitfall 1: The gambler's mistake

If a coin turns up heads six times in a row, what are the odds that it will land tails the next time? Despite the temptation to assume that chance is now on the side of tails, the odds remain exactly what they were before: 50–50. Over thousands of tosses, the heads and tails will always even out. The coin never "learns" from experience. People *can* learn, however, and can improve their chances of success far above 50–50.

Pitfall 2: Faith in small numbers

If you reached into a bag of apples and pulled out a rotten apple, would you assume that every apple was bad? Probably not, but people often assume that a small sampling is representative of a larger group. Television newscasters do this when they interview three people on the street and then announce that "the public believes thus-and-so."

Pitfall 3: The awareness trap

Most people believe that a particular event is more likely to happen if they're conscious of similar happenings in the past. For example, suppose the newspapers play up a series of muggings in a high-crime area. Everyone living there will begin to worry about being attacked. People will stay home at night, buy new locks for their doors, and ask for better police protection. In reality, the danger always existed. It was only their new awareness of the danger that changed their behavior.

Pitfall 4: Illusions of correlation

People find it easy to discover correlations (positive relationships) when they want to. Thus, someone who disapproves of divorce may notice that many juvenile delinquents come from single-parent families and jump to the conclusion that divorces *cause* delinquency. Statistics about nondelinquents from single-parent families will be conveniently ignored, as will data on delinquents who come from homes with two parents.

Pitfall 5: The P. T. Barnum effect

People often fail to evaluate information carefully before making a decision. Information that seems to be specific or that carries the weight of authority, influences people unduly. As the circus showman P. T. Barnum said, "There's a sucker born every minute." In the same spirit, advertisers use celebrities and actors playing the roles of "doctors" or "scientists" to reinforce their sales pitch.

4. *Rules* describe the relationship believed to exist between different concepts. "Honor your father and mother" is a rule, as is the statement, "Gold is expensive." In mathematics and science, you learn useful rules that establish accepted facts, such as "7 times 7 is 49," and "Matter can be neither created nor destroyed." Some rules you take for granted as part of your social or scientific heritage. Other rules, particularly those that affect your identity as a person, you'll probably want to check out for yourself.

The thinking process

What a wonderful world you carry around in your head! Without ever stirring from your chair, you can fly in space, climb Mt. Everest, or figure out a way to finance the new cassette-tape album you've been wanting. Using images, symbols, concepts, and rules, you can think about issues, decide on a course of action, or enjoy a daydream. Whatever thinking you do, some of it will be directed and some of it nondirected.

Directed thinking. Rhea is walking happily down the street, nothing much on her mind. Then she spots Ivy coming toward her. Rhea owes Ivy some money, and she's not ready to pay it back. In the few seconds left before Ivy sees her, Rhea thinks through several possible solutions to her problem. Systematically, she weighs each option, checking it out against what she knows of Ivy's personality. Finally, she has her story ready and puts on her best smile. "Oh, hi," Rhea says, "I was just thinking about you . . ."

Rhea's quick juggling of alternatives represents *directed thinking*. Some experts on thought processes also call it straight-line or vertical thinking. You start at point A, and proceed in logical fashion to points B, C, and so on, until you reach your goal. In a way, it's like working through a problem in geometry. Each step builds on the ones before. Without directed thinking, you'd have

a lot of trouble getting on with your life and solving the inevitable problems of daily existence.

Nondirected thinking. *Nondirected thinking* relies mainly on images and feelings. Lean back and daydream for a moment. Enjoy a fantasy about finding a 100-dollar bill in a letter from rich Uncle Amos. Relax and enjoy the possible ways you could spend the unexpected treasure. One image will unexpectedly lead to another, and another. Such daydreams, fantasies, and drifting thoughts are known as nondirected thinking. This type of thinking provides relief from tension and boredom. More important, nondirected thinking often gives people their most creative ideas.

No great work of art could ever grow entirely out of directed thinking. In order to paint, for example, you need to plan logically to the extent of obtaining the necessary materials. But deciding on what to paint often grows out of nondirected thinking. As you think about possible settings, a series of images will drift through your head. Then, almost without knowing why it's right, one special scene will suggest itself. Some people call this "playing a hunch," or intuition. Creative thinkers go with such feelings, for they've learned that they get better results than if they analyze each possibility step by step.

The role of language in the thinking process

At one time, scientists believed that language was the dividing line between humans and animals. Experiments in recent years have partially demolished that theory. Rats can learn to find their food under a triangle, for example, ignoring squares and circles. While a triangle isn't a word, it is a symbol that the rat learns to associate with food, just as you might associate two golden triangles with hamburgers. At a higher level of language, Lucy and other trained chimps have learned to use their limited sign-language vocabularies quite effectively. But higher levels of thinking are tied to a much more complex level of language than any chimpanzee can reach. Without language, human culture might still be at the hunting and gathering stage. With it, our species has reached toward the stars.

Language development. Thinking in infants apparently begins with simple language concepts. For example, babies learn to match the word *bottle* to the actual object. Later, they acquire the ability to recognize broader relationships. Older children recognize both milk and cereal as foods because they have learned the concept of food. As language skills increase, abstract concepts appear, along with grammar and word order. The child says, "I miss you," and understands the feelings that these three words convey.

Language expert Noam Chomsky says that only human beings are born with this inborn capacity for language. He bases his belief on the evidence that despite all the inaccurate language children hear, they still learn to express themselves in a clear and understandable way. Chomsky points out that children learn to speak at about the same age in every culture. Moreover, despite the apparent differences among languages, Chomsky states that all languages have similar concepts about sentences, subjects, and predicates. These structures provide workable rules for grammar and word usage.

Children learning to talk make many errors. Little Stan might laugh and say, "Mom sitted down." No matter. Stan has followed grammatical rules for forming the past tense. As he grows older, he'll learn the irregularities of verbs and will use them correctly. What Stan won't do is tangle up his word order. He'll never say, "Down sitted Mom," or similar scrambled usages. Chimps have learned to put the signs that make up simple sentences in proper order, but only after careful training.

Language interacts with culture. Limitations of language may also influence behavior. The traditional Hopi Indian language, for example, has no past or future tenses. Where English says, "He ran," the Hopi would use the present tense, *"Wari* (Running occurs)." For the future tense ("He will run" in English), the Hopi would say, *"Warikne* (Running occurs I daresay)." Because they did not think in future terms, schedules and future plans meant little to the people of the old Hopi culture. The Eskimos of North America, by contrast, have a number of different words to identify various types of snow. These variations make sense in a culture where snow is an overwhelming fact of life. Perhaps, if air pollution continues to worsen in this country, Americans will someday develop additional words to describe the different types of smog they must endure.

SECTION CHECKUP

1 Define thinking. Why would a dream not be considered thinking?

2 What are the differences among images, symbols, concepts, and rules? Give an example of each.

3 Describe a situation that requires directed thinking. Now add a second situation in which nondirected thinking would be useful.

4 Why is language so important to the thinking process?

10.4 HOW CAN YOU IMPROVE YOUR LEARNING AND PROBLEM-SOLVING ABILITIES?

A farmer once sent his children to the well to bring back some water. "Take these two pails," he told them, "and don't come back until you've got exactly five gallons." He handed them a two-gallon pail and a nine-gallon pail. How did they solve the problem?

Figure 10.11

The better you are as a problem solver, the better you are at thinking of possible reasons for what you see happening. Poor problem solvers accept the first one or two explanations and never look any further. Before you make a judgment about Harry Parker's sudden change of behavior, see how many possibilities you can think of to explain that change. (See page 323 for a discussion of your answers.)

THE CASE OF THE SUDDEN SPENDTHRIFT

Harry Parker has always been a thrifty person. Suddenly, however, he has begun to spend his money quite freely. How many reasons can you list to explain the sudden change in Harry's spending habits?

Here's what the clever children did. First, they filled the nine-gallon pail. Then they poured two gallons from the large pail to fill up the small pail. Next, they dumped out the two gallons from the small pail and filled it again. That left exactly five gallons in the large pail (nine gallons minus two

minus two). They dumped out the contents of the small pail, lifted the large one between them, and trudged happily home, their problem solved.

That's only a puzzle, of course, an exercise for the fun of it. But the type of logical thinking that goes into solving puzzles and riddles can also be applied to real-life problems. Perhaps the first step toward better problem solving is to use more efficient learning techniques.

Improving your ability to learn

In Section 10.1, pages 293–299, you learned something about *how* people learn. Here are some ways to make learning easier.

1. *Overlearning* is the process of repeating a skill over and over even after you've mastered it. Major-league baseball players, for example, practice every day, as do professional musicians. You can also apply the overlearning techniques to other types of learning. Anyone studying a foreign language, for example, can profit from daily practice. This may include listening to records and making up conversations in addition to reading and memorizing vocabulary.

2. *Removing negative conditions* that prevent efficient learning might mean finding a quiet place to study away from other people. It might mean turning off the radio or television. Emotional problems that interfere with your concentration can also be considered a negative condition. You might be better off dealing with the emotional problem first, then going back to the learning situation.

3. *Adjust the type of practice*, depending on the material to be learned. There are two basic types of practice: distributed practice and massed practice. Distributed practice, which divides the task into small segments, generally works best. Learning the names of the body's bones for physiology should be done in several short study sessions. It might be easier, however, to master a difficult scene in a play with massed practice. This method means working without interruption until the script has been memorized. Since each speech within the scene links to the one before, you profit from the association that builds up as you go over and over the entire scene.

4. *Verbalization* means to talk out the steps of a procedure, either to yourself or to others. Verbalization helps learning even when you're working on skills such as dancing or finishing a bookcase. Go ahead and talk to yourself. You'll get better results than with nonverbal methods. In fact, the more senses you involve whenever you're trying to learn something, the better. That's why taking notes when you read helps you learn more efficiently and why schools use so many audiovisual materials. Studies on learning efficiency show that people remember only about 10 percent of what they read and 30 percent of what they see happening around them. But they remember 90 percent of what they say while they're carrying out a particular activity.

5. *Improve your listening skills*. Dr. Robert McMillan, an expert in communications skills, estimates that 70 percent of your waking day is spent in verbal communication. Of that time, almost half is given over to listening to others. It makes sense, he concludes, to improve listening skills, since most people operate at only a 25 percent level of efficiency. Most of his suggestions for improving listening skills make good common sense, but few people work on them. For example, Dr. McMillan advises that you concentrate on what the other person is saying, as if you're determined to

learn something useful. Keep your emotions under control, for once you're emotionally aroused you'll probably stop listening. Try to pick out the speaker's main ideas, and focus on them rather than try to memorize a lot of facts. Finally, Dr. McMillan notes that people speak at about 100 words per minute, but you think at about 400 wpm. Since you can literally "think circles" around any speaker, it's easy to get distracted and go off into some nondirected thinking of your own.

Common types of problem solving

Ready for another puzzle? This one will challenge anybody. Look at the matchsticks in Figure 10.12. They've been arranged to form the Roman numerals VI = II. Obviously, six doesn't equal two in any numbering system, so your job is to take one of the matchsticks and move it to make a correct equation. (The answer can be found on page 324.) While you're thinking about that, here are the ways people generally go about solving problems.

Trial and error. Before Thomas Edison found the carbonized thread that worked as the filament in his first light bulb, he tested hundreds of materials. Animals use *trial-and-error methods* randomly, as Thorndike proved with his cats in the puzzle boxes (see page 294). Skilled problem solvers, however, use this technique in a methodical fashion. They start by ignoring possibilities that obviously won't work. Edison, for example, never tried spaghetti in his bulb. As each of the more likely possibilities is

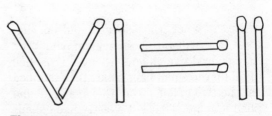

Figure 10.12

eliminated, problem solvers are left with fewer places to look for the correct answer. Mechanics call this trouble shooting. That's a short way of saying, "I've got a list of all the reasons why this machine usually stops working. Now I'm going to check out each one of them in turn until I find out what went wrong."

In the matchstick puzzle, you could use trial and error. Move each matchstick in turn to all the possible places it could go. If you have enough patience, that might work—but only if you're alert to unexpected possibilities.

Inductive and deductive reasoning. To reason is to think through a problem or situation systematically in order to make a decision. *Inductive reasoning* uses specific cases as a means of reaching a principle or generalization. Suppose, for example, that every time you see a horror movie you have trouble sleeping for the next few nights. Since you normally sleep like a log, you can reason inductively that watching horror movies interferes with your sleep. Similarly, a research psychologist might test the effects of overcrowding on rats. If time after time the rats respond to overcrowding by developing signs of neurotic behavior, such as fighting and not caring for their young, the researcher can induce the principle that overcrowding causes disturbed behavior in rats.

Deductive reasoning, in contrast, uses general principles to provide a prediction or insight into specific cases. You might deduce, for example, that going to see a Marx Brothers comedy won't interfere with your sleep because you've seen many comedies and none of them ever has. In the same way, a scientist who has taught numerous pigeons to play table tennis would deduce that Pigeon K-4 can also learn to play table tennis if given the same training.

Will either type of reasoning work with the matchstick puzzle? You can probably deduce that obvious solutions won't work, or it wouldn't be much of a puzzle. For that reason, you would stop trying to make the VI into $\frac{II}{I}$.

Insight. Have you ever had an *"Aha reaction"*? There was the problem, its solution just out of reach. You tried this and that answer, but nothing worked. Then, suddenly, you *knew* what to do. So you said, "Aha!" and did it.

That's *insight*, the sudden perception of key relationships that leads directly to the solution of the problem. Wolfgang Köhler's chimpanzee, Sultan, figured in one of the important early demonstrations of insight over sixty years ago. Köhler, a Gestalt psychologist, thought that animals were capable of more than trial-and-error learning. He gave Sultan a stick, then dropped a banana outside the cage. Sultan soon learned to rake in the banana with the stick. But then Köhler gave the chimp two shorter bamboo sticks. Only if Sultan fitted the sticks together would he be able to reach another banana. Sultan tried one stick and then the other. No luck. Frustrated, he took the sticks and sat in a corner. After a period of apparent thought, he slipped the smaller stick into the hollow end of the longer one. Then, like a flash, he raced to the side of the cage and raked in his prize.

As Sultan discovered, insight usually comes only after some hard thinking. Perhaps insight is a right-brain activity, not reachable through directed thinking. Insights often come when you're relaxed, when you've "turned off" your directed thinking for a while. One good rule in trying to use insight to solve a problem is to "sleep on it." By going over the problem just before you drift off, you can program your unconscious to work while you sleep. In many cases, the solution will appear in a dream or will be there in your conscious mind when you wake up.

Now, have you solved that matchstick puzzle? The people who do solve it report that the solution usually comes through insight. Thus, you might suddenly realize that the answer may involve mathematical signs as well as numbers.

Mind set

When a certain way of thinking becomes habitual, that mental position is called a *mind set*. If Evan is convinced that the hometown team is the best baseball team in the league, it's doubtful that he'll listen to an argument as to why they won't win the pennant. When it comes to problem solving, mind set may either help or hinder you. For example, if you believe that speed is important in solving mathematics problems, you'll probably accept a higher error rate than someone who thinks that accuracy is more important than speed.

Mind set sometimes leads people to accept limitations that aren't really there. As an example, try the problem in Figure 10.13. Copy the nine dots on a separate sheet of paper. Your task is to draw four straight, connected lines that touch all nine dots. You may not lift your pencil off the paper.

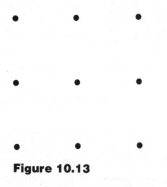

Figure 10.13

Any luck? Before you look at the solution, ask yourself, "What restrictions am I placing on myself that I don't need to make?" (The answer can be found on page 324.)

Mind set can hinder problem solving in two ways. *Rigidity* causes people to continue a behavior just because it once worked, even though it isn't right for a new situation. In World War I, for example, the generals on both sides kept ordering massed attacks of infantry across no-man's land even though the newly developed machine gun made such charges suicidal.

Functional fixedness is the inability to imagine new uses for familiar objects. As an

Figure 10.14

The problem here is to tie the two strings together. They're far enough apart, however, that you can't hold on to one and reach the other. Once you overcome functional fixedness regarding the screwdriver, the solution becomes obvious. (See page 324 for the answer.)

example of functional fixedness, look at the problem in Figure 10.14.

The woman who replaces a broken hinge pin on a pair of sunglasses with a paper clip has overcome functional fixedness. And so has the man who figured out a way to keep his coffee warm. How did he solve his problem? (See Figure 10.15.)

Figure 10.15

Problem: How can you use the one saucer to keep both cups of coffee warm? (No other equipment is available.) See page 324 for the solution.

Improving your ability to solve problems

Problem solving, it turns out, depends more upon knowing how to define a problem and search for solutions than upon an IQ score. An IQ of 160 won't help a person solve a problem if that person doesn't have a strategy for attacking it. In this section, you'll learn about two methods of solving problems. One method uses directed thinking, and the other uses nondirected thinking.

Vertical thinking. A logical, straight-line approach often works quite well. Let's say your problem is that you are determined to improve a low grade in a course. Your determination to change old behaviors is the first step. Without motivation, you probably won't be able to see the process through to completion.

1. The first step is to gather all the information you have that applies to the problem. Consider your feelings about the class. Take an objective look at your study habits. Zero in on the specific factors that contribute to your lack of success. An old misunderstanding with the teacher may be distracting you, or you may not be setting aside enough time for reading outside of class. Some of this data may turn out to be useless, but until you've fully defined the problem you can't take the next step.

2. Consider the possible alternatives. Make a list of all the ways you can improve your performance. On this list will probably be items such as extra study time, getting some help from a tutor, resolving to join in more often in class discussions, talking to the teacher about your work, and so on. Write down every possibility you can think of, then discard the weaker ideas later.

3. Now commit yourself to a plan of action. You'll probably choose the approach that seems most logical, but it's also all right to play a hunch. Check your decision out with someone you trust, perhaps the teacher or a counselor. But even now, stay flexible. Be ready to throw out what doesn't work and try something else.

4. Finally, dig in and go to work. Stop once in a while to evaluate your progress. Is your plan working? You can use your grades as a yardstick, but your own sense of progress also counts. If you don't see any change in a reasonable period of time, go back to step one and study the problem again. See if you can find another solution, and give it a try.

Lateral thinking. Edward de Bono (see BioBox, page 316) identified a nondirective type of thinking that's useful for problems that don't lend themselves to straight-line, directive thinking. He calls it *lateral thinking* and defines it as a way of freeing the mind to use its creative potential. Dr. de Bono wants you, like Sultan putting his two sticks together, to use insight to solve problems when other approaches don't work.

Look at the following puzzle, for example. The truck must get through the underpass so that the driver can deliver its load of emergency medicines to a hospital. The underpass is just inches too low, the truck can't be unloaded, and to back up and find another route will take hours. What can be done?

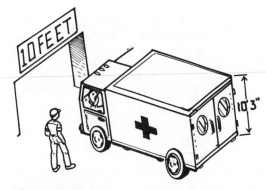

Figure 10.16

Conventional problem solving won't work here. But by breaking loose from rigid patterns of thinking, you can find a quick, neat solution. Here are some of de Bono's suggestions for lateral thinking.

BioBox

EDWARD DE BONO:
THE CASE FOR LATERAL THINKING

Dr. Edward de Bono (1933–), a man who thinks about thinking, reasons that the brain is an information processing system that does more than store data like a computer. Instead, it picks and chooses and alters the information.

A native of Malta, de Bono came to his study of thinking and brain function as both a medical doctor and a student of philosophy. He is best known for his concept of lateral thinking, a way of solving problems when neither trial and error nor logical thought (vertical thinking) will work. De Bono tells a story about himself that illustrates how easily people can allow mind set to make their lives more complicated:

I started again and with more careful direction came up to the proper second wall. There was an iron gate in this second wall and as the gate was lower than the rest of the wall and also offered better footholds I climbed the gate. As I was sitting astride the top of the gate it swung open. It had never been closed.

At that time the gates of my Oxford college were locked at twenty minutes past midnight. . . . On my first night I went off to a party in London, and knowing that I would be back late, I asked an old hand to tell me the way to get in. It seemed quite straightforward. First there was a set of railings and then one came to a wall which had to be climbed. Beyond the first wall there was a second wall which also had to be climbed.

It was late when I got back. The railings were easy. The first wall was rather more difficult. I got over it and went forward until I came to the second wall, which was about the same height as the first wall. I climbed this second wall, only to find myself outside again. My double effort had involved my climbing in and out across a corner.

How would lateral thinking have helped de Bono avoid his futile climb? If he'd started by checking out the alternatives, he would have tried the gate *before* he started climbing. De Bono learned from this experience, for he later wrote about the dangers of a closed mind:

The need to be always right . . . cannot be justified unless it is tempered with the awareness that *for some part of the time one is inevitably going to be wrong*. It is these inherent faults of the information processing system that make lateral thinking essential. Insight is so haphazard a mechanism that it cannot be expected to reduce the gap between the current arrangement of information and the best possible arrangement with any reliability. The purpose of lateral thinking is to bring about this insight type of restructuring of information.

Can you think of a problem you've faced recently that could be solved more efficiently by lateral thinking? Why not give it a try? There's no law that says life's problems can be solved only by vertical thinking.

1. *Open yourself up to alternatives*. If obvious solutions don't work, look for other possibilities. Forget for the moment about a *best* way and look at *all* ways. An old saying sums up the way of the lateral thinker: "If you can't raise the bridge, lower the river."

2. *Undo your selection process*. Avoid the logical, step-by-step approach that works so well for other types of problems. You want to make sure that no useful solution is ignored. In short, avoid mind set. You don't need to justify each step according to "rightness" or logic, as long as it works.

3. *Shift your attention*. If you can't locate a solution to the problem, perhaps you can change the problem. This is called *transfer*. A worker once decided to steal wheelbarrows from the factory where he worked. But the guards at the gate carefully checked everybody who went out. So every day the worker walked out the gate, pushing a wheelbarrow filled with a load of trash. The guards guessed that something was wrong, but they couldn't find anything hidden in the trash, so they waved him through. If they'd transferred their attention from the trash to the wheelbarrows, they'd have caught their thief.

Still working on getting that truck through the underpass? Since you can't raise the underpass, can you lower the road? (Sorry, it's reinforced concrete. Try again.)

4. *Try brainstorming*. When several people get together and start throwing out every idea they can think of, each new idea tends to spark several others. Out of the useless or bizarre proposals typical of a *brainstorming* session, a few ideas of genuine merit often emerge. The one rule of brainstorming is that no one is allowed to laugh at anybody else's ideas. A few "That's stupid" comments dampen the nondirective thinking necessary to good brainstorming.

OK, now how are you going to get that truck through the underpass? You couldn't raise the underpass or lower the road. So why not lower the truck! Perhaps you could

cut a few inches off the top, but there's an easier way. Let enough air out of the big truck tires to lower the truck. Now drive on through, pump up the tires again, and be on your way. That's lateral thinking!

Want to try another one? While changing a flat tire far from any garage, a driver lost all the lug nuts that hold the wheel to the car (Figure 10.17). What advice can you give that will solve the problem? With lateral thinking, the answer is easy. (See page 324 for the solution.)

Figure 10.17

SECTION CHECKUP

1 What advice would you give to friends who want to improve their learning skills?

2 What is the difference between trial-and-error problem solving and using insight to solve problems? Give an example of a problem that would be solved best by trial-and-error and one in which you could use insight?

3 Why does mind set get in the way of problem solving?

4 What is lateral thinking? Name some of the rules that would help you use this type of non-directed thinking.

Pro & Con: SHOULD SCHOOLS TEACH CREATIVE THOUGHT?

No one seems satisfied with what the American schools teach or with how they teach it. Along with the old "Johnny can't read" criticism, schools are also being attacked for not developing creative thought in their students. Typically, the "Pro" argument for teaching creative thought says that children start out brimming over with creative ideas but that rigid and subject-centered teaching soon discourages them. In a debate, the argument would sound like this.

Pro

1 Most schools teach traditional methods of problem solving. They apparently believe that creative thinking interferes with such teaching.

2 Children who show signs of creative thought are often singled out as "different," and pressures are placed on them to conform.

3 Creative thinkers do not always score well on IQ tests, which reward straight-line thinking. As a result, creative children are often put in slow classes that do not challenge their special skills.

4 Too many teachers treat creative children as discipline problems. Such teachers soon turn creative thinkers into either sheep or rebels.

5 Because few teachers think creatively themselves, most do not understand the needs of the creative minority. Left unchallenged and unrewarded, creativity soon dies.

Con

1 Society insists that children be taught reason and logic. Creative thought cannot be taught. Either children have it or they don't.

2 Critics often mistake lack of discipline for creative thought. Even highly creative people need to learn basic skills and study traditional subjects.

3 IQ scores are often the only valid way to place children in a class with others of the same ability level. If a creative child performs well in class, he or she will be moved to a class of students with higher abilities.

4 Schools must handle many children at a time. The so-called creative youngsters often interfere with the right of other children to learn.

5 The schools offer all students many opportunities for developing creative thought and expression. Most teachers cherish creative thinkers and give them as much attention as they can.

Can you remember any school experiences that would support either side of this argument? If you were a parent, would you want traditional subjects and strict discipline in the classroom? Or would you prefer a more open classroom where children can learn and create according to their own needs and abilities?

10.5 HOW CAN YOU IMPROVE YOUR CREATIVITY?

Have you ever made something original, useful, or beautiful? Did you ever solve a problem in an unexpected way? Perhaps you made decorations for a friend's party, scored a touchdown on a clever new play, or raised money for your club by organizing a monster-movie festival. If so, that reorganization of old ideas and processes into something novel and useful demonstrated your *creativity*.

Being creative makes people feel good. Creative thought gives you the sensation of being original, of doing something no one else has done. Psychologists estimate that only about 1 percent of the population is capable of highly creative thought. But almost all people can develop their creativity if they want to. You may never discover antigravity or write a masterpiece, but you can probably do much more than you give yourself credit for.

A creativity test

Start by trying these exercises. Allow two minutes for each item.

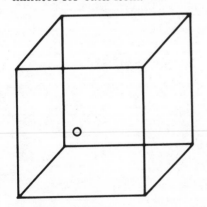

Figure 10.18

1. Look steadily at the drawing in Figure 10.18. How many times does the small circle move from back to front (or vice versa) in two minutes?

2. Name as many objects as you can that are white, soft, and edible.

3. How many uses can you think of for a piece of brown paper?

Finished? Don't look at the analysis until you've done the tests.

Test 1. Count 1 for each change in perspective. The more often the cube flips back and forth, the more flexible you are. Score: 1–3 changes, low creativity; 4–5 average; over 5, high creativity.

Test 2. Count 1 point for each answer. Score: 0–5, low creativity; 6–10, average; over 10, high. Typical answers include marshmallows, mushrooms, white bread, noodles, and yogurt. But did you think of bean curd, divinity fudge, shredded coconut, or vanilla frosting?

Test 3. Count 1 for each answer. Count 2 for truly original uses. Typical answers include wrapping a package, writing a letter, starting a fire, and making a paper airplane. More creative uses include drawing a treasure map, plugging up a sink, and mending a torn kite. Score: 0–5, low creativity; 6–10, average; over 10, high.

What does your score mean? Not a great deal, except for giving you a little more awareness of how your mind works. Neither creative nor noncreative people have a monopoly on happiness or intelligence. Some jobs reward creativity more than others, but there are just as many careers for hardworking, low-creative people as for brilliant innovators—probably more, in fact. The key point is that you had a potential for creativity when you were a child. You can still fulfill that potential if you want to work at it.

Elements of creativity

Creative thinking requires that you actively seek new answers to old questions. The elements necessary for that type of thinking include flexibility, persistence, and insight.

Flexibility. Rigid thinking defeats creativity. *Flexibility*, which is a willingness to adopt new ideas, is the opposite of functional fixedness. Flexible thinking leads to nonrigid, creative solutions. When asked what can be done with a brick, the rigid person thinks of doorstops or bookends. A flexible thinker, however, comes up with more original uses: a step for watching parades, a marker for drawing on the sidewalk, a grave marker for a buried pet animal, and so on.

Persistence. Creative solutions don't always come to mind right away. You must keep working at the problem, even after you've tried a number of ideas that didn't pay off. Almost all great inventions have been the products of *persistence* by highly creative people. If Edison hadn't persisted in his research, the electric light might not have been developed until years later.

Insight. Flexibility and persistence often combine to produce the breakthrough idea, or *insight* (see also page 313). The insight itself may come as a blinding flash of inspiration or in a dream, but it couldn't have happened if the necessary preparation had been ignored. People had been growing and eating peanuts and sweet potatoes for centuries, but it remained for George Washington Carver to see the possibilities in these simple crops. Out of the peanut, for example, he developed some three hundred synthetic products, including milk, butter, cheese, coffee, flour, breakfast food, ink, dyes, soap, wood stains, and insulating board. Such insights are really payoffs for long, hard preparation. When a creative thinker makes that type of effort, the rewards can be great, both for the individual and for society.

Improving creativity

Creativity comes in various forms. Mozart literally "heard" symphonies in his head and wrote them down. The words to "The Battle Hymn of the Republic" came to Julia Ward

Figure 10.19

One of recent history's best examples of creative thought can be seen in the design of graceful aircraft like the one shown here. A plane of this type flew more than twenty miles across the English Channel propelled only by the pilot's leg power.

Howe in a dream. Faced with "instant" creativity of this sort, many people assume that creative thought is beyond their reach and never try. This assumption might be termed the ultimate mind set, at least as far as creativity is concerned: "I know I can't do it, so I won't embarrass myself by trying." But techniques do exist for improving anyone's creative abilities.

Preschool children. With preschool children, play provides an important opportunity for creative expression. Infants in their cribs and playpens profit from an abundance of simple, colorful toys and mobiles. If you wanted to help develop creativity in three-year-old Jocelyn, for example, you could give her a "supertoy," such as a specially designed table with levers, buzzers, bells, and counting devices attached. Each time Jocelyn moves a lever, something happens. Buzzers sound, bells ring, colored discs move up and down, and so on. Jocelyn will spend a lot of time with her supertoy, because it has so many interesting things to see, hear, push, pull, touch, and investigate. If you test Jocelyn for creativity four years later, you'll probably find that she'll score higher than children who didn't have the same opportunity to develop their creativity.

Child psychologists also urge parents to allow their children to express their own views of the world. When children color the sky purple and the grass orange, adults are advised to admire their originality. Freehand drawing, no matter how simple, is better than the traditional coloring book with its preset limits on where to color. Children's fantasies should also be encouraged rather than squelched. Authority figures who insist on blue sky, green grass, and a world without imaginary animals soon convince youngsters that creativity doesn't pay off—and that conformity does.

Older children and adults. You don't have to be a child to enjoy your own "supertoy." Games and puzzles that reward insight and ingenuity are both fun and mind-stretching. Scrabble, Password, charades, handicrafts,

cooking, painting, ceramics, creative writing, chess, and other challenging activities fit into this category. The availability of microcomputers has opened up a deeply involving new field for many people. Sports, when played with a relaxed sense of freedom to try new shots and tactics, can fill the same need. Classes in college, adult school, or at a "Y" provide other opportunities to try out new ideas and learn new skills.

The important point is not to allow old messages in your head to tell you, "No, you can't do it." Maybe you'll never be a Rembrandt, an Edison, a Pelé, or a Stravinsky. But you can find your own special form of creativity if you really want to. The decision is up to you.

SECTION CHECKUP

1 How would you define creativity? Give an example of noncreative uses for a paper clip. Now give some creative uses for the same paper clip.

2 How do flexibility, persistence, and insight relate to creativity?

3 What can parents do to encourage creativity in their children?

LOOKING BACK: A SUMMARY

1 Learning is a lasting change in your behavior or performance brought about by study, training, or experience. Psychologists have two major theories about how learning occurs. Stimulus-response (S → R) theory puts emphasis on the relationship between a stimulus (any event or impulse) and the response (the resulting behavior). Successful responses are learned and become part of behavior; unsuccessful responses fade out. Edward Thorndike thought that learning is basically trial and error. B. F. Skinner added the concept of operant behaviors: those complex reactions to stimuli that the subject actively chooses in order to gain a reward or avoid a punishment. Operant behaviors can be increased by reward (positive reinforcement) and extinguished by punishment. Signals trigger operant behaviors by alerting the subject to the reward or punishment to follow. More stable operant behaviors can be obtained by a schedule of reinforcement that rewards the behavior only part of the time.

2 Cognitive-learning theorists, by contrast, believe that stimulus-response theory ignores the higher mental processes. Human learning, they feel, results from new understandings built up of individual experiences. Cognitive-learning theorists accept the influence of S → R learning, but they also believe that humans recognize the joy of learning for its own sake and can think through a problem without actually going through a conditioning process.

3 A number of factors influence the learning process. These include one's self-concept, past experiences, intelligence, motivation, emotions, rewards and punishments, feedback, guidance, and novelty. Not all of these factors need be present for learning to take place, but positive attitudes and assistance from other people contribute greatly to efficient learning.

4 The electrochemical process called *memory* seems to be located generally in the cerebral cortex. New information is stored in networks of neurons by specially coded RNA molecules. When a new stimulus triggers these neurons, you "remember" the original data. Experiments show that learning behavior can apparently be transferred by feeding or injecting untrained animals with material from the brains of trained animals.

5 Three types of memory serve your body's different needs. (a) Sensory memory receives data from the senses and almost immediately discards what you don't need. Anything important is called to your attention. (b) Short-term memory provides a twenty-second "holding tank" for processing words, numbers, sounds, and other stimuli. Anything that's not rehearsed is discarded. (c) Long-term memory stores the permanent data and experiences of a lifetime. Remembering is based on what you retain in long-term memory. Most memories are triggered by cues and stimuli from the environment, a process known as *recall* or *recollection*. Recognition is a visual form of memory retrieval, while forgetting is an inability to retrieve information from long-term memory. People forget because stored data is blocked, distorted, repressed, or fades through disuse.

6 Research shows that memory and learning can be improved through the use of drugs that improve brain function. Hormones such as ACTH and MSH show promise in aiding normal people, as well as improving the abilities of the retarded and senile. Learning-improvement drugs will not increase mental capabilities. Instead, they help people make maximum use of their abilities without interference from emotional or social factors.

7 Cognition includes thinking, remembering, problem solving, and creativity. Thinking is the process of gathering, classifying, and using the data that come into long-term memory. Images, symbols, concepts, and rules are used in the thinking process, which can be either directed or nondirected. Directed thinking moves in a straight line from point A to point B, and so on. Nondirected thinking relies on images and feelings, as in fantasies and daydreams. Images are pictorial recalls of specific objects or events. Symbols, particularly words, allow you to label objects and events so that you can deal with them when the actual objects aren't around. Concepts enable you to put things into categories and to establish relationships. Rules set up relationships between concepts. The rules establish standards for behavior and explain how things work.

8 Language plays a vital role in thinking. Babies develop language skills in predictable steps, for they are apparently born with a capacity to learn the complex structure of spoken language. Language interacts with culture, one influencing the other.

9 A problem-solving situation occurs whenever needs are blocked or a question needs answering. Good problem solvers are also good learners. They know how to use learning techniques such as overlearning, removal of negative conditions, use of different types of practice, verbalization, and improvement of listening skills. Typical methods of problem solving include trial-and-error (using all possible solutions until the right one is found), inductive reasoning (using particular facts to reach general conclusions), deductive reasoning (using general principles to solve specific cases), and insight (the sudden perception of key relationships).

10 Mind set is a person's consistent way of thinking about a particular situation or problem. Rigidity means that someone will continue using a certain behavior even when it doesn't work any longer. Functional fixedness keeps people from finding new uses for familiar objects. Vertical (directive)

thinking provides a logical, step-by-step approach to problem solving. Lateral (non-directive) thinking teaches you how to break rigid patterns of thinking by freely considering new and unexpected alternatives.

11 Creativity is the reorganization of old ideas and processes into something novel or useful. Only a few people are highly creative, but others can improve their creative thought by learning how to free their minds from self-imposed restrictions on their creativity. Creative thinking requires flexibility (the willingness to give up nonproductive ways of thinking), persistence (the willingness to keep working when the first attempts don't pay off), and insight (the breakthrough that allows for recombination of existing materials or ideas). Creativity can be nurtured or improved by encouraging creative thought in young children. Stimulating toys and games and other ways of rewarding imagination seem to help. Older children and adults can try activities that encourage creativity, such as games, handicrafts, and artistic pursuits.

Solution to Figure 10.11 (page 311)

Since Harry isn't talking, there are any number of reasons to explain his change in spending habits. Here are some sample explanations. How many more did you write down?

1. Harry just learned that he has an incurable illness and wants to enjoy his money before he dies.

2. Harry just won the New York State Lottery and is celebrating his good fortune.

3. Harry has inherited a fortune from a rich aunt and is determined to enjoy his new wealth.

4. Standard Oil found petroleum under his land and paid him a large royalty for the right to drill there.

5. Harry has had a nervous breakdown and isn't aware of what he's doing.

And so on. Try this problem with a group of friends. It's not only fun; it's a good exercise for developing your thinking abilities. Brains improve with exercise, just as muscles do.

Solution to Figure 10.12 (page 312)

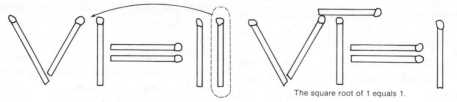

The square root of 1 equals 1.

You should also give yourself credit for either of these alternative answers:

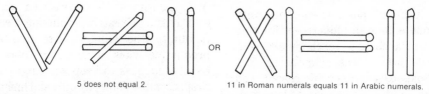

5 does not equal 2.   OR   11 in Roman numerals equals 11 in Arabic numerals.

Solution to Figure 10.13 (page 314)

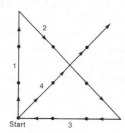

Many people make the assumption that they must stay *within* the square formed by the nine dots. Once you break free of this unnecessary mind set, a solution becomes possible.

Solution to Figure 10.14 (page 314)

As soon as you can see that the screwdriver can be used as a weight instead of a tool, the problem is solved.

Solution to Figure 10.15 (page 314)

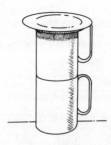

Use one of the cups to cover the other. Then put the saucer on top.

Solution to Figure 10.17 (page 317)

Borrow one nut from each of the other wheels, and drive slowly to the nearest repair shop.

PUTTING YOUR KNOWLEDGE TO WORK

Terms you should know

brainstorming

cognition

cognitive theory

concepts

creativity

deductive reasoning

directed thinking

eidetic recall

flexibility

functional fixedness

image

inductive reasoning

insight

lateral thinking

learning

long-term memory

memory

mind set

mnemonic devices

nondirected thinking

operant behavior

overlearning

positive reinforcement

punishment

recall

rehearsal

respondent behavior

rules

sensory memory

short-term memory

signals

stimulus-response theory

symbols

thinking

trial and error

verbalization

vertical thinking

Objective questions

1 Which statement best summarizes the importance of Lucy the chimp's use of sign language? (a) Lucy's thinking skills are probably equal to those of human beings. (b) Chimpanzees should be reclassified as members of the species *Homo sapiens*. (c) Lucy's language skills demonstrate an ability to think and reason at a level higher than any other animal has yet shown. (d) Lucy's "speech" is nothing more than copy-cat behavior, similar to the speech of a parrot.

2 Which of the following would *not* be considered an example of learning? (a) You touch a hot stove and instantly pull your hand away. (b) You master the art of baiting a fishing hook. (c) You travel in Mexico and become comfortable with the different customs. (d) You go backpacking on a mountain trail you've never seen before.

3 A dictator who wanted to train people to obey any order without question would be most likely to use (a) classical respondent conditioning techniques (b) operant conditioning techniques (c) the cognitive theory of learning (d) none of

these. People cannot be conditioned to behave in ways that violate basic human values.

4 If you were writing a story in which mad scientists set out to destroy people's ability to form new long-term memories, you would have them destroy (a) the hippocampus (b) the visual cortex (c) the memory center (d) any part of the old brain.

5 The process by which you can move data from short-term memory into long-term memory is (a) retrieval (b) recall (c) reinforcement (d) rehearsal.

6 Sheila says, "I don't remember anything the nuclear-power-company president said. I'm against building nuclear generating plants anyway." Her statement suggests that she's demonstrating a type of forgetting known as (a) interference effect (b) distortion (c) repression (d) decay through disuse.

7 Which of the following is an example of nondirected thinking? (a) Susan plans a hiking trip through the High Sierras. (b) Tom lies in a hammock, watching the clouds form patterns in the sky. (c) Pete works through a series of geometry problems. (d) Mrs. Thorne tries to figure out how to make the food budget stretch to the end of the month.

8 When someone solves a problem unexpectedly after working on it for a long time, the solution is said to come through (a) positive reinforcement (b) rigidity (c) assimilation (d) insight.

9 All of the following are techniques of lateral thinking *except* (a) brainstorming (b) opening up to alternatives (c) shifting attention (d) inductive reasoning.

10 Which of the following is a *true* statement regarding creativity? (a) All people have the same potential for creativity. (b) Mind set is a useful aid to creativity. (c) Creative people stick to straight-line thinking when solving problems. (d) Creative thinking can be learned and improved, at least to a degree.

Discussion questions

1 Imagine that someone has just given you a six-week-old puppy. It's your job to train the dog to be a well-behaved member of the family. How could learning theory help you? Why would stimulus-response learning theory work better in training the puppy than cognitive theory?

2 What are the three types of memory? Why do you think humans need all three? If everything people learn is stored in long-term memory, why do they still forget things?

3 How does straight-line, vertical thinking differ from lateral thinking? Which would be better for solving a problem in mathematics? Which would be better for figuring out a way to increase attendance at school dances? Why?

4 How can teachers and parents encourage creativity in a young child?

5 How does mind set inferfere with problem solving? Why would brainstorming be a useful method of overcoming rigid thinking and functional fixedness?

Activities

1 Compile a number of puzzles, some easy, some difficult. (James Fixx's two books, *Games for the Superintelligent* and *More Games for the Superintelligent* are good sources.) Give the puzzles to several friends and relatives. Pay special attention to their problem-solving techniques. Note the types of reasoning they use, how long they persist, what role insight plays in their thinking. You may find a few people who immediately say, "I can't do puzzles" and refuse to try. What does that tell you about their mind set?

2 Would your relatives or friends make reliable witnesses? Set up a test for them, following this general procedure: At a time when you have a group of people together (a family get-together would be perfect), arrange for several "actors" to put on a dramatic scene. It can involve a fight or an accident. The entire scene should not take longer than a minute. As soon as it's over, ask each witness to write an account of what he or she saw happen. Do not let the witnesses talk to one another. Collect the reports and compare them. You'll probably find a wide diversity of opinion as to what actually happened. Why?

3 Pick up a copy of A. S. Neill's famous book, *Summerhill*. Summerhill, you'll discover, is the model for the free school movement. Its philosophy is that children learn best when they are free to select their own classroom activities. In fact, the youngsters at Summerhill are free to choose whether they will go to class or not. You may not agree with all of A. S. Neill's ideas, but you'll find his school a fascinating contrast to the typical American classroom.

4 Research the current developments in the use of drugs that alter brain chemistry. Your local library would be a good place to start. Check the *Readers' Guide to Periodical Literature* for current articles in such magazines as *Psychology Today* as well as the news magazines. How close are learning-enhancing drugs to widespread use? What restrictions are being placed on their use? Report on your findings to your psychology class.

5 A simple, interesting exercise in creativity can take place either in a classroom or with a group of friends. Start telling a story by introducing a main character and a situation. Take your main character to a cliffhanging moment, and then pass the story on to the next person to

continue. Each person adds his or her own creative touches and sets up wilder adventures for the next storyteller. The experience will undoubtedly have its humorous moments. But it will also reveal unsuspected creativity in just about everyone.

6 You can set up your own learning experiment by first making a simple maze for your subjects to "run." On an 8″ x 18″ piece of wood, Celotex, or wallboard, stick thumbtacks as shown in the diagram at the top of this page. Each tack should just touch the next. Do not show the maze to your subjects (Ss). Blindfold each S and ask him or her to find a path through the maze by tracing it with a finger. As the experimenter (E), your job is to time each trial and keep a record of the number of errors each S makes during each trial. Allow ten trials for each S. Anyone who solves the maze twice in succession without an error can stop. Afterward, use your data to draw conclusions about the performance of your Ss. For example, did age or sex make any difference in their performance? Did the Ss use strictly trial-and-error learning, or did they show some cognitive learning? Did any of the Ss show more persistence than others?

For further reading

Edson, Lee. *How We Learn*. Alexandria, VA: Time-Life Books, 1975. A well-illustrated and readable introduction to what psychologists have learned about learning.

Ghiselin, Brewster, ed. *The Creative Process*. New York: New American Library, 1955. A fascinating look at creativity through the writings of thirty-eight famous people, from Mozart to Einstein.

Keyes, Daniel. *Flowers for Algernon*. New York: Harcourt Brace Jovanovich, 1966. Charly Gordon is retarded—until doctors perform an operation that turns him into a genius. You'll never think of the retarded in the same way again after reading this book, which also became a successful movie called *Charly*.

Kozol, John. *Death at an Early Age*. Boston: Houghton Mifflin, 1967. Kozol blasts American schools in general and ghetto schools in particular for taking well-motivated, creative kids and making them into turned-off, unhappy robots.

Lorayne, Harry and Jerry Lucas. *The Memory Book*. New York: Stein & Day, 1974. If you want to improve your memory, you'll find this book a useful guide.

Raudsepp, Eugene and George P. Hough. *Creative Growth Games*. New York: Harcourt Brace Jovanovich, 1977. The authors have compiled a collection of seventy-five games and puzzles guaranteed to challenge your creative talents. As a bonus, they add useful discussions on how each exercise relates to some aspect of the creative process.

Watson, James D. *The Double Helix*. New York: Atheneum, 1968. Watson's search for the riddle of DNA makes for a satisfying scientific detective story, as well as a useful insight into the process of creativity.

11

PSYCHOLOGICAL TESTING

Figure 11.1

Did you look at the picture above this paragraph before you started reading? If you're like most people, you probably glanced at it and then went on. In a moment, though, you'll be asked to take a longer look.

Is this some sort of memory test? No, it's not even one of those tricky questions psychologists sometimes spring on unwary subjects. No hidden figures lurk in the shadows, and you won't be asked to remember whether or not the woman is wearing an apron. The picture *is* part of a test, however.

Ready? Look carefully at the picture for a full minute. Think about what's happening there. When you're ready, make up a story based on what you see. Explain the events

that took place just before the picture was taken, as well as what's happening now. You can keep the picture in front of you, but concentrate on the plot. Don't worry about the descriptive details. It doesn't matter whether you write your story down on a piece of paper or just make it up in your head. When you've finished, go on to the explanation below.

You've just completed a sample item from the Michigan Picture Test, one of many personality tests used by psychologists. When interpreted by a *psychometrist* (a specialist in psychological testing), these tests provide useful clues about the test taker's emotions, interests, and ways of thinking. Interpretation can be difficult, for no two people respond exactly alike to test items such as this one. For example, eighteen-year-old Marian made up this story after seeing the picture:

> It's one o'clock, and the cop is bringing Frank home for breaking curfew again. Mrs. Smith is worried, but she feels helpless. She's just been divorced, and, without a father around, Frank won't listen to her. The cop doesn't understand the problem. He's warning her that Frank is on the way to becoming a delinquent. What is Frank thinking? I don't know. He's pretty mixed up. Maybe a good beating would help.

Marian obviously saw elements in the picture that reflected some of her own feelings. Perhaps in your story you identified with one of the people in the picture. If you took the boy's point of view, for example, it might mean that you're relating to a similar incident in your own life. In the same way, your description of the woman and the man in uniform might reveal your general attitude toward authority figures. Did you agree with Marian that the uniformed man is a police officer? Most people do, but actually the photograph is of a milkman.

The psychometrists who evaluate test responses look particularly for recurring themes, such as hostilities, fears, and anxieties. Along with negative traits, they'll also be alert to positive characteristics.

In contrast with Marian's story, this one was written by sixteen-year-old Zoë:

> Tonight will be a happy time at the Foster house! Young Sid was kidnapped four days ago, but he escaped and was rescued by the police. Officer O'Neal has just brought him home, and his mother is just about to give him a hug. Sid not only escaped; he told the police exactly where to find the kidnappers, down to the license number of their car. As soon as Sid's dad comes home, they'll have a big celebration, with all kinds of good things to eat.

Zoë's story demonstrates not only her creative imagination but also her strong sense of family unity. A psychological evaluation would also point out the lack of anxiety in Zoë's writing. If she thinks she can cope with a kidnapping, everyday life probably won't be able to frustrate her.

Personality tests represent only one type of psychological test. Even though you've probably never taken the Michigan Picture Test, your school career has exposed you to other types of testing: measures of intelligence, achievement, aptitude, and interests. This chapter will discuss each of these different types of tests, as well as some of the controversy that surrounds their use.

11.1 WHAT DO PSYCHOLOGISTS MEAN BY INTELLIGENCE AND IQ?

11.2 HOW DO PSYCHOLOGISTS MEASURE INTELLIGENCE?

11.3 DO INTELLIGENCE TESTS REALLY MEASURE INTELLIGENCE?

11.4 WHAT DO ACHIEVEMENT AND APTITUDE TESTS REVEAL?

11.5 WHAT CAN YOU LEARN FROM PERSONALITY TESTS?

11.1 WHAT DO PSYCHOLOGISTS MEAN BY INTELLIGENCE AND IQ?

Try this experiment. Ask three people to define intelligence. Everyone understands, more or less, what the word means, but it's still difficult to define exactly. Most of your subjects will probably fall back on the use of synonyms. "Intelligence? Well, you know, smart, uh . . . clever." Keep track of the definitions people give you, and compare your findings with those collected by your classmates. Which definition do you think is best?

Psychologists have been faced with the same problem for a long time. Before they could measure intelligence, they had to define it. In 1923, Professor Edwin Boring, of

Harvard University, stated flatly that "intelligence is what the tests test." Boring meant that the writers of intelligence tests were defining intelligence as what people scored on their tests. While more than fifty years have passed since Boring's criticism, psychologists still are trying to come up with a perfect definition of intelligence.

Intelligence defined

Albert Einstein stands out as a perfect example of the problems involved in defining intelligence. The Nobel Prize winner in

Figure 11.2

ALMOST EVERYONE HAS TRIED TO DEFINE INTELLIGENCE

The fact that psychologists have had trouble defining intelligence hasn't kept others from trying. Here are a few of the more interesting comments.

Intelligence consists of recognizing opportunity.

CHINESE PROVERB

Much learning does not teach a man to have intelligence.

HERACLITUS

It is the mark of intelligence, no matter what you are doing, to enjoy doing it.

ANONYMOUS

The intellect is the tool to find the truth. It's a matter of sharpening it.

SYLVIA ASHTON-WARNER

Intelligence is not something possessed once for all. It is in constant process of forming, and its retention requires constant alertness in observing consequences, an open-minded will to learn and courage in readjustment.

JOHN DEWEY

An intelligent person is one who has learned . . . that good is better than evil, that confidence should supersede fear, that love is superior to hate, that gentleness is better than cruelty, forbearance than intolerance, compassion than arrogance, and that truth has more virtue than ignorance.

J. MARTIN KLOTSCHE

The true test of intelligence is not how much we know how to do, but how we behave when we don't know what to do.

JOHN HOLT

Which definition do you like best? Try writing your own. The game is open to everyone.

physics, the man who unlocked the power of the atom, was once asked to leave school because his grades were so poor. Einstein failed his entrance examination for technical school, and the University of Zurich in Switzerland later turned down his doctoral dissertation. Even after he graduated, he had a hard time finding a job. Yet, can you find anyone who would say Albert Einstein wasn't intelligent?

If a person can be brilliant in one area and appear to be slow in another, it seems obvious that no single "thing" called intelligence exists. Instead, *intelligence is the total of all the mental abilities that allow people to solve whatever problems they think are worth working on.* In his early years, Einstein obviously did not find routine schoolwork worth concentrating on and thus did poorly.

Not all psychologists have been satisfied with this general approach. L. L. Thurstone, a pioneer in the field of mental testing, developed a catalog of seven basic mental abilities that he thought make up intelligence.

1. *Word fluency:* a measure of your ability to think of words rapidly in response to a cue consisting of initial letters or rhymes.

Write as many words as you can that begin with the letter *d* and end with *r*. The length of the words doesn't matter. You may use proper nouns or foreign words.

2. *Reasoning ability:* a measure of your ability to use deductive or inductive reasoning.

Look at the row of letters *abacada* ___. The next letter should be *e*. Now use the same procedure to complete these series: *azbycxd* ___. *mmmlllkkk* ___. *acegik* ___.

3. *Memory:* a measure of your ability to learn word lists or other material rapidly.

Study the following code: a = 2, e = 4, l = 6, m = 8. Now, without looking at the code, translate the following words: 8264, 264, 468.

4. *Spatial perception:* a measure of your ability to think in visual terms, such as interpreting drawings or recognizing a geometric figure.

The following figure is shown from a bird's-eye view, looking directly down on it. Which of the other figures represents a proper side view of the same object?

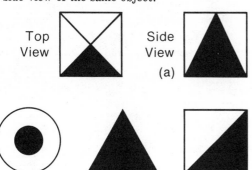

5. *Perceptual ability:* a measure of your ability to see and understand what's happening around you.

In each row of faces, one face is different from the others. Which one is it? If you guessed the first face in row (a), you're correct. Now do the same with rows (b) and (c).

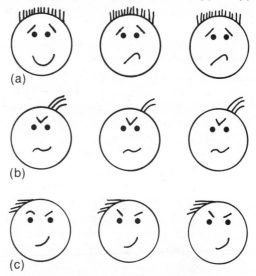

6. *Numerical skills:* a measure of your ability to use simple arithmetic.

Select the proper answer to the following problems. Don't work out the entire problem, as the correct answer is always given. Use any shortcuts that you can.

(a) $5.8681 \times 8.1197 =$ ——— (a) 47.647211
    (b) 40.824419
    (c) 19.723092
    (d) 54.098340

(b) $\sqrt{105.3468}$ = ——— (a) 8.4398295
    (b) 10.263946
    (c) 15.7836212
    (d) 32.982712

7. *Verbal relationships:* a measure of your ability to read and understand written material.

Read the following proverb: Too many cooks spoil the soup. Now, which two of the following statements have nearly the same meaning as the proverb? (a) Many hands make light work. (b) If you want a job done right, do it yourself. (c) Big oaks from little acorns grow. (d) Necessity is the mother of invention. (e) If you want to make sure a job doesn't get done, give it to a committee.

Other psychologists have gone on to modify Thurstone's list, mostly by identifying additional mental abilities. One researcher, for example, drew up a monumental list of 238 different types of intelligence. Less ambitious, but potentially more useful, is psychologist J. P. Guilford's concept. He sees intelligence as made up of 120 distinct "blocks," each identified by (1) the kind of material acted on, (2) what actions were carried out with the material, and (3) what products resulted. Sample intelligence factors in Guilford's model include the ability to identify classes of words; the ability to remember a system of numerals, symbols, or letters; the ability to state the correct deduction from given facts; and the ability to produce clever or uncommon responses.

Guilford believes that everyone has all 120 of these abilities, but in varying degrees. If Elton Y. takes one of Guilford's diagnostic tests, for example, he might find that he's strong in the ability to evaluate but weak on dealing with word meanings. Elton's counselor could then prescribe exercises that would build up his vocabulary and word-usage skills. He'll also be encouraged to look for a career where his ability to evaluate alternate choices would be useful, such as in business administration.

The concept of IQ

Most people recognize the widely used term *intelligence quotient (IQ)*. Unfortunately, many people confuse the *quality* (intelligence) with the *measure* (IQ). As defined earlier, intelligence is the basic human ability to solve problems, slowly or quickly. IQ, on the other hand, is a convenient yardstick for comparing an individual's mental abilities with those of the rest of the population.

While intelligence seems to be something you're born with, it can be influenced by a number of environmental factors. IQ is never anything more than a numerical score

derived from a specific test. Its usefulness depends on the accuracy and fairness of the test, the conditions under which the test is given, and the way people interpret the score.

As an example, look at how fifteen-year-old Dwight's IQ score is figured. Dwight will first have to take an intelligence test in order to obtain his *mental age* (MA). This number tells Dwight how he scored in relation to other fifteen-year-olds who have taken the test. To figure his IQ, Dwight's *chronological age* (CA) must also be known. The formula looks like this:

$$IQ = \frac{\text{Mental Age (MA)}}{\text{Chronological Age (CA)}} \times 100$$

Thus, if Dwight tested at an MA of sixteen years, two months, the equation works out to an IQ of 108 ($\frac{16.17}{15} \times 100 = 108$).

The basic assumption behind the IQ score is that the average person's CA and MA will be the same. By this system, therefore, the typical six-year-old would be expected to score 6/6 × 100, or 100 IQ. In actual test situations, however, it turns out that about half the population ranks above 100 and the other half falls below 100. Some people do score at exactly the 100 level, of course, but psychometrists are more interested in the general distribution of scores.

Extensive testing has established the percentage of people who will fall into any specific segment of the IQ scale. This prediction is based on a graph known as the *normal curve of distribution*. If you set up a scale and weighed every student in your school, the graph of their weights would follow a bell-shaped curve, or normal curve of distribution. A few students would fall at the extreme ends, but most people would bunch up toward the middle, or average, weight. Such a curve would look something like Figure 11.3.

What does this curve have to do with Dwight? Remember, his IQ figured out to be 108. A study of the distribution of IQ scores from a sample of 2,904 subjects

CURVE OF NORMAL DISTRIBUTION: STUDENT WEIGHTS IN A TYPICAL HIGH-SCHOOL POPULATION

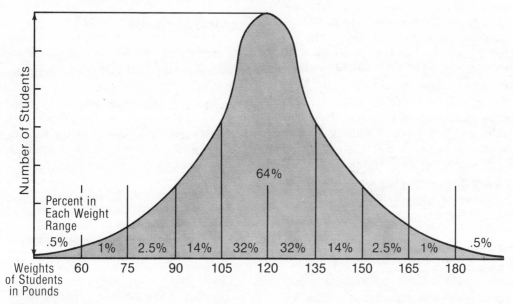

Figure 11.3

yielded a curve quite close to a perfect bell-shaped curve. (See Figure 11.4. The revised Stanford-Binet was standardized with the use of this group.) Over the years, psychologists have labeled the various categories that make up the IQ curve and the percentage of the population that falls into each category.

According to this curve, Dwight's 108 IQ score puts him toward the top end of the average category. Does that mean he's better than someone with an IQ of 98 and inferior to someone else who scored in the superior category? Psychologists are quick to point out that IQ scores don't measure a person's real-life achievements. Qualities

DISTRIBUTION OF IQ SCORES IN A TYPICAL POPULATION, AGES TWO TO EIGHTEEN

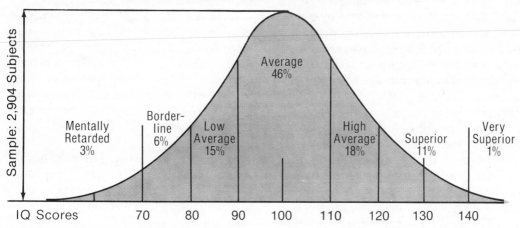

Figure 11.4

such as motivation, persistence, and stability count just as heavily as intelligence.

Perhaps Dwight wants to be a mechanic. If he's gifted with good mechanical abilities and really wants to succeed at his craft, he'll probably make a crackerjack mechanic. But Bryan, with an IQ of 128, prefers to take it easy. Bryan also would like to be a mechanic, but he can't be bothered with learning the details of his trade. He learns quickly, and he's good at bluffing his way through. (Of course, bright people are no more lazy than others. Bryan is just one particular person who is both bright and lazy.) In practical terms, many people would wonder if Bryan is really more intelligent than Dwight.

SECTION CHECKUP

1 Give a working definition of intelligence.

2 List some of the individual abilities that make up the general quality called intelligence.

3 Ursula has a mental age of twelve years, six months, and a chronological age of ten years. What is her IQ? Would you put her in the average, high average, or superior category?

4 Is Ursula's IQ a guarantee of success in life? Why or why not?

11.2 HOW DO PSYCHOLOGISTS MEASURE INTELLIGENCE?

Imagine for a moment that it's 1524 and you're the adviser to King Henry VIII of England. War with Spain seems close, and the army must be built up quickly. Henry turns to you and orders you to select only the bravest, most skillful, and most intelligent archers to support his royal knights. You swallow hard, because you know that Henry's wrath could send you to the dungeon if you make a mistake. How would you choose the best archers?

Throughout history, people have been trying to make choices like this one. Sometimes the selections have been made on the basis of observation, sometimes by guesswork, and sometimes by testing people for the qualities needed. As a clever adviser, you'd probably think up some tests for your candidates. Let the archers shoot for distance and accuracy to test their skill. Send them through an obstacle course under fire to test their bravery. And make up a set of problems relating to warfare to test their intelligence.

Although such testing and evaluation of people's abilities are nothing new, formal testing of intelligence began only in this century. The breakthrough came with the work of two French psychologists, Alfred Binet

(see BioBox, page 336) and Theodore Simon. In 1905, Binet published a series of intelligence tests intended for use with schoolchildren. Binet grouped his tests by chronological age and coined the term "mental age" to represent an individual child's achievement. Suzanne, for example, might do well on those tests usually passed by nine-year-olds but fail those passed by ten-year-olds. Whatever Suzanne's birth age, Binet believed that he had established her mental age at nine. Under the IQ formula, Suzanne has an IQ score of 113 if she's eight, but only 75 if she's twelve.

Although intelligence testing has become more complex and heavily computerized since Binet, the basic approach has changed very little. The test maker constructs questions and problems that seem appropriate for testing general intelligence. After a number of people have taken the test, the results are evaluated. Poor questions are eliminated and new ones written. Once enough data has been gathered on how typical seven-year-olds score, for example, the raw scores can be converted into mental age equivalents for all seven-year-olds who take the test.

That's basically what Dr. L. M. Terman

Figure 11.5

DOES HIGH IQ CORRELATE WITH GREAT ACHIEVEMENTS?

Do you need a genius-level IQ to do great things? That's not completely clear. But when psychologists examine the lives of famous people, they find that their intelligence puts them in the upper 1 percent of the population. The estimates shown here are based on what these high-achievers did as children, verified by their later successes.

George Washington
American President
140

Elizabeth I
Queen of England
145

George Sand
French Writer
150

George Washington Carver
American Scientist
155

Madame Marie Curie
French Scientist
160

Confucius
Chinese Philosopher
170

Sir Isaac Newton
English Scientist
190

Johann Wolfgang von Goethe
German Poet-Philosopher
210

BioBox

ALFRED BINET:
CREATOR OF THE MODERN INTELLIGENCE TEST

Intelligence testing on a scientific basis began with the French psychologist Alfred Binet (1857–1911). Binet had a background in medicine and law when he entered the relatively new field of psychology in 1886. He soon was asked by Paris school officials to design a way to classify retarded children so that they could be properly educated. Binet first tried every possible measure of intelligence available at the time. He compared head sizes, looked into palmistry, and made careful measurements of reaction time. None of those techniques seemed to work.

In the early 1900s, Binet collaborated with another psychologist, Theodore Simon, in an attempt to establish exact standards for the measurement of intelligence. They proposed that a series of tests should be developed, each test to be of increasing difficulty. The tests should start from the lowest intellectual level that could be observed and end with that of normal intelligence. These tests, when given to children, would rate the intelligence level of each individual child within his or her group.

Binet wrote about his work:

Our principal conclusion is that we actually possess an instrument which will allow us to measure the intellectual development of young children. ... Of what use is a measure of intelligence? Without

doubt one could conceive ... of a future where the social sphere would be better organized than ours; where everyone would work according to his known aptitudes in such a way that no particle of psychic force should be lost for society. That would be the ideal city. It is indeed far from us.

Binet also looked forward to a time when parents and teachers could make use of intelligence tests as a way of better understanding their children.

A father and mother who raise a child themselves, ... would have great satisfaction in knowing that the intelligence of a child can be measured and would willingly make the necessary effort to find out if their own child is intelligent. We think especially of teachers who love their profession, who interest themselves in their pupils, and who understand that the first condition of instructing them well is to know them.

What would Binet say if he heard a counselor tell a student, "I'm sorry, but with an IQ like yours, you shouldn't plan on going to college"? Why would he agree or disagree with this use of IQ scores?

did at Stanford University in 1916, when he revised the original Binet test for use in the United States. Terman set up the test, known as the Stanford-Binet, to give credit for each level passed. If Lola, age six, passes all tests rated for six-year-olds, she receives credit for an MA of six. If she also passes four of six tests at the seven-year-old level, she receives eight months additional credit. If she then cannot pass any tests at the eight-year level, she receives no additional credit. Lola, according to the Stanford-Binet, has an MA of six years, eight months, and an IQ of 111.

Criteria for constructing tests

Measuring intelligence with a carelessly constructed test would be like using a rubber ruler to lay out a new house. None of the measurements would make any sense. Before any IQ test can be used for measuring intelligence, therefore, it must meet four criteria.

Objectivity. A test achieves *objectivity* when it can be taken and evaluated without the examiner's personal feelings affecting the scores. A test made up of multiple-choice questions, for example, can be scored objectively. The scorer's likes or dislikes cannot influence the results. Tests that require interpretation of answers open the doors to *subjectivity* and put pressure on the psychometrist to remain as objective as possible. A test with good objectivity should give similar scores whenever the same person retakes the test under the same testing conditions.

Standardization. By *standardization*, psychometrists mean first that a test must be administered consistently. Time allowances, instructions, and other details of the testing situation must be handled the same every time the test is given. Standardization also refers to the establishing of *norms*—average or "normal" performance on the test. If you took a test, for example,

and scored 84, would you feel good about it? That sounds like a good score, but you'd first want to know how other people did on the same test. If the average score was 67, your 84 would be an excellent mark. But if most people got 98, your 84 would rank below average. That's why norms must be set up for standardized tests. Only after the test-maker gives the test to a cross-section of the population can raw scores be translated into meaningful results.

To make interpretation easier, test results are often given in *percentile rankings*. Perhaps your raw score of 84 puts you in the 67th percentile. That means that you scored better than 66 percent of the people who have taken the test in the past. In the same way, a score at the 34th percentile would mean that you outscored only 33 percent of the norm group.

Reliability. A test that gives consistent scores whenever a subject is retested is said to have *reliability*. To achieve reliability, test makers try to eliminate test items that can be answered correctly without knowing anything about the subject. They also stay away from items that refer to a narrow field of knowledge. A question based on chess moves, for example, would be easy for chess players but quite unfair for most other people. The test should have enough questions so as to provide a fair test of the ability being tested. A reliable test must also be written clearly and simply. Technical words, slang terms, and references to changing fads can soon make the test out of date. Even the most reliable test, however, cannot compensate for test takers who don't care about the results or who are fatigued, sick, or emotionally upset. When possible, those people should take the test at another time.

Validity. A test has *validity* if it measures what it claims to measure. Intelligence tests have been found that actually measure reading comprehension rather than intelligence. That type of test is like measuring a pound of

Figure 11.6

THE TESTS AREN'T ALWAYS PERFECT: UNFAIR TEST ITEMS

No matter how hard test makers work to make their tests perfect, some unfair items still slip through. The following items appeared in an intelligence test sold to the general public. Answer the two questions before reading further.

1. Which one of the five shapes is least like the other four?

A   Z   F   N   M

2. Which one of the five designs is least like the other four?

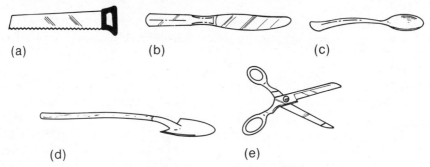

(a)   (b)   (c)

(d)   (e)

The answers and explanations given by the test makers can be found on page 359. Can you think of any answers other than those given? If so, and your logic is valid, then the questions must be classed as unfair. In a properly standardized test, items like these two would be thrown out and replaced with better ones.

---

apples with a yardstick. Test validity can be judged best by comparing the later performance of test takers with their test scores. Remember that test you were going to set up for King Henry's archers? To check its validity, select men whose scores range from low to high. Then send them into battle and rate their performance. If high-scoring archers do well in combat and low-scoring men do poorly, you can consider your test valid. If not, perhaps the King will give you another chance. (Figure 11.7 gives you a chance to make your own intelligence test, using only the dictionary as a resource.)

Types of intelligence tests

Intelligence tests fall into two categories, individual and group. Each type has its own strengths and weaknesses.

Individual intelligence tests. The most valid and reliable intelligence tests are administered on a one-to-one basis. For this reason, they are also the most expensive type to take. If you were scheduled for an individual intelligence test, the examiner might begin by chatting with you for a few minutes in order to develop a relaxed and friendly atmosphere. Then you would be asked to respond to a series of questions. Some of these questions require that you answer with a word or definition, while others ask you to solve a problem. On the Stanford-Binet, adult level, the questions and problems will include such items as these:

1. Define the following words: *brunette, corrupt, sanguine* (twenty-six words in all).
2. Finding reasons: Give three reasons why a soldier who deserts to the enemy should be punished.
3. Explaining proverbs: What does "A bird in the hand is worth two in the bush" mean?
4. Ingenuity: A child lost a valuable diamond ring in a field overgrown with weeds. What would be the most efficient way to find the ring without damaging it? (The solution is on page 359.)

The examiner records two types of data during the test: your actual answers and your emotional reactions. The answers are graded for correctness, originality, and maturity of thought. Any obvious signs of nervousness, anxiety, or lack of interest are also recorded and included in the evaluation.

The Stanford-Binet is actually a series of tests graded for twenty levels of ability. The two-year-old level starts by asking the child to identify pictures of common objects, repeat two-digit numbers, and obey simple

---

Figure 11.7

HOW TO MAKE UP YOUR OWN INTELLIGENCE TEST

Dr. L. M. Terman, who designed the Stanford-Binet Intelligence Test, wrote in 1918, "The vocabulary test has a far higher value than any other single test of the scale." He claimed that in most cases the vocabulary test alone would give an IQ score 90 percent as accurate as the complete Stanford-Binet. Terman compiled his vocabulary list by selecting words at random from a dictionary.

You can make up your own intelligence test based on the Terman model. Start with a college-level dictionary. Open the dictionary at random to the middle of the *A*'s, and write down the last word on the right-hand page. From that point, select the last word in every sixth column. When you've collected one hundred words, test yourself on your ability to define the words chosen in this random fashion. If you think you've looked at the definition as you went along, exchange your list with someone else in your class. Score yourself as follows:

Words correct	Mental age
20	Eight years
30	Ten years
40	Twelve years
50	Fourteen years
65	Average adult
75	Superior adult

Do you think that a vocabulary test provides a valid test of intelligence? Why or why not?

commands. By age six, children are also expected to define words, tell the difference between a cat and a fish, and solve a maze. Twelve-year-olds move on to questions such as "Paul's head is so big he has to put his shirt on over his feet. What's foolish about that statement?" Lower-level tests tend to be concrete and often use pictures and objects to focus the child's attention. At the upper levels, the tests emphasize abstract reasoning and verbal skills. At all levels, subjects are expected to display good recall of past experience, judgment, interpretation, a long attention span, immediate memory, and other cognitive processes.

The Wechsler Intelligence Scale for Children (WISC) and the Wechsler Adult Intelligence Scale (WAIS) differ in several ways from the Stanford-Binet. Some critics have charged that the Stanford-Binet depends too heavily on vocabulary and word usage. The Wechsler relies more upon performance tests (see Figure 11.8). If you took the WAIS, you'd be asked questions such as the following:

Figure 11.8

Individual tests such as the Wechsler Adult Intelligence Scale often seem more like a game than an examination. What do you think the examiner is looking for in this object-assembly exercise?

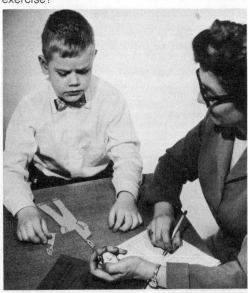

1. General information: When is Labor Day celebrated?

2. Arithmetic reasoning: If the sales tax is 6 percent, what is the total price of a sixty-cent ball-point pen?

3. Digit span: Listen carefully, and then repeat the numbers—9 4 7 2 8 3.

4. Picture completion: What important part of the picture shown here is missing?

		JULY				
S	M	T	W	T	F	S
1	2	3	4	5	6	7
8	9	10	11	12	13	14
15	16	17	18	19	20	21
22	23	24	25	26	27	28
29	30	31				

5. Block design: Use the four blocks shown here to make a design like the completed figure. (Actual blocks are provided on the Wechsler.)

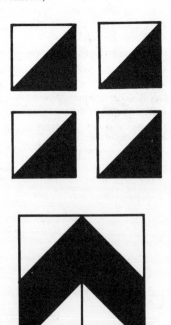

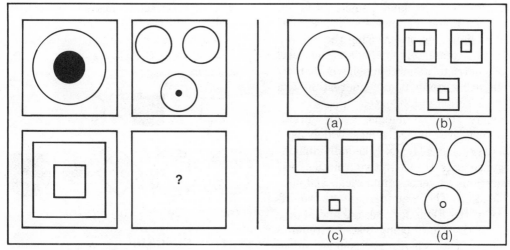

Figure 11.9

The Wechsler provides three separate IQ scores: a verbal IQ, a performance IQ, and a total IQ. Psychologists find this breakdown useful when dealing with subjects who are handicapped by language, educational, or cultural differences.

In addition to the well-known Stanford-Binet and Wechsler tests, other tests have been developed for testing special subjects. Tests of infants, for example, are based on observation of the child's behavior at a particular age. Does Suzy sit up? Walk? Does she turn to look at a new sound? Can she pick up a block? How does she react to strangers? Studies of large numbers of infants have established norms for scoring Suzy's developmental progress.

Similarly, a nonverbal test has been designed for use where language and cultural variables invalidate other tests. The Progressive Matrices Test uses sets of two-dimensional figures to test the subject's ability to perceive relationships. The figures range from relatively simple forms to complex patterns. A sample similar to the Progressive Matrices Test can be seen in Figure 11.9. Your job is to choose the proper figure to complete the relationship.

Group intelligence tests. For most people, taking an intelligence test means sitting down in a large room with a number of other people, all taking the same test at the same time. If that seems like mass production, it does have several advantages. First, by testing large groups at one time, the costs of testing can be lowered dramatically. Also, the examiners need not have extensive training. The scoring is quick and objective. Another advantage of group testing lies in the well-developed norms that have been collected over the years. The Army General Classification Test (AGCT), for example, has been given to literally millions of men and women. This forty-minute test has been extensively standardized and also has a high validity.

The disadvantages of group tests, however, cancel out some of these strengths. One problem lies in the fact that the examiner cannot make allowances for the emotional or physical health of the test takers. If you are fighting a cold or if you were up all night caring for a sick parent, you're probably not going to be at your best. A strong performance on a group test also depends heavily upon your ability to read quickly and follow directions exactly. These factors may not have much to do with your intelligence, but they can raise or lower your score considerably. Another disadvantage is that you might be "turned off" by the length and impersonal qualities of the test. After a while, some people get bored and start filling in answers at random. Finally, simple errors in using the answer sheet can completely invalidate the test. Psychometrists generally believe that IQ scores from group tests underestimate a subject's actual intelligence.

Despite these problems, group intelligence tests are among the most widely used of all psychological tests. Like individual intelligence tests, the Cognitive Abilities Test has sections on verbal, numerical, and non-verbal skills. The examiner adjusts the difficulty of the items for the age and ability range of the group being tested. Students taking the test receive a test booklet and an answer sheet. Each section of the test is timed. The Cognitive Abilities Test asks such questions as these:

1. Vocabulary: *impolite* (a) unhappy, (b) angry, (c) rude, (d) faithless, (e) talkative.
2. Verbal classification: *vulture, hawk, falcon, owl,* _____. (a) robin, (b) bat, (c) eagle, (d) parrot, (e) woodpecker.

3. Verbal analogy: *Swim* is to *pool* as *run* is to _____ (a) street, (b) meadow, (c) sand, (d) floor, (e) track.
4. Number series: 7   10   14   19 _____ (a) 22 (b) 23 (c) 24 (d) 25 (e) 26
5. Figure analogy:

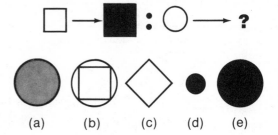

(a)   (b)   (c)   (d)   (e)

SECTION CHECKUP

1 What reasons can you think of for using intelligence tests?

2 If you wrote an IQ test to help select the next group of astronauts, how would you make sure it was reliable? Objective? Valid? Standardized?

3 Contrast the advantages and disadvantages of individual and group intelligence tests.

11.3 DO INTELLIGENCE TESTS REALLY MEASURE INTELLIGENCE?

Many well-meaning people once believed that intelligence tests truly measured basic human intelligence. From that point, it wasn't a terribly big step to the belief that a person's value to society was directly related to IQ. No one was really against low-IQ people, but it did seem as though high-IQ's were more useful and should be given preferred treatment. Jobs, benefits, opportunities—all could be allocated on the basis of IQ.

But a strange thing happened on the way to that particular brave new world. Other people began to question the validity of pigeonholing men and women on the basis of intelligence tests. After all, the critics said, there's no certain evidence that the tests truly measure anyone's actual abilities. And

even more important, they went on, it's wrong to measure a person's social worth by an IQ score. "Why not reward people who have dimples or on the basis of any other accident of heredity or environment?" they demanded.

By the mid-1960s these arguments began to have an effect. In March 1964, the New York City Board of Education banned the use of group intelligence tests in New York schools, and other large cities followed. Also alarmed by what it felt was a continuing misuse of IQ data, the state of California followed suit in 1971. The new philosophy seemed to be that children and adolescents should be judged by their performance rather than by an IQ score that far too often proved a poor predictor of future success.

This position was reinforced at the convention of the National Association of School Psychologists in 1971. There, a group of psychologists charged that intelligence tests were being used to place minority students in special education classes. The effect of this, they said, was to segregate these students from the rest of the school population.

On another front that same year, the United States Supreme Court ruled unanimously that the intelligence tests given to prospective employees by an electric-power company were unlawful. If employers want to give tests, the court said, the tests must be related directly to the skills required for that particular job. Once again, the evidence seemed to show that IQ scores had been used to penalize one group and benefit another.

Despite these attacks, defenders of intelligence tests insist that the test results are valid when properly used. Criteria for proper use include a number of safeguards. First, tests should be administered under proper conditions. Lighting, seating arrangements, phrasing of directions, and other elements must be set up so as to give test takers the best possible chance to do well. Second, test results should be used only to measure certain carefully defined abilities. A test can point out a weakness in reading comprehension, for example, but should not be used to make a final judgment about overall intelligence. Third, only specially trained people should be allowed to interpret test results. Finally, only those tests properly standardized for the particular group being tested should be used. Thus, tests standardized for white, middle-class children should not be used to test children recently arrived from Southeast Asia, and so on.

Whatever the merits of this debate, two interesting questions concerning the use of intelligence tests have developed. Can intelligence be taught? Has the problem of cultural bias in intelligence testing been fully understood? These are two of the most controversial issues in modern psychological testing.

"Teaching" intelligence

For many years, most psychologists believed that intelligence was an inborn trait. An individual has a certain amount of intelligence at birth, the theory stated, and no one can increase that amount. Supporters of this concept see little need to give special attention to children of low-IQ parents or to children who come from low-income communities. In effect, they're saying, "That's the way it is. Too bad, Mr. Bradford, but your Terry tests out at 85 IQ. You'll just have to accept the idea that he'll always be limited in what he can do."

Mr. Bradford, however, could point to an experiment that started at Milwaukee's Infant Education Center in 1966. The researchers selected twenty infants whose mothers had IQ scores of 75 or less. Earlier studies had shown that children raised by low-IQ parents tend to score low themselves. But these children were given a wide variety of stimulating play and educational experiences starting at a few weeks of age. Doctors, nurses, and social workers joined in working with the children and in training the mothers in better methods of child care. At age five, the children scored an average IQ of 124, compared to a 95 average for a carefully matched control group. Although the Milwaukee experiment was limited in size, its conclusion has been backed up by other studies: IQ scores rise when a child's early environment is enriched.

The implications of the Milwaukee findings have been backed by other studies. Psychologist H. M. Skeels obtained similar results in the 1930s when he took retarded babies from an orphanage and placed them in a home for the mentally retarded. Surrounded by loving "foster parents" and given extra attention by nurses and attendants, the babies blossomed into children with normal and above-normal IQ's. A control group left in the cold, uncaring atmo-

Figure 11.10

Educational television programs can give extra stimulation to preschool children. Here Kermit the Frog is teaching number concepts. Can such programs also affect IQ levels?

sphere of the orphanage actually decreased in IQ.

These findings suggest that intelligence tests measure learned skills, not inborn abilities. Further, intelligence is not strictly an inherited characteristic. More accurately, it seems to be a variable that is highly responsive to the experiences of infancy and childhood (see Figure 11.10). While no child will likely zoom from below-average IQ to genius level, proper stimulation and nurturing can add IQ points. One of the children in the Skeels experiment showed an increase of 58 points, and the average increase was 28 points. The sooner children receive such care after birth, the more likely it is that they will reach their full intellectual potential.

Race and intelligence

One of the great controversies in modern American social science involves the extent to which intelligence is determined by heredity. If intelligence is largely a product of genes rather than environment, as some have claimed, then special programs such as Head Start classes for low-income preschoolers cannot greatly change a child's intelligence.

Others have claimed that there are genetic differences between races that affect intelligence. Any scientific issues raised by such ideas tend to be clouded over by people who use the ideas to support their own assumptions of racial superiority.

Opposing scientists, meanwhile, have not allowed these ideas to go unchallenged.

They insist that no proof of genetically based racial differences can be found. Their arguments cover three major areas.

Cultural bias in intelligence tests. Until recent years, the people who write intelligence tests assumed that every child of a certain age had received equal exposure to the basic elements of American culture. In simple fact, that assumption is not valid. Many Americans, particularly those from low-income minority groups, do not grow up with the same educational and cultural backgrounds as do white, middle-class children. When required to take an intelligence test, minority children often begin with a built-in *cultural bias* against them. Their vocabulary, sentence structure, and general knowledge of tools, utensils, musical instruments, literature, and the like may be far different from the norms established by the test makers. In the same way, city children tend to score higher on intelligence tests than do rural children, and children of northern whites and blacks both score higher than children of both groups in the South.

As a step toward overcoming this problem, *culture-free* tests that do not depend on cultural or language skills available only to the middle class have been constructed. A question about symphony orchestras or operatic music obviously lies outside the experience of most low-income children. Similarly, the tendency to assume that Standard English is superior to Black English or other dialects has been discarded in these tests. Typically, a culture-free test modifies the usual intelligence test in three ways: (a) Language is simplified, (b) more nonverbal items are used, and (c) references are made to experiences that minority children recognize and relate to. Perhaps because of the difficulty of standardizing a

Figure 11.11

HOW BRIGHT ARE YOU? TAKE THE CBIT* AND FIND OUT

1 *¿Cuantos huevos hay en una docena?* (a) 2, (b) 6, (c) 12, (d) 18.

2 A *six-penny nail* is (a) one inch long, (b) one and a half inches long, (c) two inches long, (d) three inches long.

3 On a musical score, the *fermata* (⌢) sign means (a) play faster, (b) play softer, (c) hold the note for extra time, (d) repeat the phrase.

4 If someone says your conversation is *fatuous,* you've been (a) complimented, (b) ignored, (c) insulted, (d) misunderstood.

5 If a teammate gives you a *high five* near the end of a basketball game, you've probably (a) fouled out of the game, (b) missed an important free throw, (c) scored on a dunk to take the lead, (d) fallen down on a fast break.

6 Your host has just put a big bowl of *couscous* on the table. You know the meal is going to be (a) Japanese, (b) Swedish, (c) Algerian, (d) Brazilian.

How did you do? Most people complain that this isn't a fair intelligence test. After all, not everyone speaks Spanish or does carpentry work. And who knows that much about music or Algerian foods? Not everyone, obviously. But without meaning to, some IQ tests use culturally biased items not much different from these. When such tests are used to evaluate the IQ of people who have not had similar cultural experiences, the results are predictable.

*Green-Sanford *Culturally Biased Intelligence Test*

Answers: (c) is the correct answer to all items.

new test or because of resistance from the majority community, these tests have not yet come into widespread use. Figure 11.11 gives you a chance to try out a "counterbalance" intelligence test.

Subtle effects of discrimination. Centuries of discrimination have left their mark on black Americans. This effect can be seen in the actual test situation. When asked in one study to estimate their own IQ's, black students generally guessed lower in comparison to their actual scores than did white students. In another study, black students averaged 6 IQ points higher when tested by black examiners, as opposed to their scores when tested by a white examiner. In addi-

tion, many black children come to the test situation with a feeling that they'll do poorly. In the way of most self-fulfilling prophecies, they often do.

IQ scores can be improved. As discussed earlier in this section, IQ scores can be improved when someone reverses the environmental factors that contribute to low scores. Deficiencies can be fully remedied only if the improved health care and nurturing begin during infancy. Among the programs recommended are better nutrition and medical care, enrichment activities, and improved school services aimed at overcoming specific weaknesses. Hispanic children usually need special help with language

Pro & Con: SHOULD YOU BE GIVEN YOUR SCORES ON PSYCHOLOGICAL TESTS?

All through your school career, you've taken psychological tests of one type or another. In some schools, teachers and counselors pass on test scores to students, but in others this information is kept in a confidential file. In such cases, students usually receive interpretations of the scores but not the actual test data. Would it hurt you to know your own IQ or your scores on achievement and personality tests? Many psychologists and counselors believe it has the potential to do so. The arguments go like this:

Pro

1 The schools claim that tests are given for the benefit of the students. The scores, therefore, should belong to the people taking the tests.

2 In order to make rational decisions about school, career, marriage, and the like, students need all the available data about their abilities.

3 People are hardly ever affected in a negative way by learning that they aren't geniuses or that their abilities don't suit particular careers. Everyone should learn to live with his or her limitations.

4 Historically, schools have shared test data with teachers, parents, administrators, and law enforcement officials. Why don't they also share them with the people who take the tests?

Con

1 Psychological tests aren't the same as a quiz in math or history. The scores must remain under the control of the school because only school personnel know how to interpret them.

2 Only when they are interpreted in the light of all available data about an individual do test scores begin to serve a useful purpose. Raw test scores are useless by themselves.

3 Improperly used test scores can create a self-fulfilling prophecy. Someone who's told about a low IQ score will have a tendency to perform according to that "prophecy." Young children, particularly, tend to accept adult evaluations as fact.

4 The individuals mentioned in the Pro argument have a legal right to look at test data. The schools also recognize the right of eighteen-year-olds in many states to have access to their records.

What is the policy in your school about giving test scores to students, parents, and other people? What changes would you make in that policy, if any?

---

skills, for example. Perhaps most important of all, adults should try to give every child in every community a greater feeling of value and self-worth.

SECTION CHECKUP

1 Why have many cities and states banned the use of group IQ tests for school children?

2 If Mrs. Hammond asked you for advice on how to ensure that her new baby would grow up as intelligent as possible, what would you tell her?

3 If someone argued that blacks score lower than whites on IQ tests because of racial differences in intelligence, what counter arguments could you use?

11.4 WHAT DO ACHIEVEMENT AND APTITUDE TESTS REVEAL?

Becky K. has finished her senior year of high school. With hopes of a career in dentistry to spur her on, she carried a heavy load of math and science. Along the way, she took dozens of quizzes and exams. But when she took the Scholastic Aptitude Test (SAT), she felt rather confused.

"Look," Becky told her counselor, "I know what an *achievement test* is. That's a test that measures how much I learned in a particular course. But the SAT is called an aptitude test. I didn't see much difference between it and a general achievement test of my English and math skills."

Mr. Topping smiled. "That's understandable. Even psychologists sometimes have difficulty telling where an achievement test ends and an aptitude test begins. Achievement tests look backward to see where you've been. *Aptitude tests* look ahead to measure your chances of success in learning a new body of knowledge or a new skill."

"So if I did well on the SAT, I'll do well in college?" Becky asked. "Can't they tell from my high-school grades?"

"The colleges don't really trust your high-school grades, Becky. They don't know exactly what they mean, since every school tends to grade differently. But SAT scores are standardized. Experience shows that if you score high enough, your chances of making it through college are pretty good."

Becky relaxed. "Well, I guess that makes sense. I'll be using English and math and reasoning in college, so they want the SAT to find out if I really can handle those skills."

Mr. Topping nodded and pulled out Becky's records. "Here, let's look over your test scores for the last four years. Your high SAT score seems to correlate well with your achievement-test results."

Achievement tests

Like Becky, before you leave school you will take a number of different types of achievement tests. Your individual teachers will write tests to check up on your progress in their classes. Your school district will probably give you a standardized achievement test somewhere along the way to check up on your general progress. Before you graduate, you may be asked to take a competency test intended to make sure you've reached a minimum level of achievement in basic skills such as reading, writing, and arithmetic. Even with school behind you, your chances at a job may depend on passing an achievement test. The Civil Service merit examinations, for example, test for the specific skills you'll need on a government job.

Standardized achievement tests. When a school wants an overall picture of student progress, they turn to survey tests such as the Iowa Tests of Educational Development. This well-known test battery has been around since just after World War II, when it was written to test the educational experiences gained by veterans while in the armed forces. Today, the Iowa Tests are composed of nine subtests:

1. Understanding of basic social concepts

2. General background in the natural sciences

3. Correctness and appropriateness of expression

4. Ability to do quantitative thinking

5. Ability to interpret reading materials—social studies

6. Ability to interpret reading materials—natural sciences

7. Ability to interpret reading materials—literary

8. General vocabulary

9. Sources of information

Results from tests of this sort allow a school to compare its students with other students across the country. If the students' reading scores as a whole come in lower than the average, steps can be taken to improve the teaching of reading skills. Individual student scores can also be used to diagnose faulty skills so that remedial work can be given.

Students who plan to go to college often take a group of achievement tests prepared by the College Entrance Examination Board (CEEB). These demanding tests provide an additional checkup to go with the SAT. While you can't study specifically for the CEEB tests, you can work on three general areas.

1. *Vocabulary.* Success on most achievement tests relates closely to mastery of the language. Since vocabulary and word-usage skills play such an important part in any achievement test, anyone who plans to take such tests should begin preparation early. In fact, the following practical exercises can benefit anyone who wants to improve vocabulary skills. Start by reading a variety of books, newspapers, and magazines on a regular basis. When you run across an unfamiliar word, look it up, rehearse it, and move it into long-term memory. Use a thesaurus (a dictionary of synonyms and antonyms) when writing as a means of enriching vocabulary. Word games such as anagrams, Password, and Scrabble also build up your vocabulary. Test publishers put out study guides that give directed practice in the kinds of questions that will appear on the actual test. In some places you can take a "cram" course. Special study can give you the confidence you need to face the test when it comes.

If you were taking the vocabulary section of an achievement test today, you'd be answering questions such as these:

1. Choose the word that means the same as the word in capitals. CHRONIC (a) mild, (b) temporary, (c) healthy, (d) long-lasting, (e) regular.

2. Supply the word that best completes the sentence. No animal, with the exception of human beings, has had its _____ probed more thoroughly than the chimpanzee. (a) mental health, (b) genetic inheritance, (c) intelligence, (d) natural language, (e) sense of smell.

3. Select the pair of words that expresses a similar relationship to that expressed by the words in capital letters. PICADOR : BULL (a) heckler : speaker, (b) mote : eye, (c) executioner : victim, (d) singer : song, (e) matador : cow.

2. *Reading ability.* Both reading speed and reading comprehension count heavily in achievement tests. Typically, the test asks you to read a paragraph and answer questions about the content. Some readings are taken from literary works, others from nonfiction books. The usual reading comprehension question looks like this:

> The psychoanalyst attempts a measurement whose overhead runs into years and thousands of dollars. The brain watcher, or personality tester, as we shall see, claims that he can measure this same elusive human imponderable as easily and as accurately as counting compact cars off a Detroit assembly line. He can, he says, measure the psyche for anyone who wants to know, in as little time as five minutes, and as cheaply as $20 a head, less normal business discounts.
>
> In his attitude toward "brain watchers," the author expresses (a) uncertainty, (b) approval, (c) confidence, (d) sarcastic criticism, (e) optimism.

College admissions offices emphasize reading ability because college students usually must read three times the amount of material they did in high school. Like the flu, however, poor reading habits can be cured. Students who read at two hundred words per minute or less should consider enrolling in a reading-improvement course.

3. *Mastery of numbers.* Achievement tests also emphasize mastery of basic numerical operations. Except for those that test specific mathematics skills, achievement tests seldom ask for computa-

tions and problem solving beyond algebra and geometry. They include problems involving number series, ratios and proportion, and practical problems in area, volume, and percentages. If you took such a test, you'd answer questions like these:

1. What comes next in the series 1 3 7 15? (a) 17 (b) 21 (c) 25 (d) 31 (e) 36
2. How many digits are there to the left of the decimal point in the square root of 863722.40815? (a) 3 (b) 4 (c) 5 (d) 6 (e) none of these
3. Pilots in a cross-country race know they must cover 225 miles in exactly 45 minutes to meet a checkpoint. At what speed should they fly to do this? (a) 169 mph (b) 225 mph (c) 275 mph (d) 300 mph (e) 450 mph

Achievement tests such as the CEEB tests are also written to examine competency in a specific field. Depending on the college and your future field of study, you might be asked to take an achievement test in English composition or literature, American history, a foreign language, biology, chemistry, or physics. At this level, generalized reading and mathematics skills won't be enough. Subject-area tests demand that you demonstrate mastery of a particular body of knowledge.

Along with the pencil-and-paper achievement tests, it's not unusual for many schools or employers to ask you to take a *performance test*. The best example is the driver's test. Before you can qualify for a driver's licence, you have to prove to an examiner that you can drive a car safely. Similarly, a secretary might be asked to take a performance test in typing and shorthand and a mechanic might be given a machine to work on.

Aptitude tests

If Becky K. goes on to a successful career in a predentistry program, grades alone won't get her into dental school. As part of her application, she'll be expected to take the dental-school aptitude test. This test, like the SAT, will focus on Becky's reading

skills, reasoning ability, mathematics skills, and her knowledge of science. If the test is properly administered and interpreted, school officials will have a useful basis for judging Becky's potential as a dental student.

Areas tested. Aptitude tests have been standardized to measure your talents in such areas as language, mathematics, art, music, mechanics, clerical skills, and manual dexterity. Most people, unless they are aiming at a specific field, take *multiple aptitude batteries*. These tests provide a complete profile of aptitudes in as many as nine different areas. The General Aptitude Test Battery (GATB), developed by the U.S. Employment Service, uses both written and performance tests to make sure the test taker meets minimum standards for typical occupations.

Another popular multiple aptitude battery is called the Differential Aptitude Tests (DAT). When used for vocational counseling, the DAT provides the type of information students need to make long-range plans. The complete test takes about four hours over two separate testing sessions. You can get an idea of the DAT's eight sections by trying these sample questions:

1. Verbal Reasoning: _____ is to night as breakfast is to _____ (a) supper—corner (b) gentle—morning (c) door—corner (d) flow—enjoy (e) supper—morning.
2. Numerical Ability: $8 =$ _____ % of 24. (a) 20 (b) 25 (c) 30 (d) 33⅓ (e) none of these.
3. Abstract Reasoning: Select the figure that completes the series.

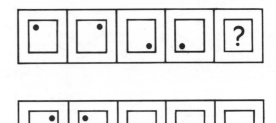

(a)   (b)   (c)   (d)   (e)

4. Clerical Speed and Accuracy: Each item is made up of five combinations of symbols, one of which is underlined. Mark the same combination on the answer sheet.

       K   bB BC <u>cB</u> bC Cf
       L.   4B <u>44</u> B4 BB 4C
Answer K. bC BC bB Cf cB
  sheet L. B4 4C 44 4B BB

5. Mechanical Reasoning: Which man has the heavier load? (If equal, mark C.)

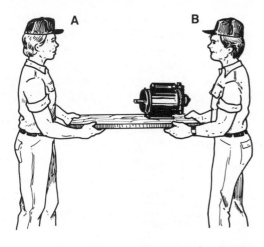

6. Space Relations: Which three-dimensional figure can be formed by folding the flat figure on top?

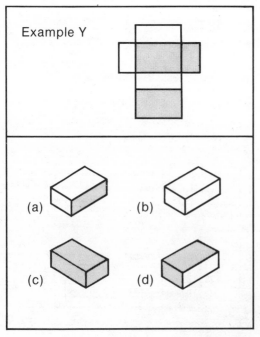

7. Spelling: Tell whether each word is spelled right or wrong by marking R for right and W for wrong. A. alot B. friend C. summary D. nervous.

8. Language Usage: Which section of the sentence contains an error?

Everyone are / invited to / the party /
    (a)   (b)   (c)
next Friday.
    (d)

Figure 11.12 shows a typical profile of DAT scores. By matching this profile to the student's career plans, a counselor can help the student judge the suitability of his or her vocational choices. The DAT also provides a Career Planning Program. This program gives each test taker a computer printout that summarizes the information from the DAT profile. Jesse, for example, scored low in Mechanical Reasoning. In polite but firm language, the Career Planning Program will tell Jesse that his plan to become a machinist probably isn't the best choice for him. At the same time, the printout will point Jesse toward careers that match his higher scores.

Keith, by contrast, scored in the 90th percentile in Mechanical Reasoning. Because he's never done well in school, Keith may not have made any career plans. Left alone, he might drift into a dead-end, unsatisfying job. The DAT results, however, can alert him to unexpected aptitudes that can pay off in greater job satisfaction. Only if Keith is willing to develop his talent with the necessary training, aptitude tests can point Keith in the right direction, but they can't do the work for him.

SECTION CHECKUP

1 What is the difference between aptitude tests and achievement tests?

2 Why do colleges put so much emphasis on tests such as the SAT? How could you prepare yourself to do the best possible job on tests of this type?

3 The counseling office is offering you a chance to take the DAT. You've already decided on a business career. Would it make any sense for you to take the test? Why or why not?

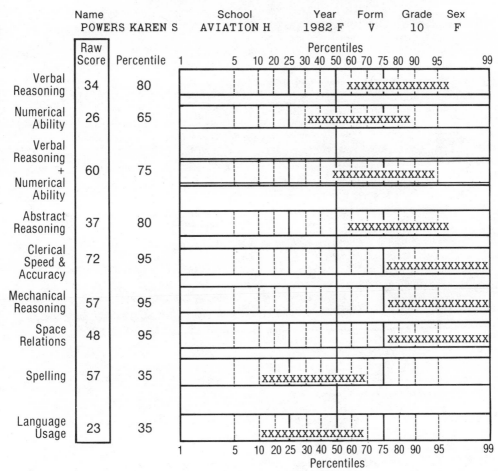

SAMPLE RATING PROFILE
FOR THE DIFFERENTIAL APTITUDE TESTS

Name	School	Year	Form	Grade	Sex
POWERS KAREN S	AVIATION H	1982 F	V	10	F

	Raw Score	Percentile
Verbal Reasoning	34	80
Numerical Ability	26	65
Verbal Reasoning + Numerical Ability	60	75
Abstract Reasoning	37	80
Clerical Speed & Accuracy	72	95
Mechanical Reasoning	57	95
Space Relations	48	95
Spelling	57	35
Language Usage	23	35

Figure 11.12

Karen just received this printout from her DAT. If you were helping her interpret it, what would you say are her strongest skills? Which are her weakest areas? What would you say about her desire to be a technical writer for an aerospace company?

Figure 11.13

HOW CAN YOU DO YOUR BEST ON A TEST?

Do you approach a test situation with a nervous, sinking feeling? A lot of people do, whether it is a mathematics examination, a driving test, a tryout for the school orchestra, or a college entrance test.

Can anything be done about this type of anxiety? First, remember that the test is meant to help you obtain something you want. Second, follow the basic principles of test taking and you'll have the confidence you need to do your best work. The following guidelines apply primarily to written tests taken in large groups.

Prepare yourself for the test

1 Follow a "business-as-usual" routine the day before the test. You won't build up an overload of nervous energy if you keep involved in your regular activities.

2 Try to get a full night's sleep. Except for achievement tests and specialized aptitude tests in which vocabulary and reading comprehension are important, no amount of study will equal being rested and relaxed for the day of the examination.

3 Wake up at least one to two hours before the time of the test. You'll want to have your body working at top efficiency when you begin the test.

4 Eat a good, balanced breakfast made up of proteins and carbohydrates for energy. Avoid heavy, starchy foods that will leave you feeling sluggish.

5 Avoid drinking too many liquids before the test. Some tests do not allow for restroom breaks.

6 Double-check to make sure you have the necessary equipment. Bring pens and pencils, a watch for keeping track of the time, a snack for energy, and a handkerchief or package of tissues. (Have you ever heard fifty people sniffling at once?)

Before the test starts

1 Arrive early. You'll want time to become accustomed to the test environment.

2 Pick out a seat that appeals to you. Look for good lighting, sufficient elbow room, and a clear view of the examiner.

3 Take some deep breaths and try to relax. Think of the test as a challenging game. It's not a matter of life or death, but you want to be slightly keyed up to do your best.

4 Listen carefully to any directions given by the examiner. If you don't understand something, ask to have it explained.

5 Survey the entire test before you begin—or as much of it as the directions allow. Check to see how much time you have for each section, so that you can budget your time.

While taking the test

1 Complete the answer sheet according to directions. The computer that scores it can't read your mind. Fill in the answer boxes fully, and erase old marks completely if you change an answer.

2 Check frequently to make sure that the number on the answer sheet corresponds to the number of the item you are working on.

3 Read the questions carefully. If you read directions too quickly, you may miss important words or phrases. Watch for qualifiers—words like *always* or *never*. Such words drastically change the meaning of a statement or question. If you run into questions that you think could be answered several ways, make a reasonable choice and move on.

4 Most tests give the same credit to every question. If you're working against the clock, skip the difficult items and go on to the easier ones. If time permits, come back to the puzzlers later.

5 Work at top speed during the entire test. When your muscles start to feel cramped, take a sixty-second break to stretch and take a few deep breaths. Relax your eyes by looking off into the distance.

6 Don't assume that questions toward the end of a section will be more difficult. Sometimes they are, but more often the hard and easy items recur in cycles. Keep going.

7 Don't be afraid to trust your "educated" guesses. If the test doesn't penalize wrong answers, you should probably guess at the correct answer after narrowing your choices down as far as possible.

When you've finished

1 Use the full time provided for the test. Even if you feel exhausted, try to save a few minutes to double-check everything.

2 After you've turned in the test, forget about it until the results come in. If you've done your best, worrying about your scores won't help.

11.5 WHAT CAN YOU LEARN FROM PERSONALITY TESTS?

Many people assume that everyone thinks and behaves just about alike. But psychologists have long recognized the uniqueness of each individual. They have used intelligence tests and achievement and aptitude tests to measure certain thinking and reasoning abilities. Along with such techniques, they also wanted a standardized method of exploring emotions. Personality testing grew out of that need. These tests are designed to measure emotions, motivations, attitudes, and the ability of people to relate to others. Properly used, they can help people bridge the gap that often exists between their self-image and the image others have of them.

Despite their widespread use, personality tests have a major weakness. To obtain valid results, the people who take the tests must report openly and honestly on their innermost feelings. Some people cannot take that risk, so they answer the way they think they should answer. In fact, the test takers who most need help are the ones most likely to give dishonest or evasive answers. Moreover, the scoring of many personality tests is quite subjective. Even the most skillful examiners find that vague and inconsistent data resist objective evaluation.

Personality tests can be divided into two general categories: interest inventories and clinical tests. *Interest inventories* help people learn more about their preferences in life-style, occupations, leisure-time activities, and friends. *Clinical personality tests*, by contrast, are designed to uncover emotional problems and tendencies toward neurotic or psychotic behavior.

The interest inventory

Most people's first experience with a personality test comes when they take an interest inventory. These tests have been developed because of two related factors. First, ability does not guarantee success in what you do. You must also be interested in that particular job or activity. The second factor is that an interest inventory can put you in touch with potential interests you didn't know you had.

A typical interest inventory. The Strong Vocational Interest Blank (SVIB) is over fifty years old and still widely used. The test begins by asking you to respond to 399 items. Under occupations, for example, you'll find architect, auctioneer, auto racer, and airplane pilot. For each item, you mark *like*, *dislike*, or *indifferent*. Later in the test, you'll be asked to respond in the same way to lists of activities and types of people. Once you've marked all the items, the test can be scored by hand or by computer.

Perhaps you have been thinking about a career in farming. With the SVIB, you can compare your interest profile to that of successful farmers. If the two profiles match, you'll probably be happy and successful in that career. The SVIB can presently be scored for more than eighty occupations, from actor to zoologist. People who enter occupations that match their SVIB scores have shown a definite tendency to stay in those jobs.

Interests and job success. Interest tests cannot take abilities and motivation into account, however. A lazy, low-ability person might show a high interest in farming but would probably not succeed in that demanding field. In contrast, high ability without a corresponding interest in the job does not necessarily work out, either. One investigation in the insurance field, for example, divided employees into three groups: *A* group, whose interests and abilities were geared to selling insurance; *B* group, whose interests were high but whose abilities were low; and *C* group, whose abilities were high but whose interests were low. The *A* group outsold the *C* group three to one, with the *B* group somewhere in between.

Psychologists conclude, therefore, that interest inventories can point you in the right direction, but you'll have to take it from there.

Clinical personality tests

Clinical personality tests measure actual or predicted behaviors. If Reggie S. makes an appointment to begin psychotherapy, Dr. Olcina might ask him to take one or more such tests. In this way the doctor will gain additional insight into Reggie's feelings. Depending on the particular test Dr. Olcina selects, rating scales can be obtained that describe a wide variety of behavior patterns. These scores, combined with a case history and Reggie's own discussions with the therapist, can build up a fairly complete picture of Reggie's attitudes, anxieties, fears, and reactions to stress.

Depending on Reggie's needs, Dr. Olcina has two basic types of clinical tests to choose from. She might prefer an *objective personality test*, or what is also known as a self-report inventory. Objective tests require a forced-choice response, usually *yes, no,* or *cannot state*. Reggie's scores will be "graded" against a norm group established by the test makers. If she isn't convinced that Reggie will benefit from an objective test, Dr. Olcina can also use a *projective personality test*. On this type of test, Reggie will respond to the test items in a free, unstructured way. The Michigan Picture Test at the beginning of this chapter is a projective test.

Objective personality tests. One of the best-known objective personality tests is the Minnesota Multiphasic Personality Inventory (MMPI). People who take the MMPI are asked to answer 550 statements as *true, false,* or *cannot say*. The items probe a variety of personal feelings and attitudes, including health, psychosomatic symptoms, marital and sexual attitudes, and occupational problems. If the subjects answer honestly, the test items also reveal evidence of phobias, hallucinations, obsessions, paranoias, and other emotional disturbances. The MMPI also contains a built-in lie detector. Scattered through the test are key items such as "I never get angry." Too many "true" answers to these statements tell the examiner that the subject is lying to create a good impression or to cover up actual feelings. Sample items from the MMPI look like this:

	T	CS	F
1. I have a good appetite	☐	☐	☐
2. I wake up fresh and rested most mornings	☐	☐	☐
3. I am easily awakened by noise.	☐	☐	☐
4. These days I find it hard not to give up hope of amounting to something	☐	☐	☐
5. At times I have very much wanted to leave home	☐	☐	☐
6. I usually have to stop and think before I act even in trifling matters	☐	☐	☐
7. Someone has been trying to poison me	☐	☐	☐
8. I think I would like the work of a librarian	☐	☐	☐

Because it's easy to use and has well-established norms, the MMPI has been used as a way of screening for personality problems in nonclinical situations. Colleges, the military, and businesses have all based personnel decisions on the test. But although the MMPI's computer printouts give a sense of objectivity and accuracy, otherwise normal people sometimes score abnormally high on one or another of the test's nine behavior scales. In such cases, the test may unfairly penalize a well-adjusted person. Ethical questions regarding such uses of the MMPI and other personality tests have been raised, much as the improper use of intelligence tests has been criticized.

Projective personality tests. Most psychologists believe that projective tests

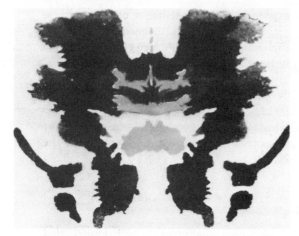

Figure 11.14

Here is an inkblot used in the Rorschach test. What does the shape suggest to you?

pretation is quite subjective. In addition, some people look on the inkblots as a challenge to their own security. They may play it safe, giving only simple, obvious responses. Psychologists who like the Rorschach, however, point out that no one knows what a specific description means, so people can't really "hide" what they're feeling.

In contrast to the Rorschach, the Thematic Apperception Test (TAT) consists of nineteen cards. Each shows a rather vague scene in which people's actions and motives might be interpreted in several different ways (see Figure 11.15). The Michigan Picture Test uses this same approach. When taking the TAT, Audrey would make up a story to describe what she sees taking place. She'll be asked to include the events that led up to the scene, what the people are doing and thinking, and what the outcome will be. The psychologist who interprets TAT stories looks at what they reveal about the subject's needs and the forces that apparently prevent satisfaction of those basic needs.

The fertile imaginations of test makers have produced a number of other projective tests. One relatively simple test uses a number of incomplete sentences, which the subject completes as he or she wishes. Typical sentence completion items include:

1. I like _____.

2. My greatest worry _____.

3. Men _____.

4. Women _____.

5. This test _____.

Other tests, particularly useful with children, use toys and art materials. Four-year-old Eva, for example, might be asked to play with a set of dolls and a well-furnished dollhouse. With the psychologist looking on, Eva would set up the furniture

tell more about a subject's personality than do objective tests. The theory behind such tests is that people will "project" their innermost thoughts, anxieties, and conflicts on the "screen" provided by the test. When Audrey D. takes a projective test, the examiner will give her only brief, general instructions. The test is designed to let Audrey's imagination operate freely, so that unconscious feelings can emerge.

Without a doubt, the most famous of all projective tests is the Rorschach Inkblot Test. Designed by Hermann Rorschach, a Swiss psychiatrist, the test simply asks the subject to look at and describe a set of ten inkblots (see Figure 11.14). If Audrey takes the test, she'll tell her psychologist what she sees in each inkblot. The psychologist will write down exactly what Audrey says, including her incidental remarks, expressions of emotion, and even the position in which she holds the cards. Next, the psychologist will question Audrey about her responses. If Audrey described one inkblot as looking like two boys on a seesaw, the examiner would ask about the location of the seesaw, whether it was in motion, the age of the boys, and other related details.

Scoring scales for the Rorschach test have been developed on the basis of responses typical of known personality types. Certain descriptions, for example, are thought to point to specific forms of disturbed behavior. Using these scoring scales requires considerable experience, and their inter-

Figure 11.15

What do you see in this picture from the Thematic Apperception Test? Show it to several people and see what different stories you can collect.

and use the dolls to create "stories" about people. In most cases, the play scene and Eva's comments will clearly relate to Eva's feelings about her own home and family.

In the Draw-a-Person test, children and adults use paper and felt pens to draw themselves, their families, and their homes. The nonverbal activity of drawing seems to open up feelings that would otherwise be repressed. If young Leo, for example, draws his father four times as big as everyone else, you immediately get a feeling that the boy feels overwhelmed by a dominating male parent.

Figure 11.16

CAN A TEST PREDICT WHO IS MOST LIKELY TO HAVE ACCIDENTS?

Psychologist J. R. Block, of Hofstra University, believes that failure to pay attention is a key ingredient in whether a person is accident-prone or not. In order to test this hypothesis, he has developed a test he calls the Attention Diagnostic Method (ADM). Block seats his subject in front of a board on which the numbers 10 to 59 appear in random order. Each row is printed in one of five colors. The experimenter asks the subject to find the numbers in sequence, and to name both the number and its color. This relatively simple procedure rates the subject's speed and accuracy. Analysis of the test data shows that the ADM is about 37 percent better than chance in predicting which people will have high accident rates.

34	19	42	54	45	(red)
26	16	39	28	57	(yellow)
40	35	14	56	30	(green)
12	29	44	51	23	(blue)
50	43	36	24	11	(white)
37	20	55	32	47	(red)
25	41	17	53	38	(yellow)
13	22	48	10	58	(green)
52	18	21	31	46	(blue)
27	49	33	15	59	(white)

You can duplicate Dr. Block's experiment by reproducing the ADM test panel on a 22" x 28" poster board. Use at least five colors (first row red, second row yellow, etc.). Rate your subjects for speed and accuracy. Then compare their scores against their driving records. There should be a positive correlation.

SECTION CHECKUP

1 What is the difference between an interest inventory and a clinical personality test? Describe a situation in which each would be useful.

2 Why is interest no guarantee of success on a job?

3 Contrast objective and projective personality tests. What are the strengths and weaknesses of each?

LOOKING BACK: A SUMMARY

1 Psychological tests are designed to measure intelligence, achievement, aptitude, interests, and personality. When properly constructed, these tests meet four well-defined standards: (a) They can be scored objectively. (b) They are standardized to norms representative of the general population. (c) They can be relied upon to give consistent results. (d) They measure what they say they will measure. Whatever the type of test used, its value depends upon proper administration and interpretation by trained psychologists, psychometrists, and counselors.

2 The concept of intelligence has never been defined to everyone's satisfaction. According to a generally accepted definition, intelligence is the total of all the mental abilities that allow an individual to solve whatever problems seem worth working on. Most psychologists today believe that intelligence is actually a number of related mental abilities, including memory, reasoning ability, perception, numerical skills, and verbal abilities. IQ can be defined more precisely. It is the ratio of a person's mental age (as measured by an intelligence test) to the chronological age multiplied by 100. Psychologists use IQ as an indication of a person's potential, not as a judgment regarding that person's value.

3 Intelligence tests may be either individual or group tests. In individual tests, an examiner administers the test directly to a single subject. Although they are expensive, individual tests generally provide a more accurate measurement than group tests. When large numbers of people must be tested, however, psychologists use the less expensive group tests. While most tests emphasize verbal abilities, several tests have been developed that measure intelligence without depending on language skills.

4 Because of increasing doubts about the validity and usefulness of intelligence testing, school boards and courts have begun to limit its use. The debate centers on several arguments. Since no firm definition of intelligence exists, how can it be properly tested? Also, some studies show that intelligence, at least as measured by the tests, can be "taught," using extra doses of nurturing and stimulation, beginning in infancy. Critics of intelligence testing have pointed out that most intelligence tests have a built-in cultural bias. That tendency of the tests to favor the majority culture, along with the effects of discrimination, seems sufficient to explain the difference in IQ scores.

5 Achievement tests look backward to measure a person's accomplishments in mastering a specific subject or skill. Most achievement tests emphasize school-related skills—vocabulary, reading comprehension, word usage, and mastery of numbers. Achievement tests are also used to screen people for jobs or entry into special programs.

6 Aptitude tests look ahead to measure the chances that an individual will succeed in learning a subject or skill. Multiple aptitude batteries can help people discover whether or not they have the abilities needed to enter various occupations. Psychologists caution, however, that having an aptitude does not guarantee success in a career. Motivation and training are also necessary.

7 Personality tests attempt to measure an individual's emotions, motivations, and attitudes. Because of the subjective nature of such tests, the results must be interpreted with great care. Interest inventories help people take stock of their preferences regarding work, leisure-time activities, and friends. A subject's test profiles can be compared with those of successful people in a particular field to see if their interests match. Interest plus ability usually leads to success, but interest without ability or ability without interest does not make for productive careers.

8 Objective personality tests such as the Minnesota Multiphasic Personality Inventory ask the subject to make forced responses to hundreds of questions covering a variety of personal feelings and attitudes. The results then give the psychologist some insight into possible problem areas in that subject's personality. Projective personality tests ask the subject to respond freely to unstructured material such as inkblots, pictures, unfinished sentences, or art

materials. Both types of personality test measure specific personality traits such as conformity, neurotic tendencies, aggression, depression, and strength of personal beliefs.

Answers to Unfair Test Items (p. 338)

1 Answer: *M*, because all the others are made with only three lines, but an *M* is made with four lines. But you could also make a case for *A*, the only vowel, or *F*, the only letter not made with a diagonal line.

2 Answer: the knife (b), because all other objects begin with the letter *S*. Knife begins with the letter *K*. You could also have chosen the spoon (c), the only item without a cutting edge, or the scissors (e), which have two parts.

Answer to Stanford-Binet Ingenuity Item (p. 339)

The best solution is to set up an efficient search pattern. A grid pattern is good, but here's a better one: Drive a stake at the center of the field. Tie a rope to the stake and use it to make a spiral search pattern of the field.

PUTTING YOUR KNOWLEDGE TO WORK

Terms you should know

achievement test	norms
aptitude test	objective personality test
chronological age	objectivity
clinical personality test	percentile ranking
cultural bias	performance test
culture-free	projective personality test
intelligence	psychometrist
intelligence quotient (IQ)	reliability
interest inventory	standardization
mental age	subjectivity
multiple-aptitude battery	validity
normal curve of distribution	

Objective questions

1 A useful definition of intelligence says that it is (*a*) a quality people are born with that never changes (*b*) a quality that is completely the result of environmental influences (*c*) the ability to solve successfully the problems people face in life (*d*) the ability to achieve economic success.

2 The IQ of six-year-old Gail, who tested at a mental age of eight, is (*a*) 75 (*b*) 100 (*c*) 133 (*d*) 180.

3 A psychological test that does *not* measure the trait or behavior it claims to measure could not be called (*a*) objective (*b*) standardized (*c*) reliable (*d*) valid.

4 If the studies that show that IQ scores of young children can be increased are valid, (*a*) the dominant role of heredity in determining intelligence would be increased (*b*) the role of environmental influences would be increased (*c*) the role of both heredity and environmental influences would be decreased (*d*) the role of both heredity and environmental influences would be increased.

5 Cultural bias in an IQ test means that (*a*) the test makers are prejudiced (*b*) the test is not valid for any group taking it (*c*) anyone from a minority group who takes the test should automatically receive 15 extra points (*d*) the test contains items outside the experience of some minority groups, and this different background will lower their scores.

6 A simple way to distinguish between achievement and aptitude tests would be to remember that (*a*) achievement tests measure inborn traits while aptitude tests measure personality (*b*) an achievement test looks back at what you've learned, while an aptitude test looks ahead at what you could learn (*c*) achievement tests measure your IQ, while aptitude tests measure your interests (*d*) achievement tests measure general vocational skills, while aptitude tests measure what you've learned in specific subject areas.

7 If Sally's test profile on the Strong Vocational Interest Blank matches that of the astronauts, (*a*) she's certain to be successful in that vocation (*b*) her interests are similar to those of astronauts, but she also must have aptitude, motivation, and education if she is to be successful in that field (*c*) she should ignore the results since scores on interest inventories have little correlation with vocational success (*d*) it means that she has an unconscious wish to become an astronaut.

8 The insights gained from a clinical personality test would not benefit (*a*) an adolescent who is having trouble keeping up with the demands of schoolwork and social adjustment (*b*) a man who cannot seem to keep a job, even though his skills fit the occupation (*c*) a woman who has been accused of repeated incidents of shoplifting (*d*) someone who gave false answers in the test.

9 Psychological tests (*a*) are useful only for those people with severe emotional problems (*b*) are too dangerous to use with people who don't have any apparent emotional problems (*c*) offer useful insights to anyone who wants to learn more about his or her own abilities, interests, and needs (*d*) have such low validity that most states have outlawed their use.

10 When taking a group test, particularly of intelligence or achievement, it is a good idea to (*a*) work as quickly as possible and then rest if you have time left (*b*) never ask for help or to have directions repeated (*c*) get a good night's sleep and eat a balanced breakfast to ensure adequate energy and alertness (*d*) leave all questions blank that you aren't sure you can answer.

Discussion questions

1 Write a definition of intelligence that makes sense to you. Why do you think your definition is a good one?

2 As you're reading the newspaper, you see an article about a woman whose IQ tested out at 67 when she entered a mental hospital. Two years later, the report says, she was retested and found to have an IQ of 118. How can you explain the difference in the two IQ scores?

3 What advantages would be gained by administering a clinical personality test to an emotionally healthy person?

4 Distinguish among the uses of intelligence, achievement, aptitude, interest, and personality tests. Describe a situation in which each one would be useful.

5 Describe your own reaction to taking a standardized group test. List some techniques that you can use next time to decrease the tension of the test experience.

6 Some people maintain that personality tests are an invasion of privacy. Do you agree or disagree? Tell why. Under what circumstances should schools and employers be allowed to give personality tests?

Activities

1 Make an appointment to see your guidance counselor for the purpose of better understanding the test results that have accumulated in your folder over the years. You'll need at least twenty minutes to explore all of the data on file. Prepare for the interview by jotting down appropriate questions ahead of time. Look for elements of consistency or inconsistency in your scores over the years, particularly in IQ and achievement results. Do you think your test scores accurately reflect your future school and career plans?

2 Invite a school psychologist or guidance counselor to visit your class to talk about the school's testing program. Ask the speaker to describe the various tests given, the ways in which the scores are recorded and used, and the programs of evaluation and follow-up that have been developed to ensure validity.

3 The magazine *Psychology Today* often prints articles about current research in the field of testing. Leaf through several recent issues until you find something in this area that interests you. Read the article and write a critique of the ideas it describes. Turn in your paper to your psychology teacher for evaluation.

4 Although the psychology profession maintains strict security on its standardized tests, you can buy several intelligence tests in bookstores. Pick up H. J. Eysenck's *Know Your Own IQ*. After taking the test and scoring your results, how would you rate the test? Does it provide information on standardization and validity? What mental abilities does it seem to emphasize? If your teacher is willing, you might share the test with other students in your class. *Remember, however, that the very fact that the test is available to anyone may prevent it from meeting proper standards. Do not take your score too seriously.*

5 You can learn something about test construction by making up your own "friendship test." This is an interest inventory that asks people to respond to questions about their likes and dislikes in music, sports, food, school, books, and other areas that are important to you. First, write the test, using questions that you think reveal important attitudes and interests. Objective questions that you can score on a point basis are best. For example, "Rate these leisure activities from 1 to 5 (5 being the highest in interest

for you): (*a*) watching TV (*b*) playing an outdoor sport (*c*) cruising in a car (*d*) going to a dance." When you have finished, make eight copies of your test. To "standardize" your test, try it out on three close friends. Their scores will give you your norms for judging the scores of your other subjects. (Remember, however, that it takes thousands of subjects to standardize a test properly.) Next, give the test to five persons you don't know very well. Did they score higher or lower than your friends did? What do you think their scores mean? Do you think you've written a valid test? Why or why not? You may even end up with several new friends at the same time that you're learning something about making tests!

For further reading

Cohen, Daniel. *Intelligence—What Is It?* New York: M. Evans, 1974. This clearly written little book explores both the general question of intelligence and the debate over the use of IQ tests. Of particular interest are the chapters on animal intelligence.

Eysenck, Hans J. *Know Your Own IQ*. London: Penguin, 1962. An expert in the field of intelligence testing gives you a chance to try an intelligence test that comes as part of his book. Watch out for cultural bias, though. Eysenck wrote his test for people familiar with a British vocabulary.

Fixx, James. *Games for the Superintelligent.* Garden City, NY: Doubleday, 1972. Don't let the title put you off. The fun and beauty of the puzzles printed in this exasperating book are that they depend more on logic than mathematical wizardry.

Harrower, Molly. *Appraising Personality: An Introduction to the Projective Technique.* New York: Simon & Schuster, 1964. Dr. Harrower writes about the basic projective personality tests in the form of a dialogue between a physician and a psychologist.

Lutterjohann, Martin. *IQ Tests for Children.* New York: Stein & Day, 1978. The tests in this book measure a child's intellectual development. The tests will also make you aware of the activities that help young minds develop to their fullest.

UNIT VI

THE INDIVIDUAL AND SOCIETY

12

BEHAVIOR IN GROUPS

Livia, a fifteen-year-old Puerto Rican girl, was brought to her high school principal's office. She was suspected of smoking on campus. Although she didn't have any previous record of troublemaking, the principal decided to suspend her.

"It wasn't what she said," he reported later. "It was simply her attitude. There was something sly and suspicious about her. She just wouldn't meet my eyes. She wouldn't look at me."

Why did the principal make that decision? A social psychologist could probably tell you quite a lot about how people make up their minds. For unlike the psychologists who work with individuals, social psychologists are more interested in the way people interact with others. After all, much of your behavior grows out of the fact that you were born into a particular culture. And no matter how independent you are, your every thought and action has been conditioned to some degree by your family, your community, and the other groups to which you belong.

One interesting insight that has come out of school psychology can be seen in the principal's interview with Livia. Researchers know that people's actions often give away what they're thinking or feeling. This type of *nonverbal communication* is known as *body language*. Once you know the "vocabulary," you can interpret a wide range of messages without hearing a single spoken word.

Figure 12.1

Can you read the body-language conversation going on between this couple? For example, who has just made a suggestion? Is the other person responsive? What clues told you how to "read" this bit of nonverbal communication?

But cultural differences can change the meaning of body language. The principal at first seemed to be on firm ground in Livia's case. During her interview, the girl had stared at the floor, apparently unable to meet the principal's eyes. Her attitude seemed to reflect a clearly guilty conscience. Moreover, Livia's mother complained to her neighbors instead of talking to the school about the problem. As a result, a group of Puerto Rican parents gathered at the school the next morning to demonstrate against Livia's suspension.

Body-language expert Julius Fast tells the rest of the story:

> Fortunately, John Flores taught Spanish literature at the school, and John lived only a few doors from Livia and her family. Summoning his own courage, John asked for an interview with the principal.
>
> "I know Livia and her parents," he told the principal. "And she's a good girl. I am sure there has been some mistake in this whole matter."
>
> "If there was a mistake," the principal said uneasily, "I'll be glad to rectify it. There are thirty mothers outside yelling for my blood. But I questioned the child myself, and if ever I saw guilt written on a face—she wouldn't even meet my eyes!"
>
> John drew a sigh of relief, and then very carefully, for he was too new in the school to want to tread on toes, he explained some basic facts of Puerto Rican culture to the principal.
>
> "In Puerto Rico a nice girl, a good girl," he explained, "does not meet the eyes of an adult. Refusing to do so is a sign of respect and obedience. It would be as difficult for Livia to look you in the eye as it would be for her to misbehave or for her mother to come to you with a complaint. In our culture, this is just not accepted behavior for a respectable family."
>
> Fortunately the principal was a man who knew how to admit that he was wrong. He called Livia and her parents and the most vocal neighbors in and once again discussed the problem. In the light of John Flores' explanation, it became obvious to him that Livia was avoiding his eyes not out of defiance but out of a basic demureness. Her slyness, he

now saw, was shyness. In fact, as the conference progressed and the parents relaxed, he realized that Livia was indeed a gentle and sweet girl.

> The outcome of the entire incident was a deeper, more meaningful relationship between the school and the community. . . . What is of particular interest in this story is the strange confusion of the principal. How did he so obviously misinterpret all the signals of Livia's behavior?
>
> Livia was using body language to say, "I am a good girl. I respect you and the school. I respect you too much to answer your questions, too much to meet your eyes with shameless boldness, too much to defend myself. But surely my very attitude tells you all this."
>
> How could such a clear-cut message be interpreted as, "I defy you. I will not answer your questions. I will not look you in the eyes because I am a deceitful child. . . ."
>
> The answer of course is a cultural one. Different cultures have different customs and, of course, different body language. They also have different looks and different meanings to the same looks.
>
> In America, for instance, a man is not supposed to look at a woman for any length of time unless she gives him her permission with a body-language signal, a smile, a backward glance, a direct meeting of his eye. . . . In other countries different rules apply.
>
> In Latin countries, though freer body movements are permissible, such a look might be a direct invitation to a physical "pass." It becomes obvious then why a girl like Livia would not look the principal in the eye.

Studies in body language and cultural differences are only two of the many areas that attract the attention of social psychologists. As society grows more complicated and stressful, these studies become even more important. Before Americans can change *what* people are doing to each other, they need to know *why* they're doing it. In that context, this chapter will examine the following aspects of social psychology:

12.1 HOW DO GROUPS INFLUENCE YOUR BEHAVIOR?

12.2 WHAT EFFECT DO SOCIAL PRESSURES HAVE ON BEHAVIOR?

12.1 HOW DO GROUPS INFLUENCE YOUR BEHAVIOR?

Lord Chesterfield, an English writer, once advised his son that true knowledge of the world can be obtained only by studying people. The record doesn't show whether the younger Chesterfield took that counsel to heart, but social psychologists have certainly done so. Using all the tools of the social scientist, from research and experimentation to observation and surveys, these psychologists study individual and group behaviors within a social setting.

Does your family have an uncle like Tim? Normally, he's a mild-mannered, quiet fellow. But whenever the family gets together, he goes into a snarling fit of bad temper. Have you ever wondered why this usually gentle person becomes bitter and aggressive? Is he reacting to the social situation, the reminder of childhood hurts, or the knowledge that he's been less successful than his brothers?

Social psychologists would see Tim as a good example of individual reaction to the family group. What motivates him? How did he learn his responses to family pressures? What does he feel about his place in the family? Given the chance, the social psychologist would study Uncle Tim in all his social roles: as a family member, as a worker, as a citizen, as a member of the bowling team, and as a church deacon. In learning more about Tim, they would also gain insight into the behavior of other people as well.

Group behavior

Most people are surprised to discover how many groups they belong to (see Figure 12.2). Take yourself, for example. Any time you join with other people who share common goals and who feel a sense of interdependence, you've become part of a group. You probably belong to a family group, a religious group, a group of students called a psychology class, an athletic team, a social club, and so on. If you examined these groups carefully, you'd find that they have two basic functions. Some groups, such as a committee set up to plan the homecoming dance, are *task-oriented. Socially oriented groups,* by contrast, have the primary purpose of providing social interactions for their members. Around most schools, for example, you might find a backpacking club, a chess club, a German club, and so on. Some groups combine both functions, as when a task-oriented soccer team puts on a pancake breakfast to raise money for a summer trip to Europe.

Most groups tend to change over the years. Even within the family, people grow up and move away, marriages take place, and feuds sometimes develop. But studies show that certain basic rules of group behavior remain fairly constant.

1. Group size greatly affects the manner in which group members interact. As groups grow larger, opportunities for people to take active leadership roles decrease, often leading to frustration and making personal contacts between group members less satisfactory. For these reasons, youth groups such as the Boy Scouts and Camp Fire Girls deliberately keep their units small so as to encourage interaction.

2. Group behavior can be conditioned by reward and punishment, just as individual behavior can be changed. When teachers punish an entire class for the misbehavior of a few, they are using this principle. Such

Figure 12.2

Although American society values individual freedom and responsibility, people
spend much of their time in groups. What does group membership contribute to
the individual? How many groups do you belong to in addition to these four?

policies can backfire, however, when the group bands together to support its members against the outside authority.

3. The ability of a group to reach its goals depends largely on how well its members work as a unit. A basketball team that refuses to follow the coach's pleas for team play will not win many games, no matter how skilled the players are as individuals.

4. In most groups, individual participation and distribution of rewards tend to be unequal. You've probably noticed how in many groups a few people do most of the work. In a similar way, rewards are often given out to only a handful of the members—and not always to those who most deserve them. All-American awards in sports, for example, often go to a few highly publicized players. Meanwhile, the team members who made their victories possible must be content with a few rays of reflected glory.

5. People are more likely to stay with groups they join voluntarily if joining requires a sacrifice of some sort. Social groups such as fraternities and sororities, for example, bind their members tightly to the organization by making initiations both difficult and painful. Similarly, the military academies make the first year of school so demanding that most of those who survive develop deep loyalties. Even communes, in which members leave their homes to begin a new life, work best when new members must give all their belongings to the commune. The rule seems to be that, if you must sacrifice to join a group, you'll find more reasons to stay.

Roles within groups

Every group assigns roles to its members. A *role* is the pattern of behavior that allows the group to fulfill its functions. Your family, for example, expects certain behaviors from you in your roles as son or daughter, brother or sister, cousin, part-time household worker, student, and so on. If you don't play these roles according to the family's rules, you'll probably feel pressure to change. Psychologists call these rules for role playing in a particular situation the *social norms* of the group. In your role as son or daughter, for example, you run into situations where the social norms vary. At a regular family meal, you probably relax your dress, speech, and table manners. But when Aunt Alice takes everyone out to an expensive restaurant, the roles change. You'll not only dress and act differently, you'll probably *feel* different.

Influence of social norms. Learning social norms for the group you belong to, a process called *socialization*, is one of your greatest tasks in growing up. Roles in recreational and work groups are the easiest to learn. If you're a tennis player or a short-order cook, you'll generally follow the social norms of the tennis court or the restaurant kitchen. Even so, the sports pages in recent years have been full of stories about tennis players who shout obscenities at officials and opponents alike. Much of the shock people feel over such antics stems from the violation of accepted social norms for tennis players.

Family roles and social roles are more challenging and differ from person to person. Think of your own roles. Outside the family, you must learn the social norms that go with belonging to clubs, teams, work crews, political organizations, and the like. As a friend, you will be expected to be loyal, affectionate, and ready to share experiences. Friends who break these social norms usually break up the friendship.

At an obvious level, your roles require that you learn different ways of dressing, speaking, and behaving. At a deeper and more important level, you must learn the emotional values that attach to certain roles. Jarvis C., for example, left home at eighteen and never bothered to keep in touch with his family. Now, twenty years later, is he still a son to that family? In a genetic sense, yes. But in a social sense, by abandoning his role as son, he "resigned" from the family group.

Leadership. Every group has a leader. Sometimes leadership is shared; sometimes it is exercised in a dictatorial fashion. But always someone within the group makes decisions, gives orders, settles conflicts, and keeps the group moving toward its goal. Psychologically, the forces that create a leader instead of a follower cannot be pinned down exactly. Many people seem to enjoy the challenge of taking over and getting things done. Their abilities and personalities fit them for this role. Others would prefer not to take a leadership role but accept it when necessary. Less positively, a smaller group of people seem to need power as a way of proving they can control their own lives.

Many leaders are chosen on the basis of their ability to do a job. If you were going to climb Mt. Everest, you'd want an expedition leader who knew how to make the climb safely and efficiently. In politics, leaders are often selected on the basis of their powerful personalities. This personal appeal, or charisma, sometimes overwhelms more objective measures of ability. The election of popular entertainers to public office may depend more on looks and style than on ability. Other leaders gain control because their jobs give them the power to do so. A President in office, for example, usually has a better chance of being reelected than does a rival for this powerful office. Finally, there are leaders who use underhanded tactics to gain power. These people are manipulators, because they'll do anything to make other group members accept their authority.

No single type of leader guarantees success for a group. Sometimes democratic processes work best, with everyone sharing in the decision making. With other groups, discipline and efficiency may require a strong leadership hand. Generally, groups work best when the members freely choose their leaders and agree upon the goals toward which they will work.

SECTION CHECKUP

1 Why are social psychologists interested in group behavior?

2 What is the difference between a task-oriented group and a socially oriented group? Give several examples of each.

3 Name some of the roles you play in the groups to which you belong. List some social norms for one of those roles. Under what conditions do these rules change?

4 List four ways in which a person can gain a leadership position in a group. Give an example of each.

5 Why would democratic processes work best when choosing a leader?

12.2 WHAT EFFECT DO SOCIAL PRESSURES HAVE ON BEHAVIOR?

You are walking with a group of friends through the zoo. Just as you pass a "Keep off the grass" sign, Rex says, "Let's cut across right here." He hops over the railing, and the others follow. What do you do?

Most people would ignore the sign and go with their friends. Social psychologists call this *conformity*, the willingness to accept the social norms of a particular group. The opposite of conformity, of course, is *nonconformity*. What if Rex said, "Let's throw rocks at the elephants and make them stampede." At that point, you would probably choose to be a nonconformist. The desire to protect the animals would be stronger than your need to keep the approval of your friends. Psychologists hesitate to make judgments about whether conformity is right or wrong. Instead, they're more interested in *why* people tend to conform.

Research shows, for example, that group pressure can cause people to deny the evidence of their own senses, as one of psychologist Solomon Asch's experiments proves. Asch starts by seating his subject in a room with five or six other so-called subjects. Actually, these other five are "stooges," who have been instructed by Asch on what they are to do. After Randy, the actual subject, sits down at the end of the table, Asch holds

up a card with an eight-inch line drawn on it. He calls it the standard line. After everyone looks at it, Asch picks up a second card with three lines of various lengths. The task, he says, is to match the standard line to the proper comparison line on each of a series of cards. In control tests, subjects pick the correct line 99 percent of the time. In the experiment, the "stooges" begin by guessing the first two cards correctly. But on the third trial they pick the longest line, even though it is clearly longer than the standard

Figure 12.3

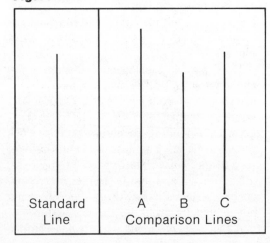

| Standard Line | A B C Comparison Lines |

Figure 12.4

Fashions in dress often reflect the type of conformity that psychologists call identification. What evidence of this kind of conformity do you see here?

line. Randy is put in a bind. He can see that line A is wrong. Should he believe his own eyes, even though that means going against the judgment of the others?

If Randy is typical, he'll stick to his own decision, but he'll show a high degree of nervousness as he does so. About one third of Asch's subjects, however, conform to the group choice. When asked about it later, some subjects rationalize by saying they didn't want to upset the group or that they felt it was all a trick anyway. But others insist that they really thought the two lines were identical. Unconsciously, they had resolved their conflict by not accepting its existence!

What other factors influence conformity? Self-confident people stand up to group demands for conformity better than those who have low self-esteem. The amount of authority behind the pressure for conformity also plays a major role. Imagine a situation in which students have littered the lunch area at school. Whose request to clean up would they be most likely to honor—one from a ninth-grader, a student council leader, or the principal? Finally, conformity also varies according to the rewards or punishments it brings. Most people pride themselves on their independence, but they readily sacrifice that pride if conformity will win social approval. That's probably the reason why Asch's subjects picked the wrong lines. In fact, as soon as someone else disagreed with the majority's choice, most subjects in Asch's experiments felt free to select the correct line.

Types of conformity

Social psychologists have identified three types of conformity: compliance, identification, and internalization.

Compliance. When you conform only long enough to gain a reward or avoid a punishment, your behavior can be called *compliance*. Elementary-school classrooms are good places to watch this type of conformity. Normally noisy, restless youngsters give in to the discipline of schoolwork and class routine in order to earn grades and approval. But as soon as they're dismissed, most of them throw compliance to the winds and run happily off to their afternoon activities.

Identification. You've probably noticed that some teenagers copy the style and mannerisms of stars of music, television, or sports. If a favorite actress appears in a new hairstyle, it won't be long before her fans begin copying the cut themselves. This type of conformity, known as *identification*, helps people feel part of a glamorous, exciting world that they admire. Sharing the identity of a successful person provides only a limited amount of satisfaction, however. By middle and late adolescence, most young people have begun to develop their own identities.

Internalization. When you make a set of values part of your own inner system of thinking and acting, psychologists call this *internalization*. You brush your teeth and comb your hair each day because you've made the values of society part of your own personality. Start the day without combing your hair and brushing your teeth and see how uncomfortable you feel! Values relating to honesty, trust, patriotism, and other important aspects of life are also internalized. Once you've made such a value part of you, it will probably remain, even when the original group associations have been left behind. People who move to another country, for example, almost always retain some of the customs of their native land.

Reasons why people conform

By now, you've probably wondered about your own degree of conformity. Some people conform more than others, and each person has different reasons for accepting the restrictions on independence that conformity imposes. Five reasons for conformity can be seen in the following listing.

Shared values. If you decide to join an organized group, it's probably because you like something about it. As a member, you understand that the group's success depends upon everyone working together and sharing common goals. But what happens when group values conflict with an individual's other needs? Belinda joined the drill team, for example, because she wanted the chance to perform at football games. Now she realizes that the practices and performances interfere with her homework. If the drill team is important enough to her, she can conform to its demands and accept lower grades. Or she can drop out of the group and concentrate on winning a scholarship.

Desire to be liked. The need to be accepted by a peer group is a powerful force for compliance. This seems especially true during adolescence, when young people lack self-confidence and need to know that other teenagers find them attractive and interesting. When Lloyd moved into a new school, he was lonely and felt left out. Anxious to find something that would help him gain acceptance, he started running cross-coun-

try. Actually, Lloyd wasn't a very good athlete, and the practices almost killed him. In addition, his father laughed at him for spending all that time running when he could have been making money at a part-time job. But Lloyd refused to give up. The chance to make new friends and to be liked was worth the pain of practice and the disapproval of his family.

Need to maintain relationships. People will often conform to maintain an important relationship. Thus, a husband will take up tennis in order to be with his wife, even though he'd rather go golfing. Such compromises are also common in sports and business. Some baseball managers, for example, insist that their players shave off beards and mustaches as a condition for playing on the team. And if your job depends upon dressing according to company policy, you'll probably conform rather than lose the employment.

Acceptance of authority. Obedience to authority represents a special type of conformity. Experiments have shown just how deeply embedded respect for authority is in most Americans (see pages 374–375).

Figure 12.5

Performing in a marching group demands long hours of practice. Why do these marchers sacrifice individual freedom and accept group discipline?

Conforming to the wishes of those who have power over you begins in infancy. The baby's demands for attention and unlimited freedom must bend to the socializing process. But even as an adult, you'll be left with an inner respect for authority. Ask anyone who has ever looked at a rear-view mirror to see the flashing light of a patrol car. Even if the individual wasn't doing anything wrong, that old childish reaction to authority probably caused a momentary feeling of guilt.

Guilt feelings over past actions. Almost everyone has felt guilty about breaking a social norm. Even if you weren't caught, the inner voice of conscience still speaks up when similar situations arise. For example, Elsa and Tony once took money from their family's grocery funds to buy treats for their friends. They were never caught, but ten years later they still remember the terrible guilt feelings they experienced. Both Elsa and Tony now conform to the family's standards of honesty more strictly than they ever did before.

Cognitive dissonance

Meet Walt Adams and Laura Vickers. They're going to demonstrate a special kind of response to pressure.

Walt smokes like a steam locomotive, three packs a day. Like just about everyone else these days, Walt knows that cigarettes can cause lung cancer. A social psychologist would call the conflict between what Walt does (smokes heavily) and what he knows to be true (the cigarette-cancer link) a *cognitive dissonance*. Listen as Walt tells his friend Laura how he handles his need to resolve this inner conflict.

Laura: Hey, Walt. I thought you were giving up smoking!

Walt: Yeah, I thought about it. But, you know, old Henry Peters is ninety years old and he still smokes a pack a day. I'm beginning to think those cancer stories are all a lot of bunk.

Laura: I don't know. The statistics look pretty scary to me. Smoking cigarettes is almost as dangerous as working in a coal mine.

Walt: Besides, I've switched to a low-tar brand. And if I stopped smoking, the stress from my job would kill me in three months. These babies are really lifesavers!

Can you see what Walt is doing? Having made up his mind to continue smoking, he has to justify that decision *to himself.* No one can live comfortably with a heavy load of cognitive dissonance. The unresolved conflict will not give you peace until it's taken care of. The amazing thing is how far people will go to reduce it.

Laura takes an extremely strong position against nuclear power. If you want her to change, talk her into taking the pronuclear side in a debate. Afterward, you'll find that her overall feelings about nuclear power will have softened. What happened? Laura hasn't sold out. But in order to debate, she had to admit that the pronuclear viewpoint might have some value. This created a cognitive dissonance with her earlier beliefs. In order to reduce this dissonance, she modified her extreme views. Otherwise, she couldn't have carried on the debate.

The lesson is that you'll often find yourself in a position where your actions won't square with your beliefs. In order to reduce dissonance, you'll find some way to justify your behavior. Sometimes you can do it by citing facts you've heard or read about, as Walt did by citing "evidence" that heavy smoking won't really cause cancer. Or you can find reasons within your own thinking, as Laura did by "discovering" unexpected values in nuclear-power plants.

Let's say that you believe profanity is wrong. But your new friends use four-letter words rather freely. You feel pressured to talk like the others, and before long you're using these formerly taboo words. Your dissonance is clear. You can either soften your antiprofanity position or give up friends who are important to you. Many people

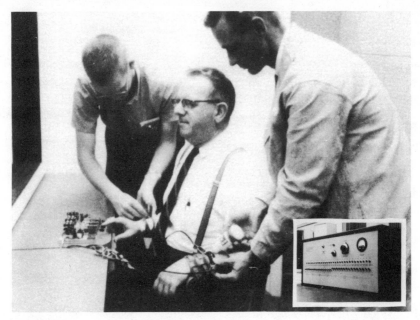

Figure 12.6

The Milgram experiment on obedience to authority puts you in front of a "shock generator." The "learner" is strapped in and hooked up to electrodes. When the "learner" makes his first mistake, would you give him the shock as instructed? [Copyright 1965 by Stanley Milgram. From the film *Obedience,* distributed by the New York University Film Library.]

would unconsciously modify their attitude toward profanity, perhaps on the grounds that "everybody talks like that these days." But reducing dissonance without examining the decision may leave you open to more compromises in the future. In time, people who take this "easy" route may not be able to admit to making mistakes at all, as the following experiment reveals.

Social dangers of conformity

Psychologist Stanley Milgram upset a lot of people with his experiments. But he upset himself as well. Milgram set out to prove that German citizens obeyed the orders of their Nazi rulers during World War II because Germans were conditioned to obedience by their culture. In contrast, he reasoned, Americans would never follow orders that would result in harm to other human beings. To test this part of his theory, Milgram ran an experiment that is still being talked about.

Imagine, if you will, that you're living in New Haven, Connecticut, in the early 1960s.

You have answered an ad offering $4.50 to take part in Milgram's learning experiment. Upon entering the laboratory, you meet the experimenter and a second subject. You learn that the experiment deals with the effect of punishment on learning. Your partner, an older man, tells you that he has a mild heart condition. The experimenter conducts a drawing to see who will be the teacher and who will be the learner. You draw a slip that assigns you to be the teacher. You watch as the learner is strapped into an "electric chair," with electrodes attached to his wrists. In a second room, the experimenter seats you in front of an impressive-looking shock generator (see Figure 12.6). You count thirty switches, ranging from 15 volts to 450 volts. The warning signs above the switches warn of "Slight shock" for the low-level voltages up to "Danger—severe shock" for the higher ones.

Now the experimenter gives you a shock. It hurts, and you're more convinced than ever that the experiment is for real. In your role as teacher, you're told that your job is to give a test to the learner. When he responds correctly, you go on to the next item. But if he answers incorrectly, you are ordered to give him an electric shock. The first shock is set at 15 volts, but for each mistake you add 15 volts. You can't see the learner, but an intercom lets you talk to each other.

Now, you're ready. You read a word, and he answers. One right. Two right. Then he makes an error. You reach for the switch. You know it hurts, for your own arm still tingles from the shock you received. What about his heart condition? You hesitate, look at the experimenter. He watches you, clipboard in hand. Your hand is on the switch. Do you flip it?

At that point, some subjects refused to continue. They got up and left the room. But Milgram found that about 65 percent of his subjects not only flip the first switch; they all go at least to the 300-volt level. As they do so, they hear the learner grunt in pain, complain, and finally scream in apparent agony. In the end, the learner lapses into silence, perhaps unconscious. Even so, at the urging of the experimenter, some subjects continue to administer heavier and heavier shocks. They break into a sweat and their hands tremble, but they keep on flipping the switches.

You've probably guessed by now that the learner is an actor. He knows when the switches are thrown so that he can react properly, but he doesn't get shocked. The subjects don't know that, however. Their responses show clearly that a majority of American men ages twenty to fifty will obey authority even when it means harming another person. Milgram concluded:

> With numbing regularity good people were seen to knuckle under the demands of authority and perform actions that were callous and severe. . . . The kind of character produced in American democratic society cannot be counted on to insulate its citizens from brutality and inhumane treatment at the direction of malevolent authority.

It's unlikely that many people will ever be put into this type of extreme situation. But you'll often run into moments when social pressures to conform will run counter to your personal values. To be a nonconformist simply to be different is a kind of game. But to be a nonconformist when it can cost you acceptance, financial gain, or personal pleasure is another matter.

As a popular sign in business offices reads, "Examine the turtle. It makes progress only when it is willing to stick its neck out." The best time to decide on the values you'll stick your neck out for is now. It may be too late if you wait until you confront the actual situation.

SECTION CHECKUP

1 What does the psychologist mean by conformity and nonconformity? Give a sample of each based on something you've experienced.

2 What are some of the reasons people conform?

3 What is the significance of Stanley Milgram's experiment on obedience to authority? Why did he think Americans wouldn't accept orders to hurt another person?

12.3 WHAT CAUSES AGGRESSION? WHAT CAN BE DONE ABOUT IT?

Almost any day's headlines tell the story:

"Terrorists Kill 47 in Bomb Attack. Strikers Dynamite Factory Trucks. Lovers' Lane Killer Strikes Again. Gang War Breaks Out in City."

And so it goes. *Aggression*, the intentional injury of another person, seems to dominate the news. Violence and disorder are as much a part of relationships between individuals as they are of relationships between groups and between nations.

Despite many animal and human studies, psychologists are divided over the causes of aggression in humans. According to the simplest explanation, aggression is instinctive, a behavior pattern that doesn't have to be learned and that appears when the proper stimulus occurs. Naturalist Konrad Lorenz, for example, described the attack behavior of the male stickleback fish. If the stickleback sees a red spot on the belly of another fish, he attacks. Move the spot to the other fish's head, and the stickleback remains calm. So instinctive is the behavior that the stickleback will attack a red-spotted wooden fish just as fiercely as he does a live rival. A few scientists have attempted to describe human aggression as instinctive, but little support for this theory has been found.

Another viewpoint suggests that people are "wired" for aggression at conception. Each person has an inborn capacity for hostility and violence, the theory says, but it is activated only when something blocks the individual's ability to satisfy his or her needs. Frustration, therefore, emerges as the triggering mechanism for aggression. If you're standing in line for concert tickets, for example, you'll probably feel relaxed and happy at the thought of hearing your favorite band. Then, just as you get to the window, it slams shut. A sold-out sign appears. You feel frustrated—and with the frustration comes anger and a desire to get even. Unlike the stickleback, however, you're not programmed to be blindly aggressive. You can shout and pound on the gates with the rest of the crowd—or you can shrug and walk away.

Finally, many modern psychologists regard aggression as a learned response to frustration. In this view, people act out their aggressions when inner tensions become unbearable. But if those tensions can be relieved, people have no built-in desire for or instinct toward hostility. Perhaps when social problems such as poverty, overcrowding, unemployment, pollution, inflation, and the like are relieved, aggression will be reduced. At the same time, parents and schools and society in general must take responsibility for teaching children nonviolent ways of coping with frustration.

Social causes of aggression

Aggression takes many forms. An angry, frustrated parent may resort to child beating. Children vandalize their schools. People loot neighborhood stores during a power blackout. A recently fired employee grabs a rifle and starts shooting.

A number of factors may be involved in such violent behavior.

Rewards to be gained. Some parents unknowingly reward aggression in their children. Children who can gain attention only by fighting, rowdiness, or other antisocial acts may carry on that pattern in later life. It's the same principle that applies to any learned behavior: If the behavior is rewarded, the behavior will be repeated. In time, it will be generalized to other situations. If Roy's father encourages him to fight when he's little, there's a good chance that Roy will use fighting as a way of solving problems when he's older.

Models of aggression. Critics charge that television, comic books, and professional sports all seem to teach the same lesson: Aggression solves problems and pays off in prestige, money, and self-esteem. A study by psychologist Albert Bandura showed how children model their behavior on that of adults. After preschool children were frustrated in a task, they saw an adult punch, kick, and shout at a Bobo clown doll. Afterward, the boys and girls copied the adult aggression against the doll. When the adult model showed no aggression, however, the children also handled their frustration more calmly.

Critics charge that TV provides a similar model for aggression. Heavy TV viewing by younger children, they claim, produces the same modeling effect demonstrated by Bandura. Violence on the screen, for

Figure 12.7

HOW QUICKLY AGGRESSION REPLACES COMPASSION

Social psychologist Philip Zimbardo's experiment in group behavior under prison conditions lasted only six days. Zimbardo had signed up a group of Stanford University men for the two-week simulation in which some of the men played the role of prison guards while others played

prisoners. But, he reports, the students almost immediately overstepped the line between role and reality. The guards, who had been chosen by random drawings, began to treat prisoners "as if they were despicable animals, taking pleasure in cruelty." The prisoners, on the other hand, became "servile, dehumanized robots who thought only of escape, of their own individual survival, and of their mounting hatred for the guards." Zimbardo concluded that people kid themselves about their ability to control aggression. Instead, he says, it lies within everyone, waiting only for the right moment to come to the surface. Another interpretation of the experiment disagrees with Zimbardo. Instead of the subjects acting out inborn behavior, according to this theory, the men had learned through TV and movies how guards and prisoners are supposed to behave. When put in the situation, they just did what they had been taught.

example, apparently has triggered a number of real-life "copycat" crimes by children and adults. TV's defenders dispute this charge, claiming that the link between television watching and aggression has not been proved.

Protection of territory. Many animals have an instinctive need to protect their territory. Some studies seem to point to a similar tendency in human beings. Rats in a closed colony live peacefully together until new births cause overcrowding. At that point fighting breaks out over living space, and their social order breaks down. Some social critics fear that similar forces may be

at work in crowded urban areas. People in cities such as Moscow and Hong Kong, however, have learned to cope with severe crowding. No one is sure just how much private space people must have in order to continue living peacefully together.

Lack of power. Poverty, prejudice, old age, and illness can cause people to feel as though they can't control their own fate. They feel "invisible," their needs ignored by the rest of the society. Lacking hope, they may turn to aggression as a means of protest. Similar feelings develop when one group believes that another group is taking advantage of it. Workers on strike, for

Figure 12.8

When a fight starts on the baseball field, both dugouts empty as players rush to help their teammates. What do you think causes this group solidarity? How could umpires prevent such mass brawls?

example, may turn their frustration into violence when their companies ignore their demands for higher pay or better working conditions. Such violence was once a common part of management-labor confrontations, but today it breaks out mostly during long strikes or when a company uses non-union workers to try to break a strike.

Reducing aggression

One solution to aggression would be to do away with the frustrations that may cause it. Elimination of overcrowding, unemployment, pollution, and substandard living conditions would help. But even if enough money could be found to do that, aggression wouldn't disappear. Hostility between groups of people is often based on learned dislike of people outside one's own group (see Figure 12.8). At a simple level, this shared group identity helps explain the hostility of sports fans for rival teams. At a more serious level, it accounts for the continuing hostility between different political, religious, and economic groups.

Break down barriers to cooperation. Problems caused by group identity can be clearly seen in the Robber's Cave experiment run during the 1950s by social psychologist Muzafer Sherif. For several years, Sherif and his assistants ran a summer camp for eleven- and twelve-year-old boys. All the campers were normal, healthy, well-adjusted children from middle-class homes.

Once there, they were separated in isolated cabins. Sherif set up tasks requiring that the boys within each group cooperate with each other, such as preparing for a campout. In a short time, the groups developed their own names (Rattlers and Eagles, for example), jokes, rules, and leadership. The boys knew and liked one another, but they knew almost nothing about the other group.

At this point, the experiment added competition between the two groups. These activities, which included tugs-of-war and ball games, offered highly desirable prizes. Almost immediately, the Rattlers took an intense dislike to the Eagles. The Eagles responded with an equal dislike for the Rattlers. At first the groups were content to call each other names. Then they stepped up hostilities by raiding the opposition's cabin. The formerly peaceful camp teetered on the edge of violence.

Sherif found that it was easier to put the groups at each other's throats than to restore harmony. Only when he set up tasks that required intergroup cooperation did the warfare lessen. When the food truck was rigged to break down, for example, the boys had to join forces to haul their dinner into camp. After a number of similar joint efforts, friendships began to form across group lines. The fighting died out.

Modify punishment. Society has traditionally used punishment as a way of dealing with criminal aggression. Psychologists point out, however, that punishment itself is a form of aggression. To a degree, the public feels better if criminals go to jail and serve long sentences. But all too often, the only lesson the prisoner learns in jail is how to be more violent the next time. Most parents know that punishing a child is effective only within a loving parent-child relationship. In a similar fashion, modern methods of dealing with lawbreakers have tried to combine punishment with programs that teach new ways of coping with frustration. Therapy and counseling, combined with vocational training, have helped many people turn their hostilities into productive ways of life.

Eliminate models for aggression. If society stops looking up to aggression as a model for behavior, people may reduce the level of individual violence. A typical proposal centers on controlling America's passion for firearms. Countries such as Great Britain and Japan, which have strict gun-control laws, report far fewer murders in relation to their population than does the United States. Japan, for example, had only 1.74 murders per 100,000 people in 1979. The United States, by contrast, recorded five times that number—9.6 murders per 100,000 people—during the same period. Another plan has been aimed at reducing violence on television and in the movies. The film rating system and the TV "family hour" are two attempts to resolve this issue without also censoring what you see on the screen.

Reward acceptable behavior. Experiments with children have reduced aggression by ignoring violent acts and rewarding more peaceful behavior. When Brad throws himself on the floor of the supermarket and screams and kicks, he's certain that his parents will respond to his tantrum. If they do, and buy his silence with a toy or candy, Brad will use the technique again. But if his mother says quietly, "Bradley, when you're finished, I'll be over at the meat counter," he'll soon learn that tantrums don't pay.

Even the frustrations of married life can be dealt with constructively. One fair-fight technique gives both parties a lightweight foam-covered club or bat. No blows to the head or midriff are allowed, but husband and wife can whack each other on the back, shoulders, arms, and legs. A few minutes of vigorous battle with such bats can work off

Figure 12.9

Nonviolent fighting with harmless bats can reduce frustrations and relieve tensions. Why is this technique a better means of resolving conflicts than the usual verbal battles between two people?

tensions and frustrations to a remarkable degree (see Figure 12.9). Afterward, the two combatants can sit down with the air cleared and deal with the real problems in their relationship.

Build understanding of others. People commit aggression more often against victims they don't see as human beings. If the other person is a symbol for frustration, as is sometimes the case with the police or wealthy people, the aggressor can more easily rationalize his or her crime. Judges sometimes require convicted criminals to visit the families of their victims in order to see the consequences of their crime. Whatever other arguments are made for school integration, the sharing of common experiences between otherwise separate racial and ethnic groups will also contribute to the same goal. Once you've worked with, eaten with, and played with members of another group, you'll find it hard to feel the same way about "them."

Assertive behavior

Hitting someone over the head is aggression. Using every possible means to con-

Figure 12.10
Martin Luther King leads a rally in support of civil rights for America's black citizens. What might have happened if King had chosen aggressive instead of assertive means to obtain his goals?

vince that person of the justice of your position is *assertive behavior*. Whereas society generally penalizes aggression, it often rewards assertive behavior. Businesses, sports teams, and political parties, among others, encourage people to be assertive. Assertive people have the energy, commitment, and ability to handle the frustration that a job or cause creates.

It's not hard to see the difference between slugging people and working to change their minds. Not all assertive behavior can be identified as readily, however. Here are the ways social psychologists describe assertive behavior.

1. Assertive behavior is directed against a real opponent, usually the cause of your frustrations. It does not strike out blindly against anyone or anything within reach.

2. Assertive behavior does not produce guilt feelings because those who use it feel their actions are justified.

3. Assertive behavior does not go too far. It uses only the pressure necessary to resolve the specific problem.

4. Assertive behavior is aimed at specific goals. It is not used to displace personal frustrations, nor is it easily provoked.

5. Assertive behavior is most often used to advance a cause you believe in deeply. It often leads to personal sacrifice so that others may be helped.

The American civil-rights movement provides a clear-cut contrast between aggression and assertive behavior. In the 1960s, organizations such as the Black Panthers promoted black power in aggressive terms that led to street violence. Worthwhile goals got lost in battles with police, and a number of lives were lost. By contrast, Dr. Martin Luther King, Jr. promoted the black cause by nonviolent demonstrations. With firm assertion, King brought black demands for equality before the nation (see Figure 12.10). If King had used aggression, the majority society would probably have refused to listen to his demands for justice. Nonviolence and civil disobedience, however, spoke to the conscience of America. The movement King led eventually helped pass federal legislation concerning civil rights, housing, education, and job opportunities. Although King's protests did touch off some violence by people outside his movement, he helped to defuse tensions that could have exploded into much wider conflict.

SECTION CHECKUP

1 Discuss the three theories that explain the process of aggression in human behavior.

2 What are some of the causes of aggression? How can some of these causes be reduced or eliminated?

3 What does the Robber's Cave experiment suggest as a way of reducing aggression between hostile racial groups in a community?

4 How does assertive behavior differ from aggression? Give some examples of assertive behavior.

Pro & Con: IS AMERICA DECLINING OR ONLY CHANGING?

For a long time now, doomsayers have warned: "Beware! The United States will collapse if the values that made it great continue to decline." The social behavior that concerns the critics is plain to see: changes in family life, loss of respect for the law, careless work habits, and a diminished faith in the goodness of the American way of life.

Social psychologists have tried to measure the effect of such change on the individual. From one point of view, needless change is equal to decay. From another, change is seen as a force for positive growth. Here are some of the arguments that have grown out of this debate:

Pro

1 Morality of every kind has declined to the point that no standards of behavior are left. Honesty, trust, and respect for one's fellow citizens have begun to disappear.

2 Laws should protect law-abiding people, not criminals. But too many citizens live in a climate of fear because criminals do not fear capture or punishment. Even when criminals do go to jail, sentences are too short and parole too easy to obtain.

3 Every institution that upholds the law is under attack, whether it is the family, the church, or the state. If America's institutions collapse, the society will drift into a disorganized period of violence and mob rule.

4 Today's permissive attitudes encourage people not to accept responsibility for their actions. Like children, many Americans seem to forget about tomorrow in a headlong quest for today's pleasures.

Con

1 Morality now reflects the basic nature of humanity, rather than artificial and impossible standards. Whatever new moral code emerges will grow out of the realities of human nature.

2 Everyone accused of a crime deserves the full protection of the law. Moreover, hard proof exists to show that punishment alone doesn't reduce crime. Only when everyone has a fair share of the good things of life will crime begin to decrease.

3 People make institutions, and people should change their institutions when necessary. Most American institutions are out of date. New systems of family organization, new rules of behavior, and a new sharing of political power are long overdue.

4 Old ideals of self-denial and hard work were set up to conceal the fact that only a few enjoyed the good things of life. Today's values say that everyone has a right to share in the pleasures of life.

Do you believe that American society has begun the long slide toward disaster? If you were President, what changes would you want to make in the way Americans think and act?

12.4 WHAT CAUSES PREJUDICE? WHAT CAN BE DONE ABOUT IT?

A picture similar to Figure 12.11 has been used in an experiment to demonstrate prejudice. Psychologists define *prejudice* as the unthinking attitudes or biases people hold about other individuals or groups. In the experiment, a group of white subjects is told that they are taking part in a study of communication. All subjects leave the room except one, who studies the picture carefully. The experimenter then removes the picture and instructs the first "witness" to describe it in as much detail as possible to a second person. In turn, the second subject repeats the description to a third, and so on. As you might guess, each witness loses some detail along the way, and often adds something new. But the important point is that by the third or fourth repetition, the knife often ends up in the black man's hand!

Why would prejudice cause some people unconsciously to transfer the knife? Social psychologists explain that the world is too complicated to think about in every detail. People, therefore, tend to reduce complex

Figure 12.11

Figure 12.12

"DON'T BOTHER ME WITH FACTS. MY MIND IS ALREADY MADE UP!"

If Martians landed tomorrow, some people would be prejudiced against them by the following day. Once such stereotyped thinking takes hold, it is hard to change. Perhaps the following dialogue will give you a taste of how prejudice works. Ms. Block is arguing with Mr. Glass about his anti-Martian prejudice.

Mr. G.: Those Martians! They landed only yesterday and they already think they own the planet. Who do they think they are, anyway?

Ms. B.: Is that fair? They've given us an antigravity device that will solve our energy crisis. And all they've asked is a chance to live here and become part of our culture.

Mr. G.: See, that shows what they're up to. They just want to worm their way into human society. I bet they've got death rays or something hidden behind that third eye!

Ms. B.: I just read that our military has investigated them, and they don't have any weapons. So far, they haven't broken a single one of our laws.

Mr. G.: Yeah, but I heard they're buying up good American farmland. How will our farmers be able to make a living if ugly green Martians spread out and grab off half of Kansas and Iowa? Next thing, they'll be wanting to move in next door and send their spores to school with my kids.

And Mr. G. is just getting warmed up. As you can see, he refuses to examine his tightly held prejudices. Since Ms. Block's facts can't really be denied, he simply ignores them and heads off in a new direction. Such thinking (or nonthinking) is all too typical of prejudiced people.

social relationships to oversimplified views of how they expect other racial, ethnic, or social groups to behave. These shorthand ways of judging people are called *stereotypes*. Most prejudices have been built up on the basis of limited and poorly evaluated information (see Figure 12.12). Many white subjects start out the experiment described in the previous paragraph with a prejudiced notion that blacks carry knives. While they're trying to remember details, it's easy for the unconscious to switch the weapon from the white hand to the black one.

Causes of prejudice

You can be prejudiced in favor of someone or something, but most prejudices tend to be negative. When a negative prejudice leads someone to take action against another person, that act is known as *discrimination*. At one level, prejudice may simply lead like-minded people to join together as a way of reinforcing their mutual dislikes and fears. At an ultimate level, these same prejudices can lead the majority group to attack the group against whom they're prejudiced. Whatever the level of prejudice and discrimination, however, the causes of this type of thinking stem from a number of sources.

Causes outside the individual. Historically, prejudice has roots in several realities of human existence. As people form a group, they tend to emphasize the similarities of skin color, religious belief, language, or customs that bind their group together. From there, it's an easy step to consider people who differ in belief or physical appearance as inferior. Slave owners, for example, found it easier to justify harsh treatment of their laborers if the enslaved peoples were thought to be less human than their masters.

The pressures of life in today's urban societies also tend to create hostility between groups. Great Britain, for example, has always prided itself on a broadminded attitude toward nonwhites. But in recent years, competition for jobs and living space in London and other British cities has created an explosive hostility on the part of whites toward West Indians, Pakistanis, and other people of "colour."

In addition, like arithmetic and reading, prejudice can be "taught." Children are born totally without any feelings of prejudice. But parents, teachers, and their peer group soon instruct them in the "right" views. Young Bess may not know why her new playmate has earned Dad's disapproval, but she can read his reaction quite clearly. Since her approval within the family depends upon holding proper prejudices, she will learn them, probably without question. All too often, by the time she's an adult, Bess will no longer wonder why she doesn't like this race or that religion. Her prejudices will have become part of her world view, and she'll unconsciously pass them along to her own children.

Governments also make—and sometimes unmake—prejudices among their citizens. American relations with the Soviet Union offer a good example. During World War II, the official policy built up American respect and admiration for the Russians and their valiant fight against the common enemy, Germany. After 1945, however, as the Soviet Union competed with the United States for world influence, old prejudices against the Communist system revived. The Cold War, as it was called, set off a wave of anti-Russian feeling. Then, as the Cold War gave way to more peaceful coexistence, attitudes toward Russia moderated. Most Americans again saw the Russians as a basically friendly and energetic people who are misused by a government determined to gain world superiority. Russians, of course, see Americans as hopelessly enslaved by their capitalist masters.

Causes inside the individual. Psychological forces also affect the development of prejudices. Social psychologists explain individual prejudices as a way of discharging hostilities built up by frustration.

The effect of frustration can be seen in the use of minority groups as convenient scapegoats for feelings of despair, anger, or hopelessness. Let's say that you're a farmer. Times are tough. Your crops are suffering from drought, the bank is demanding money, and the insects have been merciless. Just then a neighbor stops by with news that a Vietnamese family has moved in nearby. You can't do much about the weather or the local banker, but here's something you can lash out at. Without thinking of the injustice of your anger, you seize on these "foreigners" as a symbol for all that's going wrong in your world. In a way, they're a safe target since you don't know them as individuals.

The power of prejudice

It's not uncommon for a community to work together to defeat a common enemy, whether it's a flood, fire, or unwanted government action. But when the threat passes, personal fears take over once again. Whenever people feel separate, frustrated, or threatened, the seeds of prejudice are planted. In time, members of the ingroup begin to assume that all members of the outgroup will act according to the accepted stereotype. Such simplistic and incorrect ideas fill popular folklore: All Italians are lovers, all Germans obey orders, all Mexicans are lazy, all Irish drink too much. As prejudice grows, it feeds on humanity's tendency to ignore what it doesn't want to see (see Figure 12.13).

Figure 12.13

How do you account for the jogger's different reactions? What could you do to change his attitude toward the Garcias?

"Poor old Harry! He's really behind in his yardwork. Hope he's feeling OK."

"What a mess! But what can you expect of people who don't care about the neighborhood!"

Many studies have proved the harmful effects of prejudice and discrimination. Author Richard Wright described its impact in *Black Boy*, his novel about growing up in Mississippi in the 1920s. After being forced to leave a job because the white workers wouldn't accept him as an apprentice, Wright's hero said he "felt drenched in shame, naked to my soul. The whole of my being felt violated, and I knew that my own fear had helped to violate it."

Until the "black is beautiful" movement began, black children always chose to play with white dolls. They said that black dolls weren't as pretty. Psychiatrist Robert Coles found that six-year-old Ruby, a black girl, revealed the same pattern of thinking in her drawings. Her white people were larger and more lifelike than her black figures. Ruby's self-portraits often lacked a feature or two, but her white girls always had the proper number of fingers and toes.

Similarly, before the feminist movement increased their pride in being female, women tended to see men as more powerful and successful. In one study, two groups of women read an identical article in which only the name of the author was changed. As a result, one group thought the article had been written by a man, while the second group believed its author was a woman. The group reading the "Patrick N. Thomas article" rated it better in every respect than the group that read the "Patricia N. Thomas article." Only when girls began to grow up without the crippling effects of sexist prejudice did large numbers of women feel free to chose careers other than home-making.

Other results of prejudice can be equally damaging.

1. When given a choice, some minority or outgroup members deny kinship with their group. At one time, light-skinned blacks sometimes chose to "pass" as whites because they knew they would have better opportunities that way. Similarly, immigrants often changed their names when they came to the United States so that they could blend more easily into the majority society. People who leave their group to join the majority, however, often feel guilty about their desertion. The civil rights movement and increased emphasis on ethnic pride have lessened this tendency of minorities to leave their group.

2. Historically, many minority members passively accepted their inferior position. In this era of civil rights and protest movements, such attitudes have become less common. Most minority groups now use demonstrations, political campaigns, and self-pride campaigns to obtain full rights and opportunities.

3. Stereotypes can become self-fulfilling prophecies. If a minority group is thought of as lazy, cunning, or incompetent, some of its members will adopt those traits. Such behavior often causes the minority group to develop a degree of self-hate. Any indication of membership in the minority group is avoided. Children, particularly, may refuse to learn their parents' language, follow their religion, or practice their customs.

4. People who are discriminated against often compensate by developing a prejudice against some other outgroup. Perhaps this helps explain why blacks and Hispanic Americans have found it difficult to combine forces. Each sees the other as an opponent in gaining a stronger voice in the American political and economic system.

5. Outgroup members who suffer prejudice and discrimination show increased symptoms of physical and emotional illness. Stress-related illnesses such as ulcers, high blood pressure, and heart disease are found more commonly in minority populations. Drug abuse, alcoholism, depression, and other mental problems go hand in hand with the lack of opportunity and sense of hopelessness that affect many members of minority groups.

Eliminating discrimination

Since the 1960s, the United States has tried to reduce prejudice and eliminate discrimination, whether based on race, religion, sex, or any other factor. Civil-rights legislation has guaranteed equality to all minority groups. On the positive side, schools have been integrated, job opportunities have opened up, and better housing has been made available. But a negative side exists as well. Laws, speeches, and good will cannot undo overnight the built-up prejudice of centuries. For every advance in reducing prejudice, a sorry example of continued group hostilities can be found. Legal efforts can go only so far. Community programs that bring people together to cross over the boundaries between groups must also be established.

1. Despite the problems school integration has created, children who learn to work together in the classroom graduate from school with less prejudice. Even the parents who once bitterly resisted integration find that their attitudes change after school starts. Psychologists know that you can't hold two conflicting feelings at once. It's easy to hate Group X when they're somewhere else. But if your children go to school with Group X children, you're faced with a cognitive dissonance. Maybe, you say to yourself, those other kids aren't so bad after all. And in fact, experience usually shows that they're pretty much like your own kids. Communities that reinforce integration plans with study groups, cultural exhibits,

Figure 12.14

What are these people learning at this cross-cultural community fair that will help break down old prejudices?

festivals and fairs, films, and counseling programs find that much of the resistance to school integration can be overcome (see Figure 12.14).

2. Personal contacts can be encouraged at the neighborhood level. Groups that meet and work together on common projects gain feelings of mutual respect. Block parties, clean-up campaigns, youth groups, athletics, and similar activities help people see that old prejudices really aren't true. Such projects cannot be forced on people, however. Impetus must come from the people involved, perhaps with quiet, behind-the-scenes leadership from government or religious leaders.

3. Encounter groups can work to expose prejudiced thinking. Role playing, psycho-drama, and other self-awareness techniques can help people "get into someone else's shoes." These programs can be organized on a voluntary basis, with leaders trained in group techniques paid for by government agencies.

In the final analysis, however, nothing works better to reduce prejudice and eliminate discrimination than people who are aware of their own feelings. When each American takes personal responsibility for recognizing his or her own prejudices and overcoming them, the battle may finally be won.

SECTION CHECKUP

1 Name some of the reasons why almost everyone is prejudiced in some way toward people who are of a different race, religion, or ethnic origin.

2 Why are prejudice and discrimination so damaging to those who suffer their effects? Give some examples of these effects.

3 What can be done to reduce prejudice in this country? Why isn't it enough to pass tough antidiscrimination laws?

12.5 WHAT CAN PSYCHOLOGY TELL YOU ABOUT SUICIDE, AGING, AND DEATH?

If you're anything like the typical psychology student, your attitudes about suicide, aging, and death are still being formed. Unlike the energy crisis, inflation, or finding a job, these events probably seem remote from your own existence. But social psychologists have a reason for asking you to think about such topics. If you can build up a logical and positive attitude toward these facts of life, you'll be that much better prepared to deal with them when chance or the natural life processes bring you face to face with the future.

Suicide, the "decision to end all decisions"

Public officials in London a little more than a hundred years ago ordered the hanging of a man who had "come back from the dead." His crime? He had attempted suicide.

Men and women who try to kill themselves are no longer thought of as criminals. Social psychologists, in fact, see them as people who can no longer cope with the frustrations of life. In their depression, suicide seems to be the only solution. In this sense, suicide serves as their "decision to end all decisions." Whether or not people have a "right" to commit suicide is discussed in Figure 12.15.

Facts regarding suicide. Any event as emotionally disturbing as suicide creates its own mythology. Most people believe, for example, that more women commit suicide than men—but the reverse is actually true. Alfred Alvarez sums up some important understandings about suicide in his study *The Savage God.*

1. Young people attempt more suicides, but older people are more successful. Suicide rates peak at the ages fifty-five to sixty-five, with men four times more likely to end their own lives than women. But adolescent suicides have increased in recent years, as have those by women. In 1968, for example, 11 percent of all suicides were by young people between 15 and 24. By 1980, the figure was closer to 20 percent. Psychologists suspect that increased pressures to compete and succeed in a confusing and stressful society may be at the root of these statistics.

2. Suicide rates vary from country to country, with the industrialized nations reporting the highest rates. According to 1977 United Nations figures, the number of suicides per 100,000 population varies from a high of 40.3 in Hungary to a low of 1.5 in the Philippines. The United States has a rate of 12.5, relatively low for an industrial country. The suicide statistics in the Scandinavian countries show how difficult it is to pinpoint specific causes. Denmark (23.8), Sweden (19.4), and Finland (31.9) rank high, but Norway, with a similar population and economy, reports only 11.4 suicides per 100,000.

3. Anyone who threatens suicide should be taken seriously. Mental-health experts know that suicide threats are actually cries for help based on real feelings of despair, loneliness, or rejection. Suicide threats that are ignored can easily turn into the real thing. Perhaps the individual doesn't really mean to take all those pills, but the lack of response from friends or family can overwhelm the last safety margin.

4. Once a person attempts suicide, the chances are good that he or she will try again, particularly if the life situation causing the emotional distress isn't changed. This pattern of repeated attempts is often ignored by well-meaning relatives, who hush up the attempted suicide as a family embarrassment.

Preventing suicide. Few people go through life without thinking at one time or another of committing suicide. Failure, loneliness, chronic health problems, long-term depression, and a sense of being trapped in an unhappy life situation often lead to thoughts of ending one's life. The odds are good, therefore, that you'll someday come into contact with someone who seems to be thinking of suicide. If that happens, check for these danger signs:

1. Has the person ever attempted suicide before?

2. Has he or she been unusually depressed or withdrawn for a long period of time?

3. Does the person's family have a history of suicide or suicide attempts?

4. Has the individual recently suffered a severe blow, such as a death in the family, the collapse of a love affair, the loss of a job, or a severe illness?

5. Does he or she lack friends and family who provide close and loving support?

6. Does the person talk frequently about death?

Figure 12.15

DO PEOPLE HAVE THE RIGHT TO TAKE THEIR OWN LIVES?

Arthur Dyck, Professor of Population Ethics at Harvard, claims that people do not have the right to commit suicide. He challenges those who state that suicide is the ultimate expression of control over one's own destiny.

> To commit suicide is to opt out in the most final way from further contributions to the life and welfare of one's community and of the human race. In deciding to commit suicide, one decides that one will not be available to one's fellows, that one will not even be of potential benefit or service to the human community. This is the critical difference between taking one's life and giving it. Giving one's life is heroic and morally praiseworthy when it is done for someone's benefit or for the sake of humanity generally. Taking one's life is pathetic and morally blame-worthy when it is a form of withdrawal from the web of one's existence and from the human community.

Dyck doesn't think people should confuse other freedoms with freedom to commit suicide. Do you agree or disagree?

If the answer to two or more of these questions is "yes," you should enlist the help of a responsible person who can help you evaluate the problem and obtain assistance. Circumstances vary, but you can usually turn to a relative, a counselor, a member of the clergy, or a doctor. Suicide-prevention clinics and even "suicide hot lines"—24-hour-a-day emergency numbers for people who feel suicidal—can also be found in many towns and cities. The counselors there will tell you how to see that a potential suicide receives help.

Ageism, the newest prejudice

In the 1700s, people wore white wigs to make themselves look older. By contrast, a recent research study could find only one child in ten who had anything positive to say about growing old.

Social scientists are beginning to speak of this negative attitude toward aging and older people as a new form of prejudice. Some writers have called it *ageism*, the tendency to exclude the elderly from any im-portant role in American society. This trend has developed even though the number of people over sixty-five now has grown to over twenty million, an eight-fold increase since 1900. As life expectancy inches upward, that rapid increase can be expected to continue. In 1900, the average person lived for forty-seven years. By comparison, boys born in 1977 can expect to live to seventy-two, and girls to eighty-one. By the year 2000, twenty percent of the population will be over sixty-five.

Causes of ageism. Why do children carry a stereotype of the elderly as "old, wrinkled geezers, feeble and crippled by arthritis"? After all, to be prejudiced against old age is to be prejudiced against yourself, for barring accident, you too will someday be old (see Figure 12.16). The answer seems to come from social patterns that no one designed deliberately, but that contribute to ageism.

1. In a mobile society, many children don't see much of their grandparents.

Figure 12.16

Old age in a society that believes only youth is valuable can be a lonely and depressing period of life. What can you do to ensure that you won't face this sort of loneliness some day?

one third of all Americans over sixty-five live in poverty.

Facts about the elderly. Ageism, an unfair and deadly prejudice, need not exist at all. Throughout history, most cultures have treasured elderly people for their wisdom, experience, and hard-won skills. A culture that throws away the capabilities of one fifth of its people loses a national treasure. Perhaps your own attitude toward aging might change if you understood these facts about old age.

1. No one can set a specific age as the point at which a person becomes old. Sixty-five is no more a magic boundary than is twenty-one. Age is a measure of individual capacity for continued growth as a person. By that yardstick, some people are old at eighteen, and others are young at eighty-seven.

2. Old age need not be a dreaded time of sickness and inactivity. In fact, older people have fewer serious illnesses than the average population: 1.3 illnesses a year to 2.1 for all age groups. Dr. Walter Bortz, of Stanford Medical School, believes that the human body should last 120 years. If it doesn't, it's probably because people are more terrified of growing old than of dying.

3. Only 5 percent of people over sixty-five live in nursing homes. Most elderly men and women can take care of themselves, particularly if the community provides at least a minimum level of nursing and housekeeping services. True senility strikes only a few. What appears to be senility stems from two causes. Some elderly people act senile because they or other people think the elderly are supposed to act that way. Others show the symptoms of senility because of

Families move away, often to communities where everyone seems to be the same age. Without regular contact with older people, children may develop stereotyped views of age as a time of decay and unhappiness.

2. The mass media add to the prejudice against aging. Older characters on TV often appear as foolish or helpless. More important, programs and commercials alike teach viewers that it's bad not to stay young. The "Pepsi generation" never dances across the screen with gray hair and wrinkles. One survey of children's literature found that of 656 books, 544 didn't have any older characters. When old people did appear, they were portrayed as unimportant and unexciting.

3. As people grow old, many are caught in a self-fulfilling prophecy: "Old people can't take care of themselves." Expecting to be sick, feeble, and unable to work, the elderly sink into despair.

4. The financial hardships that inflation and inadequate pensions place on old people add to their burden. The occasional article about an old couple living mostly on canned dog food underlines the estimate that fully

poor nutrition. When their diet is improved, they snap back.

4. Old people do not lose intelligence or abilities. Some do slow down, but if given enough time they do as well as younger people on intelligence and achievement tests. Alex Comfort, an expert on aging, writes that old people who are physically fit are the least dangerous drivers on the road. "By seventy-plus," Comfort notes, "you have experience, and the accident-prone fraction of the population is dead or disqualified."

You will benefit if you include older relatives and friends in your life. Of course, no one would claim that all old people are saints. Just like younger people, some are difficult, cantankerous, and self-involved. But age can also provide them the time to be friendly, humorous, open, and giving. Once you recognize these qualities, you will see old age as a natural extension of your earlier life. And people who lead a rich, full, and healthy life have an excellent chance of enjoying a rich, full, and healthy old age.

Coping with death

Of all the living creatures on earth, only the human species lives with the knowledge of eventual death. Yet most people in this country do their best to ignore the fact that they will die. Instead, they cover it up with "nice" phrases. Friends and relatives "pass away," or go to their "eternal rest." In funeral homes, families visit the "deceased" in a "slumber room" with recorded music playing softly in the background.

The idea is spreading, however, that death can be an individual's last creative act. After a lifetime spent loving, working, growing, and building, death can give dignity and meaning to one's accomplishments. But that will not happen until society faces up to the need to do a better job of preparing people to face death.

Dr. Elisabeth Kübler-Ross, an expert in this field, believes that the first step must be

to allow the dying to keep their dignity and humanity. When people come face to face with approaching death, Dr. Kübler-Ross explains, they need help while they learn to accept the end of life. With time and loving care, shock and denial eventually give way to a readiness to put one's life in order. As an example of how death practices in an earlier rural society differ from those of today, read Dr. Kübler-Ross's story of a European farmer's death (BioBox, pages 392–393).

Making death less terrifying. Psychologists and other experts on death recommend that several specific steps be taken to ensure that everyone has a chance to die with dignity.

1. Although many people find thoughts of death upsetting, high-school and college curricula should be modified to include units on death and dying. Stripping away the mystery that presently surrounds death would make it less frightening and thus easier to face. Those schools which have added such elective courses report that students leave the program much better equipped to handle both the business of dying (insurance, wills, mortuaries, cemeteries) and the emotional side (grieving, comforting survivors, working through to acceptance).

2. Dying patients should receive as much information about their condition as possible. Many doctors now believe that the tradition of withholding bad news from the patient turns out to do more harm than good for all but the most immature people. As patients move from denial of their approaching death to acceptance, they feel less helpless. Not only do they face death with greater calm, but their improved emotional state lets them work with their doctors to control pain and treat their condition.

3. The hospice concept should be expanded. Hospices are special nursing homes where people can go to die in a humane way. Trained staff members provide companion-

BioBox

ELISABETH KÜBLER-ROSS:
THE DYING TEACH US TO LIVE

Swiss-born Dr. Elisabeth Kübler-Ross (1926–   ) has spent most of her life helping people. Largely because of her influence, the old taboo that kept death out of sight and out of mind has begun to disappear. In 1969, Dr. Kübler-Ross's best-seller, *On Death and Dying,* brought her ideas before the public.

Dr. Kübler-Ross first came in contact with people's reactions to death when she worked with the survivors of World War II concentration camps. After medical school she trained as a psychiatrist and treated both the retarded and the schizophrenic. It was during these years that she began to recognize the psychological steps that the dying person goes through. Understanding this progression, which begins with denial of death and moves through rage, bargaining, depression, and on to final accept-

ance, has greatly increased people's ability to cope with death and dying.

Today Dr. Kübler-Ross spends much of her time trying to arrange more humane care for the dying. She describes a death with dignity that she witnessed as a child in Switzerland:

> I remember as a child the death of a
> farmer. He fell from a tree and was

---

ship, counseling, and relief from pain. In the homelike setting, family members can visit often. Hospice staff members have the time to offer the time-consuming services not available in hospitals.

4. Families should be encouraged to allow children from age nine or ten onward to participate in funerals and other death rituals. Psychologists say that allowing a youngster to express grief along with the adults of the family gives the child a chance to begin learning to accept death as a necessary part of life. Hiding the death of a close relative or friend from children only confuses them and makes death seem doubly frightening and mysterious.

5. People should plan their own funerals ahead of time. This practice provides for a memorial service that truly expresses the individual's wishes and personality. Equally important, prior arrangements prevent funeral directors from selling a more expensive service and casket to grieving relatives than they may want or can afford.

The "right to die." As medical science develops better ways of keeping critically ill patients alive, new practical and moral questions arise to complicate the natural process of dying. At what point, for example, should a terminally ill patient be allowed to die without further suffering? In not expected to live. He asked simply to die at home, a wish that was granted without questioning. He called his daughters into the bedroom and spoke with each one of them alone for a few minutes. He arranged his affairs quietly, though he was in great pain, and distributed his belongings and his land. . . . He also asked each of his children to share in the work, duties, and tasks that he had carried on until the time of the accident. He asked his friends to visit him once more, to bid good-bye to them. Although I was a small child at the time, he did not exclude me or my siblings. We were allowed to share in the preparations of the family just as we were permitted to grieve with them until he died. When he did die, he was left at home, in his own beloved home which he had built, and among his friends and neighbors who went to take a last look at him where he lay in the midst of flowers in the place he had lived in and loved so much.

Dr. Kübler-Ross believes that grief is a normal and healthy sense of loss. Grieving, she says, "is an expression of unfinished business, hurts never healed, love unexpressed, regrets unresolved. . . . Dying people teach how to live. That's all. I mean, if I die today after having told my family 'I love you,' I've said it. If I got home and found that a loved one had died, I'd say, 'thank heavens I've said all those things I've always wanted to say.' "

As a summary of what she has learned from her patients, Dr. Kübler-Ross repeats a poem by Richard Allen:

> . . . as you face your death,
> it is only the love
> you have given
> and received
> which will count . . .
> if you have loved well
> then it will have been worth it . . .
> but if you have not
> death will always come too soon
> and be too terrible to face.

Do any of Kübler-Ross's insights regarding death strike a responsive feeling in your experience? Why is she so concerned that people "say all the things they've always wanted to say"?

their rush to save lives, doctors and nurses sometimes forget that they're dealing with human beings. The patient becomes "the heart attack in 204A," and in the flurry of expert treatment all dignity and opportunities for peaceful reflection are often lost.

Doctors have always believed that they had no choice when treating critically ill patients: They had to do everything possible to save lives. But "everything possible" can mean long days of pain for the patient and mounting expenses for the family, with no hope that the patient can ever return to a productive life. The courts have sometimes been called upon to decide at what point life-support systems should be turned off. No universal standard has been established.

Several states have recently passed laws that allow terminally ill patients to request the removal of life-support machines. People who take the opposing position, however, also make a strong case. No one should be put in a position of "playing God," they say, with responsibility for deciding who should live and who should die. Furthermore, they continue, medical miracles happen almost every day. Apparently hopeless cases recover and live for years—years they would not have had if someone had decided to let them die.

Life-and-death issues like this one arouse controversy so intense that no one can predict what decision society will eventually make. As a voter and family member who will someday face such decisions yourself, your opinions will count in this debate.

SECTION CHECKUP

1 What are some of the signals that would alert you to the possibility that a friend may be considering suicide? What can you do about it?

2 What arguments could you use to convince someone that old age need not be a time of decay and despair?

3 What advantage can be found in helping people develop more positive attitudes about death and dying? List some of the ways this can be accomplished.

LOOKING BACK: A SUMMARY

1 Social psychologists study individual and group behaviors in a social setting. The field is concerned primarily with socialization, the process by which people learn the rules of behavior for their culture and for the groups they join. Group behavior is affected by the size of the group, the type of rewards it offers its members, the way members cooperate in order to achieve group goals, and the way group tasks are distributed.

2 All groups assign roles to their members so that each person will know what to do. The rules for playing roles properly are called social norms. Learning the proper roles and social norms for group membership is one of the challenges of growing up. Group leadership grows out of the need to make decisions and to move the group toward its goals. Leaders may be chosen on the basis of ability, personality, control of rewards and punishments, or through manipulation.

3 Conformity is a measure of the extent to which people meet social norms. The degree to which people conform depends upon their self-image, whether or not they find someone else to support their position, the

group's authority, and the desire to gain approval and avoid punishment. When people conform only long enough to gain a reward or escape some sort of discomfort, the behavior is called *compliance*. Identification is a form of conformity in which people copy the behavior or life style of a hero or heroine. Internalization refers to the process of making a set of values part of one's own inner system of thinking and behaving.

4 People conform for several reasons. They may share common goals with other group members and want to work for the group's success, or they may conform so that they will be liked. People also conform in order to maintain a relationship that is important to them. Obedience to authority tends to be drilled into children and may be carried over into adult life. Guilt feelings can also cause conformity. Although nonconformity can prove costly to the individual, society will suffer if everyone conforms without question to the orders of those in power.

5 Cognitive dissonance is the internal conflict that arises when people believe one thing but do another. Unconsciously, people reduce dissonance by altering their thinking to conform to their behavior. Reducing dissonance without clearly examining the compromise it requires can lead people to abandon beliefs that are important to their self-esteem.

6 Aggression is the act of deliberately harming someone else. Most social psychologists believe that aggression grows out of frustration rather than out of instinctive behaviors. In their view, aggression results from a society that rewards it and provides numerous models for violent behavior. Other factors that trigger aggression include the need to protect one's living space and to overcome feelings of hopelessness. Studies show that aggression can be reduced when frustrating conditions are changed, when criminals are helped rather than punished, when models for aggression are eliminated, and when nonviolent behavior is rewarded. Society rewards assertive behavior that is directed toward achieving useful goals, whether in business, sports, or politics.

7 Prejudice is an unthinking, biased attitude held by one group about another. When prejudice leads to unfair acts against another group or person, it is known as discrimination. Prejudice gives people an excuse for looking down on those who are different or who threaten their security. Psychological forces that cause prejudice grow out of the need people have to blame their failures and frustrations on something or someone.

8 Prejudice has a powerful hold on people because it makes up a basic part of their identity. To reject a prejudice often means going against old beliefs and old friends. But prejudice has a harmful affect on those who feel its sting. Stereotypes of group traits and behaviors can become self-fulfilling prophecies for minority-group members. Outgroup members also suffer higher rates of physical and emotional illnesses. Before prejudices can be eliminated, people must be educated to regard all other human beings as worthy of respect.

9 People attempt suicide when depression, loneliness, or frustration overwhelm their ability to cope with these problems. All suicide threats must be taken seriously, particularly when other danger signs are present. These signals include long-term depression, a recent emotional shock, lack of family support, and a previous history of suicide attempts.

10 American society's tendency to worship youth and reject old age has tended to exclude the elderly from a fair share of economic rewards and political power. Ageism results from age segregation, the neglect of the elderly in the mass media, and a tendency of both young and old people to assume that age automatically means becoming sick, feeble, and lonely. This unfortunate prejudice can be overturned when people understand that being old is simply a natural extension of one's earlier life.

11 Efforts are being made to help people see death as a positive part of living. These programs include teaching about death in the schools, giving people a chance to die in a humane way, and asking people to help plan their own funerals. "Right-to-die" laws are also giving people a chance to decide that they do not want to be kept alive when there is no chance that they will live a normal life again.

PUTTING YOUR KNOWLEDGE TO WORK

Terms you should know

ageism

aggression

assertive behavior

body language

cognitive dissonance

compliance

conformity

discrimination

identification

internalization

nonconformity

nonverbal communication

prejudice

role

socialization

social norm

stereotype

Objective questions

1 The information conveyed by a person's posture or movement is called (*a*) personal insight (*b*) body language (*c*) verbalization (*d*) internalization.

2 Which of the following is *not* a basic rule of group behavior? (*a*) Group size greatly affects the way group members react to one another. (*b*) Group behavior can be changed by rewards or punishment. (*c*) Rewards given to group members are usually given out equally. (*d*) People are more likely to stay with groups that were difficult to join.

3 Stanley Milgram's experiment on obedience to authority proved that (*a*) everyone obeys orders without question (*b*) Americans will not harm other people even under stress (*c*) many men will obey orders even when it means inflicting harm on a fellow human being (*d*) people are less likely to harm strangers than people they know.

4 Which of the following is an example of assertive behavior as opposed to aggression? (*a*) Susan leads a student delegation to protest the principal's cancellation of the Senior Prom. (*b*) Tom throws a brick through a restaurant window after the owner refuses to serve him. (*c*) Debbie cuts off another driver after he refuses to give her room to make a lane change. (*d*) Bill steals a turkey from the supermarket to give to a hungry family at Thanksgiving.

5 A social scientist would say that the best way to cut down on aggression in American society would be to (*a*) take away all guns and knives owned by American citizens (*b*) condition children to be passive and nonaggressive (*c*) punish all acts of aggression with long jail sentences (*d*) improve the social conditions that seem to trigger most hostility and violence.

6 Which of these is *not* a reaction to prejudice found in a minority group? (*a*) Many minority group members develop prejudices against some other minority group. (*b*) Minority group members often adopt the stereotyped behaviors expected of them. (*c*) Minority group members develop few neurotic symptoms since they have nothing to prove. (*d*) Some minority group members actively deny their own heritage.

7 Social psychologists agree that (*a*) old age begins at sixty-five for everyone (*b*) old people almost always become senile if they live past seventy (*c*) the elderly do not decrease in intelligence (*d*) a person's personality in old age has little to do with earlier stages of life.

8 Suppose some believers in flying saucers sold all their belongings in preparation for being picked up to be taken to another planet. According to the theory of cognitive dissonance, what would group members be most likely to say after the saucers didn't come on the appointed day? (*a*) "The Air Force probably intercepted our saucer. It will surely come next week." (*b*) "We'll never believe in flying saucers again." (*c*) "Well, we were wrong that time." (*d*) "The joke's on us, isn't it?"

9 Which of the following is a *true* statement about suicide? (*a*) Those who talk about suicide never do anything about it. (*b*) More women commit suicide than men. (*c*) A person who tries to commit suicide but fails will very likely try again. (*d*) Suicide attempts can never be predicted in advance.

10 Teaching people to deal openly with death and dying (*a*) can only create neurotic behavior (*b*) isn't needed since American society has always done a good job of preparing people to cope with death (*c*) means that people will begin to look forward to death (*d*) will help people accept death as a natural part of life.

Discussion questions

1 Try to name all of the groups to which you belong. How much do you think each of these groups affects your behavior?

2 What are the dangers of too much conformity in a society? From your own knowledge of history and from your own experience, give some examples of useful nonconformity. When, if ever, is nonconformity dangerous?

3 What would you do to reduce aggression in our society if you had the power? Would you also try to eliminate assertive behavior? Why or why not?

4 How does prejudice get started among the members of a majority group? Why is it so hard to get rid of once it is established?

5 Suppose you were planning a curriculum for elementary-school children and you wanted to eliminate racial, age, and ethnic prejudices. What studies and experiences would you want the children to have?

6 How would you raise your children so that they would not respond, as Milgram's subjects did, to orders to harm another person?

Activities

1 Invite a panel of elderly people to talk to your psychology class about their views on aging. You and your classmates will probably be pleasantly surprised at how much you have in common with these elderly men and women. You can obtain more information about programs aimed at developing better attitudes toward aging by writing to the National Association for Humanistic Gerontology (NAHG), Claremont Office Park, 41 Tunnel Road, Berkeley, CA 94705. Another interesting organization, somewhat assertive in its policies, is the Gray Panthers, 3700 Chestnut Street, Philadelphia, PA 19104.

2 You might be interested in finding out more about "living wills." People who sign these documents are saying that they choose to die rather than allow the use of "heroic measures" to keep them alive when there is no reasonable chance of recovery. Write to Euthanasia Education Fund, 250 West 57th Street, New York, NY 10019, for a free copy of a "living will."

3 Cigarette smokers will provide you with an excellent way of demonstrating cognitive dissonance. Find a copy of an article warning about the dangers of smoking. Show it to several smokers. (Find out beforehand if the smokers are willing to discuss smoking with you.) Then ask the smokers why they still smoke even though the danger to their health has been clearly proved. You should end up with an imposing list of poorly reasoned answers and a better understanding of how far people will go to reduce a dissonance.

4 Try to arrange for a speaker to visit your psychology class from a local suicide-prevention clinic or a hot line that deals with potential suicides. Since our society tries to ignore the fact that people commit suicide, you and your classmates will probably be amazed at the seriousness of the problem. Ask the speaker especially to discuss the incidence of suicide among teenagers and young adults.

5 Write across the top of a piece of paper the names of five racial, religious, or ethnic groups different from your own. Under each name, as quickly as possible, write as many descriptive words as you can think of. When you're finished, examine the results. Is it possible that you've repeated a number of stereotypes that you've picked up without ever examining them very closely? How well do your descriptions apply to actual people you know from each of the groups? Perhaps the exercise will help you think more clearly about the nature of prejudice and its effects on people's thinking.

6 Run the Asch experiment on conformity (see page 370) to find out if you obtain similar results. You'll need to make several sets of cards with the standard and comparison lines. Be sure to coach your planted subjects carefully so as not to give the experiment away. Also, debrief your actual subjects afterward, so that they will understand what has happened. That's a tough position you'll be putting them in, and they'll need to be reassured that most people respond as they did.

For further reading

Aronson, Elliot. *The Social Animal*. New York: Viking Press, 1972. Dr. Aronson writes with wit and insight on the major questions in social psychology, including conformity, prejudice, communication, and aggression.

Downs, Hugh. *Thirty Dirty Lies About Old*. Niles, IL: Argus Communications, 1979. Downs, a TV talk-show host, writes about the "thirty myths of aging" in a witty, insightful style. His book explodes the prejudices that keep young and old alike from accepting the joys and challenges of old age.

Grollman, Earl A., ed. *Concerning Death: A Practical Guide for the Living*. Boston: Beacon Press, 1974. Experts in the field write clearly and compassionately about people's emotions and the facts they need when facing their own death or the death of a loved one.

Kübler-Ross, Elisabeth. *To Live Until We Say Goodbye*. Photos by Mal Warshaw. Englewood Cliffs, NJ: Prentice-Hall, 1978. This beautifully written and photographed book presents case histories of several cancer patients, including what they and their families wrote about dying. The book also includes a section on the hospice movement.

Morris, Desmond. *Manwatching: A Field Guide to Human Behavior*. New York: Abrams, 1977. Zoologist Morris has compiled a lively and fascinating catalog of human behavior. Excellent illustrations bring the text to life, as Morris explains the reasons behind your body language.

Readings in Social Psychology Today. Del Mar, CA: CRM Books, 1967. An excellent way to gain an overview of the type of research going on in social psychology. Most of the important people in the field are represented here.

Wright, Richard. *Black Boy*. New York: Harper & Row, 1937. Richard Wright's autobiography vividly describes the terrible weight of prejudice that blacks lived with in the South of the 1930s.

13

SEX ROLES, SEXISM, AND SEXUALITY

Revolutions change the way people feel and behave. Some revolutions are fought with guns, while others involve great changes in science or technology.

A revolution of a different sort has been taking place in this country. It goes beyond politics and economics. Before it's finished, American society will have some new definitions for sex roles, sexism, and sexuality.

As in all revolutions, many men and women are unhappy about the changes they see around them. But a major social movement cannot be ignored. Its influence can be seen in the lives of people everywhere. Here is what three of them have to say.

Liz Bennett, age forty-five. I grew up believing that finding a husband and having kids was what a woman's life was all about. So that's what I did. Fifteen years later, I started to feel really depressed. Some people wouldn't understand that. There I was, with two children, a pleasant house, and a husband who didn't run around or drink too much. I had it made, right? Only I didn't. I kept thinking, there's got to be more to life than car pools, supermarkets, and washing dishes. I could see my kids getting bigger, but I felt I was getting smaller.

So I tried to talk to Herm about it. I told him I wanted to go to work so I could make some money that was all my own. He got all upset and mumbled something about, "No wife of mine will ever have to slave as I do." That's when I signed up for a book-keeping class at the junior college. The excitement of doing something on my own made me feel alive again. I began to think about going on for a degree in business administration. Herm told me to cut it out, adding that he and the children needed me at home.

So I thought about that, and he was right. They did need me at home. But I needed something too, and they didn't seem willing to give it to me. I wanted to be Liz Bennett, not "Donny and Belle's mother" or "Herm's wife." I told Herm that. He just laughed and said, "Come on, honey, you housewives have it made. Buy yourself a new dress, get your hair fixed, and I'll take you to Las Vegas for the weekend."

I spent six months trying to make Herm understand, and then I packed up the kids and walked out. I still don't feel great about that. You can't turn your back on all those years of being a "proper" wife and mother and not feel guilty. But I'll finish my management training this spring, and for the first time in my life I feel that I'm really doing what *I* want to do. And Donny and

GRACEFUL T̶O̶U̶G̶H̶ TENDER COOL PRACTICAL TEMPERAMENTAL
STRONG E... ...EALISTIC INTELLECTUAL PASSIVE INTUITIVE
PLIANT B... ...Y POSSESSIVE AMBITIOUS LOVING GOSSIPY
SILENT I... ...H CALM SOFT DEPENDENT MEEK DOMINANT
INDEPEN... ...OUGH TENDER COOL PRACTICAL PASSIVE
TEMPERA... ...EMOTIONAL RECEPTIVE INTELLECTUAL
SHY INTI... ...ERN AGGRESSIVE AMBITIOUS CALM LOVING
SUPP... ...E COMPETITIVE SOFT ACTIVE DEPENDENT
DO... ...NDENT GRACEFUL TOUGH TENDER CLUMSY
AC... ...PERAMENTAL STRONG EMOTIONAL WISE MUS-
CU... ...SSIONATE EXCITABLE RECEPTIVE INTUITIVE
GI... ...AGGRESSIVE LOVING TALKATIVE PASSIVE
CO... ...E COMPETITIVE AMBITIOUS LOVING DOMINANT
QU... ...BELLIGERENT FIERCE GRACEFUL TOUGH TENDER
P... ...ERCURIAL EMOTIONAL GIVING GRASPING DOMINANT
L... ...EPENDENT INTUITIVE CAREFUL ATHLETIC PRACTICAL
FORMAL IDEALISTIC HUSKY GRUFF SLOW-THINKING COOL CRIMINAL

Figure 13.1

Stereotyped sex roles require that men develop certain emotional and intellectual qualities while women develop others. Does either sex have a monopoly on
any of these qualities?

Belle treat me as if I'm a real human being, not just a household convenience.

Herm? He still thinks I'll get over this
"phase" I'm going through and come running back to him. But I'm sure that won't
happen.

Emma Prescott, age twenty-three. Am I
a feminist? Don't be silly! Sure, I guess you
might get that idea because I'm a fire fight-
er, and that's supposed to be a man's job,
right? Well, the way I see it, fire fighting's a
job—period! When I applied to take the
exams, I wasn't trying to prove anything
except that women should have the same
chance as men to wear this uniform. You
probably heard about the problem I had
with the physical tests. I can see where you
have to be able to climb walls and carry
heavy loads, but the old tests weren't fair
for either men or women. One of the wom-
en's groups helped me take that to court,
and we got it changed.

Then, after I finished training and was
assigned here, some of the men's wives
signed a petition about me. I guess they

thought my big goal in life was to steal their
husbands. My own boyfriend wasn't too
happy about my sleeping here, but that's
part of the job. At first the other fire
fighters thought they'd have to take special
care of me, but I showed them I could do the
job.

A couple of the guys call me "Libber," but
that's crazy. I'm not marching for women's
rights or making speeches. I guess most
girls dream about being models or airline
stewardesses, but I always wanted to fight
fires. So here I am.

Brad Grant, age twenty-two. Hey, I can
see by your face you're wondering what I'm
doing in a laundromat. That shouldn't be too
hard. See, that's my wash, whiter than
white. Some people think this is women's
work, but in my marriage it's just a job that
needs doing. Besides, Anita's on a business
trip, so it's only fair. When I work overtime
on my job, she pitches in and does what's
necessary. That's how we work everything
out.

You see, before we got married, Anita

and I talked a lot about things like this. Neither of us wanted to repeat the mistakes our families made. I still remember seeing my folks drag in after their shifts at the plant. Dad would plop down to watch TV, but Mom just kept on going. She still had all the cooking, cleaning, laundry, and child care to do.

So Anita and I worked out a marriage contract. It's got a lot of personal stuff in it, but the important thing is that we agreed on how we'd divide up the work. And we do a lot of things together, like cooking. Later, when we have kids, we'll still share responsibilities. Anita hardly ever saw her father when she was growing up. He was so busy making money he didn't have any time to spend with his children. That's not going to happen to us. We may never get rich, but my kids will see their father a lot, especially when they're young. And my girls will get the same chances to play sports and have careers as my boys will.

You might not agree totally with the ideas that Liz, Emma, and Brad express. But the decisions people like them are making about marriage, children, and jobs will probably affect your life in the next few years. This chapter will give you some insights into this nonviolent revolution.

13.1 HOW DO PEOPLE LEARN MASCULINE AND FEMININE SEX ROLES?

13.2 WHAT ARE THE EFFECTS OF SEXISM ON WOMEN?

13.3 WHAT ARE THE GOALS OF THE FEMINIST MOVEMENT?

13.4 IF THE FEMINIST MOVEMENT SUCCEEDS, WILL MEN BE THE LOSERS?

13.5 HOW DO CHANGING PATTERNS OF SEXUALITY AFFECT SOCIETY?

13.1 HOW DO PEOPLE LEARN MASCULINE AND FEMININE SEX ROLES?

What does it mean to be male? What does it mean to be female?

Throughout most of history, people thought they knew how to answer these questions. Men were expected to be hunters and farmers, brave warriors, and stern but loving fathers. Women were supposed to be wives and mothers, keepers of the home, and guardians of the softer human virtues. Many people never did fit these stereotyped *sex roles*, of course, but these people were either ignored or dismissed as "abnormals."

Only in recent years has psychology begun to study the biological and environmental forces that create male and female behavior. The studies have reached two major conclusions: (1) The physical differences between men and women do affect behavior but not to the degree once supposed. (2) Culture, not biology, plays the major part in determining sex-role behavior.

Male-female differences

A star basketball player soars high for a rebound, then turns to throw in a twenty-footer as the game ends. The crowd surges onto the floor to greet the new national champions.

A two-year-old child, chasing a puppy across the lawn, falls and begins to cry. A neighbor quickly picks up the child, hugs it, and kisses away the tears.

Can you guess the sexes of the victorious basketball player and the kindly neighbor? Many people would assume that the basketball player is a man and the kindly neighbor a woman. Is that what you thought? If so, you were accepting old stereotypes concerning sex roles. But in this time of increased opportunities for women in sports, college women now play for national championships. And why shouldn't a man comfort a crying child with a hug and a kiss?

Despite these changing patterns, real differences still exist between men and women. Some differences are related to physical traits, others to behavior. Three theories have been advanced to explain these differences: the hereditary view, the environmental view, and a combined view.

The hereditary view. Supporters of the *hereditary view* believe that biological inheritance determines sex roles. This theory uses history as a kind of proof. Look, the argument says, man's superior size, strength, and logical mind have made him the naturally dominant sex. And just as men once excelled as hunters and tribal chieftains, they now surpass women as engineers, doctors, and political leaders. Similarly, women's role has been conditioned by their own biology. As the bearers of children, women fit naturally into their traditional task of caring for husbands and children. Their softer physique, gentler nature, and lesser strength are all caused by heredity, the argument concludes.

A careful look at human heredity, however, suggests that women may well be the superior sex. Not only do women live longer (by 7.7 years), but males experience more colorblindness, autism, speech problems, reading disabilities, and infant mortality. Although men have heavier and stronger muscles, women generally have greater stamina. Individual differences among males are also greater than among females. While these differences mean that society will have more male geniuses, they also mean that more male idiots will be born.

Where, then, did the pattern of male dominance begin? If heredity plays any part in determining sex-role differences, it probably lies in women's role as childbearers. To carry, give birth to, and nurture a child to adulthood requires an enormous investment of energy, both physical and emotional. Traditional sex roles probably started with this basic fact of life. Since women were occupied with caring for the children, men took on the task of finding food. Although hunting was hard and dangerous, it was also exciting. Even when better weapons and better food-producing methods became available, men continued to reserve the higher prestige jobs for themselves.

The environmental view. By contrast, supporters of the *environmental view* believe that sex roles result mainly from cultural pressures. The famous anthropologist Margaret Mead singled out three South Pacific tribes as proof of this theory. Among the Arapesh, she found, both men and women are similarly nonaggressive. Cooperative and gentle, these people share equally those traits that modern society has often labeled as "feminine." Unlike the Arapesh, Mundugumor men and women behave in equally aggressive, competitive ways. Mundugumor women would be considered "unfeminine" in many cultures, but their fierce behavior is expected and encouraged within their own society. Finally, the Tchámbuli reverse the usual sex roles. Tchambuli men take pride in caring for children and in producing beautiful artwork. The Tchambuli women, however, grow up domineering and independent. The females fish, trade, and produce the practical goods needed for survival.

Some critics have pointed out that these are merely three small cultures. Other studies have found that most societies follow the traditional division of labor, with men as hunters and women as housekeepers. But Dr. Mead still believed that the social environment, not heredity, dictates sex roles. In the United States, for example, only 13.4 percent of the doctors and 4.3 percent of the dentists are women. These statistics might suggest that only men have the qualities necessary to be doctors and dentists— except that in the Soviet Union 80 percent of the doctors and 87 percent of the dentists are women. Mead concluded, therefore, that personality differences between the sexes are "cultural creations to which each generation is trained to conform."

The combined view. As you might have

Figure 13.2

Anthropologist Margaret Mead refused to let traditional ideas about women's roles keep her from doing the field studies that made her famous. She also found that male/female sex roles are conditioned more by culture than by biology.

already guessed, many psychologists have concluded that both heredity and environment contribute to the development of sex roles. Male/female differences, this theory suggests, develop as a result of inborn sex differences interacting with the environment.

An example of this interaction between "nature and nurture" can be seen in the sleep patterns of infants. Since baby boys sleep one to two hours less per day than do baby girls, the boys are generally more active during the day. As a consequence, mothers spend more time holding baby boys, and encourage them to reach, grasp, pull, and stand. In this way, the biologically more active boy draws a more active response from his environment.

Similarly, women's superior verbal skills also begin in the cradle. Studies show that baby girls make more of the babbling and cooing noises typical of infants. This verbal activity causes parents to respond by talking more to their baby girls. Such stimulation encourages girls to rely on their verbal abilities to obtain rewards, just as their brothers gain approval through physical activity. Once again, an inborn trait has been strengthened and made a part of the adult personality through influence from the environment.

You will want to remember, however, that these rules apply only to the general population. You probably know some girls who are more active than some boys. Similarly, some boys will exceed some girls in their verbal abilities. In fact, Eleanor Maccoby, an expert in sex difference, believes that people perform best when they possess both male and female qualities. As proof, you probably have noted already that society often rewards the man who develops superior verbal abilities. Today, moreover, rewards are increasing for women who demonstrate superior physical abilities. Perhaps this means that American society is learning to accept both men and women for their accomplishments, without regard to stereotyped sex roles.

Communication of sex roles

Since children are not born with blueprints for male or female behavior, they must look to the people around them for information on sex roles. In primitive societies, where sex roles are often clear-cut, this process causes little confusion. Boys identify with their fathers and from childhood practice the skills of the hunter, herder, farmer, or craftsman. Girls copy the nurturing behavior of their mothers, usually defined by their society as food preparation and child care.

Today's children, however, have a more difficult time figuring out male and female roles. In a society that no longer requires sheer muscle power for most jobs, the distinction between men-only and women-only jobs has blurred (see Figure 13.3). The recent trend has been toward learning "human" roles, rather than strictly male or female roles.

Figure 13.3

Because of the feminist movement, most formerly male-only jobs have been opened up to qualified women. Why did it take so long for the army and police departments to admit women as regular soldiers and patrol officers?

Role of parents. One theory on the learning of sex roles suggests that parents and other adults have always shaped desired behavior through reward and punishment. At the obvious level, this would include such parental behavior as giving Keith approval for fighting, but scolding Gloria for doing the same thing. Similarly, you may have heard a parent react to a boy's tears with the order, "Stop that! Big boys don't cry!" Repeated incidents of this type often carry over into adult life, leaving many men unable to cry no matter how deep their grief.

An angry look or a smile can communicate as much information about "proper" behavior as a spanking or a gift. If Gloria comes into the house covered with mud, her parents don't have to punish her to let her know they disapprove. By withholding love for a little while, they'll soon convince Gloria that it's wrong to get dirty.

Children also learn sex roles by imitating the behavior of their parents. This *modeling behavior*, as it is known, seems to be a natural part of growing up. Each child tends to model on the parent of the same sex,

although the process is not identical for boys and girls. Very young boys identify strongly with their fathers, even though most men are away from home during the day. At the same time, they learn about feminine behavior from their mothers. Girls are more likely to adopt mixed male and female roles during early childhood. This weaker role identification does not last, however. Although they're surrounded by strong male models, girls model themselves more closely on women as they grow older.

Current changes in sex roles allow girls to play active sports, dress in jeans, and generally forget about being "ladylike." Once girls who enjoyed vigorous outdoor activities were called "tomboys"—rather derisively. Now girls can usually participate in athletics without being labeled in any way. Sports programs provide girls' teams along with the boys' teams. Much to the surprise of many parents, their daughters prove to be just as competitive as their sons on the soccer field or on the volleyball court.

Role of the community. The community

that surrounds the home also has a strong influence on the development of male/female behavior. Even though parental messages make the strongest impression on children, family influence can be weakened by exposure to conflicting messages from religious institutions, school, or the media. Keith's parents, for example, may allow him to play with dolls at home. Their message is one of approval, since they want him to develop nurturing qualities. But if other children laugh at Keith for being a "sissy" or if his nursery-school teacher shows disapproval, he'll probably stop playing with dolls.

In the same way, the community's standards of male/female behavior can become a self-fulfilling prophecy. In the 1950s, for instance, society defined long hair as a feminine characteristic. Boys and men, therefore, wore their hair short as part of their masculine identity. In the 1960s, how-

ever, young men began experimenting with long hairstyles. Men who grew their hair long had to endure reactions that ranged from suspicious stares to outright rejection. In time, the "rules" about hair length changed. Today, many young adults react to crew cuts as suspiciously as their parents once reacted to shoulder-length hair.

SECTION CHECKUP

1 What roles do heredity and environment play in determining male and female behavior? Give several examples.

2 How would you explain the historic tendency for men to take over the high-prestige jobs such as hunting, fishing, construction, and the like?

3 How do parents and community "teach" sex roles to children?

13.2 WHAT ARE THE EFFECTS OF SEXISM ON WOMEN?

Newborn babies look pretty much alike. Unless the first one you see is your own, you probably won't be much impressed. One look will tell you that no one could honestly see masculine or feminine qualities in such tiny, wrinkled creatures.

No one, that is, except parents. A 1974 study by psychologists Jeffrey Rubin, Frank Provenzano, and Zella Luria shows that parents of newborn girls describe them as being softer, smaller, finer-featured, and less alert than boys. If parents "see" girls as being different from boys right from the first days of life, it's not hard to predict that they will also treat girls differently in the months to come.

As the previous section showed you, that's exactly what does happen. And maybe that fact would not alarm anyone if the differences in treatment added up to a rough sort of equality. But such is not the case. By treating females as different from

males, parents open the door to a type of discrimination known as *sexism*. By definition, sexism is the social and economic domination of one sex by the other. Until recently, this practice has meant that most men *and* women have grown up believing that women are inferior to men. As a consequence, women were forced to accept a secondary role in political, economic, and family life.

Effect of sexism on self-esteem

Has this long history of sexism had an effect on women? One of many studies answering that question with a firm "yes" comes from Matina Horner, of the University of Michigan. Horner first conducted her "fear of success" study in 1968. The test is simple enough. Horner asked college-age women to finish a story about a young woman named Anne, who just found out that she had

Figure 13.4

SEXISM: THE ARGUMENT HAS BEEN GOING ON FOR A LONG TIME

The argument over the role of women in society has been going on for a long time. Some typical statements, both ancient and modern, will give you an idea of how outspoken both sides have been.

Men say:

The five worst infirmities that afflict the female are aggressiveness, discontent, false speech, jealousy, and silliness.
CONFUCIAN MARRIAGE MANUAL
(c. 500 B.C.)

In childhood a woman must be subject to her father; in youth to her husband; when her husband is dead, to her sons. A woman must never be free.
HINDU CODE OF MANU, V (c. 100 B.C.)

Wives, submit yourselves unto your own husbands as unto the Lord. For the husband is the head of the wife, even as Christ is the head of the Church.
NEW TESTAMENT, EPHESIANS 5:22–23
(c. 100 A.D.)

A woman, an asse, and a walnut tree, Bring the more fruit the more beaten they bee.
OLD ENGLISH VERSE (c. 1400)

Women say:

Remember, all men would be tyrants if they could. If particular care and attention is not paid to the ladies, we are determined to foment [stir up] a rebellion and will not hold ourselves bound by any law in which we have no voice or representation.
ABIGAIL ADAMS, IN A LETTER TO
JOHN ADAMS (1776)

The prolonged slavery of women is the darkest page in human history.
ELIZABETH CADY STANTON (1881)

Like all sciences and all valuations, the psychology of women has hitherto been considered only from the point of view of men.
KAREN HORNEY (1926)

There are two kinds of people, human beings and women. And when women start acting like human beings, they are accused of trying to be men.
SIMONE DE BEAUVOIR (1953)

---

received the highest grade in her class at the end of the first semester of medical school. Men write about an identical situation, except that their story substitutes John for Anne.

Horner's 1968 study found that a high percentage of her women subjects predicted a dim future for Anne. The men described a bright career ahead for John. A typical response for Anne often centered on the pressures of competing with men. By contrast, the males who wrote about John usually found the experience a positive one. By 1974, however, when Horner repeated the study, the number of women who gave Anne a positive chance to succeed had risen to 50 percent. Today, you'll probably find positive percentages of over 70 percent for Anne.

What conclusion can you draw from this study? If only about one college-age woman in four saw Anne in positive terms in 1968, you can assume that these women felt in-

Men say:

What a mad idea to demand equality for women! . . . Women are nothing but machines for producing children.
NAPOLEON BONAPARTE (c. 1800)

What a misfortune to be a woman! And yet the worst misfortune is not to understand what a misfortune it is.
SØREN KIERKEGAARD (c. 1840)

It would be terribly naive to suggest that a B.A. can be made as attractive to girls as a marriage license.
GRAYSON KIRK (c. 1960)

For a man there are three certainties in life: death, taxes, and women. It is often difficult to say which is the worst.
ALBERT ELLIS (c. 1970)

The shattering truth is that men outshine women in *every* field of endeavor.
WALLACE REYBORN (1972)

All right, Edith, you go right ahead and do your thing . . . but just remember that your thing is eggs over-easy and crisp bacon.
"ARCHIE BUNKER" (1976)

Women say:

The problem that has no name—which is simply the fact that American women are kept from growing to their full human capacities—is taking a far greater toll on the physical and mental health of our country than any known disease.
BETTY FRIEDAN (1963)

Those women who glom on to men so that they can collapse with relief, spend the rest of their days shining up their status symbol, and figure they never have to reach, stretch, learn, grow, face dragons or make a living again are the ones to be pitied.
HELEN GURLEY BROWN (1963)

I like men to behave like men—strong and childish.
FRANÇOISE SAGAN (1968)

Many women do not recognize themselves as discriminated against; no better proof could be found of the totality of their conditioning.
KATE MILLET (1969)

You see an awful lot of smart guys with dumb women, but you hardly ever see a smart woman with a dumb guy.
ERICA JONG (1973)

There's never been a woman Beethoven—but neither has there been a woman Hitler!
ANON.

ferior when it came to competing with men. The changing percentages, however, suggest that women's self-images have been improving in recent years.

One older study found that two thirds of the women surveyed wanted their first child to be a boy. The researchers interpreted this preference to mean that these women believed that boys had more opportunities, more fun, more freedom. The same survey today, however, finds that most women be-

lieve their daughters have as much chance to live a satisfying life as their sons.

Lost women of history

Until recently, the stories of great achievements—whether in law, religion, science, philosophy, or the arts—were mainly the stories of men, not women. Many *male chauvinists* (people who have an exaggerated notion of male superiority) have used this fact as a way of "proving" that females are inferior. *Feminists* (both men and women who work to achieve political, social, and economic equality for women), however, have been quick to point out two major flaws in this reasoning. First, the feminists argue, history emphasizes male accomplishments because men write most of the histories. Women's achievements tend to be overlooked. One history text, for example, gives five pages to the story of the six-shooter, but only five lines to the life of the frontier woman.

Further, the feminists add, sexist attitudes on the part of men have kept women locked into a position of inferiority. Without equal education and equal encouragement, women generally have not been given the same opportunities as men. As proof, the feminists point to the fields of literature and politics. In the nineteenth century, when publishers accepted women authors, women competed on even terms with men. And when politics opened up to women in this century, Great Britain, India, Israel, Bolivia, and Sri Lanka all selected women leaders.

Sexism on the job

Nowhere are the results of sexism more obvious than in the world of work. Women make only 60 percent of what men earn. In 1979, for example, full-time male workers with high-school educations earned a median salary of $18,100. Women with similar education received only $10,513. The difference is almost as great among college-educated workers. Men with four or more years of college earned a median salary of $24,007 in 1979, but women with equal training earned only $14,885.

Barbara J., age twenty-four, learned about job discrimination at first hand. A trained computer programmer, she joined the office staff of a large data-processing firm. Barbara soon learned that men hired at the same time and doing the same work were making more money than she was.

Figure 13.5

Lynn Dorgan (left) builds quality homes with an all-woman construction crew. Dorgan is like many modern women who are determined to work at jobs that challenge them. What problems do you think Dorgan had to overcome before she could work as a contractor?

Unwilling to accept this injustice, she went to see her supervisor. Mr. Hopkins stared at her. "Don't you like working here, Barbara? Surely you realize that the men make more because they're management trainees. Your job title isn't the same as theirs, is it?"

When Barbara tried to argue that she did exactly the same work as the "trainees," Hopkins rejected her. "This isn't some feminist liberation meeting," he said. "This is a business, and if you want to work here you'll have to accept the way things are." A friend told Barbara to take her case to the Equal Employment Opportunity Commission, a government agency that enforces federal fair-employment laws. But Barbara feared that while she was waiting for the slow-moving commission to act, Hopkins would fire her for making the complaint.

Pictures of women working as police officers, telephone "linepersons," stevedores, and coal miners appear regularly in the media. But for many women, their jobs are still defined by old sexist stereotypes. Social pressure and limited opportunities tend to push women into low-paying positions as domestic workers, secretaries, retail clerks, waitresses, and the like. Even in fields dominated by women, such as library science and elementary-school teaching, the top jobs are often held by men.

The housewife's double bind

The changing definition of sex roles has left some women uncertain about their future. At one time, women were conditioned to believe that a career as a wife and mother was the finest ambition a woman could have. Many women still find that role to be a deeply satisfying one, particularly while their children are young. But today's

housewife often must face scornful remarks from her working sisters. After a twelve-hour day of cooking, cleaning, shopping, gardening, caring for children, doing volunteer work, and juggling a thousand other duties, the housewife runs up against the comment, "Oh, you're a housewife? How lovely it must be to have all that free time with nothing important to do." (See Figure 13.6 for one study of a housewife's "free time.")

Psychologists know that women who stay home to care for their families can lose their identity in their limited world of kitchen, kids, and car pools. In a culture that defines people by what they "do," housewives are often identified with the achievements of their husbands and children. Women who see themselves only as wives and mothers may also suffer a severe emotional shock if

Figure 13.6

WHAT'S A HOUSEWIFE WORTH?

Most people take the work a housewife does pretty much for granted. But when the American Council of Life Insurance added up the hours typical homemakers work on each of their separate jobs, they came up with some surprising figures. What would you guess? Forty hours, after all, is a normal workweek.

Assuming that the family has small children to care for, the week looks like this:

Child care	45.1 hours
Meal planning	1.2
Meal preparation	13.1
Food buying	3.3
Dishwashing	6.2
Housekeeping	17.5
Laundry	5.9
Sewing	1.3
Maintenance	1.7
Gardening	2.3
Transportation	2.0
	99.6 hours

That 99.6-hour workweek is over twice the number of hours that leave most workers longing for the weekend! And if you had to pay this housewife on an hourly basis (figuring a minimum of $4.00 an hour), her paycheck would come to $517.00 a week, including overtime.

they lose either of these roles. Divorce, the husband's death, or children leaving home can trigger a deep depression. Suddenly cut off from the old role and anxious to find a new one, such women may find that the qualities that made them superior wives and mothers do not pay off in the job market.

Many young families are resolving this problem by combining careers and home life. Some men and women delay marriage and children until they have established themselves in their careers. Later, they may arrange their family life so that both husband and wife share equally in child care and housework. Even when these self-aware women choose to stay home with their young children, they remain involved in the outside world. They see full-time motherhood as a temporary period in a long and active life.

The costs of sexism

The price women have paid for generations of sexist discrimination can be counted in lost income, lost opportunities, and lost identity. But society has also paid a heavy price for the luxury of keeping women in a secondary role. How many potential female scientists, artists, political leaders, inventors, composers, and explorers do you think have lived and died with their talents unrecognized? Novelist Virginia Woolf illustrated this misuse of human resources in her book *A Room of One's Own* by imagining that the great dramatist William Shakespeare had a sister. But the 1500s were not ready to accept a woman's talents.

She was as adventurous, as imaginative, as agog to see the world as he was. But she was not sent to school. . . . She picked up a book now and then, one of her brother's perhaps, and read a few pages. But then her parents came in and told her to mend the stockings or mind the stew and not moon about with books and papers. . . . Perhaps she scribbled some pages up in an apple loft on the sly, but was careful to hide them or set fire to them. . . . [To avoid an unwanted marriage] She made up a small parcel of her belongings, let herself down by a rope one summer's night and took the road to London. She was not seventeen. The birds that sang in the hedge were not more musical than she was. She had the quickest fancy, a gift like her brother's, for the tune of words. Like him, she had a taste for the theater. She stood at the stage door; she wanted to act, she said. Men laughed in her face. The manager—a fat, loose-lipped man—guffawed. He bellowed something about poodles dancing and women acting—no woman, he said, could possibly be an actress. He hinted—you can imagine what. She could get no training in her craft. Could she even seek her dinner in a tavern or roam the streets at midnight? Yet her genius was for fiction and lusted to feed abundantly upon the lives of men and women and the study of their ways.

In time, Woolf writes, the young woman commits suicide, her "poet's heart caught and tangled in a woman's body." Perhaps now, with doors opening up for women of talent and determination, that story can be revised.

SECTION CHECKUP

1 What is meant by the term *sexism*? Give several examples of sexism that you have seen, experienced, or read about.

2 How would a feminist explain the failure of women to match the achievements of men in such fields as science, art, and government?

3 How has sexism affected women on the job?

4 Why is today's housewife caught in a double bind? What can be done to ease this problem?

13.3 WHAT ARE THE GOALS OF THE FEMINIST MOVEMENT?

In 411 B.C., the Greek playwright Aristophanes wrote a play called *Lysistrata*. Even though Aristophanes was a man, he had Lysistrata, the play's heroine, remark, "How is it, husband, that you men manage these affairs so foolishly?" Lysistrata believes that the long and senseless war with Sparta could be ended if the men would only be reasonable. So she persuades the Athenian women to withhold the comforts of love from their husbands until they make peace.

In the play, Lysistrata's strategy works. But in real life, men of all nationalities continued to restrict the rights and opportunities of women. Without property rights, a voice in public affairs, or even the right to choose their own husbands, women endured what they had no power to change. Even today, women in most traditional societies live in the shadow of men. The custom of *purdah*, for example, where it is still practiced in the Middle East, restricts the Muslim woman's freedom of movement, expression, and choice. These veiled women, along with their sisters in similar cultures, are still waiting for rights guaranteed to most Western women.

That progress toward equality has not come easily. In this country, the modern struggle for women's rights dates back at least to the 1800s, when feminists such as Susan B. Anthony and Elizabeth Cady Stanton fought for suffrage (the right to vote). As Anthony, honored in 1979 as the first real-life woman to appear on a United States coin, put it: "Men, their rights and nothing more; women, their rights and nothing less." That first feminist goal was not fulfilled until 1920, when the Nineteenth Amendment sent American women to voting booths alongside men. Afterward, the Great Depression and World War II delayed the pursuit of other feminist objectives.

In the 1960s a new generation of feminists revived the movement. Not all women agreed on feminist goals or methods. Some seemed willing to work within the system to bring about change; others demanded that the system itself be changed. But some goals were common to almost all feminists.

Equality under the law

Few feminists would disagree as to their top priority: passage of the *Equal Rights Amendment (ERA)*. This proposed amendment to the Constitution would ban discrimination based on sex, as its language clearly states:

> Section 1. Equality of rights under the law shall not be denied or abridged by the United States or by any State on account of sex.
>
> Section 2. The Congress shall have the power to enforce, by appropriate legislation, the provisions of this article.
>
> Section 3. This amendment shall take effect two years after the date of ratification.

The original ERA died in 1982 when the last few states needed for ratification failed to ratify the amendment.

The fight to ratify the ERA has been led by the largest of all feminist groups, the *National Organization for Women (NOW)*. NOW works within the legal system to bring about adoption and enforcement of women's rights legislation. Originally led by Betty Friedan (see BioBox, page 412), NOW has grown into a national organization with over 50,000 members. The organization's philosophy calls for women to participate fully "in the mainstream of American society now, exercising all the privileges and responsibilities thereof in *truly equal partnership with men*." NOW believed that the ERA represented a major step toward that goal.

Not all women support the ERA, however. A Stop-ERA movement, led by author

BioBox

BETTY FRIEDAN:
EXPLORER OF "THE FEMININE MYSTIQUE"

Bettye Lane

Betty Friedan (1921–   ) didn't begin the modern feminist movement in the United States. But when portions of her book *The Feminine Mystique* first appeared in magazines in 1962, she caught the attention of the nation. Friedan's scholarship and criticism were the spark the women's movement needed.

Betty Friedan graduated *summa cum laude* from Smith College. After working with the well-known psychologists Kurt Koffka and Kurt Lewin, she married, had three children, and lived the life of a suburban housewife. Publication of *The Feminine Mystique,* however, changed the course of her life. Now separated from her husband, she lectures, writes, teaches, and serves as a spokeswoman for feminist causes. One of the founders of the National Organization for Women, she served as its president until 1970.

If you asked Friedan to sum up her criticism of the role of the traditional American housewife, she'd tell you that the myth of the happy homemaker is just that—a myth. In *The Feminine Mystique,* she writes:

> If a woman had a problem in the 1950s and 1960s, she knew that something must be wrong with her marriage, or with herself. Other women were satisfied with their lives, she thought. What kind of a woman was she if she did not feel this mysterious fulfillment waxing the kitchen floor? She was so ashamed to admit her dissatisfaction that she never knew how many other women shared it. If she tried to tell her husband, he didn't understand what she was talking about. . . . When a woman went to a psychiatrist for help, as many women did, she would say, "I'm so ashamed," or "I must be hopelessly neurotic." . . .
>
> Just what was this problem that has no name? What were the words women used when they tried to express it? Sometimes a woman would say "I feel empty somehow . . . incomplete." Or she would say, "I feel as if I don't exist." Sometimes she blotted out the feeling with a tranquilizer. . . .
>
> If I am right, the problem that has no name stirring in the minds of so many American women today is not a matter of loss of femininity or too much education, or the demands of domesticity. It is far more important than anyone recognizes. . . . It may well be the key to our future as a nation and a culture. We can no longer ignore that voice within women that says: "I want something more than my husband and my children and my home."

Betty Friedan wrote in the early 1960s. How have things changed since then? Do you think there are still housewives who feel trapped by "husband, children, and home"? You might get some insight into the issue by talking to some older women—both those who work outside the home and those who work as housewives.

SHAMBLES   by FRED WAGNER

© Field Enterprises, Inc., 1979   10-27

"ERA is supposed to make you equal to me . . .
Not me equal to you!"

Figure 13.7

How would a feminist answer this husband's
complaint?

and housewife Phyllis Schlafly, emerged to
battle the amendment. Schlafly felt that
existing laws already protected women's
job, credit, and educational opportunities.
Under ERA, she said, women would not
only be forced to serve in the military but
would also lose the protection of laws that
prevent employers from assigning women
to jobs beyond their strength and endurance.

Another major feminist goal aims at ending all remaining discrimination in areas
such as credit, housing, and employment.
Title VII of the Civil Rights Act of 1964
firmly established the principle of legal
equality, but laws passed in Washington do
not always change what happens in individual schools, factories, or offices. Despite the Equal Credit Law, for example,
Pat W. was turned down when she applied
for an oil-company credit card. Angered,
she rewrote her application, concealing only
her sex. Based on the same job record and
income, the company sent her the card by
return mail. Pat took her case to court and
won. Hearings in the courts or before government agencies take time, money, and
energy, however. Feminists are working
toward the day when such actions will no
longer be necessary.

Equality in employment

The feminist goal of equal pay for equal
work has not yet been met, although the
future for women at work looks brighter.
The number of employers who think of
women as temporary workers ("As soon as
she gets pregnant, she'll quit") or as people
who cannot handle heavy or dirty jobs ("I
can't have my drivers stopping to powder
their noses") is decreasing. With federal and
state fair-employment laws on their side,
women are entering construction work, law
enforcement, skilled crafts, and other fields
once closed to them. When the Alaska pipeline was started, for example, the contrac-
tors hired only twenty-one women for heavy
construction jobs. After the U.S. Department of the Interior threatened legal action,
however, the number of women working on
the pipeline shot up to 1,700.

If you check the classified ads in a local
newspaper, you'll find that help-wanted ads
are no longer sex-segregated into "help
wanted—male" and "help wanted—female." NOW won that victory in 1968 and
went on to end sex discrimination in one of
the country's largest companies, American
Telephone and Telegraph Company
(AT&T), in 1973. In all, AT&T paid out $60
million to women and minority men to settle
discrimination complaints. Women who receive equal treatment when they apply for
loans or credit cards can thank the Equal
Credit bill of 1974. Other feminist successes
have come in improved maternity rights for
working women and in revised labor laws
that had kept women from taking well-paid
but strenuous factory jobs.

Women have also begun to make their
way into jobs where prestige, pay, and

power have belonged almost entirely to men. A new generation of professional women is challenging men for a share of society's economic and political power. More women are running for public office—and being elected. Women are taking their places as judges, professors, executives, and members of the President's cabinet. Also in the late 1970s, female crew members sailed for the first time on U.S. Navy warships. The military academies admitted their first female cadets, and space officials selected the first women astronauts. And in 1981, Sandra Day O'Connor became the first woman to sit on the U.S. Supreme Court.

Feminist leaders point out, however, that progress is not equality. Women make up 51 percent of the population and over 40 percent of the work force. But fewer than 10 percent of the nation's doctors, lawyers, legislators, and company presidents are women.

Equality in education

Feminists believe that equality in education must take two directions. First, women must be given equal access to all courses of study from elementary school to graduate school. With prodding from the federal government, the barriers that kept girls out of industrial arts and boys out of home-making have been greatly reduced. Second, textbooks and courses of study must be modified to give credit to women's contributions to society and to avoid sexist stereotyping. Some schools have added courses in women's studies as a way of helping people learn more about women's role in building American culture.

One measure of progress can be seen in the number of women entering graduate study in law, business, medicine, and engineering. One survey predicts that by 1986 one third of the nation's medical students will be women, compared to 18 percent in 1976. Business schools and some law schools

have already passed the 30 percent mark. But over 60 percent of the nation's colleges still do not meet federal standards for ending sex discrimination. You've probably noticed that women's sports programs have been improved, but few receive the same budgets as men's sports.

Eliminating sexism. Too often, feminists say, the media present a negative image of women. Television, in particular, generally pictures women as either sex objects or as brainless, passive partners in their relationships with men. A study released in 1979 showed that male characters outnumber females by over three to one in prime-time TV drama. Women on TV seemed mostly interested in marriage, romance, and family, a pattern that reinforces sexist stereotypes. Pressure from feminist groups has brought about a more fair-minded media approach to woman's role in society (see

Figure 13.8

Although there has been some improvement in recent years, sexist stereotyping still appears in advertising. Despite evidence that a feminist approach can sell a product, many advertisers try to increase sales by posing a shapely female next to their product.

THIS YEAR'S LATEST MODEL!

Figure 13.8). Some television shows now feature strong, intelligent female characters. Female newscasters also appear regularly on most news broadcasts.

A longer-range goal of the feminist movement is teaching children to accept less restrictive sex roles. This goal could lead to a world in which children have *human* models to imitate, not male or female models. The fiction that women are inferior and that sex roles are all biologically determined would be abolished.

The right to choose. Another major feminist goal can be summed up as the "right to choose." In practice, this includes such choices as having or not having children; going out to work or staying home with the children; and having a free choice of lifestyle. This goal has led to great controversy, particularly when "the right to choose" is interpreted as the right to birth control and abortion. Many feminists believe that without this right all other women's rights become unimportant, for having children almost automatically limits a woman's freedom of choice. Other women have organized to fight against more liberal abortion laws. Abortion legislation has thus become a national political issue in recent elections. Neither side seems likely to give in on what it sees as a bedrock principle.

Freedom to choose also includes the goal of setting up child-care centers for the children of working mothers. All too often, feminists say, the working mother must leave her children with inexperienced baby-sitters or at expensive nursery schools. Many school-age children are left without any supervision by mothers who must work if the family is to survive. Teachers know these boys and girls as "key children" because they come to school with their house key tied around their necks. Government-supported child-care centers would not only free mothers to work at productive jobs; they would also provide proper care for children who would otherwise be neglected.

Measuring the progress

Have the years of effort had any long-range effect? Some changes can be measured— more women working in better jobs, an increase in women legislators and judges, a lessening of sexist language and content in textbooks. But women's attitudes have also changed, and that might be the most important change of all. You can see the change in the statistics. More women than ever say they're happy with their lives. Over one third believe that they're better off than they were five years ago.

You can also see the change in the stories of individual women. A few years ago, Adrienne would have joined the pep squad to cheer for the boys' basketball team; today she's a hard-driving forward on her own winning team. Yesterday, Hope would have felt herself a failure if she weren't married by her mid-20s; today, she's so involved in her business career that she's not even thinking of marriage for at least five more years. A year or two ago, Clare would have felt that her life was over when her last child left home; today, she's taking computer training as the first step in a new career. Rhonda, meanwhile, has just given birth to her first child. Rhonda likes her technician's job with an aerospace firm, but she's going to take several years off to stay home with her daughter. She feels free to make that choice, just as other women feel free to go out to work.

SECTION CHECKUP

1 What did Susan B. Anthony mean when she said, "Men, their rights and nothing more; women, their rights and nothing less"? Do you think modern feminists would still agree with her statement? Tell why or why not.

2 Name some of the techniques feminist groups use to achieve their goals.

3 What are the basic goals of the feminist movement? Which goals do you think are closest to fulfillment?

Pro & Con: THE FEMINIST MOVEMENT IS CHANGING PEOPLE'S MINDS—EVEN DR. SPOCK'S

You've probably noticed that just about everyone has an opinion about the methods and goals of the feminist movement. You may also have noticed that people's views tend to change as they study and debate the issues. Dr. Benjamin Spock, the famous "baby doctor," whose books have helped millions of American families raise their children, is one of those who have changed their minds. If you read some of his books, you will find Spock the Male Chauvinist (1970) having different views from Spock the Feminist (1974).

Issue	Spock the male chauvinist	Spock the feminist
Careers for women	My prime concern is that, . . . parents and schools not encourage girls to be competitive with males if that is going to make them dissatisfied with raising children, their most creative job in adulthood, whether or not they go to work too. (*A Teenager's Guide to Life and Love*, 1970)	If girls are to grow up without a sense of being significantly different from boys in capabilities, and if women who want good jobs are to have an equal chance to get them, . . . parents should prepare girls for careers throughout their childhood . . . as they prepare their sons. (*Raising Children in a Difficult Time*, 1974)
Sex roles in family life	So men—whose egos depend on skill and prestige more than women's do—have been effectively deprived of their earlier sense of being uniquely important. . . . As a result, they have sometimes tried *unconsciously* to	I feel that a father during the hours when he is at home, . . . should put in as much time as the mother on child care, . . . A father's participation in child care and home care isn't simply a matter of fairness to the mother— . . . it shows

13.4 IF THE FEMINIST MOVEMENT SUCCEEDS, WILL MEN BE THE LOSERS?

Many people have recently experienced the same mild shock as the airline passengers in the Richter cartoon (page 417). You may have felt the same surprise when you first saw women writing traffic tickets, climbing telephone poles, or supervising a high-rise construction project. By the same token, you probably felt surprise when you first heard a male telephone operator or saw men working as airline stewards or kindergarten teachers.

The fact is, as you learned earlier in this chapter, people are rapidly learning new male and female roles. Most of the publicity has gone to women. But men have also been forced to examine their own notions of what makes them tick. To the surprise of many people (but not to psychologists), they

Issue	Spock the male chauvinist	Spock the feminist
	compensate by invading the wife's domestic area, doing a lot more housework and child care than men ever did before, even trying to outdo their wives in being . . . popular with the children. (*A Teenager's Guide to Life and Love*)	her that he considers these jobs just as vital, just as worthy, just as challenging as his work in the shop or office. (*Raising Children in a Difficult Time*)
Effect of dress on sex roles	In many American homes, there is relatively little difference in the way the parents treat their sons and daughters. They may dress them the same, . . . in blue jeans and sweat shirts, and expect them to play the same games together. . . . I think that treating the two sexes alike pits them against each other to some degree and increases the rivalry due to other causes. (*A Teenager's Guide to Life and Love*)	Feminists have at least half a point when they say that frilly dresses, patent-leather slippers, and permanent waves on a little girl, when boys are got up quite differently, encourage her to think of herself to some degree as a passive object for admiration. . . . She learns to see herself as someone who can get deviously what she wants out of other people . . . with her appearance. (*Raising Children in a Difficult Time*)

Why do you think Dr. Spock changed his mind? Which of his viewpoints comes closest to reflecting your own ideas about these issues? State your feelings in your own words.

"*Welcome aboard. This is your captain, Margaret Williamson, speaking.*"

Figure 13.9

"Welcome aboard. This is your captain, Margaret Williamson, speaking." [Drawing by Richter; © 1973 The New Yorker Magazine, Inc.]

are finding that giving equality to women doesn't automatically mean taking opportunities away from men.

The high price of macho

You've probably heard the term *macho* used to describe male behavior. The term comes from the Spanish word for "masculine" and has come to mean the state of mind that insists on male superiority. For Jess E., *macho* means being aggressive, dominant, ambitious, and tough. Jess's identity as a man depends on his wearing armor plates over his all-too-human emotions. To show tenderness, understanding, and affection for others might expose Jess as something less than his *macho* ideal.

Listen to Jess talking to Kate, the young woman he's been dating.

Jess: What do you mean, you're going out tonight with a bunch of girls? Friday night is our night! Call Elsa and Mira and tell them you can't make it.

Kate: What are you talking about? If you ask me about Friday night before I've made other plans, I enjoy going out with you. But you don't own me. Elsa and Mira are my friends and I want to spend some time with them.

Jess: Hey, don't get upset! I figured you knew I was coming over. I've got the van all polished up. Put on something sexy, and we'll try out that new disco on the highway.

Kate: No way, Jess! Maybe next week.

Jess: OK, then I'll call Delia! She's not spoiled by all this feminist garbage.

You can see why Jess looks on the feminist as a threat. Since he defines masculinity in light of the dominant male-submissive female, he can't cope with Kate's independence. And if Kate should choose a career over marriage, he'll be even more bewildered. Poor Jess! He wants a woman "just like the girl that married dear old dad," and he can't understand that many women no longer feel obligated to spend their lives in the kitchen and nursery.

For Jess, success means making money

and enjoying the prestige that goes with it. He'll probably turn his energies into a career, trusting that long hours and hard work will pay off. Political scientist Marc Fasteau, however, thinks that playing the *macho* role creates a limited type of human being he calls the "male machine":

> The male machine is a special kind of being, different from women, children, and men who don't measure up. He is functional, designed mainly for work. He is programmed to tackle jobs, override obstacles, attack problems, overcome difficulties, and always seize the offensive. . . .
>
> He has armor plating which is virtually impregnable. His circuits are never scrambled or overrun by irrelevant personal signals. He dominates and outperforms his fellows, . . . In fact, his internal circuitry is something of a mystery to him and is maintained primarily by humans of the opposite sex.

According to Fasteau, men who bury the emotions they think of as feminine are actually mutilating their personalities. The *macho* males come to believe that self-expression or displays of so-called softer emotions are indications of weakness. But many stress-related illnesses may stem from repressed emotions. Like powerful acids eating away at inner gears, these buried feelings can eventually cause a physical or emotional breakdown. The doctors may label it ulcers, heart attack, or severe depression. In reality, the human body wasn't designed for the stresses that go with maintaining the *macho* personality.

How a man's role might change

Some psychologists believe that the feminist movement can also lead to the liberation of men. Once men free themselves from *macho* thinking, they can develop more fully as human beings. As fifty-year-old Terry H. says:

> I never got to know my children. When they were young, I was so busy building my business I never had any time for them. And

now that I have the time, they're grown up and living their own lives. I've made a lot of money, but I'd give it all up to go back and really be a father to my kids.

But enjoying one's children is only one of the differences that can take place for men today.

Shared responsibilities. In the old system, men took full responsibility for making decisions at work and at home. This burden can now be shared with women. The energy that once went into maintaining a *macho* image can be put into creative and productive work. People can be judged on their abilities rather than on their sex. Many men feel threatened, for example, when they work for a woman boss. But new attitudes toward sex roles will also ease the feeling that masculinity is a fragile possession that disappears when men cannot always have their own way.

At home, shared responsibilities mean that men can have a true partnership with their wives. Caring for and disciplining children will be a job for both parents. As more women work outside the home, men will also be relieved of the heavy weight of being the sole breadwinner. No longer will they be forced to look to their jobs as their only means of identity.

One result of this new way of defining the male role has been that men are changing careers in mid-life. Feeling trapped in jobs they no longer enjoy, they have switched to happier pursuits. Engineers have become farmers, dentists have become artists, and mechanics have become elementary-school teachers. Even though they often make less money, most of these men report a marvelous sense of finally being in control of their own lives.

Role exchanges. A few years ago, some men made headlines by choosing to stay home and work as "househusbands" while their wives went out to work. Most people found it hard to believe that a man would make such a choice. Indeed, the custom may

never become common (see Figure 13.10). But having the freedom of choice to make such a decision is what sex-role liberation is all about. Other examples of role exchanges can be seen in career fields that were once restricted to either men or women. Today, men feel free to work as telephone operators, nurses, secretaries, and at other traditionally "female" jobs. In this sense, work becomes a human choice, not a male or female choice.

Single parents. Divorce once meant that any children of the marriage would stay with the mother. Even superior fathers were not considered capable of raising children by themselves. Now the courts recognize that men can be competent single parents. Judges and parents are thus free to make the best choice for the children. Fathers, in turn, need not always suffer the trauma of being separated from their children when a marriage fails.

Balancing the account

You've probably heard people say that opportunities and freedom for women can come only at the expense of men. To some degree, that possibility exists. If Veronica is accepted at dental school, her seat is no longer open to a man. Girls who make formerly all-male athletic teams eliminate less capable boys from those positions. On a strictly "what's-in-it-for-me" basis, the feminist movement asks that men give up some of the privileges once considered theirs by right, particularly the kingly role of having all household work done for them.

Social scientists believe that, in time, these temporary dislocations will balance out. Society will learn how to provide additional jobs, for example. More women working means more paychecks to buy more products. Tapping the creativity of one half of the population will undoubtedly lead to new ideas and techniques that will benefit everyone. Once freed from the fierce competition of the *macho* work world, men will

Figure 13.10

CONFESSIONS OF A HOUSEHUSBAND

Joel Roache found out firsthand what it means to take on the duties of a "househusband." Here he describes what happened after he and his wife, Jan, tried to share equally in the housekeeping and child-care chores:

> There was something of a shock for me in discovering the sheer quantity of the housework, and my standards of acceptable cleanliness fell rapidly. It became much easier to see my insistence on neatness as an inherited middle-class hang-up now that I had to do so much of the work myself. One of the long-standing sources of tension between Jan and me was almost immediately understood and resolved. What's more, I enjoyed it, at first.
>
> But within a few weeks that satisfaction and that enthusiasm began to erode a little more each time I woke up or walked into the house, only to find that it all needed to be done again. . . . I became lethargic, with the result that I worked less efficiently; so that even when I did "finish," it took longer and was done less well, rendering still less satisfaction. . . .
>
> Something similar happened even sooner and more dramatically to my relationship with our three children. . . . In everything I tried to do, I was frustrated by their constant demands and soon came, quite simply, to hate them; and to hate myself for hating them; and at some level, I suspect, to hate Jan for getting me into this mess. . . .
>
> I can pinpoint the place in time when we saw the necessity for a more careful adjustment of responsibilities. It was at a moment when it became clear that Jan's work was beginning to pay off and her group scored a definite and apparently unqualified success. I went around the house for a full day feeling very self-satisfied, proud of her achievement, *as if it were my own,* which was fine until I realized, somewhere near the end of the day, that much of that sense of achievement resulted from the fact that I had no achievement of my own. I was getting my sense of fulfillment, of self-esteem, *through her,* while she was getting it *through her work.* It had happened: I was a full-fledged househusband.

If Roache came to this conclusion in just eight weeks, what effect do you think years of housework and child care have on the women who get locked into such responsibilities?

Betsy Ryan, ed., *The Sexes* (Scholastic Book Services, 1975), pp. 158–60. Originally printed in *Ms.* magazine.

also have a chance to enjoy their lives more fully. Today's society provides ample leisure-time activities for people who can afford them. Closer family ties will develop as men spend more time with their children.

In general, the new sex roles leave both men and women free to make the choices that they feel will make them happy. Jenny D. likes mechanical work, so she takes responsibility for the upkeep of the family car. Meanwhile, her husband, Dexter, handles the gardening because he enjoys working with plants. Jenny and Dexter also have a special arrangement with the company where they work as engineers. When they have children later on, they will share a single job, so that one of them can always be with the children. By sharing their work and interests, they will have a chance to grow together as parents and individuals.

1 What is meant by *macho* behavior?

2 If the feminist movement succeeds, what will men be giving up?

3 If men accept the goals of "male liberation," list some ways their lives could be enriched.

13.5 HOW DO CHANGING PATTERNS OF SEXUALITY AFFECT SOCIETY?

Adolescents and young adults have always had to come to terms with their own sexuality. But the confused messages that hit them from every side today make rational decisions difficult. On the one hand, many people seem to regard sexual freedom as the most important expression of personal freedom. On the other hand, psychologists, parents, religious leaders, and other concerned observers warn that sex without affection and respect can be empty and self-destructive. As one young man put it:

> I thought that when I got to be eighteen, I'd know what's going on. But I'm more confused than ever. I've got my head on pretty straight about most things. But sex confuses me. My parents tell me one thing, my church another, and the messages I get from magazines and movies seem exactly opposite. Should I follow my instincts, or should I try to live by the rules? And just what are the rules anyway?
>
> —Walt Z.

Walt's not the only one who's confused. You might have had some of the same feelings. Perhaps the following section will help you make some sense out of the so-called *new sexuality*.

Charting the course of the new sexuality

Social psychologists hesitate to deal in terms like right or wrong. They prefer to leave such questions to philosophers, politicians, and theologians. But the psychologists do worry that rapidly changing standards can threaten people's emotional health.

Does the new sexuality increase feelings of anxiety and guilt instead of reducing them? Some people rejoice in sexual freedom, but many discover that casual sex creates a new set of problems. Peggy R., for example, drifted into a sexual relationship. But even though she enjoyed the physical part of it, Peggy often felt guilty. She worried about pregnancy, and she worried that her parents might find out. At times, she also felt used. Spence seemed to want sex all the time, but Peggy sometimes preferred simply to share a few quiet moments. She finally broke off the relationship because it was causing her more pain than pleasure.

While individual cases vary greatly, Peggy's experience turns out to be rather typical. Repressed sexual drives can cause emotional trouble, as Freud discovered. But engaging in sex without strong bonds of love and commitment can also leave people feeling lonely and anxious.

Is the new sexuality forcing young people into experimentation they're not ready for? Freud described the powerful sexual forces that help shape the personality in childhood. But this childhood sexuality is largely unconscious. Today, however, young people have sex forced upon their consciousness even before they reach puberty. Television programs and films freely portray scenes of lovemaking, rape, incest, nudity, and perversion. Magazines featuring sexually explicit stories and photos can be found on many newsstands. It seems that no matter where children go, they come into contact with a consistent message: Sex is a desirable pastime that solves most emotional problems.

Almost all psychologists agree that adults should be the judges of their own sexual choices. But they worry that exposure to sexually stimulating material may push children into feelings and experiments they're not ready for, physically or emotionally. Casual, "recreational" sex ignores the deep feelings created when two people become physically intimate. In a way, the experts say, pushing a young person into sex before he or she is ready is like handing a loaded pistol to a four-year-old. Someone is going to get hurt.

In the final analysis, parents must take the responsibility for helping their children develop a healthy attitude toward their own sexuality. Parents can begin by protecting children from exposure to experiences beyond their level of maturity. Second, parents can give their children a proper sex education. This responsibility, of course, requires that the parents themselves know how to explain the "facts of life" in a clear, honest, and unemotional way. Because many parents can't or won't do the explaining, some schools have developed sex-education programs. In the best of these schools, trained teachers at each grade level present carefully prepared information about sex as it relates to children of that age.

Controversy surrounds such efforts, however. Many communities refuse to allow sex education—perhaps on the theory that "the kids won't do it if they don't know about it." If someone tries this argument on you, you don't have to argue. Just point to the statistics. Over a million unwanted teenage pregnancies each year, along with uncounted cases of venereal disease, will make the point for you.

Is homosexual behavior a threat to society? Scientists believe that human beings are born with a hormone balance that tilts the individual toward heterosexual behavior (attraction to members of the opposite sex). Between 2 and 10 percent of the population, however, have experiences that cause them to grow up physically and emotionally attracted to people of the same sex. This sexual preference, called *homosexuality*, alarms many people. They consider homosexual behavior a danger to social stability, particularly family life. As more homosexuals come "out of the closet" and participate actively in community life, this fear has increased.

The majority of psychologists today no longer consider homosexuality as a mental disorder. Instead, they view it as an alternate life-style that puts extra emotional pressure on the individual man or woman. Sigmund Freud wrote, "homosexuality . . . is nothing to be ashamed of, no vice, no degradation. . . . We consider it to be a variation of the sexual function produced by a certain arrest of sexual development." In 1973, the American Psychiatric Association officially removed homosexuality from its list of mental disorders. Only those homosexuals who actively seek treatment are to be considered disturbed, the APA concluded.

This nonjudgmental approach to homosexual behavior has enabled psychologists to clear up a number of misunderstandings regarding *gay* behavior (as homosexuals prefer to have their life-style described). Most homosexual behavior has its roots in childhood. A boy raised by a possessive, clinging mother and a weak or absent father may grow up frightened of intimate, loving relations with women. Similarly, girls who become overly attached to immature, passive fathers may never develop their full feminine identity. Exposure to strong homosexual influences at a vulnerable age can also lead to homosexuality. You've probably already noticed, however, that many people with such family backgrounds grow up to be fully heterosexual adults.

Research has also enabled psychologists to clear up some mistaken ideas about homosexuality. Children and adolescents may have isolated homosexual experiences without becoming *gay*. The famous 1948 Kinsey study of American sex life found that almost 40 percent of the men surveyed reported at least one homosexual experience. In the same way, physical appearance or mannerisms do not provide proof of homosexual tendencies. Girls who appear masculine or boys who seem overly feminine may, however, become victims of a self-fulfilling prophecy. Teased and scorned by their peers, these young people may turn to homosexual contacts out of confusion and anxiety. Finally, forced psychotherapy cannot change homosexual behavior. Aversion therapy, hormone treatments, psychoanalysis, and group therapy have been tried with little long-term success. Therapy works only when the individual is totally committed to changing his or her sexual preferences.

Changing concepts of marriage

Until the 1960s, men and women who didn't marry and have children were often thought of as failures. Most people believed that marriage meant lasting love, personal growth, and true happiness. Perhaps that romantic ideal never existed in real life. In any event, the high divorce rates of recent years have led to a search for new ways to satisfy the human need for companionship, security, and the care of children.

The case for marriage. Despite the new alternate life-styles, many people still choose marriage as the best way to join two lives together. Even though single parents often do a good job of raising children, most experts feel that a stable marriage provides the best environment for raising children. Along with such factors as companionship and the sharing of work, married people generally enjoy better physical health than single people. Emotionally, married men and women score higher on mental-health tests and experience fewer mental breakdowns. Perhaps these factors will change with time, but even divorced people usually try again. And in many cases, the second marriage works quite well.

Living together. Increasing numbers of people live together without going through a marriage ceremony. Supporters of this arrangement believe that it gives them a chance to try out a relationship without the "until-death-do-us-part" pressures of marriage. If the arrangement doesn't work out, the partners are spared the expense and trauma of a divorce. People who choose to live together often invest as much love and commitment as others do in a traditional marriage.

Opponents of living together, however, feel that the arrangement often exploits the female. In effect, the man receives sexual and housekeeping services without any long-term obligations. Some couples solve this problem by signing a contract that spells out mutual obligations and makes arrangements for sharing income and community property. In addition, many

Figure 13.11

Many men still want to marry a woman "just like the girl that married dear old dad." Changing concepts of marriage, however, make that "old-fashioned" type of marriage less and less likely.

MEN & WOMEN　　　　　by Calman

Figure 13.12

CHILD REARING IN THE YEAR 2000

As a leader of the women's movement, Gloria Steinem has written widely about feminist goals. Here, she envisions a new approach to child raising in the year 2000:

> . . . perhaps we can predict that by then . . . there will be a concerted effort to eliminate all the giant and subtle ways in which we determine human futures according to the isolated physical differences of race or sex. . . .
>
> Hopefully, the raising of children will become both an art and a science: a chosen and a loving way of life in both cases. Whether children are born into extended families or nuclear ones, into communal groups or to single parents, they will be wanted—a major difference from a past in which, whatever the sugar coating, we have been made to feel odd or unnatural if we did not choose to be biological parents. Children will be raised by and with men as much as women; with old people, as well as with biological or chosen parents; and with other children. . . .
>
> By the year 2000 there should be no one way of raising children; there should be many ways—all of them recognizing that children have legal and social rights that may be quite separate and different from the rights or desires of the adults closest to them. At last we should be nurturing more individual talents than we suppress.

Gloria Steinem: From "Child Raising: 2000 A.D.," in *Women in the Year 2000,* edited by Maggie Tripp. Copyright © 1974, Arbor House Publishing Co. Reprinted by permission of *Ms. Magazine.*

---

parents still have difficulty accepting the fact that their son or daughter has a "roommate." Traditional moral and religious beliefs add to this conflict.

Childless marriages. A couple like Mae and Howard J. probably live in your neighborhood. You may even envy them. They live the "good life," with plenty of travel, parties, new clothes, and other expensive purchases. What makes Mae and Howard a little different is that they don't plan to have children. Ask them why, and they'll mention fears of overpopulation, concern over the environment, and the huge costs in time, money, and energy that raising children requires. They believe that by not having children, they can live a happy, fulfilling life balanced between work and pleasure. Mae and Howard may someday change their minds. Right now, however, a growing number of couples share their ideas.

Communal living and communal marriage. Experiments in *communal (group) living* date back to the dawn of the human race. The idea reached its modern peak in the 1960s and early 1970s but has not disappeared. Most modern communal arrangements are built on the concept of the extended family—the idea that everyone needs many nurturing people around to provide love and support. Thus, in most communes, children have many "parents" to turn to for comfort, advice, and companionship. While many communes have grown up in rural areas, some can be found in cities. By sharing living expenses and household tasks, the commune members believe that everyone benefits. In spite of sensational media accounts of "free love" arrangements, most communes have found that one-to-one relationships between individual men and women still work best.

Equal marriage. Even traditional mar-

Figure 13.13

NONSEXIST BOOKS TEACH A NEW LESSON

But his father was upset.
"He's a boy!" he said
to William's grandmother.
"He has a basketball
and an electric train
and a workbench
to build things with.
Why does he need a doll?"
William's grandmother smiled.
"He needs it," she said,
"to hug
and to cradle
and to take to the park
so that
when he's a father
like you,
he'll know how to
take care of his baby
and feed him
and love him
and bring him
the things he wants,
like a doll
so that he can
practice being
a father."

Children's books illustrate the changing attitudes of society regarding sex roles. Nonsexist books such as *William's Doll* by Charlotte Zolotow (Harper & Row, 1972) remind children that it's natural for boys to look forward to being nurturing parents as surely as it is for girls.

riage arrangements have been changing. Some couples have tried the concept called *equal marriage*. As the name suggests, equal marriage requires that both partners accept equal responsibility for the family's economic, social, and emotional survival. Above all, equal marriage requires that each partner value and protect the other's feelings and needs. In an equal marriage, neither person considers his or her work more important. Men join in household work and child care, while women share in producing the family income and in making major decisions.

Benefits to children of the new sex roles

Generations of parents have told their offspring to "do as we say, not as we do." And generations of children have continued to imitate the behaviors they *see*, rather than the words they hear. When parents share cooking, shopping, and cleaning chores, children will learn that these are tasks that simply need doing—not menial jobs for women only. Similarly, when children see their mothers replace a faucet washer or change an automobile tire, they will understand that mechanical skills need not remain a mystery to girls. Listening to family discussions of important issues will demonstrate that both sexes are capable of using logical thought processes. Being hugged, played with, and generally nurtured by both parents will encourage all children to express their joy and sorrow, love and anger.

Children raised according to a nonsexist philosophy will enjoy toys and reading materials without regard to what's for boys and what's for girls (see Figure 13.13). Both sexes will grow up knowing that sex does not limit their vocational choices. Girls will freely choose a career or marriage—or a combination of both. Boys will no longer fear parental rejection if they choose to be dancers, nurses, or hairdressers. Best of all, children raised in a nonsexist home will bring those same positive attitudes to their adult relationships with other people.

SECTION CHECKUP

1 Why does the new sexuality confuse and upset people? List some of its positive and some of its negative aspects.

2 Why should children be protected from excessive sexual stimulation?

3 What changes in marriage patterns are taking place?

4 What effect could nonsexist attitudes about sex roles have on children?

LOOKING BACK: A SUMMARY

1 Researchers have come up with three theories to explain the differences in male and female sex roles. In the hereditary view, biology determines sex roles; since men are stronger, they "naturally" dominate women. Research shows, however, that male dominance developed for cultural reasons, not biological ones. According to the environmental view, sex roles develop as a result of cultural influences. Most psychologists today conclude that both heredity and environment contribute to sex roles. Slight hereditary differences in physical and verbal activity between male and female infants, they say, are strengthened by the way parents respond to these sex-related behaviors.

2 Children learn sex roles when adults reward desired behaviors and punish or ignore behaviors they don't like. Children also learn through modeling their behavior on what they see others doing. Boys and girls receive their primary influence regarding sex-role modeling from same-sex adults. Society's standards of male or female behavior often establish the norms by which all behavior is judged. Thus, the community in which children live also affects sex roles.

3 The effect of sexism (the social and economic domination of one sex by the other) can be measured in many ways. As the usual victims of sexist discrimination, many women have had lower self-esteem than men. The achievements of the feminist movement (the drive to achieve political, social, and economic equality for women) have greatly improved women's self-images. Because of sexism, female accomplishments have been largely overlooked. Given equal opportunities to develop to their potential, however, women match men in intelligence and endurance.

4 Sexism shows up most clearly at work. On the average, women make only 60 percent of what men earn. Most women still work at such stereotyped, low-paid jobs as

domestic workers, secretaries, and sales-clerks. No one knows how many potential female scientists, artists, inventors, and other productive individuals never had a chance to succeed because of sexist discrimination.

5 Housewives sometimes feel that they lose their identity in the daily round of housework and child care. Self-aware women have learned to maintain control of their own lives. They work outside the home, do volunteer service, or delay the birth of their children until they're well established in their careers.

6 The feminist movement has roots deep in the past, but its greatest successes have come since the early 1960s. Voices of the movement include mainstream organizations such as the National Organization for Women (NOW). The major objective of the feminist movement is to pass laws that will end all remaining forms of sexism. Feminists see passage of the Equal Rights Amendment (ERA) as the most important step in that process. Many formerly men-only jobs are held by women, but even highly qualified women still find it difficult to enter upper-level jobs where pay and prestige are highest.

7 Schools have opened doors to women in both academics and in athletics. Textbooks are being written that give proper attention to women's achievements. Sexism in the media has been more difficult to control. Children should be allowed to develop sex roles that allow them to be the most productive person they can be.

8 Feminists also want the right to choose. This includes such decisions as having or not having children. Since this goal often includes the right to birth control and abortion, it has led to fierce political battles. Many feminists also demand child-care centers for the children of working mothers. Whether all these goals are met or not, more women than ever say they're happy to be born female.

9 The *macho* male is conditioned to repress the tender, "feminine" side of his personality. *Macho* behavior not only makes it difficult for men to relate to other people but also often leads to stress-related illness. Given a more human male sex role, men will learn to share responsibilities with the women in their lives. They will feel free to change roles and jobs without losing their feelings of masculinity.

10 More permissive attitudes toward sex (the new sexuality) leave many people confused and troubled. Some worry that liberal divorce laws and the new sex roles will disrupt family life. Others find that sexual freedom without love and commitment can lead to feelings of loneliness and guilt. Psychologists warn that too much sexual stimulation can harm young children. They advise parents to help their children learn to deal with sex in a mature and balanced way.

11 Psychologists believe that homosexual behavior may result when parents provide improper role models. Isolated homosexual experiences during childhood do not always lead to adult homosexual behavior. Because *gay* behavior is no longer considered to be a mental disorder, psychotherapy is given only when the homosexual life-style causes severe emotional disturbance to the individual.

12 Although a stable nuclear marriage is still considered the best environment in which to raise children, people are experimenting with alternate forms of marriage. More people are living together, hoping to avoid the expense and trauma of divorce if the arrangement doesn't work. More couples are also choosing to remain childless in order to concentrate on the pleasures of adult life. Others choose communal living because it provides extra companionship and emotional support. Equal marriage allows couples to develop mutual respect and to share equally in everything they do.

13 Nonsexist family life will allow children to grow up without the limitations of traditional sex roles. Girls will learn that women can do mechanical things; boys will not be afraid to express their feelings. Both sexes will be encouraged to choose jobs and a life-style that make them happy and productive.

PUTTING YOUR KNOWLEDGE TO WORK

Terms you should know

childless marriage

communal living

equal marriage

Equal Rights Amendment
(ERA)

feminists

homosexuality

macho

male chauvinists

National Organization for
Women (NOW)

new sexuality

sexism

sex roles

Objective questions

1 Most sex-role behavior results from social conditioning. One difference between men and women that seems to be definitely linked to heredity, however, is that boys show more (a) affection (b) physical activity (c) intelligence (d) emotional response to stress.

2 Which of the following has the strongest influence on the development of a child's sex role? (a) peer pressure (b) community standards (c) parental models (d) biological inheritance.

3 If children are raised in a nonsexist culture, they will probably grow up believing that (a) women are superior to men (b) men are superior to women (c) women should be housekeepers and mothers, and men should be breadwinners (d) men and women are equal in their potential talents and abilities.

4 When a male chauvinist puts women down by saying that their achievements don't match those of men, a feminist would reply that (a) male historians have largely ignored women's achievements (b) women have been denied the opportunity to compete on equal terms with men (c) women have been conditioned to think of themselves as unable to deal with high-level abstract thought (d) all of these reasons help explain the differences in male-female achievement.

5 Feminists believe that when a woman goes to work, she (a) is entitled to the same pay as a man doing the same job, if both have equal experience (b) deserves special treatment because she is a woman (c) neglects her responsibilities to her family (d) will have to act like "one of the boys" if she is to be successful.

6 The proposed Equal Rights Amendment guarantees that (a) women will have the right to work (b) men will not be obligated to support their families (c) women will become the dominant sex (d) both sexes will receive equal treatment under the law.

7 Which of the following children's books would a feminist say is a step in the right direction? (a) A brave and intelligent girl rescues her family from a gang of kidnappers. (b) A girl spends all her time playing active outdoor games while her brother stays indoors to cook and do housework. (c) A teenage girl drops out of high school to marry her boyfriend. (d) A teenage boy solves a spy case by using his girl friend's good looks to trap the enemy agent.

8 The feminist movement's top priority is to (a) establish women as dominant over men (b) establish equal rights as the legal and moral law of the land (c) remove sexist language from books and magazines (d) guarantee admission to graduate school for any woman who wants to go.

9 If a couple decides they want children, the best choice for a stable arrangement will probably be found in (a) a communal living situation (b) a single-parent family (c) living together (d) an equal marriage.

10 In an equal marriage, husband and wife will (a) carefully conceal their emotions so as not to upset the children (b) work together to push the man to the top of his career field (c) respect each other's abilities and share the work load equally (d) divide child care so that the woman nurtures the children and the man disciplines them.

Discussion questions

1 Why could the effect of the feminist movement on American society be called revolutionary? Explain some of the changes the feminists have caused.

2 In the past, women were considered the "inferior" sex. How do you explain that? What penalties have both sexes paid for the long acceptance of sexism in this society?

3 Discuss the major goals of the feminist movement. Which goals do you support? Which goals do you oppose? Explain the reasons for your decisions.

4 What effect might the success of the feminist movement have on men? Why is a nonsexist way of life so difficult for some men and women to accept?

5 Suppose you are thinking about getting married. What important agreements would you want to have with your future partner before you decided to go ahead with the marriage?

6 Why do you think the divorce rate has been steadily increasing during recent years? What—if anything—can be done to reverse this trend?

7 Would you vote for a woman as President of the United States? As Vice-President? As governor of your state? Discuss the reasons for your answers.

8 Why is it important that every young woman, whether she plans to marry or not, have job skills that will enable her to support herself?

Activities

1 Contact one of the feminist organizations in your community and see if you can schedule a speaker to discuss the current status of the feminist movement. By checking the phone book, you can probably locate chapters of the National Organization for Women, Women United, or Women's Equity Action League. Your local college probably has a women's group that will also supply speakers. If there is an antifeminist group in your community, ask for a representative to join in a debate on feminist goals.

2 You can obtain an interesting collection of feminist literature by contacting some of the national organizations. Three useful addresses to write to are:

> Women's Equity Action League
> 821 National Press Building
> Washington, D.C. 20045

> National Women's Political Caucus
> 1921 Pennsylvania Avenue
> Washington, D.C. 20006

> National Organization for Women
> Public Information Office
> 1266 National Press Building
> Washington, D.C. 20045

After you've read the literature, share it with your classmates. It will probably lead to some interesting discussion.

3 Start a collection of anecdotes gathered from interviews with men and women who feel that they have run into sexist discrimination. If you find that such incidents are common, you might want to put together a booklet for everyone in your school describing job, credit, and educational rights. The Equal Employment Opportunity Commission, 1800 G Street, N.W., Washington, D.C. 20506, will furnish the information you need.

4 On your own, or with a task force of friends, survey the textbooks used in your local elementary and secondary schools for sexist stereotypes. Your librarian can help you find guidelines for judging the books you review. It will help to look at some older textbooks and children's picture books for purposes of comparison. Elena Belotti's *What Are Little Girls Made Of?* (Schocken, 1976) will also give you some useful background.

5 Make a collection of pictures from magazines and newspapers that portray stereotyped sex roles for men and women. Label each clipping according to the particular stereotype it represents. Display your collection on a bulletin board or poster.

6 Do males really do better in mathematics, and do females really have higher verbal abilities? Ask your counseling office to help you survey achievement- and aptitude-test scores to see if the scores back up these generalizations. Your teachers can help you organize the study so as to ensure a valid sampling.

7 If you're really interested in the feminist movement, you might want to start a feminist study group on your campus. Find a faculty sponsor who shares your interests and start building your organization. Along with guest speakers and general discussions of feminist goals, your group can take on some of the following activities:

(a) Interview women in your community who have made successful careers for themselves. Find out what it took for them to succeed and what it means to compete with men for jobs and power. Ask those who are married whether or not they experience conflicts between their two roles.

(b) Survey the graduating senior class concerning their vocational choices. How do the women compare with the men in this regard? How many plan to marry? How many plan to have children? Write up your results for the local newspaper or school paper.

(c) Run your own John-Anne study (see pages 405–406).

(d) Study current TV programs for examples of sex stereotyping. Are women being portrayed in a nonsexist manner? Do women receive a fair number of important roles?

For further reading

Billings, Victoria. *The Womansbook.* New York: Fawcett, 1977. This is a witty, perceptive look at the challenges facing every woman who wants to achieve independence.

Bird, Caroline. *Everything a Woman Needs to Know to Get Paid What She's Worth.* New York: David McKay, 1973. In question-and-answer form, this useful book provides guidance for any woman who wants to find a job, get a better one, or just get ahead.

Farrell, Warren. *The Liberated Man.* New York: Random House, 1974. Farrell believes that it is time for men to stop pursuing their old *macho* image and begin acting human. This is a how-to-do-it book for improving the quality of male life and male/female relationships.

Friedan, Betty. *The Feminine Mystique.* New York: Norton, 1963. Times have changed since Friedan's book was published, but her work still has power and authority. This is one of the key books in the history of the feminist movement.

Ms. Magazine. This readable monthly magazine serves as a forum for feminist voices. *Ms.* demonstrates that a growing market for feminist ideas exists in this country.

Piercy, Marge. *Small Changes.* Garden City, NY: Doubleday, 1973. This novel deals with the lives of two young American women caught up in the sexual revolution. It provides a well-written look at the challenges women face in today's world.

Rossi, Alice S., ed. *The Feminist Papers: From Adams to de Beauvoir.* New York: Columbia Univ. Press, 1973. This collection of feminist writings provides a useful perspective on the goals and personalities of the feminist movement as it has developed over the years.

Ruddick, Sara and Pamela Daniels, eds. *Working It Out.* New York: Pantheon Books, Inc., a Division of Random House, Inc., 1977. What's it like to be a modern woman? In this book, twenty-three women writers, artists, scientists, and scholars talk honestly and openly about their successes, failures, and growing self-awareness.

NEW DIRECTIONS IN PSYCHOLOGY

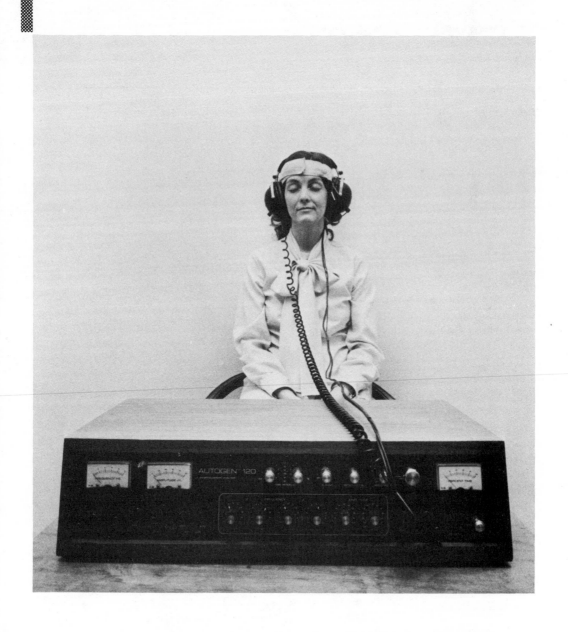

14

EXPLORING UNKNOWN WORLDS

It is quite likely that you enjoy watching stage magicians present their illusions. As you sit spellbound, rabbits pop out of hats and girls float in mid-air. But even as you marvel at the performance, you also know that the magician's art is based on clever deception.

No one, scientists agree, can violate physical laws. But what about the claims that some gifted individuals do have extraordinary powers? Can these people actually "read" someone else's mind or move objects without touching them? Skeptics warn that such performances are usually done through sleight of hand or by illusions. Others, however, believe that some men and women do possess *psychic powers* (abilities that lie outside known physical laws). As proof, they point to a small group of psychics who claim supernatural abilities.

Uri Geller, a young Israeli, became one of the most widely discussed of all psychics. Witnesses claim to have watched Geller, who once made his living as a stage magician, perform apparently impossible feats. When he was around, keys, spoons, and other metal objects seemed to bend by themselves; crystals disappeared from sealed boxes; and broken clocks suddenly started running. Geller also said he could pick up another person's thoughts, even at a distance.

Most of Geller's work, however, took place on stage or in crowded rooms. His work attracted crowds, and his assistants often ran in and out, "helping" him set up each demonstration. Viewers had trouble agreeing on exactly what happened, although most reported that *something* unusual took place whenever Geller performed.

Scientists at the Stanford Research Institution (SRI), therefore, decided to study Geller under controlled conditions. SRI is respected for its work in computer and laser technology. The scientific world watched closely. If Geller could satisfy the SRI experts, people would be more inclined to take his psychic powers seriously. Geller accepted the challenge but warned that, like most psychics, his "powers" do not always work on command.

The SRI experimenters, Harold E. Puthoff and Russell Targ, set up a series of controlled tests for Geller in 1972 and 1973. During most of the experiments, the psychic was locked in a specially designed room called a Faraday cage. This double-walled, copper-screened room totally cut off Geller from the outside world. No light, sound, or electrical signals could get through to him.

The first test zeroed in on Geller's telepathic abilities—his claim that he could receive mental images "broadcast" by

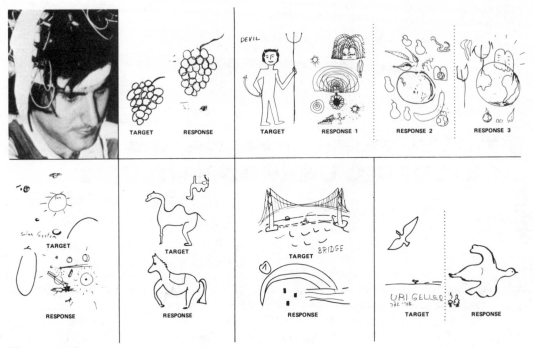

Figure 14.1

Wired to measure brain-wave activity, Uri Geller (insert) concentrates on a test of his telepathic powers. When he was asked to duplicate a scientist's target drawings, Geller made the sketches labeled "responses." Which of the responses would you score as "hits"?

another person. The scientists began the experiment by picking a target word at random from a dictionary. The first word was *grape*. One of the researchers sketched a bunch of grapes on a piece of paper. Geller soon reported over a one-way intercom that he " 'saw'. . . drops of water coming out of the picture," and he mentioned "purple circles." He then drew a bunch of grapes of his own. Both Geller's drawing and the target sketch contained the same number of grapes.

To make Geller's task more difficult, the scientists later drew the pictures on a TV-like device called a cathode-ray tube. When a computer drew a picture of a kite on the screen, Geller, still locked in the Faraday cage, responded by drawing a similar kite. The computer drew a church, and Geller sketched something that looked a little like the target. For the third test, the target was a heart with an arrow through it. Even

though the device was then turned off, Geller was able to draw the target correctly.

Geller also appeared to demonstrate another psychic ability. Eight out of ten times he called the correct number on a die (one of a pair of dice) that had been shaken in a closed steel box. This was a double-blind experiment; neither Geller nor the scientists should have been able to know ahead of time what number would show up. Finally, the psychic went twelve for twelve when asked to locate an object hidden at random in one of ten metal cans. The odds against anyone correctly guessing such random events are over a trillion to one.

Puthoff and Targ, the SRI researchers, concluded that Geller had successfully demonstrated his psychic abilities. Geller himself found it difficult to explain his success. When asked to describe what happened, he said, "I put a screen in my mind, like a television screen. Even when I talk or listen, it is still there. When I am receiving something, the image appears there as a picture. I don't feel it; I actually *see* it."

Research into psychic forces has drawn increasing public attention. Researchers have adopted the term *parapsychology* (also known as *paranormal forces,* or *psi*) to apply to the study of any event that cannot be explained by natural law. At the same time, other beliefs and superstitions have come forward to demand attention. Some Eastern religions, for example, report that their followers can control their mental and physical processes in seemingly impossible ways. Other people put their faith in *pseudosciences* (literally, false sciences such as astrology or palmistry) because of the easy answers they promise.

Although most psychologists hold to a healthy skepticism, many say that evidence to support some of parapsychology's claims

seems to be growing. Psychologists also study meditation, yoga, and other aspects of Eastern religions because these practices may add to our understanding of the mind's powers and potential. They also accept the fact that belief in the pseudosciences itself influences human behavior and therefore cannot be ignored. The questions explored in this chapter will give you a chance to make up your own mind about these challenging new frontiers.

14.1 WHY DO PEOPLE STILL BELIEVE IN THE SU-PERNATURAL?

14.2 DO THE PSEUDOSCIENCES HAVE ANY IN-SIGHTS TO OFFER?

14.3 WHAT DO EASTERN RELIGIONS TEACH ABOUT THE POWERS OF THE MIND?

14.4 WHAT IS PARAPSYCHOLOGY?

14.5 HOW CAN RESEARCH IN PARAPSYCHOL-OGY BE CONTROLLED?

14.1 WHY DO PEOPLE STILL BELIEVE IN THE SUPERNATURAL?

If a demand exists, American free enterprise will soon fill it. And a demand exists today for the supernatural.

Do you doubt that? Look at any big-city newspaper. You'll find a column of horoscopes—advice on what the day will bring you, based on your day of birth. The classified ads will probably announce the services of a palm reader or two, and you might even spot an article about a meeting of local witches. Turn to the book-review section, and the chances are good that you'll find a review of the latest best-seller on UFOs or the Bermuda Triangle. Finally, check the film listings. You'll surely see ads for movies about voodoo, werewolves, ghosts, and other supernatural forces.

Belief in magical forces

For most of human history, a belief in magical, supernatural forces ruled people's lives. But people of the twentieth century

pride themselves on their scientific attitude. Why, then, do vampires, fortune tellers, and other mystical ideas remain so popular? Psychologists point to several reasons why people hold so tightly to magical beliefs.

A search for fulfillment. Many people find little satisfaction or fulfillment in their personal lives. By turning to such mysterious forces as witchcraft or magic, believers can pretend for a little while that they're powerful and successful.

A search for answers. Many men and women feel anxious when they must make important decisions. To escape from this anxiety, they may rely on some magical power outside themselves. If "it's written in the stars" or in a magic number, how can they go wrong? Even Adolf Hitler, dictator of Nazi Germany during World War II, relied on astrology. Hitler scheduled important battles according to the positions of the

Figure 14.2

In a scientific age many people invest time, energy, and money in hopes of finding psychic knowledge. Why do you think the appeal of the unknown seems greater than ever?

A search for profit. Both the well-meaning and the less-than-honest have made profits from people's interest in the supernatural. If believers are demanding horoscopes, palm readings, lucky-number charts, and telepathy demonstrations, you can be sure someone will provide them—at a good price.

Dangers of relying on pseudoscience

A surprisingly large number of Americans believe that they have had telepathic experiences. Others happily report on their psychic adventures with ghosts, dreams that predicted the future, or mysterious runs of luck. Millions more buy expensive horoscopes, lucky charms, tea-leaf readings, magic spells, and so on. If you question them about their beliefs, they'll probably reply, "What harm does it do if someone gets a little help from the supernatural?"

The danger, psychologists believe, is not in spending money for a few words of psychic advice. The real risk arises when individuals hand over responsibility for their lives to some mystical decision-making force. These people can easily develop what some psychologists have described as a "loser's personality." Losers, they say, often see themselves as possible victims. By depending on vague, unreliable forces, they wait for good things to happen instead of going out and making them happen.

People who make their own decisions, by the same token, can be "winners." You've probably already learned how hard it is to take responsibility for important choices. When you do, you sometimes make mistakes. Some of the emotional bruises last for a long time. But you'll learn from your mistakes, and you'll grow stronger because you took responsibility for them.

stars, moon, and planets on certain "lucky" days.

A search for comfort. Some people turn to a belief in magical forces when faced with unbearable grief. Unable to accept the loss of a loved one, they may ask a spiritualist to help them contact a dead child or other relative.

A search for "kicks." People who have no serious belief in the supernatural still find it exciting to watch horror movies or to read about mysterious, unknown forces. Belief in the supernatural adds spice to their lives.

A search for belonging. Believers in the supernatural enjoy a natural bond with those who share their beliefs. "In-groups" that focus on such interests as UFO's or ESP provide otherwise lonely people with a needed sense of belonging.

SECTION CHECKUP

1 What proof exists that many people still rely on magical ideas to help them run their lives?

2 How would a psychologist explain the continued reliance on magical beliefs?

3 What is the danger of depending on the pseudosciences to help make important life decisions?

14.2 DO THE PSEUDOSCIENCES HAVE ANY INSIGHTS TO OFFER?

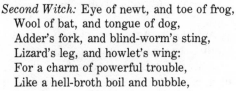

Second Witch: Eye of newt, and toe of frog,
    Wool of bat, and tongue of dog,
    Adder's fork, and blind-worm's sting,
    Lizard's leg, and howlet's wing:
    For a charm of powerful trouble,
    Like a hell-broth boil and bubble,
All Witches: Double, double toil and trouble;
    Fire, burn, and caldron, bubble.
                —*Macbeth*, Act IV, Scene i

Like most citizens of his day, Shakespeare was aware of magic and the supernatural. He spiced his plays with ghosts, magical spells, prophecy, and witchcraft. What was common belief in the 1500s, moreover, has not totally disappeared. The pseudosciences still attract both casual participants and dedicated followers. The promise that one can peek into the future or influence events exerts a powerful attraction.

Predicting the future

Divination is the magical art that tries to foretell events or discover hidden knowledge. Over the centuries, diviners have used almost every natural event you can imagine to obtain information about the future. Some claimed that the gods sent messages in the livers of freshly killed animals. Others watched the stamping of horses' hooves, or studied the smoke as it rose from a fire. Although reading tea leaves and crystal-ball gazing still exist, two of the most popular methods of divination today are the tarot cards and the *I Ching*.

The tarot. The seventy-eight cards of the *tarot* deck date back to at least the 1300s. Fifty-six of the cards make up the four suits, similar to a modern deck. The other twenty-two cards picture colorful medieval symbols with special meanings (see Figure 14.3). Among these picture cards are such universal figures as the fool, the lovers, justice, death, the sun, and the hanged man. Each card represents a number of related meanings. The fool, for example, stands for foolishness, lack of discipline, or excess. The

Figure 14.3

The meaning of the colorful picture cards used in the tarot depends on the position in which they appear. The Hanged Man often represents frustration and obstacles to success. The Lovers, as you might guess, signify beauty, temptation, and the possibility of romance.

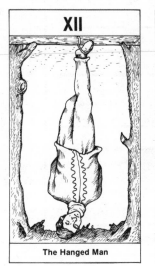

The Hanged Man

The Lovers

sun signifies more positive qualities, such as triumph, success, and happiness.

In telling the tarot, the diviner lays out the cards after the questioner has thought about his or her question. The entire deck can be used, but many diviners prefer to work only with the picture cards. As each card is turned up, the diviner relates the card to the questioner. Since each card has several meanings, the diviner can adjust the reading to the questioner's reactions. This "intuitive" response by the diviner plays a major role in the success or failure of the reading.

I Ching. More than three thousand years ago, Chinese diviners began writing a book called the *I Ching*. To use this ancient book, the diviner asks the questioner to create a hexagram by tossing sticks or coins. The six lines of the hexagram can be either solid or broken; thus, sixty-four combinations are possible. The hexagram leads the diviner into the *I Ching*, which contains general statements about the meaning of each hexagram. As in the tarot, the diviner chooses the interpretation that seems to fit the questioner best. The hexagram Tui, or Joy (see Figure 14.4), signifies progress and success. If a young man named Perry asked the *I Ching* for advice about a love affair, he would be reassured by

Tui (Joy)

Figure 14.4

Tui. The diviner would probably tell Perry, "Remain firm, and pleasurable advantage will surely come!"

The search for personal insights

Three popular pseudosciences promise personal insights to those who accept the idea that people's lives can be influenced by magical forces. Like the tarot and *I Ching*, astrology, palmistry, and numerology date back to the earliest civilizations.

Astrology. Astronomy is the science that studies the movements of the stars and planets and tries to understand the workings of the universe. *Astrology* (see also Chapter 6, page 159) is a pseudoscience that asserts that these same movements dramatically influence human affairs. Astrologers divide the sky into twelve equal segments called the zodiac. The astrologers believe that the zodiac sign under which a person is born determines that individual's personality (see Figure 14.5). Using an individual's time and place of birth, astrologers prepare a horoscope. The horoscope describes a person's character, abilities, and appearance. Some charts go so far as to say that Pisceans (Pisces is the fish) often stand with feet crossed—like a fish's tail. A horoscope also gives guidelines for making important decisions.

Detailed horoscopes take time to prepare and cost more money than most people want to invest. Newspaper readers, however, often turn to a daily table of astrological advice called "Your Horoscope" or "Astrological Forecast." These tidbits of advice might tell Virgos that "It's a good day for making new friends," or warn Scorpios that "An opponent will try to make trouble for you." If you think about it, you could write such vague predictions yourself. Isn't every day a good day for making new friends?

Palmistry. Modern medical research shows that a number of diseases and genetic disorders (liver disease and Down's syn-

THE SIGNS OF THE ZODIAC

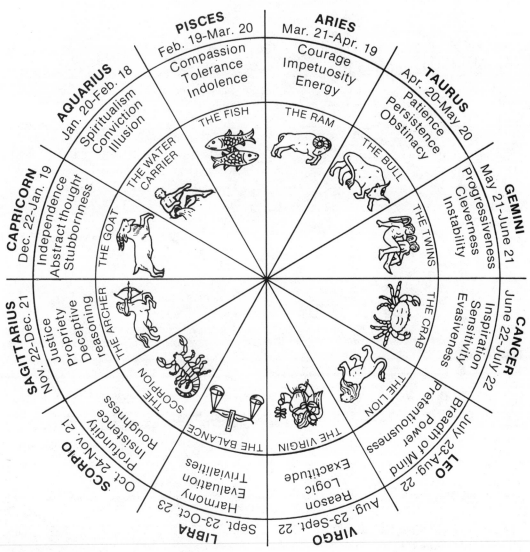

Figure 14.5

How do your own characteristics match up with those assigned by this astrological chart?

drome, for example) can be diagnosed by studying the lines in the palm of the hand. The same doctors who study the hand as a "blueprint" to the body's health, however, do not accept palmistry as a valid way of interpreting personality and divining a person's future. Even so, in cities everywhere, palmists dressed in traditional gypsy costume "read" the hand's distinctive lines,

mounts, and finger shapes (see Figure 14.6).

Palmists study the lines of the palm for clues to the individual's mental and emotional states. Breaks in the "life line," for example, are seen as predictions of future illnesses or accidents. A person with a strong "heart line" may be told to expect a happy love life. Skillful palmists adjust their reading to the questioner's reactions. Slight

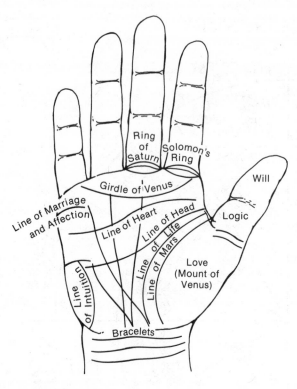

Figure 14.6

Palm readers say they can analyze character and predict a person's future from the lines and mounts of the hand. Why are so many people willing to believe in this pseudoscientific tradition?

facial movements and hints dropped in conversation are often enough to ensure a successful reading.

Numerology. Believers in the pseudoscience of *numerology* calculate their "magic number" according to a table that assigns values to each letter of a person's name. If your magic number turns out to be seven, for example, the numerologist would describe you as a "mysterious, withdrawn, scholarly person." Threes, by contrast, are supposed to be "lucky, lively, and charming." Skeptics point out that people's magic numbers seldom fit their actual personalities. Believers in numerology, however, claim that the universe "vibrates" to precise numerical relationships, such as can be found in planetary orbits and the struc-

ture of atoms. Numerology, they say, applies these same relationships to human affairs.

Spiritualism

Spiritualism is based on a belief that the living can communicate with the dead. If Benjamin wants to speak to his late Uncle Ted, for example, he would consult a *medium* (someone who claims to be able to contact the spirits of the dead). The actual attempt at contact takes place during a seance, usually held in a darkened room. The medium asks Benjamin and others who are present to join hands, then seems to fall into a trance. Soon the ghostly voice of Uncle Ted, or a messenger spirit, appears to answer Benjamin's questions. Most seances also feature knocks and raps, flickering candle flames, and ghostly objects that fly around the room.

Despite the skill with which they stage their seances, mediums achieve their ghostly effects with special props, projectors, and hidden helpers. The famous escape artist Harry Houdini (see Figure 14.7) of-

Figure 14.7

Escape artist Harry Houdini used his knowledge of stage magic to expose fake spiritualists. Here he demonstrates the tricks of the trade. Can you spot any of the props used to simulate the appearance of spirits during a seance?

Figure 14.8

DO PYRAMIDS HAVE SPECIAL POWERS? FIND OUT FOR YOURSELF

Humanity's fascination with the pyramid dates back to ancient Egypt. Since you probably don't have 13 acres of empty ground and 2,300,000 large stone blocks, however, you'll have to be content with a smaller pyramid if you want to conduct experiments.

First, make a pyramid out of poster board according to the dimensions given here. Tape the sides together, but leave the base free since you'll want to put things inside. Use a block of wood for a platform. It should be two inches high, or one third the height of the pyramid.

Locate your pyramid at a reasonable distance from electrical appliances, radios, windows, and heaters. Use a compass to find magnetic north, and line up the pyramid precisely on the north-south axis. What can be put inside the pyramid? Try dead insects, fresh meat or flowers, anything organic. It should "mummify" (dehydrate), while a control piece placed in another spot decays. You can also try the razor-sharpening experiment. A final suggestion is to buy a packet of seeds and put one half of the seeds under the pyramid for several days. Then paint the pyramidized seeds and the untreated seeds in identical soil. If pyramid power works, the treated seeds should grow faster and more vigorously than the untreated seeds.

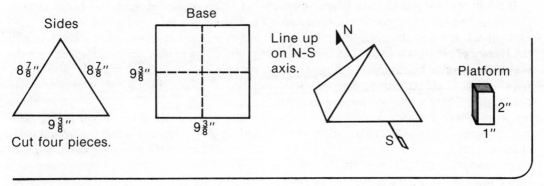

Sides — $8\frac{7}{8}''$ $8\frac{7}{8}''$ $9\frac{3}{8}''$ Cut four pieces.

Base — $9\frac{3}{8}''$ $9\frac{3}{8}''$

Line up on N-S axis. N S

Platform 2'' 1''

fered a $10,000 prize to any spiritualist he could not prove to be a fake. Houdini investigated a large number of mediums but never had to pay off on his offer. Despite the proven fakery, grieving men and women still turn to spiritualists in hopes of regaining contact with loved ones who have died. Psychologists warn that such efforts lead only to continued unhappiness. It's better, they say, to take care of relationships while the people you love are still alive.

Modern pseudosciences

Not all pseudosciences have their roots in the distant past. Pyramidology, biorhythms, and graphology all attempt to apply scientific principles to the age-old search for knowledge and control. Public interest and acceptance have given these beliefs a higher status than that achieved by divination or spiritualism.

Pyramidology. In 1959, the patent office in Prague, Czechoslovakia, issued a patent for a device that sharpened razor blades. That wasn't so unusual, except that the "sharpener" was a small pyramid. Leave a dull blade inside the pyramid, the inventor claimed, and it becomes sharp again. Today, pyramid fans believe that this basic geometrical shape works its "miracles" by focusing cosmic-ray energy. (You can try your own pyramid experiments by following the instructions given in Figure 14.8.)

BIORHYTHM CHART FOR HOLLY N.

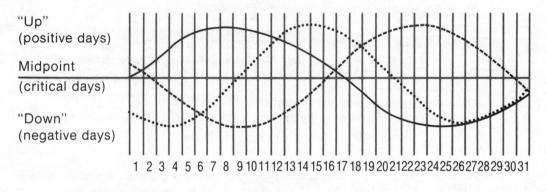

"Up"
(positive days)

Midpoint
(critical days)

"Down"
(negative days)

1 2 3 4 5 6 7 8 9 10 11 12 13 14 15 16 17 18 19 20 21 22 23 24 25 26 27 28 29 30 31

——————————— Intellectual cycle = 33 days

----------------- Emotional cycle = 28 days

················· Physical cycle = 23 days

Figure 14.9

Biorhythms. Biologists have long known that inner "body clocks" control the regular cycle of waking and sleeping. Believers in the theory of *biorhythms* say that behavior is also determined by rhythmic changes in a person's physical, emotional, and intellectual cycles. These rhythms supposedly follow a pattern that begins at birth and never varies. Some evidence has been collected to show that drivers do have more accidents on what biorhythmists call their critical days. One Japanese transport company, in fact, refuses to let its drivers work on their critical days.

To use biorhythms, you would chart your three cycles (intellectual, emotional, and physical) according to the number of days you've lived and the length of each cycle. As Holly N.'s biorhythm chart shows (see Figure 14.9), people spend one half of each cycle in an "up," or positive state, and one half in a "down," or negative state. Critical days come when a cycle crosses the midpoint between positive and negative states. Holly's chart warns that she will have a "double critical" day on the sixteenth. According to the theory, she will feel upset and have trouble concentrating on that day. It would be a poor time for her to take a test or run in a track meet.

Critics of biorhythms, however, would tell Holly to relax and go on with her life. Anyone who expects to have a bad day will probably have one, for mind set can create its own self-fulfilling prophecy. Moreover, whether biorhythms exist or not, they do not rule anyone's life. A biorhythm chart might give you an indication of your potential on any given day—but the actual decisions on how you'll live that day are up to you.

Graphology. *Graphology* uses variations in handwriting as a key to describing personality. Think about your own writing. You shape each letter almost unconsciously, for your mind is concerned with meaning and choice of words. The graphologist begins by analyzing slant and spacing, shape of loops and crossbars, end strokes, and punctuation. These elements are then correlated with common personality traits. Handwriting that slants upward, for example, is thought to indicate an optimistic frame of mind. Some psychologists feel that graphology has improved to the point that it can be used as a type of personality test. (Figure 14.10 shows how a graphologist interpreted the handwriting of singer/songwriter Janis Ian.)

YOUR HANDWRITING: DOES IT CONTAIN A CLUE TO YOUR FUTURE SUCCESS?

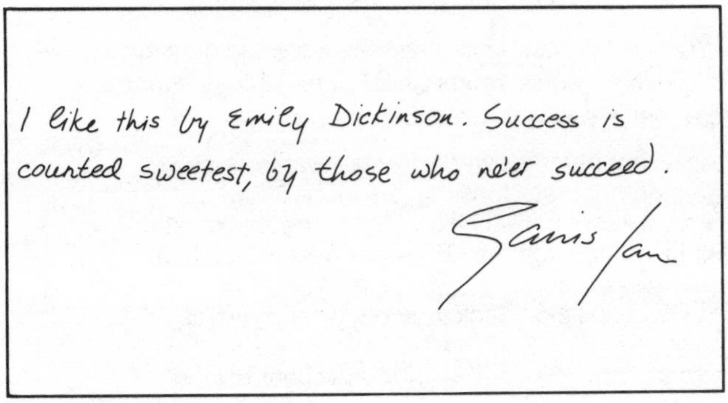

I like this by Emily Dickinson. Success is counted sweetest, by those who ne'er succeed.

Janis Ian

Figure 14.10

Graphologist Reggie Emmanuel finds confirmation of Janis Ian's success as a singer and songwriter in her handwriting. He finds "self-confidence in her capital I's. Her dramatic signature," he says, when contrasted with the small print of the message "shows a need for self-expression." Handwriting that is almost printing means that a person is "independent, witty, and creative." Does your handwriting contain similar clues to your future success?

SECTION CHECKUP

1 Describe several ways in which people try to foretell the future. Why are such pseudosciences attractive to those who believe in them?

2 Why do scientists put more faith in graphology than in astrology or palmistry?

3 Why do pyramidology and biorhythms attract people who otherwise would refuse to believe in the older pseudosciences?

14.3 WHAT DO EASTERN RELIGIONS TEACH ABOUT THE POWERS OF THE MIND?

A hint of incense hangs in the air. Legs crossed, eyes closed, eleven men and women sit quietly. In front of a small shrine, a leader chants words in a foreign language. On the wall, in a place of honor, hangs a picture of the Maharishi Mahesh Yogi. If you walked into the room, no one would notice, so deeply are they involved in group meditation.

In recent years about ten thousand people a month began similar Transcendental Meditation (TM) programs in the United States. Were they searching for religious experiences, or were they looking for a better way to relax? Whatever their reasons, new attention is being paid to Eastern (Oriental) beliefs. These teachings emphasize inner calm instead of Western society's competitive spirit. Supporters of Eastern philosophies believe that a union of East and West will free everyone to find a personal, peaceful relationship with the universe.

Concepts of Eastern philosophy

By using Eastern philosophy, religious leaders (often known as gurus, or teachers) hope to show people how to use more of their mental potential. Believers in Eastern concepts claim that most people limit themselves to a narrow range of thought that the culture defines as "normal." They believe that once the barriers of this artificial mind-state are broken the mind can move into a wider field of consciousness.

Most Westerners once ignored Eastern ideas of meditation and inner harmony, but today millions of Americans study them seriously. Famed psychologist Carl Jung believed that Western thought and Eastern religions were meant to work together, much as the left and right hands cooperate to play the guitar. The search for a more satisfying life has taken people along a path familiar to followers of Zen Buddhism, yoga, and Transcendental Meditation.

Figure 14.11

THE YOGA WAY TO THE PERFECT TENNIS SERVE

In his fascinating book *Powers of the Mind,* Adam Smith describes how the principles of Zen and yoga can be used to improve anyone's sports skills. Here Smith describes what happened when he went to a tennis pro who used Zen techniques.

> I went back to my tennis guru. My requirements were simple: I wanted a serve, that's all, with the power of a rocket, accurate to within six inches. . . .
> We went out to the court with a basket of balls. I hit a couple. The Zen master didn't say anything. Some went in, some went out. The Zen master didn't say anything. I hit some more.
> "Okay," he said. "Breathe in with your racket back, and out when it moves."
> That was easy.
> "Okay, now, where should the ball go over the net? And where should it land?"
> I pointed.
> "Okay, ask your body to send it there, and get out of the way."
> "Please, body, send it there."
> A miss.
> "It's not listening."
> "Slow it down. Visualize the whole shot before you hit it. Listen to the sound the ball makes against the string."
> It's amazing, but if you really visualize, and you really listen to the sound, you can't go racheta racheta with your mind. . . .
> We set up an empty tennis ball can in the corner of the service court. . . .
> "Slow it down more. More. Please, body, send the ball—
> "Slower, body, send the ball—
> "Slower, slower. Make time stand still. No time.
> "Please body, send the ball—"
> Zank! The empty tennis ball can went up into the air and bounced metallically.
> "Who did that?" I said.
> The tennis guru said nothing. He handed me another ball. It went into the corner of the service court, on roughly the same spot. So did the next one.
> I began to giggle wildly. I danced around a little, the scarecrow had a brain, the cowardly lion had courage. I had a serve, "I did it! I did it!" I said.
> Immediately it went away. . . .
> "Visualize. Don't use words. Don't think. Use images. In between shots, count your breath."

Adam Smith admits that he never did master his Zen serve, but that sometimes it comes back once in a while. If you'd like to apply that principle to your own tennis, try Tim Gallwey's book *The Inner Game of Tennis.* And good luck!

Zen. *Zen Buddhism,* or Zen, began in India. By the twelfth century it reached Japan, and it has now traveled to America. Zen teaches that human beings can use *meditation* (a period of quiet, focused thought) to reach true self-knowledge and a sense of unity with Ultimate Reality. This state, sometimes known as enlightenment, can be reached only through strict discipline. Zen teaches that the details of everyday life must be ignored. Intuitive knowledge, the knowledge that comes through meditation, will lead the Zen follower to the deepest and most important truths.

At the heart of Zen practices lies *zazen,* or sitting meditation. Zen teachers instruct their students in the proper posture, hand positions, and breathing. Without these techniques, the mind cannot be properly quieted. Rituals also include prayer, chanting, and stories called *koans.* Typical koans challenge the student to think about questions such as "What is the sound of one hand clapping?" and "Is it the flag or the wind that is moving?" If beginners practice these lessons faithfully, Zen Buddhists say, their worries will drop away and life will acquire new meaning.

The lengthy inward search for meaning in Zen does not always appeal to the Western mind's desire for quick results (see Figure 14.11). True followers of Zen must be willing to make it a way of life. Reading about Zen or asking questions, the Zen masters say, isn't enough. You can read a book on horseback riding, they say, but you can never fully know the reality of the experience until you grasp the reins and climb into the saddle.

Yoga. Most Westerners think of *yoga* as a complicated form of exercise. But the true yogi (one who practices yoga) believes that you can gain liberation from the prison of your body through exercise and meditation. Yoga attempts to promote the growth of physical, mental, moral, and spiritual forces. According to yoga teachings, students who follow the proper course of instruction will have a molecular change in their bodies. After about six months, personal tastes and habits will also change. Yogis claim that students stop being lonely, their fears vanish, and they experience true happiness.

Most Westerners limit themselves to the practice of yoga postures, deep breathing, and relaxation exercises. Sometimes known as *Hatha yoga*, this practice involves stretching the entire body and holding difficult postures. Yogis believe that correct posture and a flexible body help achieve a state of inner balance. Unlike more familiar exercises such as sit-ups or jogging, yoga does not require great strength nor does it strain the body. Yoga diets call for fresh fruits and raw vegetables, milk, rice, and nuts. Yogis avoid meat, coffee, onions, tobacco, alcohol, and drugs of any kind.

Transcendental Meditation. The techniques of *Transcendental Meditation* (TM) are anything but new. TM began at least 2,500 years ago in India but gained its widest popularity in the 1960s when Maharishi Mahesh Yogi set up training centers in the United States. The Maharishi claims that TM can improve people's health and emotional stability, and strengthen their ability to handle daily tasks. Lab studies have proved that TM does reduce stress and apparently increases people's ability to enjoy life—but so have other, simpler meditation techniques (see Figure 14.12).

If you were interested in TM, you would first visit a training center or attend a lecture. After this introduction, you would have a personal interview. During eight hours of individual and group training, your instructor would teach TM meditation techniques. You would also receive your personal *mantra*, a special sound used to focus your thoughts during meditation. Meditation sessions usually last about twenty minutes, and TM followers meditate twice a day. A final group ceremony completes your training. If you wished, you could return to the TM center to have your progress checked and to receive guidance in applying TM principles to your life.

Conflict has marked TM's history in the United States. Fearful that TM promotes Hindu religious teachings, parents have filed court suits to prevent its being taught in the public schools. The TM organization denies any religious intent, claiming that its only goal is to help people find a higher awareness. Critics have also complained about TM's fees. TM leaders respond that the fees pay only for necessary expenses such as rent, advertising, and teachers' salaries.

SECTION CHECKUP

1 What new ideas do Eastern religious teachings add to Western thought?

2 Describe the basic techniques used by followers of Zen, yoga, and TM to achieve greater self-fulfillment.

3 List the basic steps you would take to start meditating. Why does a person who is meditating repeat the same sound over and over?

Figure 14.12

THE RELAXATION RESPONSE: A SIMPLE GUIDE TO MEDITATION

Cardiologist Herbert Benson recommends meditation as a convenient, natural means of reducing stress and relieving the tensions of everyday life. He sees nothing wrong with TM, but he doesn't think that you need to join a TM group to receive the benefits of meditation.

Benson lists four basic requirements for successful meditation: (1) Meditate in a quiet environment, where you will be free from distraction. (2) Use a mental device—a word or sound—that you can repeat silently or aloud. (3) During meditation, adopt a passive attitude, a state of mind in which you ignore distractions and have a "let-it-happen" feeling. Don't worry about thoughts that intrude, and don't worry how well you are "doing." Simply keep repeating your sound. (4) Sit in a comfortable position, one that requires no unnecessary muscular tension. The cross-legged yoga position is fine, but do what feels best for you. Don't lie down, however, or you'll end up falling asleep.

With these principles in mind, you're ready to try the Relaxation Response:

1 Sit quietly in a comfortable position.

2 Close your eyes.

3 Deeply relax your muscles, beginning at your feet and working up to your head. Keep them relaxed.

4 Breathe through your nose. Become aware of your breathing. As you breathe out, silently say a single word such as *one* to yourself. Breathe easily and naturally. Repeat the same word each time you breathe out. This is what TM calls a mantra; it can be any word or sound of your own choosing.

5 Continue this process for ten to twenty minutes. It's OK to look at a clock, but don't set an alarm. When you finish, sit quietly for a few minutes, at first with your eyes closed. Let your mind and body return to normal activities gently.

6 Don't worry about whether you are successful. With practice, the response will come without effort. Practice the technique once or twice daily, but not within two hours of having eaten.

Most people finish a period of meditation feeling calm and relaxed. Others report feelings of pleasure, refreshment, and well-being. But each person responds differently. Try it yourself. The chances are good that you'll want to continue.

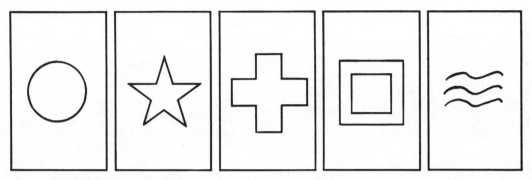

Figure 14.13

14.4 WHAT IS PARAPSYCHOLOGY?

Find a felt pen and twenty-five 3″ x 5″ index cards. Draw a circle on five of the cards. Then make five each of the other four designs shown above. When you finish, you'll have made a Zener deck of cards. Now shuffle your deck and find a volunteer. You're ready to do research in parapsychology.

What happens next? Conceal the cards from the subject. Turn them over one at a time, concentrating on the design as you (the sender) turn them. Your subject (the receiver) will write down the name of the card he or she thinks you're looking at. After you've gone through all twenty-five cards, check the results. A score of five "hits" would be no better than guessing. Scores above ten suggest that you or your subject may have telepathic powers, particularly if the high scores can be repeated.

At one time, most scientists scoffed at ideas such as telepathy and busied themselves with studies of "real" events. But reports kept coming in. In the 1880s, the Society for Psychical Research in London began looking into apparently genuine claims involving parapsychology. Modern studies began in 1927, when Duke University opened a Department of Parapsychology to carry on scientific studies. Pioneer researcher J. B. Rhine headed the new department, which has gained widespread attention for its investigations.

Extrasensory perception (ESP)

Parapsychologists define *ESP* as the ability to pick up information or to make things happen that would be impossible under normal laws of time and space. Let's say that your favorite group is playing a concert in London. If you're in the United States and "hear" the concert, is that ESP? No, if you listen to it on radio or watch it on TV. Yes, if you "listen" to it in your head, without benefit of a radio or TV receiver.

ESP usually includes four specific areas: telepathy, clairvoyance, precognition, and psychokinesis. Many scientific techniques and instruments have been used to research these mystifying phenomena. Researchers have measured brain waves, tried hypnotism, and even used animals in their studies. But for every successful demonstration of ESP in a research lab, a dozen failures have been reported. Until such inconsistent results are overcome, parapsychology will remain a stepchild to the rest of the scientific world.

Telepathy. Twins, lovers, and close relatives sometimes seem to know exactly what is happening to the other person, even over great distances. When two people communicate without using the normal senses, the phenomenon is known as *telepathy*. Uri

Figure 14.14

ESP AND DREAMS: A ROCK AUDIENCE "SENDS" A TELEPATHIC MESSAGE

Start with two psychics, a rock group, and an audience of two thousand. The result was an interesting experiment in telepathy, run in 1971 by Drs. Stanley Krippner and Montague Ullman, of the Maimonides Dream Laboratory in Brooklyn.

At exactly 11:30 each night for six nights, the audience at a Grateful Dead concert in Port Chester, New York, tried to send a picture to psychic Malcolm Bessent. Bessent slept in the Brooklyn dream lab forty-five miles away. Felicia Parise, another psychic, who served as the control, slept at her home in Manhattan. During each night's performance, a randomly selected slide was projected on a screen along with Bessent's name. While the Grateful Dead performed, the audience concentrated on the picture.

Each morning, Bessent and Parise provided dream reports to Krippner and Ullman. According to Krippner, Bessent described four of the six slides with reasonable accuracy. Parise had only one "hit," on the final night. Since Bessent apparently did not know what slides would be projected, the experiment apparently demonstrated the possibility of telepathy in these special circumstances.

Geller seemed to demonstrate telepathy in the SRI experiment reported at the beginning of this chapter, and the Zener card experiment is often used to test for this ability. (See Figure 14.14 for an unusual experiment that combines telepathy and dream research.)

Some interesting evidence has been collected concerning telepathy. In studies at Duke and at other centers, researchers have concluded: (1) Telepathy seems to be a function of the unconscious. Like all unconscious thought, telepathy is normally blocked off from the conscious mind. (2) Telepathy seems to be associated with alpha brain waves. People with telepathic abilities emit large quantities of alpha waves during telepathic experiences. (3) Distance and physical barriers do not seem to block transmission of telepathic messages. (4) Bad news tends to be communicated more easily than good news or the geometric shapes used on the Zener cards. Perhaps this explains the large number of cases in which people claim to have telepathically sensed the death or injury of a loved one.

Clairvoyance. Parapsychologists define *clairvoyance* as the power to describe objects or events outside the range of one's senses that no one else could possibly know about. For example, you'd be using telepathy if you correctly called the Zener card your sender was concentrating on. But if you could correctly name the *next* card in the stack before it's turned over, that would be clairvoyance. Controlled studies of clairvoyance, however, are difficult to set up. In a well-run experiment, no one else (including the experimenter) is allowed to know what the clairvoyant person is trying to describe. Unfortunately, such conditions can seldom be found outside the laboratory.

Two Dutch psychics, Gerard Croiset and Peter Hurkos, have used what seems to be clairvoyance to help the police. Croiset, for example, once received a phone call asking for help in finding a missing man. Croiset told the caller that the man had committed suicide by jumping into a canal. His detailed description led the police to the body that afternoon. Hurkos was similarly called in on a murder case. He first asked to hold the coat of the victim. From that, he described the murderer in detail, down to his mustache and wooden leg! Both Croiset and Hurkos, however, have recorded numerous failures also.

Precognition. How many stories have you heard about people who change their minds at the last moment before boarding a plane—and escape death when the plane crashes? In parapsychology, having knowledge of events that have not yet happened is called *precognition*. Psychic Jeane Dixon, for example, predicted in 1956 that "the 1960 election will be won by a Democrat, but he will be assassinated or die in office." President John F. Kennedy, a Democrat, was elected in 1960 and assassinated in 1963.

Psychologists caution, however, that true precognitive experiences are rare. Predictions by psychics such as Jeane Dixon do not always come true. In fact, most of what people call precognitive experiences probably relate to the work of the unconscious. Your conscious mind may be busy with a phone call, but your unconscious keeps track of everything that goes on around you. Thus, you may have a dream in which your father falls off a ladder the night before he actually does so. This could be precognition; many people would say it is. But the dream is more likely based on unconscious observation. You know the ladder is old and shaky; you know Dad uses it rather carelessly; and you heard him say earlier that he was going to do some tree trimming. Out of that data, your unconscious composed a warning dream that was useful, but not precognitive.

Psychokinesis. Gamblers often wish they could influence the roll of the dice or the spin of the roulette wheel. If they could, they'd be using *psychokinesis*, the power to move objects without physically touching them. Psychokinesis often seems to be related to crisis situations such as death or disaster. There are many stories, for example, about clocks that "stopped dead" at the moment a family member died. Psychics claim to be able to go much further. They deflect compass needles, move small objects around, bend pieces of metal, and influence the flip of a coin. Nelya Mikhailova, a Russian woman, once demonstrated what appears to be an exceptional psychokinetic talent. Along with moving cigarettes, matches, and glasses, Nelya separated a raw egg yolk from the white—from a distance of six feet!

The body's energy fields

Spiritualists and mystics have long insisted that the human body is surrounded by an energy field, or *aura*. In the early 1970s, a Russian research team learned how to take pictures of the aura. Kirlian photography, as it is called, reveals that all living bodies have a sparkling, lively energy field around them (see Figure 14.15). Some people interested in auras have suggested that old paintings of saints and angels, which often show the holy figure surrounded by a halo of light, may have had a basis in fact.

Auras have some unusual properties that scientists are only now beginning to investigate. The aura of a sick person, for example, shows noticeable changes in the area of the illness. Psychic healers, who claim to cure illness by touching the sick, show a brighter than usual aura in Kirlian photos. This aura grows dimmer when they make contact with a patient. Similarly, psychics show greatly increased energy flows during psychokinetic demonstrations, particularly around the eyes.

Exploring other mysteries

How far can you go in trusting the stories of parapsychological events that appear in books and newspapers and on TV? In many cases they're supported by what seems to be solid evidence. If you're interested in this field at all, you've probably come across accounts such as the following:

1. Ted Serios, a poorly educated laborer, stares into the lens of a Polaroid camera. When the exposed photo is developed, it shows a fuzzy building shot from a strange angle. The building turns out to be a hotel located several hundred miles away. Serios has somehow projected a mental image onto the unexposed film.

2. A girl runs her fingers over a piece of paper. Even though she is blindfolded, she "reads" the words printed there. A piece of glass is laid over a newspaper, so that she can't touch the paper itself. Again, she reads the words correctly. In what may be a parallel example, some blind children learn to recognize colors by their "feel." Red is sticky, they say, and yellow is slippery.

3. A woman sits in a psychologist's office. The psychologist writes some numbers on a slip of paper and places it on a high shelf. The woman concentrates, then reports that her "astral body" has moved around the room in spirit form and looked at the numbers written on the paper. To the psychologist's amazement, she correctly recites the five numbers he concealed from her. The odds against her guessing them correctly would be 100,000 to 1.

4. Holding only a Y-shaped hazel twig, a man walks back and forth across rough, wild country. Suddenly the twig begins to twist

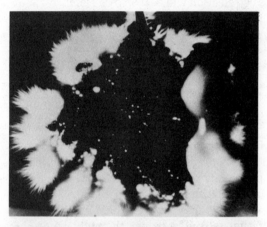

Figure 14.15

Kirlian photography provides a look at the energy field, or aura, that surrounds all living things. On the right, a leaf shows a typical aura. Below, Kirlian photos show the energy changes that seem to go with different moods. The subject's finger (left) is deeply relaxed, compared to the finger of a strongly aroused person (right).

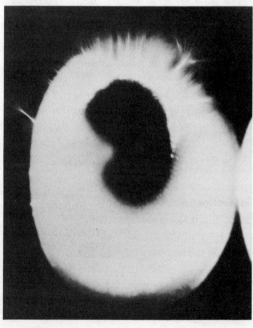

in his hands and point downward. When workers drill a well at the spot, fresh water gushes forth. The man is a dowser, and his skill has been practiced for centuries. Major oil and water companies keep dowsers on their payrolls, even though science doesn't fully understand how the process works. One guess is that dowsers somehow sense the electromagnetic fields that can be found in the presence of water, oil, or mineral deposits.

Parapsychological events such as these four can be written off as not worth investigating. But what if science had never explored the mysteries of gravity or radiation? Ignoring what doesn't seem to fit known facts adds nothing to the fund of scientific knowledge. Perhaps the best thing to do is to subject parapsychology to the same rigorous tests that are presently used in chemistry and physics labs. That's what you'll read about in the next section.

SECTION CHECKUP

1 Define the four types of ESP generally included in the study of parapsychology: telepathy, clairvoyance, precognition, and psychokinesis.

2 A friend has a dream that appears to be precognitive. How could you explain the dream-come-true in terms of the work of the unconscious?

3 What does the parapsychologist mean by an aura? What possible uses could auras have?

14.5 HOW CAN RESEARCH IN PARAPSYCHOLOGY BE CONTROLLED?

An immense amount of data has been collected that suggests that telepathy, telekinesis, and other paranormal phenomena do exist. If so, scientists can use either of two conclusions to explain the existence of ESP: (1) Parapsychological events result from unexpected applications of known scientific principles, or (2) psychic happenings belong to new and unexplored aspects of the human mind.

Asking the right questions

Believers in parapsychology often demand that people suspend their critical, show-me attitudes. After all, they say, the possibility that human beings possess psychic powers promises new and exciting days ahead. Skeptical observers, however, start with a list of questions that should be asked whenever evidence of psychic events is being studied.

Does the event seem valid only because people want to believe in it? The everyday world often seems dull and limited. People should ask themselves if the appeal of psychic mysteries doesn't tempt belief simply because it's novel and exciting. Children easily accept fairy tales and monster movies as true. Critics think that parapsychology has become an adult fairy tale, dressed up for a scientific age.

Who says it's so? Not all scientists can properly evaluate data from parapsychological experiments and events. Some scientists who study parapsychology are working outside their own fields. Others have already lost their objectivity. To make it more difficult, many psychic subjects refuse to perform under properly controlled conditions. Some telepaths, for example, see their scores fall sharply when they are tested in labs such as that run by J. B. Rhine at Duke University.

What do the data really mean? Writing up experiments and calling them valid doesn't make them so. Critics who look at the data raise such questions as, "What controls were set up? Have data been collected over

Pro & Con: CAN URI GELLER USE PSYCHIC POWERS TO BEND NITINOL WIRE?

In 1973, Uri Geller was challenged to bend a piece of nitinol wire. Bending spoons and keys was one of Geller's favorite demonstrations, so the nitinol test seemed an easy one for the Israeli psychic. But nitinol wire has an unusual property: It "remembers" the shape in which it was manufactured. You can bend, twist, or crumple nitinol, but it always springs back to its original shape when heated. Reports of the experiment appear to verify Geller's psychic powers.

Careful study of the test procedures, however, revealed that the facts may not have been fully reported. In this Pro & Con, the description of the experiment will appear in the Pro column. On the Con side, Geller's critics will point out the faults they found in the design and conduct of the experiment.

Pro: Geller's Nitinol Experiment

1 Uri Geller performed the nitinol experiment under the supervision of physical scientist Eldon Byrd in October, 1973.

2 The test took place at the Isis Center of the Naval Surface Weapons Center, Silver Spring, Maryland.

3 Nitinol at that time was not available to the general public. Byrd first gave Geller a solid block of the metal 1″ x ⅜″ square. Geller worked with the block, but could not alter its hardness nor its non-magnetic properties. Next he handled a large-diameter wire, but that wire also resisted his best efforts. Then Byrd held a smaller diameter (0.5 mm) piece of nitinol between his fingers. Geller stroked the middle of the wire. After twenty seconds a bump formed at the center of the wire. Byrd placed the wire in boiling water, which should have removed the bump. Instead, the wire bent itself into a right angle.

Con: A Critique of the Experiment

1 Eldon Byrd has a long history of involvement in parapsychological research. He further compromised his objectivity by stating that he believed "Geller is basically honest."

2 The Isis Center has no direct connection with the Navy. It's actually a meeting place for believers in the supernatural.

3 Geller could not "perform" his trick on the heavier pieces of nitinol. He explains that he cannot always control his powers—but he seems to do much better with easily bent metals.

a large number of trials? Has the statistical analysis been done properly? How did the study prevent the experimenter's own bias from influencing the results?" Pyramidologists can treat any number of razor blades with pyramid power, but until they can answer these questions, their results must be classed as unproven.

Does a cause-and-effect relationship really exist? To dedicated believers in parapsychology, coincidence doesn't exist. If Charlie is thinking about a friend and the friend calls him on the phone, Charlie immediately shouts, "Telepathy!" Baseball fan Stella has a hunch that the Red Sox will win the pennant—and they do. Has she had a

Pro: Geller's Nitinol Experiment

4 Byrd later gave Geller other nitinol wires to touch, with similar results. He writes that the changes Geller made in the nitinol normally would require a temperature of 900° F and a pair of pliers.

5 Since Byrd could not detect any marks on the surface of the wire, he concluded that Geller was using some sort of psychic power.

6 Byrd also notes that he was once an amateur magician. He does not believe that Geller tricked him in any way.

7 His article ends with a statement of "official approval" by authorities of the Naval Surface Weapons Center.

Con: A Critique of the Experiment

4 Byrd cut the smaller diameter nitinol into several pieces. He does not appear to have kept these extra pieces under tight security.

5 Conditions around Geller were quite disorganized during this time. Geller's close friend and assistant, Shipi Shtrang, could easily have substituted a previously prepared wire or could have secretly bent the one Geller eventually handled.

6 Even professional magicians cannot always detect sleight-of-hand tricks when performed by other magicians— and Geller started his career as a stage performer.

7 The endorsement by the Navy applies only to the accuracy of statements about the properties of nitinol. The Navy neither confirmed nor denied the parapsychological part of the study.

As you can see, it is difficult to pin down psychic performers like Uri Geller. Despite the criticism, many people still believe that Geller actually bent the nitinol exactly as Byrd reported. As long as any doubt remains, however, science cannot accept such clouded results.

What's your opinion? Is Geller a clever performer or a true psychic? Maybe it's best to wait until all the results are in on this intriguing new field of research.

precognitive experience—or have coincidence and her knowledge of baseball ruled her choice? Parapsychologists go by a simple rule to separate chance or coincidence from statistically valid proof. They demand that a psychic performance meet the test of *95 percent confidence.* That is, the experimenter must prove that there is only one chance in twenty that the results could have happened by chance.

Imagine, for example, that you've taken a test of clairvoyance. In the test, you were asked to guess the contents of sealed envelopes without actually looking at them. Inside each envelope is either a black or a white card. If you have one hundred guess-

BioBox

THELMA MOSS:
PIONEER IN THE STUDY OF PARAPSYCHOLOGY

At various times in her life, Thelma Moss (1920–   ) has been an actress, wife, author, mother, psychologist, and parapsychologist. Her research into human energy fields (using Kirlian photography) has brought her international attention. But she is also interested in haunted houses, precognition, psychic healing, and psychokinesis. Her energy, intelligence, and calm good sense make it difficult for critics to ignore her work.

Dr. Moss spent a number of years as a medical psychologist at UCLA's famous Neuropsychiatric Institute. At the same time, she began spending more time investigating paranormal phenomena. She traveled to Russia to learn more about Kirlian photography and also witnessed demonstrations of psychokinesis. These studies brought her into conflict with more conservative scientists. Dr. Moss finally left UCLA and today devotes herself to her research and to checking out reports of psychic happenings.

---

es, the odds are that you'll get fifty right. A score of fifty, therefore, would not meet the "95 percent confidence" test. A look at a special table of statistics, however, would tell you that a score of sixty-five or better would meet the standard.

Finally, those who study psychic happenings should ask themselves a final question:

Does it make sense? After all the statistics and descriptions have been analyzed, the data should fit into a rational, logical universe. If the data do not fit, wait for better evidence. Studies of parapsychology have been going on for a long time. No one need jump on the bandwagon right now.

Running a proper experiment in parapsychology

Proper parapsychological experiments should be double-blind whenever possible. Neither the experimenter nor the subjects should know anything about the content of the actual test. The following experiment in clairvoyance demonstrates these precautions. The test took place at Duke University under the supervision of J. B. Rhine, using the standard Zener deck described on page 447.

Preparation. The cards were shuffled and cut under controlled conditions. Neither Hubert Pearce, the test taker, nor J. G.

People often ask Dr. Moss how she can believe in forces that cannot be seen, measured, or proved. If bacteria, atoms, X rays, and other invisible organisms and particles exist, she challenges, then why can't other, undiscovered energies exist? After all, she says, inventors did not develop radar and sonar until this century; but bats and dolphins have always used these silent forms of communication.

Where do her investigations lead? Dr. Moss writes:

In the recorded history of the world, . . . certain people were considered to have the ability to detect water, or oil, beneath the ground. Others reportedly were able to detect the thoughts or happenings of people miles away. Some persons, it was claimed, could predict the outcome of a future event. Others were supposed to be able to move objects just by thinking about them.

These are all rare occurrences, obviously. And perhaps they are trivial. But it was the "trivial irregularities" of planetary orbits that led to the discovery of unknown but existing planets. Thus, possibly those . . . irregularities of human behavior may prove to have considerable significance in the study of humankind.

Do you think Dr. Moss makes a good case for parapsychology? You might like to look at some of her data before making up your mind. But whatever your final conclusion, you'll probably agree that she's a convincing voice for what she believes.

Pratt, the test giver, was present. Neither of the two young men could possibly have known the sequence of the cards ahead of time.

Setting. Pearce and Pratt met in Pratt's room to begin the experiment. After the men synchronized their watches, Pearce walked to another room 340 feet away. As he did so, Pratt shuffled and cut the cards. At no time did he look at the face side of the cards.

The test. At the zero hour, Pratt took the top card from the deck and laid it on the table face downward. One minute later he laid another card down, and so on through the deck. In his own room, thirty seconds after Pratt laid down the first card, Pearce wrote down his first guess. The process continued through two decks, with Pearce writing down his guesses every sixty seconds. Afterward, Pratt looked at the cards for the first time while he made two copies of the results. He sealed one copy and delivered it to Dr. Rhine. At the same time, Pearce sealed a duplicate copy of his guesses and also sent it to Dr. Rhine. All records were later photographed.

Results. Altogether, Pratt and Pearce took part in 1,850 trials. If only chance had been at work, Pearce's score would have been 370 hits (1 out of 5). Pearce, however, ran up a total of 558 hits, 188 better than chance. The odds against such a score happening accidentally have been figured at better than a hundred billion to one.

Since the results far exceeded the "95 percent confidence" test, Dr. Rhine's experiment appears to confirm that Pearce has clairvoyant abilities. Until science can explain how Pearce was able to guess so accurately, however, clairvoyance will remain only a fascinating mystery.

SECTION CHECKUP

1 What questions would a skeptical scientist ask someone who claimed to have psychokinetic powers?

2 What is meant by the "95 percent confidence" test in parapsychological research?

3 Describe the controls used in a double-blind test of a subject's clairvoyant powers.

LOOKING BACK: A SUMMARY

1 Belief in both parapsychology and magical, supernatural powers has increased in recent years. The following reasons may explain this increase: (1) People are searching for fulfillment in a cold, impersonal world they feel powerless to control. (2) People are looking for easy answers to hard questions. (3) People turn to magical beliefs as a way of finding comfort. (4) Some people have discovered that they can make a profit out of interest in the supernatural.

2 Dependence on mystical, psychic beliefs can lead people to forfeit responsibility for their own lives. A search for easy answers written "in the stars" or elsewhere can lead to development of a "loser's personality." Losers depend on luck and magic and often end up as victims. People who make their own decisions and take responsibility for their failures and successes have a good chance to become winners.

3 Pseudosciences (beliefs that pretend to have a factual foundation for their existence) have been part of humanity's heritage since the dawn of time. Divination, the art of foretelling the future, still attracts followers anxious to know what lies ahead of them. Two popular methods of divination are the tarot cards and the *I Ching*. The symbols on the tarot cards are believed to represent the basic life forces, and the fall of the cards determines the questioner's fortune. The *I Ching*, an ancient Chinese book of proverbs and advice, bases its divinatory wisdom on the random selection of one of sixty-four hexagrams. As with most forms of divination, the success of the reading usually depends upon the diviner's ability to interpret the reactions of the questioner.

4 Other pseudosciences attempt to provide personal insights. According to believers in astrology, each person's life is influenced by the position of the heavenly bodies at the moment of birth. In palmistry, the shape, lines, and mounts of the hand are thought to give clues to a person's past, present, and future life. Numerologists use "magic numbers" based on names and birthdates to identify personality traits and help make decisions.

5 Spiritualists claim that they can communicate with the dead. Once contact has been established, they believe that messages can be exchanged with the spirit world. Despite the total lack of evidence supporting such beliefs, some people still turn to spiritualism when they cannot cope with the death of loved ones.

6 Several pseudosciences have attempted to apply scientific principles to the age-old quest for knowledge and power. Believers in pyramidology use the pyramid shape to sharpen razor blades, mummify raw meat, and generally improve their lives. According to the biorhythm theory, each person's emotional, physical, and intellectual cycles can be plotted to predict "up," "down," and critical days. Graphologists study handwriting as a way of gaining insight into an individual's personality and emotional states. Alone among the pseudosciences, graphology has gained some status for its ability to analyze accurately the writer's mental state.

7 The search for self-fulfillment has led many people to Eastern (Oriental) beliefs. These philosophies stress meditation and inner harmony. Zen Buddhism, for example, teaches that human beings can reach true self-knowledge and peace (enlightenment) through strict mental discipline. Serious followers of Zen must devote their lives to practicing its teachings, but some of its principles can be learned and used by anyone.

8 Yoga promotes physical, mental, and spiritual growth through exercise and meditation. Most Westerners practice only the yoga exercises, which help develop good posture and body control. Transcendental Meditation (TM), in contrast, concentrates on meditation techniques. TM claims to reduce stress, improve health, and increase enjoyment. The religious and commercial aspects of TM have caused controversy, but the movement still has many adherents.

9 Parapsychology is the scientific study of forces outside the boundaries of natural law. Research in this field has grown rapidly since it first began in the 1800s. Extrasensory perception (ESP) includes telepathy, clairvoyance, precognition, and psychokinesis. Telepathy is the ability to exchange ideas with another person without using the normal methods of communication. Clairvoyance is the ability to "see" objects or events outside the range of one's own senses. A psychic who "reads" the thoughts of a person in another room is using telepathy. But if the same psychic identifies a criminal by touching the victim's clothing, that's clairvoyance.

10 Precognition is the ability to look into the future to predict events that have not yet happened. Psychologists believe that most precognitive experiences are really messages from the unconscious. Psychokinesis, unlike the other ESP abilities, works on physical objects. Someone with psychokinetic power would be able to move or influence such things as dice, pencils, compass needles, and the like. As with all paranormal powers, psychokinesis seems to fail more frequently than it works.

11 The human body is surrounded by an energy field that is known as the *aura*. The aura has long been described by psychics, but today a technique known as Kirlian photography can take pictures of it. Little is known about the aura, except that it seems to reflect the health of the individual and is found only around living matter.

12 Research in parapsychology often fails to meet the test of scientific validity because results are inconsistent and experiments poorly run. Observers should ask such questions as: (a) Does the event seem valid because people want to believe it? (b) Can the researchers be trusted? (c) Have the data been properly handled and interpreted? (d) Does a cause-and-effect relationship really exist? Before any psychic event can be considered valid, it must meet the test of "95 percent confidence." This test means that the odds are better than twenty to one that it could not have happened accidentally or by chance. (e) Finally, does the event make sense when examined in the light of known information about the universe? In time, experiments run under double-blind conditions may provide enough data so that scientists and others can make well-informed judgments about parapsychology's real meaning.

PUTTING YOUR KNOWLEDGE TO WORK

Terms you should know

astrology	meditation	psychokinesis
aura	medium	pyramidology
biorhythms	ninety-five percent confidence	spiritualism
clairvoyance	numerology	tarot cards
divination	palmistry	telepathy
extrasensory perception (ESP)	parapsychology	Transcendental Meditation (TM)
graphology	precognition	yoga
I Ching	pseudosciences	Zen Buddhism
	psychic powers	

Objective questions

1 Uri Geller's apparent ability to reproduce pictures drawn by someone in another room is called (a) precognition (b) clairvoyance (c) telepathy (d) divination.

2 Roxy C. never makes a major decision without first consulting a palm reader. Which of the following reasons best explains why Roxy depends on palmistry? (a) The accuracy and dependability of palmistry have been scientifically proved. (b) Depending on a palm reader is no worse than asking a psychologist or minister for advice. (c) Everyone believes in some form of magical power. (d) People who rely on a magical power outside themselves feel that they don't have to take responsibility for their decisions.

3 John G. believes in psychic powers. If he wants to find out what his girl friend will say when he asks her to marry him, he would most likely consult a (a) dowser (b) person with psychokinetic powers (c) tarot reader (d) pyramidologist.

4 Uncle Amos wants to make contact with his dead father to make up for not visiting him before he died. He'll be tempted to visit (a) a spiritualist (b) an astrologer (c) a graphologist (d) a psychic with clairvoyant powers.

5 A pseudoscience that charts people's emotional, intellectual, and physical cycles to spot "up," "down," and critical days is (a) numerology (b) biorhythms (c) precognition (d) graphology.

6 Research in parapsychology is complicated by the fact that (a) no capable scientists are working in the field (b) psychics cannot control their powers, and experiments cannot always be duplicated (c) the public has no interest in paranormal happenings (d) research in parapsychology did not start until the 1960s.

7 A psychic who tells police where to find a lost child after touching the youngster's favorite toys is practicing (a) telepathy (b) precognition (c) clairvoyance (d) spiritualism.

8 If Sara tells you she has forgotten her mantra, you know that she has been learning (a) telepathy (b) astrology (c) yoga exercises (d) Transcendental Meditation.

9 If an experiment in telepathy scored two hundred "hits" out of a thousand trials with the Zener cards, the results would be called (a) a successful proof of possible telepathic powers (b) incredible, since no one has ever scored that high (c) a failure, since the score did not exceed that expected under the laws of chance (d) certain proof that telepathy doesn't exist; no further tests should be made.

10 Which of the following steps would invalidate an experiment in clairvoyance? (a) The test giver stays in a room well separated from the test taker. (b) The Zener cards are randomly shuffled and sealed by a machine. (c) The test giver turns each card over and records the symbol during the test. (d) All results are delivered to the experimenter before the test giver and the test taker meet to check scores.

Discussion questions

1 Why do psychologists say that reliance on supernatural beliefs can lead to negative personality characteristics?

2 Describe the differences among the tarot, astrology, and graphology. Which comes closest to providing valid insights into personality? Why?

3 Why do the fields of parapsychology and the pseudosciences attract so many fakes? If you were introduced to someone who claimed psychic powers, what questions would you ask to prove or disprove those claims?

4 Why is meditation so important to Eastern beliefs? What can Eastern philosophies add to Western life styles?

5 Assume that your psychology teacher has asked you to set up an experiment in telepathy. How could you control the experiment so as to ensure scientific validity?

Activities

1 How common is belief in parapsychology and the supernatural in your community? Survey a cross-section of people to find out. Ask them about their beliefs in any form of parapsychology or the supernatural, and whether or not they have had any personal psychic experiences. Write up the results in a paper to share with your psychology class.

2 Using the directions printed on page 447 at the beginning of Section 14.4, make a set of Zener cards. Use heavy card stock so that the designs don't show through. Test a number of people for telepathic powers. You can be the sender or ask someone else to handle the cards so that you can watch the entire test and keep records. Most scores will cluster around five right guesses out of twenty-five, but you may get a few that exceed eight or ten. If you do, retest those people to see if they can demonstrate their "power" consistently. When you've finished, look at your data and try to draw a conclusion from the results.

3 If you're interested in carrying on your psychic experiments a little further, here are some other tests you can run:

(a) Test the claims of pyramidology. Make a pyramid (see Figure 14.8, page 441) and run controlled experiments with razor blades, seeds, raw meat, or whatever.

(b) Work out your own biorhythm chart (check your library for an instruction book), and see if the cycles correspond to your good and bad days.

(c) If you can find someone in your neighborhood who does tarot readings, *I Ching*, or any other form of divination, ask for a test reading. Be prepared with specific questions the diviner could not possibly know about. Remember that there's a tendency to forget the wrong guesses and to remember only those insights that seem accurate. Evaluate the reading in a report to your psychology class.

(d) Pick up a book on handwriting analysis and study the basic techniques. Ask a friend to gather some handwriting samples for you but to omit the names of the writers. Analyze the samples. Then see how well your readings match the actual personalities involved.

4 Watch for TV programs that claim to present honest dramatizations of psychic happenings. Do the programs meet the tests you've learned to apply to such claims? Why or why not?

5 If you've never meditated, why not give it a try? You don't have to join TM. Just use the meditation techniques described on page 446. If you want more detailed instructions, look at Herbert Benson's *The Relaxation Response*. Give yourself a week or two to get into meditation. It will take you a while to screen out all the distracting "noise" around and inside you.

For further reading

Branston, Brian. *Beyond Belief: True Tales of Psychic Phenomena*. New York: Walker, 1974. "True" stories of the paranormal world flood the market, but Branston, a British journalist, approaches his subject with healthy skepticism.

Huson, Paul. *How to Test and Develop Your ESP*. New York: Stein & Day, 1975. This is a fascinating collection of experiments and procedures for developing your abilities in telepathy, psychokinesis, and ghost hunting. A list of colleges that offer credit courses in parapsychology is included.

Moss, Thelma. *The Probability of the Impossible*. Los Angeles: J. P. Tarcher, 1974. One of the most respected names in psychic research, Dr. Moss describes the special research methods necessary in this field.

Needleman, Jacob. *The New Religions*. Garden City, NY: Doubleday, 1970. This book gives you an excellent introduction to the various Eastern philosophies and religions. Needleman interviewed numerous gurus and their students, and his book lets them speak for themselves.

Rhine, Louisa E. *Psi, What Is It?* New York: Harper & Row, 1975. A pioneer researcher in parapsychology along with her famous husband, Dr. Rhine wrote this readable book to make psychic phenomena understandable to the general public.

Watson, Lyall. *Supernature*. Garden City, NY: Doubleday, 1973. Dr. Watson's best-seller examines psychic and supernatural events with a careful, unemotional eye. Whenever possible, he relates such phenomena to known scientific law.

15

SEARCHING FOR NEW WAYS TO GROW

You've probably heard of boat shows and auto shows. The chances are good that you've been to a county fair. But what would a psychology show look like? Try to imagine it.

The banner over the entrance proclaims, "New-Life Fair." A large crowd is pushing toward the entrance. Ready? Step right this way. That's the main exhibit hall ahead.

Once inside, you see colorful booths piled high with books, leaflets, health foods, and mysterious electronic devices. The friendly people behind the displays could be selling camping trailers or hot tubs. Instead, they're pushing ideas. They think that they've found ways to make people's lives healthier and happier. Most belong to something called the self-awareness movement. Stop and check out a few of them.

Here's the Institute of Self-Development. For a small fee the institute promises to enrich your life. On Saturday you can learn meditation, and Tuesday evening you can attend a workshop on parent-child problems. Sunday the institute is sponsoring a lecture on Kirlian photography.

Across the aisle, a smiling, white-haired lady attracts your attention. "Hello," she says, "I want to invite you to our spring celebration of the healing arts. It will be a marvelous weekend of self-discovery and self-exploration." She pushes a brochure into your hand. "And all the meals will be strictly vegetarian!"

You smile at her and move on to another interesting exhibit. Green plants and flowers overflow the shelves and tables. The earnest-looking fellow behind the ivy believes that all living things need to communicate. See, he's got a plant hooked up to an EEG. Are you ready to relate to an azalea?

The auditorium is filling up for the afternoon lectures. A psychiatrist is going to speak on holistic medicine. He believes that the individual can integrate mind, body, and spirit to cure illness and maintain health. A respected woman scientist will tell about guided imagery, a mind technique to control pain. She teaches people to "give" their pain to imaginary animal friends that "live" in their minds. Before the afternoon is over, you'll also be offered a chance to learn how to increase your energy potential and how to use acupressure to cure a headache.

Ready for a snack? Sorry, you won't find any "junk food" here. Try the avocado salad on pita bread, served with organic grape juice. Not bad. While you're relaxing, wander over to where an energetic young woman is promoting an expensive seminar training program. "What's it like?" you ask.

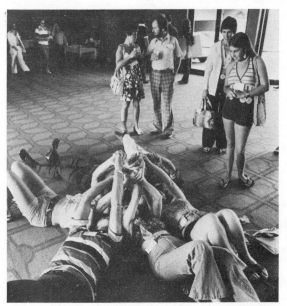

Los Angeles Times Photo

Figure 15.1

The search for new ways to grow often takes unexpected turns. A life-style convention in San Diego, California, encouraged this impromptu encounter session. What do you think people gain from such experiences?

"The seminar transforms your ability to experience living. It can't be described; you have to go through it yourself. It's about aliveness, satisfaction, and fulfillment." Her smile is radiant. "You'll experience more love, happiness, health, and self-expression than you knew existed."

That sounds pretty good. You ask for an example of what happens during the seminar.

The woman responds eagerly. "I'll tell you about one incident from my own seminar. We'd gone all day without eating. Then, late at night, the trainers gave us a free lunch: one cherry tomato, one strawberry, a daisy, and a slice of lemon. We visualized ourselves swimming inside the strawberry. Then we imagined ourselves climbing the daisy—only it was now twenty feet high! We licked the lemon, so we could really get into the acid taste. Finally, they let us eat the strawberry, the tomato, and the lemon. Some people were hungry enough by then to eat the daisy, too."

When she tells you the training costs $250, you decide that's a pretty high price for a thirty-calorie lunch. You walk over to another exhibit. Here, a man in a white lab coat is putting a space-age hookup on a woman's head. Someone in the crowd asks him what's going on.

"Marian is going to demonstrate biofeedback. This headset picks up her brain waves and displays them on that screen over there." As you watch, a green line moves up and down in a jagged pattern. "Now," he says, "watch the model train. When Marian reaches an alpha state, the train will move."

As you watch, the train jerks once, then stops. After a moment the engine moves an inch or two, then stops again. Marian seems totally relaxed. All at once, the train revs up and races around the track. The crowd applauds. Marian has apparently proved that she can control her own brain waves.

That was more like it, you think. As you move on, you see some familiar names. One group is promoting Gestalt encounter, and another is handing out information on a Zen workshop. You see signs for psychodrama training and a psychoanalytic approach to self-awareness. The different names begin to run together: Marriage Encounter, Rolfing, Family Synergy, megavitamin therapy, Bioenergetics, Silva Mind Control, and on and on. You decide it's time to leave.

Outside, you sit on a bench and wonder what the New-Life Fair means. Are all those people disturbed? Actually, most of them looked quite normal, and many seemed happy enough. As you think about it, you realize that all of those well-meaning people were trying to help other men and women cope with problems. And you know that for many people, life causes more stress, anxiety, and depression than they can handle.

As the fair suggests, many Americans have turned to the self-awareness movement for answers. Even if the fair didn't offer any remedies that appealed to you, a hundred other routes to self-help and self-discovery await you. This chapter will introduce you to some of the more interesting "ways to grow."

15.1 WHY ARE SO MANY PEOPLE SEARCHING FOR NEW WAYS TO GROW?

15.2 HOW DO BODY MOVEMENT AND MANIPULATION TECHNIQUES HELP PEOPLE?

15.3 CAN PEOPLE ATTAIN PERSONAL GROWTH THROUGH CONTROL OF THEIR MINDS AND BODIES?

15.4 WHICH THERAPIES COMBINE SELF-REALIZATION TECHNIQUES WITH TRADITIONAL PSYCHOTHERAPY?

15.5 HOW CAN TRANSACTIONAL ANALYSIS HELP PEOPLE STAY IN THE "OK" POSITION?

15.1 WHY ARE SO MANY PEOPLE SEARCHING FOR NEW WAYS TO GROW?

You don't have to go to a New-Life Fair to realize that people are looking for something. Almost everywhere you turn you'll find a new book, an encounter group, or a self-discovery experience that promises improved emotional health. Each of these is concerned with the same problem: Too many people live like emotional zombies. They think too much and feel too little.

Scientists, psychologists, religious leaders, and other experts on human behavior have been trying to improve this situation. When traditional therapies proved too slow and expensive, new-age therapists experimented with shortcuts or developed new systems. This attempt to help people reach their full potential is often called the *self-realization movement (SRM)*. The movement promotes itself with modern selling methods, but its best advertisements are the people who say that SRM techniques have improved their lives. In the age of anxiety, the promise of self-realization finds willing listeners.

The loneliness of the times

Many people who join a self-realization program are like twenty-year-old Sam M. Sam's not emotionally ill. Most of the time he functions quite well. More and more, however, he's been feeling vaguely depressed and anxious. He isn't sure his life has any meaning, and he feels cut off from his family and friends. Sam believes that he should be able to enjoy life more, to feel self-fulfilled. As he complains to his friends,

"It's a Technicolor world, but I'm living in black and white."

No two people seek out a self-realization experience for the same reason. Sam wants self-fulfillment, but Jean A. is trying to overcome angry feelings about her divorce. Here are some of the other reasons people give for joining an SRM program.

Figure 15.2

Many self-help books promise instant "cures" for emotional problems. What advice do you think the salesclerk should give this man?

© 1978 by NEA, Inc.

"Quick! Where are the self-help books?"

1. "I can't deal with life's minor problems." Small annoyances and everyday decisions leave some people upset or depressed. Life becomes a struggle against overwhelming odds.

2. "No matter how I try, I can't build a good relationship with other people." Such people feel lonely most of the time. They don't know how to build a friendship or to experience love.

3. "I'm bored with my life. Nothing exciting ever happens to me." The small pleasures of life escape these people. They may seek thrills, even when the excitement is short-lived and unhealthy.

4. "Even when my life is going well, I feel as though it can't last, that I'm doomed." Anxiety and stress overshadow every relationship and activity such people attempt.

5. "Suddenly I'm afraid to go outside. I never felt like that before." Phobic fears cripple some people's ability to enjoy life. If the fears increase, these people may not be able to carry on normal activities.

6. "I fail at everything I try. At the feast of life, I end up with the turkey neck." A negative self-image can make it impossible for some people to take charge of their lives. Because they doubt their abilities, they cannot stand up for their rights.

7. "My life is pretty solid, but it could be better. I want to develop new abilities and resources." These people sense that even a good life can be improved. They see the self-realization movement as a step in that direction.

Basic principles of self-realization

During the 1960s, rebellions against the "establishment" in politics, business, and education led to a similar revolt against traditional psychotherapy. The self-realization movement became a way of focusing on growth and self-awareness

Figure 15.3

Do you think a PSI lecture can really accomplish all it promises? Why would people fall for such an obvious come-on?

instead of on neurotic or psychotic behavior. Like mushrooms, new groups sprang up everywhere. Whatever their names, however, self-realization programs share a common set of beliefs.

1. You can make contact with your true inner self, as opposed to the social roles you've learned to play.

2. You can learn how to communicate with others on an intimate basis.

3. You can develop your full potential for growth.

4. You can benefit from taking part in self-realization experiences.

5. Your self-awareness will be raised as you get rid of old, self-defeating behaviors.

Possible dangers of SRMs

What could be wrong with a system that promises you better health, memory, vitality, and improved creativity? Such come-ons are common in the ads for some self-realization groups (see Figure 15.3). Most SRM programs will cost you money, and a few can do great damage to your mental or physical health. Poorly trained leaders can lose control of the powerful emotional forces set loose during group sessions.

Even for a basically healthy person, the SRM experience can backfire. Twenty-eight-year-old Reggie R., for example, was bored and restless. His success as a real estate salesman didn't seem enough. On impulse, he joined an SRM group he heard about through a friend. The group leader was determined that everyone should learn to express his or her anger. At each group meeting, the members took turns shouting, screaming, and punching a foam-rubber dummy "to get the anger out." Reggie felt better, but his job still frustrated him. He began using the group tactics at work. After a series of violent shouting matches with his boss, Reggie was fired. The group had taught Reggie to express his anger but hadn't helped him learn to use it constructively.

Other people lose hope and "drop out" of normal activities because their SRM program couldn't deliver its advertised miracles. A few unhappy men and women became self-realization "junkies." They move from one group to another, constantly searching for fresh experiences and easy answers. Perhaps all self-help and self-realization groups should be labeled: "Caution! If pain persists, see a therapist."

SECTION CHECKUP

1 What are the basic goals of the self-realization movement?

2 List some of the reasons people give for turning to the SRM for help. Why would a basically healthy, well-adjusted person join an SRM program?

3 Can SRM programs ever harm a person? Give some examples.

15.2 HOW DO BODY MOVEMENT AND MANIPULATION TECHNIQUES HELP PEOPLE?

You already know that what happens in your mind can affect your body. If a friend forgets to keep a date, you're likely to feel a surge of anger. Angry feelings begin in your brain, but they also trigger changes in your heart rate, stomach activity, skin temperature, and metabolic rate.

Studies have shown that emotionally disturbed people often respond to misleading messages from their bodies. Poor sleep habits, tense muscles, and high metabolic rates can turn minor anxieties into crippling neurotic reactions. The same principle applies to otherwise healthy people. Janie M., for example, feels tension in her neck and shoulder muscles whenever her boss treats her unfairly. After a few months of this, Janie's muscles stay rigid much of the time. As a result, she *feels* upset even when she's on vacation.

These findings have led to the development of therapies that treat emotional problems through body movement and manipulation. After the individual does

Pro & Con: CAN SELF-REALIZATION BE LEARNED FROM A BOOK?

Americans are great on "do-it-yourself" projects. Look in any bookstore, and you'll find titles promising to teach you how to do everything from furniture refinishing to handling your own divorce. What about self-realization? Take your pick from hundreds of titles. But can these "pop psychology" texts really help you?

Pro

1 Psychotherapists have limited time and can see only a few patients. Self-help books make their insights available to the general public.

2 Self-help books give people valuable insights into their own problems. By reading these works, they can recognize that they are not alone and that help is available.

3 Reading a self-help book can lead disturbed people to admit that they need help. The easy-to-follow advice given in most books is almost certain to lead to some psychological growth.

4 Most people cannot afford the services of a therapist or cannot bring themselves to ask for help. Reading a book may not be a perfect solution, but any understanding gained in this way will be to their benefit.

Con

1 The most important therapists seldom write for the general public. Far too many of the pop psych books are written by people without proper qualifications. Profit, not therapy, is often their prime motive.

2 The people who most need help will not or cannot read these books. In any event, reading a book can never substitute for working with a trained therapist.

3 Most self-help books simply don't deliver what they promise. Too many offer shortcuts that leave a person's deeper emotional problems untouched. Readers seldom make the life-changing commitments necessary for true psychological growth.

4 Mental-health care is available to everyone. Public agencies provide help for those who cannot afford private therapy. People who refuse to seek out therapy are unlikely to change just because a self-help book says they should.

The popularity of the self-help books on the market today suggests that many people agree with the Pro side of this argument. What do you think? If you've never looked at a book of this type, here are a few interesting titles: John Powell, *Why Am I Afraid to Tell You Who I Am?*; Mildred Newman and Bernard Berkowitz, *How to Take Charge of Your Life*; and Muriel James and Dorothy Jongeward, *Born to Win*.

some exercises or receives a special massage, the "emotional knots" are supposed to disappear. To some degree, you can think of these therapies as working backward. In order to calm and relax the mind, they first tend to the needs of the body.

Feldenkrais method

Moshe Feldenkrais, an Israeli physicist, teaches a self-realization technique that dismisses traditional psychotherapy. In its place, Feldenkrais substitutes some one thousand intricate movements and exercises, each with some forty variations. All ages, including the elderly, can enjoy the movements. Many are taken from yoga, Eastern martial arts such as aikido and jujitsu, and the dances of India. Feldenkrais believes that his slow, intricate movements allow you to tap the power inside you by altering basic patterns of thinking and feeling.

"The body only executes what the nervous system makes it do," Feldenkrais says. He believes that people are prisoners of bad habits learned while they are growing up. His exercises are designed to break those habits. His followers claim that as their posture and flexibility improve, their personal awareness and contentment also increase. Therapists have also used the Feldenkrais method to treat diseases of the nervous system such as multiple sclerosis and to combat the effects of aging.

Structural integration (rolfing)

Dr. Ida Rolf, a biochemist and physiologist, believed that people's bodies are being damaged and thrown out of alignment by painful emotional experiences. Like a car that has been in an accident, the body still moves, but in a draggy, awkward way. To counter this condition, Dr. Rolf designed a program of deep muscular manipulation and massage that she called *structural integration*. *Rolfing*, as it is more commonly known, calls for the therapist to use fingers, knuckles, and elbows to probe deeply into the patient's rigid, contracted muscles.

Rolfing theory states that the ten one-hour sessions release damaging emotional memories by relaxing and stretching muscles and tendons. The rolfing experience itself can be quite painful, for the rolfer-therapist's fingers dig into the body's soft tissue without mercy. Dr. Rolf felt that the pain arises when the rolfer must overcome resistance from tense, knotted muscles. The final three sessions concentrate on revising the body's posture so that it again moves in tune with the natural forces of gravity.

As they complete their therapy, rolfing patients say they feel physically lighter and emotionally stronger. As Leslie D. reports, "I can't deny that it was painful, but I can't dispute the fact that I felt a release of a lot of my tensions after the first four sessions." Other patients claim better posture, increased sensations of happiness, and improved confidence in dealing with problems. Because rolfing apparently produces more fluid physical movements, athletes sometimes "get rolfed" in hopes of improving their performance.

Bioenergetic analysis

Almost everyone has something to "kick about," says Dr. Alexander Lowen, a former psychoanalyst. In his approach to therapy, called *bioenergetic analysis*, Dr. Lowen encourages his patients to kick and punch their feelings literally out into the open. Bioenergetic sessions are also built around exercises that alert people to their rigid body postures and help them release repressed feelings. Dr. Lowen believes that increased ease of movement and muscle control will produce changes in self-awareness.

At a bioenergetic session, people stretch, twist, move, kick, and even scream. As patients get into these movements and postures, they say they sometimes feel intense sensations of release, "like a balloon suddenly cut loose from its anchor." Some people vividly relive the moments when they adopted the stooped, crooked body postures that Dr. Lowen thinks cover up strong, honest emotions. You may have seen a child, for example, cower in fear when scolded by an angry parent. Dr. Lowen feels that such postures eventually become part of a person's life. As he tells his patients, "You are your body—let it express itself freely and openly."

Do Lowen's techniques actually pay off in release of repressed feelings? This conversation between a mother and her nine-year-old son following a bioenergetics session might give you some insight:

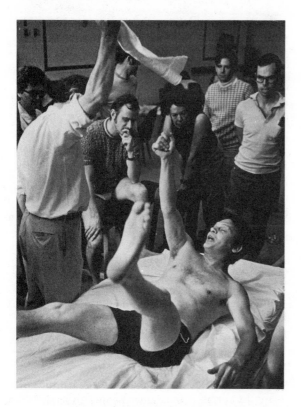

Figure 15.4

Body-movement therapies relieve stress by putting people through various physical exercises.
Do you think that pounding on your own mattress
the next time you're feeling uptight will do any
good? Why?

"How did you hurt your finger, Mommy?"
the boy asked.

"I was working out some angry feelings I
had about Grandma," his mother said.

"Why?" the boy wondered. "What did she
do to make you mad? We haven't even *seen*
her since last summer."

"It was things Grandma did a long time
ago," said the mommy. "Things she did that
made me mad when I was little like you are
now. But when I was little I didn't show my
feelings the way you do now. Getting mad, the
way you do, is better, don't you think?"

"I guess it is, Mommy," said her son. "If
people didn't know how to be angry they
wouldn't be human, would they?"

Usefulness of body therapy

You've probably discovered for yourself
that vigorous physical activity can make you
feel better when you're tense or upset.
Some people jog, while others punch a pillow or slam a tennis ball as hard as they can.
Moshe Feldenkrais, Ida Rolf, and Alexander Lowen based their therapies on that
insight. Along with many other psychologists, they believed that people have lost
awareness of their bodies. They saw emotional stress reflected in the way people sit,
stand, walk, and run. Why not remove that
stress by releasing the individual's creative
energies in a natural, physical way? A large
number of former patients think these systems work faster and with less expense than
traditional psychotherapy.

SECTION CHECKUP

1 What is the basic concept of body-movement
and manipulation therapies?

2 Contrast the Feldenkrais method with structural integration (rolfing).

3 Why does bioenergetic analysis require
patients to kick, stretch, twist, move, and
scream? What seems to happen when patients
"free" themselves of bottled-up emotions?

15.3 CAN PEOPLE ATTAIN PERSONAL GROWTH THROUGH CONTROL OF THEIR MINDS AND BODIES?

The human race has grown taller and
heavier over the centuries. Human mental
processes, however, haven't changed very
much. Perception, observation, and logical

thought work pretty much as they did for
your ancestors 80,000 generations ago.
More and more scientists, psychologists,
and other experts, however, believe that

the mind can expand beyond its present limits.

These researchers ask that people open their eyes to evidence that standard scientific logic has ignored. Why dismiss as a "trick," for example, the Amazon native who walks unharmed across a bed of broken glass? A related "trick" called biofeedback lets college students control their natural anxiety before a big exam.

Another behavioral technique, assertiveness training, can turn a shy, timid person into a strong-willed individual without months of costly therapy. And then there's the softball player who uses a mental "trick" called psychocybernetics to "pitch" a complete game without leaving the living room. Does that have anything to do with a championship performance the next day?

All these cases have one thing in common: By the laws of traditional psychology, they shouldn't happen. But they do.

Biofeedback

Would you like to be able to control your blood pressure? Stop the pain of a headache? Or even cure insomnia? *Biofeedback* training can accomplish these apparent miracles.

Yogis and other mystics long ago proved that the mind can control almost any involuntary body function. Yogis, for example, can reduce their heart rate and other autonomic body processes to almost zero. This ability allows them to stay alive for hours in sealed coffins. Biofeedback, however, provides a shortcut across the years of meditation and study required by Eastern disciplines. The process involves three steps.

1. Biofeedback devices can monitor any specific biological system, from brain waves to muscle tension. Let's assume that you have high blood pressure and wish to lower it. In this case, the technician will hook you up to a machine that measures changes in your blood pressure. Input from a hookup on your arm will translate these changes into red and green lights on a control panel.

2. You sit in a relaxed position, watching the lights. A red light means your blood pressure is too high; a green light signals that the pressure has decreased. Your job is to keep the green light on as much of the time as possible. Biofeedback experts can't describe exactly how this process works. They know that, if you receive exact data on what's happening to a particular body function, your mind can learn to control that function. Now, how are you doing with your blood pressure? After you've worked with the feedback device a few times, you should be able to keep the green light on most of the time.

3. Once you've mastered the techniques, you'll be able to control your blood pressure without the feedback from the machine. True, you won't be able to tell someone else *how* to do it, but you can do it. In biofeedback, it's the results that count.

Control of brain waves. Early biofeedback experiments centered on the control of brain waves. These waves result from the electrical activity of the brain during wakefulness. The basic waves, as measured on an EEG machine, are called alpha, beta, and theta. (Delta waves occur only during deep sleep.) All three types of brain waves are present during your waking moments, but what you're doing or thinking generally determines which wave type dominates (see Figure 15.5). Biofeedback-trained subjects have quickly learned to produce alpha waves—the same type of brain waves produced by Zen monks during meditation. Researchers believe that, if you could switch into alpha, it would help you relax and prepare for a period of creative thought.

Medical uses of biofeedback. Doctors now use biofeedback to treat chronic illnesses such as asthma, lower-back pain, migraine headaches, epilepsy, and high blood pressure. Migraine sufferers, for example, learn to raise the temperature of their hands. Diverting a heavy flow of blood into the hands at the first sign of a migraine

BRAIN WAVES AND EMOTION: THE ELECTRICAL ACTIVITY OF THE BRAIN RELATES TO HOW YOU FEEL

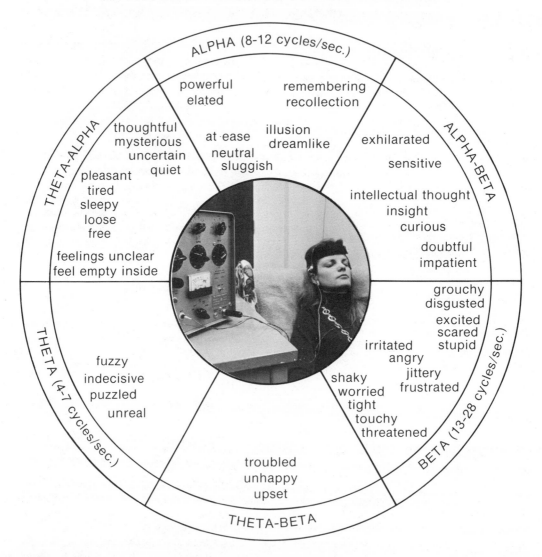

Figure 15.5

Feeling states can be related to specific brain-wave activity. What type of brain wave do you think you're producing right now? How does biofeedback train you to produce alpha waves on command?

attack apparently prevents or eases the headache. Much of this medical therapy is based on the estimate that up to 75 percent of the problems a doctor sees relate back to the patient's emotional state. If the mind can make you ill, the reasoning goes, why

can't biofeedback put the mind to work curing what it originally caused? Perhaps one day the lights and buzzers of biofeedback trainers will replace tranquilizers, pain-killers, and other medications. Doctors and patients might consider that a fair trade.

Assertiveness training (AT)

How often have you backed down when someone—a parent, friend, teacher, or salesclerk refused to give you what you felt was rightfully yours? It might have been only a promised favor or a place in line, but you probably felt frustrated when it happened. Many people run into such problems, back away from them, and gradually learn to think of themselves as inadequate. Psychologists call such reactions *nonassertive behavior*. They know that along with feelings of depression and inadequacy, nonassertive behavior can also lead to actual physical illness, such as ulcers.

Assertiveness training (AT) starts with the idea that everyone has the capacity to change nonassertive behavior. Many people, however, have never learned their Bill of Assertive Rights (see Figure 15.6). They have never developed the skills that an assertive person seems to use instinctively: persistence, reasonable compromise, rejection of unreal fears, and the ability to communicate needs to others. Assertiveness does not mean being unpleasantly aggressive, however. Aggressive people impose their will on others, often for selfish reasons. Assertive people know how to deal with others without losing either their temper or their self-respect.

Figure 15.6

YOUR BILL OF ASSERTIVE RIGHTS

The basic principle behind Assertiveness Training is that no one can manipulate your emotions or behavior unless you allow it to happen. Just as the Bill of Rights guarantees your civil rights, this Bill of Assertive Rights can free you from manipulation and guilt.

1 You have the right to judge your own behavior, thoughts, and emotions, and to take responsibility for their consequences upon yourself.

2 You have the right to offer no reasons or excuses to justify your behavior.

3 You have the right to judge whether you are responsible for finding solutions to other people's problems.

4 You have the right to change your mind.

5 You have the right to make mistakes—and be responsible for them.

6 You have the right to say, "I don't know."

7 You don't need the goodwill of other people to deal with them effectively and assertively. Save your sensitivity and nurturing for the people you're really close to.

8 You have the right to be illogical in making decisions.

9 You have the right to say, "I don't understand."

10 You have the right to say, "I don't care."

Why not give AT a try? You might find out that you can get more done with less anger and greater feelings of self-awareness.

Using AT in consumer situations. Imagine for a moment that you have returned a defective record to a music store. The clerk, however, doesn't want to give you your money back. Four basic AT skills will help you assert your rights as a customer.

1. *Broken record:* calm, persistent repetition of your position. Most people ask for something once, then give up.

Clerk: It's not our policy to give refunds on records.
You: I understand, but the record is defective, and I want my money back.
Clerk: I can't do that. It's against policy. See the sign over there on the wall?
You: Yes, but I want my money back. [You will repeat this without anger or impatience until the clerk makes the refund or calls for someone who has the authority to do so.]

2. *Fogging:* acceptance of criticism without becoming anxious or defensive. Criticism usually deflects people from their goal. AT wants you to guard against that.

Clerk: Look, the record jacket is torn.
You: That's right, it is.
Clerk: And you're holding up the other customers.
You: Yes, I know. As soon as you give me my money back, I'll be out of their way.

3. *Negative assertion:* acceptance of one's faults or errors through agreement with the criticism.

Clerk: Where's your receipt?
You: I didn't save it.
Clerk: Well! How can you expect a refund when you don't have a receipt!
You: You're right, that was a dumb thing to do. But I still want my money back.

4. *Workable compromise:* bargaining for a reasonable solution to a disagreement (but only when your own self-worth is not involved).

Clerk: Don't you understand? We never give cash refunds!
You: Well, I'd rather have my money back, but I'll settle for a record that costs the same.
Clerk: All right! Go pick one out.
You: Thanks for your help.

Using AT in social situations. Other AT skills lend themselves more readily to social situations. Many conversations die because neither person works hard enough to keep communication going. To prevent this, you can use the AT technique of *free information.* All you do is throw interesting items into the discussion that you know the other person will want to hear about. Another AT technique for improving a relationship is called *self-disclosure.* Most people wait for others to guess how they feel. Instead, you open up deeper areas of communication by expressing your own feelings openly and honestly.

Finally, *negative inquiry* requires that you encourage others to criticize you. This gives you a chance to take advantage of the criticism (if helpful) or to exhaust it (if negative). AT experts believe that practicing these techniques will quickly improve your ability to deal with whomever you meet— whether on a social, business, or personal level.

Psychocybernetics

Dr. Malcolm Maltz started his career as a plastic surgeon. He soon realized that his surgery opened up new lives for some patients but left others just as unhappy as before. Maltz concluded that people make their own success or failure. He invented the term *psychocybernetics* to describe the mechanism that creates this positive or negative self-image. In psychocybernetics, the subconscious serves as a control system made up of the brain, the nervous system, and the mind. This "creative mechanism," as Dr. Maltz calls it, takes in information, processes it, and acts upon it. If you feed negative information into your creative mechanism, you will be geared for failure. "I'm going to fail; I can't do algebra," moans Perry—and promptly fails his test. But feed in positive information and your creative mechanism will ensure success. "I know I can win this race," thinks Angela—and she goes out and runs her opponents into the ground.

Psychocybernetics depends heavily upon what has been called "the power of positive thinking." Dr. Maltz asks that you set a goal for every day and do everything you can to reach that goal. If you fail, get a good night's sleep and set a new goal tomorrow. Self-doubt, lack of faith, and destructive behaviors must be set aside. Other exercises direct you to spend thirty minutes alone every day. During this time you are told to concentrate on building a better self-image by visualizing yourself succeeding in whatever is important to you.

Imagine that you're about to go out on a job interview, for example. Dr. Maltz would tell you to "rehearse" the interview in your mind, detail by detail. Imagine what questions you might be asked, and practice answering them. Visualize the way you'll walk into the office, how you'll greet the interviewer, and what you'll do with your hands. This rehearsal will give you the self-confidence you need to convince your future boss that the business can't do without you!

If psychocybernetics sounds too good to be true, Dr. Maltz asks that you give his system three weeks to show results. In that time, he believes, you will experience improvement in your self-awareness and in the quality of your life. Saying to yourself, "I am beginning this day in a new and better way" probably can't hurt—and it might do some good.

SECTION CHECKUP

1 How does biofeedback control body processes that normally can't be influenced by the conscious mind? What uses have been found for biofeedback?

2 What is assertiveness training? How could you use AT techniques when your little brother demands that you change the channel during your favorite TV show?

3 Describe the basic theory of psychocybernetics. How could an athlete use the system to prepare to run a mile under four minutes?

15.4 WHICH THERAPIES COMBINE SELF-REALIZATION TECHNIQUES WITH TRADITIONAL PSYCHOTHERAPY?

A number of psychotherapy systems that combine traditional practices with new and experimental methods have emerged in recent years. Most of them have attracted as much criticism as acceptance. As with all new approaches in psychology, the critics counsel a "go-slow" approach—even as enthusiastic patients shout that they've found the perfect solution to their emotional problems.

These new therapies have little in common except that they all try to help disturbed people find healthier ways of coping with life. In this section you'll learn about primal therapy, reality therapy, and family therapy.

Primal therapy

The room is padded. A number of adults, young and old, are crawling around on the floor. Two of them raise their heads and scream, a terrifying blend of pain and rage. The other people pound on the floor and walls with their fists. Therapists move among them, encouraging their patients to express the long-buried feelings that torment them (see Figure 15.7).

Dr. Arthur Janov, a psychologist and psychiatric social worker, refers to this unique process as *primal therapy*. Along with Freud and other psychoanalysts, Janov believes that neurotic behavior

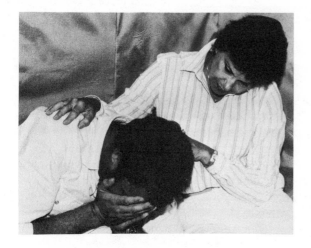

Figure 15.7

Primal Therapy as formulated by Dr. Arthur Janov allows patients to relive painful early-childhood experiences in order to resolve neurosis. How does this "primal experience" in a padded room contribute to that goal?

Dr. Janov tries to help each of his patients experience that primal moment. After they have had their "primal experience," Janov says, his patients lose their anxiety, depression, and nervous habits. Better still, he insists, they can cope successfully with their problems, free at last of the chains of the past. Janov's flat certainty that "primal therapy offers the only cure for neurosis," however, has drawn fire from a large number of psychologists. Most evidence suggests, as you have learned earlier, that no single therapy can be labeled as a certain cure or the only cure for mental illness.

develops out of the unmet needs of childhood. Most adults, he feels, build up defenses against the pain. Repressed memories, inability to feel deeply, and dependence on tobacco, drugs, and alcohol are common defense mechanisms. Unlike most traditional therapists, Dr. Janov insists that these defenses can be broken down and "primal pain" released only through screaming.

Talking about past experience in the Freudian style, the primal therapist explains, widens the gulf between thought and feeling. Primal therapy thus begins with a three-week period of almost constant therapy. Patients are asked to give up smoking, drinking, drugs, and other habits that Janov believes grow out of built-up tension. Primal therapists teach patients how to relax and also how to deepen their breathing. At the same time, patients learn to "primal"—to scream out the pain of the past. After this intensive therapy, patients join primal groups that meet two or three times a week for several months.

Primal therapy grew out of an experience Janov had with two of his patients when he was working in a Freudian clinic. When he instructed these patients to call out to their parents one day, they repeatedly shouted, "Mommy! Daddy!" Then they broke into an eerie scream. Afterward, they said that they had gone through a painful emotional experience but that they could now "see" reality.

Reality therapy

It's all right with Dr. William Glasser if Chris is a junkie and a car thief—as long as he is willing to accept the consequences of those choices. But, Dr. Glasser would also tell Chris, there must be a better way of taking care of your needs.

Dr. Glasser, a practicing psychiatrist, refers to this low-key way of helping patients as *reality therapy*. He doesn't think much of traditional psychotherapy, with its emphasis on past experiences. What's done can't be changed, he says. Instead, Dr. Glasser concentrates on improving his patients' self-awareness here and now. He refers to his formula for reality therapy as the three *R*'s: reality, responsibility, and right-and-wrong.

Reality therapists begin by setting up a close personal relationship with their patients. Once Chris trusts his therapist, the two can work together to identify the unhealthy behaviors that dominate Chris's life. The payoff starts when Chris makes a commitment to act more responsibly in one small area of his life.

Dr. Glasser makes no grand promises for reality therapy. He doesn't even claim that his therapy will make people happy. All anyone can do, Dr. Glasser explains, is to give people a fair chance of finding happiness for themselves. Even with such modest claims, reality therapy has helped many neurotics, delinquents, drug addicts, and other difficult patients return to productive lives.

Reality therapists also promote a self-realization technique that everyone can practice. Addiction is great, Dr. Glasser says, if people become addicted to things that are good for them. Dr. Glasser defines this *positive addiction (PA)* as any relaxing activity that makes you feel good. To qualify for a PA, you must set aside thirty minutes a day for "doing your thing." Depending on your skills and interests, you can choose from any number of sports or hobbies: guitar playing, painting, sewing, meditation, gardening, bicycling, model building, jogging, and so on.

It's not hard to become positively addicted. Choose an activity that you can do by yourself, so you won't have to worry about looking for a partner every day. You'll also want to choose a PA that has some physical, spiritual, or emotional value for you. Never criticize yourself for your performance, and don't set goals. The idea of PA is to let the mind relax and escape from the day's pressures. Many people depend on alcohol, coffee, cigarettes, or other negative addictions to relieve tension. PA, Dr. Glasser insists, will get you hooked on healthy habits. You'll have fun, and you'll also gain awareness of your own potential for positive growth.

Family therapy

Family therapists break many of the rules set up by traditional therapy systems. Although not all family therapists agree on methods, many share the ideas developed by therapist and teacher Virginia Satir (see BioBox, pages 476–477). Therapists who follow Satir's methods insist on treating an entire family rather than a single individual. To understand a particular situation, they often hold therapy sessions in the family home. Occasionally, they include the family dog in a group session. After all, the way a family treats its pets says a lot about the way they treat each other. Over a number of sessions the therapist will try any technique that might work: psychodrama, encounter tactics, or even a game of musical chairs (to see who ends up sitting in daddy's chair).

With American families more unstable than ever, family therapy has grown in importance. It may be Belle's withdrawn be-

Figure 15.8

What's your PA? Dr. William Glasser believes that everyone needs a totally absorbing activity that will relieve the tensions of daily life.

BioBox

VIRGINIA SATIR:
THE FAMILY CAN BE A FORCE FOR CREATIVE GROWTH

As a therapist, Virginia Satir (1916–   ) has developed a system of working with families that departs from traditional psychotherapy. As a teacher, she has trained doctors, psychologists, social workers, and counselors around the world. As a person, she is remembered in the words of famous psychologist Fritz Perls, who called Satir the most nurturing person he had known.

Satir graduated from the University of Chicago in 1948 with a degree in social work. Since then she has worked in mental-health clinics, hospitals, family-service agencies, growth centers, public-welfare agencies, and medical schools. She has also written books and articles dealing with her belief that individual emotional problems always relate back to the specific family setting. Family life is like an iceberg, Satir says. Most people are aware of only one tenth of what is going on around them. A family's success, she adds, depends on understanding the feelings and needs that lie beneath everyday family events.

In her book *Peoplemaking,* Satir describes the troubled family.

> . . . the bodies and faces tell of their plight. Bodies are either stiff and tight, or slouchy. Faces look sullen, or sad, or blank like masks. Eyes look down and past people. Ears obviously don't hear. Voices are either harsh and strident, or barely audible. There is little evidence of

havior at school that brings the family to the attention of a therapist. But family therapists believe that Belle cannot be evaluated or treated outside her home situation. One major task is to bring Belle's father into the therapy. Many men resist therapy, but once the family begins seeing a therapist they usually join in to find out what's going on. If Belle's case is typical, her problem will relate to conflicts within the home, often between her parents. In other cases, the therapist may discover that the members of the family haven't learned to value one another as people worthy of love and capable of change.

According to family therapists, everyone in the household shares in the responsibility when a family member is disturbed. Group discussions open up new lines of communication and spotlight the roles that each member plays in the family structure. To bring about change, the therapist tries to get one person started in a new direction. Then, like a line of dominoes, the other family members will be forced to fall into new ways of dealing with that one member and then with their own problems. As tensions decrease and both adults and children learn to be honest with each other, the family can heal itself.

friendship among individual family members, little joy in one another. . . . The adults are so busy telling their children what to do and what not to do that they never find out who they are, never get to enjoy them as people.

By contrast, Satir writes about the nurturing family, with its aliveness, honesty, and love. She feels that if she lived in such a family

> I would be listened to and would be interested in listening to others; . . . I could openly show my affection as well as my pain and disapproval; I wouldn't be afraid to take risks because everyone in my family would realize that some mistakes are bound to come with my risk-taking — that my mistakes are a sign that I am growing. I would feel like a per-

son in my own right—noticed, valued, loved, and clearly asked to notice, value, and love others.

Many families wear dark glasses without knowing it, Satir says. Only when they stumble and lose their glasses do they realize that it's light outside. The important thing is that families learn from their mistakes.

> If you discover that something is going wrong in your family, treat it as you would when the red light goes on in your car, indicating that the engine is overheating. . . . Stop—investigate—and see what you can do. If you can't change it, find someone you trust who can. Whatever you do, don't waste your time moaning about "poor me" and "bad you."

Can you think of a family in your neighborhood that could profit from family therapy? What signs do you see that suggest that the family is in trouble? If you're thinking about what kind of family you will create some day, pick up Virginia Satir's very readable book, *Peoplemaking*. It has some excellent awareness exercises to help you get started on the right track.

Reprinted by permission of the author and the publisher from *Peoplemaking* by Virginia Satir. Palo Alto, California. Science & Behavior Books Inc. 1972.

SECTION CHECKUP

1 Why do primal therapists insist that their patients scream?

2 How does reality therapy differ from both psychoanalysis and from primal therapy? What is the value of a positive addiction?

3 Why does the family therapist insist that all members of the family take part in the therapy sessions?

15.5 HOW CAN TRANSACTIONAL ANALYSIS HELP PEOPLE STAY IN THE "OK" POSITION?

Psychoanalyst Eric Berne didn't think that psychology should belong only to people with doctor's degrees and a habit of using long words. When Berne talked about be-

havior, he used terms everyone can understand. Even the name of his system, which he called *Transactional Analysis*, has been shortened to *TA*. Another TA psychologist,

Tom Harris, added the concept of "OK" and "not-OK." To be OK means to feel good about yourself and others; to be not-OK means that you feel bad about yourself and others. TA, in brief, gives people a nontechnical way of understanding their behavior and changing it if they want to.

The three ego states

Have you ever noticed how the same person can shift from one personality to another in a flash? For example, Mom is just sitting down to dinner with the family. Listen to her tone of voice.

"Jimmy, get your elbows off the table right now!" (Spoken like a true *parent*, right? You recognize the old shape-up-your-table-manners routine, spoken in a stern, commanding voice.)

But then Dad asks her to describe what happened when she went to pay the water bill. "The people there were very helpful," she replies. "They found the error right away, and I wrote them a check for what we owed." (Can you spot the switch? She had information to give, and she gave it in a calm, *adult* voice.)

Finally, the meal is over and Dad tells the kids to wash the dishes. He's going to take Mom to a movie. "That's great!" she beams. "I'll be ready in a minute!" (Another change. She sounds just like a *child*, bubbling over at the thought of having fun.)

Mom's different personalities during those few minutes illustrate one of Eric Berne's key insights. He said that everyone has three *ego states*, or ways of behaving and thinking. Each ego state can be recognized by what you say and how you act while you're in that ego state (see Figure 15.9). The ego states are the Parent, the Adult, and the Child (P-A-C). A newborn infant starts life with only a Child ego state, but the Parent and Adult begin to develop soon after birth.

Parent ego state. Your Parent is made up of all the messages you received from your parents and other adults when you were little. These messages are mostly instructions, advice, and commands, but children also learn Parent behavior by watching what grown-ups do. Much of your Parent information is of the "how-to" variety: how to get dressed, how to behave in church, how to change a tire. But imagine that you've received ten dollars too much change at the market. What will you do next? Your Parent voice will probably say, "Give it back. You'll feel guilty if you keep it." You can ignore that instruction, but your Parent always speaks for the moral values you learned as a child.

If you listen carefully, you'll discover that your Parent has a dual personality. It can be a *Nurturing Parent* one minute and a *Critical Parent* the next. Your Nurturing Parent takes care of people. When you say to a friend, "I know you're busy today. I'll mail those packages for you," you're in your Nurturing Parent. By contrast, your Critical Parent's job is to criticize, command, and judge other people. If you've ever raised your voice and said something like "Sherry, don't play with that dirty puppy!" you've heard your own Critical Parent speaking.

Adult ego state. You might think of your Adult ego state as your own private computer. The Adult gathers information, tests it, and files it away for later use. Your Adult also checks out the information stored away in the Parent and Child. When you were little, you were told that fires burn—but your Adult had to test out that fact to make sure.

You make your best decisions when you're in your Adult. Perhaps you've had your eye on a new stereo. Your Parent would likely say, "Save your money; you might need it later." Then your Child would jump in with, "Buy it right now! I want it!" But your Adult will analyze the purchase from all angles before making a decision. Whether you buy the stereo or not, your Adult decision will be a rational one, made without emotion.

Figure 15.9

TA'S EGO STATES: RECOGNIZING PARENT, ADULT, AND CHILD

Once you recognize the signals, you can spot ego states in yourself and in others. The chart below shows you what to look and listen for.

	EGO STATE	TYPICAL STATEMENTS	TONE OF VOICE	TYPICAL ATTITUDE
PARENT	 CRITICAL PARENT	"Don't do that." "You should..." "You must..." "You always..." "You'd better..." "Be good."	Critical Loud Disgusted Scheming Whining Superior	Judgmental Moralistic Dictatorial Rigid Comparing Demanding respect Demanding love
	 NURTURING PARENT	"I love you." "Take care." "Be happy." (and other words that are consoling, comforting, re-assuring)	Soft Comforting Concerned	Caring Understanding Giving
ADULT	 ADULT	"How, what, where, who, why?" "It seems to me..." "Let's get on with it." "Will it work?" "Here's what I think..."	Appropriate to situation and feeling. Calm Controlled Businesslike	Flexible Confident Supportive Realistic Practical Alert Open
CHILD	 FREE CHILD	"Wow!" "I hope..." "I wish..." "I can't..." "I want..." "I don't want to..." "What fun!"	Emotional Laughing Crying Loud	Impulsive Uninhibited Any feeling: happy sad, mad, scared
	 ADAPTED CHILD	"If you want..." "I guess I'll have to." "If you say so." "Is this OK?" "Do I have to?" (and other words that show compliance)	Sweet Placating Repetitive Annoying	Complaining Demanding Jealous Ashamed Seeking attention
	 REBEL CHILD	"I won't..." "Make me!" "Aw, nobody will care..." (and other defiant, rebellious words)	Angry Defiant Rebellious	Seeking power Seeking revenge Demanding own way

Child ego state. If a child has an Adult, does an adult have a Child ego state? Most definitely, says TA! Your Child is made up of all the impulses natural to children plus your childhood memories. TA says that this *Free Child* is the source of your joy, excitement, creativity, and zest for living. Everyone has a Free Child, but many adults have forgotten how to let theirs out. Instead, they become grumpy, joyless individuals. When you're in your Free Child, you smile and laugh and have fun. Games, dances, being with good friends, and other creative activities give your Free Child a chance to take over.

Along with your Free Child, parental influences and restrictions also may have given you an *Adapted Child* or a *Rebel Child*. The Adapted Child wants so desperately to gain approval that it gives up its own needs to satisfy other people. An Adapted Child does what it's told, minds its manners, and speaks only when spoken to. If you hear someone say, "I'll do that if you want me to," when really meaning, "I don't want to do that," you hear the Adapted Child. The Rebel Child, in contrast, decides

early in life that adults don't really know anything. The Rebel Child refuses to live by the rules everyone else accepts. You've possibly seen the Rebel Child in other students, as when Jim told his teacher, "No, I won't do that assignment, and you can't make me!" Carried to an extreme, an out-of-control Rebel Child can lead someone to oppose all authority—whether it means running through red lights or starting revolutions.

Transactional Analysis

When you were a baby, you needed food, warmth, dry clothes, and a great deal of love. TA refers to the love and good feelings people give each other as *strokes*. When you rub a baby's back, that's an obvious stroke. But saying something pleasant to another person ("Hey, your new haircut really looks good!") is also a stroke. Interactions with other people while in search of strokes lead to transactions, which consist of a stimulus (you say something) and a response (the other person replies). When you don't get enough strokes, you start feeling "not-OK."

Figure 15.10

The overwhelming power of parents often leaves children in what TA calls a "not-OK" position. This child will now be forced to learn unhealthy behaviors to earn the strokes so necessary to life.

(Figure 15.10 shows how easily a child can be put into a "not-OK" position.)

TA analyzes two main types of transactions.

Complementary transactions. When a transaction can be diagrammed so that the speakers' two ego states are talking directly to each other, it is a *complementary transaction*. Complementary transactions make it possible for people to get on with business. Typical transactions involve Adult-Adult exchanges of information (Figure 15.11a), Parent-Child arguments (Figure 15.11b), or Child-Child discussions about having fun (Figure 15.11c).

Crossed transactions. How many times have you said something, only to get back a response that throws the transaction off track? In TA, such breakdowns are *crossed transactions* (Figure 15.12). You may start out speaking to Paula's Adult, but, when her Child answers back, your Parent tends to take over. At that point, useful communication stops until someone switches ego states.

As you gain experience in recognizing ego states, you'll be better prepared to cope with crossed transactions. The TA rule is to go into or stay in your Adult ego state when you get into a crossed transaction. In most cases, this step will bring the other person into his or her Adult as well. If the switch doesn't work, break off the transaction. If you don't, you're probably about to get hooked into a game.

Games analysis

If a friend asks you to play a game, you'll probably answer, "Sure, I like games." But Eric Berne wasn't talking about tennis or Monopoly when he described "the games people play" in his best-selling book of the same name. When Dr. Berne speaks of *games*, he's talking about psychological games, the kind no one plays for fun.

The person who starts the game wants a payoff. If everyone in the game plays according to the rules, the good game player can collect a prize at the end of the game.

Figure 15.11

COMPLEMENTARY TRANSACTIONS

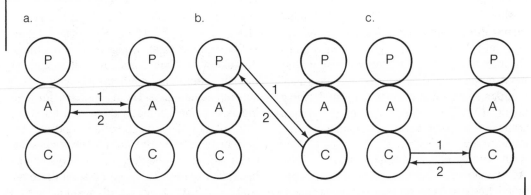

a.

b.

c.

1 *Adult:* What time is it?

2 *Adult:* It's half past two.

1 *Critical Parent:* Eat your spinach.

2 *Rebel Child:* Ycch! I hate spinach.

1 *Free Child:* Let's dance!

2 *Adapted Child:* Do you think we should?

Figure 15.12

CROSSED TRANSACTIONS

a.

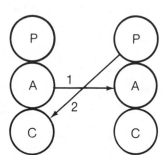

b.

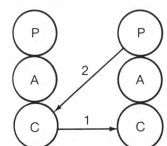

c.

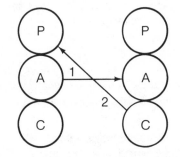

1 *Adult:* Dad, can I use the car Friday night?

2 *Critical Parent:* What's wrong with your feet? Walk! I did when I was your age.

1 *Free Child:* I can't wait 'til Christmas gets here!

2 *Nurturing Parent:* You've been so good Santa is sure to bring you lots of presents.

1 *Adult:* That cake looks lovely, but I'm on a diet.

2 *Rebel Child:* Diets are for dummies. If you don't eat it, I will.

Unlike a Superbowl win, however, psychological games pay off in negative strokes. Even worse, these games prevent honest communication.

Most people learn to play psychological games during childhood. As they grow up, they get better at carrying their games through to a payoff. Dr. Berne thought that most games serve to conceal people's real feelings, particularly those they feel guilty about. In a TA game, many of the actual transactions go on beneath the surface. In a game called "Ain't It Awful" (Figure 15.13), what sounds like a complementary Adult-Adult exchange between two older people (solid lines) covers up the actual transaction. The dotted lines represent what Harry and Joyce are really saying. Their Critical Parents don't understand the changes taking place in society. Good "Ain't It Awful" players can keep a game going for a long time.

Once you catch on to the idea, you can easily spot other games. In "Uproar," for example, husband and wife pick fights with each other so that they won't have to deal with the deeper problems of their marriage. "Kick Me" players, on the other hand, deliberately forget assignments or make mistakes so that someone will scold or punish them. This confirms their negative self-image and gives them an excuse for feeling sorry for themselves. Talented "Yes But" players set up a problem and ask for help in solving it. But no matter what solutions you offer, the response always comes back, "Yes, but . . ." You'll soon discover that "Yes But" players really want attention and sympathy, not answers. People play these games over and over, like a child who never gets tired of playing patty-cake.

It's useful to remember that gameplayers prize the negative feelings that games give them—but games will never make anyone

Figure 15.13

A GAME CALLED "AIN'T IT AWFUL"

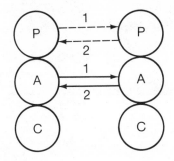

1 *Harry:* Ain't it awful how those kids listen to such terrible music?

2 *Joyce:* Yes, whatever happened to the good music we enjoyed when we were growing up?

happy or healthy. When someone starts a game, you have three choices: You can play the game; you can walk away from it; or you can try to help the person understand what he or she is doing. But don't expect anyone to appreciate your efforts to stop a game once it's started. Most people have been programmed since childhood to repeat the same behaviors over and over.

Script analysis

Imagine for a moment that you have a tiny tape recorder inside your head. You were born with it, and it's been recording everything that's happened to you ever since. Today, whenever you face a problem, that tape recorder plays back a childhood message that tells you what to do. TA refers to those messages as your *life script*. Most of your script messages were recorded during transactions between you and your parents. As a child, for example, you might have been told over and over that you were clumsy. As a result, your script now calls for you to *be* clumsy whenever agility is called for.

The first step to rewriting a poor life script is to understand just how you've been

scripted in the first place. You might find out that your Parent has convinced your Adult that you really are a clumsy person. Backed into that not-OK position, your Adult makes sure that you follow the script. Every time you stumble or hit your thumb with a hammer you're saying to the world, "See, I really am clumsy. Don't you feel sorry for me?" TA teaches that you *can* stop tripping over your own feet and write yourself a more rewarding life script. Some people can do so on their own, while others need the help of a therapist.

TA as therapy

The simplicity of TA's ideas has made it a popular part of the self-awareness movement. Books, magazine articles, TV talk shows, workshops, and TA training groups have introduced millions of people to P-A-C, games theory, stroking, and other TA concepts. The movement that Eric Berne started can be effectively applied to both simple adjustment problems and serious neuroses. Young and old alike seem to respond well to TA's nontechnical way of explaining the causes of their self-defeating

TA CONTRACT

Contract written by _Pat Garibaldi_ Date _10/7_

1. Describe the behavior pattern or attitude you wish to change:

I'd like to get more involved in my psych class.
But I feel too shy, and I never do.

2. State exactly what the new behavior will be:

When I complete this contract, I'll feel confident enough
to join in class discussions or activities at least once a day.

3. List three specific steps you will take to fulfill the contract:

(a)_I will study harder so I'll know what I'm talking about._

(b)_I'll get to know the teacher better so I won't feel so shy._

(c)_I'll raise my hand every day until I'm called on._

Set a date for completing each step: (a)_10/11_ (b) _10/14_ (c) _10/18_

4. How will you know that you've fulfilled the contract? _I'll be joining in_
without making it a specific thing to do. I'll also be more
involved in my other classes. It will feel natural.

5. Set a target date for completion of the contract: _10/28_

6. All contracts include a payoff. How will you reward yourself for completing your contract?

I'll reward myself with a special night out with my friends.

_____Pat Garibaldi_____ Signed _____10/7_____ Date

_____Mrs. Jane Carson-Smith_ Witness _____10/8_____ Date

Figure 15.14

behavior. Therapists who work with disturbed teenagers in hospitals and detention homes report particularly good results.

One common technique used in TA groups is the TA contract. A TA contract singles out a specific negative behavior and sets up a step-by-step plan to change it. Assume, for example, that Pat Garibaldi wants to get over her shyness. If Pat really wants to become more outgoing, a TA contract can show her the way. First, she must zero in on a specific situation in which her shyness keeps her from doing something she badly wants to do. Just working on shyness as a general personality trait doesn't usually accomplish much.

In this case, Pat decides that she wants to take a more active role in her psychology class. She states her goal in clear, simple language from her Adult ego state. She must be in her Adult because her Parent will promise almost anything to satisfy her Child. Pat's Child, meanwhile, loves to make resolutions it never intends to keep. Only the Adult can write a successful TA contract.

As you can see (Figure 15.14), Pat's contract spells out every step of her battle against shyness. Following through on the contract won't be easy, but success will give her enough self-confidence to tackle another area where her shyness interferes with her life. That effort may not be earthshaking, but it can make a big difference in Pat's growth as a person.

SECTION CHECKUP

1 What are the three basic ego states identified by TA? What role does each ego state play in the personality?

2 What is meant by a complementary transaction? A crossed transaction? What can you do when you run into a crossed transaction?

3 Why does TA consider gameplaying a negative behavior? Give two examples of "games people play."

4 Define the TA concept of a life script. How can a TA contract be used to change a negative script?

LOOKING BACK: A SUMMARY

1 People young and old are turning to the self-realization movement (SRM) in an effort to improve the quality of their lives. Most of these people aren't emotionally disturbed, but they are troubled by feelings of loneliness, anxiety, and insecurity. They hope that one or another of the new SRM programs can make their lives happier and more productive.

2 The self-realization movement offers growth and self-discovery rather than treatment for neurotic disorders. People are encouraged to look honestly at themselves, communicate openly with others, develop their potential for growth, and leave self-defeating behaviors behind. Seeking self-realization also carries risks, however. Some people have been hurt by groups whose leaders do not have proper training. Others are disappointed when a particular group cannot live up to its promises.

3 One segment of the self-realization movement treats emotional problems through body movement and manipulation. These groups believe that repressed emotions can be released when rigid, contracted muscles are set free. The Feldenkrais method uses intricate dance movements and exercises to improve posture and flexibility. Structural integration (rolfing) uses deep, painful massage to free the body and to release repressed emotions. In bioenergetic analysis, participants stretch, twist, kick, and scream as they "get in touch with their bodies." Followers of these body-oriented therapies believe that they reduce stress and release their natural creative energies.

4 Research shows that the mind is capable of expanding beyond its present limits. Biofeedback teaches people how to control involuntary body processes (heart rate, temperature, brain waves, blood pressure, and the like). Special biofeedback machines provide information on what's happening inside the body. After a few sessions, the subject is usually able to control the body function that the machine is monitoring. Biofeedback training has been used to control asthma, pain, migraine headaches, high blood pressure, and other chronic conditions.

5 Assertiveness training (AT) teaches people to stand up for their rights. Specific techniques include fogging, broken record, negative assertion, and self-disclosure. These and other AT methods help non-assertive people develop better communication skills and a nonviolent way of dealing with other people in business and social situations. Psychocybernetics uses positive thinking to program the mind for success. Daily practice of this technique aims at removing self-doubt and prepares people to work to their full potential.

6 Several new therapies combine self-realization ideas with conventional treatment methods. Primal therapy attempts to change neurotic behavior by forcing people to relive the pain experienced during infancy and early childhood. These repressed memories are released by screaming, a process called the *primal experience*. By contrast, reality therapy ignores the past and concentrates on building up a sense of responsibility and a positive self-image. Reality therapy doesn't claim to make people happy. Instead, it tries to give them a chance to find happiness for themselves. Reality therapists also promote positive addictions—those relaxing hobbies and sports that leave people more aware of their ability to achieve positive growth.

7 Unlike most other therapies, family therapy works with the entire family group. Family therapists believe that even if only one person in the family is disturbed, everyone shares in the problem. To bring about change, the therapist tries to get at least one family member started in a new direction. Family therapy has no set procedure; therapists will try any technique that seems useful. The goal is to break down the barriers that prevent close, loving communication among family members.

8 Eric Berne's Transactional Analysis (TA) uses simple language to explain human behavior. According to the concept of ego states, every person has a Parent, an Adult, and a Child inside. People switch from one ego state to another depending on the situations they find themselves in. Transactional Analysis shows how communication breaks down when the wrong ego state responds to a statement or question. Games analysis describes the psychological games people play. These games always involve a negative payoff and grow out of the individual's inability to gain strokes in a more positive way.

9 Script analysis looks at the life-shaping messages people are given during childhood. Negative scripts can be rewritten once people figure out the script that is controlling their lives. A common script puts people in the not-OK position, which means that they do not feel good about themselves. TA's goal is to help them move into the OK position. TA has proved effective as a therapy because it concentrates on changing self-defeating behaviors in a clear-cut, logical way.

PUTTING YOUR KNOWLEDGE TO WORK

Terms you should know

Adapted Child	bioenergetic analysis	Child ego state
Adult ego state	biofeedback	complementary transaction
assertiveness training (AT)	broken record	Critical Parent

crossed transaction

family therapy

Feldenkrais method

fogging

Free Child

free information

games

life script

negative assertion

negative inquiry

Nurturing Parent

Parent ego state

positive addiction (PA)

primal therapy

psychocybernetics

reality therapy

Rebel Child

rolfing

self-disclosure

self-realization movement (SRM)

strokes

structural integration

Transactional Analysis (TA)

workable compromise

Objective questions

1 The major goal of the self-realization movement is to (*a*) develop people's ESP abilities (*b*) cure psychotic behavior (*c*) help people make their lives happier and more productive (*d*) improve the body's posture and flexibility.

2 If you join a self-realization group, choose one that (*a*) promises quick and easy answers to difficult emotional problems (*b*) does not have a licensed or well-trained leader (*c*) requires investment of large sums of money without any guarantee of refund (*d*) is recommended by a health professional.

3 You just walked into a room where people of all ages were going through a series of slow, intricate exercises designed to break bad emotional habits. You know you're watching (*a*) a rolfing session (*b*) Feldenkrais method (*c*) primal therapy (*d*) biofeedback training.

4 If you go in for a rolfing session, be prepared to (*a*) receive deep, painful muscle manipulation (*b*) learn how to meditate (*c*) crawl around screaming like a baby (*d*) learn about brain waves.

5 The technique most directly useful for treating migraine headaches would be (*a*) psychocybernetics (*b*) assertiveness training (*c*) Transactional Analysis (*d*) biofeedback.

6 According to assertiveness training, when a waiter in a restaurant brings you a badly cooked steak, you should (*a*) eat the steak but don't leave a tip (*b*) angrily demand to see the manager right away (*c*) calmly but firmly insist that a second, properly cooked steak be brought to you (*d*) get up and leave the restaurant.

7 Primal therapy requires that patients scream out their pain in order to (*a*) achieve an alpha state (*b*) create a positive addiction (*c*) relax tense, knotted-up muscles (*d*) release the repressed pain of early life experiences.

8 Which of the following therapists would be most likely to say, "Before I can treat Tommy's neurotic behavior, I must set up a meeting that includes Tommy, his parents, and his sister"? (*a*) a family therapist (*b*) a reality therapist (*c*) a primal therapist (*d*) a psychoanalyst

9 If you hear a mother say to her child, "Come on, let's run on the beach and let the waves try to catch us," she's most likely in the ego state known as (*a*) Critical Parent (*b*) Adult (*c*) Free Child (*d*) Rebel Child.

10 In TA terms, you should avoid games because (*a*) game players always end up in the "I'm OK, You're OK" position (*b*) games prevent honest communication (*c*) game players never earn strokes of any kind (*d*) playing games is a sure sign of mental illness.

Discussion questions

1 Why have so many people been attracted to the self-realization movement in recent years? Are there any possible dangers in this search for self-fulfillment?

2 What would you say to someone who claims to have discovered the "only certain cure" for a troubled personality?

3 Contrast the treatment for neurotic behavior found in primal therapy with that used in reality therapy.

4 Describe how you could use biofeedback to control your heart rate. What uses can you think of for biofeedback techniques?

5 What do psychologists mean by "the power of positive thinking"? Describe how psycho-cybernetics and assertiveness training make use of this principle.

6 What if you read tomorrow that a psychologist had just started a new self-realization therapy based on marathon running and weight lifting? Could such a program help troubled people? Why or why not?

Activities

1 With the help of your parents and psychology teacher, arrange to visit a self-realization group. Look for notices of meetings on supermarket and library bulletin boards, in the newspaper, and at free clinics or mental-health agencies. Try to find out something about the nature of the techniques used by the group before you go. After the meeting, write a report of your impressions to share with your class.

2 Do you have a behavior pattern or an attitude that you'd like to change? Perhaps you want to improve your grades in a particular class. Or you may feel that you lose your temper too easily whenever you discuss anything with your parents. Whatever the behavior, once you've recognized the need to change, a TA contract can help you. Follow the sample contract on page 484. Copy the six steps on a sheet of paper, and then fill in the blanks in your own words. With the help of the contract, you may discover that you can change negative behaviors in a relatively short time.

3 If you're not already familiar with assertiveness training, study the AT techniques for a little while. Practice some AT dialogues with friends. You may want to look at Dr. Smith's book to learn more about AT, but the important thing is the good feeling you'll have when you stand up for yourself and assert your rights without aggression.

4 The self-realization movement often uses simple exercises to help you gain self-insight. Try the following exercise, both for the experience and as a chance to learn something about yourself. First, write the names of three people you actively dislike or avoid. Then, without hesitating or blocking out anything, write five descriptive words or phrases that come to mind when you think of each person. When you're finished, compare the lists. Do you find any similarities? Do you tend to classify people as types rather than as individuals? Do your descriptions reflect any prejudices against a particular age group, race, sex, or religion? After analyzing your lists and answering the questions as honestly as possible, sum up the results in a single sentence that also includes a statement of responsibility. For example, "I seem to have trouble getting along with older people, but I'm going to make an effort to understand them better."

5 Here's another useful self-realization exercise. Share this one with someone you feel close to. Begin by sitting quietly together. Each of you should let your mind drift. Then pick a color that fits the way you feel right now. Choose a second color that fits your partner. Share your choices. Why do you think each of you picked the colors you did? Talk about it. You can go on to choose animals, flowers, even songs or TV characters in the same way. Such fantasy exercises give your Free Child a chance to express your creativity—and you'll also find that sharing such experiences can make a relationship deeper and stronger.

For further reading

Dyer, Wayne W. *Your Erroneous Zones*. Scranton, PA: Funk & Wagnalls, 1976. Dyer's book is typical of many take-charge-of-your-own-life books. *Your Erroneous Zones* leads you step-by-step toward recognizing and overcoming the areas in your personality that block you from enjoying a free and productive life.

Greening, Tom and Dick Hobson. *Instant Relief: The Encyclopedia of Self-Help*. New York: Seaview Books, 1979. The authors believe that anxiety can be reduced "when you are shown a way of seeing your problems that gives you hope." This common-sense book covers one hundred useful topics, including anger, nightmares, stagefright, overeating, and money worries.

Harris, Thomas A. *I'm OK—You're OK: A Practical Guide to Transactional Analysis*. New York: Harper & Row, 1969. Still the best introduction to TA, Dr. Harris's book is exactly the sensible, down-to-earth guide the title promises it to be. If you'd prefer a simpler approach to TA, try Alvyn M. Freed's *TA for Teens*—easy reading, lots of pictures, and aimed right where you live.

Howard, Jane. *Please Touch: A Guided Tour of the Human Potential Movement.* New York: McGraw-Hill, 1970. The author traveled almost twenty thousand miles and took part in just about every kind of self-realization program available. She describes her experiences with humor and insight.

Lande, Nathaniel. *Mindstyles/Lifestyles.* Los Angeles: Price, Stern, Sloan, 1976. From traditional psychoanalysis to Full Moon meditation groups, this handsome book covers just about every approach to self-realization presently available. You'll also enjoy the colorful graphics by Corita Kent and R. Buckminster Fuller's thoughtful closing essay.

Maltz, Maxwell. *Power Psychocybernetics for Youth.* New York: Grosset & Dunlap, 1971. Dr. Maltz applies his positive-thinking techniques to the problems of young people. His book may be a little preachy, but Maltz is sincere in believing that psychocybernetics will help anyone change failure to success.

16

STRATEGIES FOR COPING

Figure 16.1

CATHY   by Cathy Guisewite

Cathy's problem is pretty funny, isn't it?

Or is it? Sometimes a cartoon strip can zero in on feelings you'd rather not think about. But ignoring loneliness, fear, anxiety, or any other negative emotion doesn't make it go away.

Take a moment to think about what you've read in this book. You've probably learned things about people and behavior you didn't know before. But psychology has more to offer than interesting bits of information. You can use your knowledge to help people find ways to cope with their problems. That means people like Cathy . . . and like you.

No, not everyone will have a nervous breakdown. Psychologists know, however, that sometime in your life you'll have to deal with depression, loneliness, frustration, or grief. Maybe you'll be in a position to help a friend or relative through a bad time, or maybe you'll be the one who needs help. The problem doesn't have to be anything really deep. Just living in this complex world challenges even the most self-actualizing person.

What can psychology do to help someone who can't cope? That's what you'll find out in this chapter. You'll meet eight real persons, each with a painful problem. They'll tell you about themselves and their feelings in their own words. Then a psychologist will explain what's gone wrong and how their behavior can be changed for the better. Finally, you'll be asked to try an awareness exercise related to each case history.

490

Ready? It's time to meet Marjorie, Jim, Rosa, Martin, Tammy, Ralph, Judy, and Eric. You may not know people exactly like them, but you're almost certain to recognize their problems.

CASE HISTORY 1. MARJORIE: OVERCOMING LONELINESS

Marjorie grew up in a close, loving family. On her own now, she lives in a well-furnished apartment. Her job as an assistant editor pays well enough to keep her dressed in the latest styles. When she walks down the street, men turn and take a second look. Marjorie enjoys that. Her friends would say that she's an intelligent, responsible person.

Recently turned twenty-five, she's become increasingly moody of late. When asked to describe her feelings, she remains silent for several minutes. Then she begins by talking about her parents.

"I've always been very close to my parents," she says. "They allowed me to be a child. I never had any chores to do. In college I wrote home every day. I still talk to my mother every day on the telephone. My ambition is to have the same happy married life my parents have enjoyed.

"I need to have someone to do things for," she continues. "I'm always happiest when I have a goal. I always got A's, for instance, to please my mother.

"Last year I had a boyfriend, and for a time it was serious. I was so happy I was bubbling like a kettle." Marjorie's eyes glisten with tears, but she goes on. "Maybe I scared him by coming on too strong. Anyway, he broke off the relationship. Now, not having a boyfriend is really depressing. My life is fine in every other way, except that I don't have a man of my own. That seems to take the fun out of everything else."

Marjorie sinks back into the sofa. Her voice sounds drained of energy. "In the evenings I fantasize a lot about having someone around. I've taught myself how to keep busy when I'm alone. But there's nothing to look forward to on the weekends. I'm depressed because I'm lonely."

Her tears are falling freely now. "Look," she says, "how easily I cry. Most people think I'm strong, but these days I crumble at the least little pressure."

The problem

Marjorie doesn't appear to have the feeling of rejection that sometimes goes with complaints of loneliness. She has an ongoing, loving relationship with her family.

Figure 16.2

Will Marjorie be able to overcome her feeling of loneliness?

She grew up knowing that she was loved, that she was someone rather "special." Yet she's lonely and she admits to feeling depressed.

Marjorie apparently was allowed to stay a child too long. Her closeness to her parents should also be questioned. How many young adults write or call their parents every day? She seems to be quite limited in the number of people she feels close to—and also in the manner of her closeness. You get the feeling that Marjorie lives in a state of eternal girlhood. She shows adequate intellectual development but little emotional growth.

At the same time, Marjorie appears to want someone else to set goals for her. Her attitudes apparently reflect her mother's: A young woman's role is to find an eligible man and marry him. Then she loves and cares for him and builds her life around him. Because Marjorie isn't following this pattern, she feels that she doesn't have a life of her own. When she did have a boyfriend, she smothered him with attention. As she admits, that's probably what drove him away. It might be accurate to say that she's trying to find another parent—in the form of a husband—so that she can live through him.

From a psychologist's point of view, Marjorie can be described as a friendly, intelligent, loving . . . nonperson. She believes that she cannot be complete without a man in her life. Doing things on her own can't possibly be any fun. As she says, "There's nothing to look forward to on weekends." But mature people know that good things don't happen unless they make them happen. As long as Marjorie keeps on waiting for someone else to cure her loneliness, she'll go on being unhappy.

Solutions

Before she can change, Marjorie must recognize that she's been living according to a life script that she has neither questioned nor fashioned for herself. She follows a set of rules programmed for her during childhood. In order to satisfy others, she's supposed to bubble over with good spirits, remain close to her parents, marry when she grows up, and devote the rest of her life to her husband. These aren't totally negative goals, but trying to achieve them under all circumstances will keep Marjorie from finding out who she really is. She needs some time to explore her own interests and needs without the constant pressure of a compelling need to please other people.

After she understands why she feels the way she does, Marjorie can begin a journey of self-exploration. She probably would benefit from counseling by a therapist, who could help her understand the origins of her loneliness. At the same time, she can learn how to make progress through a series of small steps.

The therapist could assure Marjorie that she has many assets to her credit. She is bright, usually cheerful, young, and not seriously neurotic. She is also healthy, loving, and generally able to find pleasure in life. During her search for self-identity, however, she will have to broaden many of her attitudes about men, marriage, and life. If she does marry with her attitudes intact, she may be in for a rude awakening.

LISTEN

If you are in conflict within your self, have the different parts talk out loud to one another.

Listen to what they have to say to each other.

Feel/find out what they/you really want to do.

—BERNARD GUNTHER

A self-awareness exercise for finding your identity

Marjorie's problem isn't unique. Many young people share her feelings of loneliness and uncertain identity. A psychologist would approach this issue by asking you to respond to four questions: Who am I? What do I want out of life? What kind of person am I? What kind of person do I want to be?

Those aren't easy questions to answer. You can make a start, however, by first tackling some smaller ones. Think about or write out your responses to the following*:

1. What activities and experiences do I find the most satisfying and enjoyable?

2. What are my standards of right and wrong?

3. How important are my religious beliefs to me?

4. What are my beliefs concerning love and sex?

5. What kind of career do I really want?

6. Do I desire to marry? To what kind of person? When?

7. Do I desire to have children? How many? When?

8. Where do I want to live?

9. What do I enjoy doing with my free time?

10. What kind of image of myself do I wish to project to others?

11. What kind of people do I enjoy being with, and why?

12. What do I hope to be doing five years from now? Ten years from now? Twenty years from now?

13. What changes do I need to make in order to achieve my personal goals? My career goals?

14. What can I do to improve the quality of my life? The lives of others?

15. What are my thoughts about death and dying?

Your answers to these questions add up to your own sense of self—your identity. You may not be ready to answer all of them now; but as you do, you'll begin making better decisions about your future. More important, you'll direct your life toward goals you've selected for yourself. If she's willing to try, it's not too late for Marjorie to do the same.

CASE HISTORY 2. JIM: MAKING CHOICES FOR THE FUTURE

Jim is a pleasant, soft-spoken young man. At seventeen, he's anxious to make a success of his life. His parents have left him alone to make his own career decisions. But Jim suffers from headaches. At times they're painful enough to put him to bed for several days.

The headaches become worse each time Jim's school counselor calls him in to talk

*Charles Zastrow, Dae Chang, *The Personal Problem Solver* © 1977, pp. 368–369. Adapted by permission of Prentice-Hall, Inc., Englewood Cliffs, N.J.

about next semester's courses or about career choices. When the counselor points out the choices to him, Jim looks angry for a moment. Then his expression softens.

"Maybe you're right," he says. "I dread making choices about my program, because I don't know what I want to do after high school. Most of my friends have already made up their minds. They're the lucky ones! I look at the schedule, though, and I feel confused. I write a few courses down, but then I worry that if I take the wrong things now I'll never catch up."

Figure 16.3

Jim has some decisions to make about his future.

Jim sighs. "I've already thought about three careers. For a while I wanted to be a carpenter, so I took shop courses when I was a freshman. That was fun. I enjoyed learning how to build and fix things. My dad let me repair things around the house. Then I realized that I wanted more from life than just working with wood. I wanted to work with people. So I decided to give up carpentry for a career. But which career?

"That's when I decided that I wanted to be a nurse. I like helping people, and I've always been interested in the body. I took biology in my sophomore year, and now I'm struggling through physiology. My supervisor at the hospital where I do volunteer work says I should take chemistry, too. But my aunt warned me about nursing. First, there's all that hard work for not much money. What's worse, nurses don't have any real power to make decisions about their patients. So, I thought about becoming a doctor. My dad warned me how hard it is to get into medical school, and I got discouraged all over again. I decided to put off the decision for a while.

"Then last semester, I switched to a business major. I mean, it made sense at the time. My friend Angelo convinced me that typing and bookkeeping will always come in handy. I didn't really like the idea of working in an office, but a good bookkeeper can always find a job. And I could work my way through college if I had to."

Jim sighs deeply. "But being a bookkeeper doesn't feel right to me." He raises his hands in mock surrender. "I just don't know what I want to do, and the days are slipping by. You're probably right. Making up my mind *does* give me a headache."

The problem

Jim has already made progress in figuring out the cause of his headaches. He's beginning to realize that his physical symptoms are probably caused by anxiety over making career decisions. This realization doesn't mean that his headaches aren't painful or that they won't recur. But in being honest with himself, Jim has taken the first step toward solving his problem.

In Jim's present state of mind, he must be careful not to overreact. Apparently he hasn't worked out his goals so as to achieve personal and career satisfaction. Other people—his aunt, his father, his friends—push him first one way and then another. Without a foundation of self-insight to build on, he cannot make a decision. But the opposite extreme would be to make a hasty decision born of desperation. His switch to a business major seems to fall into that category. As Jim is beginning to realize, either pattern is self-defeating.

To his credit, Jim seems aware of the difference between talent and training. Once he makes up his mind, he is willing to put in the necessary work to reach his goal. But he worries too much about making a mistake. In time, he'll learn that no choice is perfect. All anyone can do is to find the best alternative among all the imperfect choices. Luckily, no one need be stuck forever with the wrong career. Should Jim choose medicine now, he can still change to another field later on.

Jim also seems to be hoping that some-

LIFE IS NOW

There is no future outside of us; it lies within us, and we make it for ourselves. Rarely do we have large blocks of time in which, uninterrupted, we can start and complete a task. And so novels are read on the bus to and from work, or paintings are dabbled at in bits of time evenings. Life is now.

—IRA TANNER

thing will "turn him on." His passive approach probably will keep him from reaching the highest goal of which he is capable. Even so, Jim has eliminated several choices, and his attitude toward work seems realistic enough. His next step should be to evaluate himself, his abilities, and his goals. Otherwise, he may remain paralyzed by his fear of making a mistake. And that would be the biggest mistake of all.

Solutions

Once Jim understands what he's been doing to himself, he'll probably be ready to accept some advice. His counselor might suggest that he begin by setting aside a morning when he can be by himself. Then he should focus his thinking on four concepts: money, love, ego food, and health. After he writes these four headings on paper, he should fill in the columns as honestly as he can.

When Jim thinks about money, he should make a realistic estimate of what his adult needs will be. Many young people leave home without knowing how expensive it is to rent an apartment, buy a car, travel, and do the other things they've dreamed of. Jim should also try to project his money needs five and ten years into the future. If he's responsible for educating a younger sister, for example, his job will have to provide that level of income. At the same time, Jim cannot ignore the costs of his own education and training. He's already inclined to choose a career in medicine over a bookkeeping job because of the higher pay and greater job satisfaction. Those advantages, however, must be balanced against medicine's long and expensive training period.

Thinking about love gives Jim a chance to consider what he needs from the other people in his life. He may want to marry if the right woman comes along. Jim should also remember that after he leaves his family, he will want to find new friends with whom to share his adult life. The challenge is to accept their closeness without losing his own identity.

Ego food is a shorthand way of describing the satisfaction Jim will need from his work. In that category he should list (1) his genuine interests, (2) what he would take pride in doing with his life, (3) his present abilities and training, and (4) the steps he must take to reach his goals. Far too many people choose careers whose only attraction is a quick return for a minimum investment of effort.

Jim's friend Enrique, for example, left school to work full-time at a gas station. At age seventeen, he felt that the money was marvelous and the work more exciting than going to school. But five years from now Enrique may discover that he's caught in a dead-end job that no longer gives him much satisfaction. If helping people is really a central goal in Jim's life, he should make sure that his future career will give him the chance to do exactly that.

Because of his headaches, Jim should evaluate his health right now. With the help of his doctor, he can also look at other possible physical problems. If he smokes or drinks, is overweight or underweight, has trouble sleeping or other symptoms of potential illness, he can take action right away. The chances are good, however, that his headaches will disappear when he ends his indecision about choosing a career.

A self-awareness exercise for choosing a career

Perhaps you've been going through some of these same uncertainties about making a career choice. If so, the following exercise will help clarify your thinking.

1. If you were free and could do any kind of work you wanted, what would it be? Ignore the barriers, and write down what you *really* want to do. Be as specific as possible.

2. *Close your eyes for a few minutes.* Imagine that you are in the situation you named—doctor, engineer, farmer, secretary, homemaker, pilot, baseball player, social worker, teacher, carpenter, musician, mechanic, accountant, or whatever. Where are you? Describe the setting.

3. What are you doing? What other people are there with you? What are they doing?

4. Did you need any special training to get where you are? What skills or abilities were required?

5. What does this occupation allow you to do that's especially important to you?

6. *Now come back to the present.* How much do you really know about this occupation or activity?

7. What values, abilities, and interests do you have that relate to this type of work?

8. What related occupations would you also consider?

9. What new information do you need before actually choosing this occupation?

10. Is what you want still a dream, or is it a possibility for you?

11. What concrete steps can you take *right now* to make this dream turn into reality?

No one can guarantee that you'll be successful in your career choice. But this type of thoughtful planning and evaluation will give you a head start in the right direction. Twenty years from now, when you look in the mirror and ask who started you in the direction your life has taken, you'll have only one answer: "I made my own choices with my eyes open. For better or worse, I take full responsibility." Would you want it any other way?

CASE HISTORY 3. ROSA: LEARNING TO EXPRESS ANGER

Rosa is nineteen and in search of some answers. Although she's been in encounter groups off and on for a year, they didn't seem to help. She feels unhappy about not being able to develop close relationships with other people. As soon as she does begin to open up with someone else, Rosa complains, something happens to drive the other person away.

"I was raised to be honest about my feelings," she says. "In my family, it was OK for us to yell at one another. We slammed doors, and once my father punched his fist through the door of the kitchen cabinet. I

Figure 16.4

Rosa hasn't learned how to handle anger in a nonaggressive way.

mean, isn't that better than hitting somebody? Sure, we said things we didn't always mean, but we got over it."

Rosa clenches her fist, then slowly opens it. "It's good for you to let off steam—better than bottling it up inside. If you don't let go, it's ulcer city. When someone gets to you, you can pretend to be a nice gal and take it, or you can let them have it. That's just being honest."

"Look, if people know you and like you, it shouldn't matter if you mouth off now and then." Rosa smiles. "After all, they have the same privilege back. I think it's a pretty insecure person who can't face the truth, anyway. If two friends hang around together, one is bound to rub the other the wrong way sometimes. What I mean is, if something makes me angry, I sound off. It clears the air. It's healthy.

"And if a salesclerk is trying to high-pressure me, it makes sense to be aggressive. You come on strong, and people back down. Lots of people think that to make it in this world you have to be a goody-goody. Just take what comes and keep on smiling." Rosa taps her chest. "Not me. Never!"

The problem

Rosa is having trouble sorting out the difference between being aggressive and being assertive. She hasn't developed the inner controls that allow most people to handle their natural feelings of anger in a constructive way. Instead, Rosa gives herself the luxury of dumping her emotions on others. Her home environment apparently taught her this pattern, and her experiences in encounter groups may have reinforced it. Encounter groups encourage their members to express the feelings they normally repress so that they can learn to deal with those powerful emotions. But Rosa apparently learned only the first half of the lesson.

In time, Rosa can learn that explosive fits of anger don't allow her much room for emotional growth. Behavior that is barely acceptable in young children cannot be tolerated in adults. Rosa's anger may let her feel better about the frustrations of the moment, but when she realizes that she's driven the other person away, she probably feels guilty. Her attempt to find help in encounter groups marks a step forward. It means that she's beginning to realize that her own behavior stands between her and the friends she needs. As it now stands, Rosa can have friends only if they accept her on her terms. Despite all of Rosa's good qualities, few people are going to hang around to serve as targets for her rages.

Solutions

Anyone who has ever been overcome by a surge of anger knows how powerful that feeling can be. For Rosa to change her behavior, she'll have to practice remaining calm. This change doesn't mean that she'll become a doormat. She can still be properly assertive, but she will have to stop telling others how she feels without also listening to what they have to say.

A good starting point for Rosa would be to keep an "anger journal." Rosa's journal would be a record of each day's arguments, insults, and rages. In writing down what

ON UNDERSTANDING YOUR ANGER

The world is not necessarily just. Being good often does not pay off and there is no compensation for misfortune.

You have a responsibility to do your best nonetheless.

—SIDNEY KOPP

happens each day, she'll have a chance to think about her feelings. How often does she give in to her anger? How does she feel about it afterward? When she reviews the journal, she can also grade herself on her own honesty about the reasons behind her outbursts. Does she spot a tendency to excuse herself because "it was really hot today" or because "Steve knows I don't like being teased"? If so, Rosa will learn to recognize such self-serving rationalizations and to deal with them as they occur.

Along with her journal, Rosa can use behavioral techniques to control her aggressive outbursts. The next time she gets into an argument, for example, she might try putting herself into the role of a spectator. As she stands back and "watches" the situation, she can ask herself if the incident really deserves her angry reaction. She can also keep anger from building up by imagining the other person doing something ridiculous. Instead of blowing up when Steve teases her, Rosa should visualize Steve jumping around in a pink gorilla outfit. Silly fantasies such as this can defuse anyone's anger almost instantly.

Another approach would be for Rosa to set a mental timer on herself. She might start by giving herself two minutes for each outburst. Day by day she then chops off ten seconds from the time allowed. As an alternative, she can lengthen the time between feeling anger and expressing it. Either technique will make Rosa more

aware of her own feelings and reactions. After a while, her "anger time" will dwindle down to almost nothing. At the same time, Rosa should keep count of all the times she *could* have given in to anger during the day. At night, if it makes her feel better, she can punch her pillow several times for each incident. Finally, Rosa should watch to see how other people express anger. As she'll find out, angry people aren't so attractive.

At this point, Rosa might reasonably ask if it's ever OK to express anger. After all, if someone shoves ahead of her in line at a concert, she can't ignore it, can she? Rosa has a point. Swallowing your anger doesn't make it go away. Repressed rage eventually reappears, often as aggressive behavior aimed at an innocent third party. Over a long term, the body may also convert repressed anger into physical ailments such as headaches or ulcers.

With assertive behavior, Rosa can handle most problems that once sparked her anger (see Chapter 15, pp. 471–472). Instead of shouting at the person who shoves ahead of her in line, she can say, "Look, we all waited our turn. Go back and get in line like everyone else." If necessary, she can repeat her request several more times. This broken-record technique will cause most people to back down. If the technique doesn't work, Rosa can call for a guard or an usher to take care of the situation. In either event, she won't be left choked up with rage, unable to enjoy the evening.

A self-awareness exercise for expressing anger

Dealing with anger doesn't mean that you can't express what you're feeling. Psychologists believe that you can learn to "fight fair," especially when the conflict is with someone you're close to. For example, if you can get hold of two light, foam-covered paddles, you and your partner can release a tremendous amount of anger by whacking each other harmlessly for several minutes. Such fights have rules, of course. No hitting in areas where physical harm could result! Even the most mild-mannered and repressed person can learn to fight with foam bats—and feel good about it afterward.

Another fair-fight technique is known as the Hurt Museum. This exercise refers to the collection of little injuries and resentments people save up until one day they explode. The Hurt Museum gives you a chance to defuse that time bomb before it goes off. The exercise works as well with parents as with partners your own age. Here are the rules.

1. Both partners must agree to take part in the exercise. Each must play according to the rules.

2. No personal attacks or insults are permitted. You must stick to specific incidents which caused pain and anger. It's OK to say, "I was angry when you didn't call me last night," but not, "You have terrible taste in clothes."

3. Separate for ten minutes and write down all the hurts you've collected from the other person. Concentrate on those you haven't talked about before. You'll probably be surprised at how many little grievances you've been saving up.

4. One person begins by reading his or her list while the other person remains silent. The listener cannot question, defend, or attack what the reader is saying. When the reader finishes, the two change roles. Neither person may discuss any item on either list until both have finished.

5. You now have several options for dealing with the collection of "hurts" the two of you have uncovered:
   (a) "Bury" certain items on each list by agreeing that you'll both erase them from your thinking.
   (b) Trade off some items. For example, you might say, "I'll forget about the time you didn't call me if you'll forget about the time I pushed you off the diving board at the lake."
   (c) Agree that a few items deserve to be discussed in a fair and constructive way. These are the problem areas that could damage a relationship if they're not taken care of. If one person continually forgets to call, for example, that shouldn't be ignored.

Once you've resolved all the "hurts," don't look back. That's the time to move on to a happier, more open relationship. Like Rosa, you'll have learned that anger—whether uncontrolled or repressed—is one of humanity's most destructive emotions.

CASE HISTORY 4. MARTIN: ADJUSTING TO CHANGE

Martin is called into the counselor's office to talk about a drop in his grades. After transferring into his new school with a *B*-plus average, his first-quarter grades have fallen sharply. Seated across from the counselor, he seems small for his fifteen years. He stares at the grade card, unwilling to meet the counselor's gaze.

Finally, he blurts out, "I just don't feel like working. Back at my old school, I was involved with everything and everybody. I'd gone to school with most of the kids all through elementary school and junior high. Everybody knew who I was." Martin blushes. "Not that I was so great, you understand. But I felt I belonged."

His voice rises. "Here, no one goes out of the way to be friendly. Everyone belongs to a clique and doesn't care about anybody else. Nobody needs me, that's for sure. I tried to make friends with a couple of the guys, but it didn't work out. Back home, I lived in a small town. All the kids were interested in horses and farming. That's what I still want to do. Here, all anyone talks about is sports or souped-up cars or making money.

"I had a couple of close friends back there. I mean really close. Each of us knew what the others were thinking without even talking. Moving away from them just about killed me." Martin's smile is bitter. "Sure, they promised to write, but you know how it is. Both of them have owed me a letter for over a month."

A girl knocks on the door and hands the counselor a note. When she is gone, Martin shakes his head. "Did you see that? Betsy's in two of my classes, but she didn't even notice me. The girls are certainly different. They seem to have grown up faster, somehow. Even when they notice me, it's as if they're laughing at me. At home I had plenty of dates, but here they treat me like a punk kid."

Martin rubs his chin. His voice sounds tired. "I just feel out of everything. Sometimes it seems as though I'm invisible—to the teachers, to the guys, to everyone. I know I have to stay here until summer, because my folks won't let me leave. But come June, I'm going to split and head back to where I belong."

The problem

Martin has reacted more severely than most people to a fairly common event in today's mobile society. Uprooted from a secure

Figure 16.5

Can Martin learn to cope with the problems caused by his family's move to a new community?

environment, he's having difficulty accepting his new one. Martin shows good insight about the difference between the two communities, but his evaluations aren't always realistic. Whether he likes it or not, people will always be coming together and separating. He will always be faced with the challenge of adjusting to new situations.

For someone who was so active in his former community, Martin's attitude now tends to be passive. He seems to be expecting people to seek him out. Except for a vague statement about "trying to make new friends," he hasn't taken any positive steps to develop new relationships. At the same time, he is resisting the reality of his changed environment. If Martin really looked, he would find that opportunities for friendship and growth exist on every side. Martin also needs to understand that his dreams of returning to his old home are equally unrealistic. If he went back, he would find changes there, too. People refuse to stand still, no matter how much anyone wants them to stay the same.

Martin's low grades are only a symptom of his unconscious decision to reject his new situation. His earlier involvement in school and social life shows that he has the skills necessary for repeating those successes. As to Martin's evaluation that the girls are somehow different in the new school, the chances are that he has exaggerated small matters of style and manner. People remain basically the same, wherever you go. But you have to dig past surface appearances if you want to contact the real personalities underneath.

Solutions

Once Martin decides to become part of his new community, he has several options. Most important, he must first become an *accepting* person. Other people are quick to sense when they are being measured and rejected. When Martin sincerely reaches out to others, they will respond to him. Second, he needs to map out a program of positive activity. He can begin by checking out the groups that are open to him, such as school clubs, religious groups, athletic teams, Explorer Scouts, 4-H, and the like.

When he finds a group he likes, he should join in wholeheartedly. As he finds new friends who share his interests, he'll quickly lose the feeling that he can't enjoy an active social life.

Close friendships usually happen without too much planning. Martin will find that the activities he enjoys will attract the kind of people to whom he can relate. He will have to adopt a mature attitude about winning friends. He must be sufficiently assertive to make the first efforts at contact, but not so aggressive that people reject him for being pushy.

In time, Martin will find that his new environment isn't as alien as he thought. If he is serious about going back to farming, he will have plenty of time after graduation to complete his agricultural training. But he should also consider the career opportunities in his new community. As he finds friends and joins in new activities, he'll discover that he has much in common with the same people who seemed so different at first.

A self-awareness exercise for evaluating friendships

For most young people, friends are as important as eating and sleeping. The growth and sharing possible in a good friendship provide an important transition from family attachments to the commitments of adult life. Even the best of friendships has its ups

---

YOU CAN NEVER HAVE "ENOUGH"

The outside world can never give you "enough" if you are programmed always to want something you don't already have or more of what you do have. If you always want "more," you will never have "enough."

—KEN KEYES, JR., AND BRUCE BURKAN

and downs, however. Perhaps you're having nagging doubts about the way things are going with a particular friend. If you're ready to take an honest look at the relationship, try the following exercise*.

Directions: Select the word in each statement that *most accurately* describes your friendship. The letter X has been used here so that you can substitute the name of your friend whenever it appears.

1. When I see X, I feel (a) happy, (b) indifferent, (c) nervous.

2. My conversations with X are usually (a) exciting, (b) impersonal, (c) boring.

3. When I talk about a success of my own, X usually responds with (a) pleasure, (b) indifference, (c) envy.

4. When I think of X, I often feel (a) happy, (b) annoyed, (c) depressed.

5. When I disagree with X, it usually leads to a (a) discussion, (b) fight, (c) temporary breakup.

6. When I'm with X, we generally have (a) fun, (b) nothing to do, (c) emotional upsets.

7. When I leave X, I usually feel (a) happy, (b) tired, (c) confused.

8. When I'm working, X usually feels (a) free to let me finish, (b) irritated, (c) rejected.

9. When I'm with X and the conversation stops, X seems to feel (a) at ease with silence, (b) uncomfortable, (c) nervously talkative.

10. When I seem unusually quiet, X (a) asks me what's the matter, (b) tries to get my mind off my troubles, (c) takes my silence personally and gets upset.

11. When I'm supposed to go somewhere with X, I tend to (a) look forward to it, (b) worry about whether it will work out, (c) forget the arrangements we made.

12. When I meet X's other friends, I usually find them to be (a) good company, (b) boring, (c) unpleasant.

13. When we have plans to do something together, X tends to arrive (a) on time, (b) late, (c) with other friends I didn't know were coming.

14. When I give a gift to X, X says (a) "Thank you," (b) "You shouldn't have," (c) "When is your birthday?"

15. Regarding personal interests, X and I (a) have exactly the same ones, (b) have several in common, (c) don't like the same things at all.

16. I sometimes think that I'd like to (a) be just like X, (b) borrow some of X's traits, (c) never be like X.

17. In most ways I feel that X is my (a) equal, (b) superior, (c) inferior.

18. If I have special news to share, X is the person I (a) think of first, (b) tell the next time we meet, (c) tell only when I have to.

19. If I tell X a secret, I'm sure the secret will be (a) kept, (b) told to a few of X's friends, (c) blabbed to everyone X meets.

20. Whenever I get into an argument with someone, X (a) takes my side, (b) stays neutral, (c) tells me I'm in the wrong.

When you've finished the exercise, look at your answers. Score three points for each *a*, two for each *b*, and one for each *c*. A score of 50 or better means that you have a great relationship! Anything from 35–49 suggests that your friendship is like most people's— you have your differences, but the friendship is worth keeping. If the score is under 35, you'll want to think about what's going wrong. Your friend X may be feeling the same way!

*Adapted from Howard M. Newburger and Marjorie Lee, *Winners and Losers: The Art of Self-Image Modification* (New York: David McKay, 1974), copyright Howard M. Newburger and Marjorie Lee, pp. 88–89 and 155–156. The numerical point score in the last paragraph on this page has been added to the original exercise created by Newburger and Lee.

CASE HISTORY 5. TAMMY: COPING WITH DIVORCE

Tammy slips quietly into the counselor's office at the Free Clinic. She looks embarrassed, but she has made up her mind to talk to someone about her problem. Her parents were divorced six months ago. Tammy, an only child, is having a difficult time adjusting to the new family arrangement. After a couple of false starts, she pushes her hair back off her forehead and plunges in.

"I felt the divorce coming for a long time," she remembers. "Last year, on my sixteenth birthday, I tried to talk them out of it. Instead of trying to make their marriage work, they just gave up. They should have tried harder. They were good for each other. Now both of them are worse off. My mother won't admit it, but I'm pretty sure she'd take my father back if he asked."

Tammy brushes away a tear. "They think of divorce as a way of getting rid of problems, but the problems are still there. In fact, they used to argue a lot about money, but now there's less money than ever. Oh, they said we'd still be a family. They even tried to tell me that I'd be closer to my father because when I saw him, I'd have him all to myself. Big deal! I hardly ever see him, and when I do, we're further apart then ever."

The counselor asks Tammy to narrow her complaints down to the problem bothering her the most.

"That's easy," Tammy replies. "All at once I've had to learn to be self-sufficient. It's like things have turned upside down. I used to depend on my mother for everything, but now she leans on me. And she's so unhappy I don't feel that I can tell her my problems. So I keep my feelings to myself while she cries on my shoulder.

"And to make it worse, my father has already married another woman. She's younger than he is, and she's not at all like my mother. Instead of solving his problems, he made them worse." Tammy takes a deep breath. "How can adults be so stupid! I'd never do anything like this to my kids."*

The problem

The Free Clinic counselor describes Tammy as "an honest, mature young woman who sees life in realistic terms." Her description of the effect the divorce has had on her family seems accurate enough—although Tammy's own biases should also be taken into account. Just having a chance to talk out her feelings with a sympathetic listener will probably help her.

*Adapted from *Seventeen*® Magazine. Copyright © 1968 by Triangle Communications, Inc. All rights reserved.

WE CAN ALL HELP OURSELVES

You have a right to your feelings, your painful feelings just as much as your happier ones. To feel all that you can feel is to be truly human. But too often people cling to unpleasant feelings; they even court them. Without fully realizing what they are doing, they actually bring them about. They do things that make them feel bad, and then they say, "I couldn't help myself." What most people mean when they say that is, "I didn't help myself." But we can all help ourselves.

—MILDRED NEWMAN AND BERNARD BERKOWITZ

Figure 16.6

Tammy believes that her parents' divorce is the cause of her own unhappiness.

But a counselor can do more for Tammy than listen. Tammy needs to understand that all her unhappiness cannot be blamed on others. She should consider the possibility that her negative feelings about the divorce come at least in part from her own one-sided view of her parents. She hasn't tried to find out if they honestly believe the divorce has solved anything. At the same time, Tammy should ask herself whether she was ever close to her father, divorce or not. It might be that the separation only finalized what already existed.

Tammy also says that she resents being forced into a position of independence and responsibility. She might want to look more closely at that statement. Maybe it's time for her to repay some of the nurturing she's received from her mother all these years. Since she can't remain a child much longer anyway, she might look at her new role as a chance to grow.

In a similar way, Tammy should look at her attitude toward her father's new wife. Does the woman really deserve Tammy's scorn, or does Tammy dislike her simply because she appears to have "stolen" her father? Tammy should give the new relationship time to prove itself before she decides that her father has made a terrible mistake.

Solutions

Tammy can analyze her problems concerning the divorce if she first divides them into two categories: her feelings about the new

situation in which she finds herself, and her new relationships with the other three persons involved.

Before she can handle the effects of the divorce, Tammy should think about why people get married and divorced. Reading a book or two about divorce and continuing her talks with the counselor will help. She should also meet with other young people whose parents are divorced. Such groups exist in many communities. She can locate one through a hot line, free clinic, or other helping agency.

It would also help if Tammy thought honestly about her own reasons for opposing the divorce. After a while, she might begin to accept the fact that, for some people, divorce is a painful but necessary way of moving out of an intolerable situation and into a more rewarding situation. If nothing else, Tammy should accept the finality of the divorce. She apparently has hopes of getting her parents back together, but she can't run their lives for them.

When Tammy examines the new family relationships created by the divorce, she should focus first on herself. Thus far, she seems to have seen herself only as an extension of her parents. As a young adult, however, she has her own independence to consider. A useful step for her would be to sit down with each parent for a "gut-level" discussion of feelings. With her mother, Tammy might talk about how happy she is that they can still be close. But she could also say that she needs to know that her mother is still interested in Tammy's own feelings and problems. From her father, she might ask for time to work out her feelings about their new relationship. Right now, he probably feels hurt and confused by Tammy's coldness.

Finally, Tammy should realize that her relationship with her parents has already changed over the years. The divorce came at a difficult time, just as she was nearing the end of adolescence. She feels resentful at having this separation forced on her too soon. But as she matures, Tammy will learn that no relationship stays the same forever. Although the divorce has been difficult for her, it also gives Tammy a chance to continue her own emotional growth.

A self-awareness exercise for coping with divorce

Everyone daydreams once in a while. These fantasies do no harm and sometimes do some good. Psychologists have learned how to put fantasies to work in an organized way. In this exercise, anyone whose parents are involved in a divorce can use creative fantasies to work through the problems left behind when a home breaks up. In fact, you can adopt this technique to tackle any problem that involves human relationships.

In this exercise, you will practice saying the right things *before* you run into a possibly painful situation. Imagine yourself responding in a definite, positive way. Try to avoid saying things calculated to make people feel guilty, such as the classic, "I'd be happy if it weren't for you!"

Say your fantasy to yourself. If necessary, go over it several times until you get it right.

Situation 1: It's your birthday. For the first time since their divorce, your parents have both agreed to attend the celebration. During the party, you have a chance to talk to each of them alone. *I would say* . . .

Situation 2: You walk into your mother's room several months after the divorce, only to discover that she's been crying. It's not the first time. *I would say* . . .

Situation 3: At a get-together with several friends from school, the topic of divorce comes up. You're the only one in the group who's been in the middle of a family breakup. Everyone turns to you for an opinion. *I would say* . . .

Situation 4: Every time you see your dad, he wants to talk about all the terrible things your mother did to him during their marriage. *I would say* . . .

Situation 5: You're having dinner with your father and his new wife. When your father leaves to run an errand, an awkward silence develops. Your stepmother looks as uncomfortable as you feel. *I would say* . . .

Situation 6: All at once, your family has doubled in size. Your mother has remarried, and you now have two stepbrothers and a stepsister. Since the house is small, you'll have to share your room. Your new sibling has just walked in and is looking around the room that used to be yours alone. *I would say* . . .

You can make up as many real-life situations as you want. The important idea is to work through your feelings before you're put on the spot. Creative fantasies give you that luxury.

CASE HISTORY 6. RALPH: RESOLVING PROBLEMS WITH PARENTS

A campus guard catches Ralph drinking on campus. That comes as a surprise because Ralph has never been in trouble before. His teachers have always given positive reports on his attitude and his schoolwork. When he walks into the principal's office, however, Ralph wears a cocky grin. He doesn't wait for the principal to speak.

"So now you'll kick me out of school," he challenges. "Big deal! My father is always telling me I'll end up in the streets. He'll be pleased to find out that he's right—like always."

Ralph slouches lower in his chair. "You know, it really bugs him that I'm not just like him. He works all day in that crummy

Figure 16.7

Ralph is reacting to pressure from his parents by rebelling against all authority.

store, selling hardware to old ladies. And he expects me to follow in his footsteps!

"You want to know what really started this? My old man doesn't like it that I want to be a mechanic. He got bent all out of shape when I signed up for senior auto mechanics this year instead of those dumb business courses he's always pushing. I keep telling him that in two years I'll be making more money than he does. But all he can talk about is grease under my fingernails."

He holds up his hands for inspection. "See that? I'm proud of that grease. It's honest. But since I won't change, he's always on me about little things. Can you guess the last four major crimes he blasted me for? Tearing an elbow out of my jacket. Getting a ticket for running a red light. Coming in late—well, it was 2:30—from a date. And forgetting to buy him a season ticket for the basketball games. Does that sound like a federal case?"

The principal asks Ralph about his drinking. Ralph shrugs. "So, lately I've been hitting the booze. It makes me feel better for a while. Believe me, I'll be out of that house like a shot as soon as I get out of school and start earning my own way."

Ralph looks at the principal, pleading mixed with the defiance in his voice. "It doesn't have to be this way, does it? Why can't he let me alone? Boy, if kids could just pick their own parents!"

RESPECT

A son should respect his father
He should not have to be taught to respect his father
It is something that is natural
That's how I've brought up my son anyway.

Of course a father must be worthy of respect
He can forfeit a son's respect
But I hope at least that my son will respect me, if only for leaving him free to respect me or not.

—R. D. LAING

The problem

Ralph's problem isn't exclusively his. His father is also deeply involved. At this point, only Ralph's point of view has been heard. Later, in counseling, a psychologist would want to talk to both of Ralph's parents. But certain facts seem obvious.

First, the problem doesn't have much to do with Ralph's drinking on campus. That infraction can't be ignored, but it can be handled separately. More basic is the conflict between Ralph and his father. A no-win battle has developed over the question of Ralph's future. Along with that disagreement, the father also refuses to accept the fact that his son is now a young adult.

Ralph's father thinks of his small business as a step upward from his own family's blue-collar origins. He takes pride in what he has accomplished. But a wise father would not insist that his son carry on the tradition. Ralph needs to find his own identity, without being limited by his father's expectations.

Second, Ralph probably hasn't thought about his future very carefully. Before he jumps into any career, he should think about job satisfaction, income, opportunities for advancement, and social rewards. Working as a mechanic may be just the right choice for him—or it could be a dead-end job that will leave him unhappy and unfulfilled.

Solutions

Family counseling seems called for in Ralph's case. The therapist's first job will be to gain a commitment from all members of the family to seek help for their problems. If that hurdle can be overcome, the odds are good that harmony can be restored to the household.

Ralph has set himself up as a judge of his father's life. He has to realize that his father's values, which leave him cold, make a lot of sense to his father. With the therapist's help, Ralph may once again be able to see his father as a human being.

Right now, Ralph sees him only as a tyrant.

Ralph's father has two major adjustments to make at the same time. First, he must accept his son's growing independence. Second, he must face the fact that Ralph is determined to make his own vocational choices. On paper, these look like easy changes for anyone to make, but it takes skillful counseling to change beliefs built up over a lifetime.

Neither Ralph nor his father seem exceptionally secure in their own identities. When Ralph chose to drink on campus as his gesture of rebellion, a psychologist would guess that Ralph expected (or even hoped) he'd be caught. Perhaps he figured that if he were thrown out of school, he wouldn't have any choice but to get work as a mechanic. It also seems unreasonable that his father would insist on a career for Ralph that matches neither Ralph's interests or abilities. Both father and son have some emotional growing up to do.

A self-awareness exercise in parent-child understanding

If you'd like to start some useful dialogue within your family, this exercise should do the job. First, rate yourself on the following inventory. Be as honest as possible. Then give blank copies to your parents and ask each of them to fill in the inventory *as they see you*. When you sit down to compare your answers with theirs, you'll have the makings of thought-provoking discussion. Later, you can reverse the procedure. As other family members rate themselves in turn, they can compare the results with the evaluations made by the rest of you.

Directions: Make up a separate answer sheet for each person's inventory. If a statement is true, check column one. If it is false, check column two. If you also think that the person being rated should change his or her behavior, check column three, "Needs Change." Do not check column three unless you feel strongly about changing that particular behavior.

		True	False	Needs Change
1	Gets along with adults	☐	☐	☐
2	Relates well to children	☐	☐	☐
3	Has a good sense of humor	☐	☐	☐
4	Is interested in the outside world	☐	☐	☐
5	Is rarely sick with minor illnesses	☐	☐	☐
6	Expresses appreciation for gifts and favors	☐	☐	☐
7	Expresses anger openly but rationally	☐	☐	☐
8	Is able to ask for help	☐	☐	☐
9	Does well in school or on the job	☐	☐	☐
10	Is adaptable to new locations or a change in status	☐	☐	☐
11	Respects the possessions of others	☐	☐	☐
12	Keeps surroundings reasonably neat	☐	☐	☐
13	Isn't afraid to express personal opinions	☐	☐	☐
14	Works toward goals despite frustrations	☐	☐	☐
15	Is proud of physical and emotional growth	☐	☐	☐
16	Accepts others who are different	☐	☐	☐
17	Is fun to be with	☐	☐	☐
18	Respects the parent-child relationship	☐	☐	☐
19	Recognizes faults and works to change them	☐	☐	☐
20	Is willing to listen to advice but makes own decisions	☐	☐	☐

You'll be surprised at how often your own ratings don't match the evaluations others make of you. Once you get over the initial shock, you'll find that the exercise has given you abundant data to think about—and to act on, if you sincerely want to change.

CASE HISTORY 7. JUDY: OVERCOMING SHYNESS

Judy has ignored two requests from the counseling office to come in and plan her courses for the fall semester. Finally, in mid-August, her mother calls for an appointment. When Judy and her mother arrive at the office, Judy refuses to meet the counselor's friendly smile. Her mother settles herself into a chair and launches into a well-rehearsed speech.

"Judy has just loafed around the house all summer," she complains. "When she gets up in the morning, she has three cups of coffee before she gets moving. Then she figures out her day from an astrology book. At noon she fixes herself a sandwich for lunch, then watches soap operas on TV. She does help me fix supper, I'll say that for her, and she does the dishes without being asked. But in the evening she plops herself down in front of the TV set again, and that's it for the day."

The counselor interrupts to ask Judy if

she has any interests outside the house. In the silence that follows, the mother speaks up again. "Judy goes out shopping once in a while, and every other week she has her hair done. Aside from that, she doesn't do anything that I can see. I've tried to talk her into phoning someone or joining a dance group at the recreation center, but she always finds an excuse." She throws up her hands in despair.

Judy is sitting very still, her shoulders hunched up as if in self-protection. When it becomes obvious that she won't speak with her mother there, the counselor suggests that the older woman wait outside. When the door closes, Judy relaxes a little.

"I like the way I live," she says softly. "I don't hurt anyone. Mom thinks I should get a job, but what's the use? My dad makes enough money to take care of us. He's not pushing me. Besides, no one would hire me without any experience. As for friends, why should I try to make it with kids who don't care whether I'm alive or not? My best friend moved away this spring, and I'll never find anybody else like her."

She tosses her neatly brushed hair defiantly. "Look, maybe I'm not the happiest person in the world, but I get by. Most people work like crazy to earn enough so they can relax like me. My older brother

Figure 16.8

Judy's withdrawn behavior has its roots in her extreme shyness.

and sister are both out killing themselves to take care of their families. Who needs that?"

Judy's voice falls. "Besides, what have I got to offer? My teeth are crooked, my voice is all wrong, and the new styles look terrible on me. When someone does talk to me, I blush so badly I want to run and hide. When I finish school, things might be different. That's time enough to look for a job and to find some new friends. Right now I'm content to be by myself."

The Problem

About 40 percent of the people surveyed in one study identified themselves as suffering from shyness and lack of self-esteem. Few of them are as intensely shy as Judy, but Judy has better reasons than most. Her mother reminds her constantly that she is weak, yet she doesn't give Judy the responsibilities she needs to improve her self-image. Judy's father, on the contrary, takes a hands-off approach that seems to confirm Judy's low opinion of herself. Judy's basic needs to grow and accept new challenges are thus overruled by her fear of facing situations where she might fail.

With her parent's approval, Judy has become a passive, dependent person. She says she enjoys her predictable, repetitive life. Variety and new situations are things to be avoided. Left unchecked, this withdrawal could lead to neurosis—anxiety symptoms, depression, and phobias. Her father says, "Leave her alone; she'll grow out of it," but Judy's shyness isn't a "phase" she's going through. Even if it doesn't lead to neurotic symptoms, it can turn her life into a self-imposed prison.

At some level, Judy probably recognizes that her shyness keeps her from embracing change and growth. But she rationalizes that failure by hiding behind her imagined physical deficiencies and the loss of her one close friend. To Judy's fragile ego, these defenses are both logical and important. They make it possible for her to get out of bed to face each new day.

WHY AM I AFRAID?

I am afraid to tell you who I am, because, if I tell you who I am, you may not like who I am, and it's all that I have.

—JOHN POWELL, S.J.

Solutions

With added maturity and insight, Judy might be able to break out of her self-imposed prison on her own. Normally, however, extreme shyness cannot be overcome through self-help techniques. Her poor self-image and stubborn habits of withdrawal will need professional assistance. When she goes into therapy, Judy must admit to the need for change. She will then be encouraged to set new goals for herself, along with a strategy for reaching her objectives.

Once Judy understands that the therapist accepts her and likes her just as she is, she will feel safe enough to lower her defenses. Perhaps for the first time she will be able to look closely at her own emotions. This experience may prove painful at first. But if she sticks to her resolve, Judy will find that self-examination can be a rewarding experience. Once she begins to understand the insecurities that have caused her shyness, Judy can regain control of her life. She'll stop letting things happen *to* her.

As her self-insight increases, Judy will take more small steps. She will set realistic social and career goals for herself, and, more important, she will take risks in her personal life. As she reaches out to new friends and tries out new social roles, her fears will decrease. People will comment on the changes they see in her because she will actually look prettier, livelier, and more approachable.

One of the therapist's strategies will be to ask Judy to act as if she had great self-confidence. As Judy involves herself in gradually more difficult social situations, her new attitude can become a self-fulfilling prophecy: Each successful experience will create greater self-esteem. Although Judy will probably never be a life-of-the-party person, she can learn to stand alone, secure in her own pride and independence. Her newly found warmth and joy in living will make her a prized and supportive friend to those close to her.

A self-awareness exercise for overcoming shyness

For anyone who has suffered the pounding heart, moist hands, and shaky feeling of being truly shy, Philip Zimbardo's book will come as an eye-opener. In *Shyness: What It Is, What To Do About It*, he points out that well-known personalities such as Johnny Carson, Barbara Walters, Roosevelt Grier, and Carol Burnett have also had to fight to overcome shyness. Their success proves that the problem can be overcome.

These two exercises* are designed to help shy people cope with their feeings. Like most awareness experiences, however, the exercises are useful for all persons who want to work on their own self-image.

Exercise 1. Costs and benefits. Prepare a chart similar to the one printed below. The idea is to list the cost of what you've given up

*Philip G. Zimbardo, *Shyness: What It Is, What to Do About It*, copyright © 1977, Addison-Wesley Publishing Co., Reading, Mass. Adaptation of Chapter 8, pages 143–146. Reprinted with permission.

or lost because of shyness. The middle column stands for a valued event, action, or opportunity that you lost out on or saw diminished because of shyness. An example has been filled in to give you the idea. Add as many items as you want to write about.

SHYNESS LIABILITIES

Date	Situation/action taken or refused	Resulting loss
1. May 7	I wanted to ask Pat to the prom but couldn't get up enough nerve.	I stayed home from the prom although all my friends went. I felt miserable.
2.		
3.		

Now, think about what you've *gained* by being shy. If that suggestion sounds strange, remember that people don't adopt a behavior unless it has some sort of payoff. Examples of the benefits to be gained from shyness include avoiding criticism, preventing emotional tangles, avoiding rejection, and escaping responsibility. Add as many items to the list below as you want to write about.

SHYNESS BENEFITS

Date	Situation/action taken or refused	Resulting benefit	Resulting longterm liability (if any)
1. May 2	I saw Pat coming toward me at lunch. I turned away and pretended to be studying my math.	That way I didn't take a chance that Pat would ignore me.	At this rate Pat and I will never get together.
2.			
3.			

When you analyze your two charts, you'll understand immediately what your costs and payoffs are. Then you can ask yourself, "Is this the way I want to keep on living my life?" If your answer is "No," try the next exercise.

Exercise 2. Taking risks. Start out by listing all the important risks (chances) that you have taken in your life—whether it was learning to drive, trying out for the school play, or asking someone for a date. Decide whether each risk was wise or foolish. Complete this step before you go on to the next one.

Ready? *Now go out and take a risk.* Do something "scary" that you have wanted to do but have been avoiding. Take one such risk every day this week, but first write down what you're going to do and why it's scary for you. Remember, this step does *not* include foolhardy things like jumping off buildings or picking a fight with someone who holds a black belt in karate. Your risks should involve social challenges: speaking up in class, joining a new group at lunch, making a new friend, and so on. After a while, you'll find yourself doing these things naturally.

CASE HISTORY 8. ERIC: FINDING HAPPINESS

Eric has missed a month of school. When he returns, he is reluctant to talk about the reasons for his absence. Finally, a week later, he makes an appointment to talk to his psychology teacher. At three o'clock he drags into the classroom. He looks as if the slightest move will send him running.

"Nobody else at school knows this," he says, "but I was out of your class so long because I had a breakdown. Can you believe that? I thought only old people had breakdowns."

The teacher assures Eric that emotional problems can happen to anyone, regardless of age. Eric seems to feel a little better, and he begins to tell about his experience. His voice has a slight tremor, despite his best efforts to control it.

"I guess you could say I don't have any willpower any more. If I feel the least bit upset, I get all choked up. When this last thing started, I got so emotional I couldn't breathe. At first I thought something was wrong with my lungs. I've had what my dad calls an 'asthma condition' as long as I can remember. But this was worse. My folks took me to the hospital, and they gave me some oxygen. That helped me breathe, but the doctors couldn't find anything really wrong. They thought the news would make me feel better, but it didn't. I felt upset, ashamed. Here I was causing everyone so much trouble, and there wasn't anything the matter with me!"

Eric pulls at the thin mustache he's growing. "The doctor asked me if anything had happened to upset me, something emotional. The only thing I could think of was the time a few weeks ago when my dad missed some money from his bedroom. He accused me of taking it. I swear I didn't take it, but nothing I said could convince him that I wasn't guilty. My mother says she believes

Figure 16.9

Eric believes that something will always interfere with his chances of being happy.

HAPPINESS IS "DOING"

You can paralyze yourself with perfectionistic do-your-best nonsense. Perhaps you can give yourself some significant areas in your life in which you truly want to do your best. But in the vast majority of activities, having to do your best, or even to do well, is an obstacle to doing. . . . Try changing "Do your best" to simply "Do."

—WAYNE DYER

me, but I think she still has some doubts.

"I've been depressed ever since that night at the emergency room. My father says I can snap out of it any time I want. He thinks I'm using sickness as a way of escaping from my problems. Not that I haven't got my share of problems." Eric's smile is mocking. "I get along OK with the guys, at least I did until this business started. But I only feel really good when I have a steady girl friend. Sara and I broke up four months ago, and I haven't had a date since. Lately I've given up asking girls out. What's the use? They always turn me down."

The teacher points out that Senior Day is coming up. That seems like a good time for Eric to be with his friends. It's always easier to talk to people in a group situation, especially if everyone's relaxed and having fun.

"I don't know if I'll go on Senior Day," Eric says, shaking his head. "I don't really get a kick out of anything I do. Life seems pretty blah. I've always needed something to look forward to, like Christmas or a ski trip. But whenever I get what I've waited for, it never turns out as good as I expected. Something always goes wrong to spoil it."

He buries his face in his hands. His voice comes through clearly, however. "I'm beginning to wonder if life is worth all the trouble. What do I have to do to be happy?"

The problem

Eric is clearly unhappy. He's unhappy with himself and with life in general. His attitude

has carried him to the point of becoming neurotic, for he cannot cope with any part of his life at this point. The doctor's diagnosis that his illness is psychosomatic caused Eric more anxiety than relief. At this point, he probably cannot pull himself out of his depression and relieve his anxiety without professional help.

Somehow, Eric has managed to cast himself as a bench warmer in the game of life. Add that to his negative outlook, and his unhappiness becomes understandable. He says that he's capable of enthusiasm, but that things always go wrong. This attitude indicates that Eric doesn't really know himself very well. He has the unrealistic idea that life should be fair, when there really isn't anything fair about it. The possibility must also be considered that Eric unconsciously makes things go wrong so that his negative predictions will be fulfilled.

Almost everyone can relate to Eric's desire to find happiness. But happiness doesn't just happen to people. It grows out of a sense of purpose and accomplishment. Eric hasn't selected goals for himself, nor does he really know what will make him happy. Once he analyzes his needs, he can work with his therapist to find ways of achieving them. His father's mistrust, for example, can be overcome by setting up a series of situations in which Eric has a chance to demonstrate that he can be trusted. Right now his father may not have much reason to give his withdrawn, unhappy son the benefit of the doubt.

A complete psychiatric review should also check out the possibility that Eric's depression has physical causes. Along with psychotherapy, he might profit from treatment with one of the antidepressant medications. Whatever medical help he receives, however, Eric must still find contentment within himself. As he finds out on every birthday, happiness is not something another person can give you wrapped in red ribbons.

Solutions

Eric needs immediate help before his downward spiral of anxiety and depression carries him too far. Some suicides show a similar pattern in the beginning. While a professional psychotherapist would be best for him, but short-term, client-centered him in sorting out his conflicting emotions. Most of all, Eric needs to have his own value as a human being reinforced. No single school of therapy stands out as being best for him, but short-term, client-centered therapy, reality therapy, or an existentialist approach would all have useful insights to offer.

Once Eric and his therapist have set up a good relationship, the therapist will try to help Eric talk about his own feelings and needs. When Eric sees that happiness is a byproduct of an active, productive life, he will feel less pressured to "be happy." Eric will also feel better when he understands that his problem is not unique. Gradually, the therapist will encourage Eric to take a more active part in school life. His emotional "cramps" may not disappear immediately. Their intensity will decrease, however, as he learns to cope with failure and to handle success.

At present, Eric doesn't understand why he isn't as happy as the characters he watches on television. He desperately wants to share in their artificial happiness, but he's forgotten that only one person is responsible for Eric's life—Eric himself. Once he learns to live according to his own values and needs, he'll have a chance to find the happiness he's been looking for.

A self-awareness exercise for identifying personal values

What makes someone else happy might leave you utterly miserable. All people, young and old, have personal values and needs whose satisfaction gives them feelings of inner peace and contentment. Do you know what your own values are? Some people do; others have never stopped to think about what's really important in their lives. This exercise will give you a look at what makes you happy.

The exercise will work only if you complete each of the following items quickly and freely. Don't pause to think about "right" answers or what others would expect you to say. On a separate sheet of paper, write the first four things that pop into your mind in each category.

1. Happiness is

_____

_____

_____

2. Unhappiness is

_____

_____

_____

3. I would really like to

_____

_____

_____

4. I hate to

_____

_____

_____

5. I am proud of

_____

_____

_____

6. I have learned that

_____

_____

_____

Now look back over your answers. Do you find any recurring ideas, themes, or connections? Perhaps you'll discover that your values revolve around making other people happy. There's nothing wrong with that, as long as it makes you happy, too. But some people spend so much time taking care of others that they never tend to their own needs. You can also use different lead-ins: "A value I really admire is . . ." "My worst faults are . . ." "This year I learned that men/women . . ."

Now rate your responses. Put a C next to those that you would like to change. Writing "I hate to get up in the morning" may be how you feel, but it's also something you may want to change—especially if your job or school requires early rising. Mark a W by those items that are only wishes for the future. For example, you may have written, "Happiness is graduating from college," when that great day is still years ahead of you. Finally, put a T next to those statements that stand out as true statements about the way you feel.

Clarifying your values in such an exercise lets you see exactly where you stand. It leaves you free to keep what is right for you and to change what no longer makes sense in your life.

AFTERWORD: ON DEVELOPING A BEAUTIFUL SOUL

Not everyone can imitate Irwin the Troll's feat of flower diving. But wouldn't it be lovely if people could? In a world turned cold, where crime, hunger, poverty, illness, and anxiety are so common as to be ignored, all of us need more beautiful souls.

Can psychology do anything to help? Certainly the lessons that psychology teaches weren't meant to be confined within the covers of a book. In less than a hundred years, psychology has emerged as a living, working tool. It teaches a lesson worth repeating: *People can improve the quality of their lives*.

OK, you're probably saying, that *sounds* good. Now prove it. If Skinner can't agree with Freud, and if Maslow doesn't see eye to eye with Horney, what can the poor ama-

teur hope to gain from all the confusion? If one person's Oedipus complex is another's conditioned response, what's the point of continuing the debate?

If this entire text could be boiled down to its most important and basic concepts, four key ideas would emerge. Here they are. They speak to the importance of psychology in a world where the bad days sometimes seem to outnumber the good.

You have the power to change your life

Many aspects of your life lie beyond your personal control. You can't do much about your age, height, shape of ears, and so on. At one time psychologists also thought that

516

your emotional life was also determined by forces that you couldn't do anything about.

Today, that rather negative outlook has been greatly modified. To a degree, you *are* your parents' child. You have been shaped by the accidents of your genetic inheritance and by your childhood. *But you also have the power to change.* Most psychologists now think that it's a cop-out for a person to say, "I can't help it. That's the way I am." To the contrary, you *can* help it—if you want to. Through your own efforts or with the help of a counselor or therapist, you can overcome almost any childhood trauma.

That's not to suggest that it's easy to change behavior patterns you've built up over many years. You may carry parental messages in your head that tell you not to succeed, not to love, never to take chances, and so on. But once you recognize these messages for what they are, psychology can show you how to replace them with healthier ideas. Think of that effort as an investment in your future. Positive change will pay dividends in your own life, of course, but it will also be multiplied a hundred times through the effect you have on other people.

You are a special person

Look at the tip of your index finger for a moment. The delicate pattern of lines and loops you see there has never been duplicated on another human being. And just like your fingerprint, *you* are unique. Unless you are an identical twin, no other person can possibly share your genetic and environmental heritage. And even identical twins have different experiences in life. So stand a little straighter, and give yourself a salute. You're one of a kind!

True, everyone has faults, traumas, frustrations, fears, anxieties, compulsions, and all the other negative behavior patterns that psychologists have identified. But you also have abilities, strengths, intelligence, love, and a hundred other positive qualities. If you owned a rare orchid or a classic Rolls

Royce, you'd treat it with the care it deserves. Why not accept the help that psychology can give you in recognizing and developing your own special qualities and potential? The powers of the mind can be used to change behavior and improve the quality of your life. Are you willing to accept that responsibility? A special person like you deserves the very best!

Problems are for solving

Life on the beach of a South Seas island would be paradise for a month or two. But after a hundred identical days of sleeping, eating, and swimming, wouldn't you begin to look for a way to break up the routine? Before you knew it, you'd be inventing problems just for the fun of solving them.

Life being what it is, however, you won't have to invent problems. They'll come to you by the dozens. Some will be minor, but others will challenge every ounce of intelligence, courage, and love you possess. If you know something about human behavior, you won't have to tackle these difficult times blindly. Someday, for example, you'll have to cope with the overwhelming grief that people experience when death comes to someone they love. Psychology can't prevent that grief, nor should it. But it can prepare you to accept your feelings as a necessary part of saying "good-bye." By accepting your grief and working through it, you'll be free much more quickly to resume your own life.

People are for loving

In an age that seems to ask only, "What's in it for me?," psychology reminds us that we share our lives with other people. If we're not careful, natural selfishness can restrict our vision. More than that, some people have misread psychology. They claim that they should be allowed to say and do whatever "feels good," regardless of how their behavior affects others. Husbands and wives leave home to "find themselves";

workers tell off the boss or their customers because it's "healthy to let their feelings out"; and too many young people "go with the flow" because they believe that work, discipline, and ambition somehow prevent the full flowering of human nature.

Perhaps a grain of truth exists within each of these attitudes. But consider a greater truth. The happiest and most productive people find joy in relating to others. This won't happen if you use people for your own selfish purposes. Nor can it happen if you close yourself off to the needs and interests of those people with whom you share your life.

Try a simple experiment, if you will. Ours is not a "touching" society. You've probably noticed how careful most people are not to touch others. For a week, make a point of touching those you meet in the course of everyday life. You don't have to hug or grab or stroke people. Just use a light, quick pressure on the hand or arm or shoulder. Try it in greeting, during conversation, or when saying good-bye. See if this extra touching doesn't change your relationships with your family, friends, classmates, and the other people you come in contact with during the course of a day.

This book is only a starting place

Now that you've come to the final page of the last chapter, you probably feel that you've "learned" psychology. In fact, after five hundred or so pages, you can be for-given for thinking that you've pretty well exhausted the subject. As it turns out, however, you've only scratched the surface. For proof, check the psychology section of any library. You'll find hundreds of titles dealing with every topic covered in these pages, as well as others that lack of space prevented us from including.

We hope that your study of psychology is only beginning. A few of you may want to go on to careers in this field. If you do, your professional training will take you into the challenging world of the university, the research laboratory, and the clinic. For others who will go on to separate careers and lives far removed from the formal study of psychology, we have a slightly different message: *Stay involved.* Psychology can't answer all your questions, nor will it solve all your problems. Even so, it's the best means we have of understanding the how and why of human behavior.

Finally, we invite you to tell us how you felt about this book. Since we're human, we'd be pleased to hear positive things about your experiences with *Psychology: A Way to Grow.* But if you think something should be added or changed or dropped, we want to know that, too. Write to us in care of Amsco School Publications, 315 Hudson Street, New York, NY 10013. We want to make this book a living text that will grow with this young and vigorous science. Without your help, that can't happen.

Take good care of yourself. You deserve it.

Carl R. Green
William R. Sanford

ILLUSTRATION CREDITS

1 Frank Siteman/Stock Boston; **4** Woodfin Camp/Linda Rogers (left), Jerry Cooke (right); **6** The Iveagh Bequest; **19** Stern/Black Star; **20** Picture Cube/Frank Siteman; **22** Neal E. Miller /The Rockefeller University; **34** Shelly Katz/Black Star; **36** From a halftone of a Matthew Brady photograph; **38** Rosiland Dymond Cartwright, *Night Life: Exploration in Dreaming,* © 1977, p. 11. Adapted by permission of Prentice-Hall, Inc., Englewood Cliffs, N.J.; **40** Photo by Mark Ricker, Jr./Courtesy of Harper & Row; **46** Photo Researchers/ Jack Fields, color conversion; **49** *Broom Hilda*, by Russell Myers, Sunday Page, February 4, 1980. Reprinted by permission of the Chicago Tribune-New York News Syndicate, Inc.; **64** From *Mechanics of the Mind*, by